Strategic Survey
2002/3

AN EVALUATION AND FORECAST OF WORLD AFFAIRS

Published by

OXFORD
UNIVERSITY PRESS

for

The International Institute for Strategic Studies
Arundel House, 13–15 Arundel Street, Temple Place,
London WC2R 3DX, United Kingdom

Strategic Survey
2002/3

Published by

OXFORD
UNIVERSITY PRESS

for

The International Institute for Strategic Studies
Arundel House, 13–15 Arundel Street, Temple Place,
London WC2R 3DX, United Kingdom

Director: ....Dr John Chipman
Editor: ....Jonathan Stevenson

Assistant Editor: ....Jill Dobson
Map Editor: ....James Hackett
Editorial: ....James Green
Designer: ....Simon Nevitt
Cartographer: ....Jillian Luff

This publication has been prepared by the Director of the Institute and his Staff, who accept full responsibility for its contents, which describe and analyse events up to 7 April 2003. These do not, and indeed cannot, represent a consensus of views among the worldwide membership of the Institute as a whole.

Cover images © The Associated Press

First published ....May 2003

ISBN 0-19-852705-5
ISSN 0459-7230

Strategic Survey (ISSN 0459-7230) is published annually by Oxford University Press.

Payment is required with all orders and subscriptions. Prices include air-speeded delivery to Australia, Canada, India, Japan, New Zealand and the USA. Delivery elsewhere is by surface mail. Air-mail rates are available on request. Please add sales tax to prices quoted. Payment may be made by cheque or Eurocheque (payable to Oxford University Press), National Girobank (account 500 1056), credit card (MasterCard, Visa, American Express), direct debit (please send for details) or UNESCO coupons. Bankers: Barclays Bank plc. PO Box 333, Oxford, UK, code 20-65-18, account 00715654.

Claims for non-receipt must be made within four months of dispatch/order (whichever is later).

Please send subscription orders to the Journals Subscription Department, Oxford University Press, Great Clarendon Street, Oxford, OX2 6DP, UK. *Tel* +44 (0)1865 353907. *Fax* +44 (0)1865 353485. *e-mail* jnl.orders@oup.co.uk

Strategic Survey is distributed by Mercury International, 365 Blair Road, Avenel, NJ 07001, USA. Periodical postage paid at Rahway, New Jersey, USA, and additional entry points.

US POSTMASTER: Send address corrections to *Strategic Survey*, c/o Mercury International, 365 Blair Road, Avenel, NJ 07001, USA.

Abstracted and indexed by: Reasearch Base Online, PAIS.

PRINTED IN THE UK by Bell & Bain Ltd, Glasgow.

Contents

List of Maps

Strategic Survey Online

Members of the IISS can access *Strategic Survey 2002–2003* online via the Members area of www.iiss.org. The address for subscribers is http://www3.oup.co.uk/stsurv, where they will first need to register using their subscriber number.

Perspectives

While the 11 September 2001 attacks ushered in a new strategic epoch and established the new imperative of counter-terrorism, the subsequent American determination to forestall mass-casualty aggression of any kind elevated non-proliferation tasks to the same level of attention. Indeed, the merging of the terrorism and proliferation threats proved in 2002–03 to be one of the most controversial of the many strategic policy innovations that emerged during the year from the United States. Iraq must be disarmed, the White House argued, to deny a revanchist dictator nuclear capability that would severely impair regional and international security and to deny non-state terrorists – al-Qaeda in particular – a state supplier of weapons of mass destruction (WMD). Yet, through March 2003, American public diplomacy on these points (particularly the latter), at least outside the United States, largely failed. Most Europeans, for example, focused on the fact that no connection had been credibly established between Saddam Hussein and al-Qaeda generally or the 11 September attacks in particular. Furthermore, Europeans and others feared that a kind of risky idealism had come to dominate US foreign policy since 11 September. Few disputed the desirability, for instance, of the American vision of a groundswell of democratisation in the Gulf inspired by a reborn democratic Iraq. Many, however, justifiably questioned its plausibility in light of entrenched non-democratic traditions in Gulf politics and popular wariness of American influence in the region, and more broadly in view of its optimistic premise that nations will 'bandwagon' rather than 'balance'. There were also those who suspected that the US was cynically motivated to oust Saddam by the prospect of controlling Iraq's oil reserves, the world's second most plentiful after Saudi Arabia's.

At the same time, the United States' unilateral impulse was tempered by an element of realism, or at least by the realisation that even the world's only superpower could not do anything it wanted without prohibitive cost. Rather than strictly 'going it alone' in Iraq, in late 2002 Washington elected to build a consensus in the UN Security Council. The result was Resolution 1441, issued on 8 November 2002. The upshot of that resolution was that, in spite of Iraq's 'material breach' of multiple previous resolutions dating back to the first Gulf War in 1991, arms inspections would be given one final chance to neutralise Iraq's WMD threat before any US-led coalition resorted to force. Even after Iraq's inadequate compliance with UN disclosure and inspection requirements, the US consulted the Security Council and – with some reluctance – publicised damning intelligence to make its case for using force. When France and Russia vowed in March 2003 to veto any second resolution that would sanction the use of force, however, the US and the UK elected not to table such a resolution and to rely on Resolution 1441, and the initial authorisation to use force in Resolutions 678 and 687, to justify the legality of their action.

Once war began, on 20 March 2003, the inevitable Clausewitzean 'friction' arose. Leadership strikes did not cause the regime's immediate implosion; Saddam had materially and psychologically fortified more urban centres than expected; and irregular Iraqi recruits used guerrilla and sometimes terrorist tactics – including suicide attacks – with greater frequency and to greater effect than anticipated. 'Shock and awe' precision aerial bombardment, while certainly shocking and awful, did not intimidate the Iraqis to the extent hoped. Nevertheless, as April began, there was no doubt that US-led forces would prevail. Total allied casualties were at that time under 100, while Iraqi military casualties numbered several thousand. Although there had been some unfortunate incidents, given the amount of ordnance delivered and allowing for propagandistic Iraq exaggerations, Iraqi civilian casualties had stayed reasonably low. The stiffest challenges were not military but political, and they would come after the conflict: transforming a religiously and ethnically heterogeneous country from a dictatorship into some approximation of a liberal democracy; finding a role for the UN in post-conflict Iraq; finding and exploiting synergies between the regime change in Iraq and conflict-resolution between the Israelis and the Palestinians; reaching a better accommodation between the West and Islam; and controlling the effect of the war on transnational terrorism.

While the US and the UK's reliance on Resolution 1441 and its antecedents may have been legally credible, political legitimacy for their action was far more dubious given that most governments and populations opposed war in the absence of a second resolution. Despite an initial nod to the UN, on balance the US became obsessed with substance – regime change and disarmament – and the European powers with process – building international consensus through the UN. Thus, the Bush administration appeared to neglect alliance management. Before the first Gulf War, then US Secretary of State James Baker engaged in near-constant diplomacy with Turkey and other regional powers to ensure cooperation, making 39 visits in five major overseas missions to sign up allies and to make the case for war. During the run-up to war in February and March 2003, Secretary of State Colin Powell made only a few short foreign trips, none to key capitals in Europe or the Middle East. France and Germany, for their part, seemed distracted from the central issue of Iraqi non-compliance with Resolution 1441 in refusing to approve a resolution that merely affirmed that fact. While their purported justification was the avoidance of war, the US made it clear that their effective denial of the facts would not have that consequence. Among the principal factors that appeared to determine the French and German position was a perceived need to check American power, prompted by the Bush administration's inclusion of pre-emption in its National Security Strategy.

The US National Security Strategy

The US National Security Strategy released in September 2002 prescribed pre-emptive and preventive military action in limited circumstances. The Strategy's emphasis on pre-emption provoked considerable controversy, much of it overwrought. Contrary to many press reports, the administration was not proposing to abandon deterrence or to make pre-emption the focus of US defence policy. The Strategy acknowledged that the number of potential targets was small and that pre-emption would not be an appropriate response to all emerging threats. Moreover, practical and political obstacles would limit the actual use of such a policy – though perhaps not the benefits that arise from its deterrent effect.

The Strategy discussed pre-emption solely in the context of how to deal with 'terrorists of global reach' and 'rogue states'. It did not suggest that pre-emption had a role to play with respect to a rising China, any residual threat posed by Russia, or any other traditional security threat. The case for pre-emption was based on three claims. First, threats of retaliation would not deter terrorists and rogue states. Terrorists are often stateless, making them less vulnerable to retaliation, and many seek martyrdom. Rogue state leaders are less deterrable than the Soviet leaders the US confronted during the Cold War, because they are 'more willing to take risks'. Second, the hatred that drove the 11 September attackers, and the spread of the technologies needed to build WMD, indicated a real and immediate threat of catastrophic attack. Third, the magnitude of the potential harm that a successful attack could produce made it imprudent to rely solely on deterrence. The Strategy also noted that 'the United States has long maintained the option of pre-emptive actions to counter a sufficient threat' to its security. Like previous official discussions of the subject, it did not specify what circumstances would justify pre-emption. It merely stated that 'the United States will not use force in all cases to pre-empt emerging threats'. Nor did the Strategy specify what forms pre-emption might take. It presumably could run the gamut from air strikes against specific targets to all-out war.

The Strategy did, however, call for a broader definition of what justifies pre-emptive action. It noted that the relative weakness of terrorists and rogue states meant they would not attack in conventional fashion by openly mobilising military forces. Rather, they would attack clandestinely with 'weapons of mass destruction – weapons that can be easily concealed, delivered covertly, and used without warning'. This risk of surprise attack meant the traditional standard of international law, which holds that states can legally order pre-emptive military action only when faced with an imminent danger of attack, was too restrictive. Instead, the US had to have the right to use 'anticipatory action' to defend itself, 'even if uncertainty remains as to the time and place of the enemy's attack'. This clause reflected the notion that a state is not legally required to absorb a devastating first blow, which would make the right of self-defence meaningless. It could be read as justifying preventive wars – that is, attacking other countries simply on the suspicion that they might one day try to attack the United States.

The Strategy's arguments for pre-emption did not amount to a new doctrine, nor did they underwrite unilateralism. Indeed, it flatly stated that the US military must be able to 'deter threats against US interests, allies, and friends'. If anything, the Strategy broadened the role of deterrence by arguing that a strong military was needed not just to deter adversaries on the battlefield but also 'to dissuade potential adversaries from pursuing a military build-up in hopes of surpassing, or equalling, the power of the United States'. The Strategy also said, 'there is little of lasting consequence that the United States can accomplish without the sustained cooperation of its allies and friends in Canada and Europe'. This could be read not only as a statement of operational and political reality, but also as a broad endorsement of multilateralism. Although the US clearly did not view the formal authorisation of the UN Security Council as essential to the legality of the use of force, its efforts there in late 2002 and early 2003 indicated that it appreciated the Council's political importance.

The emphasis on pre-emption, in spite of the retention of deterrence, probably turned on the conviction of many Bush administration officials that their words can profoundly shape the behaviour of others. They would note, for instance, that tough US language since the 'axis of evil' speech had moved many US allies to intensify their efforts to stem WMD proliferation, and persuaded countries with rogue-state status partially to mend their ways. The danger with this approach was that others could hijack the arguments for pre-emption to provide themselves with cover for settling their own national-security scores.

Al-Qaeda's post-Afghanistan transformation

The Strategy's argument for pre-empting rogue states was debatable. The claim that rogue state leaders respond less to deterrence rested more on conjecture than hard evidence. Iraq and North Korea – the only countries the Strategy explicitly labelled as rogue states – have, in the past at least, both shown they understand deterrence. But the argument for pre-empting terrorists was persuasive. Al-Qaeda had already acted on its hatred of the United States, and other terrorist groups could emulate its tactics. Such groups could be impossible to deter because usually they would control no territory against which to retaliate and could embrace martyrdom. Moreover, law enforcement actions, covert operations and intelligence gathering always sought to prevent terrorist attacks, and such pre-emptive activities were well-established in international law. The debate in the United States was about whether the US government was doing enough to stop terrorists pre-emptively, not whether it had to wait for them to attack before acting.

Indeed, the most pressing and resilient American and global concern was still al-Qaeda – now reconstituted and doing business in a somewhat different manner, but more insidious and just as dangerous as in its pre-11 September incarnation. Al-Qaeda (or its successor) remained a potent transnational terrorist organisation that could take a generation to dismantle. US-led military action in Afghanistan in response to 11 September and the continued allied military presence there released the Taliban's stronghold on the country and deprived al-Qaeda leader Osama bin Laden, his inner circle and hundreds of rank-and-file al-Qaeda members of a friendly host, a recruiting 'magnet' and a comfortable and secure physical base of operations. The military campaign also killed some leaders, such as military planner Mohammed Atef, and forced others farther underground and hobbled them operationally. The global intelligence and law-enforcement mobilisation made communications, travel and financing more difficult. In numerous jurisdictions, according to US officials, about 2,700 known or suspected al-Qaeda operatives had been arrested, including al-Qaeda operations chief Abu Zubeida in March 2002, suspected conspirator Ramzi Binalshibh and logistics officer and financier Wa'el Hamza Julaidan in September 2002 and, most notably, Khalid Shaikh Mohammed, al-Qaeda's third-in-command and suspected orchestrator of the 11 September attacks. But the counter-terrorism effort also perversely impelled an already highly decentralised and elusive transnational terrorist network to become even harder to identify and neutralise. Thanks to technology and the multinational allure of jihadism, the Afghanistan camps were unnecessary.

Notwithstanding the United States' audacious targeted killing of six al-Qaeda members in Yemen in November 2002, employing a *Predator* unmanned aerial vehicle armed with *Hellfire* antitank missiles, point-targets susceptible to military action became much harder to isolate. Al-Qaeda was believed to have spread to as many as 90 countries. Intelligence agencies estimated that at least 20,000 jihadists had been trained in its Afghanistan camps since 1996. Since 11 September, military and law-enforcement efforts had resulted in the death or detention of perhaps one-third of al-Qaeda's 30 senior leaders and no more than 2,000 confirmed rank-and-file members. This left a rump leadership intact and over 18,000 potential terrorists still at large, with recruitment continuing. The group's leadership blended into the frenetic cities of Pakistan, Karachi in particular, where sympathisers abounded. The only physical infrastructure al-Qaeda required were safe-houses to assemble bombs and weapons caches. Otherwise, notebook computers, encryption, the Internet, multiple passports and the ease of global transportation enabled al-Qaeda to function as a 'virtual' entity that leveraged local assets – hence local knowledge – to full advantage in coordinating attacks in many 'fields of jihad'. Although financial institutions seized or froze some $125 million in suspected terrorist assets in the 18 months following 11 September, the informal *hawala* remittance system ensured a stream of essentially unregulated cash from diaspora to local radical Muslim groups, which also had their own ways of raising money. Bin Laden and his inner circle inspired followers via al-Jazeera and the Internet. Mid-level coordinators trained in Afghanistan and now inhabiting dozens of countries provided those followers with logistical and perhaps financial support. Al-Qaeda's leadership could leave the heavy operational lifting to the local foot-soldiers. This was the apparent modus operandi in the Bali and Kenya attacks of October 2002 and November 2002, respectively. If the minions were killed or caught, their spectacular demise in the name of Islam and al-Qaeda's audacious operational reach had moved others to take their place. The process was, in theory, self-perpetuating.

While al-Qaeda developed new angles of approach to mass-casualty terrorism to penetrate improved American and European defences, it could also content itself with softer high-value targets over a wider geographical range that fully symbolised the group's non-negotiable enmity to Western Christians and Jews. By the post-11 September record, fair game included German tourists in Tunisia; French submarine engineers in Pakistan; a French oil tanker in the Gulf of Aden; US Marines and civilian personnel in Kuwait; Australian, European and American tourists in Bali; and Israelis in Kenya. Al-Qaeda's greatest advantage was the logistical and operational flexibility afforded by having no state to defend, which allowed it to maintain a flat, transnational and clandestine organisational scheme with minimal dedicated 'bricks-and-mortar' physical infrastructure. Since al-Qaeda no longer concentrated its forces in clusters discernible and targetable from the air, the lion's share of the counter-terrorism burden rested on law-enforcement and intelligence agencies. While ideally a horizontal, multilateral network would develop to match al-Qaeda's, in practice the US – on account of its superior resources and its status as al-Qaeda's paramount 'far enemy' – would remain the central player in a set of predominantly bilateral civilian counter-terrorism relationships for the foreseeable future.

A superpower's limitations and challenges
Indeed, the United States' nod to multilateralism seemed to be premised, at bottom, on a recognition of its unequalled global security burdens.

Two factors were especially salient. First, Washington needed to maintain a broad coalition to fight a potentially trans-generational global terrorist threat with an array of tools – 'soft power' and diplomacy as well as law-enforcement, intelligence and occasionally military cooperation – and was loath to do anything to jeopardise counter-terrorism cooperation. While day-to-day counter-terrorism cooperation with the US at the intelligence and law-enforcement levels remained in the self-interest of most governments regardless of political agreement on other strategic issues, coordination and consensus on longer term diplomatic plans for addressing the root causes were needed. Second, the US remained tepid with respect to nation-building, and anticipated the need to delegate the substantial part of the task of rebuilding post-conflict Iraq (as in post-conflict Afghanistan) to those governments and organisations, including the UN, that were more willing to do it and more adept at it. Thus, selective multilateralism enabled the US to finesse its deficits on the 'political science' side of foreign policy, and leverage its strong suit of military strategy and execution.

Whether this division of labour would bear fruit in the Gulf remained to be seen. The United States faced significant and dauntingly disparate political challenges all over the world. Many of these had an important, if subsidiary, counter-terrorism function. But at least they did not appear to necessitate the use of force. While North Korea and Iran posed stiff security and counter-proliferation challenges, Bush refrained from re-branding them nodes on the 'axis of evil' in his January 2003 State of the Union address. There appeared to be reasonable chances that each could be handled through diplomacy: unlike Iraq, North Korea seemed to use WMD threats to extract economic concessions required for state (and, more importantly, regime) survival, while Iran's regional provocations seemed potentially amenable to a burgeoning domestic reform movement, with any nuclear capability several years away. For precisely those reasons, however, Pyongyang and Tehran posed more complex and subtle diplomatic challenges to Washington than did Iraq. The US could not use pre-emptive military force on North Korea without jeopardising South Korea and potentially Japan. Iran's nuclear programme – ostensibly for peaceful power-generation purposes – was thus far 'street legal', if disingenuously so.

Managing allies was almost as big a headache for the US in 2002–03 as managing adversaries. In opposing the use of force in Iraq following Hans Blix's 14 February 2002 report to the UN Security Council favouring further inspections, France and Russia deepened the transatlantic rift carved by perceived Bush administration unilateralism (over the ABM Treaty, the Kyoto accord and trade) and threatened to veto any resolution expressly authorising the use of force. To underline their opposition, France and Germany also blocked NATO from furnishing war-planning assets to

Turkey, which as a member of the alliance was entitled to them under Article 4 of the North Atlantic Treaty. Washington also faced hard financial bargaining – bordering on extortion – from Turkey itself in negotiating access to Turkish soil for US ground troops. Farther south, Ariel Sharon's easy re-election in Israel's elections in February 2003 enabled him to reinforce his hard line vis-à-vis the Palestinians, and made further Israeli settlements in the Palestinian territories more likely. This made American efforts to re-establish a framework for negotiations – for which there would likely be a nearly irresistible demand after Saddam has been swept aside – all the more fraught. The United States' confrontational approach to counter-proliferation and counter-terrorism also discomfited significant constituencies within South Korea and the Philippines.

In the realm of conflict-resolution, there were pressing needs. Despite al-Qaeda's imperviousness to compromise, resolving certain conflicts could remove some of al-Qaeda's putative justifications for terrorism, eliminate potential al-Qaeda allies by alleviating local grievances and deprive al-Qaeda of recruits. In the Middle East, with regime change in Iraq seeming unstoppable by April, the Bush administration no longer seemed able to defer proactive and focused mediation between the Israelis and the Palestinians. Yet diplomatic overstretch limited the amount of attention available for some conflicts of indisputable importance. The Kashmir conflict gave al-Qaeda a pretext and bred potential terrorists, and could lead to a nuclear confrontation between India and Pakistan, who came close to war in 2002. Nevertheless, although there was more scope for internationalising the Kashmir problem in 2002–03 than there was before 11 September, US preoccupations with Iraq, the Israeli–Palestinian conflict, Afghanistan and North Korea barred truly proactive diplomacy in South Asia, and seemed likely to do so in the near future. Al-Qaeda's political exploitation of Chechen rebels and Uighur Muslim separatists in China's Xinjiang province made Russia and China, respectively, less inclined to opt for political solutions. Meanwhile, some conflicts, though falling under the broad category of 'the war on terror', drew US attention on account of domestic American concerns other than terrorism. Following the collapse of Colombia's peace process, US operational assistance to Colombia was poised to expand beyond the anti-narcotics realm into direct counter-insurgency in early 2003, but the main objective remained the same: stemming the flow of cocaine and heroin into the US.

Fears had heightened immediately after the 11 September attacks that weak or failed states would be co-optable by terrorists. The considerable effort to establish Afghanistan as a sustainable democratic polity prompted hope that poverty alleviation and state-building in sub-Saharan Africa would get a serendipitous shot in the arm. Yet, short-term priorities dictated a coalition policy merely of prevention and containment, as in still-anarchic Somalia. While relative calm in former hot spots like the

Ethiopia/Eritrea border and Sierra Leone allowed major powers to stay on the sidelines in East and West Africa, respectively, deprivation and political decadence in Zimbabwe and an unexpectedly persistent insurgency in Côte d'Ivoire loomed as sources of instability that al-Qaeda could conceivably exploit. Though they assumed the vanguard of the ambitious New Partnership for Africa's Development in seeking large aid commitments from Western governments, South Africa and Nigeria – the latter itself plagued by Muslim–Christian tensions – still struggled to realise effective foreign policies that promised substantial improvements in security and stability. South Africa's effective diplomacy in forging three interrelated peace agreements in the Democratic Republic of Congo in 2002, however, suggested that Pretoria was finally starting to take its regional burden seriously. In other parts of the world, there were mixed results. The Sri Lankan ceasefire and peace process continued to have encouraging (and surprising) resilience, and the Indonesian government reached a welcome accommodation with separatists in Aceh and other unstable areas on the country's periphery. Nepal's communist insurgency inched closer to being tamed. The peace process in southern Sudan survived, but was bogged down by continual violations.

As the US and its partners got some purchase on the daily demands of 'hard' counter-terrorism, however, other pressing issues slowly began to draw greater attention. President Bush, in his January 2003 State of the Union message, made fighting the scourge of AIDS in Africa a major priority. After perceived American indifference to the collapse of the Argentine economy, a number of Latin American countries cooled towards the United States. Notably, Brazil turned left, electing a populist president determined to drive a hard bargain with Washington on free-trade issues that Bush had placed at the top of his pre-11 September agenda. With Hugo Chávez – a left-wing populist with anti-American instincts – stubbornly clinging to power in Venezuela (a major oil-producing state), re-establishing US bona fides in Latin America became a more important goal. But the fact that the Bush administration now had to revisit trade issues in earnest was probably more salutary than ominous. Rationalisation of US trade policy could benefit not only Latin American countries, but also African and Asian countries (Pakistan, for example) disadvantaged by protectionist American policies. Moreover, it stood to help smooth transatlantic relations hit by trade disputes over steel and agriculture as well as over persistent differences over Iraq, global warming, and arms control.

Still catching up

The 11 September attacks threw international security into disarray, and a new equilibrium has yet to be reached. The arrests of terrorist suspects in Europe and the US in late 2002 and early 2003, the success of anti-money-laundering efforts, the integrity of the coalition against terrorism built after 11 September and the ongoing coordination of counter-proliferation and counter-terrorism all suggested that the US and its counter-terrorism partners were holding their own against al-Qaeda. But these were yet, in relative terms, early days for a new strategic epoch. In particular, political and legal consensus had not yet caught up with some important strategic agendas. This shortfall was especially relevant to the war in Iraq. The legal basis, strategic rationale and moral case for that war had different roots and justifications. The legality of military intervention was based on a series of UN Security Council resolutions; yet force was used without formal UN endorsement. Strategically, the use of force was intended to pre-empt or prevent the Iraqi regime from using WMD or supplying them to terrorists; yet there remained serious unresolved questions about the legality of pre-emption or prevention in the context of Chapter VII of the UN Charter, which authorises enforcement actions. The moral objective of the Iraq war was to liberate an oppressed people; yet this humanitarian goal – central to the legality of several interventions during the 1990s – was not raised in the debate over the war's legal basis. This failure of major powers and multilateral institutions to integrate considerations of law, strategy and morality added confusion to the diplomatic acrimony that infected the public debate over Iraq. Although the UN was the logical forum for this debate and for resolving these issues, the Iraq question ultimately yielded division rather than consensus.

Yet consensus of a kind did materialise with respect to counter-terrorism – at least as narrowly construed right after 11 September. In the short-term, most states' reaction to 11 September was, appropriately, to decrease vulnerabilities by bolstering homeland security, denying al-Qaeda access to co-optable states and regions and to WMD, killing and arresting terrorists, and developing a horizontal, multinational law-enforcement and intelligence network to better cope with al-Qaeda's horizontal configuration, its virtuality and its standing threat. Not all vulnerabilities could be plugged, however. Accordingly, long-term political and economic diplomacy would be key to defeating al-Qaeda. Because its agenda was not negotiable, these instruments had to aim to outflank rather than tame al-Qaeda. Yet long-term strategies for addressing the root causes of transnational terrorism remained programmatic at best. Absolute poverty was not a major driver of Islamic terrorism, as the bulk of al-Qaeda players appeared to come from middle-class backgrounds. Recruitment seemed to turn on bin Laden's ability to sell the cultural humiliation of Islam and the malfeasance of the 'near enemies' – Egypt in making peace with Israel, Saudi Arabia in allowing US soldiers near the two most holy sites of Islam – as bases for apocalyptic violence against the US and the West. Contributing factors were rising populations and diminishing per-capita GDPs and correspondingly lower relative economic expectations in the

Muslim world, and a sense of political impotence among young Muslims vis-à-vis repressive, undemocratic regimes.

There was no firm consensus even on a general approach, however. This was in part because a tension persisted between short-term necessities – such as American support for illiberal regimes that were indispensable counter-terrorism partners, like General Musharraf's in Pakistan and several governments of the Commonwealth of Independent States – and the patience and faith required to carry out strategies involving the democratisation and economic integration of states that proved resistant to both. The Bush administration's vision of a 'MacArthur decade' in the post-Saddam Gulf could be viewed as an audacious vault from the realism of hard counter-terrorism to the idealism of addressing root causes. But even if regime change proved a relatively bloodless success, hard questions would remain. In broaching political reform in the Arab world, would it make sense to tolerate the authoritarian regimes and rentier states that defeated political Islam at the state level or directly to seek their democratic and economic reform? And in dealing with Muslim diaspora in Europe, what blend of identity politics and assimilationist policies would ensure political moderation? These questions called for concerted attention that was not yet forthcoming.

Perhaps the most immediate concern, however, was rebuilding the international institutions that were so severely buffeted in the Iraq debate. Divisions within Europe on the issue underlined the EU's inability to forge a truly common 'Common Foreign and Security Policy' and the difficulty NATO would have in agreeing on how its assets were to be used, both of which would be exacerbated by the massive planned enlargements of each organisation approved in late 2002. France's and Germany's obstruction of Turkey's access to NATO war-planning assets cast doubt over NATO's capacity to function as a transatlantic organisation. Notwithstanding the unanimous support of the UN Security Council for Resolution 1441, the subsequent split among the Permanent Five pointed to transatlantic and intra-European rifts that lay at the root of the EU's and NATO's problems. With military action against Iraq completed, the first order of strategic business in 2003–04 was to repair these three important institutions.

Strategic Policy Issues

Counter-terrorism and Military Transformation: the Impact of the Afghan Model

In the course of two months, a few hundred Special Forces soldiers and intelligence operatives, working with indigenous insurgents and backed by massive air power, brought down Afghanistan's repressive Taliban regime and denied the al-Qaeda terrorist network the use of much of the country as a safe haven. Much as the 1991 Gulf War stimulated an impending revolution in military affairs (RMA), the success of *Operation Enduring Freedom* in Afghanistan may portend radical changes in the way military units are organised and operate.

In the months that followed the campaign, the 'Afghan model' of warfare gained a growing number of adherents in the US and other governments, the press and academia. This approach to combat has four salient components.

- Special Operations Forces (SOF) acting as sentient sensors to identify targets and direct air strikes, greatly increasing the lethality of precision-guided munitions.

- A common command-control-communications-computers-intelligence- surveillance-and-reconnaissance (C^{4}ISR) grid linking the forces, alleviating (if not resolving) problems in destroying time-critical targets experienced during the Gulf War and in Bosnia and Kosovo. During the war in Afghanistan, for example, US RQ-1 *Predator* unmanned air vehicles (UAVs) beamed imagery not only to command posts in the theatre and the United States, but also directly to AC-130 Spectre gunships, whose crews used the information to improve the responsiveness and lethality of their weapons.

- UAVs such as the *Predator* and the RQ-4 *Global Hawk* gave coalition forces the ability to 'stare' at the battlefield for hours at a time, something that neither satellites nor high-flying, fast-moving reconnaissance aircraft can do.

- The use of SOF to organise, train, equip and lead local forces, with the latter doing the bulk of the fighting.

The Afghan model has become quite influential. According to press reports, it played an important role in the development of the war plan for *Operation Iraqi Freedom*. Some, such as Vice-Admiral Arthur K. Cebrowski, the Pentagon's Director of the Office of Force Transformation, have even argued that it amounts to an 'emerging American way of war'.

More evolution than revolution

The war in Afghanistan stoked rather than sparked interest in acquiring forces that are more rapid and agile. In 1996, the US Defense Science Board sponsored a study of ways to increase the effectiveness of rapidly deployable units. Arguing that in many contingencies current US forces would be too slow to arrive and vulnerable during deployment, the group called for a radical restructuring of a portion of the US military, including the fielding of light, agile ground forces connected by a robust information grid and reliant upon remote sensors and weapons. The following year the US Marine Corps conducted the Hunter Warrior Advanced Warfare Experiment, which tested the ability of dispersed, lightly armed units to hold territory in the face of a numerically superior force.

The late 1990s also saw growing interest in the concept of network-centric warfare (NCW) in the US armed forces and other militaries. NCW proponents argue that modern military forces can acquire a major battlefield advantage by interconnecting widely dispersed commanders, sensors, weapons and troops through a robust information network that would allow participants to develop a shared awareness of the battlefield and pass commands more rapidly than the adversary. As a result, networked forces would potentially be able to deny hostile forces the ability to operate coherently.

The rapid collapse of the Taliban in the face of a relatively small and lightly armed force appeared to bear out these predictions. The perceived lessons of the war have, in turn, influenced US defence priorities. Funding for UAVs, unmanned combat air vehicles (UCAVs), command-and-control systems, satellites, special operations forces and precision-guided munitions has increased. It is worth noting, however, that the campaign has not been subjected to the type of rigorous analysis that followed the 1991 Gulf War. Critics argue that the outcome of the war was idiosyncratic. They contend that it would be foolish to rely on light ground forces backed by air power in future conflicts. They note that operations in Afghanistan involved substantial close combat and that while the Taliban were not the best fighters, al-Qaeda formations frequently offered stiff resistance. Critics also envisage urban and jungle operating environments more foreboding than Afghanistan's. They also maintain that in the future it would be unwise to plan on the availability of effective local forces to carry out the bulk of fighting. As a result, they argue that it would be imprudent to reduce heavy ground forces in favour of SOF and air power. Thus, they note that the failure of US commanders to commit ground forces in sufficient numbers to stop Osama bin Laden from escaping from the Tora Bora mountains in December 2001 revealed a risk-averse culture, and that this culture can be changed only when commanders and line-soldiers alike understand that smaller units – even if protected by better technology – may inevitably be subject to greater risk. Indeed, while the 2003 Iraq intervention would involve a substantially greater reliance on UCAVs and precision-guided munitions (PGMs), the so-called 'heavy option', involving overwhelming force on the ground, was generally more in line with the 1991 Gulf War than with the Afghan model.

American visions of future warfare

In light of al-Qaeda's dispersed, transnational threat, US Secretary of Defense Donald Rumsfeld perceived a global problem that regional commanders were operationally unsuited to address. In his view, US Special Operations Command (SOCOM) – which controls the Army, Navy and Air Force's 46,000 special operations forces – was the military structure best equipped to tackle the military challenges posed by transnational terrorism, and he called for the expansion of the size, budget and responsibilities of SOCOM. The war in Afghanistan was a showcase for special operations forces such as US Army Green Berets, US Navy SEALs and US Air Force Combat Controllers, as well as SOF units from Australia, Britain, Canada, Denmark, Germany, the Netherlands, New Zealand and Norway. During the war, these units conducted reconnaissance, launched strikes, designated targets for air strikes, and trained and advised anti-Taliban forces. The success of US SOF reinforced Rumsfeld's conclusion about the suitability of SOCOM as a prime counter-terrorism instrument.

In January 2003, Rumsfeld announced a plan to increase SOCOM's budget from $4.9 billion to $6bn in the next fiscal year and to add $1bn per year for the next five years. The plan envisions increasing the size of the Special Operations community by 4,000. Some would bolster the US Army's 160th Special Operations Aviation Regiment, which operates helicopters for the special operations community; others would be used to expand the command's planning staff. It would also accelerate the development and acquisition of the controversial CV-22 *Osprey* tilt-rotor aircraft. Perhaps most significantly, the plan would give SOCOM responsibility for monitoring terrorist networks and planning and carrying out covert missions against them worldwide – a significant expansion of the command's traditional mission of supporting regional commanders.

Special operations forces are not, however, a cure-all. While the United States fields more SOF than most other countries, they still represent a scarce and precious commodity. Options for significantly expanding their ranks are limited by the demanding physical and mental qualifications of recruits as well as the extensive training that they must undergo. One approach to bridging this gap is to augment SOF with other highly skilled forces. During *Operation Enduring Freedom*, for example, Navy SEALs in Afghanistan worked closely with US Marine forces. Similarly, the Army's 10th Mountain and 101st Airborne divisions augmented the Green Berets.

Army

Another approach is to make conventional forces more 'SOF-like' by reconfiguring them into smaller, more mobile units. The US Army's interest in such an approach predated the war in Afghanistan by two years. In October 1999 Army Chief of Staff Erik Shinseki announced a goal of reconfiguring the Army into a medium-weight force capable of deploying a 5,000-strong brigade anywhere in the world within 96 hours. The Army is currently reconfiguring six brigades into Stryker Brigade Combat Teams (SBCTs). The first will achieve initial operational capability in May 2003; the Army anticipates fielding all six by the end of 2008. Designed for small regional contingencies, each team will be equipped with over 300 19-tonne Stryker wheeled fighting vehicles. Rather than closing with the enemy, the SBCTs will attempt to identify and engage hostile forces at a distance. To do this, each unit will include a reconnaissance, surveillance and target acquisition (RSTA) squadron designed to locate enemy formations at long range. They will also use information to increase their lethality and survivability. The increase in the minimum operational distance required to engage the enemy will dramatically reduce the standard size of a combat team.

Critics make two arguments against the Army's move to field medium-weight formations. First, they say that such units will lack the firepower to engage a capable adversary, particularly at close range. Second, some contend that the SBCT, even though considerably lighter than a traditional army brigade, will still be unable to meet the Army's goal of deploying anywhere in the world in four days. Moving a brigade's 3,500 troops, 309 armoured vehicles, 700 other vehicles, as well as tonnes of fuel, food, ammunition and supplies would take a heroic airlift effort.

The six SBCTs are meant to constitute an interim stage on the road to fielding what the Army terms the 'Objective Force' in 2010. The centrepiece of this force will be the Future Combat System (FCS), a set of light – possibly unmanned – vehicles that would replace tanks and self-propelled artillery in medium-weight units. The Army envisions that the system will feature a combat vehicle weighing no more than 20 tonnes (compared to the 70-tonne M1 *Abrams*) to allow it to be transported aboard the Air Force's most numerous transport aircraft, the C-130. If it is fielded, the FCS will represent a radical shift away from platforms and toward networks. Even though the Army sees the FCS as the linchpin of its future force structure, there are those who question the technical feasibility of such a system, or at least the aggressive timeline the Army has established for acquiring it. The chief FCS challenge is ensuring adequate intelligence support. Essentially, the concept trades the relative invulnerability owing to a heavy tank's armour for the speed and manoeuvrability deriving from the lighter vehicles. To exploit those qualities to lower risks to the vehicles, however, precise real-time knowledge of the threat environment is critical. Micro-UAVs offer one possible solution.

While the Army is increasingly emphasising medium-weight formations, it does not plan to abandon heavy forces. Instead, it is modernising and 'digitising' its III Corps by upgrading their M1 *Abrams* tanks and M2 Bradley fighting vehicles and modernising their command-and-control systems. The so-called 'Counterattack Corps' would be tasked with stopping an armoured attack in a future regional contingency. While such a balanced approach to change appears sensible, operational demands and budget limitations have forced the Army to shift funds earmarked for the Counterattack Corps to help pay for modernisation.

Navy

The US Navy also has an interest in deploying larger numbers of smaller, networked combatants. During the late 1990s, Admiral Cebrowski, then president of the US Naval War College, championed 'streetfighter', a family of small naval platforms designed to operate in the littorals in the face of a capable adversary. The fact that Secretary of Defense Rumsfeld tapped Cebrowski to head the newly formed Office of Force Transformation has ensured that such ideas have a prominent advocate. While the Navy has yet to fund a 'streetfighter' programme per se, it has committed itself to the Littoral Combat Ship (LCS), a small, fast, and agile craft designed for anti-submarine warfare, naval special warfare missions and mine countermeasures. The LCS will carry unmanned air, surface and subsurface vehicles, and will be networked with other naval combat vessels. Construction of the first ship is to begin in 2005, with the vessel joining the fleet by 2007. The Navy plans to buy nine ships by 2009.

The concept of 'network-centric warfare' has achieved general acceptance within the Navy. There is a widely held belief that networking the Navy's sensors, weapons and command-and-control systems can yield substantial dividends. There is less support, however, for the notion of moving from large combatants to smaller ones. Navy ship acquisition

Strategic Policy Issues

remains dominated by large platforms such as the Navy's new aircraft carrier, the CVNX. Any move towards small naval craft would depart from the US Navy's traditional approach to war in sea. It is much more in keeping with the way smaller navies have organised and trained. It is not surprising, therefore, that over the past two years the United States has sought to tap into its allies' expertise with small craft. The Defense Department has leased a fast ferry from Australia, re-christened the HSV-X1 Joint Venture, for experimentation purposes. The ship was pressed into service in support of Navy SEAL (Sea, Air, Land) teams during the war with Iraq. The Navy also hosted the Norwegian patrol craft *Skjold* for the better part of a year for exercises and experiments.

Air Force

In the air, the most prominent manifestation of the Afghan model is the increasing reliance on UAVs for reconnaissance and surveillance. The Air Force currently operates two squadrons of RQ-1A *Predator* medium-altitude and endurance UAVs. Controlled by ground-based operators, these aircraft transmit electro-optical, infrared and synthetic aperture radar imagery via satellite to ground stations in the United States or the theatre of operations. The Air Force has also tested a system to control a *Predator* from an airborne C-130 *Hercules* transport aircraft. A larger, more powerful version of the *Predator*, known as the *Predator* B, will enter service over the next year. The Air Force is also procuring the *Global Hawk* high-altitude, long-endurance UAV, an aircraft designed to fly 12,500 nautical miles at an altitude of up to 19,200 metres and remain aloft for 38–42 hours. Both saw extensive action against Iraq. The war in Afghanistan also saw the combat debut of UCAVs. During the conflict Central Intelligence Agency (CIA) and Air Force operators flew the MQ-1 *Predator*, armed with AGM-114 *Hellfire* antitank missiles, against Taliban and al-Qaeda targets. In November 2002, one blew up a vehicle identified by US intelligence as carrying a number of senior al-Qaeda commanders in Yemen. Air Force planners also envision equipping UCAVs with air-to-air missiles.

The Air Force and other services are currently developing more ambitious UCAV designs to handle missions such as strike and suppression of enemy air defences. The Air Force and the Defense Advanced Research Projects Agency (DARPA) are sponsoring Boeing's X-45 UCAV demonstrator programme. The initial model of the aircraft, the X-45A, will be able to operate at 10,700 metres and carry a 680-kilogram payload; the follow-on X-45B will be able to operate at 12,200 metres with a 900kg payload including the Joint Direct Attack Munitions (JDAM) and Small-Diameter Bomb (SDB). The X-45A made its first fight in May 2002; if successful, the programme will lead to the fielding of an Air Force UCAV as early as 2008. The Army is set to field its own unmanned combat-armed rotorcraft (UCAR) around 2008. The Navy, meanwhile, wants a naval UCAV operating off its carriers by 2015.

The Defense Department's budget for UAV and UCAV programmes doubled between 2001 and 2002. It is set to double again between 2002 and 2005, and triple between 2002 and 2007. Still, there are a number of significant hurdles that must be surmounted if unmanned systems are to be integrated into the US armed forces. Some are technological. For example, many of the technologies associated with unmanned flight are still maturing, and UAVs are much less reliable than manned aircraft. Others barriers are cultural. Air forces are built around manned flight, and some officers quite naturally see unmanned systems as a threat to their corporate identity.

Marines
The Marine Corps has a history of exploring operational concepts that lend themselves to small, mobile forces. As an expeditionary force, the Marine Corps must of necessity rely upon remote sensors and fires. It contains its own SOF in its Force Reconnaissance battalions. In late 2002, the Marine Corps signed a memorandum of understanding with SOCOM. The agreement represented a considerable shift for the service, which had strenuously resisted inclusion in SOCOM when it was formed in 1987 and had kept it at arm's length thereafter. In 2004, the first detachment of 75 Marines will augment a Naval Special Warfare squadron for a six-month deployment.

The challenge of smaller forces
Efforts to field smaller, less armoured and more mobile forces face a series of hurdles. The first arises out of the difficulty of preparing for a complex security environment. The United States and its major allies must maintain forces for a wide spectrum of potential conflicts. For the foreseeable future, the US armed forces will have to be prepared to engage in operations to track down and eliminate pockets of al-Qaeda operatives across the globe. They will also maintain a deterrent and protective presence in Afghanistan and the Balkans. Finally, they must be ready for high-intensity conflicts against capable regional foes. From January 2003, for example, the United States faced the possibility of war with Iraq and North Korea. Each of these three tasks calls for unique capabilities.

A second challenge is fiscal. Even though the US defence budget has increased markedly under the Bush administration, the US armed forces must balance the need to be ready for short-term contingencies with the need to develop the weapons, doctrine and organisations that future conflicts may require. Although the Bush administration cancelled the Army's *Crusader* self-propelled howitzer and will move a substantial part of the B-1 bomber force to the Air National Guard, such marginal changes will not yield enough savings to fund the modernisation of US forces.

Strategic Policy Issues

As a result, there is a large and growing gap between what is needed and what is funded. One recent report by the Congressional Budget Office estimates that the US defence budget will need to grow 27% over the next 15 years to fund all major programmes.

Perhaps the most formidable challenge has to do with the institutional difficulty of implementing major change. Transforming the US military will require new technology, doctrine and organisation, but also a fundamental reorientation of the culture of the armed services. Whether the US armed forces see a compelling need to change the way they do business is very much an open question. There are, at least, some hopeful signs. A recent survey of over 2,000 US officers shows considerable support for restructuring the US armed forces. Some 57% of the officers surveyed believed that the US armed forces must radically change their approach to warfare to compete effectively with future adversaries. Three-quarters felt that the increased risk to forces posed by an enemy's long-range missiles will require the US military to adopt lighter and more mobile forces and new concepts of operations. And 82% believed that threats to forward bases would require new operational models that allowed the United States to project power without reliance on fixed bases.

Eager Europeans and others

While the US armed forces have gained a lead in fielding light, networked forces, a number of other militaries are also pursuing such an approach. The Australian, British, Canadian, Singaporean and Swedish militaries have all expressed considerable interest in the concept of NCW. All have studied ways to use information technology to increase the effectiveness of their forces, and all are devoting a growing share of their defence budgets to information technology.

Another area that has attracted keen international interest is UAVs and UCAVs. France's Dassault Aviation is working on its 'Duc' series of UAV and UCAV demonstrators. A full-sized demonstrator, 'Grand Duc', could be launched by 2007, leading to a UCAV development programme in the next decade. While the US Air Force controls its UCAVs from a ground station, the French Air Force envisions controlling operational aircraft from the cockpit of a two-seat *Rafael* fighter. The German company EADS is poised to launch a UCAV demonstrator programme with the intent to fly an aircraft in 2006. Britain is interested in a UCAV capability as an element of its Future Offensive Air System programme. In July 2002, Saab Aerospace announced that it had already flown a subscale variant of the Swedish Highly Advanced Research Configuration UCAV.

The end of the Cold War and the disintegration of the Balkans forced NATO's European members to think seriously about the need to field lighter, more mobile forces. The most tangible sign of such a commitment is the Allied Command Europe Rapid Reaction Corps (ARRC), which includes contributions from a number of NATO members. The ARRC is the only NATO force structure designed for deployment outside the NATO region. Individual NATO members, though, have moved more quickly than the alliance as a whole. Britain's 1998 Strategic Defence Review (SDR) accelerated the British Army's transition from a Cold War force organised, trained and equipped for high-intensity operations in Central Europe to one geared toward power projection. The SDR requires the British Army to acquire the capability to deploy a single division for high-intensity operations or to sustain a peacekeeping brigade indefinitely while also deploying an armoured or mechanised brigade for a period of six months.

The British Army is undertaking a number of actions to increase mobility and agility of its units. It is grouping the airborne elements of 5 Airborne Brigade, including two paratroop regiments, with 24 Airmobile Brigade to form 16 Air Assault Brigade. By 2005, the brigade will include three Army Air Corps regiments with a total of 48 WAH-64 *Apache* attack helicopters. The acquisition of the *Apache* is causing the Army to rethink its doctrine. Officers are devising ways to use the helicopter's sensor capabilities, firepower, speed, range, reach and manoeuvrability. Indeed, some argue that the acquisition portends a shift away from the tank and toward the helicopter as the centrepiece of land warfare. In addition, the Army is looking to acquire a very different vehicle as a follow-on to current main-battle tanks. The Mobile Direct Fire Equipment Requirement, or MODIFIER, programme, is exploring much lighter platforms, possibly including ones armed with electromagnetic guns.

Sweden is another state that has seen its role shift since the end of the Cold War. A strategy of territorial defence has yielded to one of global peacekeeping and regional power projection. The Swedish Army's April 2000 restructuring plans call for 16 rapid-reaction battalions, an airborne battalion, an increase in intelligence resources and the establishment of information technology units. At the same time, the Army envisions radically reducing the local defence units and Home Guard that anchored its territorial defence strategy during the Cold War.

A more agile Australasia

European militaries are not the only ones seeking to implement new approaches to combat. Singapore's leadership has emphasised the importance of exploiting technology as a way of compensating for the city-state's lack of strategic depth and shortage of manpower. The Singapore Armed Forces (SAF) place great value on their technological edge. They have purchased highly capable equipment from a range of foreign suppliers as well as Singapore's own robust defence industry.

Strategic Policy Issues

The SAF have paid close attention to discussions in the United States and elsewhere of an emerging RMA. The SAF leadership views information technology as an area of comparative advantage, one of a series of 'silver bullets' it can call upon to compensate for its small size. Singapore's Ministry of Defence has emphasised the need to use information technology to integrate platforms into a unified, flexible and effective system. By harnessing information technology, SAF units will be able to locate, identify and destroy targets more effectively around the clock and in all weather.

Throughout the 1990s, the Republic of Singapore Army (RSA) moved to transform Singapore's ground units into an integrated combined-arms, active/reserve force. The RSA has now established the 21st Division as a rapid deployment force. The division includes air-mobile and amphibious brigades. The unit trains intensively with Air Force helicopter and Navy small-boat units. Still, more junior officers have been impatient, arguing for more radical changes that would flatten unit hierarchies and make them more network-centric.

The Australian Defence Force is also in the process of embracing new approaches to combat. While the raison d'être of the Australian Army has long been territorial defence, what it has actually done repeatedly in recent years is to project power: during the 1990–91 Gulf War, in East Timor and in Afghanistan. The Australian Army is a light force. Moreover, in the Australian Special Air Service–Canberra is one of the world's premier special-forces commands. The requirements of power projection have led the Army to explore new concepts for inserting and sustaining ground forces in the littoral environment. During the late 1990s, the ADF used the converted fast ferry *HMAS Jervis Bay* to support peacekeeping operations in East Timor.

Even the traditional mission of defending the maritime approaches to Australia has led to interest in new approaches to war. One particular focal point is UAV capability. In May and June 2001, the United States dispatched a developmental *Global Hawk* UAV on a trans-Pacific flight to Australia for experiments. The ADF continues to be interested in UAVs and even potentially in UCAVs.

The evolution continues

The US armed forces, together with those of key allies and friends, are adopting technology, doctrine and organisation designed to make their forces lighter and more responsive. Such a trend is a logical reaction to a changing security environment, on one hand, and the promise of new technology, on the other. At the same time, such a move incurs significant risk. Light forces will be more responsive than heavy forces, but they may be less capable in certain scenarios. Attempts to adopt new ways of war must also contend with entrenched military cultures – particularly among senior leaders, who have historically driven change in the military – that may resist radical departures. As a result, although *Operation Enduring Freedom* increased the momentum of military transformation, and despite the remarkable changes that the global security environment has undergone, such transformation will remain slow. Furthermore, the balance of both expenditure and comfort still rests dominantly with legacy systems rather than transformative ones. In any event, while the promise of the Afghan model and the rising utility of special forces in the counter-terrorism arena may accelerate transformation towards quicker and lighter military units, it has relatively little bearing on other key areas of Rumsfeld's transformation vision. These include space-based systems, ballistic missile defence and information warfare. The Pentagon may use Afghanistan as a lever to obtain more transformation funding, but use it disproportionately for these areas rather than SOF per se.

The war with Iraq may serve as a more conventional testing ground for new ways of war. Should light, mobile units prove as successful against Iraq's Special Republican Guard and Republican Guard, the United States and other militaries may accelerate the pace of this area of transformation. If not, then traditionalists in Washington and elsewhere will have new ammunition to oppose change. But even should the resource allocation shift in favour of transformation, the change in military training and culture needed to exploit transformative technologies fully is likely to lag well behind. Wholesale transformation therefore may not be evident for at least a generation.

Missile Defence After 11 September

No security issue so preoccupied the first nine months of an otherwise domestically focused Bush administration than the deployment of global missile defences. Not even the 11 September 2001 terrorist attacks dissipated the administration's enthusiasm for missile defence. If anything, supporters viewed the attacks as added justification: 11 September showed that determined adversaries would us any means available – including ballistic missiles – to threaten the American homeland and its overseas forces and allies. Advocates also feared that an exclusive American dependence on the threat of nuclear retaliation to deter rogue states from using ballistic missiles armed with weapons of mass destruction (WMD) would impede America from intervening in regional crises.

Critics of missile defence saw matters differently. The mere existence of the threat of nuclear retaliation would maintain a satisfactory level of deterrence against the ambitions of rogue states. As for the threat implications of 11 September, opponents promptly elevated al-Qaeda's low-tech yet horrifyingly effective use of jumbo jets as cruise missiles to proof positive that sophisticated means of attacking the US homeland, such as long-range ballistic missiles, were the least likely candidates for al-Qaeda's investment of relatively scarce resources. More relevant, they argued, were the urgent needs of the new Department of Homeland Security (DHS) and the vast array of local and state jurisdictions struggling to cope with unfunded first-responder responsibilities. The adverse impact of missile defences on strategic stability was no longer central to their arguments. While neither Russia nor China agreed with Bush's decision of December 2001 to withdraw six months later from the 1972 Anti-Ballistic Missile (ABM) Treaty, Washington's willingness to reduce offensive nuclear forces and its assurances that missile defences would be limited to a handful of rogue missiles and Moscow's cooperation in the war on terrorism combined to allay concerns about stability.

The corresponding diminution in the traditional salience of mutual assured destruction elevated technical, scheduling and cost issues to centre stage. President George W. Bush recognised that the details do indeed matter, in summer 2001 invoking three criteria: 'Does it work? Is it cost effective? And how does it fit into the priorities of the United States?' But when, on 17 December 2002, he announced a firm date for commencing deployment just prior to the 2004 presidential election, he left little doubt about his administration's commitment to missile defences. At the same time, he breathed new life into the missile-defence debate, leaving several technical and policy obstacles standing in the way of a smooth path towards an early missile defence deployment.

Setting the stage for a deployment decision

Early deployment of global missile defences figured prominently in George W. Bush's 2000 presidential campaign. He did nothing to hide his disdain for the Clinton administration's approach to missile defence, stating bluntly that Clinton was never really serious about missile defence and kept 'moving the goal posts' by continually re-defining deployment criteria. Moreover, Clinton's wish to make any deployment decision conditional on a revised ABM Treaty was seen by Republicans as severely constraining. The inherent limitations of Clinton's proposed land-based system of midcourse interceptors – most notably, its susceptibility to countermeasures – rendered it questionable even for an admittedly limited defence against rogue-state missile threats. Free of the restrictions associated with the ABM Treaty, the Bush administration's intention was to deploy so-called layered defences. In addition to midcourse interceptors, the eventual system would include a boost-phase layer of airborne lasers or sea-launched interceptors, as well as a terminal layer of interceptors to destroy missiles that succeeded in penetrating the other two layers.

Early Missile Defense Agency (MDA) briefings emphasised an intensive research, development, test and evaluation programme without any commitment to a single architecture. Beyond stipulating the need for a multi-layered development programme, the MDA distinguished the Bush and the Clinton programmes by drawing all missile-defence capabilities under the management of one system. Thus, a global missile-defence system would not only protect the US homeland, but allies and deployed forces, too. And given the new freedom born of the demise of the ABM Treaty, the MDA could begin seriously to explore air, sea, ground and space missile-defence concepts designed to intercept any range of missile threat. Anticipating developments, the MDA also indicated that test assets could be used as operational systems on an interim basis if so directed by the president.

Another important change in emphasis introduced by the Bush administration was the application of 'capabilities-based' as distinct from 'threat-based' planning to guide defence decision-making. Traditionally, major defence acquisition programmes required specific explication and validation of the threat in order to justify the expenditure of major resources. Secretary of Defense Donald Rumsfeld had emerged from chairing the 1998 Commission to Assess the Ballistic Missile Threat to the United States appreciative of the tendency to underestimate the tenacity, resourcefulness and determination of adversaries to acquire WMD and their means of delivery. Rumsfeld formalised the new emphasis on capabilities-based planning in the 2001 Quadrennial Defense Review. It is predicated on the belief that, since no one can know with confidence precisely what and when threats will arise, capabilities must be developed to handle a full range of likely future challenges rather than a narrow set of predictable threat scenarios. Bush's defence planners saw virtue in such an approach not only as a means of positioning the US to cope with threats before they emerge, but also in deterring adversaries from pursuing certain threat capabilities in the first place.

The Bush deployment plan

There were hints of an early deployment decision prior to the president's 17 December 2002 declaration. A year before this announcement, the administration's Nuclear Posture Review had specified a deployment of an emergency missile-defence capability sometime between 2003 and 2008. In summer 2002, the Pentagon's prestigious Defense Policy Board urged the administration to focus more sharply on the most promising missile-defence elements. Still, the Bush plan was greeted with some surprise. Critics naturally castigated the president's decision as premature, given the absence of adequate operational testing to confirm whether or not the system would actually work. Even some supporters were surprised that more time would not be devoted to exploring formerly prohibited types of interceptors and radars before moving towards early deployment. At least one consequence of the administration's narrower focus was the elimination of plans to experiment with space-based laser technology. That the president chose to declare the most advanced elements of the existing programme officially operational as of October 2004, a month before his presumed re-election run, suggests an effort to deliver on a longstanding Republican Party priority to protect the American public from ballistic-missile attacks. Just how much protection any early deployment system would furnish, however, is a matter of great debate.

Consistent with earlier MDA briefings indicating a readiness to press the system's test-bed elements into operational service, the president's plan combines existing prototype and test assets to provide what administration officials admit is only a modest ballistic-missile defence (BMD) capability in the 2004–05 timeframe. Ironically, the Bush administration has no choice but to depend upon the chief BMD legacy of the Clinton administration: ground-based interceptors (GBIs) employing exo-atmospheric kill vehicles (EKVs) that essentially are launched into space to find and destroy enemy ballistic-missile warheads by force of impact – the proverbial 'hitting a bullet with a bullet' or 'hit-to-kill' (HTK) interception. Twenty GBIs would be deployed by the end of 2005: 16 at Fort Greely, Alaska (six in 2004 and ten more in 2005); and four at Vandenberg Air Force Base, California (all in 2004). While GBIs would deal with intercontinental-range ballistic missiles (ICBMs), the Bush plan would accelerate the deployment of 20 sea-based interceptors placed on three *Aegis*-class cruisers/destroyers, as well as an unspecified number of *Patriot* PAC-3 interceptors, to deal with short- and medium-range ballistic missiles. To furnish the required target detection and tracking information to enable these interceptors to work, the system would bring together existing Defense Support Program (DSP) infrared early warning satellites, an upgraded *Cobra Dane* radar at Shemya, Alaska, a new sea-based X-band radar, SPY-1 radars based on *Aegis*-class ships and upgraded ground-based early warning radars in the UK and Greenland, which would require the approval of the British and Danish governments respectively.

The Bush plan does state that additional capabilities will be added to the 2004–05 deployment elements over time. These would complement the plan's initial emphasis on the midcourse layer. In addition to enhanced radars and space-based infrared sensors, among the most notable additional capabilities would be *Patriot* PAC-3 batteries and, eventually, the US Army's Theater High Altitude Area Defence (THAAD) system.

Relatively slow-moving *Patriot* PAC-3 interceptors would not provide any terminal defence against ICBMs operating at re-entry velocities of 7–8km per second; they would be fortunate to protect their own launch position against ICBMs. They are designed to deal primarily with slower-flying short- and medium-range missiles. Because THAAD is designed to defend against short- and medium-range missiles at significant distances from its intended target and at high altitudes (that is, just as the missiles are re-entering the atmosphere), its batteries would provide fairly broad protection of dispersed assets and population centres – an 'upper tier' capability. Short- and medium-range missiles that managed to avoid THAAD interception would then have to deal with PAC-3 interceptors. However, THAAD's test history sounds a cautionary note about the danger of rushing programmes ahead without adequate developmental and operational testing. In the mid to late 1990s, the THAAD test programme was compressed in order to furnish a prototype for early deployment. As a result, the interceptor experienced serious test difficulties leading to a major restructuring of the programme. The MDA now characterises the THAAD programme as 'disciplined development' designed to produce successful flight-test results. Viewed as a global missile defence system, PAC-3 and THAAD would constitute the Terminal Defence Segment (TDS). Although the joint US–Israeli *Arrow* is not mentioned in the president's December 2002 announcement, it too could conceivably become a part of the TDS element of a global missile-defence system, as it provides upper-tier capabilities not dissimilar to THAAD's (though *Arrow* employs an conventional warhead intercept whereas THAAD uses HTK technology).

To complement the so-called Midcourse Defense Segment (MDS), comprised mainly of GBIs, the Bush plan will add more *Aegis*-based interceptors, featuring the Standard Missile-3 (SM-3). The MDA and the US Navy have recently accelerated SM-3 flight-tests and successfully demonstrated the capability to intercept a ballistic missile (short- and medium-range missiles) in the ascent phase of flight, which is essentially the early phase of the target missile's midcourse flight. Interception during the ascent phase would, in theory, help to reduce the overall system's susceptibility to countermeasures by furnishing multiple shot opportunities during the midcourse phase of flight. Thus, GBIs and the sea-based midcourse capability on *Aegis* ships would make up the MDS element of the overall system.

Notably absent from the 2004–05 plan is any capability to cope with threats in the boost phase of the target missile's flight history – a phase lasting no longer than 3–5 minutes while the target missile is thrusting to gain the acceleration to reach the early midcourse phase outside the earth's atmosphere. Although the boost phase is short, successful interception would destroy the missile before countermeasures were deployed, regardless of the missile's range or intended aim-point. Ideally conceived, boost-phase intercept furnishes global protection against ballistic missiles. More practically, it lowers the risks due to limitations inherent in each segment of a layered missile-defence system. The Bush plan would begin to address the Boost Defense Segment (BDS) essentially with a two-pronged approach. In the directed energy area, it intends to deploy the Airborne Laser aircraft, currently configured on a wide-bodied 747-400 airplane with a multi-megawatt chemical laser, once it proves itself operationally worthy, probably late in the decade at the earliest. A common family of boost-phase and midcourse kinetic kill interceptors will also be explored as a future complement to the early plan's limited capabilities. A sea-based programme, likely involving *Aegis* ships, is focused on a high-acceleration booster coupled with a boost kill vehicle. Both the Airborne Laser aircraft and *Aegis*-based boost-phase options necessitate deploying in close proximity (say, within 800km) to the launch-point of the target ballistic missile. A more radical and longer-term concept is to detect missile launches with a satellite in a low-earth orbit and then manoeuvre the satellite closer to the launched missile in order to intercept it in its boost phase with a kinetic kill vehicle. A month after the early deployment plan was announced, the MDA said publicly that it hoped to launch 3–5 experimental satellites, beginning in 2008, and two to three more every two years after that, to form a space-based interceptor test-bed for boost-phase interception. This complementary array of programmes underscores the importance of achieving success in the critical boost phase of a missile's flight history.

Form over substance

There are good reasons to believe that the president's early deployment plan will provide a more theoretical than substantive capability to deal with emerging ballistic-missile threats. Rumsfeld called the rudimentary deployment merely 'better than nothing', and although the system appears most relevant to defeating threats emanating from North Korea, White House officials say the deployment decision was unrelated either to Pyongyang's nuclear ambitions or its threat to abrogate a missile-testing moratorium. Bush administration officials do not pretend that the 2004–05 deployment elements of a longer-term evolutionary deployment system will provide much protection.

The latest US National Intelligence Estimate (NIE), issued in January 2002, concludes that the United States most likely will face ICBM threats from North Korea and Iran before 2015. Further, George J. Tenet, Director of Central Intelligence, testified on 11 February 2003 that North Korea now possesses an untested three-stage *Taepo-dong*-2 missile that is capable of delivering a nuclear device to targets in the western United States. US intelligence officials have indicated, however, that this estimate is not based on any newly demonstrated North Korean capabilities, but rather the same evidence that led intelligence officials to conclude in the late 1990s that Pyongyang was moving closer to flight-testing the *Taepo-dong-2*.

Iran, for its part, is lagging behind North Korea in developing both nuclear weapons and their means of delivery, although recent evidence suggests progress in both fields. Western news reports indicate that Iran has accelerated its drive to produce materials needed to develop nuclear weapons. The first test of the Iranian *Shahab-4*, a two-stage, 2,000km-range ballistic missile, is expected to take place soon. Iran has experienced decidedly mixed test results with the shorter-range *Shahab-3*, and run into particular difficulty with engines, seeking help from Russia and North Korea. Iran is thought to have incorporated the *Taepo-dong-1* engine into the *Shahab-4* to enhance prospects for success. Should the *Shahab-4* be perfected, it could threaten targets in Europe and represent a possible stepping-stone to an ICBM.

The working hypothesis of the 1998 Rumsfeld Commission was that countries like North Korea and Iran would not require the same quality and frequency of missile flight testing that the US and Soviet Union practiced before declaring a missile operationally capable. Thus, North Korea would only need to achieve a rudimentary operational capability to threaten the US during a crisis. Hence, it is conceivable that North Korea could possess such a capability roughly when the Bush system is launched in late 2004. With both the offence and defence possessing marginally tested capabilities, form will truly match form. The substance of such a limited missile-defence deployment depends heavily on the nature and extent of operational testing. Because real-world missile-defence engagements occur over such short time periods, any system inevitably must be highly pre-programmed to reflect the full range of threat possibilities – including, for example, alternative missile trajectories, the use of countermeasures and details about the characteristics of the target re-entry vehicle. If, say, the North Koreans conducted only a few flight tests, information on real-world threat characteristics might be extremely limited, leaving both the offence and defence to operate with great uncertainty. Thus, the 2004–2005 rudimentary deployment system would be limited to intercepting North Korean missiles flying on pre-determined trajectories, displaying past flight conditions and carrying either no decoys or very simple ones similar to those seen prior to engagement. Not until more robust discrimination capabilities become available, especially as sea-based X-band radars and the Space-Based Infra-Red System satellites are deployed, will the missile-defence system be capable of intercepting missiles fired from the Middle East or accidental or unauthorised launches from China or Russia with confidence – a goal of the Clinton administration's initial operational capability. So to Bush's primary question – does it work? – the answer would have to be potentially, but only in a circumscribed way.

Strategic Policy Issues

Near-term technical hurdles

Only 21 months separates the president's announcement of a rudimentary deployment of missile defences and the system's intended date of operational capability in October 2004. The stiffest near-term technical hurdle is producing a reliable operational booster to launch exo-atmospheric kill vehicles into space. Thus far, the test programme has depended on surrogate boosters made from *Minuteman* II ICBMs. In the meantime, two contractors, Lockheed Martin and Orbital Sciences, which are already two years behind schedule, are feverishly trying to produce a workable operational booster. As far as meeting the desired October 2004 deployment date, two 'make-or-break' booster tests are scheduled to occur in spring and summer 2003. According to MDA Director Lieutenant General Ronald Kadish, should these critical tests reveal any problems, the deployment schedule would likely be affected. What makes these tests so critical is the need to demonstrate that the higher accelerations associated with the production booster do not adversely affect other system components.

The booster problem poses a broader difficulty arising from the conflation of research and development (R&D) and operational testing. At the conclusion of R&D testing, major weapon systems normally undergo significant operational testing before they are permitted to commence full-rate production. Having completed ten GBI tests, the current ground-based midcourse programme is roughly in the middle of its developmental testing schedule. Critics argue that developmental testing needs to be made more realistic by incorporating not just different types of decoys and countermeasures but differing target trajectories, multiple targets and unfavourable meteorological conditions. Kadish told a Senate subcommittee in March 2002 that, if test facilities were compressed into operational service, the MDA would lose some of its ability to test. This position changed after the president's late 2002 deployment decision. Now, the MDA argues that, once the MDS segment becomes operational, the US Army would assume control of all relevant facilities. Left unanswered is whether or not the tough testing conditions required to deal with the most notable technical hurdles will become central to the army's mandate. There are, of course, numerous historical precedents for deploying strategic weapon systems before initial operational testing, and even in the absence of any formal operational test phase. But, given the uncertainties and significant technical hurdles remaining, short-changing realistic operational testing would seem fundamentally inconsistent with the president's criterion of, 'does it work?'

The most substantial technical hurdle in the US missile-defence programme is achieving adequate performance against simple countermeasures. The HTK approach depends on distinguishing real enemy targets from decoys. Sceptical analysts argue that any country capable of building ICBMs armed with WMD could readily implement simple but effective countermeasures; in other words, the offence will always possess a decided advantage over the defence, particularly when the defence is handcuffed by virtue of its dependence on highly complex and fastidious HTK technology. Supporters of missile defence assert that these critics overstate the ease of developing such countermeasures, which themselves require extensive testing before they are useful. Once such countermeasures testing is detected, the defence, especially one with decided resource advantages, could readily neutralise such threats.

The offence/defence debate aside, a growing number of scientists in and out of government have privately expressed doubts about the robustness of the HTK approach. This doubt came bubbling to the surface in April 2002 when the Chairman of the Defense Science Board admitted publicly that he had received encouragement from Rumsfeld to begin exploring alternative modes of missile interception, including use of a nuclear-tipped interceptor. Russia's antiquated ABM system ringing Moscow still remains wedded to nuclear-tipped interceptors, while the US used the same approach in its short-lived *Safeguard/Sentinel* missile-defence system in the mid-1970s. Today, instead of using a fairly large-yield nuclear device that might cause collateral effects on commercial and military space assets nearby, the idea would be to marry HTK's accuracy to very small-yield nuclear devices, thereby relieving the interceptor of the difficult burden of discriminating true warheads from fake objects. HTK technology would guide the nuclear-tipped interceptor into an area surrounding a cluster of objects within which everything would be vaporised, ensuring destruction of even missile-borne biological agents. Supporters of such an approach take heart in the Bush administration's willingness to examine the utility of low-yield nuclear devices for deeply buried targets. They essentially contend that the defence community is obliged to examine all technically robust solutions to such an enduring and high-priority security requirement as protecting the American people and allies from catastrophic attacks. Still, the MDA insists that it has no requirement for such a nuclear solution, on the grounds that HTK has demonstrated that it works – even though no one would claim that it has yet demonstrated robustness in realistic operational testing environments.

Alternatives to ballistic missiles

One clear lesson of 11 September is that exclusive focus on the long-familiar threat of ballistic missiles risks neglecting more novel yet likely ways of threatening the American – or any nation's – homeland. The early stages of the war in Iraq furnished an additional lesson. *Patriot* missile-defence batteries performed well against ballistic missiles, but not against ancient *Silkworm* anti-ship cruise missiles, which succeeded in flying under *Patriot* radar. This phenomenon highlighted the dilemma of configuring the *Patriot* system to deal with both high-angle ballistic and low-flying cruise missile threats. It would mean a change in the rules of engagement. During the 1991 Gulf War, with Iraq's aircraft threat eliminated and no need for concern about low-flying threats, coalition forces could train the *Patriot* on high-angle threats (i.e., ballistic missiles) alone, and did not have to worry about distinguishing friendly returning aircraft and enemy cruise missiles. After the first cruise-missile attack on 20 March 2003, which was not detected at all and struck dangerously close to a US Marine encampment in Kuwait, coalition forces began to worry about low-fliers. That may be why a British *Tornado* fighter was mistakenly shot down by a *Patriot* – and indeed why an American F-16 fighter fired on a *Patriot* missile battery after the *Patriot*'s radar had locked onto it. The Iraqis also succeeded in flying ultra-light aircraft over a large US Army camp without detection. Fortunately, no chemical or biological agents were used, nor were any 'kamikaze' attacks executed. But the Iraqi probes underscored the need for improvements in defences against cruise missiles and other non-ballistic missile threats.

National Intelligence Estimates have routinely noted that the United States is less likely to be attacked by an ICBM than an array of other less costly, easier to acquire and more reliable means. Deputy Secretary of Defense Paul Wolfowitz has expressed concern about 'outlaw states' attempting to launch short-range ballistic missiles from a ship. There are a host of even cheaper and more reliable options. In August 2002, Rumsfeld sent a classified memorandum to the White House warning about the increasing threat of cruise missiles and unmanned aerial vehicles (UAVs), observing that terrorist groups might take existing aircraft or anti-ship cruise missiles and convert them into unmanned drones capable of WMD attacks. Such attacks could conceivably emanate from offshore commercial ships or, in the case of small UAVs, from domestic locations. By late January 2003, Bush reportedly was concerned, based on new intelligence, about Iraq's development of small, easily transportable UAVs that could be shipped into the United States or built domestically and then used to deliver biological or chemical agents. This concern may in part explain the Federal Aviation Administration (FAA)'s re-imposition of restricted air space for general aviation in the Washington DC metropolitan area in late January 2003, as well as the declaration of 'code orange', the penultimate terrorist alert, by the DHS.

In spite of the growing recognition of alternative ways to threaten the American homeland and its overseas interests, it is not clear that sufficient bureaucratic and budgetary attention has focused on these new threats – at least in comparison with the priority that ballistic-missile defence programmes continue to receive. Rumsfeld's August 2002 warning to the White House called for an intensified government-wide effort to defend against cruise missiles and armed UAVs. The cost of doing so would be significant. Even a limited defence against offshore cruise missiles would cost at least $30–40 billion. The North American Aerospace Defense Command (NORAD) is currently studying the idea of an unmanned airship operating at an altitude of 21,000 metres and carrying sensors to monitor and detect offshore low-flying cruise missiles. Several such airships would be needed together with fast-moving interceptors to cope with detected threats. A system of perhaps 100 aerostats flying at an altitude of 4,600 metres could act as a complementary or alternative system of surveillance and fire control for an interceptor fleet. But none of these measures would be adequate to address offshore cruise-missile threats without some means of warning the Coast Guard on potentially hostile ships embarking from ports of concern. In addition, sensor data on missile threats must be able to distinguish between friendly and enemy targets prior to engagement. Progress in national cruise-missile defence will not occur without corresponding improvements in respective service programmes to cope with cruise-missile threats in overseas military contingencies. But the latter efforts lack the necessary funding and are burdened by longstanding service interoperability, doctrinal and organisational constraints.

Finally, even if these costs were absorbed or the technical challenges overcome, the problem of defending against UAVs from domestic points of origin would remain unaddressed. In the aftermath of 11 September, NORAD had no internal air picture, nor were its radar assets linked with those of the FAA, which controls internal air traffic. Progress towards creating such a link has occurred since 11 September, but major holes remain, especially with respect to detecting low- and slow-flying air targets. Sophisticated lookdown radars on today's airborne sensors would not detect UAVs flying at speeds of less than 80 knots, as such sensor platforms eliminate slow-moving objects on or near the ground to prevent their data-processing and display systems from being overtaxed. In sum, missile defences against offshore cruise missiles and domestic terrorist attacks employing small aircraft will remain operationally and technically problematic as well as financially taxing for at least the next decade. The fact that cost has not been a main driver of national ballistic-missile defence only amplifies the challenge of financing cruise-missile defence.

Budgetary woes

Despite a comparative lack of concern about cost, the near-term impact of ballistic-missile defences on overall budget priorities appears manageable on the surface. While the president's overall fiscal-year (FY) 2004 budget request for defence increases by 4% to $380bn, spending for ballistic-missile defence increases by 12%, from $8.1bn to $9.1bn. Over the longer term, however, competing priorities are certain to raise questions about the relative merits of spending on ballistic-missile defences along with the rising costs of homeland security and the modernisation of conventional military forces. According to the Center for Strategic and Budgetary Assessments, since 11 September 2001, US funding for defence, homeland security and the war on terrorism has increased by roughly $145–160bn over what would have been projected in these areas over the 2001–03 time period. While Bush's proposed FY2004 budget earmarks a 9% increase for homeland security, the demands associated with the challenge are formidable. The protracted political bickering over the tardy appropriation bill for FY2003 suggests more to come. The urgent needs of first responders, together with the fiscal pressures faced by the local and state entities that employ them, assure that homeland security funding will remain politically contentious through the 2004 presidential campaign.

Fiscal pressure will also come from the growing demands on the US military to meet its increasingly overstretched obligation to help fight the war on terrorism, deal with Iraq, worry about the readiness of its overtaxed capital stock and manage a huge modernisation of its force structure. The $380bn FY2004 budget request for defence does not include the $1.6bn monthly cost of the war on terror, nor the expected cost of war and post-war obligations related to Iraq. Republicans and Democrats alike on the House Armed Services Committee reacted to the president's 2004 budget request by stating that it was $43–100bn short of the monies needed to maintain conventional forces and modernise capital stocks, build a layered missile-defence system and invest in new technologies to keep ahead of any potential peer competitor. Given that the FY2004 defence request is 16% higher than all other discretionary spending combined, and that the budget deficit is projected to grow to $307bn during that period, without considering the costs of war with Iraq, it seems clear that near-term budgetary problems will grow. Over the longer term, the costs of a layered missile-defence system will undoubtedly impinge on other defence, homeland security and discretionary domestic needs. Today's ballistic-missile defence spending, which is almost exclusively for R&D, absorbs less than 2.5% of the overall defence budget. As layers are added and procurement costs grow, defence outlays for missile defence could exceed 10% of US defence spending after 2010. Proponents naturally argue that the nation's security has no limits. But while public support for missile defence is typically close to 70%, it plummets when the question is framed in terms of alternative choices between missile defence and domestic spending programmes.

Allies aboard?

Prior to the United States' formal withdrawal from the ABM Treaty in June 2002, European attitudes toward ballistic-missile defence remained fixated on the adverse impact such a withdrawal would have on strategic stability. Yet by late November 2002, alliance officials at the NATO summit in Prague leapfrogged over tentative plans to study theatre missile defences to launch a new study to develop strategic missile-defence systems to protect the whole of European territory. The US has expressed its desire to assist European governments to deploy missile-defence systems that might become part of a truly global system of defences. However, that assistance will be manifested not in terms of US financial support but in the provision of technical insight into US development programmes and possible European industrial participation in major missile-defence development and procurement initiatives. Just how willing European governments will be to commit the huge financial sums required for any significant deployments on European soil remains doubtful.

Washington's more immediate concern was to secure the UK and Danish governments' approval to proceed with the upgrading of critically important radar-warning facilities needed to deal with ballistic missiles launched from the Middle East. Coincidentally with Bush's 17 December 2002 announcement of his 2004 deployment decision, the US government formally requested the UK and Danish governments to permit the upgrading of radars at the Royal Air Force's Fylingdales base in northeast England and in Thule, Greenland, respectively. In February 2003, London approved the upgrade; Copenhagen was expected to do so as well. The UK is particularly interested in securing an inside track on industrial participation in the US missile-defence programme and the British Ministry of Defence will probably seek to fashion a new technical memorandum of understanding with the MDA, replacing the one originally put in place during the Reagan administration's Strategic Defense Initiative.

Japan, for its part, has quietly nudged closer to making a decision to proceed beyond research to develop and deploy missile defences. During a bilateral defence ministers' meeting on 17 December 2002 in Washington, the US tested Tokyo's interest in equipping its *Aegis* destroyers with the same missile-defence interceptor it intends to deploy on its own *Aegis* vessels. Japan agreed to conduct a feasibility study, putting off any formal commitment for the immediate future. Events in North Korea, not least any abrogation by Pyongyang of its self-imposed moratorium on missile testing, undoubtedly will affect Tokyo's decision-making. Although Pyongyang may push Japan over the edge on development, several factors are destined to constrain Tokyo's longer-term plans for missile defences. Topping the list are the unwanted consequences of adding the cost of missile defences to Japan's already huge budget deficit, meshing command-and-control arrangements with Washington without violating Japanese constitutional restrictions on the use of force, and facing up to the inevitable diplomatic hammering from Beijing and other worried capitals in Asia that Tokyo would endure in the event of deployment.

Strategic Policy Issues

The way ahead

President Bush entered office promising to deploy missile defences. His 17 December 2002 announcement just before his expected run for a second term in November 2004 aims to deliver on that promise. The 11 September attacks in no way detracted from Bush's determination. In fact, the subsequent war on terrorism helped enable a relatively smooth political transition in particular, an uneventful abrogation of the ABM Treaty and the consequent elimination of its highly restrictive provisions on missile-defence testing and deployment. Technical hurdles, especially coping adequately with countermeasures in any mid-course defence layer, remain. But absent the ABM Treaty, the administration seems determined to turn the corner on boost-phase and terminal layers eventually to muster a modest and limited missile-defence system for protecting the homeland and a far more substantial one to protect against regional missile attacks.

Although not as forcefully as critics might wish, the attacks of 11 September also seem to have affected the Bush administration's strategic calculations about how potential adversaries might wish to threaten the American homeland. Protecting the homeland and overseas forces against cruise-missile attacks has become an increasingly prominent feature of the administration's defence priorities, though much more needs to be done. The same holds true for protecting the homeland from terrorist use of WMD. In that sense, 11 September has compelled the administration to take a more even-handed approach to threats to the homeland. The challenge will be paying the bill on an ever-expanding array of national security requirements. No less daunting will be the political imperative of integrating increasingly more effective global missile defences into an overarching strategic vision that maintains stable relations with Russia, China and other major powers. Missile defences have not yet seriously affected strategic stability. But, in the medium term, layered defences will likely demonstrate significantly greater performance effectiveness. Newer defences may utilise space-based systems, crossing a symbolic barrier that smacks of the 'militarisation' of space. In light of these technical prospects, the steadily expanding gap between American military capabilities and any conceivable competitor's, and a national security strategy explicitly emphasising pre-emption, global missile defences seem destined to resurrect concerns about strategic stability.

The Changing Oil Equation

Oil issues loomed large in 2002. The year began with the threat of an oil price war between Russia and Saudi Arabia, but soon gave way to a less sanguine supply reality as Iraq's struggles with the United States and United Nations over its illegal smuggling activities prompted a slowdown in Iraqi oil exports via the UN's oil-for-food programme. Tensions came to a peak on 8 April when Iraqi President Saddam Hussein announced a complete shut-off of all UN-monitored exports for 30 days, calling on other fellow Arab oil producers to follow suit in protest of Western support for Israel. Iran and Libya initially said they might favour such a boycott but later backtracked, buoying consumer confidence that the oil weapon might be harder to employ in this decade than in the past. But a renewed Organisation of Petroleum Exporting Countries (OPEC)/non-OPEC agreement on 29 December 2001 to limit flows of oil to international consumers did not bode well for prospects that oil would be readily available at cheap prices to stimulate a lagging world economy.

Moreover, unrest in Venezuela left markets shaken. Venezuela's problems simmered until 2 December 2002, when Venezuelan oil workers initiated a work stoppage designed to bring down Hugo Chavez's presidency by depriving his regime of critical oil revenues. Venezuela's oil production of almost 3 million barrels per day (b/d) was reduced to a trickle by mid-December and averaged around 400,000 b/d in early 2003, pushing oil prices above $30 per barrel. Venezuelan oil production began recovering in March 2003 to 1.5–2m b/d, but long-term damage to certain aging oil fields is likely to emerge over time, preventing restoration of Venezuela's previous exporter status. Venezuela's oil production, which might have been expected to grow to 5 or 6m b/d by the end of the decade, could easily remain static, or even decline to below 2m b/d following serious damage to its reservoirs during and in the immediate aftermath of the oil workers' strike. Extended well shut-ins, damaged infrastructure and restricted cash flow are expected to make it difficult for Venezuela to stabilise its oil production. Even foreign oil operations in Venezuela are suffering from inadequate access to transportation infrastructure and full storage facilities, and a shortage of gas supplies needed for heavy crude conversion processes. The future productivity of fields with high dependence on reservoir pressure and temperature is being called into question by the massive, strike-related lay-offs inside state-owned oil company Petroleos de Venezuela SA's technical and managerial classes. Finally, continued unrest in Venezuela has created an uncertain investment climate that is likely to deter investors for the foreseeable future. Deep social and political divisions remain, and are not likely to be easily resolved.

Strategic Policy Issues

The deterioration of Venezuela's status as a key oil supplier and exporter is likely to have deleterious consequences for the future stability of international oil markets that have yet to be fully appreciated in oil circles. Venezuela's oil minister has been touring major investment and oil trading centres to assure participants that Caracas will be able to fully restore its oil production and export rates to 3m b/d within four months, but the reality is less sanguine. In early 2003, Venezuela struggled to fend off a 25% decline in production rates in some fields. Damage to key reservoirs will make improvement difficult. Any drop in Venezuela's sustainable oil-production capacity to below 2m b/d will greatly diminish OPEC's ability to keep up with expected growth in demand in coming years, accentuating oil market volatility. The 3 November 2002 earthquake in Alaska also contributed to the sense of insecurity about oil supplies, as did unrest in oil-producing provinces in Nigeria, export disruptions in Colombia following guerrilla attacks on oil facilities and continued instability in the Middle East and Indonesia. These events, along with terrorist attacks on a French oil tanker, a failed al-Qaeda plot to sabotage oil facilities in Saudi Arabia and the US-led war with Iraq, have shaken Western consumers' sense of supply security.

The 11 September effect

The 11 September terrorist attacks changed the landscape of oil geopolitics for the coming decades. The US-led 'war on terror' has raised awareness in the US and abroad about the inherent risks of relying too heavily on Middle Eastern oil supplies. New emphasis has been placed on finding diverse alternative sources for oil supply. Very soon after 11 September, Russia offered to help the West through a concrete programme to boost its oil flows. The importance of other non-OPEC producers and non-conventional energy sources has been revisited in policy discussions, with oil diplomacy initiatives emanating not just from Washington, but also from Moscow, Tokyo, Beijing and New Delhi. Nevertheless, the near-term global dependence on Middle Eastern oil is virtually inescapable. More than 60% of the world's remaining conventional oil reserves are concentrated in the Middle East, which is currently supplying close to a third of global oil demand. A quarter of these reserves sit in Saudi Arabia alone. Iran, Iraq, Syria, Sudan and Libya – so-called 'countries of concern' to the US – produce around 8m b/d at present, or about 10% of world oil supply. Saudi Arabia alone is responsible for almost 10% of world supply and holds a unique position in oil markets. It maintains the largest share of spare idle production capacity of any other nation in the world. The Kingdom is the only oil producer that can replace single-handedly, within a short period of time, the total loss of exports for any other oil producer on the globe. Saudi Arabia demonstrated the importance of this role as 'swing producer' in the weeks running up to the military campaign in Iraq.

Given the pivotal position of Arab oil producers, developing strategies to change the oil status quo dramatically and significantly lessen dependence on the Middle East, or Saudi Arabia in particular, holds tremendous challenges. Still, US politicians and analysts are seeking options to sustain America's economic culture of oil plenitude in a manner that does not require increased dependence on the Middle East. This oil-supply conundrum has produced two distinct ideological camps in the United States energy-policy community. The first – markedly liberal in its market orientation – calls for a major grassroots initiative in energy source diversity. Proponents of this school range from serious Democratic presidential candidates such as Senator Joseph Lieberman, who is calling for a national initiative on renewable energy sources, to those who link America's fondness for fuel-guzzling vehicles and the concomitant need for close ties with Saudi Arabia to tacit support for international terrorism.

The second ideological trend, which has prominent supporters inside the Bush administration and is therefore more politically significant, is the neo-conservative game plan that would reshape Iraq in the aftermath of the US military campaign into a market-conforming economy. Under this view, regime-change in Iraq would have a domino effect on politics in the Middle East, leading eventually to positive liberalising reform throughout the region. This influential group – most notably represented by Richard Perle, a fellow at the American Enterprise Institute and formerly a leading member of the Defense Policy Board – take the position that change in Iraq could be steered to bring more democratic practices and market economy principles to the Middle East, while leveraging expanding Iraqi oil production – facilitated by the privatisation of its oil industry – to undermine the dominance of other oil producers and render OPEC less important. This is a highly optimistic and arguably unrealistic scenario. While no one can say with certainty how democratic change in Iraq might alter the region, autocracy has always been a dominant feature of the Middle Eastern political landscape. In most countries in the region, organised political parties have failed to take firm root in the political soil. Islamist elements have also developed considerable grassroots political support in several conservative Arab states. Thus, it remains unclear whether democratisation – at least in the sense of free and fair elections – would bring American-style liberalism to the region. The experience of Algeria is a cautionary example: the 1991 elections brought an Islamic party victory, prompting a controversial invalidation of the results by the existing regime, followed by a bloody civil war. An elected post-Gulf War parliament in Kuwait has voted repeatedly against suffrage for women and privatisation of the state oil industry.

Strategic Policy Issues

OPEC and post-conflict Iraq

On the economic side, many top oil analysts do agree that a change of Iraqi regime, if accompanied by a lifting of sanctions and eventual reconstruction of the country, could create more competition inside OPEC. Iraq has in the past stated a desire to more than double its oil production capacity to 6m b/d. This is geologically possible, as Iraq has the second largest proven oil reserves in the world after Saudi Arabia, and its probable reserves, at 220 billion barrels, are immense. Of Iraq's 74 discovered and evaluated oil fields, only 15 have been developed. Of 525 known oil-containing structures, only 125 have been drilled. But the nature and timing of any Iraqi decision to enlarge its oil sector are also subject to many currently unknown political variables. Iraq's oil industry and export infrastructure was badly damaged in its two wars – first with Iran in the 1980s and then with the US-led international coalition for Kuwait in 1991. A rapid increase in Iraqi oil exports will not be possible, given the limitation of Iraq's production and export facilities and the damage to facilities during the US campaign that began in March 2003. Even under the best possible circumstances, it would take Iraq at least six months to expand oil production and export rates from its current capacity of around 2.6–2.8m b/d. Expansion to 6m b/d is likely to take several years and cost tens of billions of dollars. Furthermore, it remains to be seen how eager a new Iraqi leadership will be to privatise the oil sector. For 30 years, Iraq has been a socialist, nationalist rentier state. Iraqi oil technocrats have favoured a return of foreign private investment, but a new government and a greater plurality of views may yield a consensus for Iraqi oil nationalism rather than privatisation, following the pattern of Kuwait, Mexico and Saudi Arabia. Similarly, as a founding member of OPEC, Iraq will have historical, geographical and economic reasons to remain in the cartel's fold. Many of Iraq's neighbours are OPEC members, and Iraq will have to consider its relations with them. Moreover, should Iraq choose to operate outside of OPEC, flaunting its agreements, Saudi Arabia could punish Iraq by flooding the market with Saudi oil to deprive Iraq of profits from increased production.

Most OPEC members are hawkish about short-term price levels. But competition could easily emerge within OPEC in the coming years, depending on political developments – particularly if Iraq opts to privatise its sector and invite private international investment. If prices come under pressure from rising Iraqi oil production, OPEC members may react with oil-production increases of their own. Iran is already forging ahead with capacity expansions and could reach over 5m b/d by 2008, based on investments through buy-back agreements with international oil companies (IOCs) and National Iranian Oil Company investment. However, this ambitious plan will depend on the success of major IOC field developments, including those at Azadegan, South Pars, Sirri, Gagh Saran and the Ahwaz area. Nigeria has plans to expand its offshore production, which could, if successful, raise production to over 3.5m b/d by 2006. Algerian oil production is also on the rise, and is expected to double from 800,000 b/d to 1.6m b/d through 2008. A change in Iraq's status could unleash competition among these and other OPEC producers that has been dormant for several years.

In the meantime, however, OPEC faces quite a different situation. Venezuela's capacity is constrained by well shut-ins, reservoir and infrastructure damage, a shattered management structure and restricted access to badly needed capital. In addition, new problems are emerging in Nigeria: civil unrest has already disrupted production in the Escravos area. The mid-April 2003 elections are expected to be a test of the country's stability. Since February 2003, clashes in Warri between the Urhobo–Ijaw alliance and the Itshekiri simmered over the selection of candidates for the ruling People's Democratic Party and the rearranging of political districts. The fighting has resulted in dozens of deaths. By mid-March 2003, violence in the oil-rich Delta State had escalated, resulting in intervention by government troops and a 13% cut in oil production. On 21 March, a major field was closed and the US embassy in Abuja shut due to political unrest.

As of April 2003, OPEC was producing at close to 100% capacity and had little ability to increase production to meet any near-term crisis. This reality contributed to a tremendous volatility in oil markets that could continue in 2003, depending on demand trends. OPEC capacity is estimated at around 27m b/d including Iraq, or 25m b/d if Iraq's production remains out of commission due to war. This level is very close to the expected demand call on OPEC's oil for the second quarter of 2003. An additional 1–1.5m b/d could be produced by Saudi Arabia and other Persian Gulf producers on a surge basis, potentially extended by increased investment, to offset lost Venezuelan, Nigerian or Iraqi exports.

Relief may come with a seasonal demand slump, which is typical for the early spring. Normally, the period from February to May sees the biggest drop in oil demand worldwide, sometimes averaging as much as 3–5m b/d. In 2002, demand fell by 2.6m b/d over this period versus a drop of 1.8m b/d in 2001. Some analysts are forecasting a drop of 3m b/d in demand between February and May 2003. However, any such reduction would stabilise markets only temporarily. Later in the year, prices could come under extreme upward pressure, again depending on the fate of Iraq's industry and other risk factors. Moreover, markets may remain strained due to depleted international inventory levels, which are at historic lows and will require replenishing ahead of next winter, adding to the call on OPEC oil later in the year.

Russia's role

The international politics of oil is in flux essentially because the United States is unhappy with the status quo. How the oil landscape will look in the

Strategic Policy Issues

five- to 10-year horizon is hard to predict, given the wide range of variables, including geology, global environmental politics, technological change and the shifting geopolitical relationships of the post-11 September world. There is no question that efforts are being made by Washington to locate oil allies outside of the Persian Gulf. Perhaps the most telling evidence of this was the US–Russia Energy Summit held on 1–2 October 2002 at the James A. Baker III Institute for Public Policy in Houston, Texas. This inaugural summit brought together senior government officials – led by US Secretary of Commerce Donald Evans and his Russian counterpart, Economic and Trade Minister German Greff – as well as corporate executives representing over 70 American and Russian energy companies. The aim of the meeting was to develop joint Russian–American strategies for cooperation in the energy sector, emphasising an important role for the private sector. The session led to the creation of a commercial working group, and a follow-up meeting was planned for Moscow in autumn 2003. Presidents Bush and Putin, during a meeting in St Petersburg on 22 November 2002, highlighted the Energy Summit as a key achievement that 'created new avenues for dialogue and cooperation on energy issues and led to decisions on concrete new investment projects and programs and business arrangements'.

Russia and the newly independent states of its southern flank are ranked second in undiscovered oil potential after the Persian Gulf, holding about 27% of the world's total reserves. The region ranks first globally in undiscovered natural gas. Russia itself accounts for 13% of the world's energy production, third after Saudi Arabia and the US. Planned increases in productive capacity bode well for the Commonwealth of Independent States to grow as an important supplier to Europe and Asia. The Caspian Basin countries near Russia could represent an additional 3–4% of the world's oil supply by 2010. Meanwhile, Russia itself is hoping to see its crude output rise from over 7m b/d in 2001 to 10m b/d by the end of the decade. Despite dire predictions to the contrary, Russian firms have been able to marshal capital on their own in recent years to revive the Russian oil industry. In the period September 2000–September 2002, Russian oil production rose by over 640,000 b/d, and similar gains are in store for this year. In the view of Russian leaders, this new geopolitics of energy, in which Russian oil is portrayed as a stable alternative to Middle East supply, can net Moscow both economic and political gains. Traditionally, Russian oil exports have been destined for Europe and not challenged Arab efforts to sell more oil to the US or Asia. However, the warmer diplomatic relations between Moscow and Beijing in the last few years have facilitated growing cooperation between Russian and Chinese firms in oil and gas trade. A similar improvement in relations on energy-trade issues has occurred between Moscow and Tokyo.

Oil production from Russia's Sakhalin Islands is expected to top 500,000 b/d by 2007 or 2008. Beyond Sakhalin, there are other prospects from

East Siberia. One pipeline project under examination is a \$1.7 billion Yukos–PetroChina line from Angarsk in northeastern Russia to Daqing in northeastern China, which could pump as much as 600,000 b/d of Russian crude to China. Construction of a pipeline and deep-water port at Murmansk in northern Russia could help raise Russian exports to the US to 650,000 b/d or more, according to Russian oil company officials, up from just a trickle, as of early 2003. But with total crude oil exports of 3.5m b/d, Russia has a long way to catch up with Saudi Arabia's 7m b/d-plus. Thus, although Russia will be increasingly important to the US plans to diversify oil supply, a more varied strategy is still needed.

Uncertain contributions from elsewhere

US plans to draw more heavily on nearby oil supplies from Latin America have seen serious setbacks in the past year. Venezuela's oil production, which had been expected to grow to 5–6m b/d by the end of the decade, looks almost certain to nosedive below 2m b/d following serious damage to its reservoirs during and in the immediate aftermath of the oil workers' strike. Mexico has the potential to increase production by 30% in the medium term, but capital constraints and rising domestic consumption may hinder its sustained role as a key supplier to the US market. Local politics and legal issues could continue to preclude the reintroduction of foreign investment in Mexico, preventing the country from obtaining outside capital to enhance its industry. US–Mexican relations have also been put under strain by border issues and other problems. More broadly, the rise in populism and opposition to economic liberalisation across Latin America has cast doubts on the ability of Vicente Fox's administration or other regional leaders to continue market reforms and to attract or generate the capital needed to expand the region's oil sector. Brazil was also expected to provide a boost to hemispheric oil flows, but investors may shy away from new deals given political and regulatory uncertainties created by the election of Luiz Inácio da Silva ('Lula'), the continued dominance of the Brazilian state oil company Petrobras in commercial domestic energy markets and problems with the development of markets for natural gas. Colombia's oil sector is constrained by civil war and costly and repeated guerrilla attacks on vital oil infrastructure.

All told, non-OPEC oil production, combined with rising output in natural gas liquids worldwide, added 1.7m b/d to world hydrocarbons liquid flows in 2002 and could contribute 1.4m b/d in 2003. But securing steady reliable supplies in non-OPEC countries is problematic. In 2002–03, the US turned its attention to Africa as an emerging source of increased oil and gas. Secretary of State Colin Powell assumed a visible role in responding to the HIV/AIDS issue on the African continent and several African heads of state visited Washington in 2002. African oil production

Strategic Policy Issues

could double to over 10m b/d by 2010, depending on the pace of Western investments. Angola supplies 10% of the US' oil imports. However, optimism about the end of the prolonged civil war in Angola has yet to translate into rapid development of the country's oil and gas sector. The Angolan government has been slow to approve new oil and gas development deals, hoping to press IOCs to make more lasting, onshore investments in facilities that would create jobs in the country. But the IOCs generally prefer to push for more secure and cheap offshore facilities that are less likely to be affected by general unrest in the host country. West Africa is only expected to offer an additional 100,000 b/d of oil production this year, despite its vast potential. This underachieving trickle highlights the difficulties in finding major new supply regions to replace the Middle East.

Canada added 130,000 b/d more oil to US markets, almost all of it from new synthetic oil projects. Canadian tar sands, which show no signs of waning, are considered a major potential source to meet growing US demand. Still, with so many prospective oil-supply source countries subject to actual or potential political turmoil, it is hard to see how diversified increases from around the world can make oil supplies appreciably more stable. According to the International Energy Agency, almost all of the increase in oil supplies over the next 30 years will come from the developing world, versus only 60% in the period 1971–2000. The expected decline in oil production in places like the US and the North Sea will almost certainly be made up by increases in countries where internal politics will impose major risks of interrupted production.

Relative stability in the near term

In the broader interest of reducing US dependence on oil, the US government has announced a series of presidential energy-policy and technology initiatives. These involve new technologies to capture greenhouse gas emissions, promote hydrogen as an alternative fuel and enhance nuclear-fusion research, with an eye to fostering a continuum of new energy technologies up to 2050. In addition to $500m currently planned for 'FreedomCAR' – a US government–industry programme for developing high-efficiency vehicles powered by hydrogen produced from renewable energy resources – the Bush administration recently announced a new $1.7bn budget item to develop hydrogen-powered fuel cells, hydrogen infrastructure and advanced automobile technologies. While the oil-bullish Bush team to some degree may be targeting hydrogen precisely because it is such a distant prospect, neo-conservative thinking about the Middle East also supports a genuine interest in alternative fuels that is likely increasingly to colour the American political landscape.

With upwards of $1 trillion to be spent on the application of military force and humanitarian aid in the Persian Gulf, it is a reasonable expectation that the American public will soon get around to asking: why oil? Were it to do so, an Apollo-sized project initiative instead of a relatively modest $1.7bn for hydrogen research might be justified and politically realistic. Any such concerted push towards alternative technologies would induce oil producers to try to head off new sources and technologies by making the existing ones cheaper. At the same time, mounting social, demographic and resource pressures in the oil-producing world may make it impossible for any country to allow oil prices to slip below $20 a barrel, even if that would make long-term strategic sense. Thus, prospective US efforts to unleash market forces to make Middle Eastern oil supplies more reliable and to diversify its oil imports may slow momentum behind the development of alternative fuels, but they are unlikely to reverse it.

But in any case, in the near term the Gulf will clearly remain the focal point of oil geopolitics. Even as war in Iraq was about to begin, at OPEC's 11 March 2003 meeting the group determined that it would maintain quotas and production ceilings at existing levels. While some producers expressed concern about the cartel's ability to meet demand in the event of prolonged disruptions in Iraqi production, the key member – Saudi Arabia – was reasonably certain that supplies would be sufficient. In fact, most OPEC ministers worried that a typical fall in demand during the second quarter of 2003, combined with oversupply, would cause prices to collapse as summer approached. The US-led forces' ability to take rapid control of Iraq's oilfields appeared to justify confidence in plans based on the near-term resumption of Iraqi production. At the same time, unexpectedly stiff Iraqi resistance and the Iraqi people's tentative reception of allied troops suggested that post-conflict operations would be protracted and problematic, and the restructuring of the Iraqi oil industry halting. Given the post-conflict uncertainties with respect to Iraq, the possibly long-term production disruptions in Venezuela, the gap between Russian and Saudi production capacity, and the substantial political risk affecting African sources, in April 2003 it seemed that any change in the oil equation would be slow.

State-building and the United Nations

The period 2002–03 saw four major developments in the international administration of post-conflict territories. On 20 May 2002, East Timor celebrated its independence after two-and-a-half years of administration under the United Nations (UN). Less than a month later, Afghanistan experienced the first crucial test of a more minimalist UN presence in Kabul, with the staging of an emergency *loya jirga* (national assembly). The end of 2002 saw the withdrawal of the UN's presence in Bosnia and Herzegovina, passing further responsibility for the ongoing problems there over to the European Union (EU). And, by early 2003, there was intense speculation concerning the post-conflict structures that might succeed the US-led war against Iraq that commenced on 20 March 2003. Meanwhile, the post-conflict project in Kosovo dragged on, accompanied by what was likely to be the death rattle of what remained of Yugoslavia, re-christened Serbia and Montenegro in February 2003 – an entity barely held together by that fairly weak conjunction.

These developments suggested some basic tensions concerning the appropriateness of such operations and the capacity of the United Nations to conduct them. First, the operations in East Timor and Afghanistan offered radically different models for such reconstruction processes, ranging from the maximalist operation in East Timor to the 'light footprint' in Afghanistan. Secondly, the handover of Bosnia to the EU and the discussion of a dominant role for the United States in post-conflict Iraq – perhaps even modelled on post-war Germany or Japan – raised questions about the appropriate source of authority for such operations and the actor(s) that should lead them.

Virtual trusteeship

The power of the UN Security Council to administer territory is not mentioned in the UN Charter. Nor, however, is peacekeeping, the formula that came to define UN military action. Here, as in many other areas of the Security Council's activities, practice has led theory and the Charter has been shown to be a flexible – some would say malleable – instrument. Writing in early 1995 – and chastened by the failed operation in Somalia, the failing operation in Bosnia and Herzegovina and inaction in the face of the genocide in Rwanda – Secretary-General Boutros Boutros-Ghali issued a conservative supplement to his more optimistic 1992 Agenda for Peace. The Supplement noted that a new breed of intra-state conflicts presented the UN with challenges not encountered since the Congo operation of the early 1960s. A feature of these conflicts was the collapse of state institutions, especially the police and judiciary, requiring international intervention to extend beyond military and humanitarian tasks to include the 'promotion of national reconciliation and the re-establishment of effective government'. Nevertheless, he counselled caution against the UN's assuming responsibility for law and order, or attempting to impose state institutions on unwilling combatants. General Sir Michael Rose, then commander of the United Nations Protection Force (UNPROFOR) in Bosnia, termed this form of mission creep 'crossing the Mogadishu line'.

Despite such cautious words, by the end of 1995 the UN had assumed responsibility for policing in Bosnia under the Dayton Peace Accords. The following January, a transitional administration was established with temporary civil governance functions over the last Serb-held region of Croatia in Eastern Slavonia. In June 1999, the Security Council authorised an 'interim' administration in Kosovo to govern part of what remains technically Yugoslav territory for an indefinite period; four months later, a transitional administration was created with effective sovereignty over East Timor until independence. These expanding mandates continued a trend begun with the operations in Namibia in 1989 and Cambodia in 1993 that exercised varying degrees of civilian authority in addition to supervising elections. This expansion was part of a larger growth in activism by the Security Council through the 1990s, as it showed itself willing to interpret internal armed conflicts, humanitarian crises and even disruption to democracy as 'threats to international peace and security' within the meaning of the UN Charter – and therefore warranting a military response under its auspices. This 'new interventionism' was, however, constrained by the failure of the United Nations to develop an independent military capacity. As a result, Security Council action was generally limited to circumstances that coincided with the national interests of a state or group of states that were prepared to lead.

The term 'nation-building', sometimes used in this context, is a broad, often vague, and sometimes pejorative one. In the course of the 2000 US presidential campaign, George W. Bush sometimes used it as a dismissive reference to the application of US military resources outside their traditional mandates. In addition, the term was used to conflate the circumstances in which US forces found themselves in conflict with the local population (most notably in Somalia) with complex and time-consuming operations such as those underway in Bosnia and Herzegovina, Kosovo and East Timor. Within the United Nations, the term 'peace-building' is generally preferred. In Secretary-General Boutros Boutros-Ghali's An Agenda for Peace, this was said to include 'reforming or strengthening governmental institutions'. By the time his Supplement was published, the essential goal was said to be 'the creation of structures for the institutionalisation of peace'. Nevertheless, 'peace-building' embraces a far broader range of activities than those particular operations. In fact, the term 'state-building' has evolved to refer to extended international involvement (primarily, though not exclusively, through the United Nations) that goes beyond traditional peacekeeping and peace-building mandates, and is directed towards developing the institutions of government by assuming some or all of those sovereign powers on a temporary basis.

Action in this area has been characterised by reaction and improvisation. This, together with the highly sensitive nature of the Kosovo conflict in particular, has hampered efforts to develop best practices for such operations or plan for future contingencies. In addition, many of the elements seen as crucial to the success of past operations – notably the Transitional Administration for Eastern Slavonia (UNTAES) – concern ultimately political questions of formulating the mandate and exercising command and control over the military component of a mission.

Light or heavy footprint?

Just under a month after the 11 September 2001 attacks on New York and Washington DC, a US-led coalition commenced military action in Afghanistan aimed at eliminating the al-Qaeda terrorist network and toppling the Taliban regime that had harboured al-Qaeda leaders and members. By mid-November, the Taliban had been effectively removed from power and on 5 December 2001, a UN-sponsored Afghan peace conference in Bonn, Germany, approved a broad agreement for the establishment of an interim authority pending the holding of an emergency loya jirga in June 2002. This body would, in turn, decide upon a transitional authority to lead Afghanistan until elections were held within two years from the convening of the *loya jirga*.

During the initial stages of the military action, there was considerable discussion about the role of the UN in post-conflict Afghanistan. Some feared that the UN would be handed a poisoned chalice once the United States had completed its military objectives; others eagerly looked forward to the 'next big mission' and a dominant role for the UN in rebuilding Afghanistan on the model of Kosovo and East Timor. These expectations were tempered by the challenging security environment and the decision by major states contributing forces to the International Security Assistance Force (ISAF) to limit their presence to the capital city of Kabul and its immediate vicinity. Ongoing coalition actions in eastern Afghanistan continued to provide additional coercive power – referred to as the 'B-52 factor' – but this was outside UN control. Expectations were also limited by the political context within which the UN was to operate: however dysfunctional, Afghanistan had been and remained a state with undisputed sovereignty. This was quite different from the ambiguous status of Kosovo and the embryonic sovereignty of East Timor.

Under the leadership of Lakhdar Brahimi, architect of the Bonn process, the UN mission adopted the guiding principle that it should first and foremost bolster Afghan capacity – both official and non-governmental – and rely on as limited an international presence and as many Afghan staff as possible. This came to be referred to as the 'light footprint' approach. Such a departure from the expansive mandates in Kosovo and East Timor substantially reduced the formal political role of the United Nations Assistance Mission in Afghanistan (UNAMA). This was in keeping with the limited role accorded to the United Nations in the Bonn Agreement, negotiated in December 2001 after the rout of the Taliban. But it also represented a philosophical challenge to the increasing aggregation of sovereign powers exercised in UN peace operations since the mid-1990s.

On paper, UNAMA resembled earlier assistance missions that provided governance and development support to post-conflict societies. In practice, however, the UN mission remained intimately involved with the Afghan Transitional Authority and therefore with the peace process that had put it in place. This disjunction between formal authority and practical influence posed challenges not only for the specific operation in Afghanistan, but also to accepted models of UN peace operations more generally. Senior UN staff in the mission were blunt about the reasons for the light footprint approach. A mission on the scale of East Timor's transitional administration was 'not necessary and not possible', according to Brahimi. Bolstering Afghanistan's capacity to govern itself required Afghans taking charge of their situation wherever possible, an end that would have been compromised by throwing international staff at a problem. A larger international presence would also have had negative and distorting effects on local politics and the economy. As another senior UN official put it, 'we are protecting a peace process from the hubris of the international liberal agenda as promoted by donors'. Such an agenda might include setting policy (on, for example, human rights, democracy, gender, the rule of law) in accordance with donor requirements and time-lines rather than on the basis of what was locally feasible.

In any case, armchair generals' enthusiasm for the benevolent takeover of Afghanistan was cooled by its history of resistance to foreign rule. For this reason, the Security Council-mandated ISAF was reluctant to deploy outside its original sphere of operations in and around Kabul. UN senior staff argued that expansion beyond Kabul was essential to the stability of the interim authority put in place by the emergency *loya jirga*, but were careful throughout to limit themselves to 'endorsing' Chairman Hamid Karzai's call for a wider deployment. The United States, typically reluctant to submit itself to a UN mandate, opposed any expansion of ISAF. This opposition diminished around August 2002 as mopping-up operations in search of Osama bin Laden and al-Qaeda operatives scaled down, although countries supplying ISAF personnel remained reluctant to expand its territorial coverage. In any case, a limited role for the UN had been the most politically feasible option at the time of the Bonn Agreement. But the officially passive role of the UN belies its profound political influence in state-building in Afghanistan. In making a 'procedural' decision to invite Hamid Karzai to speak at the Bonn meeting, for example, the UN was using its political clout to anoint Karzai and helped ensure his eventual appointment as chairman of the interim (later transitional) authority. A central element of the Bonn process was encouraging Afghan leaders of

Strategic Policy Issues

various stripes to see their interests as being served by buying into a political process. Asserting a lead role for the UN, it was argued, would have fatally undermined this aim; where UN influence was deemed necessary, it was played out backstage to preserve the appearance of a light UN footprint.

This hands-off approach became central to the political strategy pursued by the UN in Afghanistan – a high-risk strategy that required two conceptual leaps from the normal mould of peace operations. The first was that it would be possible to blur the customary distinction between negotiating a peace agreement ('peace-making' in UN argot) and implementing it. Thus, the Bonn Agreement was seen not as a final-status agreement but as a framework for further negotiations, mediated through the institutions that it provides for over the subsequent two-and-a-half year period (the Interim Authority appointed in December 2001; the emergency *loya jirga* that elected the Transitional Authority in June 2002; the constitutional *loya jirga* to be held by December 2003; and 'fully representative government ... elected through free and fair elections' by June 2004). The flexibility of this approach contrasts with the rigid peace agreements that locked the UN and other international actors into their roles in Bosnia and Kosovo. The Bonn Agreement avoided these pitfalls, but presumed that the UN would continue to play a meaningful role in the ongoing negotiations. Again, on paper, there was little formal authority for the UN to do so, but through high-level diplomacy and subtle interventions in its capacity as an assistance mission, it endeavoured to 'cook' the political process into a sustainable outcome.

This assumed the success of the second conceptual leap, which was that the UN could make up for its small mandate and limited resources through exercising greater than normal political influence. Brahimi went one step further, arguing that it was precisely through recognising Afghan leadership that external actors obtain credit and influence. Such an approach places extraordinary importance on the personalities involved. It is generally recognised that Brahimi was instrumental to the success of Bonn, but his continuing involvement and his personal relationship with Karzai and the three Panjshiri 'musketeers' who largely wield power (Defence Minister and Vice-President Muhammad Qassem Fahim, Foreign Affairs Minister Abdullah Abdullah and Education Minister and Special Adviser Mohammed Yunus Qanooni) are essential to the process' remaining on track. By early 2003, it seemed likely that Brahimi would soon depart Kabul. Given the centrality of his role in negotiating and implementing the Bonn Agreement, this may create a significant credibility gap in the international presence.

Prior to the June 2002 emergency *loya jirga*, there were cases of intimidation and pressure by local commanders to have themselves or their men 'elected'. This was sanguinely interpreted as confirmation and recognition of the perceived importance of the political process. In fact, few regarded the *loya jirga* as a meaningful popular consultation. The aim, rather, was to encourage those who wielded power in Afghanistan to exercise it through politics rather than through the barrel of a gun. The *loya jirga* took place peacefully on 11–19 June 2002 and did produce a somewhat more representative administration. In addition to 1,051 elected delegates, a further 450 were appointed by refugee groups, universities and other civil-society bodies, with a final hundred or so added under pressure at the last minute. Hamid Karzai, Chairman of the Interim Administration, was elected president of the Transitional Administration by an overwhelming majority, though his main opponents withdrew their candidacy not long before the *loya jirga* took place – under pressure, according to some reports. The former king, Mohammed Zahir, also stated that he would not seek election as head of state, but would support Karzai. On 19 June 2002, after extensive consultations, President Karzai announced the names of three vice-presidents and 14 ministers, whose positions were approved by the *loya jirga*. As of April 2003, the question remained whether tinkering with a few positions was enough to assuage the disgruntled Pashtun population, which sees itself as marginalised for the past sins of the Taliban. The difficulty confronting the UN was that it was neither mandated nor in a position to conduct meaningful consultations outside the power centre of Kabul.

Security remains the major concern in Afghanistan, with many analysts pointing to a 'security gap' between what is currently provided by the ISAF presence in Kabul, the coalition forces in pockets of the country and the embryonic Afghan national army. Many senior UN staff continue to see expansion of ISAF beyond Kabul as vital to the success of the larger mission, but significant expansion is now highly unlikely. Force command was transferred from Britain to Turkey on 20 June 2002, and then to Germany and The Netherlands on 10 February 2003. The number of troops remained at approximately 4,300, centred in and around Kabul. Examples of insecurity have been conspicuous: two ministers in the Afghan government have been assassinated. Aviation Minister Abdul Rahman was killed at Kabul airport on 14 February 2002. Then, soon after being appointed at the June *loya jirga*, Vice-President Haji Abdul Qadir was killed on 6 July 2002. This incident was destabilising, both as a blow against the government and especially because it removed the most prominent political leader with a political base among the Pashtuns. President Karzai himself narrowly escaped an assassination attempt on 5 September 2002, his life saved by US Special Forces acting as his bodyguards.

For the time being, Afghanistan clings to a fragile peace. Nightmare visions of the Pashtun population rising up against a Tajik-dominated Transitional Authority and their foreign abettors would require the political process spinning utterly out of control. This seems improbable. Ongoing spats between rival commanders are highly likely, though to date these have been localised. The first major tests were the staging of the emergency *loya jirga* and how the new Transitional Authority presented itself to the population. The *loya jirga* is regarded as a qualified success, but the Transitional Authority got off to an extremely bumpy start. Nevertheless, if most of those who have bought into the process achieve some of their expectations, and the Authority and the UN are seen to be facilitating the flow of assistance to the Afghan population, the fragile consensus that Afghanistan enjoys today may continue.

Less than a month before the *loya jirga* in Afghanistan, East Timor (now Timor-Leste) celebrated its independence. On 20 May 2002, UN Secretary-General Kofi Annan joined President Xanana Gusmão and the heads of state from over a dozen countries to lower the UN flag and raise the Timorese one. On 27 September 2002, Timor-Leste became the 191st member state of the United Nations. Gusmão had been elected president on 14 April 2002 by an overwhelming majority, though his powers were limited by the constitution adopted by the Constituent Assembly, dominated by the Revolutionary Front of Independent Timor, the previous month. This concluded the most expansive assertion of sovereignty by the UN in its history – in addition to administering East Timor, passing laws and overseeing the judiciary, the UN had negotiated treaties for the territory. Even so, in early December 2002, riots in Dili left two dead and Prime Minister Mari Alkatiri's house burned to the ground. It was unclear whether this was mainly student unrest or whether pro-Indonesian militia had been involved. The uncertainty led to discussion about the possibility of delaying the drawdown of UN peacekeepers, though there was little enthusiasm on the part of the states contributing troops for keeping them there. Current plans call for the phasing out of peacekeepers entirely by January 2004. By early 2003, troop strength was 4,500, down from a maximum of 9,000 during the UN transitional administration period. East Timor also immediately became the poorest country in the region. It faces a period of great economic instability, at least until tax revenues from oil taken from the Timor Gap begin to accrue – estimated at up to $3 billion over 17 years beginning in 2006.

Still, the UN was applauded for assisting the Timorese achieve long-awaited independence. Yet East Timor's small size and the fact that its future status was uncontroversial made the 'heavier' option easier to implement, both politically and operationally, than would, say, the political uncertainty of Kosovo or the complex security situation in Afghanistan. East Timor, then, was exceptional. The lighter approach used in Afghanistan is likely to be the most viable option in the vast majority of cases.

The US and state-building

During the course of the 2000 US presidential campaign, candidate Bush had been openly critical of the use of American military resources for 'nation-building' purposes. He reiterated this position once in office, and repeated it in the weeks after the 11 September attacks, when he stated that 'we're not into nation-building, we're focused on justice'. Days before the United States commenced military operations in Afghanistan, however, the president's spokesman marked a slight shift in position as it became clear that international support of the US action would in part depend on the broader consequences for the Afghan people: 'Well, to repeat what I've said many times, the United States is not engaged in nation-building in Afghanistan, but the United States will help those who seek a peaceful, economically developing Afghanistan that's free from terrorism'. The president himself elaborated this point in a news conference after military action had commenced, and endorsed a more substantial role for the United Nations in rebuilding Afghanistan:

> *I believe that the United Nations would – could – provide the framework necessary to help meet those conditions. It would be a useful function for the United Nations to take over the so-called 'nation-building' – I would call it the stabilisation of a future government – after our military mission is complete. We'll participate; other countries will participate. I've talked to many countries [that] will participate. I've talked to many countries that are interested in making sure that the post-operations Afghanistan is one that is stable, and one that doesn't become yet again a haven for terrorist criminals.*

The 11 September attacks, moreover, began to animate states with the idea that large-scale reconstruction projects may involve greater national interest than had previously been understood. Most prominently, the National Security Strategy adopted by President Bush in September 2002 stated that 'America is now threatened less by conquering states than we are by failing ones'. As the conflict in Afghanistan developed – and in particular, as the likelihood of capturing Osama bin Laden 'dead or alive' diminished – a rhetorical shift became evident in the Bush administration's war aims. 'Nation-building', something that President Bush had long derided as inappropriate for the US military, was reincorporated into the US agenda. Notably, the United Kingdom had been a more enthusiastic proponent of the centrality of such reconstruction efforts to the coalition war aims. Furthermore, with increasing frequency, the Taliban regime and its mistreatment of the Afghan civilian population were presented as the real evil, rather than as ancillary to the man and the organisation that was alleged to have attacked the United States on 11 September.

In debates within the UN and elsewhere, much attention has been focused on the unwillingness of the United States to engage in state-building. There is some evidence that the US is not well-suited to such activities. The importance of domestic politics in the exercise of US power means that it has an exceptionally short attention span – far shorter than is

Strategic Policy Issues

needed to complete the long and complicated task of rebuilding a country that has seen over two decades of war, sanctions and oppression under brutal leaders. This describes both Afghanistan and Iraq. More importantly, when the US has performed state-building, as in Afghanistan, this has been justified at home by linking it to the war on terror. US forces at times provided military and economic support for local governors not on the basis of their relations with the Karzai regime, but in exchange for their assistance in rooting out the remnants of al-Qaeda and Taliban forces. At times, this actively undermined the new regime by boosting the de facto power of the provinces at the expense of the central government. It is for this reason that the United States is described as having a military strategy in Afghanistan but not a political one. The fleeting nature of US engagement in the post-conflict reconstruction of Afghanistan was all too apparent in the initial failure to include any funds for this in the 2004 budget, though $300m was quickly added when the oversight was noticed.

State-building challenges

The American disinclination to engage in state-building, even as part of an overall counter-terrorism strategy, is unlikely to change substantially in the event of conflict with Iraq. In this light, the leaked plans to install an American-led military government in Iraq modelled on the post-war occupation of Japan begins to make sense. The speed with which such plans were denied, however, suggest that the Bush administration realises that it cannot be seen to be on an imperial quest. Kuwait, of all countries in the region, has reason to be grateful for an American military presence. Yet fatal attacks on US military and civilian personnel there on 8 October 2002 and again on 21 January 2003, respectively, suggest that such gratitude is not universal.

For the US administration to rebuild Iraq, it will have to do so together with the Europeans, probably with Russia and certainly with partners in the region. For Europe at least, the legitimacy afforded by the United Nations is likely to be a requirement for their participation. But as of early 2003, having focused on the war itself and overcoming the inconvenient diplomatic barriers to military action, the US appeared to have given little serious consideration of how such a post-conflict operation might be structured. The prospect of Iraq's descending into violent civil war is similarly underplayed. Kurdish leaders have naturally stressed that they have no intention of seceding from Iraq – anything to ensure US support against the hated Saddam Hussein. Yet the Kosovar Albanians were also persuaded to drop their demand for independence before NATO went to war on their behalf in 1999. The main barrier to resolving Kosovo's status today is that outside powers understood this pragmatic posturing as genuine renunciation; subsequent actions by Kosovar Albanians showed all too clearly that it was not. Similar problems could arise with respect to the Kurds.

An unknown quantity in projecting post-conflict operations in Iraq is the role that the United Nations might play. The organisation's humanitarian agencies will certainly be involved in any relief operation (as they already are in parts of Iraq), but it is unclear what sort of political role, if any, might fall upon the UN. The UN was selected to oversee governance of Kosovo only in the last days of NATO's air war in 1999, but it is infeasible that post-war Iraq could be patterned successfully on Kosovo or East Timor. Both territories were small, easily blanketed with international personnel and relatively benign. Iraq, like Afghanistan, is none of the above. Indeed, after a war against Iraq, a military venture loosely linked to the broader war on terror, there will be no government-in-waiting as there was (of a kind) for Afghanistan. These realities should give the Bush administration pause.

The general trend is that the success of a post-conflict UN administration depends most critically on the sustained commitment of the key actors to take decisive action to maintain the foundation of peace. When that commitment wanes, post-conflict operations become fraught. Seven years after the Dayton Accords, Bosnians elected the same politicians who had led them into ethnic conflict in the first place. On 31 December 2002, the UN Mission in Bosnia and Herzegovina (UNMIBH) transferred its police-monitoring duties to the European Union Police Mission (EUPM). Bosnia was, in the end, to become a European problem. Kosovo remains a divided non-state. In each case, the United States – the primary military prosecutor of peace – appeared to lose interest in staying the course of post-conflict reconstruction. Afghanistan clings to a precarious peace. While the continued US presence provides some insurance against wholesale failure, the slowness with which pledged international aid has materialised has strained that guarantee.

Absent a strong outside military actor, then, UN state-building efforts are likely to be frustrated. Anaemic troop commitments to operations in the Democratic Republic of the Congo and Sierra Leone suggested a lack of enthusiasm and funds to support more expansive operations. Western Sahara's long-delayed referendum on its status seemed likely to be abandoned in early 2003, in favour of an early transfer to Morocco. Under a draft plan first proposed in May 2001 by James Baker, the UN Secretary-General's personal envoy, Morocco's claims to the territory would be effectively recognised for a period of up to five years, prior to a vote on Western Sahara's future. As this would include the many Moroccans who have settled there over the past decades, integration with Morocco is the probable outcome. This process is reminiscent of the 1969 'Act of Free Choice' that saw representatives in West Papua (now Irian Jaya) vote unanimously – in questionable circumstances – in favour of integration with Indonesia.

Strategic Policy Issues

National interests still rule

It is ironic that UNAMA reached its most crucial test – the June 2002 *loya jirga* – within weeks of East Timor's independence celebrations on 20 May 2002. The UN Transitional Administration in East Timor (UNTAET) may come to represent the high-water mark of UN transitional administrations, where the UN exercised effective sovereignty over a territory for more than two years. The UN mission in Afghanistan has a fraction of UNTAET's staff and budget and operates in a country perhaps 40 times the size and 30 times the population of East Timor. Brahimi has said that people may look back at East Timor and question whether it was necessary to assert such powers. Any such evaluation may well be coloured by the fate of the UN operation in Afghanistan. Just as generals are sometimes accused of planning to re-fight their last war, so the United Nations experiments in transitional administration have reflected incremental learning. Senior UN officials now acknowledge that, to some extent, Kosovo got the operation that should have been planned for Bosnia, and East Timor got the one that should have been sent to Kosovo. Afghanistan's 'light footprint' draws, in turn, upon the outlines of what Brahimi in 1999 argued would have been appropriate for East Timor. Indeed, the combination of the frustration encountered in resolving the Israeli–Palestinian conflict and the relative lack of intrusiveness involved in the 'light footprint' model may eventually make resort to a UN trusteeship in Palestine – a dispensation increasingly discussed in some circles – politically viable.

The accepted wisdom is that a successful UN peace operation should ideally consist of three sequential stages. First, the political basis for peace must be determined. Then a suitable mandate for a UN mission should be formulated. Finally, that mission should be given all the resources necessary to complete the mandate. The accepted reality is that this usually happens in the reverse order: member states determine what resources they are prepared to commit to a problem and a mandate is cobbled together around those resources – often in the hope that a political solution will be forthcoming at some later date. Future experimentation with the models of East Timor and Afghanistan is therefore likely to pivot on the national interests at stake. In Afghanistan, the threats posed by weak states led the Bush administration to abandon its earlier threshold aversion to state- (or nation-) building. This revised position is likely to prevail in the event of a conflict in Iraq. The threat of weapons of mass destruction falling into the hands of non-state actors and the implications that a fragmenting Iraq would have for Turkey and Iran suggest that the US would remain committed to rebuilding Iraq in the event of a conflict. At the same time, the wish to avoid the appearance of imperialism in the region – as well as a residual distaste for state-building on Washington's part – may demand a formal UN umbrella for, and substantial ground-level UN involvement in, any post-conflict administration.

Post-conflict Iraq

By the time *Operation Iraqi Freedom* commenced on 20 March 2003, two discrete post-conflict scenarios were in play. The first was broadly consistent with the plans leaked by the Pentagon in October 2002 for an American-led military government in post-conflict Iraq modelled on the US occupation of Japan, with the United Nations providing humanitarian assistance. The second scenario, advanced by the United Kingdom and, to a lesser extent, by the US State Department, included a larger – if essentially undefined – role for the UN. Testifying before the Senate Foreign Relations Committee on 11 February 2003, spokesmen for the Departments of State and Defense affirmed that the United States – rather than a provisional government of Iraqi exiles – would take charge in Baghdad. Civilian tasks would be carried out under the authority of the Pentagon's Office for Reconstruction and Humanitarian Assistance (ORHA), established by President Bush on 20 January 2003. ORHA's director, retired Army Lieutenant General Jay M. Garner, would report to the President through General Tommy Franks of Central Command and Secretary of Defense Donald Rumsfeld. But there were suggestions that the State Department's top expert on Iraq, Ryan Crocker, had reservations about his own proposed role as 'ambassador' in Baghdad, given that so much power resided in the Defense Department. Lieutenant General John Abizaid, an Arab-American, also seemed likely to be given a prominent role in the post-conflict administration after being promoted to Franks's second deputy.

Discussion within the United States tended to focus on a role for the United Nations only when considering the question of how this occupation might be paid for. US, UK and UN officials had explored the possibility of transforming Iraq's oil-for-food programme, established by the Security Council in April 1995, into a more flexible arrangement to allow the UN to control goods purchased under its auspices throughout the country. (Until the suspension of the programme at the onset of hostilities, the Iraqi government had prepared distribution plans and contracts for the entire country, distributing goods itself in the centre and south; the UN distributed goods in the north.) Nevertheless, suggestions that oil revenues might actually cover military expenses incurred by the United States in administering Iraq were confined only to a few US think-tanks. A resolution giving control of the oil-for-food programme to the UN Secretary-General for an initial 45-day period was passed unanimously by the Security Council on 28 March 2003. Reference to coordination 'with the relevant authorities' was dropped from the text due to fears that this would imply UN support for either the war or a US- or UK-dominated post-war administration. Bringing the post-conflict phase of operations under UN authority had other compelling rationales. Most prominently, Chris Patten, the EU Commissioner for External Relations, stated before the war that if the US attacked Iraq without Security Council approval the EU might withhold money for reconstruction. This received vocal support from French President Jacques Chirac after military operations commenced, arguing that France would not support any UN resolution that gave retrospective legitimacy to the conflict.

The particulars of the United States and its coalition partners' virtually assured victory over Iraq – such as the level of infrastructure damage, the refugee situation and the degree of 'de-Ba'athification' politically required – will most profoundly shape any post-conflict role that the UN might play. But Kurd and Shia separatist activity and security threats on Iraq's borders could also adversely affect the security environment. Regardless of how the armed conflict terminates, appropriate post-conflict governance structures will have to be determined on an ad hoc basis, depending on the Iraqis' receptivity to a military occupation government; the attitudes of Iraq's large diaspora community, including political exiles and their US or Iranian supporters and the wider diaspora interested in rebuilding Iraq; and the possible rise of discrete regional powers within Iraq or the assumption of power by local leaders on an informal basis (i.e., warlordism). The conflict will also have significant humanitarian consequences – such as interruption to the state-controlled harvest and distribution of food as well as epidemics – that affect the distribution of power in post-conflict operations. Politically, what entity controls Iraq's natural resources – in particular its oil fields – will be an important determination. The UN would appear to be the most appropriate body, from the standpoint of both instilling in Iraqis a sense of legitimacy and quelling Arab, Muslim and some European accusations that regime-change was merely an American pretext for controlling oil. As of early April 2003, a consensus appeared to be building behind this dispensation.

Yet the prevailing attitude towards the United Nations itself, both in the region and in Western capitals, remains ambivalent. Dissatisfaction with the role of the UN in Bosnia, for example, led to the establishment of the Peace Implementation Council outside the UN framework as part of the Dayton Accords. Given the apparent frustration of the Bush administration with the Security Council process that followed the adoption of Resolution 1441 in November 2002, there were some doubts that it would be prepared to engage in the necessary negotiations to secure the Council authorisation necessary for a significant UN role. For its part, the UN engaged in only halting planning for a post-conflict role. An early planning cell was shut down in December 2002 due to concerns that its existence might be interpreted as undermining the position of UN weapons inspectors then in Iraq. An internal 'pre-planning' report was requested in February 2003; soon after it was drafted it was leaked to the press. The report apparently stressed that the UN lacked the capacity to take on the responsibility of administering Iraq, preferring a political process closer to that followed in Afghanistan. The favoured option was for an assistance mission that would provide political facilitation, consensus-building, national reconciliation and the promotion of democratic governance and the rule of law. The people of Iraq, rather than the international community, should determine national government structures, a legal framework and governance arrangements. Humanitarian contingency planning – some of which was leaked to the same journalist in December 2002 – was less controversial and more advanced.

The UN's tentativeness towards post-conflict planning reflected concerns about a role that might be thrust upon the UN as political cover for what would essentially be a US military occupation. It also reflected the tension between the different models epitomised by East Timor and Afghanistan. It will clearly not be possible to deploy a mission of comparable scale to UNTAET in Iraq, which has a population and land area approximately 30 times that of East Timor. Iraq also has far greater human capital and bureaucratic structures that may be drawn upon, compared to the former Indonesian province. Although Afghanistan is akin in size and population to Iraq, the assistance mission there depended on the existence of an alternative regime to the deposed Taliban regime. There is no Iraqi group, either domestically or in exile, that has legitimacy comparable to that of the Afghan Northern Alliance. Despite various attempts to establish such a group, the would-be 'governments-in-waiting' are divided among themselves and appear to enjoy little respect among indigenous Iraqis. Establishing a regime in post-conflict Iraq will thus require even more external management than has been necessary in Afghanistan. This reality suggests further grounds for conducting post-conflict operations under UN auspices. The Fourth Geneva Convention limits the capacity of an occupying power to change the status of public officials and to impose new laws. As the war aims in Iraq included regime change and its transformation into a 'liberal democracy', Security Council authorisation would provide a legal basis for such activities.

UN Secretary-General Kofi Annan, who had remained mostly outside the discussion on the inspections process and the countdown to war, made a plea for the restoration of Security Council unity in the post-conflict phase. As French diplomats counted the costs of their opposition to the US on a prospective Security Council resolution authorising military action to oust Saddam Hussein – ultimately never tabled by the US and the UK partially on account of that opposition – such a process seemed possible. In the short term, a central UN role would heal some of the divisions in the Security Council, just as the resolution establishing UN Interim Administration Mission in Kosovo eased tensions after NATO's Kosovo intervention in 1999. A highly visible political role for the UN, in addition to its humanitarian responsibilities, would provide the framework for wider participation in the post-conflict reconstruction. It would also aid the US in its protestations that its actions were not intended to constitute an

Strategic Policy Issues

occupation of Iraq. In the longer-term, however, following the precedent of Kosovo, the Iraq crisis may have severely, if not fatally, weakened the role of the Security Council in authorising the use of force and as the bearer of 'primary responsibility for maintaining international peace and security'. Military action under its auspices through the 1990s took place only when circumstances on the ground coincided with the national interests of a state that was prepared to act. One analyst has described the Security Council's evolved function as the equivalent of a 'law-laundering service'. Nevertheless, the UN remains an indispensable framework for the multilateral cooperation necessary to rebuild a country of the size of Iraq. The US determined that it did not need the UN going into Iraq, but it will probably require the UN to get out.

The Americas

In 2002, the administration of US President George W. Bush leveraged both its post-11 September sympathy abroad and its post-11 September popularity at home. By the time the US and the UK invaded Iraq in March 2003, without the express sanction of the UN Security Council, much of the former had been squandered. Sensitivity to mass-casualty threats induced the US to focus on consequences rather than probabilities, and the Bush team argued that the possibility that Iraq could use weapons of mass destruction (WMD) or supply them to terrorists justified the pre-emptive or preventive use of force. Unconvinced, France, Germany and Russia bitterly opposed military intervention in Iraq, instead favouring continued inspections re-introduced by UN Security Council Resolution 1441. The rest of Europe was divided on the issue, and the Arab and Muslim world solidly opposed. The US proceeded with military action without the second Security Council resolution that most governments and most populations believed was required. Perceived American unilateralism, leavened only slightly by the UK's alignment with the US, and the United States' preventive military impulse had badly damaged transatlantic solidarity, as well as the wider global counter-terrorism coalition. Only a quick and merciful war, it seemed, would bring substantial vindication for the US. As of early April 2003, whether the conflict would meet these qualifications remained in doubt.

On the domestic front, the absence of a major terrorist attack, the launch of the Department of Homeland Security and several notable arrests of terrorist suspects justified a measure of satisfaction. But a shortfall between stated homeland-security aspirations and their implementation, consistently negative news about the economy and consumer confidence, and a large and seemingly incongruous tax cut in the face of steepening defence spending and an expanding national deficit began to erode Bush's popular standing. Looking unbeatable as his popularity soared after al-Qaeda and the Taliban were expelled from Afghanistan, Bush's prospects, by April 2003, no longer appeared to turn on the war on terrorism. The US and its counter-terrorism partners continued to make arrests and thwarted several plots, and captured major terrorist figures – including senior al-Qaeda recruiter Abu Zubeida in March 2002 and al-Qaeda third-in-command Khalid Shaikh Mohammed in March 2003 – whose interrogation improved prospects for finding Osama bin Laden. Yet Bush's re-election in November 2004 appeared increasingly contingent on the success – in

Map The Americas

political, economic and security terms – of post-conflict operations in Iraq, and the recovery of the US economy. Neither appeared remotely assured.

If the Bush administration's post-11 September focus on homeland security and worldwide counter-terrorism caused its initial engagement in hemispheric affairs to flag, its post-Afghanistan preoccupation with Iraq produced an even greater lack of interest. To an extent, the coolness appeared to be reciprocated. Anti-war popular opinion coupled with hard US bargaining on free trade and immigration, respectively, made Chile and Mexico reluctant to throw unequivocal support behind a second UN Security Council resolution in support of US-led military action against Iraq in March 2003. Washington's perceived indifference to the Argentine economic crisis and a looming debt default by Brazil seemed to fuel left-wing populism there, yielding a victory in the October 2002 presidential election for former metalworker Luiz Ignácio da Silva ('Lula'). In El Salvador, former leftist guerrillas of the Farabundo Marti National Liberation Front made gains against the conservative ruling party in the March 2003 elections. Greater scepticism about American political and economic values probably also helped sustain sufficient support for Venezuelan President Hugo Chávez's increasingly dysfunctional and unpopular regime to keep him clinging to power even as unrest and perverse policies undermined the oil industry in Venezuela. Yet any leftward tilt in Argentina, akin to that of Brazil, which had seemed probable in the wake of its default on $141 billion in loans in December 2001, had not crystallised as of April 2003. Instead, although unemployment was 18% and 58.5% of Argentines lived in poverty, the traditional populist Peronists – centre-right and largely pro-American – emerged as the most favoured political group. Moreover, Brazil's lean to the left has proved far less drastic than anticipated, as Lula has opted for economic orthodoxy to preserve Brazil's credit in international markets and possibly its credibility vis-à-vis the United States in its efforts to advance free-trade negotiations.

In the Andes, Colombia's continuing insurgency did attract American attention, as it fell broadly under the heading of international terrorism. Along with counter-narcotics aid, US counter-insurgency assistance to Colombia increased and became more hands-on, as the US placed Special Forces and helicopters in-country. Washington continued to enjoy wide support among most Andean nations for stopping drug trafficking. The US, in February 2003, announced a 15% reduction in Colombia's coca crop. Yet the 'balloon effect' remained persistent, as drug production rose in Bolivia and Peru. Civil disarray in Venezuela and Chávez's passive assistance to Colombian rebels, political tensions in Bolivia and Colombia's intensifying civil war are likely to make regional narcotics and insurgency problems less tractable in the near term. Thus, economic weakness in the Southern Cone and insecurity in the Andes will continue to be the salient strategic challenges posed by and to Latin America. But, with Iraq's reconstruction,

North Korea, Iran, counter-terrorism and the recuperation of transatlantic relations high on the United States' agenda, it appears doubtful that Washington will refocus on Latin America in 2003–04.

The United States: Changed Utterly?

It was no consolation, but the tragedy of 11 September 2001 brought a catharsis of transatlantic solidarity. On 12 September 2001, America's NATO allies invoked the Alliance's central article of collective defence, declaring the attacks on New York and Washington to have constituted an attack on all 19 Alliance signatories. This solemn declaration was followed by many more offers of practical military help for the war in Afghanistan than the Pentagon was inclined to accept. By the time of the Taliban's defeat in late 2001, the United States had assembled one of history's most impressive global coalitions for the fight against transnational Islamic terrorism. A common strategic threat had forged what looked to be an enduring common purpose. Yet there was always a disturbing alternative, in which the terrorists' singular hatred of the US would bring out what was singular in the American national character, and that this process would create alienation, not solidarity, among US allies. Many of those allies were more accustomed to terrorism, which they treated as a matter of grave domestic disorder. Americans could argue, of course, that al-Qaeda represented an entirely new, strategic level of terrorist threat. From the moment that the enormity of the 11 September attacks sunk in, Americans considered themselves to be at war. As a general proposition, a state of war is more likely to sharpen than soften the national personality. This sharper American edge is not one that the rest of the world, in 2002 and early 2003, found congenial.

For several months, the differing priorities and worldviews were indeed submerged by solidarity. But over the spring and summer of 2002 this solidarity started to crack, and it was shattered by the failure of UN diplomacy and Washington's decision to go to war in Iraq. One year earlier, the United States had won a war in Afghanistan with the broadest imaginable international backing. In March 2003, it went to war again in Iraq, this time facing a near-solid wall of world opposition. The opponents included public majorities in the few states that sent forces to fight with the Americans: Australia, which sent over 2,000 troops; Poland, which contributed just 200; and the United Kingdom, sending some 45,000, whose Prime Minister Tony Blair was adamant that opposition to the US on a matter of such import would be a recipe for moral and strategic disaster. Were it not for the British government, the United States – the greatest military power in human history – would have been essentially alone.

Foreign policy: breaking the mould

The foreign policies of the administration of US president George W. Bush in the half-year after 11 September were – as Nicholas Lemann has observed – uncontroversial and, in a real sense, not optional. Faced with terrorist attacks on the scale of 11 September, any US administration would have been bound to launch a regime-changing war against the failed Afghan state that provided the terrorists with sanctuary and an operational base. While there was some international criticism of the lack of legal process accorded to captured combatants and terrorist suspects detained at the United States' Guantanamo Bay base in Cuba, there was also substantial support and cooperation from America's allies in the steady effort to break up al-Qaeda cells throughout Europe. Sometime in the spring of 2003, however, the administration started to express its own distinctive strategic vision of the post-11 September world, and of the choices, opportunities and obligations it presented. Such US officials as National Security Advisor Condoleezza Rice started speaking of a plastic moment in history, like the period 1945–49, and of the role of America's overwhelming power in shaping this plastic moment. This thinking was reflected in a series of official pronouncements issued through the spring, summer and autumn – most notably Bush's West Point speech in June 2002, and the administration's National Security Strategy released three months later. Without doubt, these appear to be radical and ambitious documents. In their overall rhetorical sweep, they state that American global military hegemony will be used to defend freedom and democracy everywhere, and they at least seem to imply that, in some cases, the best defence is a good offence.

What generated the most controversy was the notion of pre-emptive military action. Military pre-emption against an imminent attack is, in fact, a well-established right under international law. Furthermore, these Bush administration documents are very specific and limited about the instances in which pre-emptive military action would be considered: against 'rogue states' assembling arsenals of biological, chemical or nuclear weapons. If there was indeed a new Bush 'doctrine' of pre-emption, however, its first test suffered a serious conceptual flaw. The 2003 war against Iraq was not a pre-emptive war at all, but rather a 'preventive' one. Iraq, by the best available evidence, did not have a capability or any immediate intention to attack its neighbours or the US with chemical, biological or nuclear weapons. What it did have was a clear intention to acquire those weapons, an effort it had undertaken for years before its invasion of Kuwait in August 1990, and continued to pursue relentlessly even as UN inspectors

The Americas

criss-crossed the country from the end of the Gulf War in 1991 until 1998. It was very hard to imagine – as both Bush and Blair argued forcefully – that the regime of Iraqi President Saddam Hussein would have abandoned that effort in the four years after the inspectors withdrew.

In the new strategic context of 11 September, the US and Britain could make a plausible case that proliferation of weapons of mass destruction (WMD) to outlaw regimes such as Saddam's was no longer tolerable. This was not because of any particular evidence of a substantial link between Iraq's regime and al-Qaeda. Rather, it was because of the clearly documented determination on the part of al-Qaeda to acquire WMD, and the prospective logic of its eventually approaching other sworn enemies of America and the West for this purpose. (The objection that Islamic fundamentalists and secular Ba'athists were ideologically incompatible was no more reassuring than the suggestion that Nazi Germany and Stalinist Russia could never have cooperated.)

Thus, the challenge to international order posed by Saddam's continued defiance of UN prohibitions against his WMD programmes was a problem for which the Bush administration's many critics offered no convincing answer. Equally, however, the Bush administration, in its strategic pronouncements and its actual diplomacy, gave no persuasive indication that it could meet this challenge militarily and at the same time preserve the world's confidence in the benign nature of American power. The case for a preventive war was inherently difficult to make, and the case for this one was never presented clearly and forthrightly. Part of the problem was the haphazard way the administration went about deciding to go to war, torn as it was between a State Department mainly wary of a war that lacked broad international support and the alliance of neo-conservative idealists and hawk realists in the Pentagon and office of Vice-President Dick Cheney. Many of these hawks had considered Iraq to be unfinished business when they came into office in January 2001, but they made little headway in the administration until 11 September gave them powerful ammunition. Bush gave an early indication of how his own thinking had been affected in his January 2002 State of the Union address, when he classified Iraq as part of an 'axis of evil', and vowed to prevent such countries from threatening the US with the world's 'most dangerous weapons'.

By July 2002, when State Department Policy Planning Director Richard Haass, in a private meeting with Rice, suggested that there might be greater priorities in the war on terror, Rice responded that the decision for war against Iraq had already been made. The course for war may already have been set, but there were two prominent sources of dissent that played out in newspaper leaks and columns over the late summer and autumn. One involved the top ranks of the uniformed military, whose expressions of unease over administration war plans were leaked furiously to major newspapers. The second was a handful of prominent Republicans, including Nebraska Senator Chuck Hagel and some members of the administration of President George H.W. Bush: Powell himself behind the scenes; former Secretary of State James Baker and former National Security Advisor Brent Scowcroft more publicly. It was Scowcroft, for example, who warned in a 15 August 2002 *Wall Street Journal* column that 'any campaign against Iraq, whatever the strategy, costs and risks, is certain to divert us for some indefinite period from our war on terrorism' and 'result in a serious degradation in international cooperation with us against terrorism'. Such warnings poured fuel on a fire that had raged within the Republican Party since the early-to-mid 1970s, when neo-conservatives had attacked National Security Advisor and later Secretary of State Henry Kissinger for the allegedly 'amoral' basis of his strategy of détente with the Soviets. Former California Governor Ronald Reagan employed the same themes in challenging President Gerald Ford for the 1976 Republican presidential nomination. The anger flared again in reaction to the first Bush administration's decision to end the 1991 Gulf War with Saddam Hussein still in power, even standing aloof as the Iraqi Republican Guard brutally suppressed an uprising of Iraqi Shi'ites in the south. Scowcroft was one of the advisers to the elder Bush whom Republican neo-conservatives had blamed for that decision, and so his current intervention was hardly welcomed in these circles.

The dissenters did achieve one victory. Powell and Blair prevailed upon Bush – despite harsh and open scepticism from Cheney, Secretary for Defense Donald Rumsfeld and other hardliners – to address the Iraq problem in a UN framework. Bush did so in one of the most powerful speeches of his presidency, warning the General Assembly on 12 September that Saddam's 12-year defiance of Security Council resolutions threatened the credibility and fundamental viability of the UN system. The eight weeks of negotiations that followed this speech culminated, on 8 November 2002, in the Security Council's unanimous adoption of Resolution 1441, declaring Iraq to be in 'material breach' of past resolutions, and offering Baghdad one 'final opportunity' to comply. It was an impressive achievement of American and British diplomacy, but it quickly unravelled. While Saddam allowed a new team of UN inspectors into the country and granted them unhindered access, he also provided a patently false 'declaration', in sham fulfilment of the requirement under Resolution 1441 to account for past and present WMD programmes. This was followed by various other forms of active and passive dissembling, but when the US and UK claimed these as a *casus belli* under the Security Council's own terms, they encountered a solid wall of opposition from the other permanent members – namely, France, Russia and China. Owing perhaps to France's vow to veto any resolution that could support the use of force against Iraq, it proved impossible even to garner majority support from the non-permanent members.

The Americas

Washington focused its frustration on the French, who were accused of having behaved both before and after their signing on to Resolution 1441 as if they would do anything to avoid using or even endorsing military means to enforce compliance. Yet France and much of the rest of the world had reason to question the American agenda as well, as the administration had rocked back and forth between commitment to regime change and stated willingness to accept real disarmament. Logically, the administration could make a plausible case that the latter required the former. And complete scepticism about the efficacy of UN inspections did not necessarily imply bad faith in trying to make them work. But the US did appear set on an unstoppable course for war, and this impression was reinforced by a massive deployment accompanied by the buzz that so many troops in the field created their own argument for being used: summer heat would make it too hard to fight in chemical protection suits; their war-footing was too expensive to maintain until the fall; withdrawal would constitute a regime-sustaining victory for Saddam, and a corresponding loss of credibility for Bush. At the same time, it was likely that only this very mobilisation had extracted from Saddam the degree of compliance that he had shown.

The fundamental American argument, strongly backed by Britain, was that the 'final opportunity' and 'immediate' language of Resolution 1441 did not leave room for more years, or even months, of inspections. The inspectors were in Iraq only to verify Saddam's genuine and proactive determination to come clean and present the chemical and biological materials that Washington was sure he had. However, like the troops deployed on Iraq's borders, the inspectors sent to the interior created their own expectations. When Saddam was seen to be cooperating at least passively – that is, he did not block inspectors from going anywhere – and when the chief inspectors claimed to be making progress, the court of world opinion was not inclined to be a stickler about the actual wording of Resolution 1441. Nuclear weapons, in particular, would be hard for Iraq to develop secretly under these conditions. Continued containment looked, to the rest of the world, like a plausible alternative to war. American and British military intervention was perceived as unilateral. It mattered little that the Bush administration could cite over 30 governments that declaratorily approved of US and UK action in Iraq. Most of those governments were bucking domestic public opinion. The judgment as to whether a decision or act was 'multilateral' or 'unilateral' turned not on how many nations expressly supported it, but rather on the nature of the impulse behind it. To most observers, the US was imposing its will and its will alone.

Domestic disturbances

Bush's political platform for war had been strengthened by the stunning results of November 2002 midterm elections, which gave the Republican

Party solid control of the presidency and both houses of Congress for the first time since 1952. (The election results of two years earlier had left the Senate evenly divided between Republicans and Democrats; the summer 2002 defection of liberal Republican James Jeffords had handed control to the Democrats.) For the president's party to gain congressional seats in a midterm contest was almost unprecedented, and it suggested that voters' worries about national security had trumped the domestic issues and economic problems that were expected to favour the Democrats. Public-opinion surveys indicated a staggering 40% margin of preference for Republicans, when voters were asked whom they trusted to better protect national security. Bush and the Republicans exploited this reality skilfully, not to say ruthlessly, contending that Democrats were more concerned about pandering to organised labour than about fighting terrorism, because they had fought to maintain union eligibility for employees of the newly created Department of Homeland Security, which Democrats had proposed creating and the president at first had opposed. The Democrats probably also lost voters who were angered by the spectacle, just a few days before the elections, of the funeral of liberal Minnesota Senator Paul Wellstone – killed with his wife and daughter in a plane crash – which turned into a raucous anti-Republican political rally.

Wellstone's death deprived the Senate of one of its most liberal members, and one of the few unalloyed opponents of war with Iraq. Most of the likely candidates for the Democratic presidential nomination – including Senate majority leader Tom Daschle (who later decided not to run), House Minority Leader Richard Gephardt, Connecticut Senator Joseph Lieberman and North Carolina Senator John Edwards – had voted with varying degrees of enthusiasm for congressional resolutions that granted the president nearly blanket authority to wage the war. The notable exceptions were Vermont Governor Howard Dean and, somewhat surprisingly, former Vice-President Al Gore. The surprise in Gore's position was that he had a long record as a Democratic hawk, supporting interventions in the Balkans and earlier military actions against Iraq. But Gore, breaking a long political silence following the bitter dispute over the 2000 presidential election, adopted many of the same arguments as Scowcroft: this was the wrong time for a war against Iraq, which would divert energy from the struggle against al-Qaeda and shatter the anti-terrorist coalition. In the echo chamber of American punditry, Gore had long suffered from a reputation of lacking a gravity of conviction. This reputation was revived by charges that his anti-war position must have been politically motivated. A few weeks later, Gore confounded his critics by announcing that he would not seek his party's 2004 presidential nomination.

Buoyed by his political successes, Bush sought to use the momentum to make his signature tax cuts permanent, and to add an income-tax

The Americas

exemption on stock dividends. This tax-cutting programme encountered resistance from Democrats and moderate Republicans, who complained that it would disproportionately reward the rich and ruin government solvency at a time when financial resources and national solidarity were sorely needed. Bush retorted that the tax cuts were needed to stimulate a flagging economy, though he elided the fact that, in dollar terms, most of that stimulation would occur several years hence, when economic conditions could be very different. The economy, in any event, showed little sign of recovery, at least if measured in terms of job growth and stock market valuation. Unease over corporate governance also showed no sign of dissipating; a spate of scandals continued, although none were quite on the scale of the 2001 Enron collapse.

There were other political storms that the Bush administration encountered and, with some success, weathered. One occurred soon after its election triumph, when Republican Senator Trent Lott, the Senate Majority Leader, was shockingly specific in birthday greetings for 100-year-old Senator Strom Thurmond of South Carolina. Lott said he was proud that his own state of Mississippi had supported Thurmond's third-party bid for the presidency in 1948, and that, if the rest of the country had followed suit, it would have been spared 'all these problems'. The difficulty with these remarks was that Thurmond's 'Dixiecrat' campaign had involved one, and only one, issue: opposition to the relatively moderate civil-rights platform of Harry Truman's Democratic Party; and corresponding support for continued segregation and disenfranchisement of southern blacks. Lott rolled out a series of progressively more obsequious apologies, but under pressure from Democrats, neo-conservative Republicans and the Bush administration, he finally resigned his leadership post. The Bush team, through 2002, also made only limited progress in capturing and prosecuting significant al-Qaeda players. This problem was reflected in the government's overreaching presentation of its case against Zacarias Moussaoui, whom the Justice Department insistently characterised as the '20th hijacker', although there were indications that he could have been a minor, rather unstable, associate of the network. On the eve of the Iraq war, the US at last captured a key lieutenant of Osama bin Laden, third-in-command Khalid Shaikh Mohammed. Moussaoui might have provided significant information for the hunt for al-Qaeda operatives, but Attorney-General John Ashcroft was set on a death-penalty prosecution. Ashcroft was strongly committed to the death penalty on principle, having overruled federal prosecutors seeking lesser sentences. It was, in fact, a year in which the death penalty was subjected nationally to an unexpected re-examination. Breakthroughs in DNA science had proven the innocence of numerous death-row inmates. The cumulative impact of these reversals led Illinois Governor George Ryan to commute every death-sentence conviction in his state in January 2003.

State of war

The death penalty, which certainly was not going to be abolished in the United States anytime soon, was one more source of irritation between the US and its democratic allies. Of course, it was hardly a new irritant, nor was support for it limited to conservative Republicans: Arkansas Governor Bill Clinton, when he was running for president in 1992, had famously returned to Arkansas to oversee the execution of a mentally retarded convict. Such continuities provided evidence for those who argued that American 'exceptionalism' was broadly based, and not simply the result of a right-wing presidency that had been launched into office with less than a majority of votes cast. One exponent of the 'inherently different' explanation for transatlantic alienation was the American neo-conservative analyst Robert Kagan. His article 'Power and Weakness', published in the June–July 2002 issue of *Policy Review*, had become the intellectual sensation of the year. In it Kagan posited a simple explanation for America's greater readiness for military interventions: America possessed overwhelming, and historically unprecedented, military power. Europe, far weaker in military terms, was more prone to seek diplomatic solutions, even to the point of ignoring grave threats, such as the one posed by Iraq. Europe was also, in Kagan's view, the conceptual victim of its own astonishing success: having created, in the European Union, a 'post-modern' paradise of law, institutions and cooperation, it had lost touch with the Hobbesian realities of the real, and more 'modern' world. Americans operated in that world, and understood it much better.

Kagan had some muted criticism for the way that Bush's heavy-handedness had aggravated the transatlantic divide. At bottom, however, he argued that it could not have made much difference: Bush's Democratic predecessors, many of whom had come of age in the anti-war left, were themselves more likely to cite the lessons of Munich than the tragedy of Vietnam. In other words, their perspectives were deeply American. Other defenders of the Bush administration argued that its 'unilateralist' moves, which allegedly had cost the United States so much goodwill before the Iraq war, were simply more direct and honest versions of Clinton policies. Bush had rejected the Kyoto Protocol on global warming, but the Clinton administration that signed it had considered the protocol so flawed that it could not be submitted for Senate ratification. Likewise, the Bush administration's vehement opposition to the International Criminal Court (ICC) had produced the fierce resentment even of America's closest ally, Britain. Yet Clinton too had worried that it exposed American troops to unreasonable legal liability; his last-minute signing of the ICC treaty was at best a symbolic act, and at worst a poison gift for his successor. Clinton had also pursued national missile defence, hoping to reconcile it with an amended Anti-Ballistic Missile (ABM) Treaty. Bush found it simpler to leave the ABM Treaty altogether. In sum, did not comparisons of Bush

The Americas

'unilateralism' and Clinton 'multilateralism' rely more on differences of style than substance?

There was some merit to these arguments. But they did not quite capture the importance of style and national 'personality' in assessing whether the rest of the world would remain reconciled to the fact of America's global military hegemony. For those foreigners who hoped that the exercise of that hegemony would be informed by internationalist perspectives, the generational journey from Bush the father to Bush the son was not reassuring. The elder Bush, a patrician New Englander, Director of Central Intelligence, envoy to China and UN ambassador before becoming vice-president and then president, had famously coined the term 'voodoo economics' to describe the supply-side theory behind Reagan-era tax cuts. He had cultivated close relations with world leaders, and on the eve of his war against Iraq, he had assembled a truly international coalition. Bush the son, who was raised in Texas, had rarely travelled outside the United States before becoming president. Whereas his father had lost the presidency in part because of right-wing disaffection with his decision to raise taxes to offset a deficit, the younger Bush made massive tax cuts the centrepiece of his domestic policies. He was a man of religious and moral certainty, a certainty galvanised by the 11 September attacks. That certainty and self-confidence made George W. Bush a formidable, and often underestimated, politician at home. His supporters insisted that the same self-confidence and capacity for decision would vindicate his leadership abroad. As of early April 2003, roughly three weeks into the war against Iraq, it was too early to tell.

Continuing Disorder in the Northern Andes

The last eight months of 2002 witnessed the beginning of a hard-line approach by President Alvaro Uribe Velez in Colombia's decades-long civil conflict as well as the increased authoritarianism of Venezuelan President Hugo Chávez in defiance of popular opposition to his 'Bolivarian revolution'. Insurgent groups – primarily the Marxist Revolutionary Armed Forces of Colombia (FARC) – have dramatically increased their military activities, especially urban terrorism. The right-wing umbrella paramilitary organisation, the Colombia Self-Defense Forces (AUC), has engaged in continued combat with the FARC while keeping its political avenues open by suggesting it would adhere to a self-imposed ceasefire. By early 2002, the high-profile peace negotiations between the government and FARC during the term of former President Andrés Pastrana (1998–2002) had receded into history. A Colombian population frustrated with the growing levels of violence and insecurity responded, in May 2002, by overwhelmingly electing Uribe, who has promised to put security first. The Bush administration strongly supports Uribe's efforts and greater amounts of US military hardware and training will probably be forthcoming if Uribe is able to demonstrate that he is using the assistance so far provided effectively. Chávez's obliviousness to the economic decline and political dysfunction that his policies are visiting on Venezuela, however, has gratuitously created another area of instability in the northern Andes.

FARC rampage, government response

The FARC responded to the breakdown of the peace talks in February 2002 by dispatching 5,000 guerrillas to four key regions throughout Colombia. These forces received their training in the Switzerland-sized liberated zone – or *despeje* – that it provisionally ceded in 1998 as part of the peace negotiations with the Pastrana administration. It is believed that the training included instruction in bomb-making and the use of explosives as well as in other forms of urban warfare. Since this time, direct confrontations between the FARC and the AUC have increased substantially. In a particularly gruesome episode, during a FARC–AUC battle in the northwest province of Chocó in May 2002, FARC soldiers lobbed gas cylinder bombs into a church in which local residents had sought refuge; of 119 civilians killed, most were women and children. The FARC's intimidation factor is high. In what can be seen as a direct attack on democracy, in early June 2002 the FARC issued a statement that all mayors and provincial government officials were to be targeted for death if they did not stand down from their posts. More than 150 mayors have resigned, dozens have been killed and several city halls have been forced to close.

Uribe, running on a platform of 'Firm Hand, Big Heart', pledged that he would not openly negotiate with the FARC until it demonstrated a willingness to talk in good faith. Uribe's campaign was marred by the roughly two dozen attempts on his life. This included one episode on 14 April in which three people were killed and 20 injured when a bomb planted on a bus was detonated by remote control as Uribe's campaign convoy travelled through the port city of Barranquilla. In May 2002, Uribe won an unprecedented first-round victory against Liberal Party candidate Horacio Serpa. Despite intense security, during Uribe's inauguration on 5 August, the FARC fired 120mm mortar shells at the presidential palace and nearby military academy. Although the shells landed erratically, they started fires in impoverished parts of the city and killed 19 civilians.

The Americas

This attack constituted a technological and organisational leap for the insurgency and a clear indication that the FARC was taking its terrorist campaign into the cities.

Upon taking office, Uribe imposed a 'state of domestic commotion' for 90 days and renewed it in November after a constitutionally required vote by the Senate. While this designation is not as extreme as a 'stage of siege', which allows the government to impose curfews, Uribe's move was nonetheless intended to send an unequivocal message that his new administration meant business. The decree triggered governmental authority to detain individuals, search private premises and monitor phone calls without judicial warrants. It also established Rehabilitation and Consolidation Zones (RCZs) – areas under the command of a military officer empowered to impose curfews and restrict the movements of residents. Some 27 municipalities in three departments (Arauca, Bolivar and Sucre) were declared RCZs.

On 24 September 2002, Uribe travelled to Washington and met with officials from Capitol Hill, the Pentagon and the Departments of State and Treasury. Uribe indicated that his administration would do more to combat drugs and illegal groups, and said that it would launch a controversial plan to train peasant soldiers (*soldados campesinos*) and organise a network of one million civilian informants. The Uribe administration hoped by March 2003 to have enlisted 15,000 peasant soldiers, who would receive military training in order to protect their home areas once the Colombian military had cleared them of insurgent groups. Uribe also noted that, while New York City has 42,000 police officers, there are only 75,000 for Colombia's entire national territory.

In October 2002, Uribe unveiled his domestic security policy, which included a one-time security tax of 1.2% on liquid assets in excess $60,000. Total revenues from the tax are expected to reach $1 billion. Sixty percent of the revenues will be used to fund the 2002 and 2003 defence budgets, while 40% will go to increasing troops levels. Although unprecedented for Colombia, this tax will generate revenues far short of what is needed to fulfil Uribe's pledge to double combat troops and police. Uribe is also hoping to train 6,000 new elite army troops for two mobile brigades and to pay small sums to 100,000 civilian informants. Furthermore, the Colombian government has stated its intention to use a US-trained commando force to track top insurgent and paramilitary leaders. In addition to issuing security decrees and announcing enhancements to the military, Uribe ordered the military to go on the offensive against the guerrillas. Colombian military officials reported that from July to September 2002, 2,525 guerrillas and paramilitaries were captured or killed in 400 skirmishes, compared with 1,683 killed in 262 operations during the same months in 2001. Over the past year the armed groups – primarily the FARC – have continued to increase their urban activities. Between January 2001 and September 2002, the Colombian National Police recorded 409 terrorist acts committed in the country's three largest cities, Bogotá, Medellín and Cali.

Law-enforcement and political measures

While the failure of the peace process in Colombia has prompted the re-militarisation of the conflict, both the Colombian and the US governments have continued to apply ancillary criminal and diplomatic remedies. A key political development in 2002 in the ongoing war was the Colombian military's more focused and proactive attempts to rein in the AUC. Whereas in previous years the military conducted virtually no operations against the paramilitaries and often provided them with tacit support, the military has begun to treat them as the terrorist groups that they are. Greater military pressure on the paramilitaries may have been one factor behind AUC leader Carlos Castaño's 29 November 2002 call for a unilateral ceasefire to start on 1 December. In a 12-point document issued by Castaño, the AUC promised to cease offensive operations against guerrillas because the government itself was 'demonstrating its capacity and political will' against them. While few believed that the AUC would adhere to the ceasefire, Castaño's announcement did underline the link between an end to AUC military activities and greater military and political pressure on the FARC.

In early 2003, Uribe organised a six-man 'exploratory commission' that immediately held two private meetings with the AUC leadership. While these preliminary meetings do not amount to formal ceasefire negotiations, Uribe's move reinforces the perception that he is serious about ending the AUC's military activities. In this connection, the US has provided considerable diplomatic support, as the Department of State added the AUC to its list of proscribed terrorist organisations in September 2001. In late September 2002, US Attorney-General John Ashcroft announced the indictments of Castaño and two of his commanders. In the indictment, the US government accused Castaño of protecting cocaine laboratories, setting price controls on cocaine and managing shipments from Colombia's coast to maritime vessels. If captured, Castaño would presumably be tried in Washington. Then, on 13 November, the US Department of Justice indicted three FARC leaders, including Jorge Briceño Suárez, the FARC's second-in-command, on drug-trafficking and hostage-taking charges.

The limits and insufficiency of the law-enforcement approach have been illustrated in two cases. First, a Colombian judge, Pedro Suárez, ordered the release – for good behaviour – of Cali cartel kingpin Gilberto Rodríguez Orejuela. During the early to mid-1990s, Gilberto and his brother Miguel were responsible for roughly 80% of the world's cocaine exports. Gilberto Rodríguez's release came after he had served seven years of a 15-year sentence. Miguel will remain in jail to serve a four-year sentence for bribing a judge. Both the Bush and Uribe administrations

The Americas

were furious at the decision and Uribe's attorney-general ordered an investigation of the judge. Second, the trial of three members of the Irish Republican Army (IRA) arrested in August 2001 proceeded in autumn 2002. Niall Connolly, Martin McCauley and James Monaghan were arrested in Bogotá in August 2001 after arriving on a flight from the FARC's *despeje* and accused of training the insurgents in the use of explosives. In fact, the FARC's 7 February 2003 bombing of the exclusive El Nogal country club in Bogotá that killed 33 Colombians utilised technical expertise believed to have been learned from outside sources. The IRA is a likely suspect. The three men face 20 years in prison if convicted. During his 4 December visit to Bogotá, US Secretary of State Colin Powell commented that, 'When you start to see members of the IRA in Colombia sharing experiences, sharing knowledge, doing only heaven only knows what, it suggests that these kinds of organizations ... are committed to destroying democracy in our hemisphere'. But while the American, British and Colombian governments believe that the men were engaged in terrorist activity, the prosecution's case is weak due to conflicting eyewitness testimony and forensic tests showing traces of drugs and chemicals that defence lawyers have argued are contradictory. Ultimately, the men may be released due to lack of credible evidence.

American interests

With 'phase one' of the military dimension of the US-led campaign against terrorism largely completed in Afghanistan, the Bush administration is gearing up for phase two. Taming the insurgencies in Colombia is fairly high on the list of priorities. The Bush administration has had little patience with the FARC's bad faith at the negotiating table, continued involvement in drug trafficking and increasingly urban terrorist activities. It applauded Uribe's election and considers him a reliable and capable ally. Washington has, of course, made it clear to Uribe that Colombia's war will necessitate Colombian solutions and that much more needs to be done by the Colombian government before security and peace can be established. That said, the Bush administration recognised that commerce in illicit narcotics and insurgency were integrally related, and decided to fund the Colombian military's counter-insurgency efforts directly, crossing a fundamental policy boundary that had restricted American military assistance to counter-narcotics efforts.

American help will focus, in the first instance, on protecting Colombia's largest oil pipeline. Oil represents 25% of the government's annual revenues; over 1,000 guerrilla pipeline attacks since the 1980s have cost Bogotá upwards of $500 million per year. The army has deployed five of the 18th brigade's six battalions for pipeline protection – up from two battalions the year before. This has led to a drop in pipeline bombings from 170 to 30 between 2001 and 2002. In February 2002, the Bush administration announced a $98m programme to fund and train an elite Colombian counter-insurgency military battalion whose primary goal will be to guard the pipeline. The battalion will consist of approximately 1,000 soldiers and will be trained by US Special Forces (Green Berets). In January 2003, several dozen US Special Forces personnel arrived in the department of Arauca to begin training the new battalion. The troops are limited to 60 men at any one time in the areas of conflict, are barred from any military action, and will be housed in specially fortified barracks. It is likely that the hands-on training of this elite battalion will be the first step in significantly increased US counter-insurgency support over the next several years. A strong indication that this policy shift will receive bipartisan support in Washington arose in August when Congress approved a plan allowing the Colombian military to use American-supplied helicopters in counter-insurgency operations. Even Senator Patrick Leahy, a long-time critic of US policy in Colombia, backed the move.

In coordination with counter-insurgency efforts, Washington has enthusiastically continued its almost 20-year involvement in anti-drug efforts in Colombia. Despite the recent $1.2 billion 'Plan Colombia' effort that was intended to reduce the production and export of illicit drugs, in 2002 as much processed cocaine (700 tonnes) was leaving Colombia as in any previous year. Indeed, coca is apparently being cultivated in roughly twice as many parts of the country than it was a few years ago. Crop-substitution and fumigation efforts in early 2002 were frustrated by the high opportunity costs imposed on farmers, delays in government subsidies to the 3,500 farmers who did agree to stop growing coca and the intimidation tactics of drug traffickers and allied paramilitaries. Almost four times as much coca was destroyed by fumigation than by voluntary removal, and the effort was a public-relations disaster for the Colombian and US governments. In early September 2002, however, the United States started the biggest and most aggressive fumigation effort to date, aimed at wiping out coca cultivation in southern Colombia by destroying the crop before it can be replaced. Some 300,000 acres were to be fumigated by the end of the year, up 30% on the previous year; authorities hope to double the acreage fumigated in 2003. In late 2002, the US also restarted the joint programme of forcing or shooting down suspected drug trafficking planes – suspended in April 2001 when a Peruvian Air Force jet shot down a US missionary group's plane, killing an American mother and her infant daughter. In February 2003, the US announced a 15% reduction in Colombia's coca crop.

While increasingly looking for ways to ensure that its aid can be used for both anti-drug and counter-insurgency efforts, the bureaucratic inertia of the 'war on drugs' – and the political risks of a counterinsurgency effort – are likely to mean that the United States will continue to place drugs before terrorism. Yet, while pledging that the Pentagon would continue to support

The Americas

counter-narcotics programmes that 'contribute to the war on terrorism', in October 2002 US Deputy Secretary of Defense Paul Wolfowitz circulated a memo saying that the department had reviewed its existing counter-narcotics policies because of the 'changed national security environment, the corresponding shifts in the department's budget and other priorities, and evolving support requirements'. This suggests that, in the medium term, funding for the anti-drug war, especially if it continues to yield poor results, may be harder to justify. More immediately, however, Colombia will draw substantial US attention and resources. Following the 7 February 2003 bombing of the Bogotá club, Colombian Defence Minister Marta Lucia Ramirez flew to Washington to request additional counter-terrorism assistance. On 13 February, the FARC took three Pentagon employees prisoner after their Cessna crashed 400km south of Bogotá, having shot dead another American and a Colombian Army sergeant. The FARC offered to free the Americans if FARC prisoners were released from Colombian jails. On grounds of emergency, Congress permitted US troops to be deployed to Colombia for search-and-rescue, even though the new contingent would increase the total number of US troops in-country to above the congressional limit of 400. In March, another Cessna searching for the American prisoners crashed, apparently due to engine trouble; three Americans were killed.

A near-coup in Venezuela

If left-wing non-state actors in Colombia have proven that country's bane, Venezuela's left-wing government has been its scourge. The political standoff between the populist President Chávez and his political opponents continued throughout 2002 and into 2003. While he enjoyed nearly 80% support at the beginning of his term in 1999, Chávez had only around 30% backing – albeit from fiercely loyal, economically marginalised citizens – in early 2003. The national strikes of late 2002 and early 2003 temporarily paralysed the economy, and increased political violence remains likely. After surviving an April 2002 coup attempt, Chávez emerged committed to remaining in power. The growing anti-Chávez opposition is now largely resigned to pursuing electoral means to secure his removal from office. It is far from certain whether Chávez would honour such an election or referendum if the results were not in his favour. Indeed, as of April 2003, Chávez appeared to be something approaching a South American version of Zimbabwean President Robert Mugabe: against overwhelming popular opposition, he has derogated democratic political processes and dragged a country with substantial natural resources and economic potential into unnecessary weakness, all out of personal political vanity.

Chávez's grip on power began to slip in early 2002 following the 5 January election for a new congressional leadership, when Willian Lara, president of the National Assembly and a Chávez ally, was almost voted out by an increasingly confident opposition. The opposition in congress was united and even included some members of Chávez's own Fifth Republic Movement. This vote was significant, as it signalled that Chávez could no longer count on the automatic majority in the legislature that had endorsed his radical agenda and, most importantly, allowed him to rightfully claim that his administration's policies were being implemented democratically. A crisis erupted in early April 2002 as workers at the state-owned oil corporation, Petroleos de Venezuela SA (PDVSA), went on strike to protest Chávez's attempts to appoint political allies to key management positions. PDVSA had approximately 40,000 employees and generated $50bn in annual revenues. Oil accounts for half of Venezuela's tax receipts and close to 80% of its export revenues. Many workers were also upset at Chávez's policy of supplying 50,000 barrels of oil a day to Cuba at below-market prices. Shortly after the oil strike began, a national strike organised by the leading and largest labour union, Confederation of Venezuelan Workers (CTV), and supported by Fedecámaras, the leading business association, got under way. United, these groups staged large marches, some involving 250,000 to 350,000 people, and vowed not to end their protests until Chávez had left office.

On 11 April 2002, Chávez ordered the army to fire on an unarmed, peaceful march that included women, children and senior citizens. The army refused to obey what it considered to be a criminal and unconstitutional order. While the details remain murky, 17 anti-Chávez protestors were shot and killed (two more died subsequently) and hundreds were wounded by snipers and troops loyal to the president. News of the casualties spiked anti-Chávez sentiment and set in motion a military operation that had been in the making for six months and involved as many as 60 generals, 20 admirals and 3,000 officers. Army commander General Efraín Vázquez Velasco demanded that Chávez resign in order to avoid any further bloodshed. Chávez refused, but stated that he would 'abandon his functions' of office upon approval by the National Assembly, where Chávez held a slight and precarious majority. Chávez was then taken to, and held captive at, a military base on the Caribbean island of La Orchila. Reports emerged that efforts were underway to allow him to go into exile in Cuba. Armed Forces commander General Lucas Rincón Romero announced that Chávez had resigned and then announced his own resignation and that of the entire military high command; 90 minutes later Pedro Carmona Estanga, President of Fedecámaras, was named head of the transitional government. Against the advice of seasoned politicians, on 12 April, he and his team issued a decree that disbanded the National Assembly and the Supreme Court, fired the entire cabinet, the Attorney General, the Solicitor General, the Comptroller General and the Ombudsman. The decree also gave Carmona the right to appoint all governors, mayors and public officials at the state and municipal levels. While the military operation was not judged a seizure of power (the officers involved were later acquitted of military rebellion by the Supreme Court), the issuance of the decree did amount to a coup. Carmona invoked and then voided the 1999 Constitution, which had been ratified democratically by a large majority in late 1999, and swore himself in as Interim President.

The decree was vehemently rejected by most Venezuelans, people and institutions, and decried as dictatorial. Among its most vocal critics was CTV, which had accompanied Fedecamaras in leading the march towards the presidential palace a few hours earlier. CTV's representative stormed out of the room where the signing ceremony was to take place as soon as he became aware of the decree's contents, shortly before it was read publicly. The US, Spain and Colombia quickly recognised the new government. But the broad-based coalition that had marched in support of Chávez's ouster quickly broke down. Many in the trade unions, opposition parties and certain sectors of the military did not agree with Carmona's decision to dissolve the legislature and the Supreme Court and to remove elected officials whose legitimacy was not in question. Moreover, the cabinet of Carmona's interim government did not include labour leaders and, to many in the opposition, it represented a revisionist, triumphal and tiny oligarchic elite.

Carmona made another tactical mistake by naming Admiral Héctor Ramírez Pérez minister of defence, ahead of Vázquez. The Venezuelan Army is much larger than the navy and Vázquez, who had provided the crucial military support that made it possible for Carmona to become president, took it as a slap in the face when someone from the navy was appointed above him. Vázquez quickly withdrew his support for the interim government, signalling the end of Carmona's short-lived tenure as president. He stepped down at 10pm on 13 April. Air Force helicopters bearing army paratroopers from Chávez's old battalion fetched him from captivity at the naval base. In addition to issuing unpopular decrees upon taking office, Carmona underestimated the tenacity of Chávez's supporters within the Bolivarian Circles – armed militia cells that were created with Cuban assistance over the previous year. It is believed that approximately 500,000 citizens belong to 30,000 Bolivarian Circles. These well-organised cells provided crucial logistical support throughout the poorest areas of Caracas and were instrumental in maintaining civic pressure against Carmona's regime. When Chávez returned to Miraflores, the presidential palace, at 3am on 14 April, loyal troops and members of the Bolivarian Circles were there to greet him. The coup was aborted.

Chávez retrenches

After nearly being ousted, Chávez moderated his rhetoric, and appeared initially to accept the role of minority president. His first order of business was to mend fences with the armed forces. Chávez's continuous claim that the military was solidly behind him was refuted by the attempted coup.

Chávez replaced Vázquez with General Julio Garcia Montoya, an ally, and placed other unconditional supporters in control of the military. Soon after the failed coup, Chávez seemed to have pulled back from his efforts to take political control of the PDVSA. In a move designed to mollify the giant oil corporation, Chávez appointed Ali Rodríguez, Secretary-General of the Organisation of Petroleum Producing Countries (OPEC), as PDVSA's president and chairman of the board. The highly respected Rodríguez was supposed to bridge the gap between the Chávez administration and the PDVSA's management. One of Rodríguez's first acts was to approve a board of directors that included dissident executives who had remained at the company while Chávez was trying to install a new, politically loyal leadership.

Notwithstanding these gestures, by September 2002, Chávez was no longer conciliatory towards the opposition, which responded in kind by increasing activities intended to force him out of office. On 22 October 2002, 14 generals and admirals, many of whom were involved in the April events, joined about 140 other military officers who were protesting at Plaza Francia in Altamira, Caracas' mostly middle-class sector, in support of opposition groups. Relations between Chávez's government and the opposition took a turn for the worse on 16 November 2002, when Chávez ordered troops to take control of Caracas' 8,000-strong Metropolitan Police, whose members had been involved in a protracted strike. Chávez had long viewed the Metropolitan Police as a political tool of Caracas Mayor Alfredo Peña, a Chávez opponent. Street protests and disturbances led by opposition leaders erupted throughout Caracas, and an explosion in the centre of the city killed three people.

Tensions peaked on 1 December 2002, when the opposition launched an indefinite national strike. The most visible group among the strikers was the oil workers, whose walkout immediately cut Venezuela's oil production from 3m barrels per day to 300,000. The resulting losses to the Venezuelan government were $50m per day. Daily protests as large as the ones in April demanded Chávez's resignation. On 6 December 2002, shots were fired at a group of men, women and children who were attending a peaceful gathering of the opposition at Plaza Francia. Three people were killed – a 17-year old girl, a middle-aged university professor and an elderly lady – and 28 people were wounded, including a seven-year old girl. One shooter, Joao Gouveia, was overpowered by those present and handed over to the municipal authorities. Immediately after being taken into custody, he confessed to his crime. Given the high number of casualties and other evidence, it is likely that additional snipers were involved. The criminal investigation has been dilatory, and Chávez has publicly exculpated the shooter and referred to him as 'this Gentleman, Mr Gouveia'.

After clearly holding momentum during the first few weeks of the strike, by January 2003 the anti-Chávez contingent was now struggling to come

The Americas

up with reasons to defend a strike that had crippled Venezuela's economy and produced lethal violence but done nothing to remove Chávez from power. Chávez opportunistically started restoring the country's oil production and exporting ability. In late December 2002 he tightened his control over the PDVSA by suspending around 100 executives and managers whom he charged with supporting the strike. Chávez also ordered loyal forces within the military to take over oil installations. By January 2003, oil production was estimated to be back up to roughly 1.5m barrels per day. The Venezuelan Supreme Court dealt the anti-Chávez movement a severe blow when, in late January, it suspended a scheduled non-binding referendum on Chávez's rule. While this referendum would not have forced Chávez's removal, the opposition was hoping to use the results to embarrass the president. Indeed, Chávez's government has twice attempted to steal and destroy the petition forms. Nonetheless, on 2 February 2003, the date on which the referendum was to take place, the opposition gathered more than 4m signatures (almost 40% of the electorate) in support of a number of electoral and civic initiatives. This event signalled the end of the private-sector strike.

Tottering economy, political weakness

Despite Chávez's survival, permanent damage may have been done to the PDVSA. The company lost $4bn in export revenues. Chávez fired nearly 16,000 workers with an average of 17 years' experience (totalling 289,000 man-years) for participating in the strike. In February 2003, PDVSA company officials optimistically predicted that oil production would soon reach pre-strike levels of 3.1m barrels per day (b/d). However, because lack of proper maintenance has rendered some fields inoperative and may have cut production capacity by 400,000 b/d, independent analysts forecast a maximum of 2.3m b/d by the end of 2003 (including 900,000 b/d from operating agreements with third parties and extra-heavy crude joint ventures with foreign partners). This would mean that the PDVSA would be unable to take advantage of the spike in oil prices that is expected to occur in 2003, and would only take in $14.3bn – 30% less than PDVSA's crude-oil export revenues for 2001. Succumbing to the short-term financial temptation of divesting itself of its international refining facilities, which are specially outfitted to handle Venezuela's gummy variety of heavy crude, could also spell longer-term shrinkage of Venezuela's oil industry. Gasoline and basic goods remain scarce. Unable to start gasoline refining operations, the government is importing 125,000 barrels of gasoline per day at a cost of 1,000 Venezuelan bolivars (VEB) per litre and selling it at a maximum price of VEB 97 per litre, yielding losses of $11.3m per day.

Capital flight, on account of increased political risk, has occurred at a torrid pace. Venezuela's foreign reserves dropped $1.5bn within six weeks of the start of the December 2002 strike. On 23 January 2003, the government suspended all foreign exchange (FX) sales and announced the imposition of strict FX controls whereby all FX transactions were legally required to go through the Venezuelan Central Bank. President Chávez has announced that dollars will not be made available to 'coupsters' – a label he uses to describe virtually anybody who belongs to the opposition. It is widely believed that the allocation of dollars will be used with politically retaliatory intent. In early March 2003, dollars were still not available and many companies that rely on imports for raw materials were being forced to close. One episode that illustrated the dire state of the economic situation occurred on 17 January 2003, when National Guard troops armed with machine-guns and shotguns stormed a Coca-Cola and Pepsi-Cola bottling plant, confiscating bottled and canned drinks. The troops stated that they intended to distribute them to the poor. Economists have predicted a 20–30% contraction in the Venezuelan economy for 2003, and it is expected that another million jobs will be lost, in addition to the million already lost since Chávez became president.

As of March 2003, political measures to calm the situation had produced no concrete results. In a move that was largely viewed as a rebuke to Chávez, on 17 December 2003 the Organization of American States (OAS) Permanent Council passed a resolution that called for a peaceful, democratic, constitutional and politically viable electoral solution to the crisis. It also mentioned the suppression of press freedoms in Venezuela, a criticism frequently levelled against the Chávez administration. The US government quickly endorsed the resolution, which many viewed as a moderation of its more exacting and provocative previous statement of support for early 2003 elections in Venezuela. In mid-January 2003, the 'Group of Friends of Venezuela' (United States, Brazil, Mexico, Spain, Portugal and Chile) was created and will work alongside the OAS to help promote a peaceful resolution to the crisis. Chávez rhetorically welcomed the formation of the group but said, capriciously, that China, Russia, France and Cuba and several developing nations (including, among others, Libya and Algeria) needed to be included. While OAS Secretary-General César Gaviria attempted to bring the government and opposition together and establish a crisis-resolution dialogue, his efforts were met with intransigence on both on both sides. US diplomatic credibility may have been damaged by its acquiescence to the coup while it was under way – the Department of State publicly blamed the crisis on 'undemocratic actions committed or encouraged by the Chávez administration' – and Washington's further indication that it was eager to deal with a post-Chávez government. Chávez's closeness to Cuba, opposition to the Free Trade Area of the Americas and indirect support for the FARC had displeased the US, in any event.

After meeting with UN Secretary-General Kofi Annan on 16 January 2003, Chávez told a group of reporters, 'I don't have the slightest doubt of our victory. We are winning this battle and we are going to win it'.

The Americas

Chávez maintained that he was still willing to consider holding a referendum, most likely in August 2003, if 2.3m signatures – 20% of the electorate – were obtained. He indicated that he would step down if more than 3.7m people – at least one more vote than the number which he obtained when he was re-elected in May 2000 – voted in favour of removing him from office. In a January 2003 visit to Venezuela, former US President Jimmy Carter introduced a plan for holding such a referendum and both sides agreed to consider it. Even if the opposition succeeds in having a referendum held, it remains unclear whether Chávez would abide by its results.

Slow change in unstable environments

The FARC's increase in terrorist and guerrilla operations has been matched by the Uribe government's firm and resolute stand against all manifestations of terrorism. Heightened US counter-insurgency support has increased the Colombian government's effectiveness in protecting infrastructure and, to a certain extent, the population. A 'Colombian solution' to Colombia's security problems, however, is likely to require a successful offensive that deprives the FARC of territory, decimates its forces and thereby weakens it before resuming negotiations. Given that the hard-line Uribe is a natural political ally of the United States – and particularly given that the Argentina crisis and Brazil's new government have produced a Latin America broadly less enamoured of America – Colombia can probably rely on a significant level of US support in the medium term. Nevertheless, US priorities elsewhere will cap the assistance it can provide and put increasing pressure on Bogotá to carry the fight to the FARC. The continuing commitment of Bolivia, Ecuador and Peru to anti-narcotics operations and to containing cross-border insecurity posed by the FARC's remilitarisation, however, will likely help the US and Colombia in the pursuit of their objectives.

With respect to Colombia's insurgency problem, Chávez has been a minor nuisance, having offered the FARC medical supplies, transportation, safe haven and petroleum in exchange for the FARC's pledge not to operate or recruit in Venezuela. In March 2003, however, he reportedly ordered the Venezuelan Army to bomb FARC positions on the Venezuela–Colombia border. While the reconfigured post-coup military did generally demonstrate strong support for Chávez during the strike, the participation of a significant contingent of officers in the November 2002 protests indicated that all was not well within the military. Given this and Chávez's dwindling popular support, he appears to have less leeway for provocation at the regional level. At the same time, the aborted coup of April 2002 has lessened the probability of a successful military coup in the future. Further, the costly futility of the opposition's insistence on an early referendum ensured that less leverage would accrue to any future popular protest.

Although the oil sector is still committed to such a protest, the broader political opposition remains fractious. Conversely, the minority of Venezuelans who support Chávez are fiercely loyal to him and his revolution. The opposition may therefore conclude that early elections are too risky and settle for elections at a later date.

Yet even the ideologically sympathetic Brazilian President Luis Inácio Lula da Silva is nervous about Chávez's regional ambitions. Additionally, by March 2003, Chávez appeared to be getting increasingly paranoid and authoritarian as politics became more and more violent. In January, the Australian, Canadian and German embassies received bomb threats, and a grenade exploded at the residence of the Algerian ambassador, who had offered Chávez economic assistance. In late February, three dissident soldiers and one anti-government protester were murdered. A few days later, state security police placed businessman Carlos Fernandez – one of the leaders of the two-month strike – under house arrest on charges of civil rebellion and incitement to commit crimes; he was released a month after his arrest. The police also planned to arrest union (and strike) leader Carlos Ortega, who took refuge in the Costa Rican embassy and was granted asylum. On 23 February, Chávez spurned members of the OAS-linked 'Group of Friends of Venezuela', and a day later, during his weekly television and radio programme 'Hello President', warned the world to stop meddling in Venezuela's affairs, accused the US and Spain of siding with his enemies, threatened to break off diplomatic relations with Colombia and scolded the chief mediator of the OAS group for stepping 'out of line'. The next day, on 25 February, the Spanish embassy and the Colombian consulate in Caracas were bombed. Nobody claimed credit, but leaflets bearing the markings of the 'Bolivarian Liberation Front' – a theretofore unknown pro-Chávez group – were found scattered at the scene of the bombings. Directed at the OAS group, they stated that 'the revolution does not need your self-serving intervention'.

Far from seeking political reconciliation with his critics, Chávez has defiantly dubbed 2003 'the year of the offensive, the year of the attack' – unsurprising, given his military inclination to obliterate rather than negotiate with adversaries. Should the security and economic situation in Venezuela deteriorate substantially, however, Washington's hemispheric interests and Venezuela's importance as an oil producer suggest that major powers would not be as acquiescent to Venezuela's decline as they have been to Zimbabwe's. In any event, Chavez's power as a regional leader is diminished, as is the viability of his improbable project of creating a single Andean nation and that of his 'Bolivarian revolution' within Venezuela. Chávez's increasing isolation and Uribe's robust counter-insurgency may translate into net improvements for the northern Andes in the medium term. Meanwhile, though, political unrest in Venezuela and the FARC's insurgency are likely to yield greater insecurity and instability.

The Americas

Brazil: Political Optimism and Economic Restraint

Brazil's elections of October 2002, including the fourth direct presidential election since the end of its military dictatorship in 1985, confirmed the vitality of Brazilian democracy and Brazil's departure from its past elitism. Some 115 million Brazilians went to the polls to choose their leaders from 18,781 candidates running for 1,647 state and federal positions. In a rapid, efficient and peaceful process, they elected Luiz Inácio da Silva – commonly known as 'Lula' – president, as well as a vice-president, 27 governors, 54 senators (two-thirds of the Senate), 513 representatives (the entire House) and 1,024 state representatives. A former metalworker with very little formal education, from the left-wing Workers Party (PT), Lula won in a landslide after three failed attempts. In the first round of the election on 6 October, he received 46.44% of ballots cast, easily beating Brazilian Social Democrat Party (PSDB) candidate José Serra's 23.20%, Brazilian Socialist Party (PSB) candidate Anthony Garotinho with 17.87% and Popular Socialist Party (PPS) candidate Ciro Gomes with 11.97%. In the second round on 27 October, Lula received 52,793,364 votes, or 61.27% of ballots cast, against José Serra's 33,370,739 votes, or 38.73%.

Financial concerns initially dampened the campaign's affirmation of Brazil's democratic viability. During most of the electoral campaign, the international financial markets reacted nervously to the prospects of a leftist administration in Brazil – and, in particular, Lula and the PT's past advocacy of debt repudiation. Markets were wary that a PT administration might break existing financial contracts and debt obligations, pushing Brazil towards an economic disaster akin to Argentina's. Investment agencies increased risk assessments, forcing the devaluation of the Brazilian currency, the real, and helping to create the very conditions for the feared meltdown. But Lula allayed these worries, stressing that he would respect Brazil's financial obligations and maintain orthodox economic policies. The resulting political optimism was reinforced by the unprecedented smoothness of the two-month transition process. Both incumbent President Fernando Henrique Cardoso's administration and Lula's transition team made concerted efforts to further soothe markets. Lula's team was granted full access to information in all areas of government, and consulted on some critical last-minute decisions of Cardoso's administration. Indeed, every political step of Lula's transition team was taken with one eye on the political environment and the other on the reactions of the international financial market. The upshot has been an administration less populist and more conventional than anticipated, and greater economic stability.

Lula's path to power

Lula's victory resulted from a combination of his freshness and his opponent's staleness. Much of his early rhetoric was pointedly anti-American, anti-globalisation and politically retrograde. He blamed American neo-liberal economic policies for much of Latin America's and Brazil's economic woe, called the US-backed plan for a Free Trade Area of the Americas (FTAA) a plot to 'annex' Brazil and labelled international lenders 'economic terrorists'. Although Brazil renounced any intentions to develop nuclear weapons in the 1990s and ratified the Non-proliferation Treaty in 1997, Lula also seemed to suggest that Brazil should have nuclear weapons and move closer to China, which had been courting the Brazilian military and investing in Brazil's aerospace industry. The prospect of Lula's presidency also produced some anxiety in Washington. Beginning in 1990, Lula had convened the 'Forum of São Paulo', which included participants of several governments considered by the US to be sponsors of terrorism – notably Cuba, Iraq and Libya – and political representatives of some terrorist organisations, including the Provisional Irish Republican Army and the Basque separatist Euskadi ta Askatasuna. The PT had also expressed support for anti-American, left-wing Colombian guerrillas, criticised Israel, backed the Chinese government in the spy-plane crisis of April 2001, opposed US Iraqi policy and condemned the Bush administration for its 'unilateral and hegemonic vocation'.

Because the election year was an especially bad one for the Brazilian economy, it was easy for the Brazilian public to forget Cardoso's generally good economic stewardship – in the form of the complex and successful 'Real Plan' for economic stabilisation and inflation control measures – over the long term. The more urgent preoccupation with unemployment and poverty made Lula's criticisms of the Cardoso administration's 'neo-liberal' agenda and its adherence to the Washington Consensus (favouring macroeconomic discipline, the market economy and foreign trade) more compelling. Additionally, Lula's focus on social programmes and promises of doubling the minimum wage – $100 per month when Cardoso took office and currently about $60 – were extremely appealing to much of the electorate. Moreover, the dire state of the economy limited how Cardoso could help Serra's campaign and left him facing a political dilemma. If he criticised Lula or Gomes, he could exacerbate market concerns and seriously impair Brazil's economy, forsaking the considerable economic accomplishments of his eight-year administration. If, on the other hand, he did not attack Lula and Gomes, Serra's campaign would have little chance of success. Perhaps on account of realistic assessments of Serra's prospects, Cardoso nobly opted to allay market concerns.

As the election drew near, Lula diluted his rhetorical vitriol both to soothe international financial markets and to reduce the public's lofty expectations based on his earlier campaign promises. In June, he published an open letter in which he pledged to honour Brazil's financial contracts with the international community, making three substantive economic commitments: to maintain the system of inflation targets and manage monetary policy consistent with these targets; to maintain the floating exchange rate system; and to ensure the necessary primary budget surplus in order to guarantee a reduction in the ratio of public debt-to-GDP. More broadly, Lula adopted an effective marketing strategy that presented him not as the revolutionary veteran of previous campaigns but as a champion of democracy who would negotiate to achieve his agenda. 'Lulinha Paz e Amo' ('Little Lula Peace and Love') was the popular campaign slogan. In addition to the PT itself the parties included the Communist Party of Brazil (PCdoB), the Liberal Party (PL), the National Mobilization Party (PMN) and the Brazilian Communist Party (PCB). The PT's election platform was based on the generation of employment and promotion of social inclusion, buttressed by subsidiary promises to end poverty, generate a larger trade surplus, improve social services and reform the tax system. Lula's programme also included substantial redistributive mechanisms, such as doubling the minimum wage over four years and maintaining the marginal income tax rate at 27.5%. While Lula made his agenda less threatening to the middle class with sensible economic proposals, Serra was unable to convey an inventive programme for tackling the shortcomings of the Cardoso administration, especially those related to the growing national debt. In addition, Serra lacked Lula's charismatic proletarian appeal and was susceptible to being branded a candidate of the Brazilian elite. In particular, his criticism of Lula's lack of formal education backfired because Lula's strategy had been to emphasise precisely this aspect of his background.

Despite Lula's triumph in the presidential election, the PT was unable to replicate that success at other levels of government. In 27 governors' races, only three PT candidates won seats, and these only in the less significant states of Acre, Piauí and Mato Grosso do Sul. Moreover, PT candidates endured losses in the important states of São Paulo, Rio de Janeiro, Minas Gerais, Brasilia, Pernambuco and Rio Grande do Sul. The loss in São Paulo was especially shocking, given that the state was the party's demographic centre and PT member Martha Suplicy was at that time the mayor. In Rio de Janeiro, the PT incumbent, Benedita da Silva, was defeated. The PT's loss in Rio Grande do Sul ended the party's hold there. In the race for legislative seats, the PT made gains, but the party was still far from achieving a majority in the House or Senate. In the Chamber of Deputies, the PT won 91 of 513 seats and in state legislatures it captured only 147 of the 1,059 seats available. Given these legislative realities, Lula will have to negotiate feverishly to establish alliances that will grant him the necessary majority to pass major reforms in Congress.

The economy

The Brazilian economy went through 2002 like an acrobat on a tightrope, advancing step by step while being battered by the strong winds of the financial markets. The year began with the struggle to minimise the negative effects of destabilising international, regional and domestic developments in 2001. The shrinking of the global economy, the terrorist attacks against the US and the Argentine economic crisis were still causing damage. On the domestic front, an electric energy crisis had created additional inflation pressures. Compounding the lingering effects of these crises was the uncertainty surrounding the elections. Consequently, during 2002, international financial markets raised the financial burden on Brazil by greatly increasing the interest rates for foreign capital.

In September 2002, Brazil's net public debt totalled $255 billion; its net public and private foreign debt $165bn. This was largely the result of government splurging, encouraged by the financial markets' typical enthusiasm for emerging-market economies in the late 1990s. Yet Brazil's 2002 economic crisis, which led to an International Monetary Fund (IMF) emergency loan of $30bn in August 2002, cannot be explained by the standard criticisms of Brazilian fiscal policies. During the last few years of the Cardoso administration, Brazil's primary fiscal balance markedly improved. Since the 1998 launch of a fiscal directive that established annual primary budgetary surpluses, Brazil was able to exceed each targeted surplus. Additionally, in 2000 the Brazilian Congress enacted the Fiscal Responsibility Law, which established a rigorous set of guidelines and controls for public administrators (particularly state governors) regarding the management of revenues, expenditures, assets and liabilities. Thanks to this law, the federal government was finally able to tackle a chronic problem of the Brazilian economy: its lack of control over state governmental expenditures. For all levels of government, the new law established limits on public debt and personnel spending by setting fiscal targets for each year.

The Cardoso administration also implemented the largest privatisation programme in the world, committing itself to strict inflation control based on high tax rates established by the Central Bank Monetary Policy Council (COPOM). Theoretically, this should have enabled Brazil to stop the spiralling growth of its public debt-to-GDP ratio. Instead, the ratio has doubled over the last eight years from 30% of GDP in 1994 to the current 60%. The Brazilian Central Bank imputed this to high real interest rates, the devaluation of the real since 1999, small primary surpluses prior to 1998 and previously unaccounted-for 'hidden' debts in the order of 10% of GDP. Indeed, the devaluation of the real alone accounts for roughly a 15% increase in Brazil's debt. An additional factor was the further depreciation of the real due to (under-appreciated) contagion from the Argentine crisis. Central Bank officials qualify these factors as non-recurring and therefore not relevant to long-term debt projections. Their projections indicate that under present fiscal responsibility policies, current primary surpluses should keep the public debt-to-GDP ratio from growing (assuming a real GDP growth rate of 3.5 % per year and average real interest rates of 9% per year).

The Cardoso administration initially targeted the primary surplus goal by dramatically reducing investment in state-owned enterprises. Although the 2002 budget allocated R21.36bn for the investments in state-owned companies, the Finance Ministry authorised only 25% of this amount for investment. Nevertheless, the impact of these savings was relatively small, as they accounted for only about 2% of Brazil's total public debt. The bulk of the public debt was incurred by the federal and state governments, accounting for 35.4% and 18.5% of GDP respectively. An inordinately large portion of the federal government's debt was also a result of the extravagant Brazilian social security system. In 2001, the total social security deficit came to R61bn, or 4.8% of GDP. Because pensions were a highly a controversial issue, affecting a broad range of interests and lobbies, Cardoso was unable to get a social-security reform bill through Congress.

The IMF rescue

By the end of June 2002, with financial markets reacting nervously to populist presidential campaigns, the risk premium for Brazil climbed to its highest levels since just prior to the 1999 financial crisis. In July 2002, US Treasury Secretary Paul O'Neill added to the sense of crisis. During a television interview at the outset of a trip to South America, O'Neill was quoted as saying that he held little hope about the prospects for new money flowing to Brazil. He argued that as specific money comes in, Brazilian authorities should put policies in place to ensure that the 'money does some good and does not just go out of the country to Swiss bank accounts'. On the following day, the real fell more than 5% against the US dollar.

The fact that 40% of Brazil's public debt is dollar-denominated or indexed to the exchange rate compounds the risks of Brazilian currency weakness. From 26 July the real spiralled downward, losing 40% of its value against the US dollar by January 2002, which placed extraordinary pressure on Brazil's external debt. Viewed as a barometer for the market's risk appetite, the exchange rate clearly showed an increasing loss of confidence in Brazil. Additionally, investors were drawing parallels between the Brazilian and Argentine crises, regardless of the different circumstances involved. Although the Brazilian economy rested on a relatively healthy foundation (which O'Neill later acknowledged), laid during the Cardoso administration, the market's loss of confidence in Brazil's medium-term solvency capacity threatened to transform these expectations into a self-fulfilling prophecy. Therefore, it was essential for Brazil to restore confidence and regain access to external private capital through bank lending, trade finance, bond markets and foreign direct investment.

Politically, Cardoso downplayed the economic risks attending a victory of the left in Brazil. Financially, he accepted an IMF package that would disburse most of its money after the end of his tenure. On 7 August, the IMF announced the largest aid package in its history: a $30bn, 15-month agreement with the Brazilian government. After two months of slumping bond prices and weaker currency, this agreement was intended to resuscitate the market. By making most of the funding available only in 2003, pending the accomplishment of specific goals, however, the IMF agreement effectively reined in any new administration with austere economic policies. The agreement made the disbursement of new money contingent on the new administration's targeting a primary budget surplus of 3.75% of GDP. Although achieving this goal will not require additional belt tightening, since the Brazilian Congress has already approved this plan in the 2003 budget, it will still likely curb the temptation to loosen the current fiscal balance. The agreement also allowed for a reduction in the minimum reserves that the Central Bank was required to keep by $10bn. Together with $6bn of new lending, the Central Bank could count on $16bn to restore market confidence. Despite the IMF agreement, the markets remained worried that Brazil would be unable to honour $75bn worth of domestic debt obligations due in August 2003. Only after the elections were decided and emphatic affirmations of his commitment to fiscal discipline did the markets give Lula some positive feedback. After having lost 35% of its value, the real gained 9% within three months after the presidential race.

By November 2002, according to the Brazilian Institute of Geography and Statistics (IBGE) and the COPOM, most of the economic indicators showed some signs of recovery. The GDP posted growth of 0.93% for the third quarter of 2002 in comparison with the previous quarter and an accumulated growth of 0.94% compared to the same period in 2001. These indicators led the Central Bank to project an annual average growth rate of 1.26% for 2002 and 1.95% for 2003. Most importantly, the turnaround was marked by an improvement in consumer confidence, based on a perception of improved stability in the political arena. In addition, the foreign sector showed unexpectedly positive results. In large part due to the strength of the US dollar, which helped the trade balance, the current account deficit was reduced from the $20bn forecast by the government in the beginning of the year, to $14bn in September and as low as $9bn by year's end. This forecast was primarily the result of a trade surplus of $12.5bn for 2002. For 2003, the projected deficit was even lower, at $8bn, while the projected trade surplus was raised from $15.2bn to $15.5bn. However, this positive outcome was not due to the exceptional performance of exports. Rather, it was the result of a 17% year-on-year decline in imports caused by the expensive dollar and by the decline in domestic economic activity. Nevertheless, the overall effect of the reduction of the current account deficit was positive.

The Americas

Economic indicators also cast light on a more vexing development: inflation was on the rise. While the Real Plan exorcised the inflation demons in 1993, by 2001 inflation exceeded the 6.0% target set by the Extended Consumer Price Index (IPCA), reaching 7.7%. Consequently, in agreement with the inflation target regime established by the government in June 2001, the president of the Central Bank published an open letter to the Minister of Finance, in which he identified four causes of the problem: the impact of the Argentine financial crisis; pressure on the exchange rate stemming from the world economic slowdown; uncertainties in the world economy caused by the terrorist attacks against the US; and Brazil's energy crisis, which led to rationing and increases in energy tariffs. The Argentine crisis has continued to exert pressure on Brazil's economy, impairing prospects of a successful Mercosur (the trade bloc comprising Argentina, Brazil, Paraguay and Uruguay), and the world economy has not yet shown signs of recovery. While the uncertainty caused by the 11 September terrorist attacks may have been overcome, the US accounting scandals and war with Iraq produced additional uncertainty. Brazil did resolve the 2001 energy crisis, but inflationary pressure caused by elevated energy prices is still present. Some of the increase can be attributed to the depreciation of the real, which moved producers, chiefly in the food industry, to pass on the costs of the stronger dollar to consumers. Accumulated inflation for 2002 was 12.53%. In a bid to recover control over inflation, in its 17 December meeting the COPOM raised interest rates to 25%.

Lula's young presidency

In early December 2002, President-elect Lula visited Argentina, continuing on to the United States and Mexico. During his US visit, in response to an invitation from President Bush, Lula sought to improve the quality of Brazil's bilateral relations with the US, which had been somewhat harmed by his electoral rhetoric. Another aim was to further appease markets by demonstrating that he was not going to adopt a confrontational attitude towards the United States. The trip produced positive results. For example, at their 10 December meeting, Lula and President Bush agreed to hold a presidential summit in 2003, and decided to upgrade bilateral trade issues to Cabinet level. This decision was particularly important to the prospects of the FTAA, since Brazil and the US were to jointly chair FTAA negotiations over the next two years.

The appointment of Antonio Palocci as economic minister and Henrique Meirelles, a former global banking head at FleetBoston Financial Corp., as President of the Central Bank were also well received by the markets. Meirelles had won a seat in the House for the PSDB, Cardoso's party. His appointment was a clear message that a pragmatic concern with the markets had trumped left-wing ideology. The remainder of Lula's cabinet appointments reflected the President's commitments to the coalition that helped elect him and PT's efforts to reach a majority in the Congress. He appointed PT members to 14 of the 25 ministries and left seven ministries to allied parties. Former adversary Ciro Gomes was named Minister of National Integration. Miro Teixeira, from the PDT (Democratic Worker's Party), was named Minister of Communications. Roberto Amaral, from the PSB and former coordinator of Garotinho's campaign, was named Minister of Science and Technology. For the other four positions, Lula named two business leaders – Luiz Fernando Furlan as Minister of Development, Industry and Foreign Trade, and Roberto Rodrigues as Minister of Agriculture – and two diplomats with no party affiliation – Celso Amorim as Minister of Foreign Relations and José Viegas Filho as Minister of Defence.

Lula was inaugurated on 1 January 2003. His inaugural speech, as well as those of Palocci and Meirelles, reiterated assurances that the new administration would not be economically adventurous and would reinforce the current fundamentals of the Brazilian economy. A few days later, he announced the cancellation of the $760m procurement competition for new jet fighters launched during the Cardoso administration, making these resources available to the *Fome Zero* (Zero Hunger) programme. This pronouncement met with broad approval as an important and symbolic decision illustrating the new administration's focus on the social sector. Initial market responses to the Lula administration were positive.

Palocci stuck to his economic pledges. Backed by Palocci, Brazil's central bank in early 2003 twice raised interest rates – the second time to 26.5% – and thus boosted the real and restrained inflation. After the first half of January 2003, the real closed at 3.25 to the dollar – its strongest showing since September 2002. Through early April, it had maintained this rate. Most importantly, the government bond spread had narrowed to around 1250 basis points over US Treasury's, the best spread since June 2002. The risk premium for holding Brazilian debt dropped from 20 percentage points in October 2002 to ten in March 2003. Nevertheless, investors were still proceeding cautiously. On 12 January, Goldman Sachs lowered its recommendation on Brazil's equities to underweight from neutral, arguing that the market had come too far, too fast. J.P. Morgan maintained its underweight rating on Brazilian bonds, noting that 'fundamental improvements will be harder to deliver than market-friendly rhetoric'. Of substantial concern to investors are Brazil's looming short-term debt maturities and the awareness that the Brazilian Congress has a history of balking at reform initiatives, particularly controversial ones such as the reorganisation of social security. Yet because Brazilian financial institutions' government debt exposure is so high – they hold about 80% of all public debt owing to restrictions on foreign-currency holdings – they have little incentive to force the government into default.

For Brazil's debt dynamics to be controlled so as to avoid default, the economy must grow quickly enough that high interest rates do not keep increasing the economy's debt-to-GDP ratio. In that case, the ratio would decline over time, improving Brazil's risk profile and ensuring continued access to external capital. To halt the rise of its debt levels, Brazil needs to reach annual GDP growth rates of around 4–5%. The 2001 results were poor, with the real GDP growth slowing from the 4% of 2000 to 1.5%. A January 2003 Central Bank survey indicated that investors believed that Brazil would record a trade surplus of $15.3bn in 2003, lower than anticipated. This was a by-product, however, of improved expectations regarding the real, which is expected to close 2003 at 3.65 to the dollar. Inflation is expected to close 2003 around 11.23%, forcing the adjusted average rate of daily government-guaranteed financing to 20% at the end of the year. The survey also reported improved expectations towards GDP growth, from 1.93% to 1.96%, and prospects for a primary fiscal surplus of 3.80%. On balance, the reduction of the real value of debt through moderate inflation and decent prospects for managing debt-to-GDP ratio suggest that Brazil should be able to stave off a debt default, which the PT has strong political reasons for avoiding.

Regional implications

From a political standpoint, the remarkable standard of both the Brazilian elections and the transition process was a good model of democracy for the region. This is not a negligible development, considering that, until the 1990s, most Latin American countries were still under military dictatorships. From an economic standpoint, Brazil's emergence from its difficult journey in 2002 intact led markets finally to differentiate between the Brazilian and Argentine economic situations. Additionally, it may have given American policymakers some insight into the nuances of Latin American economies as well as some ideas on how to bring positive influence to bear on economic crises within the region.

Lula's ascendancy affected prospects for trade in the region. During his campaign, Lula strongly defended Mercosur while directing measured criticism at the FTAA. During the elections, PT economists were concerned that the FTAA could be wound up, based upon the North American Free Trade Agreement (NAFTA) and particularly upon NAFTA's Chapter 11, which allows the prosecution of governments for discriminatory treatment. This, they believed, would impair the PT's plans for a new Brazilian industrial policy, based on the creation of special incentives for national industries. Additionally, the economists feared that Brazil's interests would be marginalised by American efforts to impose patent provisions on FTAA associates, thereby raising the costs of critical pharmaceuticals manufactured in Brazil.

Consequently, Lula's strategy is to strengthen Mercosur in order to erect a stronger platform from which to negotiate favourable FTAA terms with the US. This strategy is not new, and indeed echoes the very impetus behind the creation of Mercosur in the early 1990s. After Brazil's 1999 crisis and the Argentine crisis in 2001, Cardoso had neither the resources nor the political support to revive it. Lula has brought political energy to the weakened organisation, prompting discussions of a common currency and a regional Parliament. He visited Argentina and Chile (which, with Bolivia, is an associate member of Mercosur), just prior to meeting with Bush in December 2002, to underscore the independence and importance of Brazil's regional agenda. Lula and other leaders of Mercosur countries have no illusions about the difficult negotiations ahead for the FTAA. In 2002, the Bush administration amplified the challenges by erecting protective trade barriers in the steel and agriculture sectors, adversely affecting some of Brazil's most important exports, including steel, citrus, meat and soy products. The ultimate fear was that trade tensions and the leftward political tilt of Venezuela and of the Southern Cone in the wake of the Argentine economic crisis and Lula's elections would result in a de facto partition of Latin America into an anti-American, anti-free trade Atlantic bloc and a pro-American, pro-free trade Pacific bloc.

The challenges ahead

So far, Lula and his PT administration have surprised their critics and even the most sceptical financial analysts. Throughout the campaign, they insisted that electing Lula would mean chaos and the dismantling of Brazil's financial architecture. They also predicted that he would push populist measures that would collide with previous policies of austerity and break financial contracts. In the event, Lula has stuck to an orthodox economic approach and his economic team has shown resolve in the face of growing pressures. As a consequence, the financial markets – although still reflecting a high degree of risk with wide debt spreads and low equity valuations – have reacted positively and are more optimistic about Brazil's current administration. In the latter part of 2003, however, attention will be more keenly directed on the future: to the progress on the reform agenda and to the prospects of economic growth, lower interest rates, less exchange-rate volatility and the continuous control of inflation.

Moreover, the markets will closely follow the way the administration handles the reaction of the electorate to Lula and the PT's failure to fulfil their more ambitious and iconoclastic campaign promises. After promising to raise the minimum wage, for example, he has now made it conditional: 'when the economic situation allows'. As of early 2003, no major programme for wealth redistribution was on stream. These circumstances may produce disquiet among Brazil's poor. Public employees have not had their wages raised in eight years, and land reform is at a standstill. In the countryside, the 'Movement of the Landless' (MST) and other dissident groups have refrained from land occupation protests in deference to the new administration. But public impatience with the lag between economic discipline and tangible ground-level improvements and with the implementation of reform caused the percentage of those rating Lula's government 'good' or 'very good' to drop from 57% in January 2003 to 45% in March. There were signs that his left-wing critics within the PT were angling for a 'Plan B' that would depart from Palocci's rigorous policies. Nevertheless, as at early 2003, Lula himself had maintained an approval rating of 75%.

The most pressing challenge is that of securing state debt obligations to the federal government. Lobbying by governors to have their debts renegotiated has so far met with a cold reception by the minister of the economy. On one hand, Lula knows that even a small lapse may lead to the collapse of fiscal responsibility that has made Brazil's current state of affairs substantially more manageable than the Argentine situation. On the other hand, Lula will also need support from the governors to pass his reforms in the Congress. A major political battle over social security system also looms. The existing system's growing deficits affect both federal and state finances, and call for reform. Yet such reform can only be made by constitutional amendment and must reduce the current inequalities between benefits for public and private sector workers while meeting strict actuarial requirements. Further, any reform in this sector must accommodate the legal presumption of rights and corresponding expectations of continued benefits. In short, meaningful social-security reform will be politically very difficult to accomplish. On 2 April 2003, however, Lula's first major economic reform – establishing autonomy for the Central Bank – was overwhelmingly approved in the lower house, 442–13. This demonstrated Lula's ability to marshal legislative support, and provided hope for more challenging reform in the tax system and public-sector pension regime.

Lula's important decision to restrain his populist instincts in favour of a degree of economic orthodoxy and his acceptance of IMF strictures, suggested that he has resisted broader social pressures on regional powers – prompted by the Argentine crisis and Washington's perceived lack of sympathy – to turn away from the United States. So, too, did his reassurances in January 2003 that notwithstanding ominously vague statements by Science and Technology Minister Amaral, Brazil had no plan to develop nuclear weapons. Lula has emerged as a trusted and diplomatically useful interlocutor for Venezuelan President Hugo Chávez. At the same time, if Lula appears to be too ideologically close to Chávez or indeed Fidel Castro, or continues Brazil's current coolness towards American anti-narcotics and counter-insurgency efforts in Colombia, Brasilia's credibility with Washington may suffer.

Lula's strategy for re-energising Mercosur as a means of increasing the Southern Cone's leverage vis-à-vis the US in free-trade negotiations may be salutary for his role as a hemispheric leader. Lula will not be as easy an interlocutor as Cardoso, and will probably strive to maintain his left-wing credentials with 'protest' diplomatic statements against some American policies; however, he will be constrained by his own divided Congress. Moreover, he cannot afford to alienate the US. Brazil is financially dependent on the IMF and, by extension, the US. Further, Brazil is one of the few nations that imports more from the US than it exports to it, and needs better access to US markets if Lula is to fulfil his goal of making Brazil an export power. An FTAA that lifted US protectionist restrictions on Brazilian steel and agricultural products could conceivably triple Brazil's US export revenues. These considerations should ensure that Lula will avoid strong or conspicuous alliances with Castro or Chávez, and dictate an approach to trade negotiations that is more pragmatic than confrontational, albeit tough and deliberate. This need to hedge will help preclude any stark ideological split in Latin America.

It may be too much to expect Brazil's foreign policy to become extroverted and pro-American in the first year of Lula's presidency, especially given the domestic economic challenges he faces. But Brazil remains the largest economy and most politically potent country in Latin America. There is plenty of scope for a more proactive and US-friendly foreign policy – for example, in supporting counter-insurgency efforts in Colombia and extending counter-terrorism cooperation in the 'Triple Frontier' between Brazil, Argentina and Paraguay, where increased transnational Islamic terrorist activity has been reported. Even with increased public pressure on Lula to scotch economic orthodoxy, the PT's 79-member national directorate endorsed Palocci's policies in March 2003. Assuming Lula's administration achieves substantial domestic economic stability, and the US and Brazil move forward on trade issues, Washington may thereafter press for a more affirmative and cooperative foreign policy. If he succumbs to populist pressure and damages Brazil's standing in international markets, however, Washington may face a reprise of the Argentine crisis of 2001–02. In that event, against the backdrop of a range of developments inimical to US interests such as Argentina's continued economic difficulties, instability in Venezuela and escalating conflict in Colombia, Washington's attention to Brazil might have to become even keener than it would otherwise be.

Europe/Russia

The Iraq crisis dominated European politics during 2002–03, and produced significant transatlantic and intra-European divisions. Among the Permanent Five members of the UN Security Council, France and Russia were aligned against the United States and the United Kingdom's decision to go to war in Iraq, precluding express Security Council backing for military intervention. Perforce NATO was divided, with France and Germany temporarily blocking the provision of surveillance and missile-defence assets to Turkey in anticipation of an Iraq war. Splits were sufficiently stark and deep that France warned that it might attempt to block the accession of hawkish eastern European countries to the European Union (EU) if they did not align their foreign policies more closely with those of core EU countries. In any case, there was no EU 'Common Foreign and Security Policy' (CFSP) on Iraq, and the institution's inability to speak in one voice on such a paramount issue cast some doubt over CFSP. Further, Iraq-related rifts only exacerbated existing difficulties that NATO was experiencing in redefining its mission in the wake of the 11 September 2001 terrorist attacks, and that the EU was enduring in striking a federal balance. Yet, through planned enlargements, both NATO and the EU reinforced their status as regional political glue, inviting seven and ten nations, respectively, to accede. NATO also established the 21,000-strong NATO Response Force and proffered the most historically significant innovation of the year in approving the Russia–NATO 'Council at 20', which gave Russia a strong voice on a number of key transatlantic policy issues.

The Iraq debate also dampened the Western vocations of Russia and Turkey. Russia's Westward foreign-policy momentum slowed, as Moscow felt compelled to register its foreboding of unchecked US power. At the same time, Russian President Vladimir Putin hedged his bets, delegating the job of delivering sharpest anti-American rhetoric to Foreign Minister Igor Ivanov. In any case, the crack in US–Russia relations and the prospect of a clash closer to home over Russian involvement in Iran's nuclear programme seemed to indicate a need for more thoughtful, candid and humble Russian policies on pre-emption and proliferation. Turkey got a new and inexperienced government with an Islamist tilt in November 2002, which stumbled in navigating Turkey's complex strategic challenges. Though offered financial 'carrots' totalling up to $26 billion for permission for the United States to deploy ground troops in Turkey, parliament disapproved and only granted the US overflight rights after war in Iraq had begun – by which time that large sum was off the table. Although Turkish

Map Europe/Russia

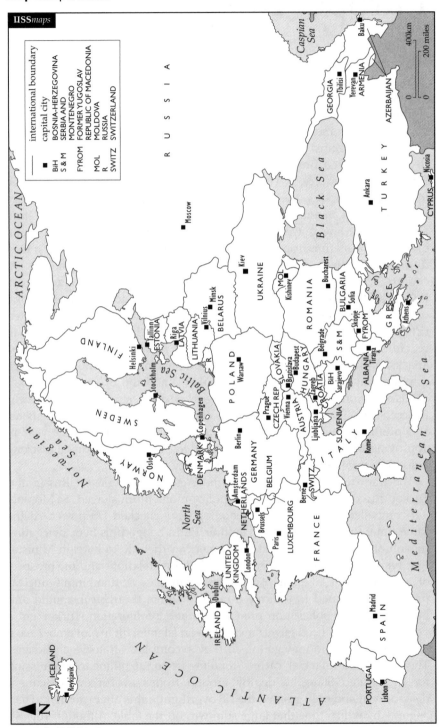

Cypriot leader Rauf Denktash remained implacable in his opposition to a UN-proposed settlement of the Cyprus problem, Ankara did not play a strong role in political negotiations, which ultimately failed, thus making Turkey's accession to the EU a more remote prospect. Turkey's stock with both the US and Europe is substantially lower than it was immediately after 11 September, and it will take time and effort to bring it back up.

The Iraq crisis revealed an almost total absence of strategic consensus between Europe and the US. In essence, Europe manifested an unhealthy preoccupation with process – i.e., multilateral dialogue – and the US an equally unhealthy myopia favouring substance – i.e., regime change in Iraq. Among the most significant victims were the institutions through which transatlantic and intra-European dialogue and consensus has been facilitated: the UN; NATO; and the EU. Rebuilding those that have been weakened via the Iraq ordeal will be a top European, as well as American, strategic priority. The three key players in this repair effort, as during the crisis, will be the US, the UK and France. The US, perceived as hegemonic and unilateralist by many Europeans, will have to show greater appreciation for the utility of European institutions. The UK, after siding with the US on Iraq, faces a challenge in re-establishing its European credentials and its effectiveness as a bridge between Europe and the US. France, having chosen to grandstand as the conscience of Europe rather than engage more candidly as an Atlanticist power, needs to strike a better balance.

Europe: Muddled Success, Dramatic Divisions

In Europe, 2002–03 generated a number of contradictory developments. On the one hand, the European Union (EU) came close to forging its first common constitution. On the other hand, the vision of a united Europe fell apart over Iraq. Economic performance and public budgets suffered in some key nations, but the EU common market and its institutions continued to radiate enormous magnetism, functioning as dominant instruments of order in and beyond Europe. Political will and leadership are in short supply, but the machinery of integration is advancing relatively undisturbed, producing more substance than appears at first sight, continuing to build a Europe of formidable pooled resources, supranational vitality and collective capabilities.

Fighting terror and crime

Unlike the US, Europeans generally have not considered themselves to be 'at war' with terrorists since the attacks of 11 September 2001. Nevertheless, they are fully aware that they too are on the target list of al-Qaeda and others, as evidenced by attacks on European tourists in Djerba, Tunisia in April 2002, and on French defence personnel in Karachi, Pakistan in May 2002, to name only two. In Europe, there has been no massive reorganisation of homeland defence, owing largely to the European tradition of relatively effective interior ministries with a generally high degree of centralisation in internal security – itself partly a response to domestic and foreign terrorist attacks that began in the 1970s. But heightened threat awareness and public concern facilitated a multitude of small steps for strengthening intelligence and law enforcement within and among nations. The neat separation between internal and external security is being eroded. In France, and increasingly in other European nations, domestic intelligence and counter-terrorism agencies are now mainly directing their efforts at transnational Islamic terrorism networks.

Among Western and Central Europe's 15 million Muslims, who come from a wide spectrum of national and religious denominations, there are believed to be some 10,000 potential terrorist activists, some with operational training received in Afghanistan or elsewhere. Given the extreme potential consequences of a mass-casualty attack, counter-terrorism authorities have, to an extent, departed from customary practices that favoured observation over interdiction, moving preventively against radical preachers and support organisations linked to religiously motivated terrorism, with a special focus on disrupting transnational finance flows for Islamic terrorism. Enhanced multinational cooperation among agencies and mutual tip-offs, also in relation with the US, Canada, Russia and other countries, have resulted in a large number of arrests and high-profile convictions in Germany (the cell that planned the attack on the World Trade Center operated out of Hamburg), Britain, Italy, Spain and Belgium.

There have been few signs of widespread anti-Muslim sentiment in European societies. Nevertheless, the existence of visible fault lines and new security threats within countries accustomed to relative social harmony has produced political stresses that may, in extreme cases, be capable of triggering violent outbursts. War in Iraq is likely to intensify the radical impulses of certain Muslims, but some of the sources of the underlying stresses predate 11 September and Iraq. Given that a plurality of the Muslims arrested on terrorist charges in Europe since 11 September have been of North African origin, the Algerian civil war of the 1990s appears to have had a pronounced radicalising effect. Against this background, France has made it a priority to develop close links with its former colonial possession across the Mediterranean – partly in the hope of intensifying joint security measures. In March 2003, President Jacques

Chirac paid the first official French state visit to Algeria since the country's independence. He was applauded by millions, who appreciated his pro-Arab stance on the Middle East, as well as France's potential to advance, by more deeply engaging in North Africa, economic progress for a population mired in poverty and unemployment. Warmer relations have also been cultivated between Spain and Morocco, in spite of friction over the Western Sahara and a highly publicised military showdown in July 2002 at Perejil, an uninhabited rock off Morocco's northern coast. After Spanish soldiers occupied the islet, the incident was quickly resolved, to the chagrin of many Europeans, not by Brussels but by US Secretary of State Colin Powell, who brokered a joint declaration that restored a complicated status quo.

The EU's 'third pillar', justice and home affairs, has benefited strongly from the growing political desire for safety and security. The most innovative initiative undertaken in the wake of 11 September is the European arrest warrant, scheduled to be in use by 2004. The Schengen arrangement for a joint European external border regime, drawing on a networked visa and immigration database, and a new fingerprint registration system for illegal immigrants and asylum seekers, known as 'Eurodac', came on stream in January 2003. Free movement within the Schengen area for nationals of the new member states, however, is still years away. Increasingly, serious attention is being paid to the establishment of European border and coast guard security regimes, to ensure that common standards are met. Also, assistance to third countries in Eastern Europe and the Balkans has been stepped up to help them control their own borders more effectively, thus allowing less restrictive travel and trade rules in their relationship with the EU. The Russian exclave of Kaliningrad, wedged between two prospective EU members Poland and Lithuania, is in many respects a test case for these developments. The recent agreement on controlled, non-bureaucratic rail transit for Russians through Lithuania, and intensified cooperation with Russian authorities in the Baltic region on border-control, customs and police issues, support the principle that the EU's future external borders, while providing reliable protection against illegal activities, should not prevent robust and legitimate commercial and social interaction that can spread the benefits of economic and societal integration to the EU's neighbours.

The Balkans

Progress has been achieved in those parts of the Balkans where the history of ethnic struggle, combined with corruption and political radicalism in elements of the security apparatus, has created strongholds of international organised crime – perceived by some to be at least as serious a transnational threat as terrorism. The EU has effectively applied the full range of instruments in its toolbox, skilfully orchestrated by High Representative and Secretary-General of the EU Council Javier Solana in close cooperation with the European Commission and NATO. In 2003, the EU's long-term agenda of stabilising southeast Europe spawned the first two operations under its European Security and Defence Policy (ESDP), established in 1999 pursuant to the Anglo-French initiative at the EU summit in St Malo. On 1 January 2003, the EU took over from the UN in running the international police mission in Bosnia-Herzegovina, which involved 480 police officers in a monitoring and advisory role, with personnel coming not only from EU member nations but also from 17 other countries. In April 2003, the first soldiers wearing the EU's blue badges with golden stars began *Operation Concordia* in Macedonia, continuing the role that NATO had played there before in monitoring the implementation of the 2001 Ohrid Agreement. The EU's 350-strong force is under the political control of the EU's Political and Security Committee (COPS) and the operational command of NATO's Deputy Supreme Allied Commander Europe (SACEUR). It is led by a French force commander in Skopje, with France acting as lead nation and a total of 27 countries providing troops.

The murder of Serbian Prime Minister Zoran Djindjic in Belgrade in March 2003, believed to have been committed by a powerful local criminal organisation engaged in narcotics trafficking throughout Europe and allegedly associated with former President Slobodan Milosevic's family, was a hard blow to Serb national confidence and to Serbia's political rehabilitation. The subsequent large-scale crackdown on organised-crime networks in Serbia–Montenegro and further measures, such as the introduction of gun-registration laws, may prove beneficial for the region as a whole. But the murder came just a few weeks after the implementation of a constitution for a new 'union' of Serbia and Montenegro completed the 12-year destruction of 'Yugoslavia'. Even that union was an uncertain proposition, since both constituent republics can exercise an 'opt-out' clause after three years. The question of Kosovo's final status was also unresolved. Michael Steiner, the German diplomat who headed Kosovo's UN administration, promulgated the slogan 'standards before status' to emphasise the reasonable point that the Albanian majority needed to earn self-rule through a demonstrated capacity for good governance and decent treatment of the dwindling Serb minority. However, international leverage over the Kosovar Albanians was perhaps a wasting asset; pressure for a decision was building, and no one could imagine the territory's return to Serb rule.

NATO continued its steady drawdown of troops in the region: down to 36,000 (including 5,000 Americans) in Kosovo; and just 12,000 (with less than 2,400 Americans) in Bosnia. With attention and resources devoted to Iraq and the broader war against terrorism, this was probably a maximum possible strength, but it was also approaching a dangerously low floor. The Djindjic murder in Serbia, low-level violence in Kosovo and disquieting

Bosnian electoral results in October 2002 – as nationalists gained among Muslim, Croat and Serb voters – suggested that instability, or even conflict, could not be safely relegated to the tragic past.

The EU: enlargement and division

The Treaty of Nice finally entered into force in March 2003, providing the legal basis for the adaptation of the EU's institutions to the current enlargement round. Ten countries – Poland, Hungary, the Czech Republic, Slovakia, Slovenia, Estonia, Latvia, Lithuania, Malta and Cyprus – are expected to join as full members in 2004 in time for the next European Parliament elections. In each candidate country, except Cyprus, a popular referendum is to be held in 2003 to authorise EU accession, in some cases also linked to the decision to join NATO. In Malta and Slovenia, governments won the required popular majority support in March 2003. The most critical votes were expected to come in Lithuania in May 2003 and in Poland and the Czech Republic in June.

In Poland, the biggest candidate, there has been concern that voter participation in the referendum may not reach the required 50% threshold. However, as of April 2003, the government remained confident that it would convincingly make the case for accession in the national interest. There has been widespread opposition to EU membership among Poland's rural population, and the Catholic Church has been reluctant to clearly endorse a 'yes' vote. Agriculture still absorbs about one-quarter of Poland's workforce, with a large segment of small landholders producing on a subsistence basis. At the EU Summit in Copenhagen in December 2002, which paved the way for the signing of accession treaties in the first half of 2003, Poland succeeded in gaining some additional financial concessions for its farmers within the EU's projected timetable for the switch from price subsidies to direct payments under a new rural-development policy. This arrangement would not affect the overall financial framework for the accession process, preset by the EU in March 1999 in Berlin within narrow limits, to prevent opposition to enlargement among existing member states. The same level of generous regional and structural aid and unchecked agricultural subsidies that boosted the economies of earlier entrants like Ireland, Greece and Spain are unlikely to be available to the new EU members. But transfers are still expected initially to amount to more than 2% of each new member's GDP. EU-funded infrastructure investments – for instance, for major new roads – are already showing major benefits, notably in Poland. More broadly, the free movement of capital and, ultimately, labour in a harmonised European legal space, after a seven-year transition phase, is likely to produce important economic advantages.

At the end of the EU's special February 2003 summit meeting in Brussels on the highly divisive Iraq issue, Chirac opened a new front when he

Europe/Russia

accused the Central and Eastern European countries, which had been openly supportive of a US-led war, of un-European manners and reminded them that any existing member state, including France, had the power to block their accession by calling a referendum. While there has been some speculation about this 'Samson option' for French European policy, there is neither a historical example nor much intelligible reason for a referendum in France in the absence of a strong chance of success, which would be highly unlikely. France certainly remains uncomfortable with the prospect of an unwieldy EU of 25 members with a wide spectrum of political preferences. As the world's biggest agro-industrial exporter, it is also still fundamentally unconvinced of the need to abolish the EU's Common Agricultural Policy that has been so profitable for it. Given France's overriding interest in an integrated Europe and a globalising world economy, however, it seems unlikely that any French leader could today assemble coherent support in France for a policy of blocking further EU enlargement.

Cyprus presented a different kind of accession glitch. The EU remains committed to admitting Cyprus as a whole to the EU. At the insistence of Greece, though, the EU has never demanded an end to the island's de facto partition as a precondition for EU accession, but required only visible progress towards a peaceful resolution. Indeed, the shape of the eventual outcome remains obvious and there seems little doubt that it will eventually materialise. The time has not yet been right. Aging Turkish Cypriot leader Rauf Denktash's stubbornness, the uncertain political transformation in Ankara after the November 2002 election and the surprising outcome of the Greek Cypriot presidential election made a solution unattainable in 2003, despite the UN's best efforts. In practical terms, the EU is likely to face a difficult balancing act. It will need to strengthen the island's unity by extending the economic benefits of membership to the Turkish Cypriot-controlled part. Yet it will have to take care not to forsake too many carrots for Cypriot political reconciliation too early or to degrade the incentives for Turkey to implement the reforms required for its accession.

The European economy: rotten at the core?
In March 2000, at the EU Summit in Lisbon, the EU announced its determination to overtake the US as the world's leading and most vibrant economy. In the meantime, dismal economic performance in some major member countries has provided a reminder of their failure to implement deep structural reforms during the growth period of the 1990s. The European Commission has increasingly scolded member states for policy inertia and backtracking, as national governments in Berlin, Paris, Brussels, Rome, Vienna and elsewhere appeared hopelessly caught amid competing interest groups, continued corporatist preferences and a marked reluctance to offend voters with determined policies. Admonitions from EU

watchdogs have so far had little resonance with the governments concerned. In 2002, overall growth at constant prices was 0.9% of GDP in the EU. Germany was close to recession at 0.2%. Only the UK, Ireland, the Scandinavian members, Spain and Greece grew by more than 1.5%, while the US reached 2.4%. Unemployment kept increasing, reaching 8.7% in the euro zone in February 2003.

Under the terms of the EU's Stability and Growth Pact, agreed at the time of the Maastricht Treaty to guarantee economic and fiscal discipline in EU governments sufficient to sustain economic and monetary union, the European Commission had to initiate punitive procedures against Germany and France for exceeding the limit, defined in the Maastricht criteria, of a 3.0% annual increase in public debt in 2002. Portugal, after a 4.2% deficit in 2001, managed to come back inside the limit through radical expenditure cuts. Germany also broke the 60% public-debt-to-GDP ratio for the first time in 2002. This procedure can ultimately lead to fines of up to 0.5% of GDP if the limit is still not met in the years following the opening of proceedings. France has suggested that its €2 billion increase in defence spending should not be counted as part of its deficit because it was in Europe's interest. Also, the Iraq war and its presumed impact on the economy have been identified by some as a possible 'special situation' that would allow setting the Stability Pact's rules aside for a limited period. As of April 2003, this argument had not won the day. But, in early 2003, France was openly pursuing a deficit-spending strategy, trying to revitalise its economy through increased public-sector demand. The French position amounts to a frontal attack on the philosophy and treaty language of the stability pact that rests on the assumptions – born of the economic experience of the 1970s – that deficits potentially drive growth-inhibiting inflation. This political challenge raises the question, not entirely unreasonable, of whether some of the key elements underpinning the euro zone's common monetary policy can survive the need for counter-cyclical fiscal policies at a time when inflation looks moribund but deflation is a real threat. Meanwhile, lagging economic performance on the continent and the UK's strategic alignment with the US over Iraq may have stalled prospects for the UK's joining the euro.

The European Convention

Headed by former French President Valery Giscard d'Estaing, the European Convention was tasked by member states to provide input on the future institutional development of the EU for the next Inter-Governmental Conference. The project has turned out to be more ambitious and appealing than many had expected. In February 2003, Giscard even presented the text of a draft constitution. The results of the Convention's work are due in time for the June 2003 European Council meeting. For the first time in many years, the atmosphere seemed to favour a major step towards a federal Europe. Factors include: the perceived need to make EU operations more transparent to the public; widespread dissatisfaction with national political establishments; realisation that the EU is often punching below its weight internationally due to its incoherent institutional make-up; and the rare blessing of a pro-European government in London. The deep divisions that emerged during the Iraq crisis, however, killed much of the sense of urgency and hope for imminent progress. Still, the enthusiastic groundwork laid by the Convention and its working groups is bound to have a strong impact on future EU institutional developments.

In early 2003, though, the colourful array of proposals and suggestions seemed to have been replaced by less productive forms of disunity. For instance, there is a proposal to embed Common Foreign and Security Policy (CFSP) into the constitution, so that member states would be constitutionally barred from contravening CFSP. Such a provision would theoretically impose unity; in practice, however, it would almost certainly be unrealistic and unenforceable. The creation of two EU presidencies – one of the European Council, to be chosen by heads of government; the other of the European Commission, elected by the European Parliament – has been suggested. France and Germany also proposed replacing the EU's rotating presidency with a permanent chair of the European Council, who would also represent the EU externally, in tandem with similar solutions for permanent chairs in the various meetings of the Council of Ministers. This proposal has already been declared unacceptable by the smaller member states in a meeting of the 'seven dwarfs' in Luxembourg. The twin-presidency idea provides something for both the federalist and intergovernmental camps, and therefore may prove more widely acceptable. Another proposal, put forward by France and Germany and others, has also found broad support. This involves the merger of the two positions of High Representative and Commissioner for External Relations, currently held by Solana and Chris Patten, to create a European 'foreign minister'. At the same time, the revival of the idea of a 'hard-core Europe', with France, Germany and a few other states moving to deeper levels of integration without the UK and the new EU members, has made smaller European countries uncomfortable. Curiously, defence has been advertised as the possible field for such an avant-garde approach, in spite of the fact that there is no discernible will to transfer sovereignty in this area even among 'core' countries, and capabilities would be quite thin without the UK.

In concrete terms, France and Germany, along with Belgium, have proposed to replace ESDP with a new 'European Security and Defence Union' that would be based on a solidarity clause with respect to security risks, including terrorism, combined with enhanced cooperation in defence matters. Specifically, these might be pursued within EU institutions, by transforming the Organisation Conjointe de Coopération en matière d'Armement (OCCAR) into the EU's armaments agency. Details remain disputed and unclear, including whether this proposal is compatible with the idea of a European Defence Capability Development Agency promoted by the UK and endorsed by France at their bilateral summit in Le Touquet in January 2003. Created in 1996 by France, Germany, Italy and the UK, OCCAR is intended to harmonise defence cooperation and procurement in member states in line with best practices; its principal objective is to consolidate and develop the European industrial and technological defence base. The European Defence Capability Development Agency, as conceived by UK officials, would be charged with identifying how capability gaps can be filled, advancing procurement projects to fill them and encouraging more open defence procurement to eliminate the costs of national protectionism. To what extent the two organisations' missions overlap, or could be coordinated, remains unclear. The fact that the European Convention's defence working group, led by Michel Barnier, drew up proposals along the same general lines has strengthened hopes that defence will be an area in which the EU as a whole can agree on new initiatives to strengthen ESDP.

An uncommon foreign policy

Customarily, the Franco-German relationship has almost always been the key to progress in the EU. But the series of bilateral proposals presented since 2002 by these two countries now seems to have proved damaging to the EU's cohesiveness. On 22 January, France and Germany in a bilateral meeting to mark the 40th anniversary of the Elysée Treaty, declared that war in Iraq had to be avoided at all costs. This prompted a letter, published a week later, by the prime ministers of the UK, Denmark, Italy, Portugal, Spain, Hungary and Poland, as well as retired Czech President Vaclav Havel, asserting that the US shared the EU's core values and that they were deeply challenged by the Iraqi regime. A week later, ten additional Central and Eastern European governments publicly added their weight to this stance.

While German Chancellor Gerhard Schröder had earlier adopted an anti-US, pro-peace position on Iraq to strengthen his coalition's election prospects at home, the French policy approach appeared more fundamental and durable. The main factors underlying the French position included fear of increased terrorism in case of war, belief that the invasion of Iraq would exacerbate rather than help settle Middle East conflicts, doubt over the legitimacy of action against Iraq and absence of an immediate threat. France was also apprehensive about the prospect of an anarchic world with a single unconstrained superpower capable of dominating international organisations and using them for its own ends. Other factors that played a role included frustration over US military and political domination and resistance to an expanded US role in the Middle East. France's leadership

Europe/Russia

also may have calculated that it had little to lose politically, given the high level of domestic anti-war sentiment. In any case, extreme governmental and public mistrust vis-à-vis the US leadership and the unconstructive polarity of the transatlantic debate on Iraq have resulted in a US–Europe rift that will be difficult to heal. Some 75% of Germans believed that the war in Iraq was against international law, and only about 10% approved of US President George W. Bush's performance. The episode was again a reminder that most European states have not developed a sense of ownership of the global strategic agenda in response to new threats, defined and shaped to a large degree by the US, yet they remain unsatisfied with merely being critical spectators.

The future of NATO

Given the transatlantic split over Iraq, many observers believe that NATO does not have much of a future. France and Germany's obstruction of NATO's *Operation Display Deterrence* to protect Turkey with surveillance aircraft and missile defences was a highly damaging episode for a collective defence alliance. In the end, the problem was resolved by taking the decision through NATO's Defence Planning Committee, in which France is not represented. Notwithstanding the NATO–Russia Council, created in May 2002, NATO's political institutions may indeed have diminishing relevance. But the integrated military structure built and maintained by the allies remains not just functional but central to their own defence efforts, and not unimportant to the US. While the UK military effort alongside that of the US in Iraq, as elsewhere, stands out as essentially national, NATO as an alliance is responding to terrorism and other challenges. In spring 2003, Germany alone had over 5,000 troops stationed in Bosnia and Kosovo, 2,500 in the German-Dutch-led International Security Assistance Force mission in Afghanistan and Uzbekistan, 1,000 in various locations east of Suez and 70 in Macedonia – less than ten years after the country's constitutional obstacle against overseas deployments had been removed.

In some ways, despite fundamental confusion about the Alliance's future role, 2002 was a productive and crucial year for NATO. Seven countries – Bulgaria, Estonia, Latvia, Lithuania, Romania, Slovakia and Slovenia – were invited to join as members and signed accession protocols in March 2003. In addition, NATO's Prague Summit in November 2002 brought agreement on crucial improvements to allied military integration, geared at fostering and supporting both improved European capabilities and a new level of network-centric interoperability with US forces. Those capabilities included the new NATO Response Force (NRF), with land, sea and air elements, expected to become operational in autumn 2004. The NRF is not meant to duplicate or replace pre-existing arrangements or initiatives but explicitly to reinforce them, in conjunction with the Prague Capabilities Commitment, the EU's related Headline Goal force development effort and the European Capabilities Action Plan. Moreover, the Alliance's new streamlined command structure will include, in addition to a single operational command at Supreme Headquarters Allied Powers Europe in Belgium, a new functional allied strategic command for military transformation co-located in Norfolk, Virginia, with the US Joint Transformation Command. This arrangement is designed to allow European forces to tap into and contribute to US doctrinal and organisational innovation.

The EU has registered concerns about whether NRF-assigned forces will remain available for EU missions, whether ESDP requirements will be reflected in NATO operations and force planning, and whether NATO's transformation agenda will be harmonised with ESDP or drain resources away from it. The resolution in December 2002 of the Greek-Turkish dispute over the ESDP–NATO relationship that led to agreement on EU access to NATO assets and conclusion of a security agreement between the EU and NATO are positive signs that such concerns will be met satisfactorily. Leaving aside French political objections, the EU and NATO appeared to have found a viable formula for mutually reinforcing their military efforts.

Clarifying the European vision

The deep split among Europeans indicates that the debate and, ultimately, the decision is nearing as to what role the EU should play and what relationship it should cultivate with the US. Fundamentally, Europe has two problems, both of which can be resolved through political decisions and leadership. The first problem is residual French resistance to integration structures that Paris cannot control. The French will need to balance their desire for national control with their need to remain a respected and influential player. The second problem, visible across the continent to various degrees, is the insufficient preparedness of European publics for the active global role that the EU needs to play, in conjunction with the US, as one of the two main pillars of the current international system. Too easily, Europe's hard-security responsibilities have been evaded in the name of peace and soft power. Too often, economic priorities have not been fully grasped in the interest of systemic stability due to inward-looking absorption with budget deficits and protectionist expectations. A convincing political language is needed to free Europe of shallow populism, insistence on corporatist harmony and 'protest' foreign policy. The process should begin with conscientious post-Iraq re-engagement with the United States and, simultaneously, a focused effort to rejuvenate the institutions that, in the past, have facilitated constructive transatlantic dialogue, but which have suffered severe strain and possibly permanent damage during the Iraq crisis.

Europe/Russia

Testing Putin's Pragmatism

Russia's active support for the US-led military campaign in Afghanistan helped to end the strategic ambiguities of the post-Cold War era. In a matter of months, Russia–US relations were transformed beyond Cold War deterrence towards a new partnership covering even sensitive areas such as intelligence sharing. In May 2002, Moscow and Washington signed a Strategic Offensive Reductions Treaty (SORT) committing the two sides to reducing their nuclear weapons to the level of 1,700–2,200 warheads by 2012. Russia's role in the global coalition against terrorism prompted a sea-change in its relations with NATO. In May 2002, 19 NATO members and Russia agreed to establish the Russia–NATO 'Council at 20', which gave Russia an equal voice, if not a formal vote, in many key transatlantic policy issues, ranging from crisis management to missile defences.

More importantly, Russian President Vladimir Putin's strategic choice to support the US after the 11 September 2001 terrorist attacks dissolved a residual myth, still pondered by some members of the country's political elite, of a Primakov-style multipolar world in which Russia could preserve its role as a great power and counterbalance US hegemony by forming alliances with other powers like China or with 'rogue' states like Iran. Instead, Russia has done what many other Central and Eastern European and Commonwealth of Independent States (CIS) countries did after the Berlin Wall came down: join the queue for integration into Western economic, political and security institutions. However, unlike its former satellites in Central and Eastern Europe, Russia's road towards integration will be much longer and open-ended.

Yet even outside any formal institutional framework, since 11 September Russia has increasingly been viewed as a 'normal' member of the transatlantic coalition. To Putin's credit, he has made a pragmatic choice not to interfere in growing transatlantic tensions on political grounds, and has tried to engage both the US and European powers in solving practical policy issues – particularly with respect to Russia's economic development and integration agenda. In short, throughout 2002, Russia's foreign policy was increasingly transparent and based on the same rules as that of Western states. On one hand, Russia toned down unnecessary political rhetoric, particularly in relation to issues on which it knew it could not win, such as the US military presence in Central Asia and in Georgia, the US decision to withdraw from the 1972 Anti-Ballistic Missile (ABM) Treaty and the accession of the Baltic states to NATO. On the other hand, the Russian government, and particularly Putin, have been engaged in active diplomacy to build political consensus with Russia's Western partners on issues of principle for Russia such as SORT, a European Union (EU)–Russia compromise on the Kaliningrad transit issue, the Russia–NATO Council (RNC), protection of Russian economic interests in negotiations with the US and the Europeans on World Trade Organisation (WTO) accession, trade sanctions and the export of Russian commodities.

Striving towards integration

It was clear from the first days of Putin's presidency that he was striving to achieve Russia's integration into the community of economically prosperous and politically stable Western states. Only after 11 September, however, did he gain an opportunity to achieve a major breakthrough and recognition of his objectives by many key members of the transatlantic community, including the US, the United Kingdom, Germany and Italy. One year after 11 September, Russia had extended its integration agenda beyond its relationship with the US. It became a full member of the G8, began actively negotiating accession to the WTO and sought membership in the Organisation for Economic Cooperation and Development (OECD). It also expanded its cooperation with the EU to European Security and Defence Policy (ESDP), and to justice and home-affairs issues. Russia became more actively involved in multilateral diplomacy in the CIS, the Organisation for Security and Cooperation in Europe (OSCE), the Shanghai Cooperation Organisation and the UN, as well as within the 'quartet' formed to address the Israeli–Palestinian problem.

The main result of these diplomatic activities has been increased confidence and trust that Russia could be a constructive institutional partner of the US and Europe in working towards international consensus. The West's most striking vote of confidence in Russia's long-term partnership was the creation of the RNC in May 2002 at the NATO–Russia Summit in Rome. Unlike its predecessor – the Permanent Joint Council (PJC), set up in 1997 under the Founding Act on Cooperation between NATO and Russia – the RNC no longer works on the '19+1' principle, under which the 19 NATO members had to agree on a common position among themselves before discussing an issue with Russia. Under the RNC format, Russia participates in all discussions and decision-making in the Council. While any NATO member has a right to remove any issue from the RNC agenda, as of April 2003, Russian fears that this would be routinely exercised had proven unfounded. Russia, in turn, has shown more interest in cooperation with NATO than it did under the PJC.

Whereas only one working group existed under the PJC, since May 2002 Russia and NATO have formed seven working groups under the RNC umbrella. They cover: terrorist threats to the Euro-Atlantic area; peacekeeping and crisis management; non-proliferation; theatre missile defence; defence reform; civil emergencies; and the Cooperative Aerospace Initiative. Substantive discussions have been held on: developing inter-

Europe/Russia

operability standards for crisis-management operations; exchanging intelligence and threat assessments on terrorist groups; and developing a common political and legal understanding of peacekeeping doctrine. As of early 2003, more words than deeds had emerged from working-group consultations. Nevertheless, they did yield a joint assessment of terrorist threats to peacekeeping forces in the Balkans. Other practical achievements included a Russia–NATO joint crisis-response exercise in Noginsk, Russia, on 25–27 September 2002 and Russia–NATO conferences hosted by the Russian Ministry of Defence in February and December 2002 on the role of the military in combating terrorism.

In the short and medium term, NATO's priority vis-à-vis Russia is to promote more military-to-military contacts. In particular, more robust confidence-building measures are required to minimise any residual reluctance on the part of the Russian military to engage in meaningful discussions with NATO on Russian defence reforms. As of early 2003, military-to-military cooperation had focused on a limited number of areas such as logistics, air transport, air-to-air refuelling and maritime search-and-rescue. One especially acute immediate challenge is to remedy Russian officers' lack of language skills (although more of them are now enrolling in training programmes in Russia and abroad). Longer-term, Putin's commitment to accelerating military reform and its objective of creating a more compact, professional, mobile and well-equipped force, is likely to produce a more open and extensive exchange of views on defence-reform issues. Russia's military restructuring and modernisation programmes lag behind not only those of NATO's existing members, but even behind those of most of the incoming members of the organisation.

Russia's wish-list for future cooperation with NATO includes more practical interaction on operational aspects of peacekeeping as well as making the RNC a platform for discussing and reaching common understandings on key global security issues. In addition, on Russia's initiative a special committee on challenges and threats to modern society was set up under the RNC framework to discuss new threats like cyber-terrorism, environmental problems and other aspects of disaster management. While these issues do not fall under NATO's usual areas of responsibility, their inclusion on the RNC agenda appears to constitute a political advance simply by virtue of the fact that they are matters on which Russia and NATO could develop a common policy. Generally, then, the most important achievement of the RNC has been that Russia and NATO have established a consensus-building culture and are acquiring groundbreaking experience in joint decision-making. According to NATO Secretary-General George Robertson, the RNC represents 'a huge change, a sea change, in the way [Russia and NATO] do business'. Testifying to the new commitment to cooperation, the work of the RNC was not affected by the divisions within the Alliance over military planning assistance to Turkey in anticipation of war in Iraq. Indeed, in March 2003, the RNC continued its work even after the launch of the US-led military campaign in Iraq. This continuity stood in sharp contrast to the Kosovo War, during which joint Russia–NATO activity was suspended.

More broadly, Russia–NATO cooperation was maintained even after the Alliance announced at its Prague summit in November 2002 that it was inviting seven countries – including the three Baltic states, whose prospective membership had long discomfited Moscow – to begin accession talks. Russia chose not to interfere in transatlantic disputes within the Alliance. In fact, it appeared in April 2003 that the RNC had fewer internal divisions than virtually any other NATO structure. This 'normality', however, should probably be read as evidence of how marginal the RNC remains to NATO's core objectives and internal transformation processes. The RNC is not seen either by Russia or NATO as central to their security needs. Over time, though, changing perceptions and greater military interoperability and bureaucratic harmonisation could lead to more important joint action. Russia–NATO peacekeeping operations are less inconceivable than they were as recently as 2001, and could become feasible in the foreseeable future.

Russia, ESDP and Kaliningrad

The only multinational operation in which Russian forces have participated outside the CIS is not under NATO auspices but under the aegis of the EU's ESDP. Russia is sending a small number of police officers to take part in the EU Police Mission (EUPM) in Bosnia and Herzegovina. At the May 2002 EU–Russia summit, Russia proposed a 'Russia–EU Action Plan in the field of European Security and Defence Policy'. As of 2002, the EU Military Staff also included a Russian liaison officer. Thus, in 2002–03, Russia's relations with the EU in the area of security and defence progressed, although, as with NATO, they remain largely symbolic and tangential to both sides' security priorities and have not yielded many practical dividends. But it remains politically significant that, after several years of Russian scepticism and apathy towards ESDP, Moscow has finally manifested its intent to cooperate. The Chairman of the EU Military Committee visited Moscow in May 2002 and met with representatives of the Russian Ministry of Defence. As of April 2003, EU–Russia cooperation covered four areas: conflict prevention; landmine clearance; possible use by the EU of Russian–Ukrainian long-haul air transportation; and Russian participation in the EUPM.

Russia and the EU have continued to discuss their strategies for crisis management and the fight against terrorism. But the only concrete example of crisis management in the EU–Russia relationship involved not ESDP but the Kaliningrad transit issue. Kaliningrad is a Russian exclave on the Baltic Sea, separated from mainland Russia. The 'Kaliningrad problem' emerged in the context of EU enlargement. Pursuant to the formal approval of EU enlargement by ten states granted at the December 2002 Copenhagen summit, Kaliningrad will be surrounded by two EU member states – Poland and Lithuania – both of which are required to introduce the strict Schengen visa regime as part of their accession agreement. This means that Russian citizens will require a Schengen visa to travel by land through Lithuania between Kaliningrad and the rest of the Russian Federation. Rather than transforming Kaliningrad into a pilot project for European–Russian cooperation by granting it special status and developing a more far-reaching economic-development plan for the region, Putin presented the issue as a challenge to Russia's sovereignty and territorial integrity as well as a crisis point in EU–Russia relations. Russia was adamant that the EU make an exception to its Schengen rules and grant Russian citizens the right of visa-free transit between Kaliningrad and mainland Russia through Lithuania. Protracted negotiations ended in compromise at the November 2002 EU–Russia summit in Brussels. Under this compromise, the EU and Russia agreed on a scheme whereby a Facilitated Travel Document (FTD), authorising transit between Kaliningrad and other parts of Russia by land, is issued to Russian citizens of Kaliningrad. The FTD is de facto no more then a surrogate visa, but the device allowed Putin – who had invested considerable political capital in this issue – to claim that he had won Russian citizens the right of visa-free travel.

After integration, the second important objective behind Putin's policy is to reassert Russia's sovereignty, territorial integrity and domestic security. But foreign-policy strategies chosen by Russia to achieve this goal – for instance, its tough stance on the Kaliningrad visa issue – have often undermined its integrationist policies vis-à-vis the US and Europe. The satisfactory resolution of the Kaliningrad problem stemmed the reversal of the forward political momentum that had built up between Russia and the West after 11 September. Nevertheless, the dispute could have a fairly durable negative impact on Russia–EU relations.

Towards a political solution in Chechnya

Contradictions between the integrationist and security agendas in Russia's foreign and security policy are even more apparent in Russia's war in Chechnya. The paradox of Russian foreign policy is that it is precisely the war against perceived terrorist threats – originally the source of the rapprochement between Russia and the West – that is now holding back Russia's progress in integrating with the Western community. In fact, Russia's participation in the US-led coalition in Afghanistan was the exception rather than the rule in Putin's foreign policy. The political objective of establishing a closer partnership with the US and Europe happened to coincide with Russia's security interests. But American and

European security worries involve mainly transnational terrorist threats. Russia's war against Chechen terrorism is essentially domestic – albeit with transnational Islamic trappings that are politically and sometimes operationally exploited by al-Qaeda. Thus, Russia's decision to pursue a unilateral security agenda in Chechnya, involving the use of force against Chechen armed groups allegedly operating from the Pankisi Gorge in neighbouring Georgia and the alleged bombing by Russia of Georgian territory – even under the pretext of counter-terrorism – has caused rifts with the US and Europe. Russia's refusal either to initiate a comprehensive political process to end the conflict in Chechnya or to cease its military campaign to suppress the Chechen resistance has deepened them. At the same time, Russia's reluctance to take on board European and American concerns over its policies in the Caucasus has been the only major problem area in its relations with the West.

In 2002, as in 2001, it was clear that Russia's continuing military campaign in Chechnya represented a key obstacle to Putin's strategy of building a political coalition with the US and Europe. Moreover, in 2002, the war in Chechnya became increasingly unpopular with the Russian public and a major domestic liability for Putin. Furthermore, the November 2002 hostage crisis at a Moscow theatre, in which more than 180 people were killed in the rescue operation, provided clear evidence that the continuation of the military operation in Chechnya would make the rest of Russia more vulnerable to terrorism. Before the hostage crisis, Moscow had started to search for a political solution to the Chechen conflict. In June 2000, Moscow established an administration in Chechnya and appointed as its head a prominent Chechen personality, Ahmad Kadyrov, a former mufti who fought Russian forces in the first Chechen war (1993–96) and declared loyalty to Moscow in the second. But the legitimacy of Kadyrov's administration remained in doubt. Moreover, there was continuing military resistance from isolated groups of Chechen rebels headed by former President Aslan Maskhadov, who was elected in 1997. Rebel forces, though significantly weakened by three years of war, in 2002 still proved capable of conducting guerrilla warfare against Russian forces and causing significant casualties. Chechen rebels also include a number of foreign mercenaries from a variety of Islamic countries. While this allows Russia to claim that it is fighting international terrorism in Chechnya, it is increasingly recognised by elites and the wider public in Russia that the conflict is fuelled not by international support from extremist Islamic organisations but by Moscow's own inability to guarantee human rights, autonomy and security to the Chechen people, as well as by excesses on the part of Russian military forces stationed in the republic.

The strategy that Putin chose for bringing a political solution to Chechnya seeks to isolate the rebel warlords who are still fighting Russian forces and orchestrating terrorist attacks. Even before the Moscow hostage crisis, the Russian government had been reluctant to negotiate a compromise with Maskhadov, the most popular Chechen rebel leader. But Moscow did make a number of attempts – through General Viktor Kazantsev, Putin's representative in Russia's Southern Federal District – to negotiate with Maskhadov's representative behind closed doors. After the Moscow siege, however, these negotiations were called off on account of the Russian government's belief that Maskhadov was involved in organising and supporting the hostage-takers. In place of negotiations, Moscow decided to follow up its original strategy of isolating and de-legitimising Maskhadov, forcing him to capitulate or face elimination at the hands of Russian forces and pro-Moscow Chechen paramilitaries. Despite criticism from the OSCE and the Council of Europe, on 23 March 2003, the Russian government held a referendum in Chechnya on a new constitution for the republic that would confirm Chechnya's status as part of the Russian Federation while promising it wider autonomy. The referendum also asked Chechens to support the election of a president and a two-chamber legislature later in 2003. Although most Western institutions refused to send observers to oversee the referendum – largely because of security concerns – it was declared valid by the Russians, who claimed that over 80% of Chechnya's residents took part and 96% of them supported the new constitution. There were clear violations of registration and voting procedures (such as allowing more than 20,000 Russian servicemen stationed in Chechnya to vote), but it was likely that the majority of people who voted supported the constitution and proposed new elections in the hope that this could lead to the cessation of violence.

For Putin, the referendum represented a major success. Most importantly, it took place without any major terrorist attacks threatened by the rebels. In addition, large numbers of Chechens voted despite threats from both sides. Finally, the referendum occurred against the background of the war in Iraq and, therefore, did not draw much criticism from the international community. Indeed, while the OSCE voiced its concerns, the Western position on the referendum could be described as cautious support. Although it was acknowledged that violations occurred, no state or institutions questioned the referendum's validity. Moreover, it was apprehended as a welcome first step towards a political solution to the war in Chechnya. Whether it will provide a lasting solution to the crisis depends on the implementation of pledges Putin outlined in his address to the Chechen people after the referendum. These included: a power-sharing treaty between Russian federal authorities and Chechnya that grants it autonomy; amnesty for Chechen fighters who did not commit grave war crimes and wish to return to civilian life; holding presidential elections in December 2003; federal financial assistance for the reconstruction of Chechnya; and reducing the number of Russian military and paramilitary forces stationed in Chechnya while transferring more responsibility for law and order to the Chechen Interior Ministry. Making good on these pledges could be an important symbolic step towards peace in Chechnya. But, apart from the amnesty, they do not offer many assurances to the rebels. Their more moderate leaders are not integrated into the peace process, while ordinary fighters have not received adequate guarantees against prosecution – especially in light of the putative absence of principled law enforcement and the Russian military's and the new Chechen police force's unfavourable record of executions and imprisonment of suspected insurgents. International organisations and non-governmental organisations could provide some guarantees, but Russia is still reluctant to internationalise the Chechen peace process.

The US–Russia partnership after Iraq

The crisis over Iraq has challenged both of Russia's central foreign-policy objectives – integration and increased security through international support and burden-sharing. The goal of Putin's integrationist policy – an economically prosperous and unified Russian–Western community – has been placed in doubt. Because the crisis has weakened NATO and the EU, Russia's new relations with NATO and the EU appeared much less important for promoting its international role. Moreover, the UN Security Council – in which Russia holds permanent membership – has been hobbled, and may remain sidelined for as long as US President George W. Bush remains in office. In the economic field, high oil prices and looming recession in the US and Europe could undermine Russia's economic reforms, including Putin's effort to diversify Russia's economy from dependency on oil and gas exports. Russia's recourse to oil revenue is likely to slow domestic structural reforms and thus jeopardise its prospects for greater integration into the global economy and for forming a common economic space with the EU. In the long run, US control over Iraqi oil reserves could compromise Russia's plans for increasing oil and gas exports to the US market.

Further, Russia's security – strengthened by the first phase of the war against terrorism in Afghanistan – is now rapidly deteriorating. Russia is facing major security concerns, including a remote possibility of US military action, along some of its non-European borders. In the east, the crisis with North Korea could escalate. In the south, the potential shift of US attention from unfinished de-Talibanisation and reconstruction of Afghanistan towards new objectives in Iraq may imperil fragile regional stability and make Russia's southern flank less secure. War in Iraq is likely to fuel Islamic terrorism, which could affect Russia's hopes for gradual stabilisation of the Caucasus. Finally, Russian politicians and experts are concerned that, after war in Iraq, the US could shift its attention to Iran, exacerbating existing tensions in Russia–US relations over Russian nuclear cooperation with Iran, which Russia claims to be purely civilian.

Europe/Russia

Russia's security concerns associated with US military action in Iraq are not purely regional. Many Russian officials see the American decision to use force without an explicit UN mandate as jeopardising the existing system of international law that incorporates institutional mechanisms to moderate US power and principles protecting the sovereignty of weaker states against external aggression. If US military action has lowered the legal and political threshold beyond which one state may use force against another, Russia's interests require that it re-elevate this threshold by helping to rebuild transatlantic relations and reinstate the role of the United Nations. However, Russia's conduct during the UN Security Council deadlock and in the period following the commencement of US military action hampered its prospects for emerging as a credible intermediary between the US-led coalition and 'old Europe'. Indeed, the diplomatic crisis over Iraq revealed the limits of Russia's pragmatic foreign policy. Putin's immediate post-11 September strategy was to focus on maintaining and strengthening relations with the US while avoiding entanglements in transatlantic disputes. In February 2003, however, he decided to side openly with France and Germany against the US and the UK, Russia's two closest partners in the West, in favour of continued inspections over military action. Following France's lead, Moscow in March 2003 also expressly pledged to veto any second resolution authorising the use of force in Iraq. Putin's decision appeared to be motivated by larger balancing and sovereignty concerns and not by economic interests in Iraqi oil contracts, as some observers suggested. If only briefly, as Russia aligned itself with France and China against the US in the Security Council, Russian dreams of building and strengthening 'multipolarity' appeared to be revived.

For Russia, however, the price of a serious break in bilateral relations with the US was too high to pay in terms of both integration and long-term security. Therefore, unlike France and Germany, which severed high-level contacts with Bush and senior administration officials, Moscow continued to conduct careful diplomacy and kept many channels of communication open to Washington and London. Moreover, unlike Paris and Berlin, Moscow refrained from megaphone diplomacy and Putin made few public statements on the crisis, delegating all public diplomacy to Foreign Minister Igor Ivanov, who was already known to play the role of 'bad cop' to Putin's 'good cop'. (Putin, for example, had overruled Ivanov's uncompromising opposition to the presence of US forces in Central Asia and Georgia.) Thus, it seems unlikely that Putin would have authorised the use of Russia's veto in the Security Council if the US and UK had decided to table a second resolution, given that such action would have risked a major rift with the US. In this sense, the Anglo-American decision to withdraw the second resolution catered to Russia's interests, leaving more room for Putin to mend bilateral relations with Washington and London. But the fact remains that Russia's opposition and the mere threat of a veto contributed to the Security Council deadlock – a fact that the Bush administration is unlikely to forget.

If Moscow's criticism of the US-led military campaign continues, trust in Russia–US relations will probably be undermined and the United States' post-11 September commitment to greater engagement with Russia dampened. Russia's concerns over US military action in Iraq stem to a significant extent from its wariness of the policy of pre-emption enunciated in the Bush administration's National Security Strategy in September 2002. Ostensibly, Moscow sees US attempts to legitimise the use of force against any sovereign nation outside the existing framework of international law as broadly destabilising, and supports the norm under which military intervention can be undertaken only on grounds of self-defence or pursuant to an explicit UN mandate. But Moscow's objections are not merely philosophical. They are also explained by its wholesale decline in military capabilities following the collapse of the Soviet Union. In that light, Russia considers any challenge to a legal system that safeguards Russian interests – particularly one lodged by the world's most powerful nation and Russia's former Cold War adversary – a threat. In certain contexts, Russia has advocated the pre-emptive use of force: against failed states like Afghanistan; and against hostile and threatening non-state forces operating against Russia from the territory of a foreign state, as Chechen rebel groups have done from the Pankisi Gorge in Georgia. In Chechnya, Russia has also used force pre-emptively against individuals and groups that do not represent a clear and immediate threat. Further, Russia, unlike European governments more comprehensively opposed to pre-emption, has no strong objections to the Israeli policy of pre-emptive (if not preventive) targeted assassinations of Palestinian terrorists. Finally, Russia did not express any major concern over the November 2002 US *Predator* strike in Yemen to eliminate al-Qaeda operatives or the 1998 US cruise-missile strikes against alleged terrorist targets in Afghanistan and Sudan.

Russia's principal concern with pre-emption, then, focuses on the pre-emptive use of force against sovereign regimes rather than against the territory of sovereign states. That concern is driven primarily by a fear that the US could coerce regime change in countries friendly to Russia. Thus, Russia might argue that it is precisely the American doctrine of pre-emption and the United States' readiness to threaten the use of military force for regime change that prompts countries like Iran and North Korea to seek nuclear capabilities. Given the Bush administration's posture on the relationship between non-proliferation and pre-emption, however, this argument is not likely to serve Russia well. Were the US to decide to launch an attack on Iranian nuclear facilities on non-proliferation grounds, to prevent Iran from acquiring nuclear weapons capabilities, the Russian attitude would be clear. In that case, Russia's special relationship with Iran, as well as the fact that Russia itself has supplied some of Iran's civilian

Europe/Russia

nuclear capabilities, could induce Russia to take a harder line on pre-emption that is not directed towards regime change. Such a policy, however, would probably imperil its relations with the US even more than the crisis over Iraq has done.

A difficult readjustment ahead

The sapping of post-11 September momentum in US–Russia relations, which to a large extent was based on personal trust between the two leaders, is likely to hinder the implementation of Russia's key policy objectives of integration and security. In the subdued environment that prevailed in early 2003, difficult issues such as US concerns over Russia's nuclear cooperation with Iran, as well as Russia's concerns over the continuing US military presence in Central Asia and its expectations regarding US support for its long-term economic interests, will be increasingly hard to resolve. Short-term economic interests in relation to oil and debt in Iraq are less momentous but still non-trivial potential sources of aggravation. Any of these issues could trigger a new crisis in US–Russia relations. If, however, Russia chooses to play a constructive and more proactive role in reinvigorating transatlantic dialogue – for which it was at least better positioned than France or Germany in early 2003 – those objectives could be not merely salvaged but significantly advanced. To do this, Russia will have to resist the post-Soviet temptation, still prevalent in some government circles, to encourage anti-American sentiment at the UN. It would be prudent for Russia to consider certain subtler and more creative diplomatic initiatives, such as hosting a UK–France–Russia summit on reconstruction, as suggested by some Russian analysts. As of April 2003, though, their voices had not yet been heard in the Kremlin.

Russia, like other second-echelon powers, wants to see US military power contained by international legal norms. Yet the United States' superior power also means that such 'containment' will be less likely to succeed if Russian policy is bluntly confrontational. Russia's arguments against pre-emption would have more credibility if it were to make a cleaner breast of its own proliferation record. In particular, Russia should use its leverage to convince Iran that it should be more cooperative with the US on nuclear non-proliferation and demonstrate that it is not pursuing a nuclear-weapons programme. This would require Russia to pressure Iran to sign an additional protocol with the International Atomic Energy Agency and a verifiable decision from Iran not to develop an indigenous uranium-enrichment capability. If Iran refuses to take such steps, Russia should seriously consider stopping all its cooperation with Iran in the nuclear sphere. However uncomfortable such a policy might be, it may be indispensable to maintaining good relations with the United States. That, in turn, is central to Putin's paramount objectives of integration and security.

Turkey: Tensions from Within and Without

The victory of the Justice and Development Party (JDP) in the 3 November 2002 Turkish general elections gave a new twist to the country's seemingly perennial quest for identity. For the first time in its 79-year history, what is often touted as the only fully functioning secular democracy in the Muslim world found itself governed by a party that had grown out of the Turkish Islamist movement. Although its supporters argued that the JDP had evolved from its Islamist roots into a party of conservative 'Muslim Democrats', its opponents remained unconvinced. Behind the scenes the powerful military, which had long seen itself as the guardian of Turkey's secularist tradition, braced itself for what it believed was the coming battle for the country's soul.

Turkish identity was not merely a domestic issue. A decade earlier, any international concerns about Turkey's being led by a potentially Islamist party would have focused primarily on the implications for internal political stability and possible changes in the country's traditionally pro-Western foreign policy. But, ever since Ankara had been named as an official candidate for EU membership in December 1999, the role of Islam in Turkey had become a significant factor in determining not only the prospects for eventual Turkish accession but even how the EU defined itself. As the JDP celebrated its election victory and publicly committed itself both to secularism and to Turkey's EU candidacy, existing members were coming under pressure, led by the Vatican, to include a reference to Christianity – or at least to God – as one of the union's defining characteristics in the new EU constitution. Even though a direct reference to religion appeared unlikely to be included in the final draft, the debate itself served as a reminder that many still saw the EU not just as a political and economic union but also as the product of a shared cultural and religious heritage. For those who held such views, the more 'Muslim' Turkey appeared, the less attractive it seemed as a potential member.

The US did not fall into this exclusionary camp. As Washington prepared to launch a military campaign to oust Iraqi President Saddam Hussein, Turkey had grown in importance – both operationally, particularly as a platform from which to strike south through northern Iraq towards Baghdad, and on the global political battlefield. Turkish support for the US campaign would enable Washington to rebut widespread suspicions in the Muslim world that its efforts to topple Saddam and its wider 'war on terrorism' were, at least partly, directed against Islam. As a result, the stronger – within reason – Turkey's Islamic credentials, the greater the political value of its support for US action against Iraq.

Europe/Russia

International and domestic speculation about the JDP's ideological agenda, however, distracted attention from other factors that were, in the end, to prove more decisive in shaping the future of Turkey's relations with its Western allies. These included the competence of the JDP administration and the rise in Turkey over the previous decade of a bruised and assertive nationalism that had accompanied, and to a large extent underpinned, the growth in electoral support for the country's Islamist movement. Inside Turkey, a persistent refusal to understand how other countries and institutions operated, particularly the EU, had been compounded by a failure to understand that it had only a limited time both to cement its closer ties with Brussels and to maximise its newfound attractiveness to the US. Nowhere was the clock ticking louder than over Cyprus, where nearly 30 years of international efforts to reunite the divided island were already deep into their endgame – with potentially devastating consequences for Turkey's foreign relations, particularly with the EU, if they failed.

Domestic politics: hubris and hope

In the first half of 2002, Turkish domestic politics appeared to have assumed many of the characteristics of an ancient Greek tragedy in which, blinded by hubris, the central character stubbornly refuses to change his ways and edges ever closer to his inevitable downfall. In 2001, the ruling tripartite coalition government had overseen a currency collapse, triggering the worst economic recession in living memory, in which the economy had contracted by 9.4% and over a million Turks had lost their jobs. But by early 2002, stability on the money markets and the first tentative signs of economic recovery encouraged the government to proclaim that its policies were finally bearing fruit. A stream of corruption allegations involving government ministers had been quietly suppressed. The coalition partners continued to procrastinate over the reforms required for Turkey's EU membership, apparently confident that Brussels would eventually settle for partial compliance in the light of what they described as Turkey's 'special conditions'. Yet the economic upturn was attributable mainly to the steadying of investors' nerves as a result of the International Monetary Fund (IMF)'s approval on 4 February 2002 of $16.3 billion in loans in addition to $15bn disbursed in 2000 and 2001, making Turkey the largest borrower in IMF history and swelling still further the country's already burgeoning foreign debt. Further, there was no indication that the Turkish public shared the government's optimism. Opinion polls suggested that the coalition's approval rating was mired in single percentage points.

Nowhere was the government's detachment from reality more evident than in the person of the 76-year old prime minister, Bulent Ecevit. Despite official denials to the contrary, Ecevit was known to have long been in poor health. In early 2002, he had appeared increasingly frail and his public statements often seemed to indicate mental confusion. On 4 May 2002, Ecevit was kept in hospital overnight after suffering a reaction to medication for Parkinson's disease. On 19 May, he was admitted to hospital again after breaking a rib in a fall at his home. For the next six weeks, Ecevit remained virtually confined to his home, with all access to him controlled by his 78-year old wife Rahsan. But he refused to listen to calls for him to step down, even from within his own Democratic Left Party (DLP), and insisted that he would remain in office until the next elections, due in April 2004. With the government effectively without a leader, tensions began to surface between the three parties in the coalition. At the beginning of July 2002, Rahsan Ecevit, who was also deputy chair of the DLP, began to purge the party of those who had been calling for her husband to step down. The result was a flurry of resignations, which halved the number of DLP seats in parliament and left the government without a majority. On 31 July parliament voted to hold early elections on 3 November.

For many Turks, Ecevit's failing health had become a metaphor for an entire generation of political leaders who, over the previous decade, had established a series of fractious coalition governments, all of which had become tainted by allegations of graft and economic mismanagement. In contrast, the JDP, which was founded in August 2001, appeared to represent a break with the past. Led by Tayyip Erdogan, the 48-year old former mayor of Istanbul, the JDP had been formed from the rump of the Islamist Virtue Party (VP), which had been closed by the Constitutional Court for alleged anti-secular activities in June 2001. However, Erdogan and the rest of the JDP leadership vigorously eschewed any religious label, portraying the party as conservative rather than Islamist and stressing its commitment both to secularism and to Turkey's pro-Western foreign policy. Such rhetoric enabled the JDP to attract votes from the conservative wings of other parties, particularly on the nationalist right. Yet its leaders' radical pedigree meant that the JDP retained the support of most Islamist voters, who saw the JDP's more moderate image as a ploy to avoid prosecution by Turkey's vigorously secularist courts.

In the elections of 3 November 2002 the JDP won 34.3% of the popular vote, giving it 363 seats in the 550-member unicameral parliament. None of the parties that had won seats in the previous elections in April 1999 were represented in the new assembly. The only other party to cross the 10% threshold for representation in parliament was the centre-left Republican People's Party, which took 178 seats with 19.4%. The remaining nine seats were won by independents. Erdogan was unable to become prime minister, as the Turkish Constitution forbade him from standing for parliament because of a 1998 conviction for a speech in which he had allegedly incited religious hatred. As a result, although Erdogan retained the leadership of the party, JDP deputy chairman Abdullah Gul, a 52-year old UK-educated economist, was officially appointed prime minister on 19 November 2002.

Europe/Russia

Following the election, stock prices rose while interest rates fell on hopes that Turkey's first single-party government in 11 years would produce a period of stability. Even the Turkish military, which remained convinced that the JDP's moderate rhetoric masked a long-term radical Islamist agenda, expected Gul to adopt a low profile, avoid antagonising the secular establishment and concentrate on passing the necessary constitutional amendments to allow Erdogan to run for parliament as soon as there was a by-election. On 13 December 2002, the government duly amended the constitution. Erdogan successfully stood for parliament in the first by-election, which was held in the town of Siirt on 9 March 2003. Gul immediately resigned and Erdogan was officially appointed prime minister on 14 March 2003. Yet far from avoiding controversy, the JDP's first four months in power had already fuelled suspicions amongst its opponents as to the party's ultimate aims, while raising doubts among even its supporters about its competence and probity.

Previous confrontations between Islamists and Turkey's secular establishment had focused on three main areas: education; the ban on women wearing Islamic headscarves in public buildings and at state occasions; and the absence of a right of appeal for officers dismissed from the military for suspected Islamist activism. On 18 November 2002, Gul nominated Besir Atalay, a former university rector who had been dismissed for alleged Islamist activism, as Education Minister. Turkish President Ahmet Necdet Sezer refused to endorse the nomination, forcing Gul to replace Atalay with Erkan Mumcu, a known moderate. On 20 November 2002, Parliamentary Speaker Bulent Arinc attended a state ceremony with his wife, who was wearing a headscarf. He was rewarded with a visit from the Turkish General Staff (TGS) warning him not to do so again. In December 2002, Gul publicly declared that dismissals from the military should be eligible for appeal and appointed Ramazan Toprak, a former officer who had been fired from the military for alleged Islamist activism, as head of the Parliamentary Defence Committee. Following behind-the-scenes pressure from the TGS, Toprak resigned on 9 January 2003.

To the Turkish military, such moves were initial probes to test their resolve as part of a long-term JDP strategy to erode secularism. But many of the government's other actions appeared more characteristic of confusion and poor planning than a coordinated campaign. The government's economic programme, which was announced by Gul on 23 November 2003, contained few concrete proposals, preferring to concentrate on targets rather than how they were going to be achieved. Perhaps more worryingly, the JDP followed the precedent set by its predecessors by offering jobs in the civil service to party supporters and appointing friends and relatives to lucrative posts in state-owned institutions. A campaign promise to limit MPs' parliamentary immunity was dropped, while in December 2002 the government blocked draft amendments prepared by the previous administration to the public procurement law that would have made the awarding of state contracts more transparent. The government itself also appeared to be poorly managed. Even while Gul was still officially prime minister, Erdogan continued to exercise overall control over both government policy and the JDP itself. Yet different ministers issued statements on the same issues, often contradicting not only their colleagues but also previous pronouncements of their own. Erdogan added to the confusion by making conflicting statements, particularly on foreign policy, which dominated the JDP's agenda during its first weeks in office and again during the first quarter of 2003.

EU: consummation postponed

When Turkey was first named as an official candidate for EU accession in Helsinki in December 1999, Prime Minister Ecevit had confidently predicted that Turkey would have fulfilled all of the criteria for membership by the time EU leaders met in Copenhagen in December 2002 to announce the next stage in the union's expansion. But the European Commission's annual progress report on Turkey's candidacy, released on 13 November 2001, clearly stated that Turkey was still far short of meeting the minimum requirements for accession, specifying restrictions on freedom of speech, inadequate minority rights, Turkey's retention of the death penalty and the political power wielded by the Turkish military. Through the first half of 2002, though, there was little sense of urgency. Both the Turkish establishment, including the military, and the ultra-nationalist Nationalist Action Party (NAP), which was the second largest partner in the coalition government, made little secret of their fear that allowing the country's 12–15m Kurds rights such as broadcasting and education in their own language would encourage them to seek a separate state. On 26 February 2002, the government was forced to shelve a proposal to abolish capital punishment following opposition from the NAP on the grounds that it would spare the life of Abdullah Ocalan, who was on death row following his conviction for leading a bloody 15-year Kurdish uprising.

Yet opinion polls continued to report overwhelming public support for Turkish membership of the EU. On 3 August 2002, three days after it had agreed to hold early elections, parliament pushed through a series of reforms, including: the abolition of the death penalty in peacetime; the lifting of bans on broadcasting and education in languages other than Turkish; and the easing of restrictions on the activities of foundations established by non-Muslim minorities. The only opposition came from the NAP, which applied unsuccessfully to have the reforms reversed by the courts. Even the military appeared to backtrack, privately arguing that the risks inherent in the reforms were outweighed by the potential benefits of EU membership. But few outside Turkey expected the reforms to be

Europe/Russia

sufficient to secure membership at the December 2002 EU Summit in Copenhagen. In its annual progress report of 9 October 2002, the European Commission welcomed the reforms, but warned that further progress still needed to be made, particularly in terms of implementation. Nevertheless, less than two weeks after the JDP's election victory, Erdogan embarked on a tour of EU countries to lobby for Turkey either to be included in the next round of EU expansion or to be given a firm date for membership.

Despite his lack of official status, Erdogan was received in European capitals as the de facto head of the Turkish government. His frustration at being unable to secure a firm accession date produced a series of outbursts that raised questions about both his understanding of international diplomacy and the motivation for his party's public commitment to EU membership, which its opponents had long argued was merely a ploy to try to remove the Turkish military from the political arena. In the week preceding the Copenhagen summit, Erdogan first accused the EU of applying 'double standards' and using purported concerns about freedoms and human rights in Turkey to mask its own anti-Muslim prejudices. He then warned that the EU would be the one to suffer if it failed to grant Turkey membership and threatened that, if Brussels was unwilling to accept it, Turkey would join the North American Free Trade Association. Privately, EU officials were infuriated by Erdogan's tone. But the Copenhagen summit nevertheless avoided an outright rejection of Turkey's demands, announcing that it would defer a decision until December 2004. On his return to Turkey, Erdogan presented the Copenhagen summit as a personal triumph, arguing that he had defended the country's national honour.

Turkey's relations with Europe deteriorated still further in early 2003. On 12 March 2003, the European Court of Human Rights (ECHR) ruled that Ocalan's 1999 conviction was unsound and that he should be retried. The announcement triggered a furious reaction from Turkish nationalists, most of whom mistakenly believed that the ECHR was an extension of the EU. On 13 March 2003, the Turkish Constitutional Court announced the closure of the Kurdish People's Democracy Party (HADEP). Within hours, the Turkish Public Prosecutor filed a case for the banning of the Democratic People's Party (DEHAP), which had served as an umbrella for pro-Kurdish parties in the 3 November 2002 elections. But the continuing dispute between the EU and Turkey over the latter's policy towards its Kurds was overshadowed by another development which threatened to deal a fatal blow to Ankara's hopes of ever joining the EU: the final collapse on 11 March 2003 of UN-brokered efforts to reunify the divided island of Cyprus.

A permanently divided Cyprus?
Time had been running out for a solution to the Cyprus problem ever since the EU decided to open accession negotiations with the Republic of Cyprus

at Luxembourg in December 1997. The island has been divided along ethnic lines since 1974, when Turkish troops landed in the north to crush an Athens-backed coup aimed at uniting Cyprus with Greece. Although the Greek Cypriot administration in Nicosia is recognised by the international community as the government of the entire island, in practice it only controls the southern 62%. The remaining 38% of the island is administered by the self-declared Turkish Republic of Northern Cyprus (TRNC), which is only recognised by Turkey and backed by 35,000 Turkish troops stationed permanently in the north. As a result, Greek Cypriot accession to the EU not only would give arguably Turkey's most implacable foe the power of veto over the union's relations with Ankara but would also mean that Turkish troops were effectively occupying EU territory. Turkish officials appeared unaware of the danger, insisting – despite repeated statements to the contrary from Brussels – that the EU would stop short of admitting the Greek Cypriots without a solution to the Cyprus problem.

Negotiations to reunite the island began almost immediately after the Turkish invasion of 1974 and have continued, through a series of direct and indirect 'proximity' negotiations, ever since. In 1997, Turkish Cypriot leader Rauf Denktash broke off direct negotiations, insisting that the Greek Cypriots recognise the TRNC's sovereignty before talks could resume. However, in autumn 2001 the Turkish military pressured Denktash into returning to the negotiating table for fear that his intransigence was damaging Turkey's own bid for EU accession. But privately they assured him that he was not expected to make any concessions from his previously stated position. Direct UN-sponsored talks between Denktash and Republic of Cyprus President Glafkos Clerides resumed on 16 January 2002, but failed to produce a settlement. Denktash insisted that a reunited Cyprus should be based on a loose confederal system in which the two communities administered their own domestic affairs, with their populations continuing to be segregated along ethnic lines. Clerides wanted an integrated single state with a large measure of freedom of movement and settlement, including the right of a substantial proportion of the Greek Cypriots displaced by the 1974 invasion to return to their properties in the north. On 12 November 2002, UN Secretary General Kofi Annan presented the two sides with draft proposals for a settlement, which became known as the 'Annan Plan'. They were based on the Swiss canton system and included: a single 'common state' government and two equal 'component states', one Greek Cypriot and the other Turkish Cypriot; a rotating presidency; the preservation of the 1960 Treaty of Guarantee, naming Greece, Turkey and the UK as guarantors of the constitution; territorial readjustments which would transfer approximately 9.5% of the island from Turkish Cypriot to Greek Cypriot administration; and limitations on migration from one component state to the other, with the emphasis on compensation for, rather than return of, property lost in 1974.

Europe/Russia

Both sides had reservations about the Annan Plan, particularly its proposals for territorial transfer and freedom of movement and settlement. For Denktash, the proposals went too far; for the Greek Cypriots, they did not go far enough. Clerides nevertheless accepted the plan as the basis for further negotiations, for fear that failure to do so would jeopardise the expected endorsement of Greek Cypriot accession to the EU at the Copenhagen summit on 12 December 2002. Opinion polls, however, suggested that over 60% of Greek Cypriots were opposed to the Annan Plan. Clerides went to Denmark expecting to have to make domestically unpopular concessions to the Turkish Cypriots in order to secure EU membership. But Denktash, who was recovering from heart surgery, checked in to a hospital in Ankara. Although a Turkish Cypriot delegation did travel to Copenhagen and engaged in negotiations, it lacked the authority to make decisions on its own and was under strict instructions from Denktash not to make any compromises. The negotiations failed. Nevertheless, the EU announced that the Republic of Cyprus would be granted accession in May 2004 as one of ten new member states. The EU set a deadline of 28 February 2003 for a solution to the Cyprus problem, which would need to be ratified by referendums in the two communities prior to the official signing of the Treaty of Accession by a single Cypriot state on 16 April 2003.

The failure to reach an agreement at Copenhagen triggered a series of mass demonstrations in northern Cyprus. On 26 December 2002, over 30,000 Turkish Cypriots – approximately one-sixth of the total population of the TRNC – took to the streets to protest Denktash's intransigence. Further demonstrations followed. On 27 February 2003, over 60,000 protestors staged a rally calling for a solution based on the Annan Plan. But Denktash remained unmoved. The continuing impasse in Cyprus also demonstrated the limitations of the government in Ankara, not only in terms of the Turkish military's continued domination of what it saw as a key security issue but also in the JDP's apparent inability to put together a coordinated, consistent policy. Traditionally, Turkish policy on Cyprus has been controlled by the TGS, working in coordination with the Ministry of Foreign Affairs (MFA) and communicating its views to the civilian government at monthly meetings of the National Security Council (NSC). On 5 November 2002, two days after the election that brought the JDP to power, Erdogan announced that the JDP favoured the Belgian model of institutionalised bicommunality as the basis for a solution to the Cyprus problem. On 6 November 2002, after a two-hour briefing at the MFA, the new Foreign Minister Yasar Yakis announced that Belgium could not be a model for a settlement and that Turkish policy on Cyprus remained unchanged. On 5 January 2003, Erdogan called for a change in policy on Cyprus. On 17 January 2003, Parliamentary Speaker Arinc announced that there would be no change. On 26 January 2003, Erdogan announced that, after so many years of fruitless negotiations, Denktash should resign, but he withdrew the suggestion on the following day. On 27 January 2003, General Aytac Yalman, the commander of the Turkish Land Forces, visited Denktash in Cyprus and assured him of the military's unconditional support. After a meeting of the NSC on 31 January 2003, Gul declared that there would be no change in policy on Cyprus and that the JDP was fully behind Denktash.

Hopes of settlement received a further blow on 16 February 2003, when the Greek Cypriots elected Tassos Papadopoulos, who had traditionally rejected any compromise with the Turkish Cypriots, as president in place of Clerides. After the 28 February 2003 deadline passed without an agreement, Annan invited the Greek and Turkish Cypriot leaders to a final meeting in The Hague on 10 March 2003. On the morning of 11 March, after chairing 16 hours of fruitless negotiations, Annan finally announced that UN attempts to broker a settlement had reached the end of the road. Later on the same day, the European Commission issued a statement declaring that the accession of the Republic of Cyprus would proceed as planned, leaving Turkey with the choice between a humiliating climb-down and the indefinite suspension of its own hopes for EU membership.

Transatlantic alliance?

In early 2002, US–Turkish relations appeared stronger than at any time since the end of the 1991 Gulf War and, for a time at least, a transatlantic alliance appeared to many Turks to offer a viable alternative to the EU. For a people who have always been highly sensitive to foreign criticism, Washington's repeated citing of Turkey as a model for other Muslim countries to follow provided a huge boost to national pride. For the US, Turkish support enabled it to argue that its 'war on terrorism' was not anti-Islamic. However, Washington's efforts to tie Turkey firmly to the West sometimes backfired. In late autumn 2002, intense US lobbying for Turkey to be given a firm date for accession at the Copenhagen EU summit merely antagonised European states such as France and Germany who were already wary of US global hegemony. But the alliance also had practical benefits. The US was instrumental in persuading the IMF to grant Turkey the package of loans that was formally approved on 4 February 2002. In May 2002, Turkey was able to go some way towards appeasing local Muslim sentiments in Afghanistan by dispatching a battalion of troops to join the International Security and Assistance Force (ISAF) and in June took over the command of the ISAF from the UK.

Turkey assumed even greater strategic and propaganda value to the US as Washington prepared to launch a military campaign to topple Saddam Hussein. US commanders were anxious to secure Turkish cooperation, including using military bases as staging points for the deployment of ground troops and armour into northern Iraq to open up a second front, in

Europe/Russia

addition to the main thrust of their attack striking northward out of the Gulf states. The Turkish military was, on balance, opposed to the war. It feared that war would further damage Turkey's already fragile economy, and that it could encourage the Kurds in northern Iraq to declare autonomy or even independence, which in turn could revive Kurdish separatism in Turkey. But the TGS was also convinced that a military campaign was virtually inevitable. As early as summer 2002, the TGS decided that, once war broke out, Turkey would have no choice but to support the US, and could even put Turkish troops on the ground in northern Iraq both to protect Turkey's alliance with Washington and to quell any Kurdish separatist aspirations. But it avoided making any explicit commitment to the US in the hope that war could still somehow be avoided and to exact as high a price as possible from the US, in terms of financial aid, in return for Turkish support. But the JDP's electoral victory of November 2002 changed the playing field. Although the Turkish military had retained ultimate control over Turkish security policy, its political leverage depended as much on its public popularity as on its ability to threaten the ultimate sanction of putting soldiers on the street. The military still consistently tops opinion polls on the most trusted institutions in Turkey. Regardless of the JDP's public rhetoric, the TGS remained convinced that the party harboured a secret radical Islamist agenda and would try to erode secularism. As it braced itself for a future confrontation with the JDP, the military was unwilling to see its public popularity eroded by explicitly advocating participation in a war that opinion polls suggested was opposed by over 94% of the Turkish population. In late 2002, despite growing frustration in Washington, the TGS was still refusing to commit itself either to allowing the US to use Turkish ports and airbases or to permitting American troops to transit Turkish soil on their way to northern Iraq, preferring to hand responsibility for the final decision to the elected JDP government.

The JDP leadership was thus faced with a dilemma. On one hand, the Turkish Islamist movement has always included a substantial nationalist element, which bridled at Turkey's being used to further US global interests. Further, most JDP supporters had grave reservations about helping what they regarded as a Christian superpower wage war on their fellow Muslims. On the other hand, the JDP leadership knew that the Turkish economy was not strong enough to risk losing the support of the US at the IMF and World Bank. To avoid unduly antagonising either the electorate or Washington, the government opted to try to delay a final decision while squeezing as much as possible out of the US in the promise of a massive aid package. On 6 February 2003, parliament passed a motion to allow US personnel into the country to upgrade Turkish military facilities in order to be able to handle 62,000 US troops in transit to northern Iraq. But the JDP was still reluctant to introduce a motion allowing the troops themselves onto Turkish soil. In mid-February 2003, after weeks of haggling, Turkey and the US finally agreed on an aid package of up to $26bn, including an estimated $6bn in grants and the cancellation of existing debts. But on 24–25 February 2003, Turkish newspapers reprinted a series of cartoons that had appeared in the foreign press, several of which depicted Turkey as a grubby bazaar merchant willing to sell his soul to the highest bidder.

Stung by public outrage at the foreign cartoons, and under intense pressure from the US, the government finally decided to submit a motion allowing US troops into Turkey to parliament on 1 March, the day after the monthly NSC meeting. The JDP appears to have hoped that the TGS would use the meeting to issue a public recommendation to parliament to pass the motion and allow the government to shift some of the responsibility onto the military. But the TGS remained silent and refused to allow any reference to the motion in the communiqué issued at the end of the meeting. On the morning of 1 March 2003, Erdogan held an informal poll of JDP MPs, which indicated that only a handful would oppose the motion. But when it was actually put to parliament that evening, the motion passed by only 264–250 with 19 abstentions, leaving the government three votes short of the constitutional requirement of a majority of those who participated in the vote. The result stunned the government but was greeted with elation by most of the Turkish public, who were proud to have defied the US and repudiated the derisive portrayal of Turkey in the foreign cartoons. Fearful that another defeat could split the party, the government initially refused to present another motion to parliament. Over the next week, the US began relocating some of its ships, which had been waiting off the Turkish coast, to the Persian Gulf. On 16 March 2003, Washington announced that the $15bn in aid was no longer 'on the table' and US Secretary of State Colin Powell bluntly warned Ankara not to deploy troops into northern Iraq following the outbreak of hostilities.

The JDP government appeared to believe, naively, that the US could not attack Iraq without its active cooperation, and therefore overestimated its leverage. The JDP was also expecting the Turkish military to pressure it into allowing US troops onto Turkish soil, but no pressure was forthcoming. In addition, neither Erdogan nor any of his inner circle seemed to understand the vast logistical operation required to send US troops to Turkey, or how much advance warning the military planners needed. As a result, they did not register the growing frustration and sense of urgency in the US. There also did not appear to be any realisation among the approximately 90 JDP MPs who failed to back the parliamentary motion allowing US troops onto Turkish soil that they were contradicting themselves. In February 2002, they had voted to allow the US into Turkey to spend over $300m upgrading military facilities that were to be used specifically to stage a strike against Iraq. Although Abdullah Gul, de jure prime minister at the time of the parliamentary vote against the US deployment, later said that he considered resigning, Erdogan appeared completely unfazed by the government's inconsistency. On 20 March, however, the Turkish parliament voted, 332–202, in favour of opening Turkish airspace to US warplanes. Shortly thereafter, Turkey sent between 1,000 and 1,500 troops into northern Iraq, citing as reasons the containment of refugees and 'Iraq's territorial integrity' – that is, to discourage any move towards independence by the Iraqi Kurds. US Secretary of Defense Donald Rumsfeld reiterated that large numbers of Turkish troops in northern Iraq would be 'notably unhelpful'.

Since the 1990s, Turkey had had a 5,000-strong brigade, including some artillery and armour, based virtually permanently in northern Iraq. The number of Turkish troops in northern Iraq increased substantially in the months leading up to the start of the US invasion in March. Thus, as of April 2003, the Turks already had a major presence there, even if it consisted mainly of lightly armed ground troops scattered throughout a strip of territory running parallel to the Turkish border. The reinforcements' primary tasks were to monitor the flow of refugees and keep an eye on the Iraqi Kurds' political ambitions. Other Turkish troops (including armour and artillery) were positioned on the Turkish side of the border, prepared to cross if necessary. The Turks probably already had enough troops on the ground in northern Iraq to control refugees.

The question was whether they would increase this number to maybe 30–40,000, to try to crush Iraqi Kurdish political ambitions. If the Iraqi Kurds attempted to declare independence, the answer would be an unequivocal 'yes'. But this seemed unlikely to happen. The most the Iraqi Kurds would probably do in the near term would be press for a federal autonomous region. The Turks have repeatedly said that this would be unacceptable unless the Turcomans were granted equal rights – that is, an autonomous region of their own. But there were some grey areas. The Turks would almost certainly apply military pressure to the Iraqi Kurds if they declared an autonomous Kurdish region that included the oilfields around Kirkuk. They might be prepared to tolerate a formula by which Iraq remained a unitary state but some way was found to give the Kurds a substantial self-government – e.g., devolution of power without official labels like 'federation' or 'autonomous region'. But if the Turks believed either that an independent Kurdish state or the foundations for one were being laid in northern Iraq, they would oppose it regardless of the US. Apart from anything else, refraining from doing so would have disastrous domestic political consequences. For the next few years at least, no Turkish government could hope to remain in office if it tolerated the creation of a Kurdish state. The Turkish military, for its part, would have difficulty spinning any withdrawal from northern Iraq in the face of US threats as anything but cowardice.

Towards an uncertain future

In mid-March 2003, perhaps only the Turkish military could look back over the JDP's first four months in power with any sense of satisfaction. There was no doubt that the JDP's popularity had been badly tarnished by the confusion and lack of coordination that had come to characterise the government. The new government also had yet to introduce any measures to strengthen Turkey's still fragile economy. Yet, if questions about the JDP's competence had made it appear less of a threat to secularism, the military nevertheless remained convinced that it still had a latent Islamist agenda. From the perspective of the secularist establishment, such fears were not entirely groundless. Even if, as they maintained, Erdogan and the rest of the JDP leadership had abandoned their former radicalism, they were still under intense pressure from their own voters to introduce measures, such as lifting the ban on headscarves, which, though apparently innocuous to the outside world, were seen by the Turkish establishment as an assault on the foundations of secularism. Although the JDP could delay for a time – particularly while public attention was diverted by the forthcoming US war against Iraq – eventually it would have to deliver. Meanwhile, any attempt to dilute the Turkish interpretation of secularism would trigger a strong adverse reaction from the military.

The military's main fear was that the JDP would be subtle and introduce incremental change. Under previous governments, the military had always used intermediaries as well as direct contacts to impose its will. But there was no one close to Erdogan with whom a Turkish commander could have a quiet word and be confident that it would be forwarded. This also meant that the military's access to inside information was more limited. For example, the military still did not know, as of March 2003, what Erdogan promised Bush when he had met him at the White House, as Erdogan had refused to take a 'military advisor' into the meeting with him. This lack of access increased the possibility of the military becoming more heavy-handed. Furthermore, the TGS was arguably less constrained by international public opinion, once the carrot of EU membership appeared more distant. Nevertheless, the military would try to apply subtle pressure first, by way of public statements, visits to government officials, tabling recommendations at the National Security Council and galvanising non-governmental organisations. If, in spite of these measures, the government attempted anything radical, however, the TGS would put troops on the streets. The government may prove so inept that it will be forced into early elections before it can do anything so dramatic as to prompt a coup. Alternatively, if the JDP listens to the military, implements only gradual change and manages to stay in power for long enough, it could make drastic action by the TGS politically awkward. But the current chief of staff is already under a considerable pressure from the lower ranks (who are even more Kemalist than the top brass) to be more assertive. If the government

Europe/Russia

tries anything radical within the next couple of years, the military is likely to force it out regardless of how unacceptable or anachronistic it might appear to the West.

The collapse of the Cyprus negotiations on 11 March 2003 also threatened to slow, if not suspend, the domestic reform process, which had always been mainly driven by the prospect of eventual EU membership. Unless that incentive could be restored, there was unlikely to be progress in democratisation or tolerance of political and cultural pluralism. Yet, although many Turks remained privately resentful of Turkish Cypriots – not least because they were suspected of not being truly 'Turkish' – the Cyprus problem has always been a matter of national honour in Turkey. Howls of outrage from Turkish nationalists greeted suggestions that Denktash should negotiate on the basis of the relatively moderate concessions contained in the Annan Plan. Given the rise of nationalism within Turkey over the last decade, it is difficult to see how any Turkish government could advocate what would now need to be even greater concessions – given that the Greek Cypriots' bargaining position has been considerably enhanced by its forthcoming membership of the EU – without facing a massive political backlash at the ballot box.

But without a settlement to the Cyprus problem, it is impossible for Turkey to realise its own ambitions for EU accession. Once this realisation sinks in, public anger is likely to be followed by a sense of betrayal and a belief that the EU, because of historical and religious prejudices, was never serious about Turkey's candidacy. Political relations between Ankara and Brussels will almost inevitably cool as a result. But Turkey has few alternatives. It also has few short-term options for repairing relations with the US over Iraq. The best it can probably do is to stop them from further deteriorating. Even this would require the US to convince Turkey that a unitary state in Iraq will be preserved, so that the Turks refrain from deploying more combat troops into northern Iraq. In any event, especially given the alarming incompetence of Turkey's new civilian government, the US will have to talk directly to the Turkish military, which will make the final decision. On 2 April 2003, Powell held discussions with Gul, Erdogan and Sezer in Ankara to dissuade Turkey from sending a large force into northern Iraq and possibly to win permission for the US to use Turkish airbases, and was scheduled to meet General Hilmi Ozkok, chief of the TGS. Now on offer from the US was up to \$8.5bn in loan guarantees.

Even if Turkey is able to repair the damage done to its relations with the US by the debacle over the deployment of US troops, Turkey's broader attractiveness to the US will probably be diminished after the war with Iraq. In late 2002, Ankara still had several high cards to play, including the possibility of concessions over Cyprus and support for the US over Iraq. By March 2003, it had none. Once the war with Iraq is over, the only inducement remaining to the JDP government to persuade the US to mend fences will be the prospect of a Turkish economic collapse – that is, an appeal to its own ineptitude. Although the JDP government's programme promised to build closer ties with other Muslim countries, the Arab states still have bitter memories of the Ottoman Empire. Other Muslim countries are either too far away or simply not rich enough to serve as a political or economic alternative to the West. In early 2002, Turkey seemed to have a soaring trajectory as the West's showcase secular Muslim partner in the war on terror. A year later, war in Iraq and the Cyprus problem had flattened Turkey's arc. Unless Ankara works hard to find some way to restore its relations with the West – most critically through keeping its hopes of eventual EU accession alive – Turkey faces a lonely and uncertain future.

Middle East/Gulf

US-led forcible regime-change in Iraq – first in prospect, then in reality – dominated the Middle East and Persian Gulf during 2002–03. The Bush administration's conviction was that America's unprecedented power provided the means to change the status quo in the region, and that it needed to be changed for four basic reasons. First, Saddam Hussein's arsenal of weapons of mass destruction (WMD) needed to be preventively destroyed to eliminate the possibility that he could supply them to terrorists. Second, removing Saddam's threat to his neighbours – in particular, Israel, Saudi Arabia and Iran – would lay the foundation for the transformation of the Arab and larger Muslim world into a more liberal, democratic and economically integrated region, better able to manage problems such as rising and increasingly young and disaffected populations and non-participatory political systems conducive to radicalisation and terrorism. Third, a more liberal Arab community and a less threatened Israel would make the Israeli–Palestinian conflict more tractable, diluting one of Osama bin Laden's key pretexts for anti-Western terrorism. Fourth, Saddam's ouster would ultimately obviate the need for a permanent US military deployment in Saudi Arabia and shrink the United States' footprint in the region, thus removing bin Laden's central grievance.

This bold and ambitious programme was questioned on a number of serious grounds. France and Germany, backed by Russia and most Arab states, feared that the precedent of pre-emptive or preventive military action – given the US' overwhelming military superiority – would be difficult to limit both legally and practically, and believed that a stable and orderly international system required that arms inspections be given one more chance to work. They also worried that military intervention could have the perverse effect of inflaming radical Muslim sensibilities – swelling al-Qaeda's ranks and increasing transnational terrorism – and fracturing the broad global coalition against terrorism that the US had worked so hard to build after the 11 September attacks. Another non-trivial argument raised was that the US should re-establish a process of political negotiation in the Israeli–Palestinian conflict before rather than after military action, to lower tensions in Israel and the Palestinian territories and thus make the region less susceptible to the popular outrage that would greet war against Iraq. In the event, these arguments were unavailing. On the basis of UN Security Council Resolution 1441, adopted on 8 November 2002, but without the second resolution that many considered necessary to fully legitimise the use of force, the US and the United Kingdom, with support from Australia and several other countries drawn from a modest 'coalition of the willing', commenced military operations against Iraq on 20 March 2003.

The precision leadership strikes on Baghdad that began the war and the further aerial attacks designed to 'shock and awe' Iraqi leadership did not produce the quick regime implosion that the Pentagon had hoped for to forestall street-to-street fighting – and politically undesirable civilian casualties – in Baghdad. US and UK military planners also had to adjust their tactics to allow for more flexible pursuit of the enemy – necessitated by unexpected Iraqi resistance in a number of urban centres in southern Iraq, often with irregular forces – and more armoured support for the main thrust towards Baghdad. Nevertheless, two weeks into the war, US-led forces were progressing towards the Iraqi capital and appeared to have severely disrupted the Iraqis' command-and-control capabilities. Coalition fatalities remained less than 100, while Iraqi military dead exceeded 5,000. Given the tonnage of explosives directed at Baghdad and other areas, civilian casualties – though difficult to ascertain with accuracy – appeared relatively low. Perhaps more than 10,000 Iraqi soldiers had defected, surrendered or been taken prisoner. Leadership strikes continued, and more stealthy options were under consideration. The US, however, was preparing to attack Baghdad with infantry, with the distinct possibility that street-to-street urban combat could not be avoided after all.

In contrast to the Gulf War of 1991, the conflict of 2003 did not directly imperil Israel. No ballistic (or other) missiles were fired at Israeli targets. The US-led action did appear to provide a somewhat gratuitous pretext for suicide attacks by Palestinian terrorists, but that was not unexpected. As of early April 2003, however, what effect the war would have on prospects for progress on the Israeli–Palestinian problem remained unclear. On 15 March 2003, at the urging of British Prime Minister Tony Blair, President Bush announced his intention to adopt a 'road map' – prepared jointly by the 'quartet' comprising the US, the European Union, the UN and Russia – towards a Palestinian state after the Palestinians chose a new prime minister. Many saw the gesture as a belated and somewhat cynical attempt to soothe nerves and win a second UN Security Council resolution in support of war, but Blair's resoluteness lent credibility to the initiative. On 19 March, Palestinian Authority President Yasser Arafat appointed Mahmoud Abbas (known as Abu Mazen) prime minister. US Secretary of State Colin Powell stated on 30 March that Israel would need to end settlement activity in the West Bank and Gaza for peace to move forward. A day later, Israeli Foreign Minister Silvan Shalom made Israeli cooperation expressly contingent on a cessation of Palestinian terrorist attacks, giving Abu Mazen a 1–2 month probation period in which to stop them.

Among Muslim countries in the region, Bahrain, Kuwait, Qatar and the United Arab Emirates offered varying degrees of support for the war. Other Arab governments opposed it. On 31 March, Egyptian President Hosni

Mubarak declared that it would produce 'a thousand bin Ladens'. This war's action, unlike that of the first Gulf War, was broadcast in real time by al-Jazeera and other Arab news outlets throughout the Arab world. Several thousand jihadis from the region were rumoured to be travelling to Iraq to fight US and British troops. The besieged Iraqi regime – though putatively secular – opportunistically exhorted fellow Arabs to take up arms against the US and the UK, proclaiming it their duty when an Islamic nation is attacked. Saddam Hussein awarded two posthumous medals to a suicide bomber who killed four American soldiers on 29 March, reportedly paying his family $34,000. Large and sometimes violent anti-American protests occurred in Amman, Cairo, Damascus, Tehran and other major Arab cities, prompting police crackdowns. While it was conceivable that positive post-conflict political developments in Iraq could eventually carry over to other Muslim countries, the war's more immediate general effect was to underline the need for the authoritarian security apparatus of the state.

As of April 2003, the US-led coalition's victory was a virtual certainty, but the human and political costs of that victory remained undetermined. The status quo was indeed about to change, but it was not yet clear whether the situation that replaced it would constitute an improvement.

War in Iraq

Middle East

The occupation and potential political reconstitution of Iraq will have profound implications not only for the Iraqi people, but for neighbouring countries as well. Depending on how deep Western commitment and stamina will prove to be in the post-war era, Iraq's population could find itself under a halting US or UN administration, or on an extended trajectory towards indigenous liberalisation and perhaps even eventual democracy.

In some respects, renewed war with Iraq was inevitable. The intertwined pressures of domestic Iraqi politics, President Saddam Hussein's self-image as leader of the Arabs, his relentless pursuit of weapons of mass destruction (WMD), Iraqi anti-Zionism and the regime's tendency to misapprehend the international environment were going to bring Baghdad into a decisive confrontation with the US sooner or later. The timing of this confrontation was determined by an event wholly outside the control of the two main protagonists, yet intimately related to the first phase of their rivalry: the emergence of a global *jihad* movement dedicated to the destruction of Islam's presumed adversaries. It was the 1991 Gulf War that galvanised this movement, provided its animating imagery, and refocused jihadist wrath from Arab governments to the 'far enemy', a favoured euphemism for the United States. The Gulf War also revivified a popular Islamic eschatological literature that had surged after the Six-Day War of 1967, in which apocalyptic dreams of the destruction of New York City were a staple feature. The successful attempt by al-Qaeda to transform this dream of the night into the reality of the day on 11 September 2001 catapulted Iraq from the bottom of a new American administration's agenda to the top and put Baghdad and Washington on a collision course.

The administration of President Bill Clinton expressly favoured regime change, but considered its cost prohibitive. But veterans of the first Bush Administration who formed George W. Bush's foreign and defence policy advisory team during his presidential campaign and now constitute his national security cabinet had argued throughout the 1990s that the American declaratory position on regime change should be forcefully implemented. Setting aside the normative issues that regime change raised, the Bush team's assessment of the Clinton administration's commitment to removing Saddam by force was correct. For Clinton's team, the disincentives were considerable. The Iraqi opposition was feckless and disconnected from events on the ground, basing countries were unenthusiastic, European allies uncooperative, other priorities such as the Middle East peace process and the Balkans crisis too pressing, economic uncertainties too great, and the military options unappetising to both the Joint Chiefs of Staff and civilians in the White House and Pentagon. Moreover, sanctions enforcement, although clearly weakening, was far from disintegration. The administration could plausibly argue that the UN escrow scheme and oil-for-food programme effectively deprived Saddam of the resources to reconstitute his military strength, while reducing the adverse effect of sanctions on the lives of ordinary Iraqis. Saddam, as administration spokespersons routinely stressed, was 'in the box'.

These arguments were challenged not only by Republicans, but also by powerful Democratic critics, including Senator Joseph Lieberman who would become the candidate for the vice-presidency in 2000. The Iraq Liberation Act was championed by a bipartisan coalition in Congress, but signed reluctantly by Clinton in October 1998, and only after extensive wrangling over its scope and funding. The Iraqi opposition that was so appealing to its friends in Congress was not so persuasive to the White House, or to the Central Intelligence Agency (CIA), which was saddled with responsibility for undermining the Iraqi regime through covert action. In the wake of the debacle of 1996, in which the CIA infrastructure in northern Iraq was dismantled in an Iraqi incursion that the US military was powerless to prevent, the CIA was not overly eager to start again. Accordingly, despite significant political pressure from both sides of the congressional aisle and Iraq's increasing non-cooperation with UN Special Commission weapons inspectors in 1998 and their eventual withdrawal, the Clinton team put Iraq on the back-burner after the large-scale *Operation Desert Fox* air strikes of November 1998, which Republican critics dubbed 'the pinprick'.

Once in office, however, the Bush administration perpetuated its predecessor's approach. The new team had higher priorities than forcing regime change in Iraq. The testing and deployment of large-scale missile defences, which would require American withdrawal from the 1972 Anti-Ballistic Missile (ABM) Treaty, threatened to recapitulate the intra-Alliance crisis of the mid-1980s over the deployment of nuclear-tipped intermediate-range ballistic and cruise missiles to Europe. US–Russia relations were entering a delicate phase and no one could be confident that Moscow would acquiesce in Washington's stated intention to scrap the detritus of the Cold War and transcend its reliance on mutual assured destruction. China was branded a strategic competitor by the administration, which quickly became embroiled in a succession of small crises involving, *inter alia*, a presidential pledge to do whatever was necessary to defend Taiwan against Chinese aggression and a subsequent collision off the Chinese coast between a US spy plane and Chinese tactical aircraft. While the administration was able to withdraw from the ABM Treaty without disrupting relations with Russia or destabilising those with China, the intensive diplomacy required to accomplish this crowded out efforts to move forward on regime change in Iraq.

In keeping with its perception that the world had changed in a way that demanded a new strategic paradigm, the White House and the civilian Pentagon leadership embarked on an audacious restructuring of entrenched military planning, programming and budgeting practices. Given the apparent absence of immediate adversaries and the emergence of rapid technological advances over which the US seemed to have a monopoly, the new team saw an opportunity to skip a generation of weapons and take a fresh look at the missions and structure of American forces. The uniformed services opposed these initiatives, however, and precipitated a crisis that was widely thought to presage the resignation of Secretary of Defense Donald Rumsfeld and his cadre of reform-minded appointees. At home, the White House was focused on an exhaustive study of American energy options, based on a stated belief that a crisis was looming, and on lobbying for a large, multi-year tax cut in an economy that was edging toward recession. With its hands so full, there would be scant opportunity or motivation to put Republican campaign rhetoric on Iraq into action.

Philosophically as well as pragmatically, there was no urgent interest in the Middle East among foreign-policy managers who believed that American interests were bound up with the actions of other major powers, rather than small countries on the periphery of world affairs. From the new administration's perspective, key alliances – particularly NATO and treaty ties to Korea and Japan – had been neglected and there had been a failure to focus on potential adversaries, such as China and Russia, which truly

Middle East

had the capacity to challenge American interests in the future. Other countries, with the possible exception of India, were marginal to a worldview that was disciplined, realistic and disinclined to see foreign policy as 'social work'. The Israeli–Palestinian front was not seen as ripe for intervention, while the main Persian Gulf player, Saudi Arabia, was perceived as unreliable and potentially hostile. Indeed, the administration's determination to diversify domestic and foreign energy sources was not unrelated to its distrust of Saudi Arabia and scepticism about the long-term prospects of its rulers.

The 11 September effect

The attacks of 11 September did not completely overturn the administration's existing priorities or neutralise its prior instincts. Nevertheless, the sudden, shocking apprehension of the vulnerability of the United States to a devastating attack on its territory made it hard not to think about other adversaries that might have the will and ability to hit Americans in the same way. Al-Qaeda's objective was to cause mass casualties. Looking at the carnage in lower Manhattan – especially in aerial photographs – Americans could not help but think that New York looked as though it had been hit with a nuclear weapon. The terrorists were known to be flirting with WMD, a fact confirmed shortly afterward by evidence recovered from Taliban and al-Qaeda installations in Afghanistan. The scale and brutality of the attacks suggested that if al-Qaeda had possessed a nuclear device on 11 September, it would have used it. The anthrax attacks that followed (and remain unsolved) reinforced the burgeoning public perception of the threat posed by WMD.

Administration officials and a small number of influential outside advisors seized the opportunity to raise the profile of Iraq by intimating that Saddam Hussein was linked to one or another of these attacks. Although the Kurdish opposition has argued that the regime in Baghdad had worked with Ansar al-Islam and Jund al-Islam, two jihadist groups in northern Iraq that have connections with al-Qaeda, and US Secretary of State Colin Powell offered circumstantial evidence of the link between Baghdad and Ansar al-Islam before the UN Security Council in February 2003, a review of intelligence failed to turn up specific information showing that Saddam was complicit in either attack. Reports that Mohammad Atta, the ringleader of the 11 September attacks, had met with the chief Iraqi intelligence officer in Prague were unconvincingly documented by the Czech intelligence service and ultimately repudiated by the Czech government. Convinced that the CIA was withholding relevant reports on contacts between Iraq and al-Qaeda, the Pentagon created its own intelligence cell in which state-of-the-art data-mining software is being used to re-examine all-source reporting on this issue.

The absence of a 'smoking gun' has not mattered, however, because decision-makers and the public soon focused not on the question of Saddam Hussein's culpability for 11 September, but on the possibility that he might at some point transfer WMD materials or components to al-Qaeda or a similarly motivated group. Iraq's enormous stocks of anthrax in this context were like the proverbial elephant in the living room. They could not be ignored despite the lack of evidence that Iraq had been directly involved in terrorism against the US. The point was, rather, that Iraq was a place where terrorists could possibly obtain WMD. The vast ideological gap between the secular Ba'athist regime in Baghdad and the fundamentalist salafist orientation of the terrorists, as well as Saddam's obsession with control over his WMD assets, suggested that transfer of such materials would be unlikely, or at best made only in the fog of war. But the bulk of informed American opinion coalesced not around probabilities, but consequences. Thus, cooperation between al-Qaeda and Iraq on WMD might be unlikely, but if it took place, the risk to America's population would be unacceptably grave. As Bush's national security advisor phrased the problem, the United States could not afford for the smoking gun to be a mushroom cloud.

Within the US administration, these developments coincided with – and helped to shape – an ongoing process of strategic reinvention. The unwillingness to rely exclusively on deterrence that had underwritten the administration's commitment to ballistic-missile defence was leading US planners to explore the other strategic option in a world where deterrence was no longer deemed credible: pre-emption. What these thinkers meant was something more preventive than pre-emptive, inasmuch as they were contemplating the need to deprive an adversary of a dangerous capability well before a crisis had materialised in which it might actually be brought to bear. In the flow of post-11 September events, Iraq naturally emerged as the first candidate for preventive attack. Decision-makers who had seen 47 senators vote against US military intervention in Kuwait in 1991 for fear of high casualties asked how the Senate would vote in a future contingency involving war against a nuclear-armed Iraq. Would America be deterred from defending its interests in such a situation? Analysts conceded that Saddam was deterrable – he had, after all, refrained from using WMD in the 1991 Gulf War – but feared that his tendency to misjudge his adversaries would result in his future disregard for American threats of retaliation. It was not so much that deterrence no longer worked, but that Saddam might not 'get it'.

A slow political build-up

Despite the momentum developing towards war, an administration decision to forge ahead was not forthcoming. In early 2002, proponents of robust regime change had made considerable progress but had not yet won the day. The president made clear that military operations in Iraq would

Middle East

have to await the stabilisation of the situation in Afghanistan. Military planners endorsed this step-by-step approach, asserting that the US was already overstretched, munition stocks were low and intelligence collection platforms over-committed. The State Department also favoured a go-slow approach to gain time for the difficult diplomacy that war preparations would entail. Against a backdrop of Israeli–Palestinian violence for which the US was (and is still) judged by many in the region to be responsible, the State Department would have to win basing, access and overflight rights to many countries; foster a semblance of unity among disparate opposition groups; and prepare the ground in New York and in capitals for a possible presidential decision to attack Iraq.

Nearly two years after the Bush administration took office and over a year after the 11 September attacks, war had not broken out. The president's decision to seek a UN Security Council resolution was foreordained, although Powell used his influence skilfully to bring the drama to a close by persuading the president that an imminent decision would work to Washington's advantage by short-circuiting brewing opposition both at home and abroad. Public-opinion polls were clear about American willingness to support a war within the framework of UN authorisation and their corresponding reluctance to approve a unilateral battle. Indeed, US and European attitudes tended to converge on this point. The outcome was UN Security Council Resolution 1441, unanimously adopted on 8 November 2002. The upshot of that resolution was that, in spite of Iraq's 'material breach' of multiple previous resolutions dating back to the first Gulf War, arms inspections would be given one final chance to neutralise Iraq's WMD threat before any US-led coalition resorted to force.

The inspections themselves, however, produced discord within the Security Council and among the Permanent Five members. Iraq's December 2002 declarations concerning its WMD stocks were widely regarded – by the US, by the United Nations Monitoring and Verification Commission (UNMOVIC), and even by France – as inadequate and evasive. In several reports to the Council in the first three months of 2003, UNMOVIC Executive Chairman Hans Blix stated that, while the Iraqi regime was cooperating procedurally with inspectors, compliance in terms of substance was lacking. The US and the UK came to view this continued humiliation of the UN as intolerable. The US, in particular, had postulated that a bold move like regime change in Iraq was needed to catalyse positive political change in the Gulf that would ultimately condition a better accommodation between Islam and the West and enervate transnational terrorism. In time, the UK leadership also began to see regime change and the liberation of Iraq as both a moral good and a strategic objective. But France and others believed, *inter alia*, that coercive regime change would recklessly risk inflaming terrorists against what would be perceived (perhaps rightly) as unconstrained US power and fracture the post-11 September global coalition against terrorism. In early March 2003, it became clear that while the US and the UK considered gaps in Iraq's declaration borne out by UNMOVIC to be evidence of continuing material breach and therefore *casus belli*, France, followed by Russia and China, believed that the inspectors' very capacity to ferret out discrepancies proved that inspections were working and war was unnecessary. World public opinion was solidly opposed to war. When France, backed by Russia, vowed in mid-March to veto any second UN resolution that would implicitly authorise the use of force against Iraq, and the prospect of majority support dimmed, the US and the UK elected not to present any such resolution. As for Saddam himself: either out of the conviction that the US intended to unseat him regardless of his efforts to cooperate with inspections, or because he thought that he could drive a paralysing wedge among the Permanent Five by adopting a posture of ambiguous cooperation and a propaganda campaign aimed at publics in surrounding countries, he miscalculated.

On 17 March, Bush issued a final ultimatum to Saddam Hussein, offering him 48 hours to either flee the country or face the consequences of war. Saddam declined. In the meantime, diplomatic protest, national debate and some serious complications with the original war strategy arose. The Arab League (with the exception of Kuwait) expressed its discontent with the ultimatum, and planned a last-minute peacemaking visit to Iraq. The trip was cancelled on 18 March, as UN weapons inspectors and international personnel completed their withdrawal from Iraq on the same day. France refused a US request to allies on 19 March to expel Iraqi diplomats. Despite its opposition to the war, Germany accepted this request, expelling four Iraqi diplomats believed to be involved in activities incompatible with their diplomatic status and, furthermore, allowed the US overflight rights during the conflict. But the Russian, German and French foreign ministers at the United Nations in New York repeated their opposition to hostilities in Iraq. After a historic move in the UK to open up the war debate to a vote in the House of Commons in hopes of establishing greater legitimacy for military action, UK Prime Minister Tony Blair gained almost two-thirds majority approval for UK participation. But this move also exacted a heavy political cost in the form of a backbench rebellion that yielded 217 'no' votes, 139 of which came from MPs of the ruling Labour Party itself. In addition, Robin Cook, Leader of the House of Commons and a member of Blair's cabinet, resigned in protest. Finally, it became clear that Turkey would not permit 62,000 US troops to deploy in Turkish territory, which rendered the US military unable to open a northern front from which Baghdad could be threatened from a second direction. The ground war, in its opening stages, would proceed only from the south, out of Kuwait.

Middle East

War's progress

Bush's ultimatum expired on the evening of 19 March. Along with the fairly routine bombing of targets in the southern no-fly zone, the war began with precision strikes on leadership targets in Baghdad. Approximately 40 cruise missiles were used in these strikes, along with F-117 stealth fighters. This tactic was surprising, as the Pentagon had signalled that it would commence the campaign with massive aerial strikes designed to 'shock and awe' the Iraqi military and ultimately the regime into submission. It soon became clear that the United States was acting on fresh intelligence regarding the whereabouts of Saddam and his sons, in the hope of truncating the war by 'decapitating' the regime at the outset and forestalling a number of politically unattractive eventualities. These included: a protracted conflict that would tax domestic support; US and UK military casualties to the same effect; and heavy Iraqi civilian casualties as a result of street-to-street fighting in Baghdad that could inspire Islamic terrorism worldwide and turn world opinion even more acutely against the war. But the leadership strikes appeared not to find their targets. While a televised address by Saddam was aired the next day, it was unclear whether or not the statement was recorded before the strikes occurred. Reports surfaced that Saddam had been carried out of one of the bombed buildings, as rumours spread that the US intelligence community had intercepted communications to other countries asking for medical help for the president. Up to 7 April 2003, the US continued to remain publicly agnostic about Saddam's fate, though there were indications that some American officials believed that Saddam was killed in the initial strikes. In any case, the Iraqi regime did not immediately crumble. Neither did it offer a serious military riposte. While several Iraqi ballistic missiles were fired at Kuwait on 20 March, two were destroyed by US *Patriot* missiles and the others fell harmlessly onto the desert. Israel, which Iraq attacked with *Scud* ballistic missiles during the 1991 Gulf War, was not targeted. Coalition air supremacy was virtually immediate.

The war began in earnest on 20 March. In spite of large-scale global opposition to the war, the United States was able to cite a coalition of 40 nations that rhetorically supported it. The fact remained that only two nations – the US and the UK – were providing substantial contingents of combat troops, while Australia contributed a not insignificant 2,000 soldiers, Poland 200 soldiers and South Korea 700 non-combat personnel. Having failed to demonstrably oust Saddam Hussein in the precision strikes, the coalition's avowed policy was to attack the Ba'athist regime and not the Iraqi people, in hope of winning their 'hearts and minds'. Several tactics were adopted to this end: the dropping of leaflets with instructions on how to surrender and telling civilians how to avoid becoming targets; the precision targeting and bombing of Ba'athist Party and government buildings; and preserving the civilian infrastructure as much as possible.

At the outset, an estimated 250,000 US personnel were deployed in the Gulf theatre of operations, a number that was expected to rise during the course of the conflict to over 300,000. Of these, a total of 130,000 US troops – about 64,000 Marines and 66,000 Army and other armed forces personnel – were stationed in Kuwait, which was the main base of operations for invading Iraq. There were also US deployments in Jordan, estimated at between 2,000 and 7,000 troops. UK personnel deployed to the region numbered some 45,000 troops, of which 26,000 were ground forces. An estimated 90,000 US ground troops would take part in initial combat operations in Iraq. The original strategy relied heavily on the rapid advance of ground troops towards Baghdad, and on their encountering little resistance. UK forces were primarily responsible for southeastern Iraq, including securing Basra, Iraq's 'second city'. Meanwhile, the Americans' main task was to establish military control of southwestern areas of Iraq, including the city of Nasiriyah, and to secure airfields further west to prevent their being used by the Iraqis to launch an attack against Israel.

In the initial ground assault, the US 3rd Infantry Division (Mechanised) advanced rapidly north from Kuwait towards Baghdad with its leading column, supported by AH-64 *Apache* helicopters, some 120 kilometres inside Iraq. The objective was to secure Nasiriyah, and subsequently to secure strategically important bridges across the Euphrates River. Protecting the 3rd Infantry's right flank, the US 1st Marine Division advanced slowly from northern Kuwait into Iraq with flank protection provided by the UK 7th Armoured Brigade. The objective was to secure Basra and move north towards Baghdad. Greater resistance was met in the south and around Basra than originally anticipated, and the UK 7th Armoured Brigade was left to secure the town. The US 1st Marine Division, meanwhile, moved north to try to establish a northeastern dimension to the coalition assault on Baghdad. The UK 3rd Commando Brigade (with two regiments of Royal Marines), along with the US 15th Marine Expeditionary Unit were deployed on 21 March to secure the port town of Umm Qasr along with the oilfields and oil infrastructure of the Al Faw peninsula. While an initially surprising target for many commentators – the port would have to be dredged before any large ships could enter – Umm Qasr became the staging point for humanitarian aid and operations. UK Ministry of Defence officials initially stated that the port could be open in as little as 72 hours. However, clearing the port of mines (in which specially trained dolphins were used) would take considerably longer, while pockets of Iraqi resistance emerged. The port was declared open on 25 March, and humanitarian aid began moving through it on 28 March. As the Al Faw peninsula was being secured, the UK 16 Air Assault Brigade deployed to take control of the oilfields around Rumaylah. When Turkey finally granted the United States overflight rights on 21 March, the process of stabilising Northern Iraq started and 2,500 troops from the US 173rd Airborne Infantry Brigade began

Middle East

deploying on 26 March out of Italy. Elements of the US 101st Airborne Division deployed into southern Iraq to secure the town of Najaf – of logistical value because it is situated along a key supply route, and political value because of its importance as a holy city to Shi'ite Muslims and the fact that its majority Shi'ite population suffered oppression under Saddam.

On the night of 21 March 2003, the US and UK conducted over 1,000 precision bombing strikes on Baghdad that displayed impressive and unprecedented accuracy and firepower. But if it produced 'shock and awe' in the Iraqi leadership, it did not immediately cause its implosion. The aerial operations were not accompanied by the rapid approach to Baghdad that some anticipated. Iraqi forces did not desert en masse, citizens were not cheering for US troops and coalition forces were facing stiff resistance from Iraqi soldiers, *fedayeen* paramilitary militia controlled by Saddam's son Qusay and irregulars – including some suicide bombers – either under duress or inspired by Iraqi nationalism or Islam. US forces were held up in Nasiriyah, while UK forces also came under fire in Basra. Both towns were strategically important for staging an invasion of Baghdad, but 'pockets of resistance' were arising in territories previously claimed to be secure. Saddam was broadcast over Iraqi television – whether pre-recorded or live remained unclear – claiming that Iraq would eventually defeat the invading 'crusaders'. The 24 March capture of several non-combat US supply convoy personnel behind the vanguard of the main manoeuvre forces seemed to highlight weaknesses in the security of coalition supply lines and some neglect for the clearance of urban areas en route to Baghdad. (News revelations that several of the Americans taken prisoner may have been executed amplified the possibility of mistakes in the public mind.) It also appeared that *Apache* helicopters may have been used for inappropriate missions. Designed to hover several kilometres from the ground battle and to launch *Hellfire* missiles at enemy tanks, on 24 March, 32 *Apaches* were sent in close to an armoured Republican Guard formation at Karbala and virtually all were damaged by small-arms fire.

These glitches in the original war plans were minor, and did not substantially impede operational progress. Nevertheless, by late March they began to spark criticism – some from retired military officers who had served in the 1991 Gulf War – that the 'overwhelming force' doctrine had been too readily discarded and that US and UK forces initiated the conflict prematurely and should not have made a 'rolling start' whereby combat operations were commenced before reinforcements were in place. It was clear that, in fortifying more urban centres than expected and cleverly controlling propaganda from Baghdad, the Iraqi regime had conditioned a population that was more resilient than expected. By 5 April, however, most recriminations had been quelled. The UK Royal Marines occupied parts of Basra and played soccer with a local Iraqi team in Umm Khayyal, the US 3rd Infantry Division had taken control of Saddam Hussein

International Airport – which they renamed 'Baghdad International' – and followed up with a dramatic advance by 60 of its M1 *Abrams* tanks and *Bradley* fighting vehicles into downtown Baghdad. On 6 April, combined British forces, with US air support, commenced operations to secure Basra, and root out remaining Ba'ath and *fedeyeen* elements while on 7 April, US advances into central Baghdad resulted in film footage of US vehicles parked near Saddam's 'truimphal arch' of crossed swords. Coalition troops had reached and penetrated Baghdad and Basra with breathtaking Patton-esque speed and relatively few casualties. In the first 21 days of war, roughly 70 American and British troops had been killed, many of them in non-combat or 'friendly fire' incidents. In contrast, over 5,000 Iraqi soldiers had been killed and over 10,000 had surrendered or been captured. The coalition had executed some 18,000 precision airstrikes. Oilfields had been secured with very little environmental or infrastructure damage, only seven of roughly 1,400 oil wells having been set alight by the Iraqis. Iraqi authorities reported some 500 civilians killed and 4,000 injured, but these figures were unreliable.

While US forces had rendered at least two of six Iraqi Republican Guard divisions – the Baghdad and the Medina – combat-ineffective, it was clear that many of Iraq's elite soldiers had fallen back to Baghdad in contemplation of forcing coalition forces into urban warfare, in which their technological superiority would be compromised by physical impediments, asymmetrical techniques and the Iraqis' local knowledge. The idea was doubtless to provoke as many civilian casualties as possible, to inflame international opinion against the war and to portray Saddam as a heroic David to the United States' Goliath. Two discomfiting questions remained: whether the 15–20,000 Republican Guard and Special Republican Guard troops defending Baghdad would hold fast, necessitating a full-bore coalition onslaught on the city involving street-to-street fighting; and whether an increasingly desperate Saddam would unleash WMD on coalition troops. The US appeared intent on finding a 'third way' to deliver the *coup de grace* – something between a siege and an urban invasion. The massive tank incursion into Baghdad by the 3rd Infantry on 5 April was intended as an intimidating show of force to confuse and panic the Iraqis. Initial estimates stated that over 2,000 Iraqi soldiers and paramilitary fighters were killed. Additional means available included continued precision leadership strikes and stealth options involving the deployment of small US Special Forces or Navy SEAL teams or British Special Air Service soldiers to capture key Iraqi figures. While coalition forces still intended to exploit their precision-guided aerial munitions, the urban environment forced them to be far more selective. Fallback options short of street-to-street combat included seizure of part of the city for use as a base of operations and armoured thrusts coupled with light-infantry raids on government command centres. The firmest hope

Middle East

from a political point of view remained that of psychological attrition: that the spectre of stunning and overwhelming American firepower and forces on the edge of the city, coupled with an obvious presence in the city centre at times of the coalition's choosing, would induce surrender without a fight to the finish.

Risk and uncertainty

A major land war in the heart of the Middle East, aimed at the elimination of a 32-year regime and undertaken in the strategic context of a global *jihad* against the US and its allies will have unforeseeable effects on the interests of the combatants themselves and the region as a whole. Thus, though in April 2003 it appeared that the war would be a military success, the undertaking remained a serious political risk. The Bush administration had sought to change the status quo in the Gulf, and undoubtedly would do so. How, and to positive or negative effect, was not so clear. Immediate problems were considerable. In early April, tensions surfaced between the US and Syria, which appeared to be providing material support to the Iraqi regime, and between the US and Iran, which considered permitting an incursion by an Iranian-trained Iraqi Shi'ite Badr Corps militia into Iraq in support of its Shi'ite population. Early indications were that the US might not yield substantial political control over post-conflict Iraq to the UN, even though doing so would take the political heat off Washington and ease the release of aid from anti-war donors. In the run-up to the conflict, consultation and coordination between coalition governments and non-governmental organisations (NGOs) appeared inadequate, posing the threat that aid would not be efficiently distributed, and that refugees and internally displaced persons might not be sufficiently accommodated. On 28 March, the UN Security Council re-activated the oil-for-food programme, to be administered by the UN, which would facilitate the distribution of 450,000 tonnes of food per month. An estimated 60% of Iraq's 26 million people rely entirely on the oil-for-food programme. The UN also requested $2 billion in aid for Iraq. But, as of April 2003, there continued to be friction between the Pentagon's Office of Reconstruction and Humanitarian Assistance for Iraq – headed by retired US Army Lieutenant-General Jay Garner – and relief NGOs. Garner reported to General Tommy Franks, commander-in-chief of US Central Command and the US war commander in Iraq; the NGOs complained that a military-led relief effort would compromise the safety and independence of relief workers and complicate burden-sharing among UN agencies and governments.

More broadly, American attempts to warm the world to its cause by portraying the Iraq campaign as a war of liberation did not appear to be taking hold. As of 7 April, no WMD stocks had been found, which for the moment made the prime justification for the war less convincing.

That, however, was likely to change as coalition forces expanded and consolidated their control of Iraq territory. There had been several incidents in which coalition strikes appeared to cause large numbers of civilian casualties. Human-rights organisations impugned the US and UK's use of cluster bombs. Although there was no spike in major terrorist incidents outside of Iraq during the first three weeks of the conflict, on 31 March, Egyptian President Hosni Mubarak declared that it would produce 'a thousand bin Ladens'. Large and sometimes violent anti-American protests occurred in Amman, Cairo, Damascus, Tehran and other major Arab cities. This war's action, unlike that of the first Gulf War, was broadcast in real time by Al-Jazeera and other Arab news outlets, which often exaggerated Iraqi successes and downplayed coalition military domination. The besieged Iraqi regime – while putatively secular – opportunistically exhorted fellow Arabs to take up arms against the US and the UK, proclaiming it their duty when an Islamic nation is attacked. Saddam Hussein awarded two posthumous medals to a suicide bomber who killed four American soldiers on 29 March, reportedly paying his family $34,000. Several thousand jihadists from throughout the region were rumoured to be travelling to Iraq to fight US and British troops. Thus, the prospect of terrorist-style violence in post-war Iraq, directed at coalition soldiers and possibly civilian workers, became more salient. The Bush administration itself was also divided about what larger strategic message it wanted to send by way of military intervention in Iraq. Hawkish idealists suggested that Iraq was a peremptory warning to leaders contemplating the acquisition of WMD that they had best refrain or suffer the same fate as Saddam. More pragmatic realists held that Iraq had best be cast as a single case rather than precedent, lest rogue regimes accelerate WMD programmes to make the cost of conflict too high even for the US.

Of course, the war could be vindicated even in the eyes of many Arabs and Muslims if the US and its partners were able to remake Iraq into a unitary democratic polity that provided for its people in a palpably better way than did the former regime. But that is one of the stiffest of post-conflict challenges. The Kurds, anxious to retain the benefits that their *de facto* autonomy and oil-for-food payments have yielded, could face marginalisation in a new Iraq and pressure from a Turkish government that will not tolerate an independent Iraqi Kurdistan. The oppressed majority Shi'ite Muslim community is not a monolithic bloc, and may be over-eager for political clout long denied it. As a means of maintaining its iron grip, the Ba'ath Party atomised Iraqi society by making individuals dependent on the state. Then, in the face of sanctions, it exacerbated divisions by exploiting tribalism to retain control over the population. And Tikritis who may remain loyal to, or at least inspired by, Saddam pervade Iraq's military, political and civil institutions. Against this background, it appeared unlikely that indigenous Iraqis would be receptive to the solution favoured by some

Middle East

neo-conservatives in the Bush administration: an interim administration quickly established by the US and run by prominent Iraqi exiles in the Iraqi National Congress. The State Department's preferred solution of a regime built from the ground up at a Baghdad conference – loosely modelled on the Bonn Conference on Afghanistan – to be held four to six weeks after the war's end, seemed more promising.

By April 2003, the diplomatic debate about how post-conflict Iraq would be administered and reconstructed was beginning to take more definite shape. That debate centred on the interrelationships among four different authorities: coalition military forces charged with security and disarmament; the Pentagon's Office of Reconstruction and Humanitarian Assistance for Iraq, under Garner; Iraq's interim government, presumptively composed of some combination of exiles and indigenous Iraqis; and the UN. The US wanted, during a relatively short transition period, to maintain tight control over all major security, disarmament, reconstruction, commercial and civil administration tasks. The Iraqi administration would have essentially a decorative consultative role while its members worked among themselves to establish political harmony sufficient to govern the country, and the UN would administer humanitarian assistance and merely support the US transitional authority. European capitals – including London – and the UN itself contemplated a more central coordinative state-building role for the UN, based on the 'Afghan model' under which the UN oversaw the Bonn Conference that established an interim government for Afghanistan, as well as a strong day-to-day bureaucratic function. Whatever the procedural dispensation, forging unity and democracy in substance in Iraq will be difficult. Overseeing Iraq's rebirth as a pluralistic democracy is likely to require exposure and staying power in the Middle East, and a taste for nation-building generally, that have not distinguished US policy in the past. Yet, these are prerequisites of the propagation of liberalisation – the 'MacArthur decade' – envisaged by the Bush administration for the region, or even of any lesser facsimile thereof.

The War's Regional Impacts

Following President George W. Bush's identification of Iraq, North Korea and Iran as an 'axis of evil' in his 29 January 2002 State of the Union address, the US in September 2002 launched a National Security Strategy that includes military pre-emption and prevention and has engaged in a preventive war against Iraq. The immediate strategic objective of that war was to deprive Saddam Hussein of weapons of mass destruction (WMD) that he would use to threaten other states and destabilise the region and, perhaps, supply to transnational Islamic terrorists. A longer-term objective was to create a democratic polity in Iraq that would demonstrate its merits to Muslim populations and hasten democratisation and political liberalisation of the Gulf: in the 2002 State of the Union address, Bush also committed the United States to delivering to the Middle East and elsewhere the rule of law, respect for women, free speech, equal justice and religious tolerance. These are bold and laudable goals. Realising them, however, will be difficult and fraught with risks.

Prelude to war against Iraq

Osama bin Laden was not located or apprehended in 2002 or early 2003, but intelligence gleaned by US authorities following the 1 March 2003 capture of Khalid Shaikh Mohammed – al-Qaeda's third-in-command and suspected mastermind of the 11 September attacks – suggested that bin Laden was hiding in the 'tribal areas' of western Pakistan near the Afghan border. In a 12 November 2002 Al-Jazeera broadcast – authenticated to a high degree of certainty by American intelligence experts – bin Laden made references to various terrorist activities undertaken by his supporters in Bali, Indonesia, the Chechen siege in Moscow and the assassination of an American diplomat in Jordan. He promised retribution for military action in Iraq and warned Westerners: 'You will be killed as you kill, and you will be bombed as you bomb'. Equally important, bin Laden threatened US allies, including Britain, France, Israel, Italy, Canada, Germany and Australia. Shortly after the tape surfaced, simultaneous attacks occurred on Israeli tourists at a hotel in Mombasa, Kenya (suicide car-bomb), and on an Israeli airliner departing from Mombasa (surface-to-air missile); al-Qaeda later claimed credit for the operation on the Internet. Bin Laden also chastised Arab regimes allied with Western powers, most of which, for a variety of reasons, fear that his message has a receptive audience among their politically and economically marginalised populations. Without exception, then, Iraq's neighbours are worried that regime change in Baghdad will increase radical, and potentially terrorist, activity.

Moreover, most Gulf countries remain dubious of the capacity of the US and its Western partners to engineer a smooth political transition in Iraq that produces a stable, unitary nation, and are therefore sceptical that regime change will give rise to greater regional stability even in the medium term. Iraq is an ethnic, religious, social, economic and military cauldron. The country has a significant Kurdish population that may form a bridge to Baghdad. But an autonomous, semi-independent Iraqi Kurdistan, even if safely nestled in a federated arrangement, could re-ignite

Kurdish nationalist aspirations in Turkey or Iran. Moreover, the liberation of Iraq's Shi'ite Muslim population, which constitutes a 60% majority but has been repressed by Saddam's secular and largely Sunni Ba'ath regime, could give rise to a theocracy in Baghdad that could align itself with Tehran. Any such alliance would be perceived as a genuine regional challenge by a number of governments – in particular, Turkey and Saudi Arabia. Within Iraq, equally problematic are the many social repercussions of rapid political change, including the disruptive opportunities for revenge against repressive state agents and the difficulties that Iraqis who have grown financially dependent on a rentier state will have in adjusting to a more market-based economy. On balance, however, handling the impact of war has been of less concern to Western planners than the prosecution of the war itself.

Saudi Arabia's constructive manoeuvres

Washington seems to have failed to convince regional powers that Iraq posed a permanent or a semi-permanent threat to any of them. At the spring 2002 League of Arab States summit in Beirut, Crown Prince Abdullah bin Abdulaziz, the Saudi heir apparent, embraced the Iraqi second-in-command, Ezzat Ibrahim, thus registering the Al Saud's serious doubts about coercive regime change in Baghdad. Indeed, calls for an American withdrawal from Saudi Arabia, perhaps uttered in public to regain the Al Saud's battered legitimacy, accelerated in 2002. Talal bin Abdulaziz, a confidant of Prince Abdullah, articulated the view that Saudis would prefer to see the departure of the American troops permanently deployed in Saudi Arabia since the Gulf War. Since 11 September 2001, the American–Saudi security relationship, under attentive construction and care since the 1950s, had been under severe strain. The willingness of senior Al Saud officials to rupture a core alliance was an indication of intense internal pressure from increasingly powerful Islamists. Several prayer leaders in Riyadh, Jeddah and Burayda resigned their posts in January 2002 to display their opposition to the continued US military presence.

Washington itself did not, for the better part of 2002, ease Abdullah's political burden. After hesitating to accept President Bush's invitation to Washington, Abdullah finally visited Bush at his ranch in Crawford, Texas in late April 2002. Having characterised Israeli Prime Minister Ariel Sharon as 'a man of peace', Bush appeared insensitive to the need to factor Arab public opinion into the content and conduct of US Middle East policy. Abdullah's priority was to salvage what was left of US–Saudi relations, no matter how unpalatable Bush's agenda (e.g., to embark on a common fight against 'Saudi fundamentalism') may well have sounded. Abdullah left empty-handed. Visibly shaken, he displayed his anger with the US

IISS*maps*
Strategic Geography 2002/3

——	international boundaries		attack(s)/incident(s) and skirmishes
– – –	province or state boundaries		
-------	disputed and other boundaries	*Dar El Beida* ⊕	international airport/airfield
══	roads	*Gudermes*	air base
LOFA	province or state		
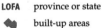	built-up areas	⌒	rivers
▣	capital cities	⬭	lakes
•	cities/towns	▲	mountain peaks (height in metres)

The Americas Major US peacetime military dispositions

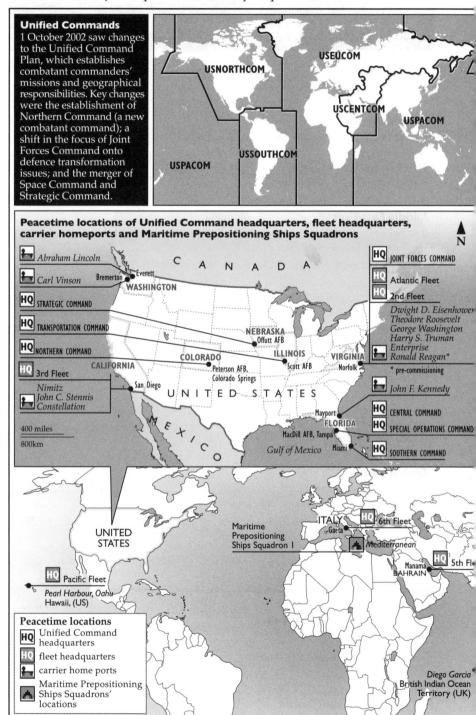

Unified Commands
1 October 2002 saw changes to the Unified Command Plan, which establishes combatant commanders' missions and geographical responsibilities. Key changes were the establishment of Northern Command (a new combatant command); a shift in the focus of Joint Forces Command onto defence transformation issues; and the merger of Space Command and Strategic Command.

USNORTHCOM
USEUCOM
USCENTCOM
USPACOM
USSOUTHCOM
USPACOM

Peacetime locations of Unified Command headquarters, fleet headquarters, carrier homeports and Maritime Prepositioning Ships Squadrons

N

C A N A D A

Abraham Lincoln
Carl Vinson — Bremerton ● Everett
WASHINGTON

HQ STRATEGIC COMMAND

HQ TRANSPORTATION COMMAND

HQ NORTHERN COMMAND

HQ 3rd Fleet
CALIFORNIA
Nimitz
John C. Stennis
Constellation
● San Diego

U N I T E D   S T A T E S

NEBRASKA
Offutt AFB

COLORADO
Peterson AFB,
Colorado Springs

ILLINOIS
Scott AFB

VIRGINIA
Norfolk ●

Mayport ●
FLORIDA
MacDill AFB, Tampa
Gulf of Mexico Miami ●

400 miles
800km

M E X I C O

HQ JOINT FORCES COMMAND

HQ Atlantic Fleet

HQ 2nd Fleet

Dwight D. Eisenhower
Theodore Roosevelt
George Washington
Harry S. Truman
Enterprise
Ronald Reagan*

* pre-commissioning

John F. Kennedy

HQ CENTRAL COMMAND

HQ SPECIAL OPERATIONS COMMAND

HQ SOUTHERN COMMAND

UNITED
STATES

Maritime
Prepositioning
Ships Squadron I

ITALY HQ 6th Fleet
Gaeta ●
Mediterranean

Manama ● HQ 5th Fl
BAHRAIN

HQ Pacific Fleet
Pearl Harbour, Oahu
Hawaii, (US)

Diego Garcia
British Indian Ocean
Territory (UK)

Peacetime locations
HQ Unified Command headquarters
HQ fleet headquarters
carrier home ports
Maritime Prepositioning Ships Squadrons' locations

Department of Defense Budget by component

TOTAL $bn 365 380 400 420 441 462 484

(line chart showing discretionary budget authority $bn, y-axis 50 to 150)

- Navy/Marine Corps
- Air Force
- Army
- Defence-wide*

'03 '04 '05 '06 '07 '08 '09
fiscal year

* Includes Defense Health Program

Selected US airlift capabilities

Type	Payload capacity (maximum normal)	Unrefuelled range (nm)	Minimum takeoff distance (m)*	Minimum landing distance (m)*
C-5 Galaxy	122,472kg	6,320nm (empty) 2,150nm (max payload)	2,530m	1,493m
C-17 Globemaster	77,519kg	2,400nm (with 72,575kg)	2,360m	915m
C-141B Starlifter	31,239kg	5,500nm (ferry) 2,550nm (max payload)	1,768m	1,128m
C-130 Hercules	17,605kg (C130J-30)	2,517nm	930m 540m (max effort)	427m

under optimum operational and climatic conditions

HQ 7th Fleet

Yokosuka Kitty Hawk

JAPAN

Maritime Prepositioning Ships Squadron 3

Guam (US)/Saipan
Northern Mariana
Islands (US)

PACIFIC OCEAN

Maritime Prepositioning Ships Squadron 2

INDIAN OCEAN

Global supply line

Since the 1980s, the US has maintained its Afloat Prepositioning Force, to provide a ready force-multiplier and reduce reaction times for crises requiring military attention. These vessels are deployed to form part of three Maritime Prepositioning Ship Squadrons. The present composition is:

- 16 Maritime Prepositioning Ships (MPS), organised in squadrons, are designed to provide a Marine Expeditionary Brigade with the equipment and stores necessary to sustain operations for 30 days, in concert with strategic airlift operations
- 13 Combat Prepositioning Force ships (Afloat Prepositioning Squadron 4) to provide equipment and CSS to army brigade (heavy)
- 12 Logistic Prepositioning ships, containing fuel, air force and navy munitions, and Marine Corps aviation support facilities.

Fleet aircraft carriers

The US navy has 12 major fleet aircraft carriers, one pre-commissioning, and one more under construction. Each is usually deployed as part of a Carrier Battle Group (CVBG). Locations listed on the map are peacetime locations. Each CVBG usually consists of the following:

- 1 aircraft carrier with embarked air wing (c. 70 aircraft usually containing 3 FA/18 *Hornet* squadrons; 1 F-14 *Tomcat* squadron; 1 S-3 *Viking* squadron; 1 E2-C *Hawkeye* squadron and 1 helicopter squadron)
- 2 cruisers
- 2 destroyers
- 1 frigate
- 2 nuclear powered attack submarines
- 2 supply ships.

Amphibious Forces

US amphibious forces are composed of a naval element – an Amphibious Task Force (ATF) – and a Landing Force (LF) of Marines. In most cases, the ATF will be deployed under the umbrella of a CVBG. Aggregated amphibious forces (Marine air-ground task forces) can be deployed on the nine naval Amphibious Squadrons (Amphibious Ready Groups), as:

- 7 Marine Expeditionary Units (some Special Operations Capable) (approx. 2,200 strong)
- 3 Marine Expeditionary Brigades (approx. 17,000 strong; and another, 4th MEB (anti-terrorism))
- 3 active Marine Expeditionary Forces (approx. 50,000 strong).

IISSmaps

Europe/Russia Cyprus: reunification hopes falter

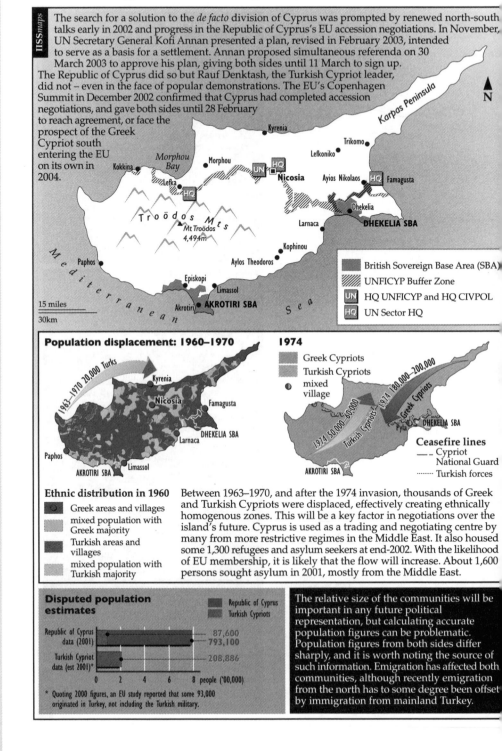

IISS*maps*

The search for a solution to the *de facto* division of Cyprus was prompted by renewed north-south talks early in 2002 and progress in the Republic of Cyprus's EU accession negotiations. In November, UN Secretary General Kofi Annan presented a plan, revised in February 2003, intended to serve as a basis for a settlement. Annan proposed simultaneous referenda on 30 March 2003 to approve his plan, giving both sides until 11 March to sign up. The Republic of Cyprus did so but Rauf Denktash, the Turkish Cypriot leader, did not – even in the face of popular demonstrations. The EU's Copenhagen Summit in December 2002 confirmed that Cyprus had completed accession negotiations, and gave both sides until 28 February to reach agreement, or face the prospect of the Greek Cypriot south entering the EU on its own in 2004.

N

Karpas Peninsula

Kyrenia
Trikomo
Lefkoniko
Morphou Bay
Morphou
Kokkina
Kokkina
Lefka
UN HQ
Nicosia
Ayios Nikolaos   HQ   Famagusta
HQ
Dhekelia
Troödos Mts
Mt Troödos 4,494m
Larnaca
DHEKELIA SBA
Kophinou
Paphos
Aylos Theodoros
Episkopi
Limassol
Mediterranean
15 miles
30km
Akrotiri   AKROTIRI SBA
Sea

	British Sovereign Base Area (SBA)
	UNFICYP Buffer Zone
UN	HQ UNFICYP and HQ CIVPOL
HQ	UN Sector HQ

Population displacement: 1960–1970

1963–1970 20,000 Turks
Kyrenia
Nicosia
Famagusta
DHEKELIA SBA
Larnaca
Paphos
AKROTIRI SBA   Limassol

1974

	Greek Cypriots
	Turkish Cypriots
⊙	mixed village

1974 180,000–200,000
1974 50,000–60,000
1974 Turkish Cypriots
Greek Cypriots
Pyla   DHEKELIA SBA
AKROTIRI SBA

Ceasefire lines
– – Cypriot National Guard
········ Turkish forces

Ethnic distribution in 1960

	Greek areas and villages
	mixed population with Greek majority
	Turkish areas and villages
	mixed population with Turkish majority

Between 1963–1970, and after the 1974 invasion, thousands of Greek and Turkish Cypriots were displaced, effectively creating ethnically homogenous zones. This will be a key factor in negotiations over the island's future. Cyprus is used as a trading and negotiating centre by many from more restrictive regimes in the Middle East. It also housed some 1,300 refugees and asylum seekers at end-2002. With the likelihood of EU membership, it is likely that the flow will increase. About 1,600 persons sought asylum in 2001, mostly from the Middle East.

Disputed population estimates

	Republic of Cyprus
	Turkish Cypriots

	0	2	4	6	8 people ('00,000)
Republic of Cyprus data (2001)					87,600
					793,100
Turkish Cypriot data (est 2001)*			208,886		

* Quoting 2000 figures, an EU study reported that some 93,000 originated in Turkey, not including the Turkish military.

The relative size of the communities will be important in any future political representation, but calculating accurate population figures can be problematic. Population figures from both sides differ sharply, and it is worth noting the source of such information. Emigration has affected both communities, although recently emigration from the north has to some degree been offset by immigration from mainland Turkey.

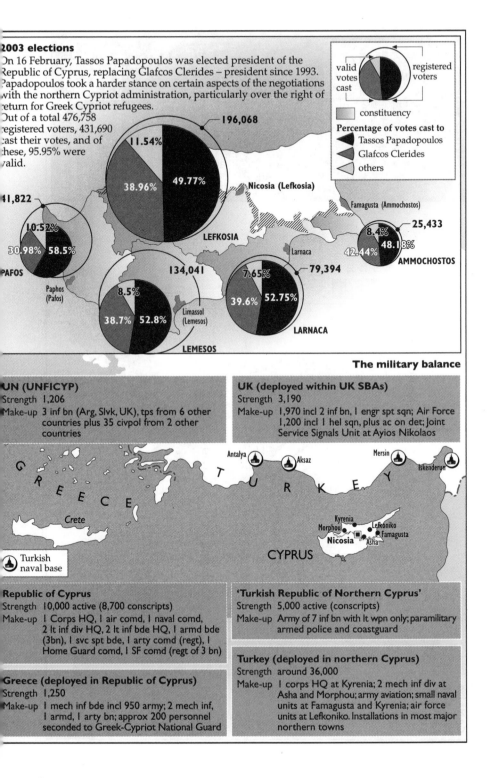

2003 elections

On 16 February, Tassos Papadopoulos was elected president of the Republic of Cyprus, replacing Glafcos Clerides – president since 1993. Papadopoulos took a harder stance on certain aspects of the negotiations with the northern Cypriot administration, particularly over the right of return for Greek Cypriot refugees.

Out of a total 476,758 registered voters, 431,690 cast their votes, and of these, 95.95% were valid.

valid votes cast — registered voters

constituency

Percentage of votes cast to
- Tassos Papadopoulos
- Glafcos Clerides
- others

196,068 — Nicosia (Lefkosia) — **LEFKOSIA**
11.54% / 38.96% / 49.77%

41,822 — **PAFOS** — Paphos (Pafos)
10.52% / 30.98% / 58.5%

134,041 — **LEMESOS** — Limassol (Lemesos)
8.5% / 38.7% / 52.8%

79,394 — **LARNACA** — Larnaca
7.65% / 39.6% / 52.75%

25,433 — Famagusta (Ammochostos) — **AMMOCHOSTOS**
8.4% / 42.44% / 48.18%

The military balance

UN (UNFICYP)
Strength 1,206
Make-up 3 inf bn (Arg, Slvk, UK), tps from 6 other countries plus 35 civpol from 2 other countries

UK (deployed within UK SBAs)
Strength 3,190
Make-up 1,970 incl 2 inf bn, 1 engr spt sqn; Air Force 1,200 incl 1 hel sqn, plus ac on det; Joint Service Signals Unit at Ayios Nikolaos

Turkish naval base — GREECE — Crete — TURKEY — Antalya — Aksaz — Mersin — Iskenderun — Kyrenia — Morphou — Lefkoniko — Nicosia — Asha — Famagusta — CYPRUS

Republic of Cyprus
Strength 10,000 active (8,700 conscripts)
Make-up 1 Corps HQ, 1 air comd, 1 naval comd, 2 lt inf div HQ, 2 lt inf bde HQ, 1 armd bde (3bn), 1 svc spt bde, 1 arty comd (regt), 1 Home Guard comd, 1 SF comd (regt of 3 bn)

Greece (deployed in Republic of Cyprus)
Strength 1,250
Make-up 1 mech inf bde incl 950 army; 2 mech inf, 1 armd, 1 arty bn; approx 200 personnel seconded to Greek-Cypriot National Guard

'Turkish Republic of Northern Cyprus'
Strength 5,000 active (conscripts)
Make-up Army of 7 inf bn with lt wpn only; paramilitary armed police and coastguard

Turkey (deployed in northern Cyprus)
Strength around 36,000
Make-up 1 corps HQ at Kyrenia; 2 mech inf div at Asha and Morphou; army aviation; small naval units at Famagusta and Kyrenia; air force units at Lefkoniko. Installations in most major northern towns

Europe/Russia NATO moves east

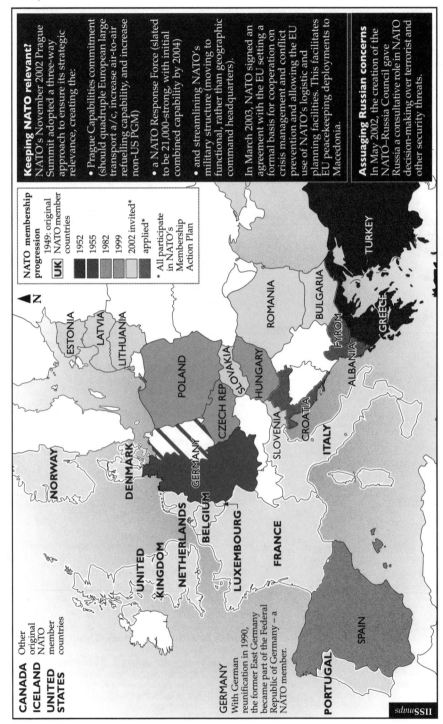

Keeping NATO relevant?
NATO's November 2002 Prague Summit adopted a three-way approach to ensure its strategic relevance, creating the:

• Prague Capabilities commitment (should quadruple European large transport a/c, increase air-to-air refuelling capability, and increase non-US PGM)

• a NATO Response Force (slated to be 21,000-strong, with initial combined capability by 2004)

• and streamlining NATO's military structure (moving to functional, rather than geographic command headquarters).

In March 2003, NATO signed an agreement with the EU setting a formal basis for cooperation on crisis management and conflict prevention and allowing the EU use of NATO's logistic and planning facilities. This facilitates EU peacekeeping deployments to Macedonia.

Assuaging Russian concerns
In May 2002, the creation of the NATO–Russia Council gave Russia a consultative role in NATO decision-making over terrorist and other security threats.

NATO membership progression

UK 1949: original NATO member countries

1952
1955
1982
1999
2002 invited*
applied*

* All participate in NATO's Membership Action Plan

N

CANADA
ICELAND
UNITED
STATES

Other original NATO member countries

GERMANY
With German reunification in 1990, the former East Germany became part of the Federal Republic of Germany – a NATO member.

NORWAY
ESTONIA
LATVIA
LITHUANIA
DENMARK
GERMANY
POLAND
CZECH REP
SLOVAKIA
HUNGARY
ROMANIA
SLOVENIA
CROATIA
BULGARIA
FYROM
ALBANIA
GREECE
TURKEY
ITALY
UNITED KINGDOM
NETHERLANDS
BELGIUM
LUXEMBOURG
FRANCE
SPAIN
PORTUGAL

IISS*maps*

Europe/Russia The EU: expansion and agriculture

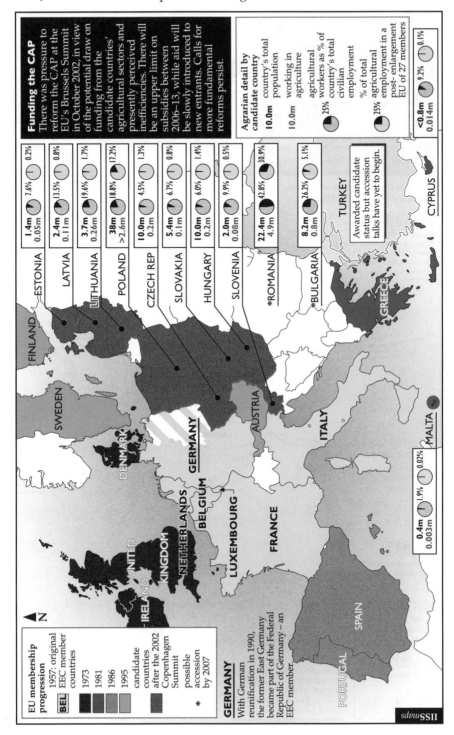

Funding the CAP

There was pressure to reform the CAP at the EU's Brussels Summit in October 2002, in view of the potential draw on funding from the candidate countries' agricultural sectors and presently perceived inefficiencies. There will be an upper limit on subsidies between 2006–13, while aid will be slowly introduced to new entrants. Calls for more fundamental reforms persist.

Agrarian detail by candidate country

- 10.0m country's total population
- 10.0m working in agriculture
- 25% agricultural workers as % of country's total population
- 25% agricultural employment % of total civilian employment
- agricultural employment in a post-enlargement EU of 27 members

Country	Population	Agriculture	% pop	% emp
ESTONIA	1.4m	0.05m	7.6%	0.2%
LATVIA	2.4m	0.11m	13.5%	0.8%
LITHUANIA	3.7m	0.26m	19.6%	1.7%
POLAND	38m	>2.6m	18.8%	17.2%
CZECH REP	10.0m	0.2m	4.5%	1.3%
SLOVAKIA	5.4m	0.1m	6.7%	0.8%
HUNGARY	10.0m	0.2m	6.0%	1.4%
SLOVENIA	2.0m	0.08m	9.9%	0.5%
*ROMANIA	22.4m	4.9m	42.8%	30.9%
*BULGARIA	8.2m	0.8m	26.2%	5.1%
FRANCE	0.4m	0.003m	1.9%	0.02%
MALTA	<0.8m	0.014m	9.2%	0.1%

TURKEY
Awarded candidate status but accession talks have yet to begin.

CYPRUS

EU membership progression

BEL 1957: original EEC member countries
1973
1981
1986
1995
candidate countries after the 2002 Copenhagen Summit
* possible accession by 2007

GERMANY
With German reunification in 1990, the former East Germany became part of the Federal Republic of Germany – an EEC member.

N

IISS sdvumaps

(Map labels: FINLAND, SWEDEN, DENMARK, UNITED KINGDOM, IRELAND, NETHERLANDS, BELGIUM, LUXEMBOURG, GERMANY, AUSTRIA, FRANCE, SPAIN, PORTUGAL, ITALY, GREECE, MALTA)

Europe/Russia A political solution for Chechnya?

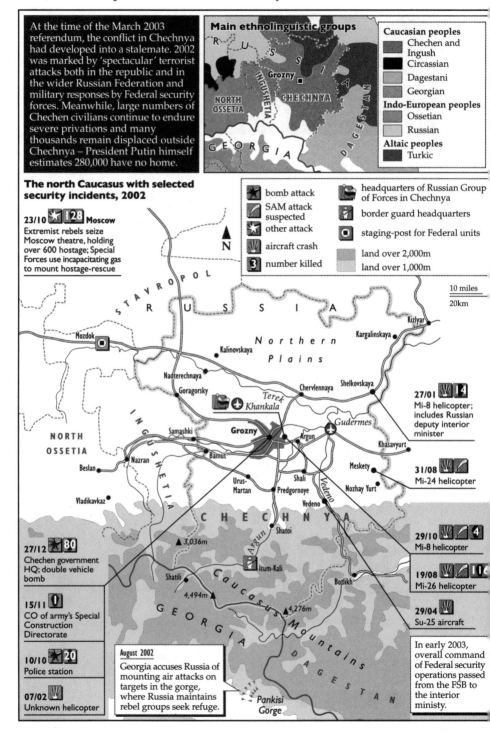

At the time of the March 2003 referendum, the conflict in Chechnya had developed into a stalemate. 2002 was marked by 'spectacular' terrorist attacks both in the republic and in the wider Russian Federation and military responses by Federal security forces. Meanwhile, large numbers of Chechen civilians continue to endure severe privations and many thousands remain displaced outside Chechnya – President Putin himself estimates 280,000 have no home.

Main ethnolinguistic groups

Caucasian peoples
- Chechen and Ingush
- Circassian
- Dagestani
- Georgian

Indo-European peoples
- Ossetian
- Russian

Altaic peoples
- Turkic

The north Caucasus with selected security incidents, 2002

23/10 Moscow **128**
Extremist rebels seize Moscow theatre, holding over 600 hostage; Special Forces use incapacitating gas to mount hostage-rescue

- bomb attack
- SAM attack suspected
- other attack
- aircraft crash
- **3** number killed
- headquarters of Russian Group of Forces in Chechnya
- border guard headquarters
- staging-post for Federal units
- land over 2,000m
- land over 1,000m

27/01 Mi-8 helicopter; includes Russian deputy interior minister **14**

31/08 Mi-24 helicopter

29/10 Mi-8 helicopter **4**

19/08 Mi-26 helicopter

29/04 Su-25 aircraft

27/12 Chechen government HQ; double vehicle bomb **80**

15/11 CO of army's Special Construction Directorate

10/10 Police station **20**

07/02 Unknown helicopter

August 2002
Georgia accuses Russia of mounting air attacks on targets in the gorge, where Russia maintains rebel groups seek refuge.

In early 2003, overall command of Federal security operations passed from the FSB to the interior ministy.

1999 to end-2002

Russian armed forces in Chechnya lost 4,572 personnel killed and 15,149 wounded, according to the Russian defence ministry

the defence ministry itself lost 2,750 killed and 6,569 wounded.

During 2002

It was reported that interior ministry troops

- killed 383 rebels during 'special operations' and 'search operations'
- arrested more than 27,000 people on suspicion of membership of armed groups
- confiscated 1,200 weapons, 680,000 pieces of ammunition and 700kg of explosives. (More weapons and equipment, including MANPAD systems have also been seized by other units.)
- Destroyed over 520 landmines and IEDs, as well as 2280 illegal oil processing facilities.

In the year to November 2002

- a reported 133 interior ministry troops had been killed in Chechnya.

As of late-December 2002

- the Russian Group of Forces in Chechnya was about 80,000 strong.

It included

- 42 Motor-rifle Division (Garrison Division, at its wartime strength of 15,000 troops)
- 70th, 71st, 72nd and 291st Motor-rifle Regiments and the 50th SP Arty Regt.
- 3,000 airborne troops
- regimental and battalion groupings from other military districts total 22,000 and are rotated through Chechnya
- 46th Brigade (interior ministry) 10,000 strong; Garrison Brigade
- 10,000 border guards on the border with Georgia
- interior ministry OMON (special force) and SOBR (rapid deployment) troops are also rotated from other regions
- other Federal security units.

New political structure

A 23 March 2003 referendum was intended to provide the basis for a political settlement that would secure Chechnya's status within the Russian Federation.

Moscow rejected calls to postpone the referendum, which had three ballots: firstly, on a constitution; secondly, on a law regarding presidential elections; and thirdly, relating to the formation of a new regional assembly. The overall objective is to hold parliamentary and presidential elections in Chechnya; under a new constitution. A parliament will consist of two houses – a Council of the Republic (with 21 deputies), and a People's Assembly (with 40 deputies).

Although conduct of the poll was questioned by some observers, Russian officials said that over 90% of voters had backed the changes, including the new constitution.

IDPs in Ingushetia
as at 15 December 2002

in tent camps **20,400**

with host families **55,950**

in spontaneous settlements **28,050**

Total: **104,400**

IDPs in Chechnya
as at 15 December 2002

Total: **141,800**

'vulnerable' groups **125,750**

IDP camps – Autumn 2002

Some camps were closed in late 2002, in a bid to encourage returns to Chechnya.

Food aid estimates for 2003
(as of November 2002)

School feeding and food-for-work in Chechnya **37,500**

Food-insecure vulnerable groups in Chechnya **143,000**

IDPs in Ingushetia **110,000**

IISS*maps*

Middle East/Gulf Iraq: before the battle

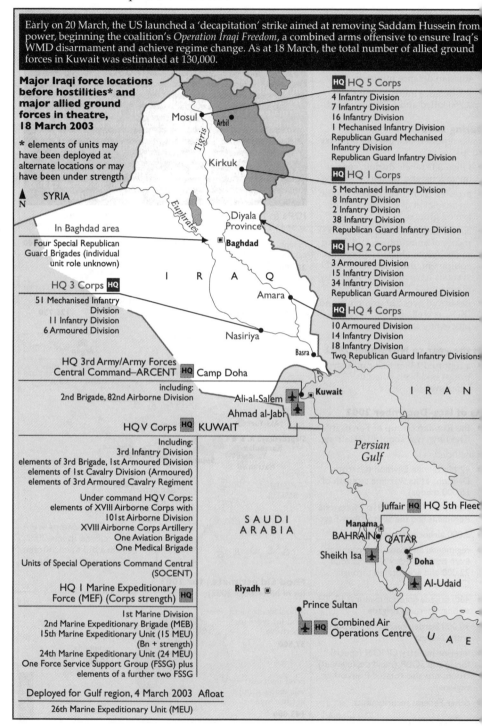

Early on 20 March, the US launched a 'decapitation' strike aimed at removing Saddam Hussein from power, beginning the coalition's *Operation Iraqi Freedom*, a combined arms offensive to ensure Iraq's WMD disarmament and achieve regime change. As at 18 March, the total number of allied ground forces in Kuwait was estimated at 130,000.

Major Iraqi force locations before hostilities* and major allied ground forces in theatre, 18 March 2003

* elements of units may have been deployed at alternate locations or may have been under strength

SYRIA

N

In Baghdad area

Four Special Republican Guard Brigades (individual unit role unknown)

HQ 3 Corps **HQ**

51 Mechanised Infantry Division
11 Infantry Division
6 Armoured Division

HQ 3rd Army/Army Forces Central Command–ARCENT **HQ** Camp Doha

including:
2nd Brigade, 82nd Airborne Division

HQ V Corps **HQ** KUWAIT

Including:
3rd Infantry Division
elements of 3rd Brigade, 1st Armoured Division
elements of 1st Cavalry Division (Armoured)
elements of 3rd Armoured Cavalry Regiment

Under command HQ V Corps:
elements of XVIII Airborne Corps with
101st Airborne Division
XVIII Airborne Corps Artillery
One Aviation Brigade
One Medical Brigade

Units of Special Operations Command Central (SOCENT)

HQ 1 Marine Expeditionary Force (MEF) (Corps strength) **HQ**

1st Marine Division
2nd Marine Expeditionary Brigade (MEB)
15th Marine Expeditionary Unit (15 MEU) (Bn + strength)
24th Marine Expeditionary Unit (24 MEU)
One Force Service Support Group (FSSG) plus elements of a further two FSSG

Deployed for Gulf region, 4 March 2003 Afloat

26th Marine Expeditionary Unit (MEU)

HQ HQ 5 Corps

4 Infantry Division
7 Infantry Division
16 Infantry Division
1 Mechanised Infantry Division
Republican Guard Mechanised Infantry Division
Republican Guard Infantry Division

HQ HQ 1 Corps

5 Mechanised Infantry Division
8 Infantry Division
2 Infantry Division
38 Infantry Division
Republican Guard Infantry Division

HQ HQ 2 Corps

3 Armoured Division
15 Infantry Division
34 Infantry Division
Republican Guard Armoured Division

HQ HQ 4 Corps

10 Armoured Division
14 Infantry Division
18 Infantry Division
Two Republican Guard Infantry Divisions

Mosul
Arbil
Tigris
Kirkuk
Euphrates
Diyala Province
Baghdad
I R A Q
Amara
Nasiriya
Basra
Ali-al-Salem
Ahmad al-Jabr
Kuwait
I R A N
Persian Gulf
Juffair **HQ** HQ 5th Fleet
S A U D I A R A B I A
Manama
BAHRAIN
QATAR
Sheikh Isa
Doha
Riyadh
Prince Sultan
Combined Air Operations Centre **HQ**
Al-Udaid
U A E
KUWAIT

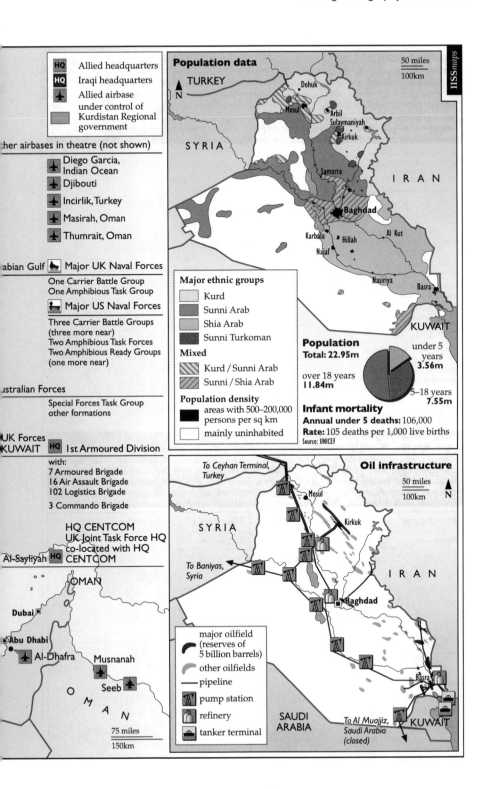

Legend / Key:

HQ	Allied headquarters
HQ	Iraqi headquarters
✈	Allied airbase
	under control of Kurdistan Regional government

...her airbases in theatre (not shown)

- ✈ Diego Garcia, Indian Ocean
- ✈ Djibouti
- ✈ Incirlik, Turkey
- ✈ Masirah, Oman
- ✈ Thumrait, Oman

...abian Gulf Major UK Naval Forces

One Carrier Battle Group
One Amphibious Task Group

 Major US Naval Forces

Three Carrier Battle Groups
(three more near)
Two Amphibious Task Forces
Two Amphibious Ready Groups
(one more near)

...ustralian Forces

Special Forces Task Group
other formations

...UK Forces
...KUWAIT HQ 1st Armoured Division

with:
7 Armoured Brigade
16 Air Assault Brigade
102 Logistics Brigade
3 Commando Brigade

HQ CENTCOM
UK Joint Task Force HQ
co-located with HQ
Al-Sayliyah HQ CENTCOM

OMAN

Dubai

Abu Dhabi
✈ Al-Dhafra   Musnanah

✈ Seeb

O M A N

75 miles
150km

Population data

TURKEY
N
Dohuk
Mosul
Arbil
Sulaymaniyah
Kirkuk
SYRIA
Samarra
I R A N
Baghdad
Karbala   Al Kut
Najaf   Hillah
Nasiriya
Basra
KUWAIT

50 miles
100km
IISSmaps

Major ethnic groups

	Kurd
	Sunni Arab
	Shia Arab
	Sunni Turkoman

Mixed

	Kurd / Sunni Arab
	Sunni / Shia Arab

Population density

■	areas with 500–200,000 persons per sq km
□	mainly uninhabited

Population
Total: 22.95m

over 18 years
11.84m

under 5 years
3.56m

5–18 years
7.55m

Infant mortality
Annual under 5 deaths: 106,000
Rate: 105 deaths per 1,000 live births
Source: UNICEF

Oil infrastructure

To Ceyhan Terminal, Turkey
Mosul
Kirkuk
SYRIA
To Baniyas, Syria
I R A N
Baghdad
Basra
SAUDI ARABIA
To Al Muajjiz, Saudi Arabia (closed)
KUWAIT

50 miles
100km
N

	major oilfield (reserves of 5 billion barrels)
	other oilfields
—	pipeline
	pump station
	refinery
	tanker terminal

Middle East/Gulf Iraq: before the battle

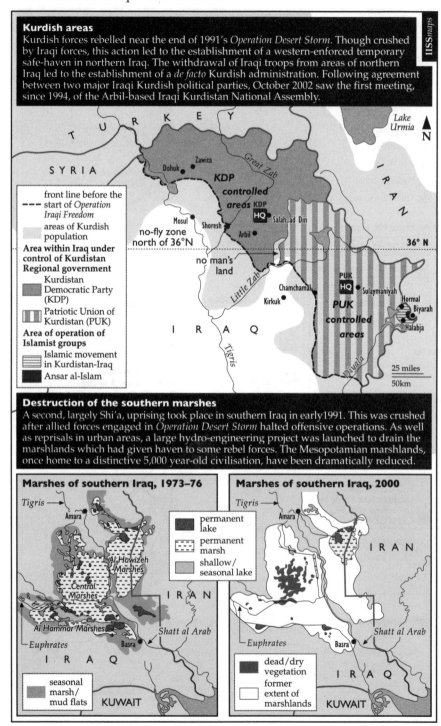

Kurdish areas

Kurdish forces rebelled near the end of 1991's *Operation Desert Storm*. Though crushed by Iraqi forces, this action led to the establishment of a western-enforced temporary safe-haven in northern Iraq. The withdrawal of Iraqi troops from areas of northern Iraq led to the establishment of a *de facto* Kurdish administration. Following agreement between two major Iraqi Kurdish political parties, October 2002 saw the first meeting, since 1994, of the Arbil-based Iraqi Kurdistan National Assembly.

IISS maps

Legend:

- front line before the start of *Operation Iraqi Freedom*
- areas of Kurdish population
- **Area within Iraq under control of Kurdistan Regional government**
  - Kurdistan Democratic Party (KDP)
  - Patriotic Union of Kurdistan (PUK)
- **Area of operation of Islamist groups**
  - Islamic movement in Kurdistan-Iraq
  - Ansar al-Islam

Map labels: TURKEY, SYRIA, IRAN, Lake Urmia, N, Dohuk, Zawita, Great Zab, KDP controlled areas, KDP HQ, Salah ad Din, Mosul, Shoresh, Arbil, no-fly zone north of 36°N, 36° N, no man's land, Little Zab, PUK HQ, Chamchamal, Sulaymaniyah, Hormal, Biyarah, Kirkuk, PUK controlled areas, Halabja, I R A Q, Tigris, Diyala, 25 miles / 50km

Destruction of the southern marshes

A second, largely Shi'a, uprising took place in southern Iraq in early 1991. This was crushed after allied forces engaged in *Operation Desert Storm* halted offensive operations. As well as reprisals in urban areas, a large hydro-engineering project was launched to drain the marshlands which had given haven to some rebel forces. The Mesopotamian marshlands, once home to a distinctive 5,000 year-old civilisation, have been dramatically reduced.

Marshes of southern Iraq, 1973–76

Labels: Tigris, Amara, Al Hawizeh Marshes, Central Marshes, Al Hammar Marshes, Shatt al Arab, Euphrates, Basra, IRAN, IRAQ, KUWAIT

Legend: seasonal marsh/ mud flats; permanent lake; permanent marsh; shallow/ seasonal lake

Marshes of southern Iraq, 2000

Labels: Tigris, Amara, IRAN, Shatt al Arab, Euphrates, Basra, IRAQ, KUWAIT

Legend: dead/dry vegetation; former extent of marshlands

Middle East/Gulf Iraq: before the battle

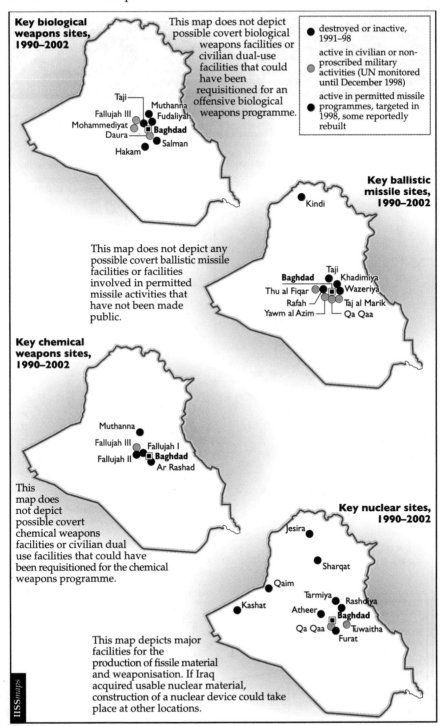

Key biological weapons sites, 1990–2002

This map does not depict possible covert biological weapons facilities or civilian dual-use facilities that could have been requisitioned for an offensive biological weapons programme.

● destroyed or inactive, 1991–98

◐ active in civilian or non-proscribed military activities (UN monitored until December 1998)

● active in permitted missile programmes, targeted in 1998, some reportedly rebuilt

Taji
Muthanna
Fallujah III
Fudaliyah
Mohammediyat
Daura
Baghdad
Salman
Hakam

Key ballistic missile sites, 1990–2002

Kindi

This map does not depict any possible covert ballistic missile facilities or facilities involved in permitted missile activities that have not been made public.

Taji
Baghdad Khadimiya
Thu al Fiqar Wazeriya
Rafah Taj al Marik
Yawm al Azim Qa Qaa

Key chemical weapons sites, 1990–2002

Muthanna
Fallujah III Fallujah I
Fallujah II **Baghdad**
Ar Rashad

This map does not depict possible covert chemical weapons facilities or civilian dual use facilities that could have been requisitioned for the chemical weapons programme.

Key nuclear sites, 1990–2002

Jesira
Sharqat
Qaim
Tarmiya
Kashat Rashdiya
Atheer
Baghdad
Qa Qaa Tuwaitha
Furat

This map depicts major facilities for the production of fissile material and weaponisation. If Iraq acquired usable nuclear material, construction of a nuclear device could take place at other locations.

IISS*maps*

Middle East/Gulf Iran's nuclear ambitions

Iran has pursued nuclear technology since the early 1970s. In the 1980s, Tehran sought to revive its nuclear power and research programme – disrupted by the 1979 revolution. Recently disclosed facilities could reportedly be configured to produce enough highly-enriched uranium for several nuclear weapons per year, once they are completed in a few years. Although Tehran says these facilities are intended for peaceful use, analysts argue that they are incompatible with Iran's nuclear power programme as presently pursued.

The intended use of the Arak facility has been questioned. Bushehr does not use heavy water and it is argued that Iran's existing research reactors also do not use heavy water, or use too little of it, to justify a production facility.

At the Natanz plant, Iran has already assembled a pilot scale 'cascade' of 160 centrifuge machines of relatively advanced design. Iran has sufficient parts for 1,000 centrifuge machines and plans to install about 5,000 by 2005.

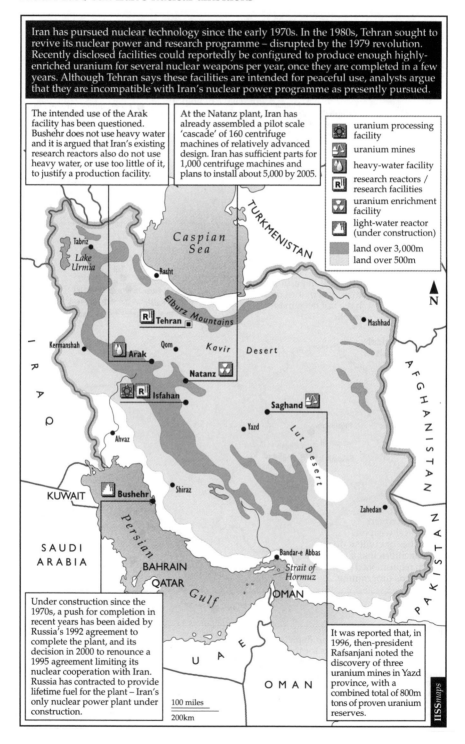

- uranium processing facility
- uranium mines
- heavy-water facility
- research reactors / research facilities
- uranium enrichment facility
- light-water reactor (under construction)
- land over 3,000m
- land over 500m

Under construction since the 1970s, a push for completion in recent years has been aided by Russia's 1992 agreement to complete the plant, and its decision in 2000 to renounce a 1995 agreement limiting its nuclear cooperation with Iran. Russia has contracted to provide lifetime fuel for the plant – Iran's only nuclear power plant under construction.

It was reported that, in 1996, then-president Rafsanjani noted the discovery of three uranium mines in Yazd province, with a combined total of 800m tons of proven uranium reserves.

100 miles
200km

IISSmaps

Asia Another troubled year in Kashmir

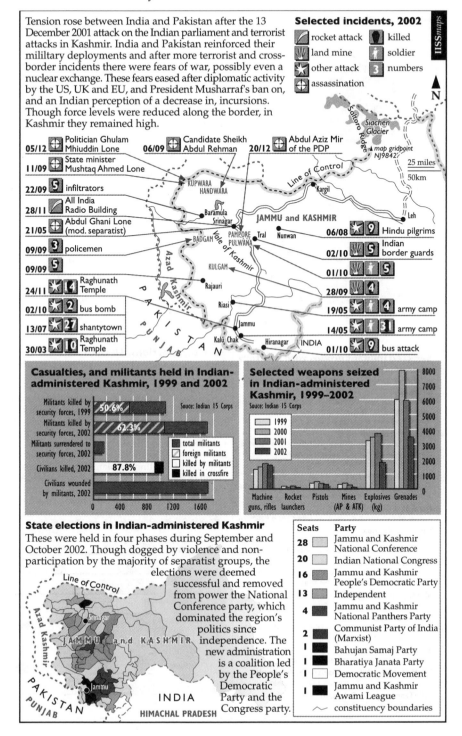

Tension rose between India and Pakistan after the 13 December 2001 attack on the Indian parliament and terrorist attacks in Kashmir. India and Pakistan reinforced their military deployments and after more terrorist and cross-border incidents there were fears of war, possibly even a nuclear exchange. These fears eased after diplomatic activity by the US, UK and EU, and President Musharraf's ban on, and an Indian perception of a decrease in, incursions. Though force levels were reduced along the border, in Kashmir they remained high.

Selected incidents, 2002

rocket attack — killed
land mine — soldier
other attack — numbers
assassination

IISSmaps

N
25 miles
50km

05/12 Politician Ghulam Mhiuddin Lone
06/09 Candidate Sheikh Abdul Rehman
20/12 Abdul Aziz Mir of the PDP
11/09 State minister Mushtaq Ahmed Lone
22/09 infiltrators
28/11 All India Radio Building
21/05 Abdul Ghani Lone (mod. separatist)
09/09 3 policemen
09/09 5
24/11 4 Raghunath Temple
02/10 2 bus bomb
13/07 27 shantytown
30/03 10 Raghunath Temple

06/08 9 Hindu pilgrims
02/10 5 Indian border guards
01/10 5
28/09 4
19/05 4 army camp
14/05 31 army camp
01/10 9 bus attack

JAMMU and KASHMIR
Siachen Glacier
Saltoro Ridge
map gridpoint NJ9842
Line of Control
KUPWARA
HANDWARA
Kargil
Baramula
Srinagar
Leh
BADGAM PAMPORE Tral Nunwan
PULWAMA
Vale of Kashmir
Azad Kashmir
KULGAM
Rajauri
Riasi
Jammu
Kalu Chak
Hiranagar
INDIA
PAKISTAN PUNJAB

Casualties, and militants held in Indian-administered Kashmir, 1999 and 2002

Source: Indian 15 Corps

Militants killed by security forces, 1999 — 50.6%
Militants killed by security forces, 2002 — 62.3%
Militants surrendered to security forces, 2002
Civilians killed, 2002 — 87.8%
Civilians wounded by militants, 2002

total militants
foreign militants
killed by militants
killed in crossfire

0   400   800   1200   1600

Selected weapons seized in Indian-administered Kashmir, 1999–2002

Source: Indian 15 Corps

1999
2000
2001
2002

Machine guns, rifles — Rocket launchers — Pistols — Mines (AP & ATK) — Explosives (kg) — Grenades

8000
7000
6000
5000
4000
3000
2000
1000
0

State elections in Indian-administered Kashmir

These were held in four phases during September and October 2002. Though dogged by violence and non-participation by the majority of separatist groups, the elections were deemed successful and removed from power the National Conference party, which dominated the region's politics since independence. The new administration is a coalition led by the People's Democratic Party and the Congress party.

Line of Control
Azad Kashmir
Srinagar
JAMMU and KASHMIR
Jammu
PAKISTAN PUNJAB
INDIA
HIMACHAL PRADESH

Seats	Party
28	Jammu and Kashmir National Conference
20	Indian National Congress
16	Jammu and Kashmir People's Democratic Party
13	Independent
4	Jammu and Kashmir National Panthers Party
2	Communist Party of India (Marxist)
1	Bahujan Samaj Party
1	Bharatiya Janata Party
1	Democratic Movement
1	Jammu and Kashmir Awami League
~	constituency boundaries

Asia Pakistan: security challenges persist

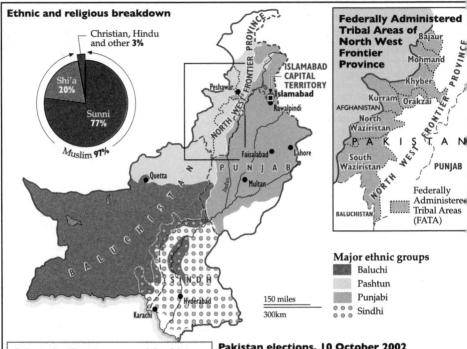

Ethnic and religious breakdown

Christian, Hindu and other **3%**

Shi'a **20%**

Sunni **77%**

Muslim **97%**

Federally Administered Tribal Areas of North West Frontier Province

Federally Administered Tribal Areas (FATA)

Major ethnic groups
- Baluchi
- Pashtun
- Punjabi
- Sindhi

150 miles
300km

Selected militant groups with a history of activity in Pakistan or Indian-administered Kashmir (Sunni unless stated)

al-Qaeda (al-Q)
Transnational focus; based in Afghanistan until ouster of Taliban; elements remain in Afghanistan and Pakistan border areas and cities; leadership elements apprehended in Pakistan in 2002.

Jaish-e Mohammed (J-e M)
Banned in Pakistan. Operates in Pakistan and Kashmir (was in Afghanistan); offshoot of Harakat al-Mujahiddin; suspected of involvement in December 2001 attack on Indian parliament compound.

Lashkar-e Jhangvi (L-e J)
Banned in Pakistan 14/8/01; breakaway from Sipah-e Sahaba; suspected of involvement in the Daniel Pearl murder.

Harakat ul-Jihad-I-Islami (H ul-J)
Deobandi extremist; operates in Pakistan and Kashmir (was in Afghanistan).

Lashkar-e Tayyiba
Banned in Pakistan 14/08/01; active in Kashmir and Pakistan; suspected of involvement in December 2001 attack on Indian parliament compound.

Harakat ul-Mujahiddin (H ul-M)
Active in Kashmir, Pakistan (was in Afghanistan); believed related to al-Qaeda; parent organisation of Jaish-e Mohammed.

al-Intiqami al-Pakistani (al-I al-P)
Name used to claim responsibility for Muree school killings. New group.

Sipah-e Sahaba
Politico-military organisation banned in Pakistan 12/01/02; pressing for religious state in Pakistan.

Sipah-e-Muhammad
Banned in Pakistan 14/08/01; Shi'a extremist group.

TNSM (Tehrik-e Nifaz-e Shariat-e Muhammedi)
Banned in Pakistan 12/01/02; had been active in Afghanistan.

TJP (Tehrik-e Jafria Pakistan)
Banned in Pakistan 12/01/02; Shi'a extremist group.

Pakistan elections, 10 October 2002

The elections were the first since then army chief-of-staff now president, Pervez Musharraf seized control in 199? Although Pakistan now has its first civilian-led government since that time, constitutional changes made in June 2002 give Musharraf the right to sack the prime minister and national assembly. He has also been accorded an extra five-year term as president, following April's near-98% referendum victory. In October, the emergence of the MMA (a coalition of six Islamist parties with the objective of creating an Islamic system) created some alarm in the West. At time of press, the MMA controls the North-West Frontier Provincial Assembly, and is a governing partner in the Baluchistan Assembly.

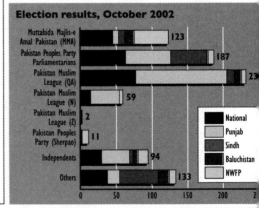

Election results, October 2002

	National	Punjab	Sindh	Baluchistan	NWFP
Muttahida Majlis-e Amal Pakistan (MMA)	123				
Pakistan Peoples Party Parliamentarians	187				
Pakistan Muslim League (QA)	23?				
Pakistan Muslim League (N)	59				
Pakistan Muslim League (Z)	2				
Pakistan Peoples Party (Sherpao)	11				
Independents	94				
Others	133				

0   50   100   150   200   2?

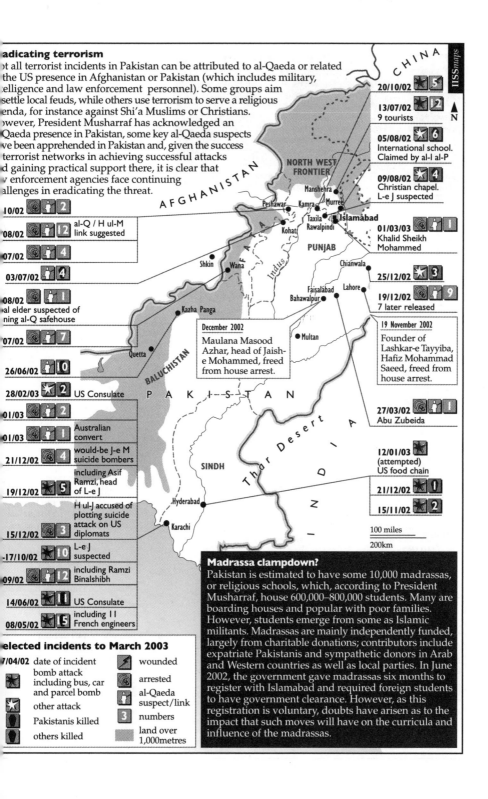

IISS*maps*

...adicating terrorism

...t all terrorist incidents in Pakistan can be attributed to al-Qaeda or related ...the US presence in Afghanistan or Pakistan (which includes military, ...elligence and law enforcement personnel). Some groups aim ...settle local feuds, while others use terrorism to serve a religious ...enda, for instance against Shi'a Muslims or Christians. ...wever, President Musharraf has acknowledged an ...Qaeda presence in Pakistan, some key al-Qaeda suspects ...ve been apprehended in Pakistan and, given the success ...terrorist networks in achieving successful attacks ...d gaining practical support there, it is clear that ...v enforcement agencies face continuing ...allenges in eradicating the threat.

CHINA

AFGHANISTAN

NORTH WEST FRONTIER

Peshawar • Kamra • Murree • Manshehra
Taxila • Islamabad
Kohat • Rawalpindi
PUNJAB
Shkin • Wana
Chianwala
Faisalabad • Lahore
Bahawalpur •
Kazha Panga
• Multan
Quetta
BALUCHISTAN
P A K I S T A N
SINDH
Thar Desert
Hyderabad •
Karachi •
I N D I A

20/10/02 ☀ 5
13/07/02 ☀ 12 — 9 tourists — N
05/08/02 ☀ 6 — International school. Claimed by al-I al-P
09/08/02 ☀ 4 — Christian chapel. L-e J suspected
01/03/03 — Khalid Sheikh Mohammed
25/12/02 ☀ 3
19/12/02 9 — 7 later released

December 2002
Maulana Masood Azhar, head of Jaish-e Mohammed, freed from house arrest.

19 November 2002
Founder of Lashkar-e Tayyiba, Hafiz Mohammad Saeed, freed from house arrest.

27/03/02 — Abu Zubeida
12/01/03 — (attempted) US food chain
21/12/02 ☀ 0
15/11/02 ☀ 2

100 miles
200km

10/02 2
'08/02 12 — al-Q / H ul-M link suggested
'07/02 4
03/07/02 4
08/02 1 — ...al elder suspected of ...ning al-Q safehouse
'07/02 7
26/06/02 10
28/02/03 2 — US Consulate
01/03 2
01/03 1 — Australian convert
21/12/02 4 — would-be J-e M suicide bombers
19/12/02 5 — including Asif Ramzi, head of L-e J
15/12/02 3 — H ul-J accused of plotting suicide attack on US diplomats
-17/10/02 10 — L-e J suspected
09/02 12 — including Ramzi Binalshibh
14/06/02 11 — US Consulate
08/05/02 5 — including 11 French engineers

...elected incidents to March 2003

7/04/02	date of incident	✦ wounded
☀	bomb attack including bus, car and parcel bomb	⊙ arrested
✦	other attack	al-Qaeda suspect/link
●	Pakistanis killed	3 numbers
●	others killed	land over 1,000metres

Madrassa clampdown?

Pakistan is estimated to have some 10,000 madrassas, or religious schools, which, according to President Musharraf, house 600,000–800,000 students. Many are boarding houses and popular with poor families. However, students emerge from some as Islamic militants. Madrassas are mainly independently funded, largely from charitable donations; contributors include expatriate Pakistanis and sympathetic donors in Arab and Western countries as well as local parties. In June 2002, the government gave madrassas six months to register with Islamabad and required foreign students to have government clearance. However, as this registration is voluntary, doubts have arisen as to the impact that such moves will have on the curricula and influence of the madrassas.

Asia Slow progress in Afghanistan

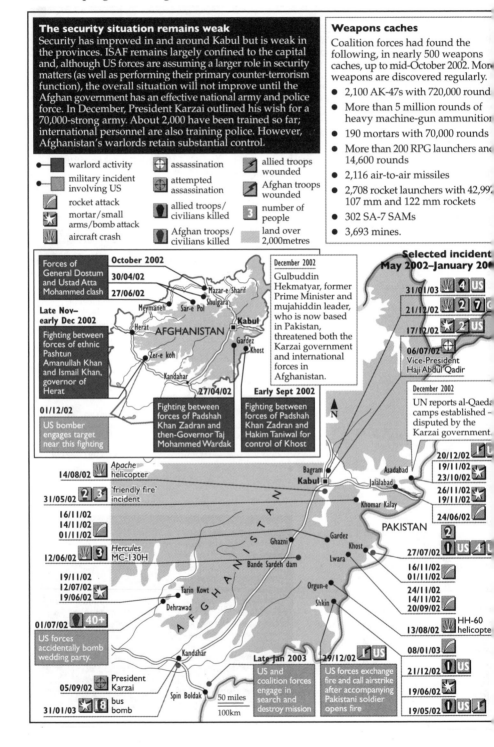

The security situation remains weak

Security has improved in and around Kabul but is weak in the provinces. ISAF remains largely confined to the capital and, although US forces are assuming a larger role in security matters (as well as performing their primary counter-terrorism function), the overall situation will not improve until the Afghan government has an effective national army and police force. In December, President Karzai outlined his wish for a 70,000-strong army. About 2,000 have been trained so far; international personnel are also training police. However, Afghanistan's warlords retain substantial control.

warlord activity

military incident involving US

rocket attack

mortar/small arms/bomb attack

aircraft crash

assassination

attempted assassination

allied troops/ civilians killed

Afghan troops/ civilians killed

allied troops wounded

Afghan troops wounded

number of people **3**

land over 2,000metres

Weapons caches

Coalition forces had found the following, in nearly 500 weapons caches, up to mid-October 2002. More weapons are discovered regularly.

- 2,100 AK-47s with 720,000 round
- More than 5 million rounds of heavy machine-gun ammunition
- 190 mortars with 70,000 rounds
- More than 200 RPG launchers and 14,600 rounds
- 2,116 air-to-air missiles
- 2,708 rocket launchers with 42,99 107 mm and 122 mm rockets
- 302 SA-7 SAMs
- 3,693 mines.

Forces of General Dostum and Ustad Atta Mohammed clash

October 2002
30/04/02
27/06/02

Late Nov– early Dec 2002

Fighting between forces of ethnic Pashtun Amanullah Khan and Ismail Khan, governor of Herat

01/12/02
US bomber engages target near this fighting

Mazar-e Sharif
Shulgara
Meymaneh
Sar-e Pol
Herat AFGHANISTAN
Zer-e koh
Kandahar
Kabul
Gardez
Khost

27/04/02

Fighting between forces of Padshah Khan Zadran and then-Governor Taj Mohammed Wardak

Early Sept 2002

Fighting between forces of Padshah Khan Zadran and Hakim Taniwal for control of Khost

December 2002

Gulbuddin Hekmatyar, former Prime Minister and mujahiddin leader, who is now based in Pakistan, threatened both the Karzai government and international forces in Afghanistan.

Selected incident May 2002–January 20

31/01/03 **4 US**
21/12/02 **2 7**
17/12/02 **2 US**
06/07/02
Vice-President Haji Abdul Qadir

December 2002

UN reports al-Qaeda camps established – disputed by the Karzai government.

14/08/02 Apache helicopter

31/05/02 'friendly fire' incident

16/11/02
14/11/02
01/11/02

12/06/02 Hercules MC-130H

19/11/02
12/07/02
19/06/02

01/07/02 **40+**
US forces accidentally bomb wedding party.

Bagram
Kabul
Ghazni
Bande Sardeh dam
Tarin Kowt
Dehrawad
Kandahar

Asadabad
Jalalabad
Khomar Kalay

Gardez
Khost
Lwara
Orgun-e
Shkin

20/12/02
19/11/02
23/10/02
26/11/02
19/11/02
24/06/02

PAKISTAN
2
27/07/02 **0 US 4**
16/11/02
01/11/02
24/11/02
14/11/02
20/09/02
13/08/02 HH-60 helicopte
08/01/03
21/12/02 **0 US**
19/06/02
19/05/02 **0 US**

Late Jan 2003
US and coalition forces engage in search and destroy mission

29/12/02 **US**
US forces exchange fire and call airstrike after accompanying Pakistani soldier opens fire

05/09/02 President Karzai

31/01/03 **8** bus bomb

Spin Boldak
50 miles
100km

N

IISSmaps

efugee and IDP returns

ast year, *Strategic Survey* noted the vast nternally displaced person (IDP) and refugee roblem that Afghanistan's political and conomic difficulties had generated. Many eople have returned to their home provinces his year, assisted by surrounding countries nd international aid agencies. However, those eturning face difficulties, and the UNHCR stimate was that 550,000 would suffer severe ardship during the cold season.

onthly returns, 2002

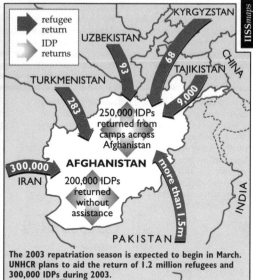

The 2003 repatriation season is expected to begin in March. UNHCR plans to aid the return of 1.2 million refugees and 300,000 IDPs during 2003.

pium production increases in 2002

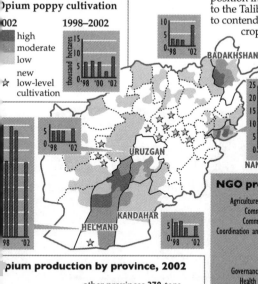

Since late 2001, Afghanistan has returned to a central position in global opium production, after a drop due to the Taliban's 2000 cultivation ban. Farmers, having to contend with poor soil and low returns for alternate crops and seeing minimal central control, have viewed opium poppies as a sure cash crop – particularly after prices rose following the 2000 ban. Efforts to stamp-out production, increasingly supported by the international community, have had mixed results and, in the context of a challenging security environment, have often served to generate resentment among a local population for whom opium seems to offer the best livelihood.

pium production by province, 2002

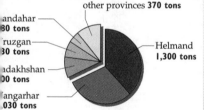

NGO proliferation by sector

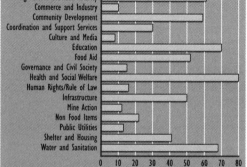

NB: Some NGOs may be active in more than one sector

number of NGOs operating by sector, as at 2 January 2003

Asia North Korea: problems accumulate

In 1994, the US and North Korea signed the 'Agreed Framework' after a crisis provoked by North Korea's near-withdrawal from the nuclear Non-Proliferation Treaty (NPT). Pyongyang agreed to freeze and eventually dismantle its plutonium-production reactor and facilities at Yongbyon, abide by NPT obligations (which include not to receive, manufacture or otherwise acquire nuclear explosives) and account for its nuclear material and associated shipments. In return, North Korea would receive fuel-oil shipments until the construction of two light-water reactors at Kumho. This deal effectively collapsed in late 2002 with the disclosure of North Korea's covert uranium enrichment plans.

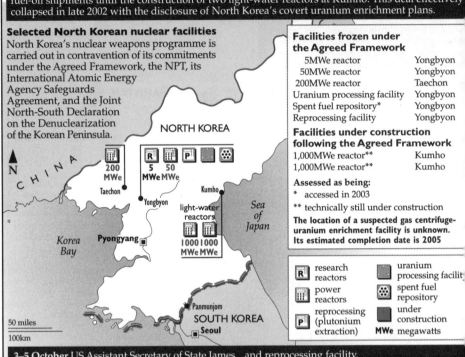

Selected North Korean nuclear facilities

North Korea's nuclear weapons programme is carried out in contravention of its commitments under the Agreed Framework, the NPT, its International Atomic Energy Agency Safeguards Agreement, and the Joint North-South Declaration on the Denuclearization of the Korean Peninsula.

Facilities frozen under the Agreed Framework

5MWe reactor	Yongbyon
50MWe reactor	Yongbyon
200MWe reactor	Taechon
Uranium processing facility	Yongbyon
Spent fuel repository*	Yongbyon
Reprocessing facility	Yongbyon

Facilities under construction following the Agreed Framework

1,000MWe reactor**	Kumho
1,000MWe reactor**	Kumho

Assessed as being:

* accessed in 2003

** technically still under construction

The location of a suspected gas centrifuge-uranium enrichment facility is unknown. Its estimated completion date is 2005

R research reactors	uranium processing facility
power reactors	spent fuel repository
P reprocessing (plutonium extraction)	under construction
	MWe megawatts

3–5 October US Assistant Secretary of State James Kelly visits Pyongyang; tells North Korea US has evidence of secret uranium enrichment programme.

16 October Washington announces Pyongyang admitted to covert nuclear programme.

14 November The Korean Peninsula Energy Development Organization (KEDO) announces oil shipments will halt after November if North Korea doesn't agree to halt covert programme.

12 December IAEA receives letter asking for removal of its seals and monitoring cameras on all North Korea's nuclear facilities.

21 December North Korea cuts seals and interferes with monitoring equipment at Yongbyon's 5-MWe reactor.

22 December North Korea removes seals at Yongbyon's spent fuel pond (containing some 8,000 irradiated fuel rods) & impedes other surveillance equipment.

23–24 December North Korea cuts most seals and impedes the functioning of surveillance equipment installed at Yongbyon's fuel rod fabrication plant and reprocessing facility.

31 December IAEA inspectors leave in response to North Korean request.

10 January Pyongyang announces NPT withdrawal; argues this is effective on 11 January

4 February US considers strengthening forces in Western Pacific area.

5 February North Korea announces reactivation of its 'nuclear facilities'.

13 February IAEA declares North Korea in breach of IAEA nuclear safeguards and refers issue to th UN Security Council.

18 February North Korea threatens to withdraw from 1953 Armistice Agreement.

25 February North Korea tests short-range land-to-ship missile on same day as South Korean presidential inauguration.

2 March US surveillance aircraft intercepted by North Korea fighters in international airspace.

10 March North Korea tests short-range land-to-ship missile.

10 April Formal expiry of 90-day notice period for NPT withdrawal.

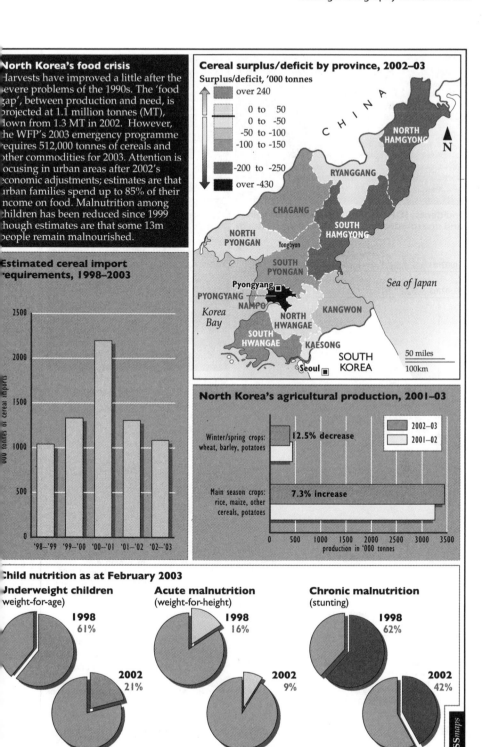

North Korea's food crisis

Harvests have improved a little after the severe problems of the 1990s. The 'food gap', between production and need, is projected at 1.1 million tonnes (MT), down from 1.3 MT in 2002. However, the WFP's 2003 emergency programme requires 512,000 tonnes of cereals and other commodities for 2003. Attention is focusing in urban areas after 2002's economic adjustments; estimates are that urban families spend up to 85% of their income on food. Malnutrition among children has been reduced since 1999 though estimates are that some 13m people remain malnourished.

Estimated cereal import requirements, 1998–2003

'000 tonnes of cereal imports

2500
2000
1500
1000
500
0

'98–'99 '99–'00 '00–'01 '01–'02 '02–'03

Cereal surplus/deficit by province, 2002–03

Surplus/deficit, '000 tonnes

- over 240
- 0 to 50
- 0 to -50
- -50 to -100
- -100 to -150
- -200 to -250
- over -430

CHINA

NORTH HAMGYONG

N

RYANGGANG

CHAGANG

SOUTH HAMGYONG

NORTH PYONGAN

Yongbyon

SOUTH PYONGAN

Pyongyang

Sea of Japan

PYONGYANG

NAMPO

KANGWON

Korea Bay

NORTH HWANGAE

SOUTH HWANGAE

KAESONG

SOUTH KOREA

Seoul

50 miles
100km

North Korea's agricultural production, 2001–03

- 2002–03
- 2001–02

Winter/spring crops: wheat, barley, potatoes **12.5% decrease**

Main season crops: rice, maize, other cereals, potatoes **7.3% increase**

0 500 1000 1500 2000 2500 3000 3500
production in '000 tonnes

Child nutrition as at February 2003

Underweight children (weight-for-age)

1998 **61%**
2002 **21%**

Acute malnutrition (weight-for-height)

1998 **16%**
2002 **9%**

Chronic malnutrition (stunting)

1998 **62%**
2002 **42%**

IISS*maps*

Asia Sri Lanka's peace process

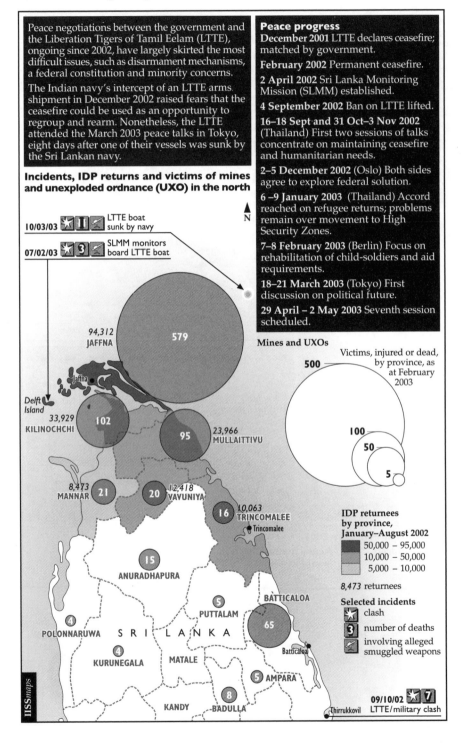

Peace negotiations between the government and the Liberation Tigers of Tamil Eelam (LTTE), ongoing since 2002, have largely skirted the most difficult issues, such as disarmament mechanisms, a federal constitution and minority concerns.

The Indian navy's intercept of an LTTE arms shipment in December 2002 raised fears that the ceasefire could be used as an opportunity to regroup and rearm. Nonetheless, the LTTE attended the March 2003 peace talks in Tokyo, eight days after one of their vessels was sunk by the Sri Lankan navy.

Peace progress
December 2001 LTTE declares ceasefire; matched by government.

February 2002 Permanent ceasefire.

2 April 2002 Sri Lanka Monitoring Mission (SLMM) established.

4 September 2002 Ban on LTTE lifted.

16–18 Sept and 31 Oct–3 Nov 2002 (Thailand) First two sessions of talks concentrate on maintaining ceasefire and humanitarian needs.

2–5 December 2002 (Oslo) Both sides agree to explore federal solution.

6 –9 January 2003 (Thailand) Accord reached on refugee returns; problems remain over movement to High Security Zones.

7–8 February 2003 (Berlin) Focus on rehabilitation of child-soldiers and aid requirements.

18–21 March 2003 (Tokyo) First discussion on political future.

29 April – 2 May 2003 Seventh session scheduled.

Incidents, IDP returns and victims of mines and unexploded ordnance (UXO) in the north

N

10/03/03 ✦ I ◿ LTTE boat sunk by navy

07/02/03 ✦ 3 ◿ SLMM monitors board LTTE boat

94,312 JAFFNA 579

Jaffna

Delft Island

33,929 KILINOCHCHI 102

95 23,966 MULLAITTIVU

8,473 MANNAR 21

20 12,418 VAVUNIYA

16 10,063 TRINCOMALEE

Trincomalee

15 ANURADHAPURA

BATTICALOA

5 PUTTALAM

65

4 POLONNARUWA S R I L A N K A

Batticaloa

4 KURUNEGALA MATALE

5 AMPARA

8 KANDY BADULLA

Thirrukkovil

Mines and UXOs

Victims, injured or dead, by province, as at February 2003

500

100

50

5

IDP returnees by province, January–August 2002
■ 50,000 – 95,000
■ 10,000 – 50,000
□ 5,000 – 10,000

8,473 returnees

Selected incidents
✦ clash
3 number of deaths
◿ involving alleged smuggled weapons

09/10/02 ✦ 7 LTTE/military clash

IISSmaps

Africa Angola after Savimbi

After the death of UNITA leader Jonas Savimbi in February 2002, and the peace deal between the government and UNITA, Angola's long-term prospects have markedly brightened. But the country remains damaged after 30 years of conflict. The WFP estimates that only 3% of arable land is under cultivation, while 2,232 minefields and UXO locations were reportedly registered in 2001. UNITA soldiers, many quartered in transit camps, remain to be resettled and reintegrated. Some 2m Angolans face serious food shortages. IDP movement across unfamiliar areas may lead to more mine accidents. Meanwhile, in the oil-rich Cabinda province, separatists are continuing to fight for independence.

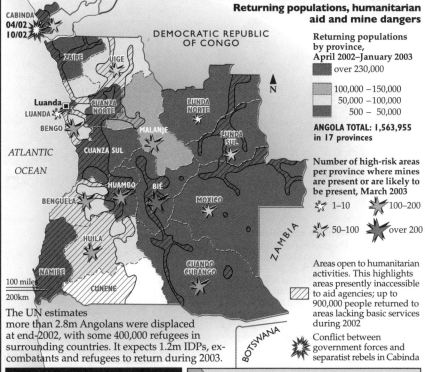

Returning populations, humanitarian aid and mine dangers

Returning populations by province, April 2002–January 2003

- over 230,000
- 100,000 – 150,000
- 50,000 – 100,000
- 500 – 50,000

ANGOLA TOTAL: 1,563,955 in 17 provinces

Number of high-risk areas per province where mines are present or are likely to be present, March 2003

- 1–10
- 100–200
- 50–100
- over 200

Areas open to humanitarian activities. This highlights areas presently inaccessible to aid agencies; up to 900,000 people returned to areas lacking basic services during 2002

Conflict between government forces and separatist rebels in Cabinda

The UN estimates more than 2.8m Angolans were displaced at end-2002, with some 400,000 refugees in surrounding countries. It expects 1.2m IDPs, ex-combatants and refugees to return during 2003.

Reintegrating UNITA

By end-January 2003, 90,000 ex-combatants were registered as part of the government's resettlement and reintegration plan, and a further 15,000 were waiting to move to their designated reception areas. Several factors have complicated the reintegration process. Over 100,000 UNITA fighters – twice as many as expected – arrived for registration, along with their dependants; delays occurred in the distribution of resettlement payments and kits; and climatic factors were a hindrance. The reception areas were scheduled for closure by 31 December 2002, but by 7 February 2003 only four out of 38 had been closed.

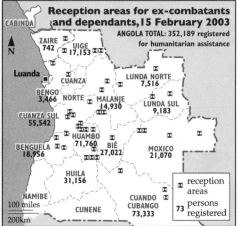

Reception areas for ex-combatants and dependants, 15 February 2003

ANGOLA TOTAL: 352,189 registered for humanitarian assistance

ZAIRE 742	UIGE 17,153
CUANZA	LUNDA NORTE 7,516
BENGO 3,466	NORTE MALANJE 14,930
CUANZA SUL 55,542	LUNDA SUL 9,183
HUAMBO 71,760	BIÉ 27,022
BENGUELA 18,956	MOXICO 21,070
HUILA 31,156	
NAMIBE	CUANDO CUBANGO 73,333
CUNENE	

reception areas

73 persons registered

IISSmaps

Africa Food and health crises in Africa

Food insecurity is again causing hardship in many parts of Africa. Although drought is a contributory factor, along with livestock deaths and agricultural pest outbreaks, civil strife and political difficulties also play a substantial role. In southern Africa, HIV/AIDS is especially pervasive, with high proportions of the working-age populations falling victim. International assistance is being mobilised, but the scale of the continent's problems remains daunting.

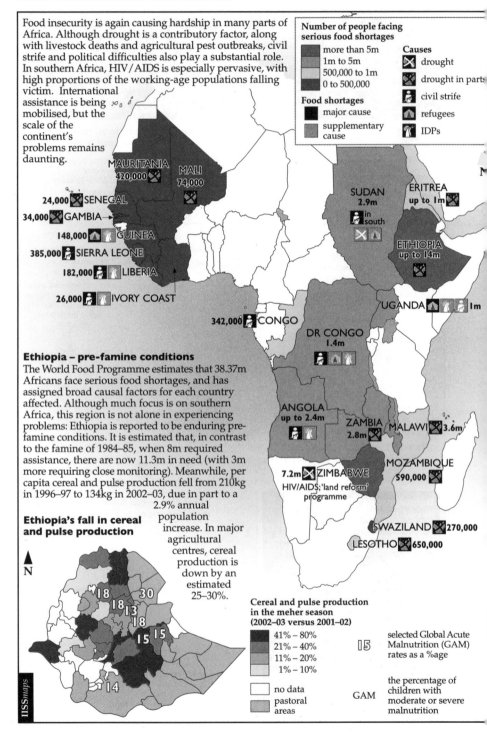

Number of people facing serious food shortages
- more than 5m
- 1m to 5m
- 500,000 to 1m
- 0 to 500,000

Food shortages
- major cause
- supplementary cause

Causes
- drought
- drought in parts
- civil strife
- refugees
- IDPs

MAURITANIA 420,000
MALI 74,000
24,000 SENEGAL
34,000 GAMBIA→
148,000 GUINEA
385,000 SIERRA LEONE
182,000 LIBERIA
26,000 IVORY COAST
342,000 CONGO

SUDAN 2.9m — in south
ERITREA up to 1m
ETHIOPIA up to 14m
UGANDA 1m
DR CONGO 1.4m
ANGOLA up to 2.4m
ZAMBIA 2.8m
MALAWI 3.6m
MOZAMBIQUE 590,000
7.2m ZIMBABWE HIV/AIDS; 'land reform' programme
SWAZILAND 270,000
LESOTHO 650,000

Ethiopia – pre-famine conditions

The World Food Programme estimates that 38.37m Africans face serious food shortages, and has assigned broad causal factors for each country affected. Although much focus is on southern Africa, this region is not alone in experiencing problems: Ethiopia is reported to be enduring pre-famine conditions. It is estimated that, in contrast to the famine of 1984–85, when 8m required assistance, there are now 11.3m in need (with 3m more requiring close monitoring). Meanwhile, per capita cereal and pulse production fell from 210kg in 1996–97 to 134kg in 2002–03, due in part to a 2.9% annual population increase. In major agricultural centres, cereal production is down by an estimated 25–30%.

Ethiopia's fall in cereal and pulse production

N

18 30
18 13
18
15 15
14

Cereal and pulse production in the meher season (2002–03 versus 2001–02)
- 41% – 80%
- 21% – 40%
- 11% – 20%
- 1% – 10%
- no data
- pastoral areas

15 — selected Global Acute Malnutrition (GAM) rates as a %age

GAM — the percentage of children with moderate or severe malnutrition

IISS*maps*

Rainfall and crop production

Food insecurity is heightened by climatic effects. In southern Africa, rains to feed the 2003 harvest started well, but a reduction from mid-November to mid-December withered many young plants and affected termination. It is open to question how many farmers affected will have been able to replant. In South Africa, 2002–03 maize production is forecast at .35MT, down from the last five-year average of 8.43MT.

Rainfall deviation from normal, end 2002

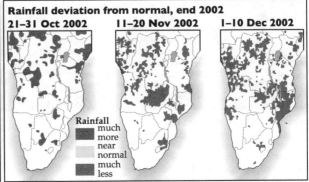

| 21–31 Oct 2002 | 11–20 Nov 2002 | 1–10 Dec 2002 |

Rainfall
- much more
- near normal
- much less

Estimated maximum population requiring food aid by district (to March 2003)

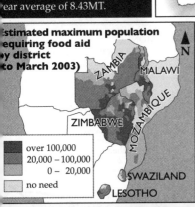

- over 100,000
- 20,000 – 100,000
- 0 – 20,000
- no need

People in need of food aid, June '02–March '03

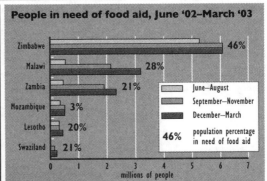

Zimbabwe	46%
Malawi	28%
Zambia	21%
Mozambique	3%
Lesotho	20%
Swaziland	21%

- June–August
- September–November
- December–March

46% population percentage in need of food aid

millions of people

The impact of HIV/AIDS in southern Africa

Sub-Saharan Africa is suffering a devastating HIV/AIDS pandemic. In southern Africa, this is having a more insidious impact than food problems. At end-2002, it was estimated that of a global total of 42m people with HIV/AIDS, 29.4m were in Sub-Saharan Africa. As well as issues of treatment and care, for orphans as well as the sick, the crisis is affecting economic and food security – the FAO has warned that 16m agricultural workers in severely affected African countries could die in the next 20 years unless large-scale programmes are mounted. However, reports note that HIV rates for pregnant women in South Africa fell to 15.4% in 2001 (from 21% in 1998). Also, 19 African countries have set up HIV/AIDS bodies at senior government levels.

Current adult prevalence

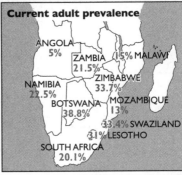

- ANGOLA 5%
- ZAMBIA 21.5%
- MALAWI 15%
- NAMIBIA 22.5%
- ZIMBABWE 33.7%
- BOTSWANA 38.8%
- MOZAMBIQUE 13%
- SWAZILAND 33.4%
- LESOTHO 31%
- SOUTH AFRICA 20.1%

Adults with HIV in Sub-Saharan Africa, 1986–2001

Percentage of adult population

- 20% – 40%
- 10% – 20%
- 5% – 10%
- 1% – 5%
- 0% – 1%
- no data

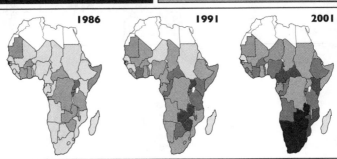

| 1986 | 1991 | 2001 |

Africa Peace in the DRC?

Fighting in the DRC involved forces from seven African nations. It has, when added to the legacy of the Mobutu years, retarded economic and political development, depriving the DRC – and Africa generally – of the benefits of vast mineral resources, and it split central African countries and the SADC along anti- and pro-Kinshasa lines. Multilateral and bilateral economic pressure, with a change in Kinshasa's attitude and South Africa's willingness to push a regional solution, led in 2002 to bilateral peace negotiations and finally, in December, the Inter-Congolese Dialogue agreement in Pretoria between the Kinshasa government and some of the rebel groups. This provides that elections should be held after a 24-month transition period. Although security has improved, renewed fighting in the east and north-east is cause for concern.

Foreign military withdrawals

The overt military presence of other African countries was reduced by late 2002. Effective extension of control from Kinshasa is vital if eastern communities are to look to the capital for security, rather than to Kigali and Kampala. Until this occurs, MONUC – the UN peacekeeping force – remains key, but is hamstrung by lack of troops. As of April 2003, MONUC's strength had not reached 5,000 and even at its authorised maximum strength of 8,700 (as of December 2002), the force would be inadequate to establish security and centralised control in a country the size of Western Europe. By way of comparison, 20,000 peacekeepers were deployed in Sierra Leone.

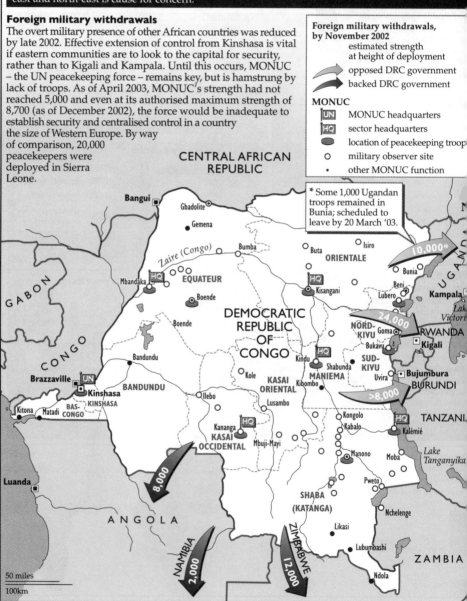

Foreign military withdrawals, by November 2002

estimated strength at height of deployment

opposed DRC government

backed DRC government

MONUC

- UN — MONUC headquarters
- HQ — sector headquarters
- location of peacekeeping troops
- O military observer site
- · other MONUC function

* Some 1,000 Ugandan troops remained in Bunia; scheduled to leave by 20 March '03.

UN criticises resource exploitation

The attitudes of countries hitherto militarily and economically involved in the conflict remain key to the DRC's future. Although all have now lessened their military presence, the continued threat of proxy forces, and a desire to preserve residual economic interests in the DRC's natural resources could lead some countries to conclude that instability is preferable to an extension of Kinshasa's control. In October 2002, the UN released a report by its Panel of Experts investigating illegal resource and wealth exploitation in the DRC. It argued that commercial gain by rebel factions and their regional backers Rwanda and Uganda, as well as Zimbabwe – the DRC's military ally – had become a driving force in the conflict. The panel recommended financial and travel restrictions on individuals and companies it identified as playing a lead role in exploitation.

Origin of companies considered by Panel to be in violation of OECD Guidelines for Multinational Enterprises

Country	Number	OECD Guideline signatory
South Africa	12	✗
UK	12	✔
Belgium	21	✔
US	9	✔
Germany	5	✔
Canada	5	✔
Zimbabwe	4	✗
16 others*	19	

* Ghana 1; Netherlands 1; Thailand 1; DRC 2; Switzerland 2; St Kitts 2; Kazakhstan 1; Bermuda 1; Malaysia 1; China 1; France 1; Finland 1; UAE 1; Hong Kong 1; Israel 1; British Virgin Islands 1

Companies on which the UN Panel recommends placing financial restrictions

Company type	Number
Diamond-related businesses	5
General resource exploitation & trading	14
Airlines	3
General services	5
Undefined	3

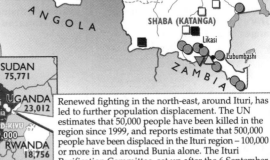

DRC's mineral and energy resources

Energy rich areas
- ■ coal
- △ oil
- ▽ uranium

Mineral rich areas
- ● copper
- ◇ diamonds
- ● gold
- △ lead/zinc
- ■ manganese
- □ tin

0 miles
00km

IDPs and refugees

SUDAN	75,771
ORIENTALE	641,000
Ituri Bunia	23,012
UGANDA	
EQUATEUR	167,629
NORD-KIVU	929,000
RWANDA	18,756
BANDUNDU	
KASAI ORIENTAL	180,000
MANIEMA	180,000
SUD-KIVU	271,000
BAS-CONGO	28,000
KINSHASA	
KASAI OCCIDENTAL	71,500
SHABA (KATANGA)	347,364
ANGOLA	184,201

IDPs by province
- ■ 500,001 – 930,000
- ■ 100,001 – 500,000
- ■ 25,000 – 100,000
- 929,000 IDPs
- 184,201 refugees

Renewed fighting in the north-east, around Ituri, has led to further population displacement. The UN estimates that 50,000 people have been killed in the region since 1999, and reports estimate that 500,000 people have been displaced in the Ituri region – 100,000 or more in and around Bunia alone. The Ituri Pacification Committee, set up after the 6 September 2002 Luanda accord, is intended to improve security, but slow implementation in an environment of shifting allegiances has only assisted continuing instability.

IISSmaps

Global trends The ballistic missile threat

Land-based ballistic missiles

Although over 30 countries are estimated to possess ballistic missiles, generally only a limited number give the international community cause for concern – magnified in recent years given the spread of WMD know-how. Ballistic missiles are seen by some as the WMD delivery system of choice. Agreements to limit the spread of ballistic missiles – and the technology needed to create them – are in place. However, as these tend to be voluntary or non-binding, a state may opt not to subscribe to an agreement, or to employ avoidance or circumvention to evade international controls – the latter as vendor as well as recipient.

Major international regulation regimes

Missile Technology Control Regime (MTCR) 1987

A voluntary arrangement designed to restrict the proliferation of missiles, unmanned aerial vehicles (UAVs), and related technology for those systems capable of carrying a 500kg payload at least 300km, as well as systems intended to deliver WMD. Seeks to coordinate national export licensing efforts to prevent proliferation. MTCR controls apply to such systems as ballistic missiles, space launch vehicles, sounding rockets, UAVs, cruise missiles, drones and remotely piloted vehicles. However, the MTCR is hampered by the increasing ability of countries to indigenously manufacture missiles, and has been criticised for its focus on the non-proliferation of missiles, rather than counter-proliferation.

International Code of Conduct against Ballistic Missile Proliferation (ICOC) 2002

The ICOC calls for restraint in the development, testing, use, and proliferation of ballistic missiles. The ICOC does not seek to prohibit possession; rather it seeks to improve transparency with the use of confidence-building measures, such as prior notification of missile launches. Although not binding, the ICOC does call for subscribing states 'not to contribute to, support or assist any Ballistic Missile programme in countries which might be developing or acquiring weapons of mass destruction...'.

Wassenaar Arrangement (WA) 1995

The WA is a multilateral arrangement concerning export controls for conventional weapons and sensitive dual-use goods and technologies. However, the decision to transfer or deny transfer of any item is the sole responsibility of each state party to the Arrangement.

India, Iran, Iraq, North Korea and Pakistan have not signed any of these agreements.

Iran's major land-based ballistic missile systems with estimated ranges of 150–2,000km

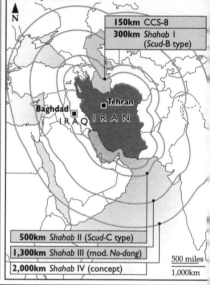

150km	CCS-8
300km	Shahab I (Scud-B type)
500km	Shahab II (Scud-C type)
1,300km	Shahab III (mod. No-dong)
2,000km	Shahab IV (concept)

Iraq's ballistic missile and major UAV systems with estimated ranges of 200–1,200km

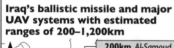
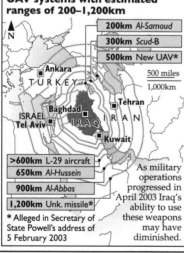

200km	Al-Samoud
300km	Scud-B
500km	New UAV*
>600km	L-29 aircraft
650km	Al-Hussein
900km	Al-Abbas
1,200km	Unk. missile*

* Alleged in Secretary of State Powell's address of 5 February 2003

As military operations progressed in April 2003 Iraq's ability to use these weapons may have diminished.

Pakistan's major land-based ballistic missile systems with estimated ranges of 180–2,500km

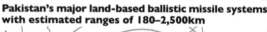
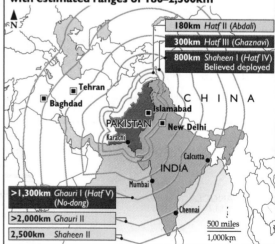

180km	Hatf II (Abdali)
300km	Hatf III (Ghaznavi)
800km	Shaheen I (Hatf IV) Believed deployed
>1,300km	Ghauri I (Hatf V) (No-dong)
>2,000km	Ghauri II
2,500km	Shaheen II

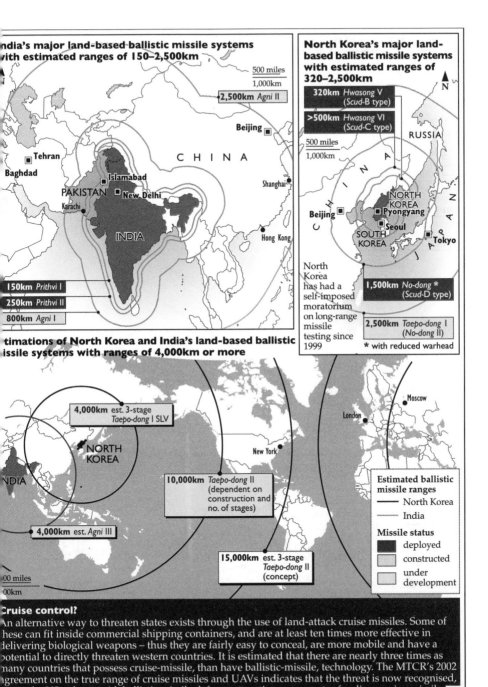

ndia's major land-based ballistic missile systems with estimated ranges of 150–2,500km

500 miles
1,000km

2,500km *Agni* II

Beijing

Tehran

Baghdad

Islamabad

PAKISTAN New Delhi

Karachi

C H I N A

Shanghai

Hong Kong

INDIA

150km *Prithvi* I

250km *Prithvi* II

800km *Agni* I

North Korea's major land-based ballistic missile systems with estimated ranges of 320–2,500km

320km *Hwasong* V (*Scud*-B type)

>500km *Hwasong* VI (*Scud*-C type)

500 miles
1,000km

RUSSIA

NORTH KOREA
Pyongyang
Beijing
Seoul
SOUTH KOREA
Tokyo

North Korea has had a self-imposed moratorium on long-range missile testing since 1999

1,500km *No-dong* * (*Scud*-D type)

2,500km *Taepo-dong* I (*No-dong* II)

* with reduced warhead

timations of North Korea and India's land-based ballistic issile systems with ranges of 4,000km or more

4,000km est. 3-stage *Taepo-dong* I SLV

NORTH KOREA

Moscow

London

New York

NDIA

10,000km *Taepo-dong* II (dependent on construction and no. of stages)

4,000km est. *Agni* III

15,000km est. 3-stage *Taepo-dong* II (concept)

Estimated ballistic missile ranges
— North Korea
- - - India

Missile status
deployed
constructed
under development

00 miles
00km

Cruise control?

An alternative way to threaten states exists through the use of land-attack cruise missiles. Some of these can fit inside commercial shipping containers, and are at least ten times more effective in delivering biological weapons – thus they are fairly easy to conceal, are more mobile and have a potential to directly threaten western countries. It is estimated that there are nearly three times as many countries that possess cruise-missile, than have ballistic-missile, technology. The MTCR's 2002 agreement on the true range of cruise missiles and UAVs indicates that the threat is now recognised, but in the US at least, with ballistic missile defence attracting ever greater funding, cruise-missile defence programmes remain hamstrung by inter-service rivalries. All the nations highlighted on these maps possess cruise missiles (designed or improvised), UAVs, or aerial vehicles that can be remotely piloted or can operate with autonomous-control flight management systems.

IISSmaps

Global trends International terrorism: striking softer targets

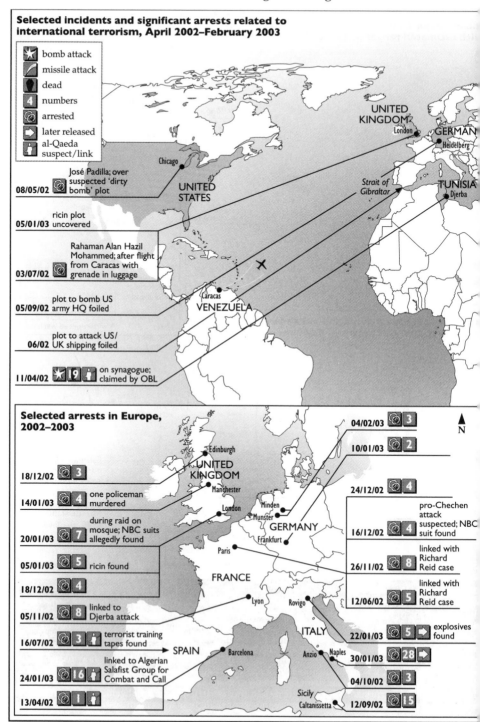

Selected incidents and significant arrests related to international terrorism, April 2002–February 2003

- ⭐ bomb attack
- ◢ missile attack
- 🕴 dead
- **4** numbers
- ◎ arrested
- ➡ later released
- 🔲 al-Qaeda suspect/link

08/05/02 ◎ José Padilla; over suspected 'dirty bomb' plot

05/01/03 ricin plot uncovered

03/07/02 ◎ Rahaman Alan Hazil Mohammed; after flight from Caracas with grenade in luggage

05/09/02 plot to bomb US army HQ foiled

06/02 plot to attack US/UK shipping foiled

11/04/02 ⭐ **9** 🕴 on synagogue; claimed by OBL

Chicago — UNITED STATES — Caracas — VENEZUELA

UNITED KINGDOM — London — GERMAN — Heidelberg — Strait of Gibraltar — TUNISIA — Djerba

Selected arrests in Europe, 2002–2003

18/12/02 ◎ **3**

14/01/03 ◎ **4** one policeman murdered

20/01/03 ◎ **7** during raid on mosque; NBC suits allegedly found

05/01/03 ◎ **5** ricin found

18/12/02 ◎ **4**

05/11/02 ◎ **8** linked to Djerba attack

16/07/02 ◎ **3** 🔲 terrorist training tapes found

24/01/03 ◎ **16** 🔲 linked to Algerian Salafist Group for Combat and Call

13/04/02 ◎ **1** 🔲

04/02/03 ◎ **3**

10/01/03 ◎ **2**

24/12/02 ◎ **4**

16/12/02 ◎ **4** pro-Chechen attack suspected; NBC suit found

26/11/02 ◎ **8** linked with Richard Reid case

12/06/02 ◎ **5** linked with Richard Reid case

22/01/03 ◎ **5** ➡ explosives found

30/01/03 ◎ **28** ➡

04/10/02 ◎ **3**

12/09/02 ◎ **15**

Edinburgh — UNITED KINGDOM — Manchester — London — Minden — Munster — GERMANY — Frankfurt — Paris — FRANCE — Lyon — Rovigo — ITALY — SPAIN — Barcelona — Anzio — Naples — Sicily — Caltanissetta

N

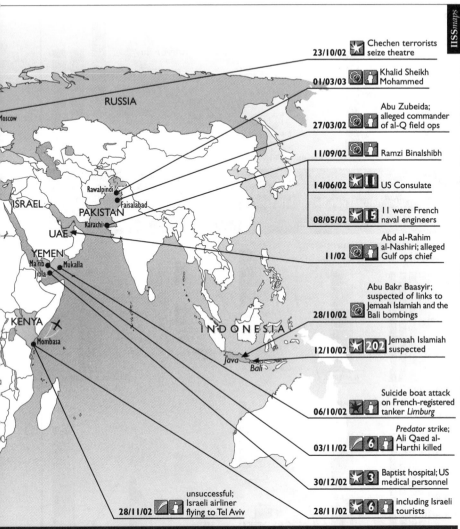

23/10/02 Chechen terrorists seize theatre

01/03/03 Khalid Sheikh Mohammed

27/03/02 Abu Zubeida; alleged commander of al-Q field ops

11/09/02 Ramzi Binalshibh

14/06/02 US Consulate

08/05/02 11 were French naval engineers

11/02 Abd al-Rahim al-Nashiri; alleged Gulf ops chief

28/10/02 Abu Bakr Baasyir; suspected of links to Jemaah Islamiah and the Bali bombings

12/10/02 Jemaah Islamiah suspected

06/10/02 Suicide boat attack on French-registered tanker *Limburg*

03/11/02 *Predator* strike; Ali Qaed al-Harthi killed

30/12/02 Baptist hospital; US medical personnel

28/11/02 unsuccessful; Israeli airliner flying to Tel Aviv

28/11/02 including Israeli tourists

The past year has seen a continuation of global Islamic terrorist activity. Interrogation of suspects held in Afghanistan and at Guantanamo Bay – and those in the custody of other governments – has yielded valuable information. But the military intervention in Afghanistan also made al-Qaeda an even more decentralised organisation, and a series of arrests both indicated and exacerbated breaches in operational security that are likely to prompt further changes in al-Qaeda's *modus operandi*. Al-Qaeda apparently must now rely more on local affiliates or sympathisers – some with their own logistical or financial means and organisational infrastructure – to plan and carry out terrorist attacks, with al-Qaeda itself supplying assistance ranging from mere inspiration or blessing to advice, coordination and funding. This manner of doing business has been termed 'franchised terrorism'.

Probably in response to more robust counter-terrorism in the United States and Europe, as well as to shore up support throughout the Islamic world, al-Qaeda has also extended its *jihad* to other regions and softer targets. The attacks on German tourists in Tunisia, Israeli tourists in Mombasa, and Australian, European and American tourists in the Bali bombing, as well as bin Laden's attempts – though his media outbursts – to inspire terrorist activity by exploiting pro-Palestinian feelings and anti-war sentiment with respect to Iraq, can be seen in this light.

Global trends World energy

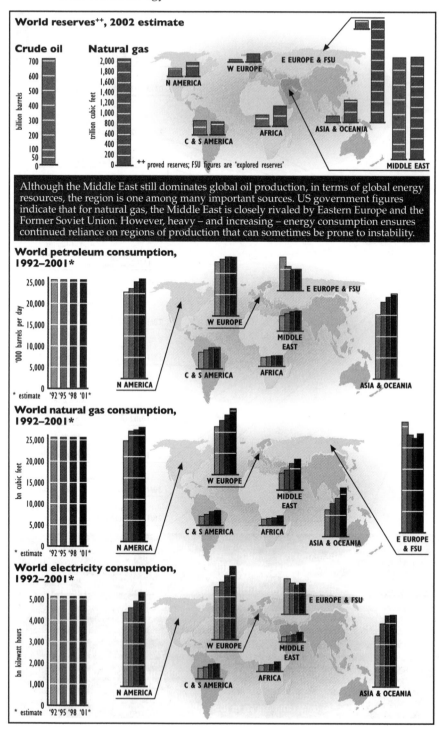

World reserves++, 2002 estimate

Crude oil — Natural gas

++ proved reserves; FSU figures are 'explored reserves'

Although the Middle East still dominates global oil production, in terms of global energy resources, the region is one among many important sources. US government figures indicate that for natural gas, the Middle East is closely rivaled by Eastern Europe and the Former Soviet Union. However, heavy – and increasing – energy consumption ensures continued reliance on regions of production that can sometimes be prone to instability.

World petroleum consumption, 1992–2001*

* estimate   '92 '95 '98 '01*

World natural gas consumption, 1992–2001*

* estimate   '92 '95 '98 '01*

World electricity consumption, 1992–2001*

* estimate   '92 '95 '98 '01*

approach by authorising a leak to the *New York Times* shortly after the Crawford visit. Unnamed Saudi sources declared that 'it is a mistake to think that our people will not do what is necessary to survive. And if that means we move to the right of bin Laden, so be it; to the left of Gaddafi, so be it; or fly to Baghdad and embrace Saddam like a brother, so be it'. Exacerbating this tension was a 10 July 2002 briefing by a RAND Corporation analyst to the Pentagon's Defense Policy Board describing Saudi Arabia as an enemy of the United States – 'the kernel of evil' – and recommending that Washington issue an ultimatum to the Al Saud to stop supporting terrorists or face the seizure of their oil fields and all financial assets in the US. The US government distanced itself from the analyst's view and RAND subsequently dismissed him. Nevertheless, US troops and equipment steadily redeployed out of Prince Sultan Air Base near Riyadh to Al Udeid Air Base near Doha, Qatar, in mid- to late 2002.

Abdullah took unprecedented steps to encourage debate and explore liberalising reforms in anticipation of war in Iraq. His guiding rule of thumb appeared to be that liberalising change was the best way to ensure the Kingdom's survival amid the turmoil an Iraqi war might cause and, equally important, to solidify Riyadh's key legitimising role within the larger Muslim world. Throughout 2002, he bluntly admitted to some failings on the counter-terrorism front, thereby gaining respect abroad. Taking note of the huge funeral procession for Sheikh Hamud bin-Uqla al-Shuaibi, the author of the 1991 *fatwa* against the Al Saud for siding with infidels against Muslims in the Gulf War, Abdullah spoke out. He warned leading Islamists to tone down their rhetoric, pointing out that their vitriolic statements were only nourishing Washington's inclination to go to war. Public discourse subsequently became more moderate. In Burayda, a city famed for its puritanism, Muhsin al-Awaji – once jailed for religious extremism – called for the development of a 'modern, tolerant, and inclusive interpretation of faith'. As of 2002, even Saudi Shias were finally considered to be Muslims, although Saudi courts continued to enforce the Hanbali (Sunni) code on all Muslims. In March 2002, 15 young girls died in a school fire in Mecca when *mutawaeen* (religious police) prevented rescue teams from entering the facility because the children were not properly veiled. This afforded Abdullah a unique moment. In the outrage that followed the fire, the control of girls' education shifted from the clerical establishment to the government. Abdullah also issued a rare public 'lecture' to senior members of the *ulema*, or religious leadership – who were not accustomed to being on the receiving end of such dictates to take a more moderate and reasonable tone in their legalistic pronouncements.

The domestic challenge confronting Abdullah is whether small political advances would become permanent or whether these would wither away once domestic and foreign crises passed. Certain modest reforms were sustainable. For example, Saudi women were issued separate identification

Middle East

cards, with unveiled photographs of the face. Issued by the Interior Ministry to women 22 years of age and above (but with written consent from a woman's guardians, as well as a letter from an employer if she was working), ostensibly 'to combat fraud and forgery', the measure nonetheless was a significant stride towards allowing women an independent social identity. But other more substantial reforms – including Washington's long list of demands, such as changing the country's religious curriculum and crushing fundamentalist elements – were not yet realistic. Such actions, were they to be undertaken, would further jeopardise the ruling Al Saud's tense relationship with the religious establishment. Abdullah did take note of the steep rise of violent crime and drug-trafficking in spite of the harsh repercussions prescribed by *sharia* law for those caught in the act, as further signs of a breakdown of law and order and the need for change. Saudi authorities also arrested several al-Qaeda lieutenants.

As of early 2003, wholesale liberalisation – an independent judiciary, civil and human rights institutions, constitutional reforms, elections to a national consultative council and freedom of expression – was not feasible. Through modest, judicious reform, however, Abdullah had considerably strengthened his power to advance further incremental change, especially if the Saudi role in the war against Iraq were minimal. In the event, while Riyadh remained wary of Saddam's aggression, it allowed only the use of bases by a small number of US military ground personnel and did not permit the United States to use Saudi bases for tactical air operations against Iraq. Riyadh released Said bin Zuair, one of the Al Saud's most vocal opponents, and allowed the Saudi people to voice their opposition to the war and to the US, but Abdullah also encouraged the *ulema* to condemn war-inspired attacks on non-Muslims as a form of religious 'deviancy'. Given Abdullah's reformist leanings, these balancing efforts make the prospects for significant post-Saddam liberalisation in Saudi Arabia reasonably bright. Indeed, the Al Saud and Washington broadly share an objective that regime change could facilitate: the withdrawal of US troops from Saudi Arabia. Such a move would remove bin Laden's most potent pretext for terrorism – the presence of the 'infidel' or the 'crusader' in the land of the two most holy Muslim sites – and provide the Al Saud with substantially greater latitude for exploring domestic social and political change. In early February 2003, senior members of the Al Saud were reported as saying that Abdullah would request the withdrawal of all US armed forces from the country once the US-led Iraq campaign were completed. According to these reports, this would set the stage for the advent of democratic elections (initially without women's suffrage) to provincial assemblies and then, over the course of six years, a national assembly. But such proposals were floated in the past by various Saudi monarchs who abandoned their declared plans upon fuller reflection.

Yemen's helpful authoritarianism

Yemen's cooperation with American authorities after the bombing of the *USS Cole* by al-Qaeda operatives in October 2000 had been grudging. Although the Yemeni government proclaimed its counter-terrorism solidarity with the United States shortly after the 11 September 2001 attacks, in early 2002 US intelligence services regarded Yemen – on account of its history of extremism, lack of central government control and rugged terrain – as a weak counter-terrorism partner and a potential host for al-Qaeda members fleeing Afghanistan. Sana'a was considered unable or unwilling to impede or neutralise al-Qaeda operatives. In fact, Yemeni authorities did little in the way of counter-terrorism enforcement in early 2002. President Ali Abdullah Saleh had recruited many mujahideen, who had proven useful to him during the 1994 civil war and his subsequent assault on South Yemeni Marxist separatists holding the port city of Aden. Indeed, Saleh appointed Abdel Majid al-Zindani, a former associate of bin Laden's who helped form the Muslim Brotherhood in Yemen, as a presidential councillor. Zindani recruited key tribal leaders to support Saleh, and was not muzzled. Furthermore, in the 1990s, the Yemeni Islamist network set up its own school system and Taliban-style moral security forces that attacked wedding parties and, in one instance, torched a brewery; as of early 2003, that network had not been dismantled.

Given the need to keep such leaders on a manageable leash, Saleh seemed to be pursuing a policy of integration rather than suppression. Ironically, democratisation both enabled and constrained him in this agenda. Because the Islah, Yemen's largest opposition and leading Islamist party, held 64 of 301 seats in parliament, the president had to take them into account. Islah members have probably infiltrated the Political Security Office – Yemen's intelligence service – as well as the army. The US attempted to remedy this situation. In early February 2002, General Tommy Franks, commander-in-chief of US Central Command, successfully negotiated the deployment of a substantial FBI contingent, along with an equally substantial group of military advisors. Their mission was to train Yemeni coast guard and security forces in counter-terrorism, so as to eliminate the vulnerabilities that had permitted the bombing of the *USS Cole*. Washington also successfully pressured Saleh to strip Islah of the estimated $80 million it received from the state to run various religious schools in 2002. Saleh also expelled scores of 'foreign students' enrolled in leading Islah religious institutions. These were positive steps, but the government failed to hire school inspectors to ensure that the state's secular syllabus was being followed, and so the gains were not consolidated. Moreover, in 2002, neither the Islah nor Zindani were challenged directly. The latter's theology book was still part of the current syllabus, and taped sermons of preachers who clearly sympathised with al-Qaeda were widely available throughout Yemen.

Middle East

In August 2002, Yemeni security forces revealed that they had uncovered a group calling itself 'Sympathizers of al-Qaeda', which was armed with 14 boxes of C-4 plastic explosives. Whether they were involved on the October 2002 attack on a French oil tanker, the *Limburg*, in the Gulf of Aden was not clear, but it became evident that Sana'a could not gain the upper hand against freelance terrorists or rebel tribes. *Stinger* surface-to-air missiles were fired at the helicopter of the president's son, Colonel Ahmed Saleh, the Commander of Yemen's Republican Guard. In September 2002, shots were also fired at the president's own helicopter convoy. Accordingly, the government acquiesced in US counter-terrorism efforts in Yemen. On 3 November 2002, a CIA-controlled *Predator* unmanned aerial vehicle fired two *Hellfire* anti-tank missiles at a pick-up truck travelling on a remote desert road in Yemen, killing Qaed Salim Sinan al-Harithi, a top associate of bin Laden's and the suspected orchestrator of the *USS Cole* operation, along with five other suspected al-Qaeda members. The strike occurred in the same area where Yemeni forces in December 2001 had attempted to capture al-Harithi, but had failed when local tribes protected him; 25 people had died in the hostilities.

By the end of 2002, the computer tracking systems installed in Yemeni ports and airports were linked to American command facilities. Further, Saleh's clear support for the US-led global campaign against terrorism had an intimidating effect on local actors, allowing the government to extend control over key tribal regions, often through ruthless counter-insurgency operations that included taking the relatives of tribal rebels hostage. Saleh appeared to be leveraging US support for aggressive internal security to strengthen his own authoritarian power. As of early 2003, for example, two-thirds of senior government posts in Aden were in the hands of non-militant northerners, including the key post of chief of police. Saleh has also complained vocally that Aden is bloated with Marxist-Leninist civil servants – allegedly 700,000 of South Yemen's population of two million held government posts before unification in 1990 – which suggests an inclination to purge Aden and Hadramawt, bin Laden's ancestral home, of tribal or religious institutions. But, as of early 2003, Saleh could not ban the Islah, criminalise its activities or muzzle socialist/secessionist leaders, as Washington would prefer, without jeopardising his legitimacy.

Yemen was one of the few Arab countries that made steady progress towards genuine democratisation in the 1990s. The campaign against terrorism – as much as regime change in Iraq – has impelled Sana'a to backtrack. Thus, Washington's relationship with the Yemeni regime resembles its relationship with the Pakistani government: notwithstanding the Bush administration's overarching goal of exporting liberal democracy to authoritarian regimes, including most in the Arab and larger Muslim world, in the particular case of Sana'a, authoritarianism better serves US counter-terrorism objectives. Indeed, Yemen's counter-terrorism cooperation appeared to yield it a WMD dividend in December 2002, when the US asked Spain to release to Yemen a ship intercepted by the Spanish Navy in the Arabian Sea containing 15 *Scud* missiles and 15 conventional warheads that North Korea had sold to Yemen. Although Sana'a agreed not to purchase any more *Scuds*, it had also denied having purchased any in the first place. Regime change in Iraq is likely to increase radical Islamic anti-government activity in Yemen. The larger US regional presence will make Yemeni counter-terrorism cooperation even more critical in staving off intrusive US impingements on Yemen's sovereignty. On balance, therefore, war in Iraq is likely to have an anti-democratic effect on Yemen.

Egypt: status quo likely

The year 2002 saw Egypt slide into economic gloom – the result of its falling exchange rates, significant losses in share prices as well as property values, and capital flight. Egyptian unemployment, unofficially standing at 20% and poised to increase as 800,000 new job seekers entered the market each year, could not be offset even by a healthy government-projected economic growth of 4.9% in 2001. In any case, independent analysts questioned the validity of official statistics, and after 11 September even government sources indicated marked declines in income generated from tourism, fees collected in Suez Canal crossings, remittances from migrant workers and oil sales. Worse still, Cairo did not expect any of its foreign debt to be forgiven in the aftermath of a new war in the Middle East, as it had been after the Gulf War in 1991. To be sure, an estimated $60 billion in foreign savings were repatriated in the mid-1990s, but the 1997 Asian financial crisis and terrorist activities against tourists in 1998 deflated whatever economic cushion may have been generated. For all the misgivings that Egyptian radical elements and their numerous public acolytes may have had about 'political Islam', the bin Laden phenomenon – with its undeniable ability to strike at the heart of the world's most powerful military state – seemed to recapture the imagination of many ordinary Egyptians after 11 September. There remains a resilient anti-American strain in Egypt, even among middle-class professionals with beneficial Western connections.

Cairo responded with a major law-enforcement crackdown in 2002. Moreover, Islamists were, perhaps for the first time, challenged effectively on the ideological front. Prolific Egyptian writers have now produced several treatises that excoriated bin Laden for harming Islam. Several including Khaled al-Guindi – a popular preacher – have drawn on the *sharia* to explain why peaceful means were in the interest of the faith. Amr Khaled, a Cairo accountant turned popular televangelist, had the greatest public impact and – wearing a jacket and tie and sporting a slim moustache – established a new, urbane image of the Egyptian Muslim activist. A

Middle East

conservative theologian, Khaled distinguished himself from scores of others by avoiding fiery militant rhetoric and refusing to patronise or hector approving audiences. Broadcasting throughout the Muslim world, Khaled spoke of sacrifice and martyrdom but condemned terrorism outright, not because it alienated the mainstream or Western powers but because *sharia* forbade it. To like effect, some of the 10,000 or so Egyptian Islamists jailed for militant anti-government activities were paraded on television seeking to apologise 'for crimes committed' and 'horrible mistakes'.

While Cairo was not ready to release Gamaa Islamiya leaders from jail or to trust fully the televangelists, its willingness to relax authoritarianism to encourage religious moderation seemed salutary. In late July 2002, however, Saad Eddin Ibrahim, a prominent academic, was sentenced in a retrial to seven years in prison for criticising the government. The secular Ibrahim was once a popular figure, with his own television show, and headed a sociological research institute on whose board a slew of government officials served. When he decided to monitor elections, encourage voter registration and examine the conditions of Egypt's Christian minorities, however, Cairo disapproved and had him arrested and charged. Ibrahim's case starkly illustrated the limits of Cairo's commitment to democratisation. The manner in which President Hosni Mubarak's son, 39-year old Gamal Mubarak, who was appointed to the National Democratic Party (NDP)'s 25-member secretariat two years ago, is being groomed for succession also shows the regime's uneasy relationship with democracy. Gamal is quietly rising to the top of the NDP, aided by ongoing purges.

Much like Syria in 2000, Egypt appeared in 2002 to be institutionalising an orderly succession, but the effort was reminiscent of monarchical or pharaonic rather than democratic traditions. The process was well in train before hostilities commenced in Iraq. During the war, the Muslim Brotherhood issued calls for Islam to 'resist' the US and UK's drive for regional hegemony, and there were massive anti-war demonstrations throughout Egypt. Mubarak, while opposed to the war, stated that he could do little to stop it or end it on terms substantially different from those dictated by Washington and London, demonstrating his incapacity to mollify or sway Egyptian public opinion. Post-Saddam, the US will be under international pressure to re-engage more deeply in the Israel–Palestinian conflict. These factors will disincline Washington to risk Egyptian non-cooperation by leaning too heavily on Cairo to democratise, despite the Bush administration's general indications that foreign assistance will be laden with political and economic conditionality. Beyond the standing $2bn Egypt receives annually in US military assistance – deemed necessary to guarantee that Egypt will keep peace with Israel – Egypt cannot expect overwhelming financial inducements towards major political reform. These circumstances suggest that while Egypt may be more open to liberalisation at the margins – to the extent that it can control

Islamic extremism – it will remain relatively unamenable to wholesale democratisation, notwithstanding regime change in Iraq.

Security challenges in Jordan

King Abdullah II carefully cast himself as a reformer throughout 2002, but was confronted with several disruptive events that highlighted the fragility of his rule and prompted greater royal authoritarianism. Despite Abdullah's 'Jordan First' agenda launched in November 2002 – which, among other things, encourages national pride as an engine of participatory democracy – over 100 new temporary laws that restricted various freedoms were enacted in 2001 and 2002 via royal decrees. For example, unauthorised public meetings were banned and journalists were subject to imprisonment if the government deemed that they 'sowed the seeds of hatred'. Although parliament could reverse royal decrees, Abdullah II dissolved the legislative body and did not seem eager to re-assemble it, twice postponing elections. Throughout 2002, Jordanian Islamists were detained by the hundreds, often on charges of belonging to illegal organisations. Secular activists were not spared, either. Toujan Faisal, Jordan's first female member of parliament, was sentenced in May 2002 to 18 months in prison for an internet article alleging that the prime minister benefited from a decree doubling car insurance rates. But Faisal won the support of *Sabil*, the Islamist newspaper, and in July 2002, after three months in jail, received a royal pardon. Indicating the limits on Abdullah's magnanimity, the pardon extended not to liability for the crime itself but only to the sentence.

Amman's tilt towards illiberality was reinforced by terrorist threats. Starting in summer 2002, a number of Jordanian Islamists were said to have returned from Afghanistan to plot attacks on Western targets. On 20 October 2002, Lawrence Foley, a 60-year old USAID director, was assassinated in his driveway as he was preparing to leave for work. This act, according to US Secretary of State Colin Powell in his address to the UN Security Council on 5 February 2003, was abetted by al-Qaeda operatives even though the 'Honourable Men of Jordan' – an obscure organisation – claimed responsibility. This information originated from the Jordanian security services, which have been among the US' most reliable counter-terrorism partners in the Gulf region since well before 11 September 2001.

The Foley assassination prompted Abdullah to launch a major counter-terrorism operation in the town of Ma'an, 200km south of Amman – a centre of Islamist, anti-Israeli, pro-Iraq, anti-economic reform sentiment, which had rebelled against Amman's authority at least four times in the previous 13 years. On 8–14 November 2002, Jordanian troops occupied Ma'an, while heavy machine-guns fired on homes from which gunfire had emanated. King Abdullah imposed a six-day total curfew, subject to

Middle East

exception only with written permission to go to mosque on Friday. Troops disarmed hundreds of residents; six were killed and over 140 arrested. Ostensibly, the principal objective of the Ma'an operation was to apprehend Muhammad Shalabi, a cleric allegedly implicated in Foley's assassination. Shalabi, a member of Takfir wal-Hijra, a banned religious party, had declared the young monarch a kafir (sinner) and, unlike traditional Islamists, was not integrated in the country's political structure. Abdullah's harsh security tactics probably reflected his wish to avoid Yemen's fate and forestall any American intrusion into Jordanian internal security by sending an unmistakable signal to the clerical establishment that *jihad* against Americans – proclaimed in regularly issued *fatwas* – was not acceptable. Further, he may have wanted to signal Iraq and Saudi Arabia (where Shalabi may have sought and received refuge) not to disrupt Jordan's delicate ethnic balance. Finally, the November operation reiterated to the people of Ma'an that insurrection did not pay.

Given Jordan's proximity to the West Bank, Abdullah was extremely sensitive to the destabilising effect that war in Iraq could have on the Israeli–Palestinian conflict, and with most other Arab leaders registered his opposition to war absent UN backing. At the same time, he wanted to avoid being punished for lack of support for the US in 2003 by the withdrawal of American aid, which had occurred when Jordan failed to support the 1991 Gulf War. By early February 2003, Amman had calculated that US military action against Iraq was all but inevitable, had been promised roughly $1bn by the US for the use of Jordanian territory by US forces and had quietly agreed to provide it. Jordan pushed for a formal UN resolution that, among other things, offered Saddam Hussein exile. Although the Jordanian government did not expect him to accept, it regarded his likely rejection as an inducement to others in the Iraqi hierarchy to kill or otherwise depose him. That, in turn, would at least minimise, if not forestall, military and civilian casualties. Especially interesting was the Jordanians' political gloss. Provided the war was quick and merciful, the Iraqi people welcomed US-led troops once Saddam was decisively removed, and the Americans' post-conflict presence in Iraq was reasonably brief (ideally no more than three months), they reasoned, sceptical popular Arab opinion as to the merits of regime change might reverse rapidly.

Jordan permitted several thousand US and UK special operations troops to deploy at an airbase on the Jordan–Iraq border, from which they staged operations inside Iraq. Although Amman kept much of the war news out of its media, the Jordanian branch of the Muslim Brotherhood demanded the expulsion of all coalition troops by all Arab governments. Abdullah was quick to unleash his secret police, and hundreds of demonstrators were arrested.

Unlike the Saudis, however, the Jordanians did not expressly link regime change and US withdrawal with liberalisation in Jordan itself.

This is unsurprising. Jordan has less to prove to the West: it is not as illiberal as Saudi Arabia and is viewed as a much surer counter-terrorism partner, and it has made peace with Israel. For the same reasons, war in Iraq is unlikely to have pronounced democratisation effects on Jordan. Indeed, identity politics – of the Palestinian majority, the Saudi- and Iraqi-related Transjordanians and various tribal and religious minorities – and its associated divisions can be expected to intensify in the immediate aftermath of the war against Iraq. The same goes for Islamic militancy. Such developments would tend to lead to Abdullah's continuation of rigid internal security policies and restrictions of civil liberties. A fast war could lead to greater regional stability, broadly less stressful Arab–American relations and better conditions for lessening Israeli–Palestinian tensions. While these results could strengthen democratising forces in Jordan, there is an equal chance that they could reinforce illiberal impulses in Amman, as they are likely to do in Cairo.

Iran's halting reform

Iran's inclusion in Washington's 'axis of evil' was yet another wedge in the increasingly bitter schism that characterised American–European differences. To be sure, Americans and Europeans alike aimed to persuade Iran to desist from making mischief in the Persian Gulf region and, for that matter, throughout the Muslim world. However, the preferred means of persuasion differed sharply. European powers noted that Tehran had a long tradition of obeying various international treaties and agreements and, therefore, could be trusted with diplomacy and trade. American officials have not forgotten the 444-day long hostage crisis in 1979. While the Bush administration was initially inclined to explore a rapprochement for strategic reasons, the December 2001 *Karine-A* affair – in which Israelis interdicted a large cache of Iranian weapons on a ship intended for the Palestinian Authority – pushed the US back to a policy of economic and diplomatic isolation. Neither of these approaches affected Iranian policies in 2002 due to the regime's pre-occupation with a significant internal power struggle between its elected reformist government under President Mohammed Khatami and the unelected but institutionally entrenched religious conservatives surrounding the 'Supreme Leader', Ayatollah Ali Khamenei, and in the Council of Guardians, a 12-member advisory body that leans strongly towards the Supreme Leader.

As the stalemate persisted between the conservative establishment and the reformist government, the paralysis of the Iranian regime deepened throughout 2002. At its core, the dispute was between those who were attempting to rule in the name of their constituents through elections and other forms of participatory government, and those who were portending to guide the masses in the name of God. President Khatami, first elected in

1997 and re-elected by a greater margin in 2002 – both times on political reform platforms – saw all his initiatives ridiculed or sabotaged by his opponents. Khamenei's supporters also infiltrated the judiciary, seeking the strictest interpretation of *sharia*, along with the state's security apparatus. They held veto power over all government decisions through the Council of Guardians. Thus, a frustrated Khatami could do little when newspapers were shut down, writers and activists attacked, protests repressed and 'liberal' members of parliament (presumptively enjoying immunity) sentenced to jail terms for various offences.

Nevertheless, there were indications in 2002 that at least some conservative forces were bending to the gravity of the reform movement. In July 2002, Ayatollah Jalaluddin Taheri, who resigned his post as a prayer leader in Isfahan, issued a vitriolic statement inveighing against 'despair, unemployment, inflation and high prices, the hellish gap between poverty and wealth, the deep and daily growing distance between the classes, the stagnation and decline of national revenue, a sick economy, bureaucratic corruption, desperately weak administrators, the growing flaws in the country's political structure, embezzlement, bribery and addiction'. These were powerful words that discomfited leading Iranian clerics. Some, including Ayatollah Yusef Saanei, were openly critical of the country's slow democratisation pace, and called for Grand Ayatollah Montazeri's release from virtual house arrest. Montazeri, who outranks Ali Khamenei in religious terms, helped write the 1979 Constitution but fell out of grace with Ayatollah Ruhollah Khomeini two months before the latter's death in 1989. Montazeri was emboldened by Khatami's victory election in 1997 to publicly favour greater religious tolerance. Both his ideas and his plight gained prominence among Iran's intellectuals, who pointed out that Khamenei could not justify how Montazeri had been treated between 1997 and 2003. His release had been rather narrowly ruled out, 161–129, in 2001 by the Majlis (national assembly). To placate a public increasingly mobilised behind reform, on 9 February 2003 Khamenei ordered Montazeri's release.

There were, of course, limits on the degree of dissent that the conservative establishment would tolerate. Hashem Aghajari, a dissident academic, challenged the clerical claim to the divine right to rule and called for reform. He was found guilty of blasphemy on 6 November 2002 and sentenced to imprisonment, flogging and death. A few years earlier, dissidents who voiced similar views were merely jailed. The Iranians' adverse popular reaction was confrontational. University administrations and students demonstrated against the regime, and protests occurred in major cities. Opposition forces mobilised around Abdolkarim Soroush who, while believing that religious and worldly powers were better left separate, nevertheless endorsed the notion that Islam and democracy were linked. While conservatives generally disliked him, they could not deny that he was devout. Consequently, he was far less vulnerable than, say, Aghajari. Thus, it may be safe to conclude that in early 2003, the Iranian opposition was turbaned, relatively legitimate (at least in the eyes of the state) and firmly located within the ruling class. But it remained unable to institutionalise government reform. In September 2002, Khatami submitted two bills to the Majlis that would curtail the Council of Guardians' veto power and empower the president to impose constitutional limits on Islamic courts. As of early 2003, the bills were still pending and may not be passed. Khatami threatened to resign but, as of April 2003, had not stepped down and was not likely to do so.

Perhaps owing to Iran's internal political restiveness, Iranian foreign policy became more moderate in 2002. On one hand, Tehran supported Washington during the Afghanistan campaign to oust the Taliban and, as a further sign of compliance, closed down the Iranian offices of the fundamentalist Pushtun leader, Gulbuddin Hekmatyar. Iran also expanded trade with Saudi Arabia. On the other hand, the US raised suspicions that Iran was harbouring al-Qaeda terrorists, and Europe and the US still opposed Iran's efforts to develop WMD. From Iran's perspective, the recent strategic trauma of the Iran–Iraq War and its strategic encirclement by Pakistan, Turkey and Iraq and prospectively the United States itself justifies a robust strategic capability. Therefore, it is not surprising that Tehran has repeatedly tested its *Shahab-3* ballistic missile, with a range of up to 1,500 kilometres – a successful test in May 2002 was followed by an unsuccessful one in July 2002 – and may be working on longer-range and higher-payload missiles. Government claims that Iran's development of nuclear power is strictly for civilian purposes are unconvincing in light of its ample oil and gas resources. Iran's nuclear programme is likely to receive additional Russian and Ukrainian support, and may accelerate in 2003 and 2004, hastening its acquisition of significant offensive capabilities. So far, however, its known activities are largely 'street legal'. It remains to be seen whether Iran will honour various nuclear, chemical and biological weapons treaties.

On the whole, the expansion of civil institutions and the robustness of reformist protest appeared to be slowly weakening Iran's theocracy. The country's structural economic weakness and declining per-capita GDP and its consequent need for foreign credit has also made it more responsive to the economic conditionality of international financial institutions, which has loosened the grip (legal and otherwise) of the clerics on the economy. Although the Iranian political leadership has expressed fears that the US might take pre-emptive action against Tehran as against Baghdad, and thus regards regime change as a 'dangerous precedent', the Bush administration made it clear that no such action is intended and that Iran is regarded as primarily a political and diplomatic challenge. That challenge would be eased considerably by a more democratic state that would allow constitutional change whereby the reform movement would become more institutionalised. Democratisation in Iran remains more internally than externally driven, and the events of 2002 suggest that it may prevail over religious conservatism. Whether regime change in Iraq encourages or discourages such democratisation depends on the duration of the post-conflict American presence and the nature of the new Iraqi regime. Suggestions that Iran was tacitly cooperating with the US plans for Iraq weakened Khatami politically. If the US finds resurrecting an Iraqi unitary state a protracted and problematic affair, is forced to maintain a large military presence right next door to Iran and intensifies its intolerance of Iran's nuclear programme, Iranian conservatives may close ranks against a proximate enemy and delay the process of reform. But if the US withdraws its major military presence fairly quickly, Iranian leaders will perceive less of a threat and enjoy more leeway for reform. And if the new Iraq appears to remedy Saddam's oppression of Iraq's Shia majority through democratic structures, that may recommend incremental moves towards democracy in Iran, rendering the ongoing political contest between conservatives and reformers more manageable.

A political anticlimax?

Regime change in Iraq, if accomplished neatly and quickly, may encourage democratisation in a few Gulf states, including Iran and Saudi Arabia. But, despite the visions of Bush administration 'idealists', the American public's disinclination to expend the resources or energy required to nurture friendly democracies could produce something closer to a 'realist' or 'minimalist' post-Saddam US Middle East policy. The meagre sum of $29m initially allocated to the US–Middle East Partnership Initiative launched in December 2002 to encourage moderate opposition voices – against the reality that most opposition movements in the Middle East are Islamist and reject US influence in the Muslim world – indicated as much. Such token attention to the region's deep-seated political under-development – sourced in a broad lack of freedoms, chronically low levels of modern secular education and limits on the role of women in society – is not likely to make a serious impact on such problems. Furthermore, at least in the short term, US military intervention in the Arab world is also likely to inflame terrorist motivations. Regimes like those in Egypt, Jordan and Yemen therefore will continue to place a premium on security, and therefore authoritarianism, over democratisation. This impulse will only be strengthened and prolonged if the US footprint in the region, enlarged via the Iraq intervention, remains in place in the medium term. Continued US failure to directly link Saddam and al-Qaeda, the discovery of a relatively small or unthreatening stock of WMD in Iraq, or a fraught process of political rehabilitation there would also make it more difficult for Arab governments to sell their more radical and anti-American elements any political or economic agendas perceived to be US-driven. In addition, the conservatism of the US government and its need for Arab support for any re-invigorated Israeli–Palestinian peace process will still dictate continuing close, risk-averse relationships with Cairo, Amman and Riyadh that are unlikely to involve heavy pressure towards internal political reform. Democratisation, though perhaps marginally advanced by regime change in Iraq, may have to wait a long while.

The Israeli–Palestinian Conflict: Utopianism vs Realism

War against Iraq has raised questions about the underpinnings of America's approach to the Middle East. Traditionally, US policy has focused on US interests, avoiding grandiose, values-based ambitions to transform the region. The 1991 Gulf War led to the first outburst of 'utopianism' – the belief that the defeat of Iraq's Ba'athist regime, combined with the proper application of US political power elsewhere, would unleash sweeping change in the region. Having gone into abeyance during the Clinton administration, with the important exception of the push for an Israeli–Palestinian settlement at Camp David in 2000, this impulse has returned. The US is no longer perceived as a status-quo power in the Middle East, and in some ways and by some parties is apprehended as revolutionary. On balance, however, it is likely that the realist approach that dictated a reluctant and mostly hands-off posture during the Cold War will reassert itself – even if Iraqi President Saddam Hussein is toppled.

Late arrival
The US came late to the Middle East and largely remained aloof until the 1973 Yom Kippur War. A concern for the regional power balance, and a distaste for imperialist adventures, led the US to compel Britain's withdrawal from Egypt after its Suez campaign of 1956. In the 1960s, preoccupied with surging Soviet influence, Washington first tried to woo Egypt with the promise of aid and then, in June 1967 under the Johnson administration, declined to intervene militarily or diplomatically on Israel's behalf during the Six-Day War. The change came with the Nixon administration. Initially reluctant to offer Israel military assistance during the 1969–70 war of attrition, Nixon authorised a huge aid package during

Middle East

the 1973 war. This shift hinged on the conviction that Soviet credibility, especially in Egypt and Syria, would best be challenged by a quick and decisive Israeli victory – an outcome that would have otherwise eluded Israel. Nonetheless, Washington remained disinclined to become too directly involved in regional politics. To protect US interests in the Gulf, Nixon deputised the Saudi Arabian and Iranian regimes as a first line of defence against Soviet aggression, rather than deploy globally stretched US forces to the area.

Soviet assertiveness under Leonid Brezhnev, and the emergence of President Anwar Sadat in Egypt, spurred the first significant deepening of US regional engagement. Intelligence suggesting that Soviet military planners contemplated a campaign through Iran, aimed at seizing the Khuzestan oilfields, impelled the Carter administration to declare the Gulf of vital national interest and to form a new unified military command for southwest Asia. Almost simultaneously, the Camp David Accords made the US a security guarantor and economic benefactor for both Israel and Egypt, while the 1979 Iranian revolution presaged the need for a continuous military presence in the Gulf. Under the Reagan administration, these trends gathered momentum. A growing Soviet aerial threat to the US Mediterranean fleet dictated a reliance on Israel as a 'strategic partner', and Reagan instructed the Department of Defense to strengthen its capabilities for coalition warfare in the Gulf. Tehran's post-revolutionary hostility to the US complicated American strategy, resulting in the bizarre juxtaposition of limited military assistance to Iraq and the provision of anti-tank weaponry to Iran. US policy in this period was thus motivated not by a sentimental attachment to the region or its Arab and Jewish inhabitants, but by strategic calculations concerning oil and the threat of Soviet domination. Interests, not values, shaped policy choices. Decision-makers strove for maximal leverage from minimal intervention. The Cold War context endowed this approach with strong bipartisan congressional support.

Grander plans emerge

Free of the constraints of Cold War competition, the administration of George H.W. Bush adopted more ambitious policies. After Iraq's invasion of Kuwait in 1990, planners viewed the imminent war against Iraq as the opportunity to rid the region of its last 'radical alternative'. With the revisionist Ba'athist regime eliminated, the region would embrace a progressive, pro-American agenda. US military power would, as in post-war Europe, guarantee regional security, and hesitant local states would be lured into cooperative arrangements. Eight months after the end of the war, Washington used its newly won clout to force Israel and its neighbours to the Madrid peace conference, where the presence of Saudis, Israelis, Syrians and Palestinians marked a dramatic advance. Israel's Likud government was forced to acknowledge Palestinians as having an independent stake in the outcome; Syria had to recognise Israel as a legitimate interlocutor; and the Saudis were manoeuvred into a public, if lukewarm, endorsement of peace with Israel. Washington signed agreements with all of the Gulf Cooperation Council countries (except Saudi Arabia) that fell just short of explicit security guarantees. Meanwhile, the Defense Department pressed for an enormous training facility in Saudi Arabia and a large permanent ground presence. Formalised US military ties to regional states, the Madrid conference and a strong push for a regional missile non-proliferation regime, signified goals that went far beyond the ejection of Iraqi forces from Kuwait. The US was aiming to reshape the region.

Reduced opportunities, constricted aims

These ambitions cooled under the Clinton administration. The Arab–Israeli peace process stalled with the 1995 assassination of Israeli Prime Minister Yitzhak Rabin, the ascendance of a new Likud government in Israel and the durability of an increasingly ineffectual Palestinian Authority (PA) President Yasser Arafat. Saddam defied expectation that he would not survive Iraq's defeat, while Iran pursued a covert war against the US, culminating in the terrorist attack on the US Air Force Khobar Towers complex in Dhahran, Saudi Arabia, in June 1996. Reduced opportunities and the constricted aims of the new administration were summed up by the name of its regional strategy: 'dual containment'. This policy evolved into a more belligerent posture toward Iraq and a more conciliatory one toward Iran, where Muhammad Khatami, a moderate, was popularly elected president in 1997. On the Arab–Israeli front, President Bill Clinton's commitment foundered on his miscalculation of Syrian President Hafiz al-Assad's willingness, during negotiations over the Golan Heights, to surrender Syria's claim to a sliver of land along the northeast edge of the Sea of Galilee and Arafat's summary rejection of Israeli proposals regarding the repatriation of Palestinian refugees and distribution of sovereignty within and around Jerusalem.

US Republicans developed a deep contempt for Clinton's perceived failure to use America's remarkable leverage in a unique 'unipolar moment'. Paul Wolfowitz, who had been Undersecretary of Defense for Policy in the first Bush administration and would become Deputy Secretary of Defense in George W. Bush's administration, pressed for Saddam's overthrow. In Wolfowitz's view, the US had the pieces in place to launch an insurrection within Iraq, which American military power could shield from Saddam. He was deeply troubled by US failure to back Iraqi rebellions after the Gulf War, and believed that Washington had a moral obligation to compensate for its putative betrayal of Kurdish and Shi'ite aspirations.

Middle East

The Saudis, meanwhile, were increasingly regarded as unreliable allies, whose style of governance and subordination to conservative clerics was bound to bring them into conflict with America's regional agenda. An Iraq liberated from the brutal tyranny of Saddam Hussein seemed the ideal substitute for the sour partnership with Riyadh. Iraq has a secular political tradition, an abundance of technocrats and a sound conventional military organisation. Its Islamic legacy is both Shi'ite and orthodox Sunni in orientation, in contrast to the xenophobic Wahhabism of Saudi Arabia. Its enormous oil reserves – second only to Saudia Arabia's – provided reasonable hope that Baghdad could challenge Saudi Arabia's role of 'swing producer' and, if its production capacity were modernised, even break the power of OPEC. Freed from tyranny, globally integrated, technologically advanced and under US protection, Iraq would no longer view weapons of mass destruction (WMD) as a strategic priority and would be ready to make peace with Israel – the other secular, advanced democracy in the region. The emergence, within the heartland of historical Islam, of an Arab state committed to broad political participation, universal suffrage and parliamentary democracy, would galvanise civil society throughout the Middle East.

Competing impulses

This somewhat utopian urge to refashion the region has co-existed with a narrower Republican interpretation of US interests. During the 2000 presidential campaign, Condoleezza Rice published a manifesto arguing for a strict national interest standard for US foreign policy – one that would not necessarily encompass societal engineering on the vast scale envisioned by the neo-conservative Iraq 'hawks'. Indeed, this concept would not even have focused on the Middle East, which is mentioned only once in this articulation of the vision of the soon-to-be Assistant to the President for National Security Affairs. In Rice's view, Clinton's foreign policy failed to distinguish the vital from the trivial. Rather than concentrating on powers with the ability to shape the international order, such as Russia and China, or on key alliances, especially in northeast Asia, Clinton frittered away American credibility and military prowess on peripheral matters. In this worldview, the Middle East would be very much on the strategic periphery.

Rice's construction was much in evidence during the first nine months of the Bush administration, which focused on withdrawal from the 1972 Anti-Ballistic Missile Treaty, deployment of ballistic-missile defences and challenging China's perceived pretensions to regional leadership. Senior civilian appointees at the Defense Department began the painful process of reordering budgetary priorities and attempting to persuade military chiefs to accept a realignment of procurement priorities and redistribution of roles and missions. The Israeli–Palestinian dispute was considered beyond effective US action. Under pressure to demonstrate awareness that the worsening conflict was a matter of concern for regional allies, Bush declared in June 2002 that the US favoured the establishment of a Palestinian state within three years. Yet no action was taken to implement this objective.

The Iraq hawks could scarcely make themselves heard. In the welter of conflicting policy priorities, the White House was not ready to begin preparing the ground for war with Iraq. As under Clinton, 'regime change' was promulgated only as an eventual goal. By late summer 2001, Washington's customary caution towards the Middle East had returned. Officials who had experienced the excitement of 1991 and sensed the potential for radical transformation had to agitate from the sidelines.

The events of 11 September 2001 provided hawks, including those of a 'utopian' persuasion, with the opportunity to push Iraq to the top of the agenda. They successfully exploited the belief in the upper tier of government immediately after the attacks that there was a better than even chance that Iraq had been involved, and the more broadly held concern that Baghdad might in future supply WMD to terrorists. In bureaucratic terms, this resulted in the insertion of a single provision, at the end of a presidential guidance document otherwise dedicated to the government's response to 11 September, instructing the military to prepare for war with Iraq. However contingent the evolution of this policy objective, the stage was set for eventual confrontation with Iraq over its WMD ambitions, which ultimately would lead to war.

Return of the realists

War with Iraq commenced on 20 March 2003, and by 5 April, American and British troops had taken several Iraqi cities and the US Army's Third Infantry Division and US Marine Corps units had amassed on the outskirts of Baghdad. But Washington and London's decision to proceed against Saddam without the express backing of the UN Security Council and against the positions of key European allies and the balance of world opinion has opened up America's subsequent Middle East policy to intense scrutiny and, potentially, acute criticism. On one hand, the United States' need to repair alliances and partnerships and to resurrect international institutions – especially the UN and NATO – damaged by the Iraq crisis could be construed as compelling motivation to re-engage robustly in a renewed Israeli–Palestinian peace process and to pressure the government of Ariel Sharon. Such an aggressive approach would be in line with the views of European powers like France and Germany, which also vehemently opposed war in Iraq, and the UK, which views proactive engagement as essential to re-establishing its bona fides with Europe after having aligned itself with the US on Iraq and demonstrating its own 'balanced' approach to the Middle East. Nevertheless, a number of factors are likely to favour the return of the realist approach to the region.

Middle East

Democratisation depends on a gradual accumulation of trust between reformers in government and the opposition. After the war, this dynamic is likely to unfold more quickly precisely because repressive structures will be swept away. Yet the necessity of maintaining Iraq's unity will require that power remains centralised. The control of any new government – whether a transitional administration run by the US or the UN or an indigenous Iraqi government nurtured by outside powers – over oil will be vital here. It will also impede democratisation, as rentier systems do in other settings. But Iraqi oil production is not likely to increase quickly enough to pose a serious threat to OPEC cohesion or Saudi Arabia's primacy as a swing producer. Thus, in the meantime, US strategic and economic interests and the conservatism of the US government will dictate continuing close relations between the US and Saudi Arabia. On top of this, severe structural defects in the political economies of regional states, including galloping population growth, water shortages, crumbling infrastructures, inadequate literacy rates and ineffective educational systems, along with low domestic and foreign investment rates, will undercut whatever traction democratisation in Iraq might gain in neighbouring countries.

Considerable hard security threats will probably also persist in post-war Iraq. During the war, Iraqi nationalism proved to be a source of resistance to the US that was more potent than expected, as paramilitary irregulars – including the occasional suicide bomber – complemented Iraqi troops. Further, the US–UK intervention has angered Arab populations and governments, and as of early April 2003, had shown signs of generating regional support for residual Iraqi resistance. If indigenous terrorist threats materialise and persist in post-war Iraq, and draw American blood, domestic opinion in the US will tilt away from ambitious engagement in the Middle East – as it did following Hizbullah's devastating 1983 attack on the US Marine barracks in Lebanon, which killed 241 soldiers. More broadly, Iraqi nationalism is likely to find focus through anti-Zionism. On the regional level, opposition movements in the Middle East are nearly all Islamist and reject US influence in the Muslim world. Washington recognises this, as Secretary of State Colin Powell indicated in his December 2002 remarks on the new US–Middle East Partnership Initiative, designed to encourage a moderate opposition voice in the Muslim world. The paltry sum allocated to this important project – $29 million – illustrates the most substantial reason for the triumph of conservatism in America's approach to the region after the war: the American public will not want to expend the energy and resources, or accept the substantial risks, that would be required to realise the utopian vision of the hawks. Finally, in Israel and the Palestinian territories, the recalcitrant hard-line policies of Sharon's government, the absence of any strong moderating voice from the Israeli left, Bush's tendency to equate Israel's local and regional terrorism concerns with transnational terrorist threats to the US, and the continuing radicalisation of Palestinian terrorist groups are all likely to inhibit aggressive US diplomacy.

A daunting year in Israel and Palestine

The year 2002 began with the most violent confrontation between Jews and Arabs in Palestine since the partition of the territory west of the Jordan River in 1947. The al-Aqsa intifada had already caused roughly 2,000 deaths – more than three-quarters of them Palestinian – in a lopsided confrontation over the previous 18 months. Following a four-month period in which Israeli civilian casualties spiked sharply – inside the Green Line, where 98 were killed, and in the occupied territories, where 40 died – the Israel Defense Force (IDF) initiated a coordinated air, sea and ground assault against PA installations and locations believed to be staging bases for suicide bombers known as *Operation Defensive Shield*. During this period, 241 Palestinians were killed by Israeli forces. In the ensuing 90 days, Israeli forces entered virtually all of the significant towns on the West Bank, including Nablus, Ramallah, Jenin, Tulkarm, Qalqilya and Bethlehem. As *Operation Defensive Shield* wound down in early summer, the West Bank had in effect been re-occupied. The IDF called up 30,000 reservists for this campaign, which took the fighting down narrow lanes in a house-to-house search for Palestinians believed to be middle- and senior-ranking members of Hamas, Islamic Jihad and the al-Aqsa Martyrs Brigade. Israel's stated objectives were to destroy terrorist infrastructure, apprehend suspected terrorists and create 'a new strategic reality' by reinforcing deterrence.

The military logic, as the UK showed in Northern Ireland in the 1980s, was that terrorists find it difficult to operate when their neighbourhoods are saturated with enemy forces. As anticipated, the operation led to a 50% decline in average monthly Israeli fatalities during the year that followed. In broader terms, Israel's demonstration of will in entering the casbahs of West Bank towns may have intensified a growing sense among Palestinians that the *intifada* had been a disaster. Yet survey data seem to show that many Palestinians believe that the uprising advanced their national interest, even as attacks against Israelis continue to be launched even under more unfavourable tactical conditions. In any case, as of April 2003, there was no way to prove or disprove that deterrence was reinforced. The chief political result of *Defensive Shield* was the elimination of boundaries established under the two Oslo agreements between areas A (controlled by the Palestinian Authority) and B (controlled jointly by Palestinian and Israeli authorities), and between those two areas and the Green Line. This effectively concluded the dissolution of the peace process begun at the Madrid conference of 1991.

Indeed, the burial of the Oslo process was probably Sharon's unstated objective in ordering the assault. His party, Likud, had never believed that

Middle East

the process served Israel's interests. By abrogating the key territorial arrangements set up under the Oslo Accords, Sharon considered himself to be unshackling Israel from an unwanted commitment. Ironically, he simultaneously fulfilled the wishes of a younger generation of Palestinian activists who saw the Oslo Accords as a mechanism for the never-ending deferral of Palestinian statehood through a series of unachievable interim procedural requirements. This new generation of post-1967 born-and-bred Palestinians – the 'insiders' – had borne the brunt of occupation while the elders of the movement postured in Tunisian villas. They held that the 'outsiders' used the Accords to reinforce their influence, privilege and wealth. From this perspective, the apparent complicity of the old guard – mainly the Fatah leadership under Arafat – with the Israelis in perpetuating the agreements was galling. For this cohort, the uprising was as much an expression of independence and quest for leadership within Palestine as it was an attempt to bleed an occupying power.

The Tanzim, an offshoot of Arafat's Fatah party, had been established in the early Oslo period as part of Arafat's strategy to co-opt young insiders. It was an effective approach for containing their fervour and resentment, and gave Arafat a tool to suppress opposition to Fatah, primarily from the Islamists and especially from Hamas. The leader of the Tanzim, Marwan Bargouti, was emblematic of his constituency. He was young, well educated, and fluent in Hebrew, which he had acquired as a prisoner in Israeli jails. By the late 1990s, the Tanzim, though still loyal to Arafat, was slipping from his grasp. Its leaders had grown increasingly impatient with their exclusion from power within the PA and repelled by the towering corruption of the old guard, abuse by security forces and Fatah's failure to advance the cause of Palestinian independence. The radicalisation of the Tanzim not only made them more difficult for Arafat to control – graffiti in Tanzim-dominated neighbourhoods in West Bank town occasionally mocked Arafat in vicious terms – but made them ripe for partnership with erstwhile rivals on the Islamist right. One of the more striking developments during the past year was the convergence of Fatah and Islamist militancy. In early 2001, Tanzim members, many of whom were employed by the plethora of PA security agencies and police forces, formed the al-Aqsa Martyrs Brigade and stepped up their participation in the anti-Israeli insurgency. In part because of religious overtones that have crept into Palestinian justification for violence against Israelis and in part as a way for this Fatah-related group to compete with Hamas, the al-Aqsa Martyrs Brigade adopted suicide bombing as a tactic, soon surpassing the damage that Hamas was inflicting on Israel. The success of these attacks – especially those that followed Israel's January 2002 assassination of Raed Karmi, the group's leader – buoyed Fatah's credibility and was probably a factor in Hamas's failure to overtake Fatah's narrow lead in popularity.

The operational difference between Hamas's and Fatah's political objectives is difficult to pinpoint. The declaratory differences are less obscure. Hamas seeks to establish an Islamic state over all of mandatory Palestine, beginning with the West Bank and Gaza. Its doctrine rejects a peace deal along the lines that Israel and the Palestinians were negotiating at Taba in January 2001 and which Arafat subsequently stated that he would accept in some form. Yet Hamas has displayed substantial pragmatism in dealing with its more powerful rival, despite its leadership's refusal to participate in elections that would endow Fatah with Hamas's tacit recognition. Hamas has proffered truces in its campaign against Israel, albeit at times when the group was under severe pressure and needed breathing room. In November 2002, Fatah and Hamas met in Cairo under President Hosni Mubarak's auspices to explore the possibility of closer cooperation during the *intifada*. While that meeting was unsuccessful, their respective military wings appear to have coordinated some of their operations. Some analysts believe that Hamas will eventually be drawn into the gradual political process of forging Palestinian statehood, and that its religious fundamentalism and political irredentism will recede over time. Other observers do not foresee Hamas's tactical flexibility evolving into long-term accommodation of a secular Palestinian state confined to the West Bank and Gaza.

Whether the organisation can mount a meaningful challenge will depend on the strength of Palestinian political institutions and their ability to provide employment, social services, medical assistance and public safety. If these goods are not delivered, Hamas will have the manoeuvring room to compete for leadership in the new state. In the meantime, however, Arafat's popularity remains at roughly 35%, according to a reliable November 2002 survey. The nearest second is 43-year old Marwan Barghouti, whose commitment to a two-state solution is well known, at 12%. Barghouti was arrested by the IDF in the West Bank in March 2002 for allegedly orchestrating terrorist al-Aqsa Martyrs Brigade attacks and subsequently imprisoned, and in March 2003 was still on trial in Israel. Thus, the old and young guard of the secular resistance together command the approval of nearly half of the survey's respondents, while the leader of Hamas, Sheikh Ahmed Yassin, hovers at 14%. Others who enjoy sufficient name recognition to register in public-opinion surveys are all affiliated with Fatah or other secular arms of the Palestine Liberation Organisation (PLO). As parties, however, Fatah and Hamas are evenly matched in public-opinion polls, which suggests that a charismatic leader might be able to catapult Hamas to prominence, especially if a political and security crisis persists. This survey data indicated that there is a large swing vote to be captured. They also reflected the call on the Palestinian street for responsible government. Public opinion is nearly unanimous regarding the corruption and inefficiency of Arafat's PA. In this respect, the Palestinian street is in accord with both Washington and Jerusalem.

Middle East

When Bush, under pressure from London and Riyadh, presented the US plan on 24 June 2002 for restarting the peace process, he focused on internal Palestinian reform as the prerequisite for American engagement. Without naming Arafat, Bush urged Palestinians to vote for a new leadership and implied strongly that Arafat had disqualified himself as a legitimate interlocutor. This was farther than most Palestinians themselves wanted to take reform and, in consequence, Bush inadvertently boosted Arafat's popularity. Arafat was not unaware of this and sought to press the idea of presidential elections, which he would surely win, rather than local or legislative elections that would open doors to the insider generation. The Bush administration's wishful notion that the barrier Arafat posed to progress could simply be bypassed was widely criticised, primarily because the proposal seemed to be dictating the results of elections and was therefore intrinsically undemocratic. Beneath the roar of denunciation, however, the European Union (EU) – which has generously supported the PA – quietly endorsed the priority of reform, while think-tanks advocated arrangements that would retain Arafat as a figurehead and endow a prime minister with real political authority and responsibility.

Sharon, too, picked up the idea, taking it beyond the American formulation in two significant directions. First, he authorised the IDF's siege of the Mukata, Arafat's headquarters in Ramallah, in autumn 2002 and publicised documents found there which tended to implicate Arafat himself, or his office, in terrorist attacks carried out by the al-Aqsa Martyrs Brigade. Outside parties – including the US and European and Arab states – envisaged and, more importantly, preferred Arafat's gentle transition to symbolic leadership, which they hoped would emerge naturally from the Palestinian community's growing dissatisfaction combined with delicate diplomatic and financial pressure from the US and from European and Arab donors. But Sharon suddenly and brutally forced the outcome that all these other parties thought would be achieved slowly and softly by demonstrating as savagely and publicly as possible Arafat's operational impotence and political irrelevance. The publication of the documents relating to terrorism added the quasi-legal condemnation of Arafat to the appalling humiliation inherent in the pillaging of the Mukata. In short, Sharon induced trauma when others wanted merely slow decline and made a more nuanced incarnation of American, European and Arab Middle East diplomacy considerably more difficult to realise. Further, the disclosure of incriminating documents enabled Sharon to exploit Bush's perception that the US and Israel faced an identical terrorist challenge.

These developments combined in March 2003 to bring about the biggest change in Palestinian politics since the establishment of the Palestinian Authority in the wake of the first Oslo agreement. Arafat appointed a prime minister, Mahmud Abbas (also known as Abu Mazen). Abbas is committed to political reform and a negotiated solution to the Israeli–Palestinian conflict. He has worked closely in the past with Israeli Labour Party negotiators, especially Yossi Beilin, with whom he developed an imaginative peace plan that, in the event, was never tabled. Abbas was also one of the founders of the PLO and an old comrade of Arafat's. He is a transitional figure, one of the last of a passing generation. Yet he is not expected to make a substantive difference for several reasons. He is unequivocally an 'outsider' and therefore is unlikely to command the respect of the younger 'insiders'. He also participated heavily in the Oslo process and is thus associated with a failed project. And it remains uncertain whether he is psychologically able to act in a manner that is truly independent of Arafat's influence. In any event, authority over the security and police services still rests with Arafat, who has also reserved to himself responsibility for external affairs, including negotiations with Israel. Thus, the three areas requiring action – control over a consolidated security service, suppression of violence against Israelis and development of a negotiating strategy vis-à-vis the US and Israel – are likely to remain moribund.

Israeli politics have also developed in ways that do not appear conducive to productive negotiations. In the February 2003 elections, for which there was a low (by Israeli standards) turnout of 68.5%, Labour was smashed, suffering its worst defeat in 30 years. For demographic reasons – declining ratio of Ashkenazi Jews to overall voting-age population – some Labour decline was to be expected. But its crippling diminution from 25 seats in the outgoing Knesset to 19 turned on more emergent factors. Amram Mitzna, the Labour leader who replaced former Defence Minister Binyamin Ben-Eliezer, seemed to voters to be out of touch with reality, insisting on defining Arafat as a negotiating partner when even the US president had ruled Arafat out of bounds. Labour was also inextricably identified with the thoroughly discredited Oslo process. It did not matter that Mitzna was a former senior IDF general who had been commanding officer of Central Command (West Bank) during the first *intifada*. He struck many as an Arab absolver, when survey data indicated that most Israelis did not believe that a solution was achievable in the foreseeable future. Against such perceptions, Mitzna argued that, as a former mayor of Haifa – a substantially integrated port city in northern Israel, and the only one that most Arabs did not leave in 1948 – he knew how to bring disparate groups together. He also aimed to regain the Israeli Arab vote that Ehud Barak had squandered. But the key development since the beginning of the second *intifada* has been the irreversible alienation of Palestinians within the Green Line from Israel. While they had once formed tactical alliances with Israeli mainstream parties, during the current *intifada* the government attempted to bar them from taking their Knesset seats due to their vocal sympathy with Palestinian militants.

Mitzna's other sin was to insist that he would not join a unity government with Sharon – that Labour's place was in the opposition to

Middle East

provide an alternative to Sharon's policies. In his view, Labour had simply provided political cover for Sharon's harsh policies. While Mitzna may have had the long-run integrity and viability of the Labour Party in mind, the short-run costs of this stance were high. Most Israeli Labourites are more pragmatic than Mitzna appeared to understand. While despite their pessimism they want an agreement with the Palestinians on the understanding that this would entail statehood, they see the necessity for the right-wing implementation of this essentially left-wing policy preference. After the election, the rejected Labour leaders – Haim Ramon and Ben Eliezer – were manoeuvring to unseat Mitzna as party leader. Many Labourites unhappy with the party's exclusion from government are sympathetic with this agenda.

The other development that badly damaged Labour was the emergence of a once-obscure free-trade and secular government party called Shinui. The leader of Shinui is Tommy Lapid, a 72-year old Hungarian refugee, who came to Israel as a child. He has been a television commentator, had his own show – *Pop-Politika* – that savaged Israeli politicians, and was head of the Israel Broadcasting Authority. He single-handedly took an utterly marginal party to 15 seats in the Knesset, making Shinui Sharon's largest coalition partner. Shinui's secular agenda – Lapid considers the religious parties budgetary parasites that are corrupting the soul of the state – appealed to Labour voters who were looking for a cause worth voting for when peace-process issues were off the agenda. In early 2003, Shinui was known as the 'unidentified flying object' in Israeli politics, as it was unclear how it would use its leverage within the current coalition. But despite this wildcard, the governing coalition that emerged from the election held 68 seats – Likud (40), Shinui (15), National Union–Israel Beteinu (7) and National Religious Party (6) – which constitutes a very sizable majority in Israeli terms. For the first time since 1974, no ultra-orthodox parties were participating in government. More notably, the cabinet includes two extreme right-wingers: Defence Minister Avigdor Lieberman and National Infrastructure Minister Effi Eitam, the latter a decorated veteran of the legendary 1976 raid on Entebbe. Both favour Palestinian expulsion – or, in Israeli parlance, 'transfer' – from the West Bank.

Early soundings in the US

Even before the Iraq war was concluded, realist impulses in US Middle East policy had begun to surface. On 30 March 2003, Powell and Rice gave speeches in Washington before 3,000 members of the American Israel Public Affairs Committee. Their language regarding America's commitment to Israel was resolute and emotionally powerful, with attendees reporting tears flowing down the faces of some listeners. Amid this rhetoric was the substantive policy statement that 'settlement activity is simply inconsistent with President Bush's two state vision' and 'as progress is made toward peace, settlement activity in the Occupied Territories must end'. Rice added that the seven-page 'roadmap', arrived at by the 'quartet' engaged in restarting the Middle East peace process – the US, the UN, Russia and the EU – and requiring the cessation of settlement activity and expansion by 'natural growth' is 'non-negotiable'.

The roadmap envisages a comprehensive final settlement by 2005, to be achieved in three phases. The initial phase, which would extend through the first half of 2003, entails the PA's meeting performance-based criteria for comprehensive security reform, Israeli withdrawals to the positions of September 2000 as security improves and support for the Palestinians to hold free, fair and credible elections early in 2003. The first phase would also include a ministerial-level meeting of an 'Ad Hoc Liaison Committee' to review the humanitarian situation and prospects for economic development in the West Bank and Gaza, and to identify priority areas for donor assistance, including support for the reform process, before the end of 2003. The second phase would focus on the creation of a Palestinian state with provisional borders based on a new constitution, as a transition to a permanent-status settlement. The third phase, in 2004–05, contemplates Israeli–Palestinian negotiations aimed at a permanent-status solution in 2005. Specifically, any such solution would involve the end of the Israeli occupation that began in 1967 by virtue of a settlement negotiated between the parties and based on UN Security Council Resolutions 242 and 338, with Israeli withdrawal to secure and recognised borders.

Sharon, however, had already stated that Israel had numerous reservations regarding the roadmap. While Sharon broadly endorsed Bush's June 2002 framework in a major December 2002 speech in Herzliyah, he laid even greater emphasis than Bush on Palestinian political reform, an exclusively symbolic role for Arafat and an interim Palestinian state that includes only areas A and B – that is, about 42% of the West Bank and Gaza. Moreover, the Israelis are moving forward on the construction of a security wall. This will have political consequences insofar as it will shape perceptions of final borders. Furthermore, the fact that the Sharon government is proceeding with construction indicates that it is serious about the separation of Israel and any Palestinian state. Thus, the wall could seriously curtail economic interaction between Israel and a notional Palestinian state. This has negative implications for such a state's viability – and, more immediately, for the Palestinians' inclination to bargain.

The pressing question is whether Powell and Rice's statements signal a focused post-Iraq war effort on the part of the US administration to implement the roadmap and push Sharon to the wall, or whether they were intended mainly to placate UK Prime Minister Tony Blair, who felt that more explicit engagement of the US and the UK on the Israeli–Palestinian problem would generate domestic political support in the UK for the Blair government's alignment with the US on Iraq. Circumstances suggested the latter: Bush agreed to publish the roadmap only after Blair had exerted intense pressure on him in mid-March. The choice of venue also seemed both curious and telling. The overwhelmingly Jewish audience did not receive the Bush team's statements as portents of radical change, but rather, understood them as the articulation of a 'vision' embedded in a sentimental appreciation of a truly special relationship between Israel and the US. Indeed, the speakers gave the Bush administration an escape route from deeper engagement in admonishing that the Palestinians would have to be 'a real partner for peace with Israel' and embrace 'transformed leaderships and institutions that end terror'. These conditions, consistent with the June 2002 speech in which Bush articulated his vision, leave plenty of room for the administration to keep any confrontation with Sharon well into the visionary future if it wishes to do so: as of April 2003, political decadence and support for terrorism as a strategy remained resilient among the Palestinians.

Indications are that the Bush administration will take little domestic political risk for progress on the Israeli–Palestinian front. A speech by Attorney-General John Ashcroft at the convention of a Christian Zionist group called 'Stand for Israel' on 2 April 2003, in which he stated that the United States and Israel were 'united by common virtues' and a common threat, seemed to underscore this point. Ashcroft's clear emphasis was hard counter-terrorism; conflict-resolution was barely, and then only vaguely, mentioned. The Palestinians are likely to reinforce US risk-aversion by hamstringing Abu Mazen as terrorist attacks continue to be launched. The irony is that Sharon may be both vulnerable to US leverage and in a position to get coalition backing for some degree of cooperation in roadmap implementation precisely on the pretext of American pressure. With Shinui in the government, the ultra-orthodox Shas Party out of it and Labour anxious to get back in, the possibility exists of a centre-right unity government that would not be dependent on small extreme parties or the ultra-orthodox. Such a government would be ripe for some form of compromise. While there is a chance that the utopians, girded by a salutary outcome in Iraq, will prevail and induce Bush to put pressure on Sharon, in the uncertain moments of early April 2003, it appeared at least as likely that realist caution would win the day and that another opportunity would be missed.

The Maghreb: Juggling International and Local Opinion

The Maghreb may be the western outpost of the Arab world, but popular feelings have run high over developments in the Middle East, particularly over the fate of the Palestinians and, more recently, the Iraqis. During the first Gulf War of 1991, Morocco hosted the region's largest pro-Iraqi demonstrations, replicated during the current conflict. On 31 March 2003, an estimated 150,000–200,000 people took to the streets in the capital Rabat, despite earlier official attempts to discourage public opposition to the war. Allowing populations periodically to let off steam has been part of a complex juggling act for the region's governments, all of whom have an interest in maintaining good relations with their European and American partners.

Even Libyan President Muammar Gaddafi has shown greater docility since 11 September 2001, with a view above all to reaching a settlement with the US over compensation to the victims of the 1988 bombing of Pan Am Flight 103 over Lockerbie, Scotland. Despite his opposition to war in Iraq – shared in muted terms by governments across the region – Gaddafi continued in March 2003 to negotiate with US officials to lift sanctions and agree terms for compensating the families of victims. Realpolitik rather than rhetoric appears to reflect Gaddafi's new mood, conditioned increasingly by his disenchantment with the Arab world's inability to resolve its own problems without outside interference.

Elsewhere in the Maghreb, governments have taken pains to be seen as good global citizens in the fight against terror since September 2001. Algerian President Abdelaziz Bouteflika gained access to the White House in November 2001 for the second time that year. In producing a list of 350 terrorist suspects, he also claimed vindication for Algeria's own 'single-handed' struggle against terrorism since 1992. Not all the named suspects were convincing to the State Department, and Algeria's requests for counter-terrorist equipment from the US had failed by early 2003 to produce the materiel expected. Nevertheless, against a rising tide of accusations that Algeria's senior generals have themselves been guilty of torture and human-rights abuses, Bouteflika's main success has been to move Algeria's still-volatile domestic situation out of the diplomatic limelight.

Less successful was President Zine El Abidine Ben Ali of Tunisia's initial attempt to cover up as an accident the suicide terrorist attack that killed 10 Germans and one French tourist in Djerba in April 2002. Only pressure from the French and German authorities succeeded in uncovering a trail that led to arrests of Tunisians related to a bomber in France and linkage of the incident to al-Qaeda. For both Morocco and Tunisia, protecting valuable tourist industries from 11 September fallout, and subsequently fears over war in Iraq, has been a key preoccupation. In June 2002, Moroccan police arrested three Saudis and their Moroccan wives on charges of conspiring to attack Western shipping in the Straits of Gibraltar. This pre-emptive act, resulting in the conviction and imprisonment of all the suspects in February 2003, has complemented higher levels of cooperation across the region with European and American police and intelligence agencies since 11 September. A disproportionate number of North African nationals (or Europeans of North African descent) have featured among those arrested in Europe and North America on al-Qaeda-related terrorist charges. Maghreb governments have been swift to stress that most were recruited abroad, but the appeal of Islamist violence has at least some roots in local frustrations that have driven large numbers of young North Africans to migrate, largely illegally, out of the region.

Political, economic and social discontent
The source of their impatience stems from the slow pace of economic and political change across the region and the diminishing standards of living, graphically outlined in the UN's first Arab Human Development Index, published in July 2002. The Maghreb has won International Monetary Fund and World Bank plaudits for macroeconomic reform, but it has lagged in translating this success into gains at the microeconomic level – whether in housing, public services or jobs.

With the exception of Libya, the region's trade and development plans hinge on the success of the Barcelona process set in train by the European Union in 1995. The main aim of this initiative has been to integrate the Mediterranean region into global markets through the establishment of a regional free-trade zone by 2010. This date now looks perilously close for economies that have long been shielded from open competition by tariff barriers and local protectionism.

Despite the promise of European investment, economic reforms vigorously pursued in Tunisia and Morocco have in practice led to higher levels of unemployment and under-employment, with growth rates unable to keep pace with the high numbers of graduates reaching the job market each year. As of 2003, Algeria had the world's third-highest level of unemployment, at 30%, mostly among the young. This is the volatile sector of the region's population: increasingly susceptible to approaches by grassroots Islamist groups, such as Al-Adl wal Ihsane in Morocco, which has campaigned for a more equitable distribution of wealth and political influence.

In Tunisia, the official response has been to tighten political controls – over the press and freedom of association – in inverse proportion to its accelerated economic liberalisation. This approach may become unsustainably counter-productive if free enterprise also continues to be stifled at the local level. In the interim, however, Ben Ali's constitutional coup of May 2002, by which – gaining a referendum vote of over 99% – he extended his term in office for 12 years and gained judicial immunity for life, provoked very little international comment. Morocco's political restrictions have eased considerably since the accession of King Mohammed VI in 1999, but the official political system has remained archaic and sluggish, with Islamist alternatives gaining 15% of the official vote in the September 2002 general elections.

The UN attempted this year to bring the Western Sahara dispute to an end. As in previous years, these efforts seemed half-hearted at best. Although a ceasefire agreement was signed in 1991, no referendum on the future status of the territory was held. Disagreement continued over who should be allowed to vote. Alternatives set out by the UN envoy, former US Secretary of State James Baker, have tilted in the direction of granting Morocco ultimate sovereignty while giving the local population wide-ranging autonomy. By February 2003, it became clear that these efforts would be rejected by the Polisario Front, which continues to insist upon a referendum as the basis for a definitive settlement. The conflict was further exacerbated this year by reports of the discovery of oil deposits off the Western Sahara coastline. Moroccan officials began awarding contracts for the drilling of these deposits, much to the chagrin of the Polisario Front and local Saharawis who were hoping to use the deposits to finance the creation of their own state. The Moroccans, however, found little oil.

The hydrocarbon-rich states of Algeria and Libya have done little to address youth unemployment, relying in the case of Libya on the palliative effects of oil rents, but local discontent remains high. Algeria, almost unnoticed, remained at war with itself after a decade of internal conflict, even though overall levels of violence have dropped since the late 1990s. Since 2001, a new form of instability has taken over from the Islamist-backed terrorism of the 1990s, in the shape of widespread public disorder in the Berber region of Kabylia. Sparked by the death of a young Kabyle at the hands of the local gendarmerie in April 2001, the region has experienced intermittent riots directed at local security forces, with little sign that protesters' demands for political and economic reforms will be met. Worse, a series of floods and droughts from late 2001 has provoked an increase in popular protests elsewhere in Algeria, directed against local authorities whose repair of collapsing local infrastructures has been slow.

A delicate balance

Some respite has been found across the region through flourishing informal economies that keep the worst effects of long-term joblessness at bay. In escaping both fiscal and legal nets, however, black-market activities are only a small step from criminality, which in Algeria has become increasingly enmeshed with the low-level violence. For governments that are themselves exposed to accusations of self-enrichment and corruption, tackling the black market head-on carries its own risks of instability. Not only are the governments' own interests often at stake, but their inability to create alternative sources of employment could provoke further unrest. There is also a rising tide of opinion – voiced loudly in the liberalised press of Algeria and Morocco – that cooperation with the US and Europe over terrorism has shielded governments from international criticism over crackdowns on political opposition groups at home. The prevailing official choice is therefore a finely balanced juggling act between local and international opinion, and attempts to distract the attention of both from stalling reform programmes and – in Algeria's case – unresolved violence. Maghreb governments' biggest fear is that a prolonged or messy outcome to war in Iraq could upset that balance.

Asia

Nuclear proliferation and terrorism problems made the headlines in Asia in 2002–03. Pyongyang's provocative revelation of a secret programme for producing highly enriched uranium for nuclear weapons led to the collapse of the Agreed Framework, reached in 1994, whereby North Korea's nuclear production and proliferation activities had putatively been controlled. While it was clear that the United States as well as regional powers (South Korea, Japan, China and Russia) considered any military pre-emption option unattractive, the US alone sought to diplomatically internationalise the problem through the UN Security Council to maximise pressure on North Korea. In December 2002, North Korea escalated tensions by breaking the seals on its five-megawatt plutonium-production reactor at Yongbyon and transporting spent fuel rods back into the reactor. There was no imminent threat, since the Yongbyon reactor would take almost a year to produce a significant quantity of plutonium, and larger 50- and 200-MW reactors were years from completion. As of April 2003, this crisis had essentially been put on hold pending the completion of the US-led war in Iraq, which Japan supported and China (unsurprisingly) opposed.

Increasing transnational terrorist activity in Southeast Asia was not so much a crisis as an intensifying standing security challenge. In October 2002, a car-bomb killed over 200 people – most of them Western tourists, a plurality of them Australian – at a nightclub on the island of Bali in Indonesia. Suspicions fell on Jemaah Islamiya (JI), a group with al-Qaeda links that seeks to establish a *sharia*-governed Islamic caliphate in Indonesia, Malaysia, Singapore and the southern Philippines. Pressured by the US, Australia and other external actors, Indonesian intelligence and law-enforcement authorities – theretofore politically compromised by influential Islamist elements in domestic politics – finally admitted that there was an indigenous Islamic terrorist threat and made a number of arrests. Any links between al-Qaeda and local JI operatives remained uncertain. But it became broadly clear that al-Qaeda leadership enjoyed relative freedom of action in the 'tribal areas' of Pakistan near the Afghan border and in some Pakistani cities, and that, now operationally hindered following *Operation Enduring Freedom*, was seeking soft targets of opportunity and increasingly utilising local affiliates and sympathisers over an expanded geographical range of 'fields of *jihad*'. The security situation in warlord-ridden Afghanistan itself presented itself as an ongoing problem. Hamid Karzai's government appeared dependent on a sustained US military presence, which continued to engage in counter-

Map Asia

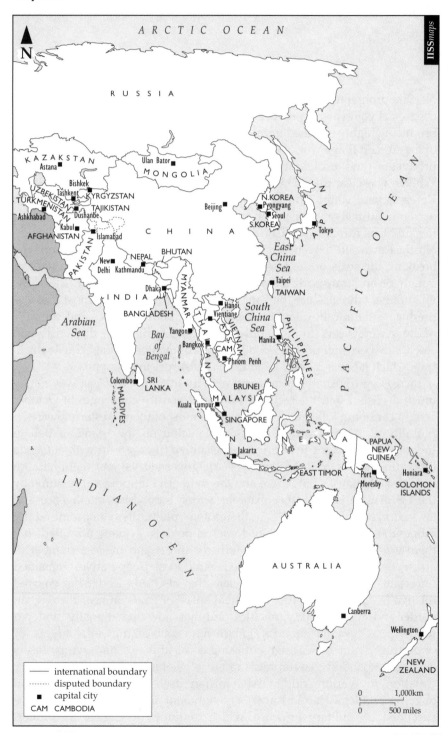

terrorist operations. Central authority stood to be strengthened in spring 2003, when large-scale international funding was scheduled to be released to facilitate the build-up of the Afghan army and the acceleration of infrastructure construction.

North Korea, Bali and Afghanistan obscured a number of positive developments and trends in Asia. A complex domestic leadership transition, and the consequent need to avoid crises that might shake economic confidence at home, induced China to adopt a less passive and rigid approach to foreign affairs. Warmer relations with the US reinforced this choice. Japan, while becoming more extroverted in its security policy in light of clear regional threats, struck a delicate balance between a reliance on its alliance with the United States and an appreciation for regional ties with countries such as China and South Korea. With the exception of Indonesia, Southeast Asian nations proved to be robust counter-terrorism partners. The Pakistani government, though hampered by domestic Islamist sensitivities and Islamist sympathies within the security apparatus, was also helpful. With American assistance Pakistani authorities arrested two key al-Qaeda leaders – recruiter Abu Zubeida and al-Qaeda third-in-command Khalid Shaikh Mohammed – and turned them over to the US.

The military confrontation between India and Pakistan stemming from the 13 December 2001 attack by Pakistan-based terrorists on the Indian parliament in New Delhi slowly defused, while elections in Kashmir brightened prospects for conflict-resolution in that potential nuclear flashpoint and source of Islamic terrorist recruitment. The first International Institute for Strategic Studies (IISS) Asia Security Conference on 31 May–2 June 2002 – to be an annual event at the request of the participants – provided a new forum for bilateral defence discussions, as US Deputy Secretary of Defense Paul Wolfowitz and Indian Defence Minister George Fernandes met there to positive effect at a crucial moment in the India–Pakistan crisis. The cease-fires in Sri Lanka largely held, and the process of political reconciliation moved forward, albeit haltingly. Even Nepal, where the Maoist insurgency and government resistance became increasingly lethal in 2001 and 2002, witnessed a cease fire in January 2003.

Though Asia's security challenges are abundant, the US' near-term preoccupations there are largely limited to counter-terrorism, counter-proliferation and crisis-management. Projects requiring deeper engagement, such as conflict-resolution in Kashmir, collective security, while certainly on the US' longer-term agenda, have been sidelined in deference to Iraq and North Korea. At the same time, major Asian US partners such as Japan and India, and to a lesser degree Indonesia, have enjoyed generally improved relations with the US, while newly elected South Korean President Roh Moo Hyun – outgoing President Kim Dae Jung's handpicked successor and a surprise victor in the December 2002 election – has moderated his sometimes anti-American views. Meanwhile, China has adopted a relatively

Asia

quiet regional foreign-policy stance, including Taiwan matters, and for the time being appears oriented towards the status quo. Thus, 2003–04 may shape up as a year in which Asian powers seek to better harmonise their policies with those of the US – first on North Korea and subsequently in other areas – in anticipation of deeper US engagement once it has weathered emergent crises elsewhere.

The Koreas: Dangerous Defiance

As of April 2003, six months after North Korea startled everyone by admitting the truth of the US accusation that it was pursuing a continuing secret nuclear programme in spite of the 1994 agreement that it would desist, there was still no consensus on Pyongyang's motivation. North Korea's admission could have been a rash act by the erratic autocratic ruler of a dangerous 'rogue' nation, or a cool-headed tactical move by the shrewd leader of a desperate nation exploiting his opponent's preoccupation with a build-up to war a hemisphere away to squeeze more economic aid from a worried world. There was no doubt, however, that North Korea's gambit had rudely, and comprehensively, grabbed the attention of its neighbours, and more importantly, from its viewpoint, the United States.

The administration of US President George W. Bush was caught off-guard. Although its suspicions concerning the true state of affairs had been sharpened by newly acquired evidence, Washington hardly expected a blatant admission of guilt. With the possibility of quiet behind-the-scenes negotiations conclusively removed, and with its attention and a large portion of its military might devoted to Iraq, the US was left with few palatable options. Refusing to recognise the gathering storm as a 'crisis', ruling out the use of military force, insisting that diplomacy could solve the dilemma while declining to negotiate with North Korea, and trying to assemble a coterie of concerned nations that did not agree with the basic US position did not add up to an effective policy.

China and Russia, which the US tried to convince to apply pressure to North Korea, both counselled that the US negotiate with Pyongyang and offer security reassurances and increased economic aid in exchange for verifiable confirmation that North Korea would abandon its nuclear-weapons pretensions. Equally disappointing to the US was the position taken by South Korea's newly elected president, Roh Moo Hyun, the candidate of the incumbent Millennium Democracy Party (MDC) who had surged from behind on a tide of anti-Americanism to win a narrow victory over Washington's preferred candidate, Lee Hoi Chang. He insisted that the proper route to take was a continuation, if not an augmentation, of outgoing South Korean President Kim Dae Jung's 'sunshine policy' towards the North, which Roh renamed the 'peace and prosperity policy'. North Korea's intransigent drive toward the acquisition of a nuclear-weapons capability, and the lack of a concerted policy by the US and other nations, had created the most serious security crisis in Asia since 1994.

The spectre of proliferation

North Korea had developed the fundamentals of a nuclear-weapons programme before finally signing a 'full scope safeguards agreement' with the International Atomic Energy Agency (IAEA) in March 1992. It had a functioning plutonium production facility at Yongbyon, a well-advanced programme for separating plutonium from nuclear waste and the technical ability to turn that plutonium into weapons. The administration of US President Bill Clinton considered the situation serious enough to develop plans for a military attack on North Korea and to begin shifting forces to the area to ensure its success. The crisis was averted only at the last moment when negotiations between the US and North Korea resulted in the Agreed Framework in October 1994. In brief, the Agreed Framework required North Korea to freeze and eventually dismantle its nuclear programme, shut its Yongbyon nuclear plant and reprocessing facility, put the fuel rods from this plant under observable control and allow verification through IAEA surveillance that it was doing what it promised. In return, the US, South Korea and Japan agreed to provide two light-water nuclear reactors (which are less amenable to the creation of weapons-grade plutonium), and to supply 500,000 tonnes of heavy fuel oil per year until the reactors were functioning and developing electricity.

The Agreed Framework worked reasonably well, up to a point. North Korea did halt work at the Yongbyon plant in October 1994, but the Central Intelligence Agency (CIA) estimates that, before then, it had accumulated sufficient plutonium to make one or two bombs. The US and its allies prudently assumed that it had done so. Nevertheless, they supplied the promised fuel oil and slowly began the work necessary to construct the two light-water nuclear reactors. Both sides, however, had complaints about the implementation of the Agreed Framework. Work on the foundations for the replacement nuclear plants had fallen far behind schedule. North Korea, of course, blamed the US for this, and the US blamed North Korean obstructionism. North Korea, meanwhile, dragged its feet on preparing for the necessary inspections by the IAEA to ensure that it was harbouring no additional plutonium. These inspections could take at least three years and were required before reactor components could be delivered. In September

1999, North Korea agreed to a moratorium on additional long-range missile tests in exchange for an end to US economic sanctions. By the end of the Clinton administration, the two sides came close to completing a comprehensive agreement to limit North Korea's indigenous missile programme and end missile-related exports.

When the Bush administration came to office in January 2001, it cancelled talks that the previous administration had been holding with Pyongyang, citing the need for an overall review of US Asian policy. It completed that review in June 2001, concluding that North Korea needed to improve implementation of its side of the Agreed Framework, adopt verifiable constraints on its missile programmes and a ban on missile exports, and assume a less threatening conventional military posture, in exchange for rather vague benefits. Offering less for more, Washington proposed to send Assistant Secretary of State for East Asia and the Pacific James Kelly to Pyongyang for face-to-face talks. The North Koreans turned this offer down flat, partly out of pique at the unusually contemptuous terms that had emanated from Washington since the new administration had arrived (President Bush had characterised North Korean Leader Kim Jong Il as a 'pygmy' whom he 'loathed') and partially because they regarded the preconditions Washington had laid down for the talks as unacceptable. Bush also labelled North Korea part of the 'axis of evil' in his January 2002 State of the Union address. By April 2002, however, Pyongyang made an overture of its own and talks were scheduled for July. In late June, however, a naval battle between South Korean ships and a North Korean vessel that had intruded into South Korean waters left four South Korean sailors dead and 19 wounded. The US cancelled the July 2002 talks, noting that the atmosphere was not propitious. More seriously, beginning in the late 1990s, suspicions arose that Pyongyang was working on a new clandestine nuclear programme. In mid-2002, US intelligence agencies reportedly acquired solid evidence that North Korea had obtained large quantities of materials needed for the construction of a gas centrifuge facility from Pakistan between 1997 and 1998 in exchange for *No-dong* missiles. According to a CIA report, North Korea was constructing such a facility, capable of producing enough weapons-grade uranium for two bombs a year, which would be in operation within a couple of years. It was clear that the Agreed Framework had, at best, merely postponed the crisis.

Preoccupied by Iraq, Washington initially deferred acting on the damning intelligence. At the 17 September 2002 Japanese-North Korean summit, however, Kim Jong Il reversed another record of rigid denials by admitting to Japanese Prime Minister Junichiro Koizumi that, 25–30 years earlier, North Korea had abducted young Japanese citizens to be used as teachers for North Korean spies. Most of these Japanese had since died, but five were still alive and Kim was now willing to allow them to visit Japan. For a brief period, this acknowledgement looked as though it would provide an impetus for Japanese-North Korean talks on normalisation of relations and greater aid from Japan for the suffering North Korean economy. The prospect of such an ill-founded normalisation compelled Washington to confront Pyongyang. When Kelly finally sat down with North Korean Vice-Foreign Minister Kang Sok Ju in October 2002, he immediately presented the US accusation that North Korea was making a clandestine effort to build nuclear weapons, involving uranium enrichment. Reportedly, Kang dismissed the US position at the first meeting, but the next day astonished the US delegation by admitting that it was true. In public, however, the North Korean regime never made the same admission; on the contrary, it maintained that the US had invented both the evidence and its admission. In any case, Japanese-North Korean relations cooled. Further, as of April 2003, North Korea continued to insist that it was 'entitled' to acquire a nuclear-weapons capability, particularly since it considered itself threatened by a 'bloodthirsty imperialist' United States, which was armed to the teeth with nuclear weapons and which maintained a large military force on its border.

Although North Korea's insular leaders clearly tend towards alarmism, it was not wholly surprising that they might feel threatened at this time. While the Clinton administration did not believe that the communist regime in North Korea was a fully trustworthy interlocutor, the administration was willing to negotiate concerning its nuclear-weapons threat and to go along with Kim Dae Jung's 'sunshine policy'. Before 2001, the US was committed to an effort to bring North Korea into the existing international system in hopes that Pyongyang's leaders would recognise that adherence to accepted rules of behaviour would repay them handsomely. Despite Washington's efforts, however, Pyongyang apparently decided that it needed to maintain a secret nuclear hedge and decided to begin a secret enrichment programme in violation of the Agreed Framework. Unlike the Clinton administration, the Bush team felt that this 'rogue' regime should not be rewarded in any way. It continued to supply food for starving North Koreans as a humanitarian gesture, and agreed to honour the previous administration's commitment to supply fuel oil until the new nuclear power plants could come into production. But, in addition to including North Korea in the 'axis of evil', the Bush administration made its distaste for the regime known in other ways. Under its new national security doctrine, set forth in September 2002, the US asserted that it could pre-emptively attack a would-be proliferator of weapons of mass destruction. The preparations that were underway to topple Saddam Hussein may have convinced the hermetic North Korean leadership that their country was next on the US target list. Thus, Pyongyang could have concluded that building a serious nuclear-weapons capability was a necessary strategic-defensive manoeuvre, although efforts to create a new avenue to nuclear-weapons proliferation had begun before Bush took office.

Asia

From bad to worse

In uncharacteristically acknowledging in October 2002 that the US evidence was accurate, it is conceivable that Kim Jong Il decided that, since the Americans had all the proof, there was little use in denying it. But it is more likely that, as with his other 'confession diplomacy' gambit involving the Japanese abductees, his aim was co-optation rather than capitulation. Kim Jong Il probably believed that admitting the existence of the clandestine programme was the best way open to him to engage a United States consumed by Iraq in negotiations and to gain more aid, as the US would be unwilling to face two difficult foreign crises simultaneously. Washington, for its part, had few options with which to force Pyongyang to forego its ambitions. Any attack on the North, whether in the form of a quick surgical strike against nuclear facilities or an invasion across the border, would result in many thousands of casualties. While most of the language employed by the North in its dialogue with other countries is bombast with little substance, its continual threat to create 'a sea of fire' in Seoul must be taken more seriously. It has always maintained between 8,000 and 10,000 artillery pieces, rocket launchers and long-range guns within range of Seoul, and estimates are that these weapons could unleash up to 300,000 shells an hour onto Seoul and other population centres in the South. As a last resort, it must be assumed that North Korea would use whatever nuclear weapons it might now have to increase the damage. Its huge army has been weakened by years of economic deprivation, but it is still a formidable force and most of it is on alert close to the armistice line that has separated the two Koreas since 1953. No one doubts that, in the end, the US and South Korea would prevail in a shooting war. Costs, though, would be very high. Like the Clinton administration, Bush advisors concluded that some form of peaceful resolution was the best possible outcome. But unlike Clinton, Bush was unwilling to negotiate with North Korea. Instead the US promised increased economic and political measure to 'improve the lives of North Koreans,' but only on condition that Pyongyang first 'eliminate its nuclear weapons program in a verifiable manner'.

On 26 October 2002, the North responded by denying that it was engaged in developing a new uranium enrichment programme, asserting that all of its nuclear efforts were devoted to the production of electricity, necessary because the US had failed to complete the reactors it had promised under the Agreed Framework. Nevertheless, it maintained that it was prepared to settle 'the nuclear issue' as soon as the US gave it legally binding assurances of US non-aggression, including the use, or threat to use, nuclear weapons. With neither side willing to budge, the situation deteriorated in an ascending spiral of actions that turned an impasse into a crisis. The US first attempted to put diplomatic pressure on North Korea by enlisting those nations that have been keeping the tiny North Korean economy afloat: China, Japan, South Korea and Russia. It wanted them to make their displeasure with Pyongyang's behaviour known and to threaten to reduce or withdraw their aid. Much to its chagrin, Washington found that it had less than full support from those nations. China privately decried the North's action while noting that its own influence was limited. Beijing's public position was to call for a peaceful resolution of the dispute; it believed that direct negotiations between Washington and Pyongyang were the best way to handle the crisis. Japan did inform North Korea that bilateral normalisation was contingent on resolution of the nuclear issue, but was wary of putting pressure on North Korea for fear of jeopardising the release of the family members of the Japanese abductees. Kim Dae Jung noted that pressure and isolation had never been used successfully against communist countries and he argued that his engagement policy could still work. Russia, which was unwilling to curb its arms sales to North Korea, argued that efforts to coerce the North into concessions would only lead to a new escalation of tension.

This prediction was soon borne out. In mid-November 2002, the US decided to halt the oil shipments that were part of the Agreed Framework. It maintained that North Korea's continued development of an enrichment programme had abrogated the Agreed Framework, and that the US and its allies therefore were no longer obliged to abide by its terms. In deference to South Korea and Japan, the US announced that it would allow the November shipment of 42,500 tonnes of oil. On 13 December, North Korea announced that it was immediately reactivating the Yongbyon reactor in order to make up for the suspension of fuel-oil deliveries. Pyongyang asked the IAEA to remove its seals and monitoring cameras. A week later the Director General of the IAEA, Dr Mohamed ElBaradei, accused North Korea of 'nuclear brinkmanship' after North Korean technicians broke open the sealed doors of the reactor and moved 1,000 fuel rods back into the reactor. North Korea insisted that it needed the reactor for nuclear fuel; ElBaradei noted that the five-megawatt (MW) reactor was a research reactor, irrelevant to the North's ability to produce electricity. While discussing North Korea's intransigence on this question, US Secretary of Defense Donald Rumsfeld pointedly noted that the US was fully capable of fighting and winning two regional wars at the same time. On 27 December, North Korea announced that it was expelling all international nuclear inspectors. It noted that this was in reaction to the US suspension of construction of the two light-water reactors under the Agreed Framework, and to the designation of North Korea as a member of the 'axis of evil' and a 'target for a nuclear pre-emptive strike'. On 10 January 2003, Pyongyang upped the ante by formally withdrawing from the 1970 Non-Proliferation Treaty (NPT). In mid-January 2003, satellite intelligence showed trucks that could have been moving the spent fuel rods previously stored and secured by the IAEA. There is enough plutonium in these rods to make an estimated five or six more nuclear weapons.

In practical terms, the threat presented was not immediate, as the Yongbyon reactor would require nearly a year of operation to produce a significant quantity of plutonium and the larger 50- and 200-MW reactors were years from completion. Yet Washington seemed at a loss for an effective response. It hoped that the IAEA report of the North's non-compliance to the UN Security Council in early February would induce other nations to join the US in what it termed 'tailored containment', a policy of economic pressure, threats to seize shipments of North Korean missiles to other countries and encouragement to North Korea's neighbours and suppliers to publicly criticise the North's policies. It is doubtful that such measures would be very effective. The US, South Korea and Japan had already suspended oil deliveries. Japan also suspended its food shipments, and the US curtailed its food contribution. There are not many other actions that would seriously affect North Korea's already anaemic economy. The US had also suffered an embarrassment in December 2002 when Spain, whose ships were patrolling the Arabian Sea, stopped a ship that had originated from North Korea, discovered missiles hidden under other cargo and asked what it should do to prevent them from landing. At this point Yemen announced that it had bought the missiles from North Korea. Since the sale and purchase were legal, and the US did not want to annoy Yemen, a putative supporter of its counter-terrorism and Iraq policies, Washington decided to allow the vessel and its cargo to continue to port. With little else working, US Secretary of State Colin Powell set out on a four-day visit to Northeast Asia on 22 February, a trip that would culminate in his attendance at the inauguration of Roh Moo Hyun on 25 February, in an effort to swing China, Japan and South Korea behind the US diplomatic position.

Changes in South Korea

Roh Moo Hyun, candidate of the ruling MDC, won a surprising, if close, victory over Lee Hoi Chang, candidate of the opposition Grand National Party in the 19 December presidential election. Roh had to overcome a number of obstacles on his way to elective office. He is considered to be much further to the left of the political spectrum than was Kim Dae Jung and, by the standards of a country that reveres age, at 56 he is a young political leader. Throughout much of the year's campaign, he ran a dismal third in the race for president; until the last days, Lee unfailingly led the pack. Part of Roh's problem was that he was a relatively untried, and unusual, candidate. A civil-rights lawyer, who had studied law as an apprentice and not at university, he had only served a single term in the legislature. His other major difficulty was that he represented a party that had consistently lost favour with the public. Kim's poll numbers had fallen below 18% in mid-summer 2002. Whatever lustre Roh might have had was tarnished by association. Kim had come to office promising to run a squeaky-clean administration that would uproot corruption. During 2002, however, both of his sons were jailed on corruption charges. His party also came under attack for using large amounts of cash to acquire nominations. Towards the end of the year, the opposition charged that, in 2000, the administration had encouraged the payment of up to $400 million to North Korea to ensure that Kim Jong Il would take part in a summit meeting with Kim Dae Jung. Furthermore, while Kim was much praised for his handling of the economic crisis that he faced when he came to office, the economy stuttered in 2001 and stalled in 2002. Finally, North Korea's failure to make a serious substantive effort to improve inter-Korean relations had soured the people on his 'sunshine policy'.

Kim's weakness was underlined in mid-summer 2002, when he made a large number of changes in his cabinet in hopes of recovering some political standing. As part of his comprehensive juggling act, Kim nominated Chang Sang to be the first female prime minister. Kim was probably seeking to gain the support of women and younger voters, but the choice did not pay political dividends. Chang, who is president of Ehwa University and had never played any role in politics, came under heavy attack from conservatives for what they claimed were shady real-estate dealings, her son's becoming an American citizen and allegedly falsifying her academic credentials. The National Assembly, which is dominated by the Grand National Party, and will continue to be so until at least 2004 when general elections are to be held, rejected her nomination on 31 July and went on to refuse another of Kim's choices for prime minister. It was not until early October that a new prime minister, Kim Suk Soo, a former Supreme Court judge, was accepted by Parliament. Parliament is certain to continue to thwart President Roh in the same way that it has his predecessor.

While Kim's efforts to generate support for Roh met with little success, two other developments made all the difference. In early September 2002, Chung Mong Joon, the multimillionaire heir to the Hyundai conglomerate, decided to join the race for president. Chung heads the South Korean Football Association and was widely admired for his efforts to make South Korea the co-host, with Japan, of the 2002 World Cup. Even more important was Korea's extraordinary success in the tournament, when it became the first Asian nation to get to the semi-finals. Those who suggested that he was then so popular he could run for president may have been half-joking, but Chung, a four-term assemblyman, seemed to take the suggestion seriously. It soon became clear, however, that with both Chung and Roh in the race the conservative candidate, Lee Hoi Chang, would be assured of a shoo-in victory. Chung tried first to convince Roh that he should stand aside and allow him to run as a 'unity' candidate. When that failed, the two men reached an unusual political agreement. Whichever of the two garnered the least support in the polls – to be taken immediately

Asia

after a planned three-way television debate on 22 November – would step aside and support the other. In the event, Chung had the lowest rating, and true to his word he withdrew from the contest, throwing his support behind Roh.

The second significant factor in the dynamics of the presidential race was a surge of anti-Americanism. This was fuelled in part by an unfortunate accident in June 2002, when an American armoured personnel carrier accidentally crushed two teenage Korean girls who were on their way to a birthday party. When an American military court acquitted the soldiers in late November, South Korean anger boiled over. In addition to demonstrations in major cities, more than 50 protestors carrying signs that demanded the withdrawal of US troops from South Korea managed to break into Camp Red Cloud, the large US base several miles north of Seoul. South Korean police removed them after about 30 minutes, but not before they had made a loud and significant point that represented the views of growing numbers of South Koreans. Subsequently, American soldiers were physically attacked on the street and signs began to appear in the windows of restaurants and shops saying that Americans were not welcome.

The wave of anti-American sentiment coincided with a new sense of self-confidence in South Korea, a result both of its success in the World Cup and a belief that, of all the East Asian nations that had suffered from the economic crisis of 1996, South Korea had done best in managing to overcome the difficulties. This particularly affected younger voters, who had no personal memory of the US role in freeing Korea from Japanese rule and then driving North Korean troops back after they poured over the border in 1950. Roh Moo Hyun was the clear beneficiary. Although the US had, of course, been careful not to back any candidate publicly, it was no secret that Lee Hoi Chang was Washington's choice. Lee had condemned the anti-US demonstrations; Roh had not, although he recommended demonstrators tone down their demands until he had an opportunity to negotiate new arrangements with the US. Lee backed the US position on North Korea, while Roh insisted that, despite North Korea's nuclear ambitions, the best way forward was to continue, and perhaps strengthen, Kim Dae Jung's engagement policy. By choosing Roh and his policies, South Korean voters were asserting a belief that the country had matured politically and economically to the point that it should move from the subordinate position vis-à-vis the US that it has assumed since 1953 to what Roh has called a more 'balanced' relationship. Roh himself has shown signs of moderating his views. While he once publicly advocated the expulsion of US troops, he has since said that he was wrong. Some American officials appear to regard Roh as something of a Pollyanna with respect to North Korea, but there also seems to be a minority view that – having little experience in foreign policy – he is open to revising some of his positions.

Struggling to find a policy

Powell's trip to Asia in February 2003 was apparently a late decision, suggesting that the Bush administration had realised that it indeed had a crisis on its hands, as opposed to the euphemistic 'serious situation' to which it had referred in previous months. Powell had a number of goals in mind. While the administration was clearly focussing most of its attention on the Persian Gulf, he hoped: to reflect the seriousness with which Washington was viewing developments in North Korea; to convince China and other countries to support a US call for a 'multilateral forum', during which the attending nations (including the European Union [EU] nations as well as Russia) could all pressure North Korea to back away from its nuclear threats, as the best way to handle the problem; to demonstrate to Roh that the US wanted to re-knit the unravelling US–South Korea relationship; and to solidify Japanese support for the US position.

Although the US has said that it would be willing to meet with North Korea in a side venue as part of the multilateral forum, and has also said that it would be prepared to give North Korea considerable economic aid were it to 'step back' from its nuclear programme, the North has declined to meet on a multilateral basis. It insists on face-to-face negotiations with the United States, without any other country present, and demands a non-aggression pact, among other things. Senior American policymakers, including Bush on many occasions, have asserted that the US has no intention of attacking North Korea and that they wish to deal with the impasse diplomatically. But Bush has not been willing to hold direct talks with Pyongyang, a procedure that he has characterised as giving in to 'blackmail'. Yet most of the leaders Powell met on his trip felt that the forum idea was a non-starter and argued that direct US–North Korea negotiations were the only viable solution.

The concerted opposition of Asian and other nations to Washington's preferred strategy has had the perverse effect of increasing tensions in the region at a time when the US would like to concentrate on Iraq. It has very few palatable options left. North Korea has continued to insist that it does not want to develop nuclear weapons, but that it is 'entitled' to, and may have to, because the US, in its unwillingness to discuss a non-aggression pact, has shown that it could attack North Korea after it deals with Iraq. Pyongyang clearly believes that the best way to change the status quo on the peninsula, as well as to gain substantial new economic and food aid, is to increase the pressure. Just before Powell set out on his February trip, a North Korean military aircraft flew a sortie over territory South Korea considers to be under its jurisdiction. On the day Powell arrived in Seoul for the presidential inauguration, North Korea tested a shore-to-ship cruise missile. South Korean jets easily chased the plane away, and the missile splashed down harmlessly in the Sea of Japan. On 10 March, Pyongyang fired another anti-ship missile into the Sea of Japan, and subsequently alerted countries whose ships use that area that it intended to test more missiles in the coming weeks. These actions could not be considered serious, but they were obviously meant as symbolic gestures. The same goes for the shadowing by four North Korean fighters of a US surveillance plane in international airspace and a second anti-ship missile test in early March. As a precaution, the US deployed 12 B-1 and 12 B-52 bombers to Guam.

On 22 March, North Korea suspended the economic talks that were to have taken place with South Korea over the weekend. These discussions were to have covered completion of the road and rail links that the two countries had been restoring and to arrange for shipping and fishing in each other's waters. North Korea claimed that South Korea's participation in military exercises with the US and its heightened military alert made the talks impossible. On 25 March, Pyongyang stated that it would no longer send liaison officers to conduct routine border consultations with the US-led UN group that handles the armistice that ended the Korean War. More serious was a 27 February report that satellite intelligence showed that North Korea had restarted the nuclear plant at Yongbyon. There was also evidence that North Korea was preparing to put its reprocessing facility at Yongbyon back into operation – a move that would allow the country to produce several more nuclear weapons within a few months. Indeed, it seemed likely that Pyongyang would take advantage of the war in Iraq to begin reprocessing operations.

North Korea's march to the precipice left the United States in a quandary. Washington is unlikely to draw 'red lines' against reprocessing, since doing so probably would not win the support of Seoul or Tokyo and the US does not want to face the choice of backing down should the lines be crossed, or attacking militarily. Backing down would mean an embarrassing loss of credibility, and the use of military force is widely considered too risky. Establishing the production of nuclear weapons as a threshold would be largely meaningless, given the difficulty of verification. The multilateral forum idea has gathered little support. The effort to bring pressure to bear on North Korea through the IAEA complaint to the UN Security Council has had little effect. The UN has only two clear punitive diplomatic options. It can impose sanctions – a measure that would be ineffective without the participation of China, South Korea, Russia and other countries. Not only have these countries argued against sanctions, they assert that further engagement with, and assistance to, North Korea is the proper policy to follow. Alternatively, it could declare North Korea's possession of weapons of mass destruction materials illegal. Other measures to isolate North Korea can hardly work against a country that is already isolated.

What seems to be left is the least unpalatable of all the unpalatable options. Pyongyang will want to get as much as possible for as little as possible. The US may need to swallow its pride and find some creative way to talk directly to North Korea without appearing to be 'negotiating'. With such an approach, Washington would hope to create a deal that would mean the resumption of oil shipments and work on the light-water reactors, and greatly increased economic aid, in exchange for North Korean steps towards giving up its nuclear programme and allowing intrusive inspections as assurance that it will not again pursue a nuclear weapons option. In principle, both countries would gain by such an agreement, but negotiations are likely to be difficult and protracted. The Bush administration will demand a tougher pact than the Agreed Framework, but Pyongyang is almost certain to resist more intrusive inspections and insist on retaining a nuclear hedge for the time being. North Korea appears to see its nuclear-weapons capability as both a bargaining chip and as an essential tool of regime survival. Thus, it has been willing to accept limits on its nuclear weapons but not to give them up completely. Whether it would forsake them if the price were right is unknown. In any case, multilateral talks are most likely to yield an effective formula for security guarantees and economic assistance. But bona fide US–North Korea bilateral talks under the umbrella of multilateral discussions also appear necessary. As of April 2003, Washington would not agree to such talks. If negotiations stall or collapse, Washington may reinvigorate efforts to isolate and punish Pyongyang, hoping to undercut the survival of the regime. The result could be a dangerously unpredictable state with a good-sized nuclear arsenal that might be prepared to sell plutonium and scientific know-how to non-state terrorist actors or a 'rogue' state.

Asia

The Delicate Strategic Balance in South Asia

India and Pakistan narrowly escaped war in 2002, but internal developments in both countries could lead to further and repeated crises in the region. The year 2002 began with the two rivals poised for conflict. Accusing Pakistan of abetting terrorism that culminated in the attack on the Indian parliament on 13 December 2001, India mounted its biggest military mobilisation since the 1971 war. The crisis escalated during the next five months. Another terrorist attack in Kashmir on 14 May 2002 on Indian soldiers and their families, killing 31, almost precipitated war in May and June. With nuclear threats being exchanged and missile tests taking place, several Western governments and Japan asked their citizens to depart both countries. These diplomatic efforts and travel advisories prompted India to step back from its war footing, especially since New Delhi's threats had succeeded in inducing Washington and London to pressure Islamabad to cut off military assistance to the Kashmiri uprising. The crisis dissipated, although the Indian military mobilisation continued for several months, partly to ensure a peaceful election in the troubled state of Jammu and Kashmir in September–October 2002.

The crisis demonstrated that military deterrence – albeit fragile – was viable in the region. New Delhi concluded that the risks and the potential costs of a general conflict and possible nuclear exchange trumped any desire to resolve the Kashmir dispute by force. For its part, the Pakistani military regime temporarily curtailed the infiltration of militants into India. At the peak of the crisis, on new year's day 2002, India and Pakistan exchanged lists of nuclear facilities, an annual ritual that is part of a 1988 agreement to refrain from attacking each other's nuclear installations. They repeated the ritual at the start of 2003, though the animosity between the two countries, and especially their regimes, has remained. New Delhi refuses to engage in any bilateral talks with Islamabad, and another high-profile terrorist attack in India could usher in another crisis.

In both states, domestic problems gave a new edge to strategic and foreign policy. In February 2002, a Muslim mob in the town of Godhra, Gujarat, reportedly torched a train carriage of Hindu fundamentalists, killing 59 persons. Hindu mobs took revenge over the next three months, resulting in the deaths of between 1,000 and 5,000 Muslims. Tens of thousands of Muslims were made homeless, and there were rumours of rape and torture. It appeared that the state government, which controls the police, allowed the carnage to occur. The violence called into question India's secularism and the safety of the country's 140 million Muslims. The violence did not spread beyond Gujarat, however, and in September– October 2002 India held the first successful elections in Kashmir in two decades.

In Pakistan, the military regime re-engineered the constitution and Pakistan's enfeebled political institutions, according itself a veto over the political process for the indefinite future. The regime held controlled elections that installed a pliable prime minister and cabinet, further deferring democratisation in Pakistan. Although the regime's defenders argue that real democracy might bring radical Islamists to power, the lack of democracy in Pakistan could lead to a coalescence of pro-democratisation activism and religious fundamentalism, creating force for a more powerful explosion.

Domestic developments in each country have been troubling, and carry implications for South Asia's peace and stability. Both insurgent violence in Nepal, which grew significantly in 2002, and the incipient peace process in Sri Lanka called for greater attention from India, the ranking regional power. If tensions with Pakistan persist at the level reached in 2002, India will be unable to turn its attention to such other matters. The more immediate concern is crisis stability, to which the mobilisation and escalation strategies of the two states are central.

India's pre-11 September ascendancy

Before the 11 September attacks in New York and Washington, India was the region's rising power while Pakistan was on the verge of economic and political collapse. Islamabad's economy was in shambles, its society increasingly divided along ideological and religious lines. Its core civilian institutions had been debilitated since the army seized power in October 1999. The systematic assassination of Shia physicians by sectarian Sunni extremists had led to an exodus of many talented professionals, and even the army could not stem the increase in domestic terrorism. Pakistan's support for the Taliban regime in Afghanistan alienated the United States, China and Iran, and a wide range of American sanctions remained in place.

By comparison, India had doubled its GDP during the 1990s. Its software industry and the growing Indian community in the US were increasingly influential. Then US President Bill Clinton's visit to the region in 2000 accelerated the transformation of the US–India relationship. He spent five days touring India and five gloomy hours in the Islamabad airport lecturing the army chief, General Pervez Musharraf, and by extension, the people of Pakistan on the need to reject fundamentalism and move towards democracy. President George W. Bush built on the legacy of the Clinton visit by sending a close foreign-policy advisor, Robert Blackwill, to New Delhi as ambassador, charging him with consolidating the bilateral relationship. Many in Republican circles held dear the notion that India might one day be a strategic counter-weight to China, and they adopted the Indian locution that India was a 'natural' ally of the US in Asia.

The Kargil War in 1999 cast a pall over India–Pakistan relations. Not only did Pakistan lose the conflict, but the defeat also set in motion the military coup that brought Musharraf to power. The presence of a regime in Pakistan led by the 'father of Kargil' set back the possibility of any rapprochement between the rivals, and the subsequent summit between Musharraf and Indian Prime Minister Atal Behari Vajpayee was easily derailed by Indian hawks. Pakistan lost internationally as well. For the first time in 50 years, the US openly and unequivocally sided with India against Pakistan. After Kargil, both countries expanded their nuclear and missile capabilities. Pakistan tested intermediate-range missiles that put all of India within range of its nuclear weapons, and India continued developing long-range missile systems intended to threaten Beijing.

The subcontinent's war on terror

The 11 September 2001 terrorist attacks changed the subcontinent's strategic calculus. As the primary backer of the Taliban in Afghanistan, Pakistan faced a choice between abandoning the Islamic fundamentalist regime and facing the wrath of the US. Musharraf opted for the former, denouncing the Taliban and Osama bin Laden, and allowing US military forces to use Pakistani bases and airspace in their operations in Afghanistan. As US forces deployed to the region and the second Afghan war proceeded, Pakistan received almost a billion dollars in aid and a much-needed reprieve from action by its international creditors. An infusion of capital saved the regime from financial collapse. Musharraf thought that the revived relationship with Washington might also lead the latter to pressure India on Kashmir. Across the border, New Delhi was dismayed by the revival of US–Pakistan ties, which hearkened back to the 1980s and the Cold War. From New Delhi's point of view, Pakistan was part of the problem. Islamabad's support for the Kashmir insurgency emanated from the same system and beliefs that had installed the Taliban in Afghanistan and facilitated the rise of al-Qaeda. The radical fighters in Afghanistan, Chechnya, Kashmir and elsewhere, reasoned India, trained and fought together; for the US to target only one part of the network was to allow the underlying system to survive. The exigencies of the war in Afghanistan, however, compelled a new American pragmatism, balancing US bilateral relations with India and Pakistan. As in the past, Washington sought to de-link its relations with the two countries, calling them both 'close allies' in the war on terror.

US policy changed once again after the terrorist attack on the Indian parliament on 13 December 2001. Although no members of the parliament or the cabinet were seriously injured, the attack stunned the nation. Investigations revealed a detailed plan to take the parliament hostage. India blamed the attack on the Lashkar-e-Taiba (LeT) and the Jaish-e-Mohammed (JeM), two Pakistan-based fundamentalist organisations. Indeed, New Delhi had long held that the Kashmiri insurgency had slipped out of indigenous hands and into those of groups such as the LeT, which comprised the most radical elements from Pakistan, and included veterans of other Islamic *jihads*. Indian Defence Minister George Fernandes argued that the Pakistani government bore ultimate responsibility for the actions of groups like the LeT. The day after the attack, India sent Pakistan a formal diplomatic demand to close down the LeT. India then proceeded to withdraw its high commissioner to Pakistan and reduce the size of its mission. The only other time New Delhi had taken such a step was during the 1971 war. India also banned overflights of Pakistan's national airline, cut all bus and train links, and produced a list of 20 terrorists and criminals it wanted Pakistan to hand over. Midway through the crisis there was talk of abrogating the 1960 Indus Water Treaty, the only bilateral agreement that has survived past wars and difficulties. Washington declared the LeT and JeM to be terrorist organisations, thus restricting their ability to raise funds in, or to travel to, the US, and Blackwill backed India's position that the 11 September and 13 December attacks had emerged from the same source – and, by implication, warranted similar responses. Most importantly, New Delhi threatened to retaliate directly against Pakistan for the terrorist attack. The situation on the India–Pakistan border heated up rapidly and both countries deployed ballistic missiles in forward positions. For the next five months, there was continual shelling on the border.

India on the attack

The war on terror, along with the Kargil conflict, provided India with a way out of a decade-long bind. In 1990, Pakistan had used its newly acquired (if untested) nuclear capability to force India to back down from its threat of a conventional attack that was designed to relieve the pressure of the Kashmiri insurgency, then in its infancy. Several subsequent crises proved that Pakistan's nuclear weapons deterred a vigorous Indian response to Pakistan's support for the insurgents. India was caught in a stability–instability paradox: its security situation had deteriorated as a result of Pakistani help to the Kashmir insurgency, but New Delhi was unable to escalate for fear of a nuclear attack. The Kargil conflict showed that a limited war – that is, something more than an insurgency, but less than an all-out conventional battle – was not necessarily going to lead to a nuclear exchange. India quickly developed and began propounding a theory of limited war, by which it could retaliate directly against Pakistan and was morally justified in doing so. Henceforth it was up to the Islamabad regime to decide whether it wanted further escalation. The 11 September attacks and the consequent US counter-terrorism posture bolstered this Indian stance. In mobilising its troops in December 2001, therefore, India was in a better political position to pursue a compellence strategy than it had been in a decade.

Though outside observers can never be certain of whether the Indian government was truly prepared to go to war, its toughening stance during the crisis period lent considerable credibility to its threat of retaliation. The Indian government seemed to calculate that 'hot pursuit' action – hitting terrorist training camps in Pakistani territory – might catalyse a larger war, but that such a war was unlikely to escalate beyond a manageable point across the Line of Control in Kashmir. India's overwhelming retaliatory capacity and the presence of US troops and interests in the region were believed to sufficiently deter a conventional attack by Pakistan across the international border or its first use of nuclear weapons. New Delhi also shifted the onus of escalation to Islamabad as Indian leaders maintained a constant refrain that it was up to Pakistan to decide what it wanted. When

Pakistan did threaten nuclear escalation, signalling its seriousness with three consecutive missile tests during the peak of the crisis in late May 2002, India accused it of 'nuclear terrorism'.

India's compellence strategy also addressed the US and the UK, prompting them to put pressure on Musharraf to destroy the infrastructure of the Kashmiri insurgency. New Delhi feared that the Pakistani regime might leave Kashmiri terrorist insurgency operations in place even as it dismantled the structure that sustained the Taliban and the al-Qaeda network. By threatening war in the east, India forced Pakistan to reconsider its own efforts to close down the escape routes of the Taliban and al-Qaeda fighters in support of the American effort in Afghanistan. Later in the crisis, Pakistan even asked US forces to leave the Jacobabad air base. This was not ultimately necessary. But to mollify India, Washington was compelled to extract a public promise from Musharraf to permanently close down facilities that supported the infiltration of militants into India. This increased domestic pressure on Musharraf. While India later accused Musharraf of going back on his word, verifying the ebb and flow of infiltration is notoriously difficult. Musharraf publicly dedicated himself to stopping cross-border terrorism when he joined the war on terror, but as the threat of war with India faded, Islamabad appeared to relax its efforts to prevent assistance to the Kashmiri insurgency. The fact that India would mobilise its forces to retaliate directly against Pakistan in the event of terrorist attack makes the region prone to instability: in future, any terrorist group could initiate a crisis.

India's brinkmanship was motivated by two other strategic purposes. First, the crisis established a direct link between Pakistan's support for the insurgency in Kashmir and nuclear war. It demonstrated that the chain of nuclear escalation began not with an Indian conventional attack, but earlier, with Pakistan's proxy war. Hitherto, this connection was not evident to the international community, and crisis-management efforts had focused on preventing a conventional war. New Delhi hoped that henceforth war-avoidance measures would refocus on forcing Pakistan to cease its support to the Kashmiri insurgency. In effect, this strategy would extend deterrence to sub-conventional conflict.

Second, repeated mobilisation and fast-paced military rearmament might precipitate Pakistan's internal failure. India's national security policymakers tried to replicate the lessons of the fall of the Soviet Union: they believed that the United States won the Cold War not by using its nuclear arsenal, but by forcing the Soviets to build one they could not afford. Similarly, India's growing economic power and technological ability was going to absorb the costs of such a strategy, while the gross mismanagement of the economy in Pakistan made it particularly vulnerable. Indeed, India is likely to continue this strategy. Its economy was one of the world's best performers in the latter part of 2002, and was estimated to grow by more than 5% for the full year despite severe drought conditions and the global economic slowdown. For the strategy to work, however, Pakistan would have to be cut off from Western assistance, which has been a primary objective of Indian diplomacy in the last year. Owing to Pakistan's centrality to counter-terrorism, that aim has been frustrated. Also, Pakistan's unofficial economy has shown resilience, even as its official one grew at a rate of only around 3.5% during Musharraf's tenure – down from an average of roughly 5% for 1988–99. The Pakistani diaspora, especially in the Middle East, has in the past shored up a failing economy long enough for the country to ride out crises. These factors suggest that technical economic collapse would not be tantamount to Pakistan's functional failure. Any risk that Pakistan might attempt a pre-failure nuclear strike against India to deny it the ability to influence its reconstruction is remote. But advancing the implosion of the Pakistani state does make the possibility that nuclear weapons could fall into the hands of Islamic radicals more salient.

Pakistan's riposte

Despite keeping the initiative through the crisis, India failed to force Pakistan to close down the radical groups and their training camps. Pakistan successfully resisted Indian military and diplomatic pressure for three reasons. First, the reality of Pakistan's military capabilities kept Indian belligerence in check. Notwithstanding the limited war theory, New Delhi could not strike inside Pakistani territory without risking a major conventional conflict and risk of nuclear escalation. Pakistan's own military mobilisation robbed the Indian forces of any quick strike-and-withdrawal option that might prevent escalation. With both militaries called up and deployed, any conflict was going to become a war of attrition. The reality of such a war – or worse, the possibility of escalation into a nuclear exchange – loomed large not just in India, but also in the rest of the world. The potential for nuclear conflict ensured that world attention remained focused on avoiding war in the region. During the period December 2001 to June 2002, when the crisis was finally defused, one senior member of the Bush administration visited the region every month, and there were frequent visits by European, Russian and Japanese officials.

Second, the US, while clearly believing that the equities were all with India with respect to the attack on the Indian parliament, resisted edging back toward the broader pro-India tilt that was evident before 11 September. While Washington understood the interconnections between terrorism in Kashmir and Afghanistan, its own concern was primarily with al-Qaeda terrorists rather than Kashmiri ones. The success of the US campaign in Afghanistan and within Pakistan, where many al-Qaeda leaders had escaped, hinged on Pakistan's cooperation on intelligence and access. An implicit condition of Pakistan's participation in the war on terror was that

Asia

the US was going to take a more 'balanced' approach to the India–Pakistan rivalry. Thus, for instance, Washington allowed Pakistan some leeway on the issue of infiltration. As senior US officials pressed Musharraf to stop the infiltration into India, they pointed out that Islamabad did not have the capability to stop the movement even if it fully wanted to do so. In effect, this allowed the Pakistani government to control American and Indian pressure on the issue of infiltration by selectively providing and withholding cooperation.

Initially, Pakistan complied with the US and Indian demands, banning five fundamentalist organisations, including the LeT and JeM, as well as the militant Sunni organisation, Sipah-e-Sahiba, and its Shia rival, Tehrik-e-Jafria, and promised to closely regulate the Islamic schools that had become the breeding grounds of radicalism. Musharraf arrested the leaders of the LeT and JeM, promising to freeze their bank accounts and close down their offices and other facilities, such as training camps. However, he refused to hand over the 20 individuals demanded by India as terrorists and criminals. By April 2002, he had freed the arrested leaders and allowed the banned organisations to go back to business under new names. The latter moves signalled to Washington and New Delhi that Islamabad would not make one-sided concessions, and Islamabad reiterated its impatience with India's refusal to restart bilateral negotiations.

Third, and perhaps most importantly, Pakistan's return to the role of a frontline state brought the country a reprieve from debt repayments and imminent fiscal collapse. The country's debt repayment was renegotiated. The fiscal assistance made available by the US, other Western nations and Japan stabilised the country's economy. Astonishingly, the Karachi stock market outperformed most other Asian bourses, even as the country was faced with war on both of its main borders. What remains from the crisis is Pakistan's grudging recognition that it can no longer freely support the Kashmiri insurgency. In 2002, unlike the 1990s, the new global security environment had created the political space for a limited Indo-Pakistani war. The fact that a limited war may not actually occur or that such action would have little lasting impact did not mean that India was going to eschew this course of action or not find international support for a tougher policy. Pakistan would also have to match each Indian mobilisation for fear that India might go through with an attack if it saw an opening. Not only would this raise the direct costs of supporting the Kashmiri insurgency, but it would also put Pakistan in a precarious international position. Pakistan could not depend forever on external financial support. The most dramatic reversal could occur if the US lost interest in Pakistan as it gained a decisive upper hand in the war on terror, and returned to its strategic tilt towards India. In late 2002 and early 2003, Islamabad attempted to secure new partners through high-level dialogues with Moscow and Tehran and paid its customary homage to Beijing.

Colliding internal mobilisations

Washington's long-term engagement with Islamabad could be strained if Pakistan's fundamentalist parties won a massive electoral victory and were able to prevent the military from having a direct role in politics. The army's exit would destroy the deal that has facilitated the US counter-terrorism war in return for the financial assistance to revive Pakistan's economy. The country's growing fundamentalist forces, with their ties to the Taliban, al-Qaeda and the Kashmiri insurgency, have opposed the military regime's alliance politics. Reportedly there were at least six attempts to assassinate Musharraf in 2002. Their victory in a general election would make the US presence in Pakistan untenable.

The war on terror had triggered fears that Pakistani people would explode in a fury against the United States and the Musharraf regime. Led by the Islamisation initiated in support of the first Afghan war, Pakistan had become increasingly divided along ideological and religious lines. The Afghan *jihad* ideology enabled the rise of the Taliban from the religious schools that had spread across Pakistan, generated endemic Shia–Sunni violence and underpinned the Kashmir insurgency. A black market whose wares included light weapons and drugs gave hardline religious leaders access to new resources and power. The close relations between the fundamentalists in Pakistan and the Taliban regime made Musharraf's decision to ally with the West dramatic. However, tight military control and, arguably, Pakistan's moderate but silent majority belied the worst fears of revolutionary violence during the early days of the bombing campaign in Afghanistan. The protests that materialised in areas in the North West Frontier Province (NWFP) and the Federally Administered Tribal Areas (FATA) – where radical influences have been strong – were small and sporadic. After Musharraf's 12 January 2002 speech condemning terrorism 'under any pretext', there were a series of highly publicised murders of foreigners. Sectarian violence in Pakistan continued. Evidence also mounted that al-Qaeda and the Taliban had made Pakistan their new home base. On 1 March 2003, Pakistani authorities with US assistance arrested al-Qaeda third-in-command Khalid Shaikh Mohammed in Rawalpindi. Mohammed was swiftly turned over to the US, and the hunt for bin Laden in Pakistan intensified. Nevertheless, there was still no explosive public protest.

What may have hurt Musharraf the most was the referendum he held on 30 April 2002 on his own presidency. After being billed as a first step toward the return of democracy, the referendum turned out to be the rubber-stamp ratification of Musharraf's authority as president for the subsequent five years. According to Pakistan's Election Commissioner, 70% of the country's voters cast ballots, compared to under 36% for parliamentary elections in 1997, and 97.7% voted in favour of his continuing as president. The process alienated every constituency in Pakistan except the army. It also amplified the opposition of fundamentalist and mainstream political parties, leading to the formation of the fundamentalist coalition, the Muttahida Majlis-e-Amal (MMA). The MMA's main component is the Jamaat-e-Islami, Pakistan's largest and best organised Islamic political party, which draws strong support among middle-class urban professionals. The Jamaat leadership, however, defers to Ahmed Shah Noorani, the head of the Jamiat-e-Ulema-e-Pakistan, a more fundamentalist and sectarian Sunni organisation. The coalition's most extreme elements are two factions of the Jamiat-e-Ulema-e-Islam, a movement of the Deobandi Sunni school of Islam, which became virulent by adopting the militant principles of the Wahhabi school of Saudi Arabia. One faction is led by Sami ul Haq, who ran the string of madrassas that fuelled the Taliban and was a confidant of Taliban leader Mullah Omar. The other, led by Fazlur Rahman, emerged as the most popular single fundamentalist force in Pakistan according to October 2002 parliamentary election results. The coalition tried to neutralise its Sunni bias by including the Shia Tehrik-e-Islami-e-Pakistan.

The referendum and Musharraf's arrogation of power made the subsequent parliamentary elections on 10 October 2002 less important in terms of allocating governmental power. Prior to the elections, Musharraf had decreed constitutional changes that made it impossible for a political party to remain in power without the constant support of the military. The new rules allowed the army chief, as the head of Pakistan's National Security Council (NSC), to dismiss governments. The NSC itself was to be a body nominated by the military rather than directly elected or appointed by elected officials. This institutionalised a political role for the Pakistani Army similar to that of the Turkish Army. But the elections were politically and symbolically significant in that they confirmed the strength of the religious parties. Despite electoral rules designed to disadvantage religious parties, the MMA won 45 of 272 elected seats in the National Assembly – an unprecedentedly high number for religious parties. They formed the government in the NWFP, and led the coalition that formed the one in Baluchistan, on the Afghan border. The Pakistan Muslim League–Quaid-i-Azam faction (PML-QA) formed Pakistan's new national government, as well as the provincial government in Punjab, the country's largest state. The PML-QA was referred to as the 'king's party', owing to Musharraf's support, and may have the most seats (77) due to the support it had received from the military regime. In late February 2003, the PML-QA consolidated its dominance by winning well over half the seats in the Senate, Pakistan's upper house of parliament. The continuing lack of true democracy in Pakistan poses the danger of further rallying fundamentalist groups to the cause of democratisation, which will tend to legitimise them and bring them further into the mainstream within Pakistan.

Pakistan's rising Islamic fundamentalism has also been on a collision course with Hindu fundamentalism in India. A Hindu backlash against

Islamic terrorism is likely to put into office increasingly hardline leaders in India, who might allow the violence of Gujarat to be replicated elsewhere. While the violence in Gujarat did not spread beyond the state and prompted widespread condemnation by the state and national governments – both run by the Hindu nationalist Bharatiya Janata Party (BJP) – it cast doubt on India's future as a secular state that could peacefully embrace the second-largest Muslim population in the world. In 2002, Hindu support grew for leaders who promised to provide security at all costs, including that of alienating the country's large Muslim population. In Gujarat itself, for example, Chief Minister Narendra Modi of the BJP, who was ultimately responsible for the violence that occurred under his rule, was re-elected in December 2002. The BJP also increased its majority from 117 to 126 of 182 seats in the state assembly.

Modi's campaign, which asserted Hindu pride and security, resonated not only in Gujarat but also in other parts of the country. Unless public safety improves, Indians are likely to elect leaders like Modi, who advocate the creation of a Hindu-ised, if not exclusively Hindu, India to ensure the country's security. The ascent of such leaders to national office would further hurt the prospect of an India–Pakistan détente. Indeed, as terrorism at home increases, there will be a temptation for the government to resolve the problem by 'teaching Pakistan a lesson'. Yet further Indo-Pakistani violence or tension is unlikely to resolve India's terrorism problem. The rise of Islamic terrorism outside Kashmir has been exacerbated by the rise of Hindu nationalism under the BJP. As the only national political party, the BJP looks poised to continue in government for the near future. Though being in power has moderated the BJP – or at least allowed the moderates within the party to remain dominant – the core of the organisation remains Hindu nationalist.

One bright spot in 2002 appeared improbably in the perennially troubled state of Jammu and Kashmir. For the first time in two decades, India successfully held elections, over a three-week period that ended on 8 October 2002. They were far from inclusive, however. The All-Parties Hurriyat Conference, the umbrella organisation of the separatists, chose not to participate, albeit after an extensive internal debate. Abdul Ghani Lone, the most moderate among Hurriyat leaders, seemed willing not only to participate in the elections but also to negotiate with New Delhi within the limits of the Indian constitution. He was shot dead on 21 May 2002 in Srinagar by unidentified gunmen. Field commanders of the Hizbul Mujahideen, the last indigenous group to control the insurgency, had expressed willingness to talk with the Indian government, but the Pakistan-based central leadership of the group had overruled them. In the run up to the elections, Musharraf articulated Pakistan's position that it could not support any elections that would be used by New Delhi to legitimise its rule over the disputed state. In Kashmir, the leaders of the LeT and JeM threatened retaliation against those who participated in the

Asia

elections. There were assassinations and substantial communal violence – indeed, some 800 people, including 50 political activists, were killed during the two-month campaign period – but the elections were conducted with observable fairness.

The voter turnout of 46% was considered outstanding, though in separatist strongholds the figure was much lower. Even more remarkably, the elections threw out the Abdullah family, which had conspired to remain in power in the state and was responsible for the corruption and misgovernance that led to the beginning of the insurgency in 1989. The Abdullah family's National Conference, which had held a comfortable majority of 57 of 87 seats, won only 28 seats and party leader Omar Abdullah – hand-picked heir apparent to the departing Chief Minister Farooq Abdullah, his father – lost his seat. The Congress Party won 21 seats and the fledgling People's Democratic Party (PDP), whose support in Muslim areas surged, 16. The new coalition state government – consisting of three Congress members, two from the PDP, two independents and one from the Hindu-dominated Panther Party – showed a healing touch. It offered an amnesty to the rebels and invited them to talks, raising hopes of a political settlement. It remains to be seen, however, whether New Delhi is willing to negotiate a political arrangement with the new government in Srinagar that could replace the autonomy arrangements that collapsed in 1989 and led to the insurgency.

The strategic future

With India and Pakistan embarked on nuclear and military rearmament, South Asia's strategic future is precarious. India is likely to set the pace of this remilitarisation and use its own procurement capacity and resources as strategic weapons. India has declared its intention to field a seaborne nuclear deterrent and, in January 2003, inked a deal with Russia worth nearly $3 billion for military hardware and the lease of two *Akula*-class nuclear submarines. Pakistan has the option to play catch up, at the cost of hurting its economy, which is already strained by the need to maintain a standing army of over half a million. But it could also keep India off balance with deliberate unpredictability in its nuclear policies and deployments, which would increase the risk of nuclear accidents. Moreover, another terrorist attack could bring a new crisis. So long as Pakistan does not shut down the infrastructure that supports the Kashmir insurgency and India wants to retaliate directly against Pakistan, the initiative for another crisis is in the hands of extremist groups. Islamabad is likely to be blamed for allowing the use of its territory even if it does not specifically authorise an attack. India might also launch repeated mobilisations in order to exhaust the smaller forces of Pakistan, which might then consider a pre-emptive strike on India.

Any hope of a continued 'hot peace', therefore, would depend on the robustness of deterrence on both sides, the ability of the regimes to neutralise their most radical elements and, ultimately, the willingness of the United States to step in should crises recur. The nature and tone of US involvement would be deeply contingent on the pursuit of its own primary national interest in South Asia – the war on terror – but will have to take into account the dynamics of the regional rivalry. Of durable importance is the growing security relationship between the US and India. In 2002, their two militaries conducted a series of high-profile exercises that included special operations forces. Though separate from the military-to-military relationship, cooperation and training arrangements between Indian and US law-enforcement and intelligence agencies have grown. India also may buy the *Arrow* missile-defence system from Israel, although the required US approval did not appear to be forthcoming in early 2003. American companies are also selling surveillance equipment that will allow Indian forces to better prevent terrorist infiltration. After many years, the United States has finally yielded to India's requests for high technology transfers, including those with dual-use possibility. Following the expansion of US–India ties and the nuclear tests, China's policy towards South Asia has become less certain. Beijing holds on to its time-tested and close relationship with Islamabad, but has also pursued a range of subjects in talks with New Delhi.

The future of South Asia, however, will be decided within India and Pakistan. The internal contradictions in the two main countries of the region threaten the possibility of rapprochement. The inability of the Pakistani state to meet popular demands for meaningful democratisation, political accountability and development make it difficult for the regime to acquire the legitimacy required to neutralise growing Islamic fundamentalism, particularly in Kashmir. Given the omnipresence of the military in politics, in the medium term Pakistan will likely remain a national security state, driven by security objectives to the neglect of development and accountability. A substantial muting of American influence there may be a necessary condition for successful democratisation in Pakistan. While any democratisation process could elevate those figures and groups inimical to US interests in the short term, the continued imposition of US security priorities on Musharraf at the cost of democratisation affords Islamic radicals the opportunity to seize democratisation as a popular cause whereby they could foster a potent internal mobilisation comparable to the Iranian revolution. The attendant possibility of full rejection of the West and the availability of nuclear weapons to anti-Western radicals is a prospect that demands consideration even if it is unlikely. Greater US emphasis on social and economic development, and less on the military, could have a leavening effect. Possible measures include lifting US trade quotas to improve market access for Pakistani cotton and textile exports, which make up 65% of Pakistan's exports, and targeting more economic assistance towards social welfare.

Meanwhile, the Hindu–Muslim conflict within India may dampen Pakistan's current inclination to negotiate with India. More dangerously, the portrayal of vengeful Hindu intentions could encourage radical groups both in Pakistan and India to escalate the struggle, precipitating further and more acute religious violence in India, including widespread use of suicide bombers as in the Middle East. The corresponding prospect of civil war is likely to receive full play in the election platform of the BJP, which is up for re-election at the national level in 2004 and fighting for power in a number of states. The party's victory in the Gujarat polls in 2002 amply demonstrated the appeal of a domestic security agenda to the majority Hindu population.

Progress towards resolving the Kashmir dispute – both a key source of regional sectarianism and the main nuclear flashpoint – would help counteract these dangerous portents. Arguably, there had rarely been a more propitious time for making such progress than early 2003. The Kashmiri elections produced a broad-based government inclined towards conflict resolution. The 11 September attacks brought the US and Pakistan closer together and made Musharraf a US ally. And the distance between the US and India produced by the US–Pakistan post-11 September rapprochement had been closed by Washington's post-13 December 2001 admonitions to Islamabad and its careful nurturing of broader bilateral ties with New Delhi. Thus, political conditions appeared ripe for India's dropping its insistence on treating Kashmir as a strictly bilateral problem and accepting the US as a 'facilitator' in establishing the key building blocks for a settlement, if not as a direct mediator. Since 11 September, however, Washington has regarded Kashmir primarily as a counter-terrorism and crisis-management problem rather than a diplomatic challenge, and is likely to be strategically preoccupied by Iraq, related Gulf issues and North Korea in 2003 and 2004.

Further, New Delhi blamed Pakistan for the 24 March 2003 terrorist attack that killed 24 Hindus in a village near Srinagar. Washington counselled calm, but its suggestion of India–Pakistan talks was met with derision in New Delhi. Indian Foreign Minister Yashwant Sinha said: 'Advice to India about resuming dialogue with Pakistan in the aftermath of the killings of Hindus in Kashmir this week was just as gratuitous and misplaced as [our] asking [the Americans] to open a dialogue with Osama bin Laden and Saddam Hussein'. While India's response prompted the US to call for an end to terrorist infiltration from Pakistan yet again, Washington is likely to continue with a degree of equivocation in the interest of counter-terrorism. Continued Pakistani cooperation is considered essential to containing terrorist threats. India's hard-line position and US strategic preoccupations elsewhere may lead Washington to adopt an even less proactive policy in the region, which could make crisis management more difficult. Meanwhile, events are likely to test the Indian government's ability to resist pressure to retaliate and the resiliency of the new Jammu and Kashmir state government's policy of accommodation with the rebels. By the time tempers cool and the US sees fit to turn its attention to South Asia, the opportunity for significant political advances may be gone.

Indonesian Security and Countering Terrorism in Southeast Asia

There was significant amelioration of several of Indonesia's separatist and ethnic security problems during 2002. Terrorism, however, developed into a bigger problem after the Bali bombing in October 2002, when it became clear that Indonesia was a major source as well as a target of transnational Islamic terrorism. While Indonesian counter-terrorism efforts and those of other regional powers were ramped up accordingly, institutional weakness, the ineffectualness of the Association of Southeast Asian Nations (ASEAN) and the currency of radical Islam in the region suggest that terrorists will continue to focus attention on Southeast Asia.

Attenuated insurgencies

Government-sponsored peace talks resulted in Muslim and Christian factions in Maluku and Central Sulawesi agreeing to ceasefires and disarmament under the terms of the 'Malino agreements' for each province, signed in December 2001 and February 2002, respectively. Though resentments simmered and there were sporadic eruptions of violence, in general a tense peace subsequently prevailed in both provinces. By March 2003, in North Maluku province, where there had also been bitter Muslim–Christian conflict, the government was planning to revoke the local state of emergency.

In the two provinces, Aceh and Papua (formerly Irian Jaya), where armed separatist struggles challenged Jakarta's rule, 'special autonomy' arrangements came into force in January 2002. A key provision in both cases is a massive increase in the provincial governments' share of revenues from natural resource exploitation. In Aceh, the local administration is also

Asia

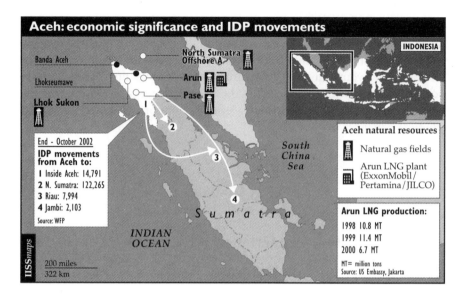

Aceh: economic significance and IDP movements

Banda Aceh
Lhokseumawe
Lhok Sukon

North Sumatra Offshore A
Arun
Pase

INDONESIA

End - October 2002
IDP movements from Aceh to:
1 Inside Aceh: 14,791
2 N. Sumatra: 122,265
3 Riau: 7,994
4 Jambi: 2,103
Source: WFP

South China Sea

Sumatra

INDIAN OCEAN

200 miles
322 km

IISSmaps

Aceh natural resources
Natural gas fields
Arun LNG plant (ExxonMobil/ Pertamina/JILCO)

Arun LNG production:
1998 10.8 MT
1999 11.4 MT
2000 6.7 MT

MT= million tons
Source: US Embassy, Jakarta

allowed to introduce elements of *sharia* law. However, Gerakan Aceh Merdeka (GAM), the Acehnese independence movement, initially rejected the new legislation and in early 2002 the Indonesian Armed Forces (TNI) escalated military operations against the rebels. Nevertheless, growing recognition by both GAM and Jakarta, combined with international pressure (particularly from the US) energised peace talks. In February, GAM accepted autonomy as a starting point for new negotiations, and in August the Henry Dunant Centre – the Swiss-based NGO sponsoring the talks – designated retired US Army General Anthony Zinni, backed by the US Department of State, as chief mediator. In early December, the two sides signed a Cessation of Hostilities Framework Agreement calling for not only a permanent ceasefire but also for a Joint Security Committee (JSC) to investigate truce violations and oversee GAM's disarmament and the withdrawal of non-garrison Indonesian troops. 'Peace zones' established by the JSC would become foci for humanitarian and reconstruction assistance, funded largely by an international donors' group. The Agreement also prescribed an All-Inclusive Dialogue between all sections of Acehnese society, leading to provincial elections in 2004. Although there was a dramatic reduction in violence after the negotiations began, several weeks into the Agreement's demilitarisation phase that began in early February 2003, neither GAM nor the TNI had begun fulfilling their obligations. More fundamentally, having been alienated from Indonesian authority by widespread human-rights abuses since 1989, the great majority of Acehnese continue to favour independence. This also remains GAM's ultimate objective but, because present Indonesian legislation effectively bars parties without widespread national membership from elections, no political route is open to the movement. In these circumstances, continuing reluctance on GAM's part to disarm, leading to renewed armed conflict, remained distinctly possible.

In Papua, the majority of the indigenous population rejected special autonomy as an adequate solution to their dispute with Jakarta. Armed resistance to Indonesian rule took the form of small-scale, localised violence. But the tolerated presence in the province of hundreds of militiamen belonging to Laskar Jihad, an extremist Islamic paramilitary group whose intervention contributed significantly to the intensity of conflict in Maluku and Central Sulawesi, and the creation of a pro-Indonesian militia amongst non-Papuan immigrants, suggested that the TNI was cultivating proxy forces in case demands for independence escalated. By February 2003, Laskar Jihad units, allegedly trained by Indonesian special forces, were operating against Papua Freedom Organisation (OPM) insurgents on Papua's border with Papua New Guinea. The division of Papua into three provinces – apparently part of a central government strategy aimed at undermining the independence movement – provoked strong local opposition. In sum, the outlook for a peaceful settlement remained unpromising but, in the absence of significant international support, Papuan independence remained a remote prospect.

Elsewhere in Indonesia, the devolution of administrative and fiscal authority to sub-provincial administrations helped defuse some of the widespread centre–periphery tensions that had arisen during the 1990s. Overall, Indonesia's potential territorial disintegration became a dimmer prospect. However, Indonesia's democratisation since President Suharto's ouster in 1998, combined with economic hardship and widespread popular disillusionment with the mainstream political elite, has encouraged the emergence of a wide range of radical Islamic groups. These include some advocating violence as a means of establishing an Islamic state, a trend that threatens the stability of Indonesia's political evolution and, in the longer term, its national cohesion. Political Islam's growing prominence also complicated Jakarta's response to the challenges posed by Islamic terrorist groups based in Indonesia.

Islamic extremism and terrorism in Indonesia

On 12 October 2002, terrorist bombings in Bali killed 202 people (predominantly Australian and other foreign tourists) and injured approximately 300. The incident dramatically highlighted the failure of the Indonesian President Megawati Sukarnoputri's government to act decisively against militant Islamic groups (some possibly connected with al-Qaeda) or to collaborate effectively in the US-led international campaign against terrorism. Since late 2001, other Southeast Asian states (notably Singapore, but also Malaysia and the Philippines) and Western governments (primarily the United States) have expressed concern that Indonesia is the weakest link in regional cooperation against international terrorism. In the months preceding the Bali attacks, there had been growing unease in the region and farther afield over the serious threat posed by internationally connected local terrorists to Indonesia's own security, to neighbouring Southeast Asian states and to Western interests. In March 2002, US intelligence sources claimed that 'dozens' of al-Qaeda personnel had found safe haven in Indonesia after escaping from Afghanistan. The following month, a Singaporean press report revealed that at least five radical Islamic groups in Indonesia – Majelis Mujahidin Indonesia (MMI), Laskar Jihad, Darul Islam, Front Pembela Islam (FPI) and Gerakan Pemuda Islam (GPI) – had received funds from al-Qaeda, in some cases subsequent to 11 September 2001. Other Indonesian groups, including Laskar Jundullah and Laskar Hizbullah, were also reported to be communicating with al-Qaeda.

Since May 2001, vigorous counter-terrorist policies in Malaysia, Singapore and the Philippines have led to the arrest of almost 100 members of Jemaah Islamiah (JI). The clandestine region-wide network of militants, known to be intent on creating a pan-Southeast Asian sovereign Islamic archipelago, were accused of plotting terrorist activities, including large-scale bomb attacks. By way of contrast, despite voicing the rhetoric of counter-terrorist cooperation, Megawati's government had proved unwilling to respond firmly in the face of either domestic Islamic militants advocating violence or the growing evidence of their regional and international terrorist connections. Concerned governments had pressed Jakarta to arrest Abu Bakar Bashir, co-founder and head of a religious boarding school near Solo in central Java – known as an important breeding-ground for Islamic radicalism and the hub of a network of Indonesians suspected of links with al-Qaeda – and chairman of the above-ground MMI, which he established in 2000. Singaporean and Malaysian authorities consider Abu Bakar the leader of JI. In early 2002, the Indonesian police had questioned and quickly released him, though he was kept under surveillance and reportedly remained in regular contact with JI members. Another key figure was JI's alleged operational commander, Riduan Isamuddin, also known as Hambali, who is reputed to act as the organisation's main intermediary with al-Qaeda. Despite supposed efforts to track him down in connection with attacks on churches across Indonesia in December 2000, as well as bombings in Malaysia, he apparently operated with impunity from Indonesia.

As reasons for failing to arrest terrorist suspects, Indonesian officials cited the need to protect human rights, the absence of anti-terrorism legislation comparable to the Internal Security Acts available in Malaysia and Singapore, and Indonesia's vast and unwieldy geography. More importantly, though, Megawati increasingly found herself trapped between international pressure to crack down on indigenous terrorist networks and widespread domestic scepticism (even within the government and TNI) regarding the seriousness of the terrorist threat. In the context of Indonesia's multi-dimensional economic, political and security crisis since 1997–98, terrorism hardly seemed a pressing issue for most Indonesians. Delicate domestic political realities were also a major factor. Before the Bali bombing, Megawati was unwilling to jeopardise the stability of the coalition between secular-nationalist and Islamist political forces on which her government rested to appease critics of Indonesia's counter-terrorism performance. Despite a widespread trend towards greater religious observance, the majority of Indonesia's Muslim population remained tolerant in their outlook and adhered to Nahdlatul Ulama (NU) or Muhammadiyah – essentially moderate social movements together claiming more than 70 million followers. Nevertheless, leading Muslim politicians including Vice-President Hamzah Haz, leader of the Partai Persatuan Pembangunan (PPP), one of the two largest Muslim parties in parliament, and Upper House Speaker Amien Rais, leader of Partai Amanat Nasional (PAN), often felt it necessary to defer to extremist and anti-Western viewpoints in order to bolster their political support from more radical 'street Islam' – particularly the numerous Islamic militias – that had flourished since Suharto's ouster in 1998. Not only did Hamzah Haz propose amending Indonesia's constitution to apply *sharia* law to all Muslims, he also maintained friendly relations with both Abu Bakar Bashir and Jafaar Umar Thalib, leader of Laskar Jihad. Megawati, in turn, needed the support or at least the acquiescence of Muslim political leaders if she was to remain in power until the next elections in 2004.

Nevertheless, during 2002 there were signs of increased willingness on the part of elements of Indonesia's law-and-order apparatus (particularly BIN, the national intelligence agency led by retired Lieutenant-General A.M. Hendropriyono) to tackle the problem of terrorism more vigorously. Such efforts, though, often encountered resistance from within the government and the wider political establishment. In March 2002, after a tip from BIN, Philippine authorities arrested three alleged Indonesian terrorists including Agus Dwikarna, a leading figure in JI and the closely-related Laskar Jundullah, which had reportedly provided training facilities in central Sulawesi for al-Qaeda. However, two of the suspects detained in Manila were soon freed, apparently as a result of intervention by Megawati, who was in turn responding to pressure from Muslim political leaders. Manila, however, refused to release Dwikarna because of his stature in JI. In April, state prosecutors outlined plans to force Abu Bakar Bashir to serve a nine-year prison sentence for subversion, dating from 1985, but the intervention of Justice Minister Yusril Ihza Mahendra – leader of the hardline Islamic Partai Bulan Bintang (PBB) – ensured that no action was taken. In early May, Jafaar Umar Thalib was arrested and charged with inciting sectarian violence in Maluku and threatening Megawati's life, and the government ordered Laskar Jihad to withdraw from Maluku.

Remarkably, though, on the following day Vice-President Hamzah Haz visited Jafaar in the police headquarters where he was held, with the justification 'we Muslims are brothers'. Meanwhile, the government continued to refine a draft anti-terrorism bill, which would provide a legal basis for TNI as well as police action against terrorist suspects even in the absence of clear evidence against them. But fear that tabling the bill would allow parliamentary opponents to accuse her administration of capitulating to US pressure persuaded Megawati to delay enacting this legislation.

During the weeks immediately before the Bali bombings, Western governments became increasingly apprehensive over intelligence reports (based largely on intercepted communications 'chatter') warning of imminent terrorist attacks against their interests in Indonesia. On 10 September a security alert forced the US embassy in Jakarta and the consulate in Surabaya to close for almost a week, and later that month the US and other Western governments issued warnings over potential anti-Western violence in Yogyakarta and Solo, both home to extremist Islamic groups. A grenade explosion outside a US embassy property in Jakarta exacerbated security concerns. On 11 October, US Ambassador Ralph L. Boyce had warned the Indonesian authorities of an imminent terrorist attack.

Outside pressure for firmer action against terrorist networks continued to provoke hostility from Indonesian Muslim leaders, particularly after *Time* magazine published an article based partially on a leaked CIA report concerning Omar al-Faruq, a Kuwaiti terrorist suspect arrested in Indonesia in June 2002. Al-Faruq was rapidly transferred to US custody and taken to Bagram air base in Afghanistan, where he revealed new information on terrorist operations in Indonesia. Al-Faruq confessed that he had been al-Qaeda's senior Southeast Asian representative since the late 1990s and had helped Agus Dwikarna to establish Laskar Jundullah. He admitted to plotting to assassinate Megawati during the 1999 election campaign and to blow up the US embassy in Jakarta during 2000, to masterminding a wave of bombings of Indonesian churches in December 2000 (in which 19 people were killed), and to conspiring to attack US navy vessels visiting Surabaya during May 2002. He further confessed to planning, under orders from senior al-Qaeda officials, large-scale car- and truck-bomb attacks on US interests (particularly embassies) in not only Indonesia, but also Cambodia, Malaysia, the Philippines, Singapore, Taiwan, Thailand and Vietnam to coincide with the first anniversary of the 11 September attacks. Finally, al-Faruq implicated Abu Bakar Bashir in planning the bombing of Jakarta's largest mosque in December 1999 and providing JI with personnel and logistical support for the planned attacks in 2002.

There were signs, though, that Indonesia's government was becoming less complacent. In late September 2002, TNI Commander-in-Chief General Endriartono Sutarto acknowledged that an internationally linked terrorist network existed in Indonesia, while denying any evidence of connections with al-Qaeda. Within days, however, Coordinating Minister for Politics and Security Susilo Bambang Yudhoyono announced that Indonesia would work closely with the US to investigate whether or not there was an al-Qaeda presence in the country. (In a further instance of influence from Muslim politicians, however, within 24 hours Susilo felt compelled to stress that though Indonesia would cooperate with the US, there would be no joint investigation.) In early October, the government announced that it would establish a National Security Council to advise the president on domestic and international matters, anticipating that this broadly based body would facilitate counter-terrorism efforts by reassuring Muslim parliamentarians (who would be assigned a formal role in its deliberations) that measures against violent extremists were not part of a wider campaign against political Islam. Because of these developments, only four days before the attacks in Bali the US ambassador praised Jakarta's more assertive counter-terrorist posture.

Jakarta's response to the Bali bombing

Despite widespread anticipation of a major terrorist incident, the fact that the 12 October attacks occurred on Hindu-majority Bali, which had retained its reputation as a haven from Indonesia's political, religious and communal turmoil since Suharto's overthrow, shocked Indonesian and foreign observers alike. No group immediately claimed responsibility for the attack, which involved near-simultaneous explosions at two nightclubs in the Kuta tourist area and the US consulate in Denpasar; a 450kg bomb detonated in a van outside the Sari Club caused the great majority of the deaths and injuries. The Bali attacks constituted the most serious terrorist incident anywhere since 11 September 2001, and seemed to form part of an upsurge in Islamic terrorism that also included a suicide attack on a French oil tanker off Yemen and the shooting of US Marines in Kuwait. There was some speculation, both in Indonesia and internationally, that Indonesian military elements might have engineered the bombings, to avenge the Australian-led, UN-backed military intervention in East Timor in 1999, or to undermine civilian government and restore the TNI's political fortunes. However, evidence quickly emerged indicating that the bombings were most probably the work of JI acting jointly with al-Qaeda.

Given the dire consequences for Indonesia's economy if the confidence of foreign investors and the tourist industry were further degraded, Megawati and her government were impelled to treat the issue of terrorism considerably more seriously. The government's previous rejection of the notion that Indonesians were involved in a region-wide terrorist conspiracy, possibly linked to al-Qaeda, began to crumble. The cabinet's centre of gravity shifted away from Muslim hardliners such as Hamzah Haz and towards those like Susilo, who favoured a tough response and were now backed by Megawati. In the days immediately after the bombings, amid warnings by Jakarta and Western governments of possible further attacks in Indonesia, Indonesian authorities mobilised to arrest the perpetrators of the Bali bombings. They also applied somewhat more energy to determining the extent of the terrorist network in Indonesia and its international connections. It became clear that, in addition to a lack of political resolve on the government's part, bitter rivalry among the BIN, the police and the TNI had impaired Jakarta's intelligence capabilities regarding the terrorist threat, thus helping to create the conditions in which JI could thrive and the Bali incident could occur.

Megawati pressured the three security bodies to work more closely together and resisted efforts by General Endriartono to assert military control over the new counter-terrorism initiative. In the continuing absence of definitive counter-terrorism legislation, a week after the Bali bombings the government enacted an emergency presidential decree that established an inter-ministerial agency led by the police to handle terrorism, allowed the detention of terrorist suspects without charge, permitted the use of intelligence agencies' evidence in court, and sanctioned life prison sentences and the death penalty for terrorist acts. A second decree allowed the retrospective application of the first decree to the Bali case. Importantly, both NU and Muhammadiyah expressed support for these decrees, which became normal laws after receiving parliamentary approval in March 2003. Nevertheless, weaknesses in coordination were apparent during the Bali investigation, prompting the government to announce in late November 2002 an overhaul of the intelligence community that included increasing BIN's budget and personnel strength to allow it to assume greater responsibility for provincial intelligence from the TNI.

Crucially, concern over the Bali bombings' repercussions for Indonesia's international reputation led the government to allow foreign participation in the investigation into the incident. Though led by Indonesian police under the command of a senior ethnic Balinese officer, the investigation task force also included forensic and counter-terrorism officers from the Australian Federal Police, the US Federal Bureau of Investigation and Britain's Metropolitan Police. Ultimately, more than 100 Australian officers joined the probe, their roles included crucial technical and intelligence support for Indonesian investigators as they moved to arrest key suspects. The first breakthrough in the case came in early November, when the owner of the van used in the Sari Club bombing was arrested in East Java. Amrozi, a mechanic who had studied under Abu Bakar Bashir, quickly confessed to having helped organise the bombing as part of a ten-member terrorist cell. According to Amrozi, the aim had been to 'kill Americans' in revenge for US attacks against Iraq and Afghanistan. In late November, police arrested Imam Samudra, who confessed to acting as JI's operational commander for the Bali bombings and implicated Abu Bakar in the plot. A third key conspirator, Ali Gufron (alias Mukhlas), reputedly JI's chief of operations for the whole of Southeast Asia, was apprehended in early December. By that stage, 29 arrests had been made and the chief police investigator claimed that his task force had completed 90% of the Bali investigation. Files on 14 of those detained were sent to state prosecutors in February 2003, and it was anticipated that trials would be held during 2003.

Despite BIN chief Hendropriyono's claim in February 2003 that Indonesia's terrorist networks were 'a spent force', followed by the US ambassador's observation that the security situation had 'dramatically improved', there was no compelling evidence that the JI network in Indonesia had been comprehensively unravelled, let alone destroyed, that its leadership had been neutralised, or that its international connections had been mapped comprehensively. Indeed, the authorities seemed to be wary of probing the overall JI network (as opposed to the cell specifically linked to the Bali incident), for fear of inflaming wider Indonesian Muslim opinion. Despite what had happened on Bali, popular scepticism over the existence of an Indonesian-based terrorist network remained widespread. Indeed, many Indonesians believed that the Bali bombings might be part of a 'foreign' (in other words, Western) plot to discredit political Islam. Police attempts to search Islamic boarding schools for suspects during November provoked Hamzah Haz into accusing investigators of being 'heavy-handed'.

Initially, it appeared that militant Islamic groups in Indonesia in addition to JI might be substantially suppressed in the post-Bali security backlash, particularly in light of claims concerning their al-Qaeda connections. Though it denied involvement, Laskar Jihad announced three days after the bombings that it would not only withdraw from Maluku but also disband. While funding problems and internal disputes helped to explain these decisions, the group evidently wished to avoid being caught in any law-enforcement or military crackdown against Islamic extremism. The following day, FPI leader Habib Muhammad Rizieq Shihab was arrested and charged with instigating violence and vandalism, and in early November, the FPI announced the suspension of its activities. However, as the impact of the Bali incident receded over the following months, extremist groups resurfaced. In January 2003, a judge commended Laskar Jihad leader Jafaar Umar Thalib for seeking to 'maintain national unity' and found him not guilty on all charges levelled against him. In February, the FPI revived its paramilitary wing. It also appeared that Laskar Jihad was regrouping in Papua.

Abu Bakar Bashir's arrest after the Bali incident spearheaded the government's post-Bali offensive against terrorism, but did not result in his unmasking and prosecution as Indonesia's terrorist puppet-master. While it was widely acknowledged inside the Indonesian security apparatus that Abu Bakar was JI's 'emir' or leader, he may still have benefited from the protection of Muslim hardliners within the government. His connection to the Bali bombings remained obscure. While national police chief Da'i Bachtiar claimed that Abu Bakar not only approved the Bali bombings but also met with the terrorists before and after the attacks, a widely reported independent assessment stressed that Abu Bakar had argued strenuously against the Bali bombings for tactical reasons and had consequently precipitated a schism within JI, with more impetuous members deciding to proceed with the attacks. Initially detained in hospital, Abu Bakar was taken into police custody in October for questioning, mainly about the alleged plot to assassinate Megawati and the Christmas 2000 church bombings. By March 2003, it seemed likely that he would eventually face the less serious charge of seeking to overthrow the government. But Jafaar Umar Thalib's acquittal may have set a tone of leniency, and it would not be altogether surprising if Abu Bakar were ultimately exculpated and released. In mid-March, he filed a lawsuit against the police, claiming that his detention had been unlawfully prolonged.

While Abu Bakar's detention implied that he was probably unable to exercise any substantive operational role in JI, at least for the time being, other important JI figures – Including Hambali and the bomb-maker Dulmatin (probably responsible for many other bombings besides those in Bali) – remained on the loose. There were further bomb attacks after Bali. In December 2002, an attack on a McDonald's restaurant in Makassar that killed three people was blamed on Laskar Jundullah. In February 2003, bombers struck the national police headquarters in Jakarta. Diplomatic sources suggested that further attacks against Western targets and assassinations in Indonesia were probably still being planned in response to a US-led attack on Iraq under the cover of widely expected large-scale popular anti-war protests. Yet the question of the Bali bombers' operational and ideological international links also remained unresolved. Days after the attack, Defence Minister Matori Abdul Djalil pointed to al-Qaeda involvement. This was also the US and Australian view. It was reported that Omar al-Faruq claimed that 'a Saudi' sent $74,000 to Abu Bakar Bashir for the purchase of the explosives used in the bombings. Initially, Indonesian intelligence sources claimed that a team of seven 'foreigners' led by a Yemeni (later identified as Syahfullah) and a Malaysian (Zubair) was responsible for planning and executing the bombings. Mohamed Mansur Jabara, an al-Qaeda activist held by the US, claimed that al-Qaeda bomb-making skills were key to the Bali incident, and that the attacks on 'soft targets' in Southeast Asia had been planned at a meeting between Saad, an al-Qaeda operative, and JI leaders in southern Thailand in January 2002. However, the picture began to change after Amrozi's arrest. Though the BIN continued to claim al-Qaeda involvement through Syahfullah and Zubair (neither of whom was apprehended), the police were reluctant to concede any foreign role. The suspects insisted that JI had acted without al-Qaeda's help, and there seemed to be evidence that funding for the Bali attack derived from misdirected charitable contributions and the proceeds from robbing a jeweller's shop.

Megawati and her government are open to criticism for not wholeheartedly pursuing investigations into the wider domestic and international network that supported the Bali bombers, and for failing to restrict the freedoms of other militant groups, which some intelligence sources suggested were more closely related to JI than was once assumed. But Indonesia's domestic political context meant there was a danger that Megawati's acquiescence in what many Muslims saw as a Western-led 'crusade' against terrorism might further strengthen Indonesia's already growing and increasingly militant Islamist movements, encouraging moderate Muslims to support hardline parties such as Hamzah Haz's PPP. At the same time, more of those who wish to see the implementation of *sharia* law or the establishment of an Islamic state might gravitate towards extremist militias. The growing sway of militant Islam was highlighted in January 2003, when Muslim student groups took the lead in demonstrations against government plans to cut subsidies for fuel, electricity and telephone charges, successfully coercing Megawati into postponing and reducing the price rises. Fear of a populist and more coherent Islamic opposition bloc coalescing is a critical consideration in the run-up to the mid-2004 parliamentary elections and the presidential poll later that year. For this reason, the depth of Indonesia's commitment to the cause of counter-terrorism remains questionable, particularly as the furore over the Bali attack subsides.

Restoring Indonesia's military links with the US?

US assistance to the TNI under the International Military Education and Training (IMET) scheme was halted after Indonesian troops massacred unarmed demonstrators in East Timor in 1991. Virtually all military ties were subsequently severed in September 1999 as TNI-controlled militias terrorised East Timor's population, following the pro-independence vote in the UN-organised plebiscite. In late 1999, the US Congress enacted into law the 'Leahy conditions', which made the allocation of future funding to support military training and arms sales conditional on the prosecution of military and militia personnel responsible for human-rights violations as well as TNI personnel who had assisted militias, the repatriation of East Timorese refugees, an audit of the TNI's finances, access for human-rights monitors to conflict zones such as Aceh, Papua and Maluku, and the release of political detainees. Because most of these conditions had not been satisfied as of October 2002, before the Bali attack there seemed little chance that military-to-military ties would be restored in the foreseeable future. Nevertheless, when Presidents Bush and Megawati met in Washington in

September 2001 they agreed on periodic consultation between the US and Indonesian defence departments. At the first Indonesia–US Security Dialogue in April 2002, officials discussed national and regional defence and security issues, but the only apparent outcome was a vague statement on the 'need to focus on joint efforts to fight international terrorism and other trans-national threats'. Simultaneously, the US and Indonesian marine corps held a three-day seminar on non-lethal weapons – part of a US Department of Defense effort to develop links with one of the TNI's more professional branches in a manner calculated to minimise objections from the human-rights lobby.

Even before the Bali incident, there was considerable debate in the US over whether resuming assistance to the TNI would boost Indonesia's capacity for counter-terrorism. This issue provided a new dimension to the widely held view in some Western defence establishments that the Indonesian military constituted the main force capable of holding Indonesia together. It was also argued that military-to-military ties were important if the West was to maintain any influence over the future evolution of the TNI's role. The new twist to the argument was that the TNI's extensive territorial network could provide invaluable detailed intelligence on terrorist suspects and networks throughout the archipelago. These views were countered by those who argued that, despite superficial reforms since Suharto's ousting (including the separation of the police from the armed forces in 1999), the TNI remained an irresponsible and even subversive force, its senior officers inordinately interested in promoting their own financial and political interests. Deriving most of its funding from un-audited commercial enterprises, the military retained considerable freedom from civilian political control. Since 1999, its relations with the police have often degenerated into provincial turf wars, and sometimes armed conflict. There was also considerable evidence that the army's counter-insurgency role, involving widespread flagrant human-rights abuses, had proved counter-productive in Aceh and Papua, that it had often acted with partiality (where it had acted at all) in communal conflicts in Maluku and elsewhere, and that the shadowy ties of some senior officers with militant Islamic groups, such as Laskar Jihad, appeared to implicate it in the very type of extremism that US policy should be trying to preclude.

Nevertheless, the Bali attack boosted the conviction of those US officials (notably Deputy Secretary of Defense Paul Wolfowitz, a former ambassador to Indonesia) who argued that restoring military ties with Indonesia would support US policy in Southeast Asia. But there seemed little chance that the administration could overcome congressional objections. Though the Senate approved $400,000 in IMET funding for Indonesia in January 2003, these funds were aimed mainly at educating civilian officials. While a Jakarta court on 12 March 2003 did convict

Brigadier General Noer Muis of failing to prevent two massacres of civilians in East Timor, sentencing him to five years in prison, the Leahy conditions remained a significant obstacle to the restoration of military-to-military assistance in the absence of far-reaching TNI reforms and more convictions. Further, it was clear that under Megawati's presidency there had been little progress in reforming the TNI. Indeed, the military was attempting to bolster its political influence ahead of the 2004 elections, particularly through an Article 19 of the proposed Armed Forces Bill, which would permit the TNI commander to deploy forces during an emergency without the president's prior approval. Specific new evidence of the armed forces' nefarious activities, such as the involvement of Indonesian soldiers in the killing of three people, including two US teachers, near the Freeport mine in Papua in August 2002, and the TNI's continued resistance to reform, strengthened the case for the continued application of the Leahy conditions. Moreover, the creditable role of the police in the Bali investigation and the move to strengthen the BIN at the expense of the military intelligence agency compromised the argument that the TNI might play a central role in counter-terrorism.

Internal security and terrorism in the wider region

Several other Southeast Asian governments have continued to confront serious internal security threats. In Singapore, after arresting 13 suspects in December 2001 in connection with a JI plot to target US, British, Australian and Israeli assets, the authorities arrested a further 21 terrorist suspects in August 2002. Those arrested allegedly belonged to or were linked with JI cells that had been planning to attack local targets, including water pipelines, Changi Airport and the defence ministry, with the aim of provoking conflict between Singapore and Malaysia as well as communal clashes between Muslims and non-Muslims. Most of the suspects were arrested under the Internal Security Act (ISA), which allows initially for up to two years' detention. In January 2003, the government released a White Paper examining the nature and extent of the JI network in Southeast Asia and explaining the reasons for detaining the JI suspects (including those arrested in December 2001). The paper included a detailed assessment of the specific JI plots aimed against Singapore. The authorities also continued to implement a wide range of security measures aimed at protecting Singapore's highly concentrated population and infrastructure against terrorist attacks.

In Malaysia, where 90 militants belonging to JI and the closely related Kumpulan Mujahideen Malaysia (KMM) had been detained by early 2003, there was relatively little transparency in the way the ISA was applied. Nevertheless, some detainees were reportedly linked to the JI cells that had planned attacks in Singapore. In January 2003, six suspects were arrested in

Asia

the Borneo state of Sabah, where a local cell had provided logistical support for JI recruits travelling to camps run by the Muslim insurgent Moro Islamic Liberation Front (MILF) in the southern Philippines for training. Worryingly for the government, several of those arrested since 2001 were serving or retired military officers, raising questions over the armed forces' dependability.

Fearful of deterring investors and tourists, and reluctant to highlight the depth of its counter-terrorism cooperation with the US against international terrorism, Prime Minister Mahathir Mohamad's government remained wary of linking local extremists to al-Qaeda. It had little hesitation, though, about using the issue of terrorism in attempts to discredit the Partai Islam Se-Malaysia (PAS), the largest opposition force, which already held power in two Malaysian states. One of those arrested in 2001 was the KMM's alleged leader, Nik Adli Nik Aziz, the son of the spiritual leader of PAS. In June 2002, Mahathir argued that some young PAS members did not believe in democracy and were turning to violence as a means of achieving their objective of an Islamic state. Government supporters privately referred to the KMM as the 'military wing of PAS'. Responding to such allegations, the acting president of PAS, Abdul Hadi Awang, claimed that the government had manufactured the alleged JI and KMM conspiracy as a means of justifying the repression of political Islam. Embarrassingly for Abdul Hadi Awang, though, in February 2003 the government revealed that during 2000 he had attended a meeting of Islamic radical groups in Indonesia alongside Abu Bakar Bashir and Agus Dwikarna.

Like Singapore, the Philippines government (without a majority-Muslim population to appease) was not shy about investigating and publicising JI and al-Qaeda activity. In April 2002, Fathur Rahman al-Ghozi, an Indonesian JI bomb-maker implicated in the December 2000 bombing of a Manila rail station that killed 22, as well as in the planning for bombings in Singapore during 2001, was arrested in Manila in January 2002 and sentenced to 12 years in prison. In November, the Philippine police claimed that local Muslim groups were linked to JI through an Asia-wide alliance, Rabitatul Mujahedeen. Concern over JI and al-Qaeda links sharpened the concerns of both Manila and the US over the seemingly intractable problem of rebellion in the Muslim south, where the immediate challenge was the small, Muslim but increasingly mercenary Abu Sayyaf group, whose hostages still included an American missionary couple in early 2002. The much larger MILF, estimated to field 12,500 fighters, was involved in peace talks with Manila. But the lack of funds for rehabilitating war-ravaged Muslim-dominated areas, continuing armed clashes, growing concerns within the Philippine security establishment over rebel links with al-Qaeda and Abu Sayyaf, and allegations concerning the MILF's role in incidents such as the December 2000 Manila bombing and another in General Santos City in April 2002, complicated negotiations.

A major problem for Manila in dealing with Abu Sayyaf – with which al-Qaeda was reportedly attempting to revive links in late 2002 – was the weakness of the Armed Forces of the Philippines (AFP). Particularly acute deficits included the absence of an intelligence network among the local Muslim population and some officers' willingness to strike deals with rebel commanders. However, the involvement of more than 1,000 US troops, including special forces, in *Exercise Balikatan* 02-1 in Zamboanga and Basilan (the island where Abu Sayyaf was based) for six months from January 2002 substantially boosted AFP morale and capabilities, if temporarily. In early June, Philippine forces supported by US troops attempted to rescue Abu Sayyaf's three hostages, but only one – an American – survived. Search-and-destroy operations over the following weeks again involved US forces in supporting roles, but for constitutional reasons Philippine President Gloria Arroyo refused to allow them to engage directly in combat. Nevertheless, in late June Philippine Navy commandos supported by US airborne surveillance and helicopters killed Abu Sayyaf's leader, Abu Sabaya, during a clash at sea off the island of Mindanao. Subsequently, the AFP captured four Abu Sayyaf camps on the islands of Basilan and Jolo and it seemed that the organisation might have been crippled as a fighting force.

After all but 300 of the US troops deployed for *Exercise Balikatan* had been withdrawn as scheduled at the end of July 2002, Abu Sayyaf's seizure of more hostages in August demonstrated that it had not been defeated. The focus of the AFP's struggle against Abu Sayyaf was now the island of Jolo, where there were fierce battles during October, but Abu Sayyaf operatives, possibly trained by JI, were responsible for a series of bombings in Zamboanga in October. In February 2003, the Philippines expelled the senior Iraqi diplomat in Manila because of his alleged role in sponsoring a bombing that killed a US soldier. Against a background of threats by Abu Sayyaf to attack civilian targets and in the context of intensifying bilateral defence cooperation between Washington and Manila that included plans for at least 17 joint exercises during 2003, in late 2002 the US and Philippine defence departments began planning another major joint exercise in the south, on Jolo, involving 750 US troops deployed in combat patrols. Controversy erupted over the plan in February 2003, though, with the Philippine government insisting that a combat role was out of the question. By early March, Philippine and US defence officials were revising exercise plans to avoid provoking nationalist and Muslim opinion.

Though Manila and the MILF had agreed to a ceasefire in August 2001 and contacts continued through a back-channel provided by Malaysia, there was no sign that the two sides could establish a durable peace. Amid allegations by the Philippine military that the MILF was harbouring a kidnapping gang in its ranks and massing forces for 'retaliatory attacks' in the event of a US–Iraq war, in early February 2003 Philippine forces

Asia

launched a major offensive against a rebel concentration in the Liguasan Marshes region of central Mindanao. Several hundred MILF guerrillas were killed and more than 40,000 civilians displaced. In mid-February 2003, President Arroyo approved a final draft of the government's proposed peace agreement, but the rebels demanded that government forces withdraw from recently occupied territory before talks could proceed. Malaysia and Libya offered to mediate, but MILF chairman Salamat Hashim called for a 'fight till death'. In late February, the AFP blamed the MILF for a bold sabotage attack on power transmission towers, leaving 18m people on Mindanao temporarily without electricity. The attack – and another on Davao Airport in early March that killed 21 people – apparently reflected a split within the MILF between hardline and pro-peace factions. Nevertheless, exploratory talks in Kuala Lumpur in late March resulted in an agreement to work towards a resumption of peace negotiations. The MILF denied responsibility for a bomb in Davao on 2 April 2003 that killed 16 people.

Regional cooperation against terrorism

An important aspect of Southeast Asian states' responses to the terrorist threat has been their much greater emphasis on strengthening counter-terrorism coordination (particularly in the area of intelligence sharing) not only among domestic agencies, but also with regional neighbours and interested extra-regional powers. However, the path to counter-terrorism cooperation within Southeast Asia has been rocky, and the agreements reached of questionable value, in light of regional states' mutual suspicions and divergent perspectives as well as shortcomings in national policies and capabilities. It remains to be seen whether counter-terrorism cooperation between certain Southeast Asian countries and the US will be affected by the war in Iraq. But the lack of a common Southeast Asian position on the war with Iraq was striking. While Indonesia and Malaysia rejected US requests to cut their ties with Iraq and close the Iraqi embassies in their capitals, the Philippines and Singapore both agreed to join the coalition. Thailand's stance was equivocal, but it nevertheless allowed US military aircraft enroute to the Gulf to refuel at the U-Tapao air base.

As in other dimensions of security, bilateral relationships (between regional states as well as between extra-regional and regional partners) continue to provide the most effective forms of counter-terrorism collaboration in Southeast Asia. Singapore's bilateral link with the Philippines has been particularly fruitful. The city-state's counter-terrorism collaboration with Indonesia was showing signs of progress by February 2003, when a tip-off from Singapore led Indonesian police to arrest Mas Selamat Kastari, the fugitive leader of JI's Singapore network. Singapore's cooperation with Malaysia has clearly played an important part in disrupting JI's networks in both states, but the deterioration in bilateral relations over unrelated issues in late 2002 and early 2003 threatened to undermine joint counter-terrorism efforts. Most Southeast Asian states have intensified their bilateral cooperation with the US on counter-terrorism, but Singapore's collaboration has been especially robust. In January 2003, Singapore jointly hosted with the US a workshop on suppressing finance for terrorism. Both Singapore and Malaysia have joined the US Container Security Initiative. However, Malaysian objections to US plans to base intelligence officers at a proposed counter-terrorism centre in Kuala Lumpur held up anticipated US funding for the enterprise. In another regional example of a difficult partnership, by late 2002 relations between the FBI and the Thai police were severely strained due to different perceptions of how Bangkok should handle the JI presence in Thailand's southern region. Like the United States, Australia has also enhanced its counter-terrorism links throughout Southeast Asia, particularly since the Bali attack, although Prime Minister John Howard's suggestion in December that Australia might strike pre-emptively at terrorists in the region caused widespread concern.

At the multilateral level, in May 2002 Indonesia, Malaysia and the Philippines signed an Agreement on Information Exchange and Establishment of Communication Procedures, aimed against terrorism and other transnational crime and covering 23 areas of cooperation ranging from intelligence exchanges (such as sharing airline passenger lists) and establishing hotlines to combined counter-terrorist operations. However, though Thailand and Cambodia subsequently joined the pact, its catch-all and ill-defined provisions, many not even vaguely related to terrorism, deterred Singapore from participating. In addition, during 2002 the ten ASEAN home affairs ministers adopted an 'action plan' more carefully focussed on terrorism, emphasising intelligence-sharing and harmonisation of relevant laws.

In July 2002, the ministerial meeting of ASEAN and the follow-up meetings of ASEAN dialogue partners and the ASEAN Regional Forum (ARF) in Brunei took regional counter-terrorism cooperation a stage further, at least in declaratory terms. Despite initial Indonesian and Vietnamese objections that it might permit the US to deploy troops in regional states on counter-terrorist missions, ASEAN and the US signed a Joint Declaration for Cooperation to Combat International Terrorism. The agreement allows for increased US technical assistance against terrorism, greater intelligence-sharing and closer relations between US and Southeast Asian law-enforcement agencies. Also in Brunei, the 23 ARF members agreed on measures to undermine terrorist funding. The effectiveness of these agreements has yet to be properly tested. However, the problem remains that while grand regional declarations may help counter-terrorism efforts by providing programmatic frameworks for cooperation, regional

Asia

states' views on terrorism often diverge widely from one another and from the attitudes of interested extra-regional powers. Some Southeast Asian states will be able and willing to collaborate much more effectively than others. Rapid progress towards multilateral action against terrorism in Southeast Asia is unlikely, however desirable it might be.

Change and Continuity in China

Throughout much of 2002 and the early part of 2003, Beijing was preoccupied by the need to manage China's most far-reaching leadership transition in over a decade. It had to do so not only against the backdrop of accelerating – and potentially destabilising – economic and social change at home, but also in the context of an unusually dynamic strategic environment characterised by increasing uncertainty and risk.

The leadership changes initiated at the ruling Communist Party's 16th five-yearly congress of November 2002, and completed at the annual National People's Congress in March 2003, carried immense symbolic as well as practical significance. Instead of providing proof of the extent to which China's political system was becoming more institutionalised and predictable, with procedures gradually mattering more to the exercise of power than personalities, the leadership changes underscored the often mystifying opacity of Chinese politics. The sweeping, if ultimately partial, nature of the transition was implicitly justified on the grounds that China needed firm and experienced hands on the national tiller at a time of domestic and foreign uncertainty. But the new and more complicated configuration of power also pointed to an increased risk of instability: China's leaders now face various new constraints in responding to unanticipated emergencies and to existing challenges posed by systemic economic difficulties and daunting social problems.

These preoccupations reinforced Beijing's tendency towards introspection and introversion, and increased its premium on maintaining external stability. However, Beijing found it hard to sustain such a posture in the face of a strategically more extroverted United States, the demands of the 'war on terror', the international tensions precipitated by the American-led confrontation with Iraq and the gathering crisis over neighbouring North Korea's reactivated nuclear facilities. Beijing's response was complex and inconsistent. In some areas, Chinese foreign policy became more active and pragmatic. China's desire to maximise economic opportunities and minimise diplomatic tensions led it to proactively strengthen its engagement of Southeast Asia on trade matters and outstanding territorial disputes. Its greater pragmatism was evident in its request for a dialogue with NATO – a military alliance whose very existence Beijing in the past has found highly objectionable. Beijing's reluctance to confront the United States at a time of sensitive domestic transitions was reciprocated by an equally distracted Washington, allowing bilateral relations to become sufficiently cordial for the two sides to deflect inevitable differences over American pronouncements on strategic doctrine and Washington's determination to deploy ballistic-missile defence (BMD) systems. Increased Chinese confidence about the general direction of the US–China relationship, combined with a growing recognition of the complex political realities with respect to Taiwan, also helped to introduce a somewhat greater degree of flexibility into China's approach to the cross-strait dispute.

Washington, for its part, was beginning to invest its relationship with Beijing with certain hopes and expectations. Yet, on the two most pressing strategic questions of the day – whether Iraq should be forcibly disarmed, and how the North Korean nuclear conundrum should be tackled – China and the United States approached the issues from opposite directions. While Beijing was queasy about the prospect of US freedom of action towards Iraq outside of the constraints and authorisations of the United Nations, it urged Washington to deal bilaterally with a North Korea that, in its bid to extort economic and political benefits from the outside world, was climbing the escalation ladder. Both of these issues carried the potential to unbalance a Sino-American relationship long prone to abrupt mood-swings.

The significance of the 16th Party Congress

The preparations for changes in China's leadership intensified in the months immediately preceding the November 2002 16th Communist Party Congress (CPC), when new party and military leaders were to be named. But the process of political bargaining and intrigue had begun much earlier. During the 15th CPC of 1997, Jiang Zemin – the state president, Communist Party general-secretary and chairman of the Central Military Commission – had brokered an agreement between Party factions and key players that considerably enhanced his authority. The deal stipulated that nobody aged 70 or over was entitled to sit on the Party's powerful Politburo. This provision, ostensibly designed to rejuvenate the Party leadership, effectively disqualified Jiang's leading rival, Qiao Shi, from holding any position of power. It would have similarly disbarred Jiang (then 71), had he not succeeded in exempting himself from the age limit in return for a commitment that he would stand down at the 16th CPC. This settlement marked a major tactical accomplishment for Jiang. In the years following the 15th CPC, Jiang worked successfully, with the crucial help of key lieutenants, such as Zeng Qinghong, to consolidate and further expand his power base. By the time of the 1999 celebrations to mark the 50th anniversary of the founding of the People's Republic of China, the image of Jiang that his allies sought to portray to the public had evolved – not without controversy – from that of a mere balancer of party factions within an explicitly collective leadership to something aspiring to the grander public personas of former leaders Deng Xiaoping and Mao Zedong. A continuing close association with foreign policy, and the gradual development of a convoluted but politically significant theoretical canon, were used to try to enhance Jiang's profile and credentials still further.

In addition to the timetable for succession affecting Jiang and the majority of members of the Politburo's Standing Committee – the supreme decision-making body – and the term limits applying to government posts, pressure for change came from a 'Fourth Generation' of communist leaders in their 50s and 60s to replace the 'Third Generation' headed by Jiang. The 'core' of the 'Fourth Generation', Hu Jintao, owed his position to the late paramount leader Deng Xiaoping, who had elevated him to the Politburo Standing Committee in 1992, following stints as governor of Tibet and Guizhou. In the ten years that followed, the unassuming Hu played the role of heir-apparent with consummate virtuosity. He displayed deference and loyalty to Jiang and other leaders; sought to offend no one; developed wide contacts in the Party through his association with the Party Secretariat, Communist Youth League and Central Party School; and steadily accumulated official positions – including the vice-presidency (1998) and vice-chairmanship of the Central Military Commission (CMC) (1999) – in accord with his implicit status. While Hu was never Jiang's choice of successor, Jiang could neither flout Deng's wishes nor find egregious fault with Hu.

To satisfy the Party's expectations regarding succession and at the same time preserve his hard-won influence and secure his political legacy, Jiang settled on a strategy that would allow him to play a role similar to that enjoyed by Deng Xiaoping until his death in 1997. In modified form, this would involve a withdrawal from some but not all formal positions of office and the retention of much informal power that would enable him to influence policy and protect interests from behind the scenes. In practical terms, the succession issue came to centre on the extent to which Jiang felt comfortable in relinquishing the Communist Party general-secretaryship and state presidency, and the degree to which he felt able to justify a continuing hold on the chairmanship of the CMC. At the 16th CPC, Hu Jintao was given the most senior party post of general-secretary, becoming the only surviving member and head of an otherwise wholly reconstituted and expanded Politburo Standing Committee. Yet, of its nine members, up to six – Wu Bangguo, Jia Qinglin, Zeng Qinghong, Huang Ju, Wu Guanzheng and Li Changchun, in order of seniority – could be counted as individuals who owed their positions and loyalty to Jiang rather than Hu. As members of the dominant 'Shanghai faction', many of them had associations with Jiang stretching back to the late 1980s. Although he ranked only fifth in the new Politburo Standing Committee's overall formal hierarchy, Zeng Qinghong instantly emerged as the anointed leader of Jiang's faction within it and therefore as a leader of major consequence. Zeng is widely regarded to be the chief architect of Jiang's successful bid to consolidate power throughout the 1990s. He is also an important articulator of Jiang's political theories.

The Jiang faction, then, dominates the Politburo Standing Committee. In an apparent further victory for the Jiang camp, the outspoken, liberally inclined Jiang critic Li Ruihuan was removed from the Politburo Standing Committee and his post as leader of the largely symbolic Chinese People's Political Consultative Conference. This was despite firm expectations among some Chinese and foreign commentators that Li would be elevated to the second-highest rank in the Party. Li Ruihuan's appointment would have generated a sense of anticipation concerning the possibility of a less glacial pace of political reform. While some figures in the new Politburo – including Zeng Qinghong – are said to favour an extension of village elections to the township level and some relaxation of press restrictions, the leadership will move with extreme caution, if at all. Meanwhile, a reassessment of the Party's verdict on the Tiananmen Square protests is highly unlikely to come about while so many leaders associated with that episode and its aftermath remain on the scene.

Jiang's instalment of protégés in the Politburo Standing Committee has given him significant indirect influence on policy. But his controversial retention of the chairmanship of the Central Military Commission, making him commander-in-chief, has assured him of a much more immediate and critical role in all matters of national security and the maintenance of public order. Jiang's retention of the post raised eyebrows not only because he was again exempted from the generational changeover, but also because it involved the explicit divorce of Party and military leaderships. Although Hu Jintao is the second most senior member of the CMC, his relations with the People's Liberation Army (PLA) are not intimate. Whereas Zeng Qinghong has served in the PLA and has at various times over the last ten years represented Jiang on the CMC, Hu has no military experience and his involvement in policy matters has largely been restricted to the punitive – and resented – role of supervising a programme in the late 1990s to strip the PLA of its sprawling and often illicit business empire. Within the streamlined eight-member CMC, Hu is surrounded by generals – headed by Vice-Chairmen Guo Boxiong and Cao Gangchuan – who are steadfastly loyal to Jiang, who has been personally responsible for the promotion of around 80% of the generals since 1988. The composition of the CMC he heads points to a continuing policy emphasis on technological modernisation, doctrinal innovation and a further diminution in the armed forces' formal political role.

Asia

Completing Jiang's sweep of successes at the 16th CPC was the inclusion of his 'Three Represents' theory in the Communist Party constitution alongside 'Marxism-Leninism, Mao Zedong Thought and Deng Xiaoping Theory'. The 'Three Represents' correspond to: the development trends of China's advanced productive forces; the orientation of China's advanced culture; and the fundamental interests of the overwhelming majority of the Chinese people. The theory holds that the Communist Party is the sole representative of these essential elements of the Chinese polity. This obscure and simplistic-sounding theory in fact constitutes a pragmatic response to the Communist Party's declining relevance to China's fast-changing economy and society. It recognises that the process of economic reform, now over 20 years old, has, through the rationalisation of the state enterprise sector and introduction of market mechanisms, forced the retreat of the party-state from many areas of life and promoted the growth of new interest groups and constituencies into which the Communist Party's tentacles do not reach. Key among these is the burgeoning private sector, on which China's future economic prospects hinge. The 'Three Represents' theory calls for the inclusion of private entrepreneurs in the Party's ranks – a policy first announced by Jiang amid great controversy on the eightieth anniversary of the Chinese Communist Party in July 2001. While it has faced resistance from conservative cadres, the theory's adoption suggests that China's leaders feel they have little choice but to try to co-opt powerful groups in society and subsume them within the Party rather than risk confrontation between the Party and groups outside it.

With the new party and military leadership having been established in November at the 16th Party Congress, changes in government posts were completed at the two-week long National People's Congress in March 2003. The most notable – but by then, expected – developments included the transfer of the state presidency from Jiang Zemin to Hu Jintao and the vice-presidency from Hu to Zeng Qinghong – a position that gave Zeng a formal and legitimate role in foreign policy and promised to raise his international profile. While Hu had collected a second top title, there was little indication that he was amassing commensurate influence. The options open to him in putting his stamp on the government appeared very limited. Hu had to contend with a predecessor who showed little interest in quitting the scene in the short term and claimed special prerogatives in policy-making. On top of this, he headed a Politburo Standing Committee populated by people not of his choosing, faced an astute and resourceful implicit rival in Zeng Qinghong, and lacked a senior sponsor or patron who might intervene on his behalf. It became clear that the attributes of modesty and deference that had served Hu so well as an heir-apparent did not necessarily equip him for the political battles to come. Hu may be inclined to follow his natural tendency to play a long game, using the five-year run-up to the 17th Party Congress to consolidate his position slowly, while calculating that Jiang – lacking the immense authority and personal standing of Deng Xiaoping – would see his influence quickly fade.

Yet, with Zeng waiting in the wings, it is unlikely that Hu can afford to take a relatively leisurely and complacent course. Should Hu decide to adopt a less passive approach, two factors could work to his advantage. The first is a feeling of resentment in parts of the Communist Party over Jiang and his faction's perceived grab for power in derogation of the tradition prescribing a more equitable division of the spoils. The second factor is the emerging division of labour between Jiang and Hu. With Jiang holding sway over foreign policy, a focus on the domestic issues that are more immediately relevant to the everyday lives of China's citizens provides Hu with considerable opportunities. Indeed, in his early public statements and visits to economically distressed parts of China, Hu has adopted a remarkably populist tone, addressing head-on concerns about growing economic inequalities and the risk that too many are losing out in dislocations associated with World Trade Organisation (WTO) accession. By requiring timetabled measures to liberalise the economy and implying a much reduced role for the state in economic affairs, WTO membership will involve a qualitative shift in China's reforms. The government is likely to lose the initiative in many areas, including the ability to fine-tune and manipulate the pace of reform in the interests of social stability. Hu's stance does not imply that he favours policies of retrenchment, but rather points to an appreciation of the need for urgent government action on welfare reform, social policy and the creation of regulatory authorities to guard against the perceived excesses of freewheeling capitalism. From Hu's perspective, a lack of progress in these areas could jeopardise the rule of a Communist Party whose coherence, standing and legitimacy has already been battered by extensive corruption.

China is still settling into its new and more complicated domestic political environment. Key players in Beijing are hunkering down, consolidating positions and showing little interest for the time being in matters of policy, where broad continuity can be expected as a direct function of the distribution of power. Wen Jiabao, who in March 2003 took over the post of prime minister from the uncompromising and often confrontational economic 'czar' Zhu Rongji, is expected to tread more delicately in managing economic reforms than his predecessor. However, this lull on policy matters can only temporarily obscure two related concerns: that the new pattern of power will inevitably have a detrimental impact on the efficiency of China's already cumbersome decision-making process; and that further paralysis will be caused by confusion about where, among China's many informal and formal power centres, executive powers actually reside.

Asia

Relations with the United States

Jiang Zemin's retention of the chairmanship of the CMC was often justified in China on grounds of his experience in foreign affairs. Yet US officials also registered the awkwardness and confusion inherent in the move. They realised, for example, that President Hu Jintao would for reasons of protocol have to be their primary point of contact, but suspected that it might be more practical to talk to Jiang. In substantive terms, however, the leadership changes did not have an appreciable impact on the US–China relationship. The relationship itself had improved notably over the course of 2002 and the early months of 2003. Both Washington and Beijing worked hard to keep relations on an even keel, and to move beyond the mutual suspicions and recriminations that had grown out of the Bush administration's campaign-trail characterisation of China as a 'strategic competitor' of the US; the April 2001 crisis over the collision of a US surveillance aircraft and a Chinese fighter jet; and Chinese indignation at Washington's decision to offer Taiwan increased rhetorical support and arms in response to China's continuing military build-up. Although the events of 11 September 2001 encouraged unrealistic expectations – mainly on the Chinese side – that the war on terror would provide a cooperative framework and the basis for a new strategic accommodation, the improvements in atmosphere that were achieved have been far from trivial. The positive tone has been sustained for longer than expected, and has been strong enough to allay, if perhaps only temporarily, some of China's long-held fears of 'strategic encirclement' by a US that is reaching into South and Southeast Asia and has moved closer to Russia. Over 2002 and early 2003, the two sides have ridden out some differences that in other circumstances might have had a more destabilising effect on the relationship.

The improved atmosphere between Beijing and Washington is attributable mainly to a convergence of interests. With its attention drawn primarily to the domestic political transition and economic-reform agenda, Beijing wishes to minimise external distractions to the greatest degree feasible. In this moment of uncertainty, it has little wish to confront the United States – even on the most highly charged strategic issues of the day, such as Iraq – and believes that maintaining positive commercial relations with the US is vital to sustaining the rapid pace of economic growth on which the Communist Party's domestic legitimacy has come to be based. Even if Beijing wanted to confront the US, moreover, the fact that the global campaign against terrorism lends moral reinforcement to some aspects of US foreign policy would limit China's room for manoeuvre. For its part, Washington realises that the efficacy with which that campaign is waged will be heavily influenced by the number and calibre of states it can draw into its coalition, as well as by the amount of attention Washington can devote to achieving the destruction of al-Qaeda. Other US goals, such as the elimination of Iraq's weapons of mass destruction (WMD), also call for fewer distractions elsewhere.

At senior levels, interaction between Washington and Beijing was comparatively intense in 2002. US President George W. Bush, having already met with Chinese leaders at the October 2001 Asia-Pacific Economic Cooperation summit in Shanghai, made a successful visit to China in February 2002. In addition to highlighting the value of anti-terrorism cooperation with China, he also sought greater activism from Beijing in halting the spread of WMD-related technologies and in public remarks called for greater religious and political rights in China. In April, Hu Jintao toured the US and held a flurry of meetings with Bush, Vice-President Dick Cheney, Secretary of Defense Donald Rumsfeld and Secretary of State Colin Powell, among others. These encounters were largely non-substantive, but provided a valuable opportunity for the Bush administration to familiarise itself with Hu prior to his assumption of the Communist Party leadership and state presidency. In October, on the eve of the 16th CPC, Jiang Zemin was accorded the politically useful honour of a summit with Bush at his ranch in Crawford, Texas. This meeting produced little beyond a demonstration of the new cordiality of US–China relations, but the run-up to the summit had witnessed a number of Chinese initiatives on non-proliferation and other US concerns designed to ensure a warm summit ambience. In addition, exchanges among senior officials were regular, most notably over the matter of North Korea's resumed nuclear activities, which in late 2002 and early 2003 brought many US diplomats – including Powell and Assistant Secretary of State for East Asian and Pacific Affairs James Kelly – to Beijing for consultations. At the same time, lower-level delegations made exchange visits to discuss bilateral counter-terrorism and non-proliferation initiatives, as well as to investigate a possible resumption of military-to-military exchanges that had been suspended in April 2001.

There were bumps in the road, however. The contents of the congressionally mandated US Nuclear Posture Review (NPR), finalised in January 2002 and partially leaked to the press in March that year, drew strong protests from Beijing on two grounds. First, the NPR discussed, for the first time, the conceivable use of nuclear weapons by the United States if it were drawn into any future military conflict between China and Taiwan. Second, the attention paid in the NPR to the need to develop new, earth-penetrating tactical nuclear weapons – to be used against WMD facilities in the context of an otherwise conventional conflict – raised concern in China that the Bush administration foresaw a greater role for nuclear weapons in future wars extending beyond the putatively exclusive purpose of deterrence. To these concerns were added Beijing's dismay at Washington's decision – with Russian acquiescence – to withdraw from the 1972 Anti-Ballistic Missile (ABM) Treaty in June 2002. This brought

Asia

closer the prospective deployment of a US ballistic-missile defence (BMD) shield, which China has, despite US reassurances, tended to see as aimed at neutralising its minimal nuclear deterrence rather than guarding against missile launches by North Korea and other rogue states.

Although doubts have persisted among Chinese strategists and others about the technical feasibility of BMD, the Bush administration's December 2002 announcement that it would deploy a limited capability by 2004 added urgency to the debates in Beijing concerning how it should react. The weak second-strike capability of China's relatively small and silo-based nuclear deterrent argues for a reinforcement of the existing trend towards developing a larger, more mobile nuclear force, featuring counter-measure technology and multiple independently targetable re-entry vehicles, to overcome any missile shield. A US National Intelligence Estimate (NIE) released in January 2002 suggested that China could, by 2015, have 75–100 long-range warheads that could be deployed against the United States. It argued that China is developing a road-mobile, 8,000 kilometre-range *Dong-Feng*-31 intercontinental ballistic missile (ICBM); attempting to extend the range of the DF-31; and developing a JL-2 submarine-based ballistic missile that would also be less vulnerable to detection and attack.

Further US concerns about advances in China's military capabilities were detailed in July 2002 by the Department of Defense (DoD) in its 'Annual Report on the Military Power of the People's Republic of China'. The report estimated that Chinese military expenditure, which officially stood at $20 billion in 2002, in reality amounted to $65bn, and went on to project that annual outlays could rise in real terms by a factor of three or four by 2020. It complained about the lack of Chinese military transparency, arguing that military-to-military exchanges between the United States and China yielded few valuable insights into the workings and priorities of the PLA. In terms of Chinese military doctrine, the DoD noted an increasing trend towards 'pre-emption and surprise', together with the accumulation of capabilities that could be used to coerce Taiwan into a political settlement and deter outside intervention on its behalf, including that by the US. It noted particularly the continuing build-up of short-range ballistic missiles at a rate of approximately 50 per year and advances made in ICBM technology. The report suggested that PLA exercises are increasingly driven by the need both to deploy and sustain forces and to devise responses to US technologies and tactics. Emphasis is also being given to asymmetrical warfare capabilities. Meanwhile, the report noted the continuing strategic importance to China's overall capabilities of transfers of fighter jets and guided-missile destroyers from Russia.

Closely following the DoD survey was the publication in July 2002 of the US–China Security Review Commission's first report to Congress on the national security implications of the economic relationship between the two countries. From China's perspective, the tone of this document, which stressed factors dividing Washington and Beijing and recommended proactive use of economic tools to pressure China to act in greater conformity with US national security goals, was both unsettling and confusing. By contrast, Beijing's reaction to the Bush administration's National Security Strategy, released in September 2002, was ambivalent. The strategy document's discussion of the pre-emptive use of force and the utility, under certain circumstances, of a preventive war unsurprisingly troubled China. While the document criticised China's military build-up and stressed that the country would only find 'greatness' in political and social freedoms, Beijing was reassured by the otherwise positive tone – and by the emphasis placed on the necessity for the global 'centres of power' to cooperate in dealing with the new strategic challenges posed by international terrorism and the spread of disorder. Indeed, these sentiments were reciprocated in the Defence White Paper published by Beijing in December 2002, which also stressed the increasing opportunities for coordination and cooperation among states. China's defence white papers have traditionally been used to make doctrinaire statements of principle regarding China's foreign-policy posture, and have never been especially illuminating on defence matters. It is a measure of Beijing's current willingness to answer some of the concerns of the US and others that the 2002 paper for the first time contained an account of the structure of the PLA and addressed the issue of Chinese military spending.

Although the details provided were far from revelatory, the expansion of the defence white paper in this direction marked at least a symbolically important step. It might also help to contribute to the resumption of meaningful military-to-military exchanges between the United States and China, which were cut off following the military aircraft collision crisis of April 2001. The Pentagon has stressed that such exchanges must be based on the principle of reciprocal openness, alleging that China has tended only to allow US defence officials and military personnel access to 'showcase' facilities. As the weaker military power, China has always felt it had an incentive not to expose the PLA to a high degree of outside scrutiny. Both sides, however, recognise that military exchanges potentially offer important confidence-building benefits and opportunities to reduce the scope for misunderstanding. Following their meeting at the Pentagon in April 2002, Hu and Rumsfeld agreed that the two sides would to look into the possibility of restoring military-to-military exchanges. In June 2002, Assistant Secretary of Defense for International Security Peter Rodman travelled to Beijing to discuss the issue further, and the matter loomed large in the fifth US–China Defense Consultative Talks – the first since 2001 – held on 9 December 2002 in Washington between General Xiong Guangkai, deputy chief of staff of the PLA, and Undersecretary for Policy Douglas Feith. Xiong used the occasion to deliver a number of proposals regarding future exchanges, which are now under review, as well as to present formally a copy of the 2002 Defence White Paper. With the political will now present on both sides, resumption of contacts depends on whether satisfactory modalities can be worked out.

Gradual progress was also made in 2002 in resolving bilateral differences on transfers of WMD-related material and technologies by Chinese firms and entities. On 16 January 2002, Washington imposed sanctions under the Iran Non-proliferation Act of 2000 on two Chinese firms, alleging transfers of technologies that could be used in the production of biological and chemical weapons, and which violated the norms of the Australia Group multilateral export control system. On 9 May, Washington imposed sanctions on a further eight Chinese entities for chemical and biological-related transfers to Iran, as well as the export of technologies restricted by the Missile Technology Control Regime (MTCR) – of which China is not a member. On 9 July, nine Chinese entities were penalised under the 1991 Chemical and Biological Weapons Control and Warfare Elimination Act and 1992 Iran–Iraq Arms Non-proliferation Act, again for transfers to Iran. While China criticised these initiatives, it stepped up efforts to satisfy US demands for tighter controls on the flow of WMD-related technologies to unstable regimes and took pains to sequence its policy announcements for maximum political effect. On 25 August, on the eve of a visit to Beijing by Deputy Secretary of State Richard Armitage, Beijing unveiled a law designed to restrict exports of missile and relevant dual-use technology through a control list, as well as licensing and end-use guarantee requirements. Broadly adhering to the MTCR, the Chinese regulations apply to ballistic missiles able to carry payloads of 500 kilograms over a range of 300km. These controls were promised by China in November 2000, having previously been held up by Beijing's unmet demand that Washington first lift the prohibition on Chinese commercial launches of US satellites. Meanwhile, shortly prior to Jiang Zemin's summit with Bush at Crawford, Beijing enacted export-control laws restricting transfers of chemical and biological weapons-related and dual-use technologies.

China's actions do not only mark a response to the application in specific instances of pressure by the United States, but also reflect an appreciation of the extent to which proliferation behaviour has become a key benchmark for Washington in evaluating a bilateral relationship. What is not yet clear is whether there has been a complete reversal in China's calculations regarding transfers of sensitive technologies, which in the past have been driven by the pursuit of distinct commercial and strategic advantages or linked in policy terms to such issues as US arms sales to Taiwan. Sceptics argue that, rather than having unconditionally digested international non-proliferation norms, China has learned to leverage the issue to keep relations with the United States on track.

Iraq and North Korea

If Sino-US relations were in reasonably robust health throughout much of 2002, by the first quarter of 2003 it was also clear that two major tests lay ahead. Washington and Beijing differed in their approaches to the disarmament of Iraq and in their responses to North Korea's renewed nuclear activities.

After Washington signalled its determination to ensure – through diplomatic means or military intervention – the elimination of Iraq's WMD and ballistic-missile programmes, China struggled to perform a difficult balancing act. It backed the general goal of disarmament, and on 8 November 2002 cast its vote in favour of UN Security Council Resolution 1441, giving Iraq a final opportunity to come into compliance with its disarmament obligations. China's decision not merely to abstain in the vote raised certain hopes in Washington that Beijing was prepared to assume more fully the responsibilities of permanent membership of the Security Council, trading its historically passive stance for an active and constructive role. In fact, China's position was more nuanced. China did not want the US to see it as equivocating on the Iraq issue, undermining the unanimity of the Security Council or squandering the steady gains that had been made in US–China relations. But Beijing – like France, Russia and others – saw even a slow and only partially successful UN weapons-inspections process as a means of containing and disarming the regime of Iraqi President Saddam Hussein. Inspections obviated the need for a war that might destabilise the Middle East and radicalise international terrorist groups. Beyond these immediate concerns, Beijing feared that an American-led war against Iraq would reinforce the tendency towards US military interventionism already witnessed in Kosovo and Afghanistan, and imply a further loosening of constraints on the United States. A rapid US victory in Iraq, moreover, might have the effect of hugely emboldening Washington in its approach to other foreign-policy issues, including the status of Taiwan.

As US patience with the UN weapons-inspection process evaporated, and London and Washington signalled their willingness to proceed with an invasion of Iraq even in the absence of a further UN resolution, Beijing found itself in a deep quandary. It could use its status as a permanent member of the Security Council to try to block or condemn military action, risking both impaired bilateral relations with the US and a critical reassessment by Washington of the UN's utility and relevance. Alternatively, China could offer reluctant support for US policy, in the hope of minimising damage to the UN and preserving at least some of its restraining influences. Neither option appeared particularly attractive. Happily for Beijing, the decision of the US and UK to withdraw their further UN Security Council resolution obviated the need for China to take a public stand.

Asia

Beijing's insistence that Washington work through the UN system in crafting its policy towards Iraq contrasted sharply with the emphasis China placed on bilateral talks between Washington and Pyongyang as the only means of resolving the North Korean nuclear crisis. This contrast did not go unnoticed in Washington. In the wake of North Korea's October 2002 admission, under US pressure, that it was pursuing a clandestine uranium-enrichment programme, its subsequent expulsion of International Atomic Energy Agency (IAEA) inspectors, its withdrawal from the 1970 Nuclear Non-Proliferation Treaty and its reactivation of plutonium-based nuclear facilities at Yongbyon, Chinese calls for a US–North Korea dialogue grew more insistent. This came as a disappointment to Washington, which did not wish to be forced to the negotiating table by what it saw as an extortionist Pyongyang trying again to fray the delicate nerves of America's regional partners and allies. Only by multilateralising the dispute and adopting a common front against Pyongyang, Washington believed, could North Korea be induced to desist in its attempts to acquire a nuclear arsenal. Washington argued that Beijing, an indispensable source of fuel and food aid for North Korea, was uniquely placed to exert pressure on Pyongyang. With no such action forthcoming, however, there were signs of increasing impatience with Beijing in Washington. While China insisted that it was working hard towards a solution behind the scenes, US officials perceived a lack of commitment in China's half-hearted and somewhat unwelcome offers to host North Korean–US talks in Beijing.

Beijing's position reflected the extent to which it saw itself as facing only unfavourable outcomes. China realised that a nuclear North Korea would be much more difficult to influence, would provide justification for the extended presence of US forces in East Asia, and would constitute a ready pretext for the deployment of US BMD systems that could in time be extended to Taiwan. It might also induce greater extroversion in the posture and doctrines of Japan's armed forces. At the same time, however, Beijing had little confidence in its ability to calibrate pressure in such a way as to produce desired responses from Pyongyang's notoriously erratic leadership. It feared that attempts to pressure North Korea could lead to a regionally destabilising regime collapse or spark an immensely destructive war on the Korean Peninsula. The disappearance of North Korea from the political map, moreover, would remove a strategic buffer between China and the US in East Asia.

Three factors gave Washington hope that a shift in China's position was still within reach. First, given China's traditional reluctance to conduct its policy towards North Korea in the glare of publicity, the IAEA's referral of the nuclear dispute to the UN Security Council for deliberation might provide China with an incentive to intensify behind-the-scenes pressure on Pyongyang. Second, further escalatory action by North Korea might eventually alienate Beijing. Finally, the US sought to impress on China that a high degree of cooperation and coordination between Washington and Beijing might exert a potentially 'transformational' effect on their overall relationship – a proposition that also made plain that there were circumstances under which currently cordial relations could suffer setbacks.

Cross-strait relations

The absence of significant antagonisms between China and the United States throughout much of 2002 and early 2003 contributed to a greater degree of confidence in Beijing regarding American intentions towards Taiwan. This provided Beijing increased scope to pursue a more active and flexible policy vis-a-vis Taipei. Meanwhile, the need to manage difficult leadership changes in China without major distraction, as well as to adjust to an increasing complicated political scene in Taiwan, also argued for rhetorical moderation and greater pragmatism.

Until the end of 2001, Beijing's approach to Taiwan had been informed by the belief that three key factors were working in its favour: the growth in China's coercive military capabilities; the increasing economic pull exerted by the Chinese economy on Taiwanese traders and investors; and the persistent political weakness of Taiwanese President Chen Shui-bian, who hailed from the pro-independence Democratic Progressive Party (DPP). As a result, Chinese policy was largely passive, consisting mainly of restatements of its 'One China' policy. However, dented by the large arms package that the Bush administration offered Taiwan in April 2001, Beijing's confidence was dealt a further blow by the DPP's electoral gains in the December 2001 elections to Taiwan's legislature. Beijing's response was to moderate its tone, publicly making a distinction in January 2002 between more and less radical elements of the DPP. Presented as an overture, the remarks – while technically correct – were received in Taipei as an attempt to create divisions within the ruling party.

Although it felt rebuffed, Beijing continued to act on the belief that, for strategic reasons, it should try to bring Taiwan more tightly into China's economic orbit. Throughout 2002, it was ready to talk about direct cross-strait transportation links and increasing economic exchanges between China and Taiwan. In October 2002, Chinese Vice-Premier Qian Qichen, while discussing proposals put forward by a Taiwan opposition party legislator regarding the establishment of temporary direct air routes for the Lunar New Year, said that economic issues should be separated from political considerations. Qian also noted that the flights could be designated 'cross-strait' rather than 'domestic'. Amid public excitement on both sides, direct flights to Shanghai commenced on 26 January 2003 and continued for 15 days. Taipei's attitude to deepening economic contacts, however, was ambivalent and cautious. While Taiwan's business community enthusiastically seeks such contacts, the government has long realised that these links will, in the long-term, only provide Beijing with

Asia

greater political leverage over the island. Taipei's position is that increased contacts can only be established in a way that reinforces, rather than blurs or undermines, Taiwan's status. Therefore, whereas Taipei in mid-2002 indicated that private bodies and individuals could represent it in any discussions on establishing permanent direct cross-strait transport routes, in January 2003 it reverted to the position that only government officials could represent the government.

Taipei's suspicions about Beijing's economic overtures have been reinforced by continuing Chinese attempts to restrict Taipei's diplomatic relationships. In addition, Chen has been frustrated by what he regards as Beijing's intransigence in refusing to reciprocate the moderation and restraint exercised by his administration. On 21 July 2002, it was announced that the Pacific island state of Nauru had switched diplomatic recognition from Taiwan to China. Coming on the day on which he was appointed the new chairman of the DPP, this announcement prompted an indignant Chen to warn on 22 July that Taiwan was willing to 'take its own path' and call on Beijing to enter into serious dialogue. Then, on 3 August, Chen went a step further, declaring that there was 'one state on each side' of the Taiwan Strait – a position essentially identical to former President Lee Teng-hui's controversial 1999 characterisation of cross-strait ties as 'state-to-state' relations. Beijing was further alarmed by Chen's suggestion that Taiwan 'urgently' consider putting into place legislation to allow referendums to be held – a necessary precondition to any future attempts to hold a plebiscite on Taiwan's status. These comments caused concern in Washington as well as in Beijing, and during a series of consultations the US made it clear that neither side in the cross-strait dispute should act in a provocative manner. The developments added to a sense in Washington that Taipei was pushing too far its attempts to capitalise on the instinctive sympathies harboured by some in the Bush administration towards the island. US pressure and the discomfort of important domestic political constituencies induced Chen to refrain from pushing the issue further.

Apparently satisfied with the role the US had played in this episode, Beijing restricted itself to a relatively moderate condemnation of Chen's remarks. But it also stepped up attempts to put distance between the United States and Taiwan, particularly in the area of defence ties. During his October 2002 summit with Bush, Jiang outlined a proposal under which China might freeze and/or withdraw short-range ballistic missiles deployed opposite Taiwan – currently estimated at 350–400, and rising at a rate of 50 per year – in return for a reduction in or cessation of US arms sales to Taiwan. Never publicly unveiled, this proposal was revealed in November 2002 by the Taiwanese representative to the US, Chen Chien-jen. Washington rebuffed the bargain. In doing so, it seems to have been motivated by two key factors. First, the bargain appeared to place the onus on the US to act first, which could precipitate a sharp and destabilising decline in Taiwan's confidence. Second, because China's short-range missiles can be positioned with relative ease, their withdrawal would do little to diminish the missiles' role as a possible instrument of coercion. Nevertheless, the proposal did demonstrate a new degree of flexibility on Beijing's part.

As Beijing looked ahead to the 2004 Taiwanese presidential election, there was little it could predict with great confidence. The DPP, while strengthened by the 2001 legislative elections, lacked an overall majority and therefore the means by which it could unilaterally advance its agenda. Yet, precisely this fact also made the DPP reliant on the support of the Taiwan Solidarity Union (TSU). Founded by Lee Teng-hui to carry forward his political legacy after his acrimonious split with the former ruling Kuomintang (KMT), the TSU is forceful in its support for a distinctly Taiwanese identity. With Chen having already used rhetoric resembling that of Lee on cross-strait relations, Beijing worried that the association between the two parties would push Chen towards a still more assertive stance. Even so, the TSU and DPP argued noisily about aspects of domestic policy.

Problems were arguably more acute, however, among opposition parties favouring closer ties with China. Since losing power in 2000 the KMT had been reduced by defections to Lee's TSU and the People First Party (PFP) of another former senior KMT official, James Soong. Recognising that electoral competition between Soong and KMT Chairman Lien Chan had handed victory to Chen in 2000, the two parties, in February 2003, confirmed that they would be standing on a joint ticket in the 2004 poll. But this was clearly more a marriage of convenience than of conviction. Members of the PFP were uneasy about a close alliance with a KMT that had not fully reformed and was still fending off allegations of corruption. At the same time, the balance of power within the alliance had not yet been settled. Although the KMT remained the larger party, it stood to lose votes to both the TSU and PFP in 2004. Moreover, some within the KMT believed that a shift in the balance of power towards Soong could only be averted if the KMT fielded a more charismatic presidential candidate than Lien. Many hoped that the popular KMT mayor of Taipei, Ma Ying-jeou, could be induced to make a bid for that role. Beyond continuing to hold out the prospect of continuing economic engagement, it was not clear to Beijing how it could most advantageously respond to these developments.

Selective outreach

A more forward posture was evident in China's relations with the ten-member Association of Southeast Asian Nations (ASEAN). Here, the common theme of wishing to minimise diplomatic tensions and expand economic opportunities mingled with sensitivities about America's success in reinforcing its Southeast Asian ties in the war on terror. On 3–4 November 2002, China and ASEAN reached agreement to move towards a common

Free Trade Area (FTA), with the lowering of Southeast Asian tariff barriers staggered between the most developed economies (in 2010) and the least advanced (in 2015). Although the deal appears to open up a vast market to ASEAN members, the two sides produce a similar range of goods and compete in similar markets. If anything, China, with its low-cost business environment, now stands to benefit from increased Southeast Asian investment. As this process gathers momentum, ASEAN members will probably need to offset the flight of low-cost industries to China by moving towards value-added manufacturing and service businesses. Meanwhile, in the context of China's wider strategic objectives, a further significant aspect of the FTA is its intrusion into the historically close economic relationship between ASEAN and Japan. The second agreement reached in November 2002 concerned the creation of a code of conduct between China and ASEAN regarding disputed territories in the South China Sea. A loose statement of principle rather than a legally binding treaty, this code serves the political purpose of reassuring China's neighbours about its increasing power. It did not, however, foreclose any options through which Beijing might pursue its interests and territorial claims in future.

China also showed greater confidence in other areas of its foreign and security policy. On 10 October 2002, during a meeting with NATO Secretary-General George Robertson in Brussels, Chinese officials for the first time requested the establishment of a strategic dialogue with an alliance. This marked a major reversal in China's prior opposition to military alliances, its derision of NATO as the plaything of the United States, and its castigation of NATO for its 1999 intervention in Kosovo (which involved the accidental destruction of the Chinese embassy in Belgrade). Beyond a general improvement in relations with the United States, the change in position has been determined by several other factors. America's strategic engagement in Central Asia as part of the counter-terrorism campaign has allowed it to deepen ties with countries on China's periphery that are already associated with NATO through its Partnership for Peace programme. While the Shanghai Cooperation Organisation – grouping China, Russia and Central Asian republics in counter-terrorism efforts – has largely floundered, NATO itself has assumed a greater operational and planning role in Afghanistan. Finally, the enhanced strategic dialogue between Russia and NATO has provided Beijing with both a rationale and the required political cover to engage the alliance. By developing these contacts, China and NATO should be able to foster greater mutual confidence and explore areas for cooperation. It is also true, however, that China is now better positioned to interpret and assess the long-term implications of recent splits within NATO over policy towards Iraq.

Throughout 2002 and early 2003, China's foreign and security policy was shaped by relatively benign forces. The need to focus on a complex leadership transition, and to avoid crises that might shake economic confidence at home, provided Beijing with a strong incentive to broadcast soothing and reassuring noises. Warmer relations with Washington provided some compensation for US incursions into regions and friendships that China had long cultivated. Beijing felt comfortable in experimenting with a less passive and rigid approach to foreign affairs. Yet there were few reasons to believe that these trends were permanent. Should tensions over the leadership transition break out into the open, or social and economic problems intensify, knock-on effects for foreign policy can be expected. While severe domestic difficulties of this kind might contribute to further Chinese introversion, it is more likely that – in an attempt to dispel the impression of vulnerability, galvanise public opinion and paper over Party cracks – foreign-policy issues will come to the fore. Any sudden reversal in US–China relations could similarly vault foreign affairs to centre-stage, and could also influence the way in which the leadership transition ultimately plays out. Under any of these scenarios, Beijing could revert to a less flexible and confident posture.

Japan: Strategic Dynamism, Domestic Stasis

The year 2002–03 has proven to be an unusually difficult one for the administration of Japanese Prime Minister Junichiro Koizumi. The ruling Liberal Democratic Party (LDP) coalition has had to confront the twin challenges of persistent economic stagnation and deflation at home and an unpredictable international environment dominated by the post-11 September counter-terrorism campaign, the looming war with Iraq and the nuclear-weapons crisis on the Korean Peninsula. Overall, the government's scorecard has been varied. Performance on the economic front has been poor, with little sign of improvement in either the medium or long term. Conversely, developments in terms of foreign and security policy have been more encouraging, with evidence of a more proactive style of decision-making, a readiness on the part of the government to address its national interests more coherently and noted improvements in some (though by no means all) of its key bilateral relationships, most notably those with the United States and South Korea. These changes have taken place against a background of fluctuating, generally declining public support for the government and rumours of possible leadership challenges to Koizumi from within the LDP. In spite of these political pressures, the prime minister's position remains relatively secure, bolstered by his option to call an early general election, the low public profile of his LDP rivals and the general weakness of the country's opposition parties.

New security problems

In terms of developing a credible response to national security threats, the first half of the year involved setbacks and frustrations. During a specially extended session of the Diet in July 2002, the government was forced to shelve efforts to pass legislation intended to strengthen the country's defence against a major external attack. The legislation included: measures to strengthen the decision-making authority of the prime minister, particularly in relation to local government and utility services; changes to the country's Self-Defense Forces (SDF) Law governing the operations of Japan's military in contingencies in and around Japan; and plans to strengthen support for US forces based in Japan.

These proposals quickly ran into opposition from a number of quarters. Bureaucratic disagreements between the Japanese Defense Agency (JDA) and the National Police Agency (NPA) prevented the new legislation from addressing the risks posed by indirect subversion and terrorist-backed attacks. As a consequence, opposition critics and some members of the governing coalition charged that the definition of 'external attack' had been too vaguely worded and highlighted the risk that Japanese forces could be inadvertently drawn into a conflict through a conflation of the proposed new measures with existing legislation, passed in 1999, allowing Japanese logistical support for US forces outside Japanese territory. Local government representatives also questioned the central government's ability to guarantee adequately the civil liberties and security of individuals, while revelations in June 2002 of illegal JDA surveillance of private citizens seriously compromised the reputation of the defence community. Most damaging of all, perhaps, was the willingness of senior LDP politicians to exploit their opposition to aspects of the government's economic reform agenda, especially in the area of postal deregulation, to help delay the security legislation. The government may have found some consolation in passing legislation in June enabling it to punish and seize the assets of Japanese individuals and organisations found to be supporting terrorist organisations. However, this represented relatively modest progress at a time when most domestic debate seemed focused, perhaps complacently, on economic issues and party politics rather than risks to national security.

A more mature security debate

Six months later, with the possibility of war with Iraq intensifying and North Korea's covert nuclear ambitions revealed, the Koizumi cabinet faced a new opportunity to revisit some of these security issues. On 4 December 2002, the government announced its intention, much to the delight of the Bush administration, to dispatch an Aegis-equipped destroyer to the Indian Ocean to provide additional surveillance and logistical support to US and UK naval forces under the terms of counter-terrorism legislation passed in October 2001. This legislation had represented a step-change in Japan's defence policy in allowing overseas deployment of naval forces by shifting the terms of Japan's security debate away from the traditional question of the country's defence capabilities to operational issues. At the same time, the 2001 law came with a two-year time limit and required ship deployments to be semi-annually re-authorised (which they were, in May and November 2002). Thus, these measures were a temporary response rather than a permanent redefinition of the country's defence policy. By the end of 2002, it was becoming increasingly clear to senior officials in Japan that the country needed a more durable and internally coherent security framework that would allow it to address a diversity of security challenges without resorting to ad hoc responses, and that was consistent with both the country's constitution and its existing alliance obligations with the United States.

In contemplating how best to respond to a US-led war with Iraq, the Koizumi administration had – particularly in the wake of the terrorist attacks in New York and Washington – been inclined to cooperate with its American ally, acutely aware that Japan had to avoid the diplomatic and political damage it suffered in the first Gulf War in 1991. At that time, Japan was widely accused of providing economic assistance grudgingly and of failing to demonstrate a tangible commitment to the allied campaign. However, Japan's traditional non-offensive defence posture (symbolised by Article 9 of the country's constitution), and the interpretation by successive cabinets since 1981 that this prohibits Japanese participation in collective security initiatives, seriously limits the government's policy options. To provide even limited logistical support to American combat forces in the Gulf, the government would need to be assured of two things: an unambiguous linkage between Iraq and al-Qaeda to justify cooperation consistent with existing counter-terrorism legislation, and United Nations support for a second resolution authorising force. Absent these conditions, the government limited its attention to possible options for Japanese SDF involvement in a post-conflict Iraq, while providing, in March 2003, rhetorical backing for US military action against Baghdad even if Washington chose to act without a second UN resolution. This verbal commitment represented no small concession, given widespread Japanese public rejection (78% according to a February 2003 poll) of such action, as well as opposition from the leaders of the government's two coalition partners (the New Conservative Party and the New Komei Party) and non-mainstream factions within the LDP itself. After hostilities in Iraq began,

Asia

Koizumi swung firmly behind the US and the UK. This stance was widely expected to cost him up to ten percentage points in the opinion polls, but this drop failed to materialise, suggesting a certain resignation in public opinion.

The effort to reconcile Japan's alliance commitment to the US and its constitutional constraints has reflected a subtle and gradual, but nonetheless very important, philosophical shift in the terms of the Japanese security debate. When he took office as prime minister in 2001, Koizumi established, in strictest secrecy, a high-level study group to consider the possibility of removing the ban on participation in collective security initiatives. The group produced a confidential report in the summer of 2001, and in 2002 the issue was taken up again and in a far more public manner. In August, the JDA's annual white paper stressed the importance of SDF multinational participation in combating terrorism and suggested the possibility of a review of the country's medium and long-term defence doctrine, the National Defense Program Outline (NDPO), last articulated in 1995. In December 2002, a prime ministerial private advisory Task Force on Foreign Relations, headed by Yukio Okamoto, called for a more independent Japanese foreign policy stance while maintaining the importance of the US–Japan alliance. (Okamoto has personally suggested that Japan's maritime forces might play a much more extensive role, including deployment to the Western Pacific.) Moreover, in December the government's Advisory Group on International Cooperation for Peace, headed by former UN Undersecretary-General Yasushi Akashi, called for new legislation to allow regular SDF participation in UN multinational peacekeeping and removal of the stringent restrictions, in place since 1992, on overseas deployment of Japanese forces. Such changes would effectively remove the collective security ban, allow Japanese forces to carry firearms in the course of their duties and ensure that Japan's security norms are more explicitly consistent with international peacekeeping standards. Underscoring Japan's positive predisposition towards active involvement in peacekeeping initiatives were: its decision in May 2002 to despatch 690 SDF personnel to participate in the United Nations Mission of Support in East Timor (UNMISET); its pledge of $35 million of an expanded $50m international assistance package at the February 2003 Conference on Consolidation of Peace in Afghanistan in Tokyo; and its $270m loan to Sri Lanka in February 2003 for post-war reconstruction, in addition to the $300m Japan has annually provided.

In an effort to develop a coherent response to a likely war with Iraq and its wider consequences, the government, beginning in January 2003, actively considered a range of new legislative initiatives, including a comprehensive anti-terrorism bill, intended to bolster its intelligence capabilities and combat terrorism at home. At the same time, the government sought to introduce new legislation enabling the SDF to be despatched to the Gulf to guard Japanese ships (particularly oil tankers) and to assist in the post-conflict situation, primarily in providing social infrastructure, medical support, refugee relief, transportation and the disposal of weapons of mass destruction. Such legislation will take time to enact. May 2003 is the earliest likely time for the dispatch of Japanese forces. In the interim, the cabinet has planned to convene Japan's Security Council from the onset of war and is likely to establish a dedicated, centralised headquarters to coordinate Japan's response. Reports in early March 2003 suggested also that the government had devised emergency economic measures involving currency-market intervention, an easing of monetary policy and the possible release of the country's oil reserves to offset any marked increase in international oil prices.

Alongside the new legislative initiatives, there were a number of indications during the year of a more forthright debate over the nation's security priorities, including:

- an informal proposal in February 2002 by then-JDA chief Gen Nakatani for the establishment of a new regional collective security organisation, an 'Asian NATO', repeated in essence in May 2002 at the inaugural IISS Asia Security Conference (Shangri-La Dialogue) held in Singapore;

- controversial (given Japan's historical nuclear sensitivities) public statements by prominent politicians, in particular Chief Cabinet Secretary Yasuo Fukuda, in May 2002 hinting at a possible qualification (subsequently retracted) of Japan's long-standing ban on nuclear weapons;

- an unexpected December 2002 coalition agreement in principle on transforming the JDA into a fully-fledged government ministry;

- SDF internal discussions in January 2003 on measures to combat possible bio-terrorism against Japan;

- joint exercises between NPA and JDA officials in February 2003 to counter terrorist and subversive activities in Japan;

- pressure from young, conservative lawmakers in early February 2003 to introduce new legislation allowing for the confiscation of private-sector financial disbursements to North Korea and measures to prevent North Korean ships from entering Japanese ports; and

- cabinet approval in March 2003 of legislation that would strengthen the legal rights and temporary residency entitlements of asylum seekers.

Asia

An enhanced US–Japan relationship

Interaction between Washington and Tokyo was positive throughout 2002, encouraged by the Bush administration's continuing emphasis on developing the security dimension of the bilateral relationship – a priority highlighted in the White House's National Security Strategy released in September 2002. By contrast, economic issues have been comparatively under-emphasised, as the White House seems to have become resigned to the slow pace of Japanese recovery. President Bush was quick to praise Koizumi's reforming instincts during his February visit to Tokyo, while pushing in private for further reform. By late June 2002, when the two leaders met at the G8 summit in Kananaskis, Canada, the tone was much more muted. In part, this may reflect the US administration's desire to deprive the prime minister's domestic opponents of political ammunition; it may also reflect Washington's desire to win valuable diplomatic support from the Japanese leader in other unrelated contexts. At the summit, for example, Koizumi backed Bush's Middle East policy, including the suggestion that Yasser Arafat be replaced as Palestinian leader – a policy at odds with the official position of the Japanese Foreign Ministry.

Economic irritants

Downplaying the reform issue did not mean that economic concerns were not periodically a source of disagreement. US Trade Representative Robert Zoellick has continued unsuccessfully to persuade Japan to limit agricultural protection at home. In contrast to such free-trade instincts, the White House's decision on 5 March to impose three-year 30% tariffs on Japanese steel provoked a sharp response from Tokyo, prompting the Japanese government's announcement, via the WTO, that it intended to retaliate with its own tariffs on American exports. A June 2002 decision by the US to exempt some 250,000 tonnes of Japanese steel from US tariffs eased tensions, but did not eliminate them. Similarly, a long-festering disagreement over international and Japanese whaling practices that threatened to intensify in May 2002, following clashes between US and Japanese representatives at the International Whaling Commission, was only partially resolved by Japan's acceptance in June of a US-backed compromise, allowing limited whaling off Alaska. Notwithstanding the importance of these issues, they were offset by more positive developments, including an unprecedented bilateral tourism pact in April 2002 that focused on boosting tourism between the two countries by 20% over five years.

Minor political discord

Tension over economic issues was paralleled by small bilateral ructions over political and strategic issues, although here much of the disharmony was the result of misunderstandings and personal differences rather than fundamental clashes of interest. In February 2002, the US Defense Department published a list of contributors to the Afghanistan conflict that failed to mention Japan's substantial financial commitment, but soon corrected the omission. In late August 2002, Deputy Secretary of State Richard Armitage and New Komeito Secretary-General Tetsuzo Fuyushiba reportedly exchanged strong words over the legitimacy of individual and collective-security measures during discussions in Tokyo. This, however, was offset by a regular pattern of extensive and active consultation between senior figures from the two administrations. Prominent among such consultations during 2002–03 were:

- the regular and successful meetings of the Trilateral Co-ordination and Oversight Group (TCOG) bringing together US, Japanese and South Korean defence and diplomatic personnel;

- separate visits to Tokyo by Assistant Secretary of State for East Asia and the Pacific James Kelly, Undersecretary of Defense Douglas Feith as well as Armitage;

- the September 2002 visit to New York by Koizumi in which the prime minister stressed the importance of cooperation with the United States in resolving regional tension; and

- the reconvening (in Washington), after a two-year hiatus, of the Japan–US Security Consultative Committee – the '2+2' grouping bringing together the foreign and defence ministers of the US and Japan.

Military basing issues have continued to prove a source of irritation, but without the intensity of past episodes. Tokyo governor Shintaro Ishihara has continued to call for the closure of the US airbase at Yokota, but his views are not shared by the national government. In Okinawa, a couple of high-profile rape incidents (one confirmed and a second alleged) involving American servicemen underlined the persistent problem associated with the US military presence, and in one instance prompted calls from Okinawa Governor Keiichi Inamine for a revision of the Status of Forces Agreement (SOFA) governing the jurisdictional rights and responsibilities of the two governments. Despite these distressing incidents, Okinawa-related tensions have been partially alleviated by a willingness, in principle, on the part of the Okinawa-based US marines to train outside the islands, away from their permanent bases, and also by progress in relocating a controversial heliport at Futenma to a new reclaimed land base at Nago. Troublesome issues remain regarding the environmental impact of such a

Asia

move and the duration of the US presence at the new airfield, but agreement between central and local Japanese governments over the terms of the plan represents a significant positive achievement.

Strategic fundamentals

In gauging the strength of bilateral relations between Tokyo and Washington, the most telling marker has been the two capitals' cooperative strategic instincts. On Iraq, Koizumi stressed on various occasions the importance of advancing an international, multilateral solution, but nonetheless accepted by March 2003 the legitimacy of the more unilateralist US position. Similarly, in the wake of Tokyo's surprise announcement in August 2002 of the prime minister's planned summit meeting in Pyongyang, there was much media speculation that Japan had acted independently without consulting or informing its American ally. In fact, a detailed reading of the Korea situation suggests a pattern of close coordination between the US and Japan. Japan informed the United States relatively quickly of North Korea's invitation to the Japanese prime minister and when Koizumi met on 17 September with the North Korean leader, Kim Jong Il, he delivered a personal letter from President Bush.

There have, however, been differences between Washington and Tokyo on how best to handle the Korean situation as well as substantial strategic 'asymmetries' that might complicate coordination between these two allies. Publicly, Washington has staunchly resisted Pyongyang's demand to engage in direct bilateral talks, stressing instead the importance of a multilateral solution, while Tokyo, along with Seoul, has appeared more exercised by the need to lower regional tensions by opening a door to direct bilateral US–North Korea talks. At the same time, behind the scenes, the Americans were careful to brief Tokyo about North Korea's covert nuclear programme, while also privately finding opportunities to talk to the North Koreans (for instance, in Berlin in February 2003). In addition, Washington has apparently supported Japanese multilateral initiatives to engage with North Korea, such as Tokyo's push in December 2002 to craft a seven-nation initiative (comprising France, Britain, the US, Russia, China and the two Koreas) to defuse nuclear tensions. On balance, in fact, the US has accorded Japan remarkable freedom of action in regional security matters. This may be in part a function of the US preoccupation with Iraq. It may also reflect the US' recognition that Japan's unavoidable strategic reliance on US military support to protect against a possible North Korean ballistic-missile attack limits the degree to which Japan can diverge from the US on the Korean issue.

The pace of collaboration on theatre missile defence (TMD) has also quickened. At the so-called '2+2' US–Japanese ministerial meeting in Washington in December 2002, Defence Minister Shigeru Ishiba indicated

Japan's willingness to move from studying TMD to active joint development and deployment with the Americans. The shift was confirmed in late February 2003, when the two governments announced their intention from 2004 to begin joint exercises off the coast of Hawaii to test technology for intercepting ballistic missiles. For Japan, TMD will be a lengthy and costly procedure with important constitutional implications. In the meantime, the Koizumi government has sought to hedge against the growing North Korean missile threat by considering purchasing advanced PAC-3 *Patriot* missile systems from the US and by launching its own surveillance satellites (two launches occurred in March 2003 and a further two were scheduled for August). The new satellites will enhance Japan's monitoring capabilities, but the country will remain heavily dependent on the United States for intelligence, not least because it lacks, at present, the large number of trained personnel needed to analyse the complex information provided by satellite imaging. Underscoring the enhanced cooperation between Washington and Tokyo, press reports in March 2003 indicated that both governments were planning extensive talks aimed at strengthening the military alliance, allowing a greater role for the SDF in providing logistical support to the US and in assisting in counter-terrorism initiatives. There is some speculation that these discussions will provide a foundation for an autumn 2003 joint declaration by Bush and Koizumi as significant as the Joint Declaration of 1996, which substantially expanded bilateral defence cooperation.

Volatile relations with North Korea

In the immediate run-up to the 17 September 2002 summit between Koizumi and Kim Jong Il, internal Japanese cabinet memoranda suggested that Koizumi's visit might prove as momentous as former US President Richard Nixon's visit to China in 1972, with the possibility of securing full bilateral normalisation within three months. In many respects, the meeting did represent an unprecedented breakthrough. In the face of emerging concerns about a possible covert North Korean nuclear programme, Kim reassured Koizumi that the North would abide by all past international agreements on nuclear issues, including inspections by the International Atomic Energy Agency (IAEA). Moreover, Kim surprised many observers by offering a number of unexpected concessions, including an agreement to continue North Korea's suspension (in place since 1999) of ballistic-missile tests throughout and 'beyond' 2003; the cessation of intrusions by North Korean spy vessels into Japanese waters; and, most dramatically, an admission that the North had been responsible for abducting at least 13 Japanese nationals during the 1970s and 1980s. The five surviving abductees were allowed to visit Japan. For his part, Koizumi expressed Japan's regret and apologies for its past action towards Korea, and indicated a willingness to provide substantial economic assistance (not to be viewed officially as 'compensation') as a means of encouraging normalisation.

Hopes of rapid progress in bilateral relations, however, were quickly eclipsed by the revelations, following Kelly's October 2002 visit to Pyongyang, of the North's secret highly enriched uranium programme. Tokyo issued strong warnings to Pyongyang that any move to proceed with the reprocessing of nuclear material – under whatever pretext – would nullify Kim's and Koizumi's Pyongyang declaration, including anticipated benefits to Pyongyang. Further, public opinion in Japan became stridently critical of the North following news of the abductions, and was further agitated by North Korea's refusal to allow relatives of the five surviving abductees to rejoin them in Japan. Rumours of a possible further 80 abductions of Japanese citizens by the North did nothing to improve its image. Relations worsened appreciably in February following the arrest of a 72-year old North Korean agent in Japan. This was in addition to reports of a possible 100-strong North Korean spy network in Japan, actively involved in narcotics smuggling and espionage, and the revelation that a Tokyo-based engineering company had illegally supplied the North with sophisticated jet mill technology used to produce missile fuel in 1994.

Against this background, the Japanese government enjoyed little policy flexibility. The Asian Winter Games, held in Aomori in January 2003, in which a modest North Korean athletic delegation participated, may have offered an opportunity for cultural bridge-building, but the public and political reaction in Japan was almost uniformly hostile, with some in the LDP going so far as to call in mid-March for the resignation of Japanese Foreign Minister Yoriko Kawaguchi because of her perceived softness towards Pyongyang. Tokyo's concern over the North's high-profile nuclear violations post-October 2002 persuaded the Koizumi government to join with the United States in agreeing in November to suspend heavy fuel-oil shipments to the North, and by February, it was actively considering halting its participation in the Korean Peninsula Energy Development Organisation. Growing worries that the North might be on the point of test-firing a *No-dong* ballistic missile capable of reaching Japan prompted the government in March to consider imposing economic sanctions. Given that North Korean residents associations in Japan provide annually some 20 billion yen's worth of remittances to North Korea, and that Japan accounts for 18% of North Korea's trade as its second-largest trading partner, sanctions would have a major impact on North Korea. Recognising Washington's unwillingness to engage in bilateral talks with Pyongyang, as of early April 2003 Tokyo was focusing heavily on gaining support for six-party talks including the US, North Korea, South Korea, China, Japan and Russia and on enlisting China's help in persuading Pyongyang to take part. Yet the problem for Tokyo was that Pyongyang would only enter into multilateral talks that were in effect a pretext for bilateral talks with the US, while Washington was not interested in multilateral talks that were seen as implicitly bilateral.

Improving cooperation and dialogue with South Korea

Mutual concern over Pyongyang's provocations has, not surprisingly, bolstered security cooperation between Tokyo and Seoul, much of it taking place through the regular TCOG 'mini-lateral' framework. This has been encouraged in part by a general improvement in bilateral ties, highlighted by a Bilateral Investment Agreement in March 2002, the beginning of talks on a free trade accord, and the establishment of a two-year study programme entailing discussions between South Korean and Japanese academics of contentious historical issues. Although the jointly hosted World Cup highlighted the historical rivalry between two countries, the event also set the tone for important practical cooperation. Japan and South Korea signed a bilateral criminal extradition treaty in April 2002, and, following the unexpected exchange of hostile fire between North and South Korean naval vessels in June, Tokyo was quick to signal its continuing support for the 'sunshine' policy of then President Kim Dae Jung.

The South Korean presidential transition does not appear to have disturbed this generally positive trend, despite South Korean President-elect Roh Moo Hyun's limited exposure to Japan. In December 2002, Roh publicly called for close cooperation among South Korea, Japan and the US in managing the North Korean nuclear crisis, and Roh and Koizumi reportedly got on well at their first face-to-face meeting at the presidential inauguration in Seoul on 25 February. History continues to remain a divisive issue, although Koizumi's visits to Japan's Yasukuni shrine (a symbol of Japan's wartime aggression) in April 2002 and January 2003 were 'managed' without de-railing the bilateral relationship. Indeed, signs on bilateral relations in early 2003 were relatively encouraging. Talks in Seoul between the South Korean and Japanese defence ministers on 29 March, and South Korean Foreign Affairs and Trade Minister Yoon Young Kwan's visit to Tokyo on 30 March indicated the urgent need felt by both governments to jointly address their mutual security concerns. Close ties between South Korea and Japan may prove especially important in 2003–04, with Tokyo and Seoul both eager to impress on Washington the importance of minimising the risk of military conflict with North Korea. Japan, given its strong alliance relationship with the US, may be able to play a mediating role in this connection.

Sino-Japanese ambivalence

While Japan's links with South Korea have generally improved in the face of the growing crisis with North Korea, relations with China have remained

Asia

more uncertain. Superficially, 2002 began on a promising note with the planned thirtieth anniversary celebrations of the Sino–Japanese normalisation of September 1972. In January 2002, representatives from 53 Japanese non-governmental organisations met Chinese President Jiang Zemin in Beijing and underlined their commitment to bilateral dialogue, and on 10 January, Japanese and Chinese officials signed a Memorandum of Understanding committing both countries to cooperation in the communications field. In a similar vein, Koizumi, meeting with Premier Zhu Rongji in early April 2002 at the Boao Forum for Asia on China's Hainan Island, went out of his way to counter Japanese public misgivings about the rapidly expanding Chinese economy, stressing China's development was an opportunity rather than a threat and signalling the commitment of both countries to regular vice-ministerial talks on a comprehensive range of bilateral economic issues. Such talks, modelled on existing US–Japan economic discussions, reflect an effort, dating from the beginning of 2002, to enhance internal Japanese ministerial coordination on trade and investment policy towards China.

Economic coordination was paralleled in the security field by meetings in January 2002 between Chinese and Japanese police officials in Beijing to deal with illegal immigration, smuggling and organised crime, and by similar dialogue between Chinese and Japanese defence personnel in March 2002. Bilateral cooperation during the year in managing the potentially awkward sovereignty issues associated with Japanese efforts to salvage a suspected North Korean spy vessel, scuttled in December 2001 in China's Exclusive Economic Zone, indicated a mature approach to the North Korean issue, reinforced by China's support for Koizumi's September 2002 visit to Pyongyang.

Notwithstanding these positive developments, relations were complicated by the failure to advance bilateral human-rights discussions and persistent Japanese concerns over China's perceived lack of transparency in military spending. More seriously and dramatically, in early May 2002 the Chinese authorities' removal of five North Korean asylum seekers from the Japanese consulate in Shenyang prompted a serious public row between the two governments. The Koizumi government accused the Chinese of violating the 1961 Vienna Convention and demanded that the asylum seekers be handed back to Japan. Beijing, for its part, claimed that it had received tacit approval for its actions from local Japanese officials (including the Japanese ambassador to China). Disagreement between the two governments was resolved following a compromise decision in late May 2002 to allow the North Koreans to be deported to South Korea. But this eventual accommodation did not forestall damaging and bitter criticism of the Japanese Foreign Ministry by conservative LDP and opposition politicians along with calls for a cancellation or curtailment of Japanese Overseas Development Assistance to China. In general, and in the wake of Jiang's sharp and repeated denunciation of Koizumi's 21 April 2002 Yasukuni shrine visit, the impression was of a Japanese government mishandling its relations with China and guilty of excessive optimism about China's attitude towards sensitive historical issues. By August, Koizumi had decided not to attend the normalisation anniversary celebrations, leaving the representation of Japan to a group of senior LDP politicians that included former Prime Minister Ryutaro Hashimoto and LDP Secretary General and close Koizumi ally Taku Yamasaki.

Notwithstanding the symbolic significance of Koizumi's non-attendance, the rift between the two governments was not unbridgeable. Koizumi found time to talk to senior Chinese officials in other contexts, meeting Zhu Rongji in September 2002 at the Asia Europe Meeting (ASEM) in Copenhagen and Jiang Zemin in October 2002 at the Asia-Pacific Economic Cooperation gathering in Los Cabos, Mexico – although in the latter instance Jiang revisited the Yasukuni issue no fewer than three times. Dialogue and a pragmatic leavening of differences are increasingly likely developments as China experiences a major leadership transition. Both Hu Jintao and Wen Jiabao, the replacements respectively for Jiang and Zhu, are of a generation that did not directly experience the 1930s war with Japan, and appear less likely to be preoccupied with historical issues. An important *People's Daily* article in December 2002, for instance, criticised some Chinese as 'irrationally hostile' towards Japan and strongly suggested that Koizumi's 2001 Marco Polo Bridge apology for Japan's past deeds might be sufficient to put historical recriminations to rest. There remain critical attitudes towards China in the Japanese establishment, and Japanese public opinion has also grown somewhat more sceptical towards China, with only 37% of respondents in a *Yomiuri Shimbun* August survey expressing confidence in China – a substantial decline from the 76% figure recorded in 1988. Nevertheless, in November 2002, Japan defused tensions caused by the detention of a Japanese military attaché caught off-limits in a Chinese naval base by voluntarily agreeing to recall the official in question. Similarly, a potential row with Beijing over a planned visit to Japan by former Taiwanese President Lee Teng-hui was deflected following the unexpected and swift decision of the Japanese authorities on 11 November not to issue Lee a visa.

Economic engagement offers perhaps the most compelling reason for bilateral accommodation, since both countries view one another as their second largest trading partner and corporate Japan is heavily committed to investing in the Chinese market. This is not to say that economic friction may not occasionally complicate relations. In 2002, there were a number of disagreements between the two governments. Tokyo criticised Beijing for steel tariffs and patent violations, while Beijing objected to Tokyo's restrictions on imports of Chinese dietary supplements and guidelines for appropriate levels of pesticide residue on Chinese vegetable and fruit exports to Japan. Both countries, however, are likely to experience regional

Asia

pressure for reduced rather than increased trade restrictions. Indeed, China has stolen a march on Japan in its bid to secure an extensive free trade agreement with the Association of Southeast Asian Nations (ASEAN) by 2005, at least five years ahead of Japan's plans for a similar arrangement. While Koizumi made a rhetorical pitch in January 2002 to develop a regional economic community with Southeast Asia, he has achieved precious little in terms of substance, despite a high-profile second tour of the region – taking in Vietnam, East Timor and Australasia – in April–May 2002. The Japanese government remains hamstrung by bureaucratic differences between the Japanese Foreign Ministry, which favours negotiating a series of bilateral free-trade agreements with other East Asian countries, and the Ministry of Economy, Trade and Industry, which backs a more comprehensive Japan–ASEAN free trade agreement. In addition, Japan labours under the burden of importing a far higher proportion of agricultural commodities from Southeast Asia than does China. The LDP's continuing political dependence on a farming lobby that has long enjoyed high levels of import protection does not augur well for a rapid lowering of Japan's agricultural trade barriers.

Russo-Japanese inertia

Domestic political issues have also played a role in another of Japan's important bilateral relationships. Ties with Russia remain stymied by a general absence of any political commitment from either Moscow or Tokyo to resolve the long-standing post-1945 territorial dispute surrounding islands to the north of Hokkaido. After a year in which Russo-Japanese relations remained essentially frozen, Koizumi travelled to Moscow in January 2003 for a three-day visit, the first by a Japanese premier since 1998. In a meeting with Russian President Vladimir Putin on 10 January, Koizumi announced the launch of a joint six-part action plan intended to improve political dialogue and cultural exchanges, strengthen trade and investment ties, boost bilateral security cooperation and participation in regional and international initiatives, and ultimately secure the elusive goal of a peace treaty between the two powers – an unresolved holdover from the Second World War. Yet the initiative remained long on rhetoric and short on substance.

Japan lacks the economic resources to woo Russian elite and popular opinion. Despite Koizumi's floating of the idea of Japanese–Russian cooperation to build from 2006 a pipeline linking the oil fields of Eastern Siberia with Nakhodka on Russia's Far Eastern coast, the inducements offered by Tokyo are tentative and unlikely to prompt an immediate breakthrough in bilateral relations. Japanese firms remain reluctant to commit themselves in Russia without substantial public support from the Japanese government and increasingly find themselves overshadowed by rival foreign corporate interest in the Russian Far East, most notably from

China, which is both steadily expanding its trade interests in the region and proposing a rival oil pipeline initiative with the Russians, extending from Siberia to Khabarovsk. Tokyo has looked to Moscow for help in pressuring Pyongyang to provide further clarification on the fate of Japanese abductees, and the North Korean issue is a source of common concern to Japan and Russia – reflected in the willingness of both governments to support a six-country initiative (embracing China, Russia, Japan, the US and the two Koreas) to help broker the nuclear crisis. This, however, is only a partial basis for cooperation and there appears little prospect of significant improvement in bilateral relations in the immediate future.

Domestic difficulties

The fluidity of Japanese foreign policy has been thrown into relief by the relatively static political and economic conditions within Japan throughout 2002–03. The high expectations surrounding Koizumi's elevation to the premiership in 2001 have not been realised and the prime minister's public and international standing has suffered from his apparent inability to resolve the country's deep-seated economic problems. Four successive years of persistent deflationary pressures, non-performing bank loans in excess of $1 trillion, seemingly intractable obstacles impeding deregulation and structural reform, as well as a ballooning government debt of more than 150% of annual national income, add up to a very gloomy economic situation. Cabinet Office statistics released in mid-February 2003 offered a glimmer of good news in highlighting a better-than-expected fourth-quarter increase in GDP of 0.5% in 2002. Yet this resulted mainly from strong export growth rather than long-term improvement of economic fundamentals. Consumer spending has remained sluggish, held back by pessimism at home and cuts in winter wage bonuses, and there has been no discernible rise in capital investment. The anticipation and eventual outbreak of war in Iraq further dented corporate expectations, pushing the Nikkei index below 8,000 on 10 March, the lowest level in 20 years, and fuelling fears for the second year in a row of a 'March crisis' at the end of the fiscal year.

The prime minister's difficulties in grappling with these complex challenges have emerged in a number of contexts. In October 2002, Economics and Financial Services Minister Heizo Takenaka unveiled a much-anticipated plan to deal with the bad loan problem, by injecting substantial amounts of government capital into Japan's banks and establishing conditions for the nationalisation of the country's most inefficient financial institutions. However, in the face of strenuous opposition from conservative LDP politicians afraid of a 'hard landing' and the knock-on effects of corporate bankruptcies and increased unemployment, Takenaka revised the proposal to avoid capping the deferred assets that banks could count as core capital. By failing to impose a specific timetable for adjustments by the banks, he also discouraged individual institutions from applying for public funds. As a consequence, the government appeared irresolute and incapable of matching aggressive reform rhetoric with substantive policy. Even where the government put its weight behind detailed reform initiatives – e.g., increasing employee responsibility for medical expenses, privatising public highway construction corporations and lowering rice tariffs – it ran into strong opposition from within its own ranks and from a wide collection of influential and vocal interest groups. Even the government's relatively imaginative initiative to create special structural reform zones, allowing for selective but more ambitious deregulation proposals, faced difficulties as a result of direct opposition from individual government ministries wary of haemorrhaging authority.

Koizumi defended himself in the face of criticism by claiming that the reform process would take time. Recent developments, such as the appointment in February 2003 of Toshihiko Fukui as governor of the Bank of Japan, may offer an escape route from the current economic predicament. Fukui is a respected and experienced central banker and, together with his two newly appointed deputies, Kazumasa Iwata and Toshiro Muto, may be more willing to sanction an expansionist monetary policy – to many observers the only viable means of countering deflationary expectations and re-stimulating the economy. Similarly, the planned launch of the Industrial Rehabilitation Corporation (IRC) in April 2003 may help to deal with the non-performing loans problem while minimising the financial burden on individual taxpayers. Nonetheless, the government's policy options are limited and in some instances confused. Koizumi, for example, has abandoned his long-standing commitment to cap government bond issues at 30 trillion yen, while also refusing for political reasons to sanction any increase in the country's consumption tax as means of meeting the rising pension and welfare costs of an aging population.

Amid these difficulties, Koizumi may take limited comfort in the absence of any serious political challengers. But there is little doubt that his rivals within the LDP, such as Takami Eto, Shizuka Kamei, Taro Aso, Masahiko Komura and Takeo Hiranuma, would be happy to unseat him. Indeed, there was some speculation during 2002 that some of his opponents favoured the establishment of a rival conservative party, headed by maverick Tokyo governor Shintaro Ishihara, to directly challenge the government. However, Ishihara chose to run for re-election in the April 2003 gubernatorial elections and, therefore, was not an immediate threat. In the past, the prime minister has been able to restrain his rivals by threatening to dissolve the Lower House of the Diet and call a snap election. Given the uncertainty caused by war in Iraq and the faltering economy, this prospect appeared increasingly unlikely in April 2003. The next general election may be delayed until June 2004, and timed to coincide with the fixed term elections for the Upper House. Such 'double elections' tend to favour the government by ensuring a high turn-out among conservative voters.

For Koizumi, the next immediate political test will come with local elections on 13 April and a House of Representatives by-election in Yamanashi on 27 April. The government has reason to be worried, having lost two important contests in 2002 – a mayoral election in Yokohama and an Upper House by-election in Niigata when the LDP was defeated by an independent candidate. In March 2002, the cabinet's popularity stood at 49%, significantly down from the 61% figure it enjoyed in September 2002 following the success of the Pyonygang summit, while Koizumi's active wartime support for Washington remained deeply unpopular at home. Moreover, a string of corruption scandals tarnished the LDP's credibility and raised serious doubts about Koizumi's vaunted commitment to political reform. In June 2002, senior LDP politician Muneo Suzuki was forced to resign from the LDP in the face of serious corruption charges, while Makiko Tanaka, the once-popular former foreign minister, was forced to quit the party following allegations of misuse of financial resources. The image of LDP venality has persisted into 2003. In February, it was revealed that the Nagasaki prefectural chapter of the LDP had been illegally strong-arming private sector construction companies for political donations. At the end of March, Agriculture, Forestry and Fisheries Minister Tadamori Oshima was pilloried and forced to resign from the cabinet for allegedly receiving financial support in exchange for illegally providing a government contract to a construction company. Further, in the same month, LDP representative Takanori Sakai was arrested on suspicion of falsifying political funds reports.

The government attempted to regain some credibility by announcing on 24 March its intention to reform the rules governing corporate political donations, but this is unlikely to reassure an already very sceptical public. Perhaps the most reliable insurance policy for the government is the continuing weakness of the main opposition party, the Democratic Party of Japan (DPJ). In September 2002, the party re-elected Yukio Hatoyama as its leader, but barely two months later he was forced to step down following sharp internal discord at his plans – ultimately unsuccessful – to broker an alliance with the smaller opposition Liberal Party, headed by Ichiro Ozawa. Naoto Kan, Hatoyama's replacement, is considered more effective publicly than Hatoyama, and has outperformed Koizumi in Diet debates. However, support for the DPJ continues to flat-line at an unimpressive 15%, and the party remains divided on policy and was weakened by the defection to the governing coalition of five of its members in late December 2002.

Looking ahead

Koizumi's immediate political hurdle is securing re-election to the party presidency in the regular two-year contest, scheduled for September 2003.

Asia

He is likely to win the grudging support of the old guard, who in turn will expect important concessions – probably in the form of a cabinet reshuffle, an expansion of government spending directed at reinforcing politically advantageous pork-barrel projects and a slowing of the pace of structural reform. All of these compromises, by jeopardising his reform credentials, risk seriously weakening Koizumi's image. He will face a major challenge in addressing the growing list of unresolved reform issues at home while managing the country's increasingly complex and tension-fraught foreign and security priorities. Koizumi's government has shown, and probably will continue to show, greater decisiveness on the latter. Japan's support for US Iraq policy, in particular, will bolster his credentials on security policy in Washington and help cement an already positive personal relationship with Bush. Koizumi may be able to leverage this to persuade Bush to adopt a more flexible policy towards Pyongyang. More broadly, Japan's strategic alignment with the US on North Korea as well as Iraq, its progress on TMD and the crystallisation of an extroverted policy in the areas of peacekeeping, collective security and maritime operations suggest that its break from a minimalist security policy is real, though slow and duly limited by historical sensitivities and by its deference to the US.

Afghanistan's Unsteady Fledgling Government

The year 2002 began with a fragile, fledgling post-Taliban government in power in Afghanistan and the Taliban and al-Qaeda movements shattered and in disarray. The United States, as well as the other coalition members in *Operation Enduring Freedom*, had committed themselves to stabilising the new government, by helping to build its institutions and by stimulating economic growth, and to hunting down and eliminating the Taliban leadership and remaining elements of al-Qaeda. While optimism was pervasive, the key questions were whether the new Afghan leadership could avoid the mistakes that had tipped the country into civil war in the early 1990s and whether the US and the coalition had the skill and agility to navigate the troubled politics of post-war Afghanistan and to control the continuing ambitions of neighbouring powers.

The challenge of consolidating the power of the new government in Kabul had five distinct facets. First, the remnants of the Taliban regime and al-Qaeda had to be prevented from threatening the new political order.

Second, the central government needed to be stabilised. Third, with regional warlords controlling most of the country, the central government's authority had to be extended to the provinces. Fourth, assistance would be needed to prevent a humanitarian catastrophe and to rebuild the economy. Fifth, interventions by assertive regional powers – Pakistan, Iran, Russia and India – had to be held in check until the Afghan government was sufficiently strong to thwart efforts to destabilise its rule.

Eliminating the Taliban and al-Qaeda

The theatre of war against the Taliban and al-Qaeda centred on the eastern and southern provinces of Afghanistan and the tribal areas of western Pakistan, a region over which Islamabad exercised few, if any, police powers by agreement with local Pushtun tribes. As the Taliban regime collapsed, its leadership fled into the mountains and across the border into Pakistan. When the US bombed the mountain redoubt of Tora Bora in December 2001, it did so before Pakistani forces had positioned themselves to seal myriad escape routes. The battle therefore resulted in hundreds of al-Qaeda leaders and fighters scattering into eastern Afghanistan and western Pakistan, with a smaller number filtering into Pakistani cities. Although the threat in Afghanistan diminished, the challenge of conclusively defeating the enemy became in some ways more challenging.

By early 2002, the US had developed a new regional basing system to support approximately 10,000 coalition troops in Afghanistan. US air forces and logistics systems were deployed in Central Asia, with bases or access to bases established in Tajikistan, Kyrgyzstan and Uzbekistan and supply routes extending by rail to the Russian Far East. The US continued to use a handful of bases in Pakistan, ostensibly for non-combat operations, and maintained at first two and then later one aircraft carrier in the Indian Ocean. Aircraft based in the Persian Gulf provided additional support for air operations. Naval forces monitored maritime traffic to prevent al-Qaeda from escaping by sea. In Afghanistan, US and coalition forces were based at Bagram, north of Kabul, and Kandahar, as well as at a variety of small and shifting forward bases in areas where enemy fighters were believed to operate.

In the first half of 2002, coalition operations involved raids in search of Taliban or al-Qaeda leaders, as well as the systematic harvesting of documents and other intelligence information at former enemy bases. US forces raided compounds in several provinces bordering on Pakistan, destroyed cave complexes at Zawar Khili, and conducted selected air strikes on suspected enemy targets. The only larger military undertaking – *Operation Anaconda* – involved a 17-day battle at Shah-e Kot. The engagement, in which eight Americans and several hundred al-Qaeda fighters died, was launched as a result of intelligence that enemy fighters were gathering in the

Asia

mountains of Paktia province. The battle began inauspiciously, when local Afghan forces accompanied by US troops failed to arrive at designated positions and caused US troop transport helicopters to land amid enemy fighters. Soon thereafter, the al-Qaeda fighters were surrounded and pummelled with air strikes from B-52 and B-1 bombers and other aircraft. In the aftermath of *Operation Anaconda*, al-Qaeda kept its fighters widely dispersed and increasingly resorted to guerrilla tactics. British, Canadian, Australian and American forces conducted sweep operations through mountainous terrain along the Pakistan border. However, these efforts – such as *Operation Mountain Lion, Operation Snipe, Operation Iron Mountain* and *Operation Condor* – were frustrated by the determination of al-Qaeda fighters to avoid engagement on the coalition's terms.

Gradually, the US and its coalition partners developed more refined tactics to pursue the enemy on both sides of the 2,900 kilometre-long Afghanistan–Pakistan border. On the Afghan side, US and coalition forces worked with local militias, and utilised high-technology assets like the *Predator* drone, to monitor border crossings and to raid suspected Taliban or al-Qaeda facilities. Questions surfaced about the quality of intelligence, or the trustworthiness of Afghan allies, when a series of strikes mistakenly killed civilians and failed to result in the apprehension of enemy leaders or troops. Even though US troops aggressively patrolled and deployed in small firebases, the number of enemy killed or captured appeared relatively small. On the Pakistani side of the border, small numbers of US troops began accompanying Pakistani patrols to search for al-Qaeda fighters. More than 50,000 Pakistani paramilitaries and border police were stationed in the tribal areas. Over the course of months, Pakistan captured several hundred suspected al-Qaeda members in the border areas. In addition, a handful of senior al-Qaeda members were arrested in Pakistani cities. At the same time, al-Qaeda picked up an Afghan ally. Hekmatyar Gulbuddin, a radical Islamist militia leader, returned from Iran to mobilise forces against the US and the coalition. The US targeted him, apparently barely missing him with a *Hellfire* missile fired from an unmanned aerial vehicle. Later in the year, reports indicated that he had formed a coalition with remnants of the Taliban and al-Qaeda to wage a holy war against the US and the government of President Hamid Karzai.

Stabilising the Kabul government

Formed at the November 2001 Bonn Conference, the Afghan Interim Administration was an unstable coalition led by Karzai but dominated by the leadership of the Northern Alliance. It was scheduled to rule for six months until an emergency *loya jirga*, or national assembly, would create a Transitional Administration that would write a new constitution by late 2003 and prepare for national elections in 2004. Defence Minister

Mohammed Qasim Fahim – who had succeed the slain Ahmad Shah Massoud – aggressively sought to consolidate his faction's position and to intimidate those who did not belong to his Islamist and predominantly Tajik faction. The Bonn Conference had given this faction control over all of the power ministries: defence; interior; foreign affairs; and intelligence. Moreover, Fahim's men controlled most of the sub-cabinet positions in other ministries. Few analysts disputed the fact that one faction dominated about two-thirds of the cabinet and that Pushtuns, the country's largest ethnic group, were significantly underrepresented in the cabinet and throughout the government. In January 2002, the Minister of Tourism and Civil Aviation, Abdul Rahman, was assassinated. Karzai accused several senior Northern Alliance officials of complicity in the killing. In addition, the politics of Kabul were marked by raids and round-ups of perceived Northern Alliance rivals.

The International Security Assistance Force (ISAF) was intended to prevent violent political competition in Kabul. The UK had had to press hard to strike a deal to deploy the ISAF, with Fahim strongly resisting a force above 1,000 troops or one permitted to operate independently of Northern Alliance units. Ultimately, a compromise agreement was concluded: the ISAF would number 4,500 and would conduct independent patrols, while Fahim's militias would be allowed to remain in garrisons around Kabul. By mid-January, the early elements of the ISAF began to arrive, with the UK slated to lead the multinational force. A central question was how to create a national – not a factional – government in Kabul and how to build the state's instruments of force. US officials strongly believed in the importance of maintaining a small military footprint and in not allowing the new Afghan government to become dependent on foreign forces for security. Discussions quickly focused on the creation of a new 70,000-strong Afghan National Army (ANA) and a 74,000-strong national police force. Eventually, major coalition members assumed leading roles in assisting the Interim Administration in different spheres of security policy. The US took the lead on the national army, Germany on the national police, Italy on the judiciary and Britain on counter-narcotics. ISAF, under British leadership, conducted basic training of the first ANA battalion. The US opened the Kabul Military Training Center in late spring 2002 and, with French support, began to train five more battalions by the end of the year.

Under the Bonn process, initial imbalances in the Interim Authority were to be corrected in the next stage – the emergency *loya jirga*. The former king of Afghanistan, Zahir Shah, was scheduled to open this assembly. His return to Afghanistan was postponed twice because of credible information about conspiracies to kill him. Zahir Shah had the support and admiration of millions of Afghans, who looked back fondly on the 40-plus years of stability and peace under his leadership. He was still considered the

Asia

nation's leader by many local elders and tribal chiefs in Afghanistan's traditional social structure. However, to the radical Islamists, he was anathema and a major political threat. In this political scene, Karzai cut an ambiguous figure. On one hand, the vast majority of Afghans invested their hopes in him, clearly appreciating the values he articulated and his personal civility. They also understood that the US and the international community endorsed and supported him. On the other hand, he appeared to believe that he could bring peace to his country in the absence of countervailing power to Fahim's dominance of the security organs. His legitimacy depended on creating a genuinely national government and economic prosperity. Yet, problematically, the power to create those outcomes was largely in the hands of Fahim and international community.

Coping with the warlords

Part of the strategy to defeat the Taliban in 2001 involved providing resources to commanders who had been major warlords in the early 1990s, in order to raise anti-Taliban militias in the provinces. In the aftermath of the war, the warlords had no intention of quietly ceding power to the central government. The dilemma was that they were at once the de facto government in the provinces, filling the vacuum created by the fall of the Taliban, and also the source of great insecurity for the Afghan people. The warlords made up a rogues' gallery: Gul Agha Shirzai in Kandahar; Abdul Rashid Dostam in Mazar-e Sharif; Haji Abdul Qadir in Jalalabad; and Ismail Khan in Herat, to name a few. In many cases, these were the very same men whose misrule and abuses of the populace had caused many Afghans to turn to the Taliban movement in the early 1990s, in a desperate attempt to obtain basic personal security. Each warlord now exploited his militia to create a local power base. Some enhanced their power by controlling border customs posts, with Ismail Khan reportedly reaping more than $80 million per year in duties. Many profited from poppy crops and the drug trade. All imposed myriad checkpoints to extract internal 'tariffs' and extorted money and goods from local people. Arbitrary arrests, assassinations and other abuses became common. In northern Afghanistan, the warlords were involved in depredations against ethnic Pushtuns. Armed clashes among warlords were common, particularly around Gardez, Mazar-e Sharif and Herat. As in the early 1990s, warlordism was deeply entrenched; the warlords themselves simultaneously hated and feared.

Karzai and the US struggled to develop an approach to the warlord problem. Karzai vacillated, sometimes denouncing the warlords but never challenging their roles as governors or corps commanders who in theory served at his pleasure. Their continuing rule steadily undercut Karzai's authority, making him appear at best weak or at worse complicit in their abuses. US officials appeared to believe that warlord rule was unfortunate but inevitable under the circumstances, and that it was better than anarchy. Washington resolved to avoid involvement in clashes among warlords, adopting a policy against involvement in 'green-on-green' violence. In the face of this problem, many advocated expansion of the ISAF to the major cities of Afghanistan. Karzai, European leaders, UN officials, non-governmental organisations and many analysts and commentators backed such a move. US officials rejected the idea in March 2002, but later indicated that they were open to it, offering to provide needed logistical and other support but not to send US troops. Even after this change in position, however, no country stepped up to accept the offer.

Stimulating post-war economic recovery

Devastated by 25 years of war and economic mismanagement, virtually nothing remained of the Afghan economy, with the population in many regions on the verge of famine. In the course of the war against the Taliban regime, US President George W. Bush and leaders of the coalition had committed themselves to improving the lives of the Afghan people. At the post-war Tokyo donors' conference, more than $4.5 billion was pledged for humanitarian and reconstruction assistance. Yet, the results after a year were decidedly mixed. The greatest success was the humanitarian assistance programme, which likely saved millions of lives from drought- and war-induced famine. The opening of schools, the introduction of a new currency, and the distribution of some improved wheat seed were also significant achievements. However, reconstruction of infrastructure or economic production capacity hardly took place in 2002. US civil-affairs teams rebuilt schools, dug wells and undertook other small projects costing about $10m in total. Major multilateral or bilateral aid programmes were stymied by bureaucratic and budgetary processes. The most glaring failure was the international community's inability to move forward in the rebuilding of the country's primary roads.

In the absence of economic reconstruction, the opium economy returned with a vengeance. The Taliban had banned poppy production during its last year in power, leading to a drop in production from 3,600 tonnes in 2000 (75% of world supply) to 206 tonnes in 2001. Because farmers could earn exponentially more money from poppies in comparison to wheat, production in 2002 rose to an estimated 3,000 tonnes, which meant that Afghanistan regained its previous title as the world's leading producer of opium. Efforts to pay farmers not to plant poppies, as well as eradication programmes, failed badly. The danger of an emerging mafia or drug economy became a real one. At same time, the most hopeful sign was that Afghan refugees were voting with their feet by returning to their country. UN officials expected 800,000 to return. By the end of the year, two million had come home.

Asia

Curbing regional meddling

The cycle of civil war that began with the Soviet-backed communist coup in April 1978 had an underlying logic that had to be broken to create enduring peace. Afghan internal politics were driven by a vicious competition for power among political radicals, both leftist and Islamist. Meanwhile, Russia, Iran, Pakistan and India established relationships with favoured Afghan factions, hoping to propel their clients into power in Kabul and thereby achieve a dominant position in Afghanistan and an advantage over regional competitors. The interaction of these bilateral dynamics created a vortex of armed conflict: as soon as one regional power achieved dominance in Kabul through the victory of its client, rival powers would arm their clients to destabilise the new government. After the inception of the Interim Administration, the key question was whether this 'great game' among the regional powers would continue. At first, Pakistan was forced to the sidelines by the defeat of their Taliban clients. Pakistani President Pervez Musharraf changed the top leadership of the Inter-Services Intelligence (ISI) directorate and claimed to disband the bureaus that supported pro-Islamist ISI activities in Afghanistan and Kashmir. In January, faced with the confrontation with India over cross-border terrorism, Musharraf pledged to end the *jihad* culture, reform the *madrassas*, arrest militants and ban groups associated with terrorism and insurgency.

Pakistan's restraint was not reciprocated by Russia, Iran, or India. The Northern Alliance had been a client of Russia and Iran, and both countries took advantage of their client's dominance in Kabul to seek a geopolitical edge. Russia formed a tight relationship with Fahim, as well as his Northern Alliance colleagues. Tehran, despite warnings from the US, supported Northern Alliance leaders and established close ties with Ismail Khan in Herat. India, pleased at Pakistan's geopolitical reversal, sought to build its position in Afghanistan through ties with Fahim's faction.

Emergency *loya jirga*

The most important political event of 2002 was the emergency *loya jirga* in mid-June. In March 2002, Afghans begun to meet in each district to select 40–60 representatives, who later met at regional centres to select actual delegates to the assembly. About 1,500 delegates were to be picked, with two-thirds chosen by the people and approximately one-third designated to represent special groups such as women and refugees. The stage was set for a confrontation over the future of Afghanistan: would the *loya jirga* result in moderation represented by Karzai and Zahir Shah, the radical Islamism of the Northern Alliance, or the violence and self-enrichment of warlordism? On account of prevailing circumstances, the process for selecting delegates was far from perfect. Although the rules required that delegates had no links to terrorist groups, no record of killing innocent people and no connections to drug trafficking, these were not enforced. Also, at both the district and regional levels, there were many reports of manipulation, intimidation, bribery, vote rigging and other abuses. Eight people were killed in disputes surrounding the voting, and warlords detained or harassed electors and delegates. Observers estimated that only one-third to one-half of the delegates were selected in reasonably clean contests.

As the *loya jirga* drew near in early June, there was a consensus that stability required better political and ethnic balance in the government. A common statement made by Afghans was that the country could not be ruled by one valley, a reference to the fact that leading members of the Northern Alliance all came from the Panjshir Valley. The expectation was that Fahim's faction would need to yield two of the power ministries for the country to be set on a path to stability. When the delegates began arriving in Kabul, however, it was clear that an overwhelming majority wanted more dramatic change. A grassroots movement in favour of selecting Zahir Shah as head of state gathered steam, quickly attracting the signatures of more than 800 delegates and probably capable of mobilising support from 80% of the total delegation. The former king's popularity reflected most Afghans' desire to return to moderate government and their rejection of the rule of the radical factions that had dominated political life for 25 years.

Fahim and his colleagues responded quickly, reportedly threatening to disrupt the *loya jirga* and by some accounts to take the country back into civil war unless Zahir Shah withdrew from consideration. US officials intervened and consulted the king, and then announced that he would not be a candidate. Ultimately, Karzai was selected as head of state, securing 80% of the votes against weak opposition. For most Afghans, the real shock came when Karzai announced his cabinet: it not only preserved the power of Fahim's faction, but also put warlords and their cronies in major positions. All three vice presidents named at the *loya jirga* – Fahim, Karim Khalili and Haji Qadir – were warlords. Fahim's faction ceded the position of minister of interior, though it retained all of the senior staff posts in the ministry. Afghan moderates had been routed, with none of the supporters of the former king receiving a significant position.

A brittle political stability

After the *loya jirga*, the Afghan political and military situation settled into a deceptive stability. Improvements were made in the ethnic, if not the political, balance of the cabinet by expanding the number of ministries. ISAF, under Turkish military leadership, patrolled Kabul's streets largely undisturbed. There was continuing political violence, such as urban bombings, the July 2002 assassination of Haji Qadir, and the attempted assassination of Karzai. But politics largely stagnated. Fahim's faction consolidated its control over institutions. Warlords kept their grip on major regional towns, with those in control of customs revenues strengthening their positions. Karzai failed to mount any successful challenge to the status quo. The slowness of reconstruction assistance meant that no new dynamic was introduced into the system.

In January 2002, Bush had asserted that the US would remain committed and involved in Afghanistan for 'as long as it takes', alluding to the fact that its abandonment of the country after the Soviet withdrawal in 1989 had contributed to the outbreak of civil war. US and coalition forces continued to conduct patrols that captured caches of arms but few enemy fighters, while experiencing light opposition. Yet, as long as Karzai and the international community do not address underlying political and economic problems in Afghanistan, it will remain unclear whether time is working for or against stability. As of April 2003, the key to Afghanistan's future lay in several unanswered questions.

- First, how long will the Pushtuns accept the discrimination and second-class status that Fahim's faction has imposed on them without going into hostile opposition or rebellion?

- Second, given his inability to curb Fahim's power and ambition, how long will Karzai maintain his legitimacy in the eyes of the moderate majority of Afghans?

- Third, how long will the central government be able to maintain credibility in light of its continuing failure to bring the warlords to heel and, conversely, how long will the Afghan people endure warlordism before turning again to a movement promising basic security?

- Fourth, how long will Pakistan continue to exercise restraint in intervening in Afghanistan while Russia, Iran, and India simultaneously consolidate their positions, particularly after radical Pakistani parties gained major ground in national and provincial elections?

This unfinished business has created several potentially troubling scenarios that could put the coalition in the position of defending a narrowly based and unpopular regime against widespread hostility or opposition. During the period before the constitutional *loya jirga* in late 2003 or, at the outside, before the general elections tentatively scheduled for June 2004, it will be critical for Karzai and his foreign supporters to address the problems of ethnic inequity, weak central government, warlordism and foreign intervention if they are to place the country on a trajectory to longer-term and more enduring stability.

Local Conflicts: Hope in Sri Lanka, Positive Signs in Nepal

In a region afflicted with transnational terrorism and acute strategic tensions between two nuclear powers, a couple of smaller South Asian conflicts tend to be obscured. Neither the Sri Lankan civil war nor the Nepalese insurgency involve Muslim terrorists, and neither has recently had significant cross-border or regional ramifications. Nevertheless, in the new strategic environment all sources of instability are significant insofar as they can be exploited by non-state actors. In 2002, tentative political progress occurred in Sri Lanka. While Nepal's situation deteriorated throughout most of 2002, early 2003 brought a ceasefire and greater potential for resolving the conflict.

Sri Lanka's tenuous peace

Between early 2002 and early 2003, peace negotiations to end the 20-year Sri Lankan civil war appeared to come a long way. An incident that took place on 7 February 2003 indicates that they still have a long way to go. Off the coast of Sri Lanka, the Hindu separatist Liberation Tigers of Tamil Eelam (LTTE or Tamil Tigers) staged a suicide bombing of a cargo of arms that the Sri Lankan Navy and members of the Sri Lankan Monitoring Mission (SLMM) – set up to maintain the December 2001 ceasefire – were about to seize. This incident cast a long shadow over the fifth round of talks between the Sri Lankan government and the LTTE, then taking place in Berlin, which opted for early suspension. It also symbolised the principal uncertainty that has beset the negotiations from the beginning: whether the Tamil Tigers were serious in their pursuit of a peace settlement with the Sinhalese majority within the framework of a unitary state; or whether (as in the past) they have merely agreed to talks as a tactic for regrouping and strengthening their position in pursuit of a separate Tamil state and partition of the island.

By 2001, a military stalemate between the LTTE and the predominantly Sinhalese government had been reached. Military expenditures constituted nearly half the government's total outlay, weakening its external financial position (to the point of a rapid depreciation of the rupee) and crippling the economy. In 2001, the economy experienced negative growth (-0.6%) for the first time since independence in 1947. The present peace process effectively began in December 2001, with the election of a new United National Front (UNF) government led by the United National Party (UNP). In the run-up to the polls, UNP leader Ranil Wickremasinghe had made clear his intention to pursue an immediate ceasefire with the LTTE and to invite a

Asia

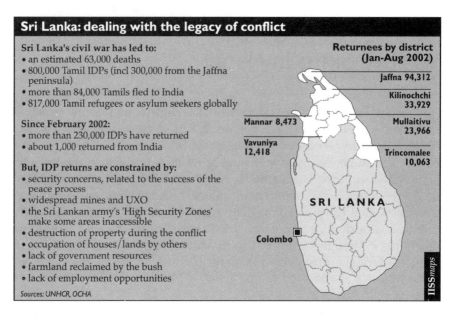

Sri Lanka: dealing with the legacy of conflict

Sri Lanka's civil war has led to:
- an estimated 63,000 deaths
- 800,000 Tamil IDPs (incl 300,000 from the Jaffna peninsula)
- more than 84,000 Tamils fled to India
- 817,000 Tamil refugees or asylum seekers globally

Since February 2002:
- more than 230,000 IDPs have returned
- about 1,000 returned from India

But, IDP returns are constrained by:
- security concerns, related to the success of the peace process
- widespread mines and UXO
- the Sri Lankan army's 'High Security Zones' make some areas inaccessible
- destruction of property during the conflict
- occupation of houses/lands by others
- lack of government resources
- farmland reclaimed by the bush
- lack of employment opportunities

Sources: UNHCR, OCHA

Returnees by district (Jan-Aug 2002)

Jaffna	94,312
Kilinochchi	33,929
Mannar	8,473
Mullaitivu	23,966
Vavuniya	12,418
Trincomalee	10,063

SRI LANKA

Colombo

peace team formed by the Norwegian government to broker talks. This contrasted sharply with the policy of the departing Sri Lanka People's Alliance (SLPA) government, led by President Chandrika Bandaranaike Kumaratunga. The SLPA had also won the 1994 presidential and general elections on a pledge of pursuing peace and, subsequently, Kumaratunga had even sketched out a new federal constitution – providing a high degree of regional autonomy – to overcome the fears of the Tamil minority. But peace talks with the LTTE broke down in 1995, whereupon Kumaratunga lay increasing emphasis on a military strategy aimed at defeating the LTTE on the battlefield. An LTTE attempt on her life in December 1999 – in which she was wounded – hardened her position. She spurned the offer of Norwegian (and all international) mediation, which had been on the table since 1998 and, in the last days of her parliamentary government, had moved closer to Janatha Vimukthi Peramuna (JVP), which preaches an extreme form of Sinhalese nationalism and opposes any concessions to the LTTE.

Shortly before the general election – and presumably in the hope of influencing its result – the LTTE declared a ceasefire. Wickremasinghe, on forming his government, immediately seized upon this initiative and sought to expand it into a full-blown peace process. By February 2002, with the help of the Norwegians, a broad plan had been agreed for winding down hostilities and commencing direct negotiations between the government and the LTTE, which remained an illegal organisation. Both sides would hold their present military positions, which included High Security Zones (HSZs) occupied by the Sri Lankan Army inside what was generally regarded as LTTE territory, such as the city of Jaffna.

But a joint ceasefire monitoring mission, consisting of members of both the government and the LTTE together with international (mostly Scandinavian) members would be created to oversee the ceasefire and arbitrate any disputes that might spark wider conflagration. Trade in non-military materiel would also be opened up between the two militarily occupied zones and restricted movement of unarmed personnel permitted. Talks began in Oslo in May 2002. Before continuing negotiations, the LTTE insisted on being deemed a legal organisation. In a highly controversial move, the government lifted the proscription in September 2002. Talks occurred in Thailand in September and December 2002, and in Berlin in February 2003. Additional sessions were slated for Japan in March and Thailand later in 2003.

In perpetuating the ceasefire – from the perspective of most Sri Lankans, an unequivocal benefit in itself – the peace process has been a clear success. It has been less successful in advancing a sustainable political settlement. In December 2002, Anton Balasingham, the LTTE's chief negotiator, conceded that a separate Eelam national state was not the sole objective of the LTTE and that it would consider 'self-determination' within a unitary Sri Lanka, providing that the degree of regional autonomy offered was adequate. This overcame perhaps the most serious obstacle to the progress of talks: the unwillingness of most Sinhalese to contemplate partition. But the euphoria dissipated when, a few days later, LTTE leader Velupillai Prabhakaran suggested in a speech that the actual degree of autonomy that he expected amounted to a separate Eelam state. Prabakharan also publicly rejected an invitation from US President George W. Bush to foreswear a reversion to armed struggle in the future. Proposals to design a new federal (or, as the LTTE would require, confederal) constitution are still at a rudimentary stage. Ironically, the only concrete proposals on the table are from Kumaratunga's scheme for greater regional autonomy, which had been rejected earlier.

Progress towards finding solutions to more basic problems of governance has also been slow. Since February 2002, the negotiation teams have consistently suggested that the best way to consolidate the ceasefire would be to extend the principle of joint administration, on which the SLMM was based, into wider spheres of government. However, scope for this development has been severely limited by conflicts within the Sri Lankan government. Although Kumaratunga's party lost the parliamentary elections of December 2001, she herself won a second term as president in the separate presidential election held the previous October, and continues to enjoy substantial powers. While not completely opposed to a peace settlement, she is intent on defending the prerogatives of the Sri Lankan state (and, by implication, the majority Sinhalese population) against encroachments of 'minorities' and 'foreigners' in the search for a solution. This stance has produced repeated clashes with both

Asia

Wickremasinghe and the Norwegians over points of 'sovereignty'. In summer 2002, Wickremasinghe appealed to the Supreme Court to reduce the executive powers of the presidency within the constitution. The court upheld Kumaratunga's existing position.

As a result of this intra-governmental disagreement, the effective re-organisation of government along the lines of a joint administration, especially in the critical northern and eastern provinces, has been attenuated. Nevertheless, the principle of joint administration has been extended de facto – albeit surreptitiously and perhaps illegally – into a number of specific areas of governance, including women's rights, the resettlement of refugees and, in the east, relations between the Tamil and Muslim communities. But its application has been slow and subject to setbacks. The administration of large quantities of foreign aid, pledged by many members of the international community for the economic reconstruction of the region, could speed up the process. As of April 2003, however, little of this promised aid had actually materialised. Consequently, there has been scant incentive to act on proposals for its joint administration.

On balance, efforts over the first year of the peace process concentrated more on preventing the derailment of talks than on finding lasting solutions to the most serious problems. The most pressing of these are disarmament and demilitarisation. The concordat reached in February 2002 permitted both sides not only to hold their existing military positions, but also to maintain their existing arms and even to continue recruiting for their military forces. Subsequently, this has brought charges (especially from Kumaratunga's followers) that the LTTE has been acquiring new weapons and continuing to recruit child soldiers. On the other side, the LTTE has started to demand the government's demilitarisation and evacuation of the HSZs. But the government has refused to comply unless disarmament is mutual, which the LTTE has refused to contemplate. Given the deep suspicion on both sides, it remains to be seen how a suitable logistical arrangement for the laying down of arms can be devised. Other fraught issues include what the subsequent relationship of former LTTE cadres might be to a Sri Lankan national army and what their status would be even in an autonomous Tamil province within a confederal Sri Lankan state.

Several other issues, too, have raised knotty problems. In eastern province, the position of the Muslim community is especially difficult. In February 2002, the LTTE refused to deal with the Sri Lanka Muslim Conference (SLMC) – the main party of the Muslims – in national-level negotiations. Muslims constitute less than 10% of Sri Lanka's population, and the SLMC itself is split, with only half its parliamentary members supporting the Wickremasinghe government. The LTTE did concede that it would be prepared to work with SLMC members in joint committees to resolve local problems in the east. But, over the summer of 2002, relations became strained, as Muslims – who have suffered severely at the hands of the Tamil Tigers in the past – complained that LTTE cadres were attempting to dominate them. In September 2002, Prabakharan dismissed several members of the LTTE's high command in the east in an effort to restore the balance, but it is not clear that this has solved the problem or calmed Muslim fears that the government would sacrifice their interests.

Perhaps of greatest concern have been the possible reactions of the Sinhalese majority to any peace, which appears to many to be 'without honour'. Although most Sinhalese would like to end political and economic debility through peace, many draw the line at the effective partition of the island. Indeed, SLPA members posted a 'no-confidence motion' in parliament in December 2002 on account of concessions that Wickremasinghe has already made to the LTTE; his government only narrowly survived. Further, the Supreme Court validated Kumaratunga's presidential prerogative to dissolve parliament and to call a new general election, which she might exercise if she considers Wickremasinghe's negotiations to jeopardise national integrity. More worrying still are signs of growing popular support for the JVP, which has twice launched insurrections against the state. Proscribed in the late 1980s, it was rehabilitated in the mid-1990s under the SLPA government and has enjoyed increasing parliamentary representation at successive elections. Although its leadership has proclaimed its abandonment of armed struggle in favour the constitutional process, its rhetoric remains militant and it has particular appeal among younger, male sections of the Sinhalese population. Kumaratunga is sensitive to the possibility that an 'unjust' peace could prompt the JVP to return to its old ways and unleash a wider Sinhalese backlash against both the Tamil population and the state.

At the same time, the ambitions of the LTTE are still not wholly clear. There were sound tactical reasons why, in December 2001, Prabakharan should have sought a ceasefire. The strain of maintaining the war effort was depleting his forces and, in the face of tightening international restrictions on the funding of terrorism after the 11 September attacks, his finances as well. The LTTE has always drawn heavily on the funding support of Sri Lankan Tamil diaspora and, even before 11 September, host countries like the US, the UK and Canada were starting to crack down on conduits of arms and money. Indeed, in 1999, Prabakharan's annual 'Heroes' Day' addresses – his principal channel of communication with the outside world – began to note the need to rehabilitate the image of LTTE to an increasingly unsympathetic international audience. The December 2001 ceasefire inaugurated this rehabilitation, and it has paid diplomatic dividends. India – which holds the LTTE responsible for the 1991 assassination of Indian Prime Minister Rajiv Gandhi – has remained too sensitive to permit requests for peace negotiations to be held on its own soil, but it has ceased to press its own demands for leading members of the LTTE to be extradited. Further, now that it is no longer officially banned in Sri Lanka, the LTTE may eventually be removed from other states' lists of proscribed terrorist organisations, whose funding activities are presumptively prohibited, and regain some international respectability.

Within Sri Lanka, the Tamil Tigers have consolidated their political position. The relative failure of attempts to create forms of joint administration has meant, in effect, that the LTTE has been left to govern the areas that it occupies, establishing a full parallel government complete with official titles – including a 'Chief Justice' whose appointment Kumaratunga has protested vociferously – and a powerful radio station dubbed the 'Voice of Eelam'. The LTTE has also imposed its own system of local taxation to raise an estimated $30 million a year. In addition, with the agreement of the government and the Norwegians, it has increasingly dominated other Tamil groups and interests – for example, compelling the competing Eelam People's Democratic Party to disarm.

In sum, the LTTE appears to be effectively employing a hedging strategy: while offering to negotiate on the basis of maintaining a unitary Sri Lanka, the LTTE has been building the infrastructure of what could be declared a separate Tamil Eelam state. For all of the LTTE's advances in legitimacy, loopholes in the February 2002 concordat have enabled it to continue recruiting and, judging by the maritime incident of 7 February, to evade the SLMM and to re-build and re-arm its own military forces. Should, in future, the LTTE decide to break the ceasefire and revert to its original demand for the partition of Sri Lanka – which it has not foresworn – it would be in a much stronger position than it was before December 2001. Of course, the current global anti-terrorism climate still makes that a problematic option. But, in substantive terms, the LTTE has done nothing more than make a vague gesture towards confederalism. A year of truce is, no doubt, a valuable benefit for the island in and of itself. But a year of peace negotiations may not necessarily have brought the prospects of a lasting peace settlement much closer. On 10 March, a week before talks were scheduled to resume in Japan, the Sri Lankan Navy sank an LTTE vessel that it claimed was carrying arms, killing 11 crew members. Balasingham protested that it was carrying only fuel and threatened to suspend participation in the negotiations. Over the course of March 2003, the naval security issue became increasingly tense, as the LTTE mistakenly sank a Chinese ship.

Nepal's civil crisis

Violence between government and insurgent forces in Nepal spiralled during much of 2002, but a ceasefire between the government and the 'Maoist' rebels, reached on 29 January 2003, furnished some hope for ending a seven-year conflict.

The insurgency – led by Pushpa Kamal Dahal, known as Comrade 'Prachanda' (which means 'awesome') under the banner of the Communist Party of Nepal (CPN) – has been in progress since February 1996 and had already cost 2,000 lives through November 2001. Until then parliamentary governments had attempted to contain it using only the police. Underlying this state of affairs, however, was considerable tension between the monarchy and the government. According to Nepal's 1990 constitution, the Royal Nepal Army (RNA) remains under royal authority. King Gyanendra – like his predecessor, King Birendra – was loath to concede that his country was actually in a state of civil war and risk a constitutional confrontation with elected politicians. In turn, the parliamentary governments were reluctant to call in the RNA for fear that it might lead to a re-assertion of royal authority over their own. Instead, in July 2001, then Prime Minister Girija Prasad Koirala resigned to protest Gyanendra's failure to act. On 26 November 2001, following the breakdown of talks between the government and Prachanda and four days of violence in which over 100 people died, Prime Minister Sher Bahadur Deuba abandoned his predecessor's circumspection and declared a State of Emergency and called the Royal Nepal Army into the conflict. Since then, fighting has intensified, with casualties rising to over 7,000. Significant claims of human-rights abuses on the part of both insurgents and soldiers have also increased.

As matters have turned out, Koirala was wise to have been cautious. Deuba's decision to accept the prime ministerial office in succession to Koirala split the ruling Nepali Congress Party (NCP), led to Deuba's expulsion and left him running a minority government backed mainly by members of the Communist Party of India–United Marxist-Leninist (UML). Unlike the CPN, the UML – the product of a previous split in communist ranks – prefers constitutionalism over revolution and includes some of Prachanda's bitterest enemies. By May 2002, however, strains between Deuba and the UML were beginning to show and, in seeking a renewal of the State of Emergency order, he invited the king to dissolve parliament, which would allow him a six-month grace period before new elections had to be called. King Gyanendra agreed to this proposal. But Gyanendra's accession to power made him feel insecure in the throne. His brother, King Birendra, along with his wife and several other family members, was murdered in June 2001 by his son in a family dispute. King Gyanendra therefore felt compelled to assert royal power decisively to legitimate his own branch of the royal family. On 4 October 2002, he exploited a breaking corruption scandal to dismiss Deuba, postpone the November elections indefinitely and, under the provision of the 1990 constitution vesting him with emergency powers, appointed a new ruling Council of Ministers answerable to him. Nepal thus reverted to de facto monarchical rule, which is executed by new Prime Minister Lokendra Bahadur Chand of the royalist Rashtriya Prajatantra Party (RPP) and sustained by the RNA.

Asia

The 1990 constitution is both a cause and a casualty of the civil war. Nepal is mainly Hindu. Nepal's monarchy still claims (and is widely regarded to possess) a divine dispensation. In 1960, King Mahendra took an earlier opportunity to dispose of constitutional constraints – previously imposed mainly by neighbouring India – to dismiss his parliament and restore a more direct form of monarchical rule. Under Mahendra, conventional political parties were banned, but considerable local power was devolved to *panchayats* (councils) in the rural areas, which administered their own affairs and dispensed patronage. While these *panchayats* – and royal rule more generally – undoubtedly favoured traditional elites and made no appreciable dent in the country's deep endemic poverty, they did provide for a more equitable distribution of power between the capital, Kathmandu, and Nepal's vast and mountainous hinterland. But, in 1990, Mahendra's system was overthrown by a popular movement, strongly backed by India, calling for the modernisation of government and the restoration of a parliamentary constitution. The new 1990 constitution re-legitimised the party political process and transferred substantial power from the king to elected ministers.

The present civil war is largely the product of local resentment of the over-development of Kathmandu, the overweening power of its political elite and the poverty and sense of deprivation afflicting the bulk of the rural population that have intensified since the 1990 constitution came into effect. (Although there is a small ethnic dimension – Nepal's minority Tibeto-Burman Buddhists are over-represented within insurgent cadres in protest against the preponderantly Indo-Aryan composition of power in Kathmandu – most of its leaders, such as Prachanda, are Indo-Aryan.) The first governments under the constitution espoused fashionable models of development, which favoured the centralisation of power and set out to attract maximum quantities of investment and aid from abroad. Nearly half of Nepal's current development budget comes from foreign aid, of which some $2.5 billion was pledged in February 2002. Power and wealth has become heavily concentrated around the capital, where most of the development budget stays. The hinterland has felt the effects mainly through increased taxation and increasingly dysfunctional schemes to harness Nepal's vast hydroelectric potential, regardless of social and environmental costs, and to sell it cheaply to India. Traditional rural elites also more broadly lament the *panchayats'* loss of authority at the hands of the 'modern' politicians in Kathmandu. Adding fuel to the fire, corruption within the Kathmandu political elite is legendary. The October 2002 dismissal of Deuba was premised on his refusal to dismiss five ministers against whom major corruption charges had been proven. Finally, the Kathmandu elite has also failed to provide even minimal political stability. Factional conflicts within both the main NCP and the opposition communist parties brought about 12 changes of government in 12 years.

Though inspired by events in Chinese history, the so-called 'Maoist' insurgents have gained very little support from contemporary China. Insofar as they are connected to international forces at all, it is through the Revolutionary International Movement, which also has contacts with the 'Shining Path' in Peru. In the early days of the insurgency, they may have enjoyed some cross-border protection from India, whose traditional interests in Nepal have centred on keeping its government weak and susceptible to New Delhi's influence. But recently this position has changed and New Delhi has shown hostility to the insurgency. There are three reasons: the changed international climate after 11 September; the insurgency's unexpected military success; and growing evidence of its links with minor 'Naxalite' insurgencies in regions of India itself. Nepal's insurgency, then, is essentially rural and homegrown. As of April 2003, it operated committees of government in 22 of Nepal's 75 districts, mainly in the west. Moreover, its revolutionary tactics (following the classic Maoist model) have focused on taking the countryside away from the central government and gradually encircling the Kathmandu valley.

King Gyanendra appears to have the strong backing of the RNA and the RPP, which are sceptical of elected governments. But whether he can use his newly assumed powers to tame the insurgency, and what kind of political settlement could eventuate, remain to be seen. It is improbable that the RNA can defeat the Maoists in the field. Yet the insurgents' political demands are stiff. One reason for the breakdown of the talks between Prachanda and Deuba's government in November 2001 was the former's insistence on the abolition of the monarchy and establishment of a republic. It is possible that the Kathmandu politicians and the Maoists will seek a rapprochement at the expense of the monarchy and the RNA. Behind their military front, the Maoists could claim to administer their territories on principles of social democracy (albeit of a radical kind) to which the constitutional political parties might be able to accommodate themselves. But this prospect remains unlikely. Ironically, the more probable way forward for Nepal may lie in an alliance of Maoism and monarchism against constitutional modernity. Many members of the constitutional parties have shown signs of wanting to jump ship to join King Gyanendra's Council of Ministers. Gyanendra may seek to scupper the 1990 constitution entirely and devise a new model that re-establishes, at least in part, the 1960 settlement whereby local rural *panchayats* were directly empowered, shifting a measure of power back from Kathmandu to the provinces. This would have to be accompanied by the legitimisation of political parties and the creation of some kind of representative assembly in Kathmandu, which did not occur in 1960–90. Perhaps in anticipation of such a possibility, Prachanda in early 2003 did not re-assert his long-standing insistence on a republic and the abolition of the monarchy, and opened the way for negotiations directly with the throne.

Asia

Despite the relative insularity of the Nepalese conflict, outside actors may influence outcomes. The US has tended to view counter-insurgency in Nepal as part of the global campaign against terrorism, and has added the CPN to two of its three lists of proscribed terrorist organisations. US Secretary of State Colin Powell visited Kathmandu in January 2002 to support the government. For 2002, the US provided $35m in development assistance and $17m in military aid to Nepal. The UK and India have not been far behind. India views the CPN as having arisen from resentful perceptions of Indian hegemony, and is wary of links between Nepalese and Indian Maoist insurgents. New Delhi also regards Nepal as a buffer against China. In April 2002, India started to provide Nepal with small arms, trucks and helicopters, and to provide RNA commandos with counter-insurgency training. The UK has a keen, if limited, historical and practical interest in stabilising Nepal: since 1816, Nepal has been an ally and, with the Gurkhas, has supplied the British Army with some of its best soldiers. Rebels are hostile to the Gurkha–UK relationship and reportedly have attempted to subvert the British Army's recruiting operations. Further, about 50,000 retired Gurkha soldiers live in Nepal. After Admiral Sir Michael Boyce, Chief of the UK Defence Staff, visited Nepal with a team of specialists to assess Nepal's military requirements in May 2002, the UK authorised 'non-lethal military hardware assistance', including two helicopters.

Gyanendra's takeover of 4 October, however, caused some embarrassment to these powers, and as of April 2003 only China had openly recognised the reversion to monarchical autocracy. India, which helped to write the 1990 constitution, has voiced the need to restore constitutional government as quickly as possible. The US encouraged the restoration of democracy but subsequently appeared to diplomatically acquiesce to the coup. King Gyanendra has claimed, under the reserve powers granted to him by the constitution, that his actions were 'constitutional'. As of early 2003, the NCP was contesting this claim before the Nepal Supreme Court. Both sides agreed to a ceasefire on 29 January 2003, and on 30 March a Maoist delegation under deputy rebel leader Dr Babaram Bhattarai offered to begin political negotiations. Given India's current strategic concerns about terrorism, New Delhi is unlikely to do anything to de-stabilise Gyanendra or to upset the US. US policy in South Asia, in turn, is likely to be less politically idealistic than elsewhere and to focus narrowly on counter-terrorism – as suggested by continued American military support for the Nepalese government. Accordingly, an accommodation between the monarchy and the insurgency could be sustainable.

Post-11 September dividends?

Heightened intolerance for terrorism and insurgency generally has constrained the LTTE's military options in Sri Lanka and ensured a measure of US support for government anti-insurgency efforts in Nepal. While neither the Tamil Tigers nor the Maoists of the CPN are logical partners of transnational Islamic terrorists, an awareness among outside powers that active armed non-state groups are susceptible to alliances of convenience should sustain pragmatic international support for peace processes in both countries.

Africa

Sub-Saharan Africa undoubtedly took a turn for the better in 2002. South Africa finally began to implement a constructive, forward-looking foreign policy worthy of its economic and political status in brokering fairly promising peace accords in the Democratic Republic of Congo (DRC). Pretoria also provided 750 troops to consolidate a peace deal that former South African President Nelson Mandela had brokered in Burundi. South Africa and Nigeria took the lead roles in launching the New Partnership for African Development (NEPAD), the continent's massive multilateral poverty-reduction initiative – a sign that major African states are beginning to work together effectively. Against the expectations of some, Kenya managed a smooth political transition from President Daniel arap Moi's 25-year rule to a new political era by way of a genuine and reasonably fair multiparty election in December 2002. In Angola, the death of rebel leader Jonas Savimbi in February 2002 and an end to the fighting spawned a peace process that has borne fruit. The process of resettling and reintegrating former rebel combatants and their families proceeded, if slowly, and Luanda began to assert itself at the regional level. The political and economic prospects of Angola and São Tomé & Principe improved as the US sought to cultivate them as sources of non-OPEC oil. Ethiopia and Eritrea's rather cold peace held. The peace process in Sierra Leone stayed on track, as President Ahmad Tejan Kabbah won a second five-year term in the May 2002 election – though the government will need to focus more sharply on security to ensure stability and the economy needs to be revived if the underlying stresses that caused the war are to be addressed. In Sudan's more tentative peace process there are key unresolved substantive issues, including executive power-sharing, the level of southern representation in national bodies, the extent of the Sudanese People's Liberation Movement/Army's constitutional authority in the south, the legal status of the national capital, ceasefire monitoring, the role of militias and wealth sharing. But the process itself remained reasonably robust.

Madagascar had been a divided country, with two presidents, two capitals and two economies, since the disputed presidential election of December 2001. On 29 April 2002, the High Constitutional Court ruled that Marc Ravalomanana had won the December 2001 poll by 51% compared to incumbent President Didier Ratsiraka's 36%, and Western donors – including the US – recognised Ravalomanana as president in June 2002. But Ratsiraka did not accept the ruling and sought exile in France

Map Africa

in July 2002. Although the African Union (AU) – the successor to the Organisation for African Unity – stated in August 2002 that it would not recognise Ravalomanana's legitimacy until legislative elections were held to confirm his popularity, in September the UN invited him to the World Summit on Sustainable Development and legally consolidated his authority. In any case, on 15 December 2002, Ravalomanana's 'I Love Madagascar' party won a parliamentary majority in peaceful elections.

Yet there also remained multiple sources of instability, insecurity and human misery. Political progress in the DRC and the substantial withdrawal of the forces of several of the seven nations involved in the conflict did not mean the absence of hostilities on the ground, and UN forces were not sufficient to enforce peace. In principle, all foreign troops have left, although some Ugandans have stayed at the UN's request, and it is alleged that about 5,000 Rwandans are still there covertly. Côte d'Ivoire hurtled towards civil war in spite of France's and the Economic Community of West African States' military and political involvement at the end of 2002, which led to the Marcoussis agreement in early 2003. Charles Taylor's regime in Liberia came under heavy pressure from an increasingly hostile insurgency. Zimbabwean President Robert Mugabe continued to fiddle – with coercive 'land reform' policies and repression of legitimate political opposition – while Zimbabwe burned in drought and looming famine. Regional powers remained reluctant to pressure Mugabe to moderate his cynical policies. The EU–Africa summit scheduled for 5 April was cancelled over African nations' refusal to attend unless Mugabe was invited. Notwithstanding the efforts of regional powers – notably Kenya – Somalia came no closer to having a functioning civil government and continued to be a source of insecurity in the form of arms trafficking and refugees and, potentially, transnational Islamic terrorism. Al-Qaeda appeared to step up terrorist activities in East Africa, as an Israeli-owned hotel and airliner were simultaneously targeted in Mombasa, Kenya in November 2002. Nigeria continued to endure Muslim–Christian problems and political unrest that imperilled both oil production and the integrity of elections scheduled for 19 April 2003.

Other developments were ambiguous. On 15 March 2003, General François Bozizé and 1,000 troops – who had been unpaid for several months – seized the airport and presidential palace on Bangui, Central African Republic, while President Ange-Félix Patassé was at a conference in Niger. Fifteen people died in the coup, which sparked looting. Patassé's ten-year rule had been marked by ineptitude, greed and brutality. As Bozizé imposed a curfew and had looters executed, he pledged to hold a 'national dialogue' with an eye towards a return to civil rule, and to secure fresh loans from the International Monetary Fund and the World Bank. Whether he makes good on these promises will be a test for the new orthodoxy in Africa that rulers who come to power by force will not be recognised. Burundi faced a crucial test with trepidation on May Day 2003, when President Pierre Buyoya, a member of the politically and economically dominant Tutsi minority, was scheduled to cede power to Domitien Ndayizeye of the majority Hutu tribe under the power-sharing deal brokered by Mandela. The last time he stood down in favour of a Hutu, in 1993, a civil war ensued in which 300,000 were killed and 1.2 million displaced. The AU planned to send 43 observers to pave the way for peace enforcement including the disarmament of roughly 70,000 rebel fighters – involving up to 5,000 soldiers.

Sub-Saharan Africa enjoyed greater global strategic resonance in early 2003 because Angola, Cameroon and Guinea, as non-permanent members of the UN Security Council, emerged as key potential 'swing votes' on a second resolution that would sanction military action in Iraq. In the event, the resolution was never tabled. But the prominence of the debate and the reluctance of the three to support war highlighted Africa's acute fear of marginalisation in the post-11 September strategic environment. On 4 February 2003, the AU expressed plain opposition to military action. The Southern African Development Community endorsed the AU's position. Later in February, 41 out of 42 heads of state attending the Franco–African Summit in Paris supported a French-drafted statement that military action should be a last resort. Africa's worries centred on the prospect of religious violence in the event of war in Iraq (nearly 50% of the continent's inhabitants are Muslims); potential refugee problems for regions already over-burdened by local conflicts; the negative economic effect of higher oil prices (except on high-production countries like Angola, Guinea and Nigeria); the diversion of trade and investment away from Africa towards the Middle East; and the longer term consequences of unrestrained US power. As unexpected military and political challenges began to surface in Iraq in March and April 2003, Africa's fear did not seem misplaced. After 11 September, the prospect of greater major-power attention to saving failed and failing states in Africa to deter terrorist co-optation gave way to more limited preventive measures, such as airborne and maritime surveillance and quick-reaction forces in East Africa and the Horn. After a highly controversial military operation that is designed to change the status quo in the Middle East, Africa is likely to command even less attention from Washington and European capitals. But at least there were stronger signs in 2002 that Africa was taking firmer charge of its own destiny.

Southern Africa: New Look, Persistent Problems

Southern Africa witnessed several salutary developments in 2002, but faces at least as many stiff challenges to marked improvement in its prospects as a region. On the plus side, Angola's long-running civil war ended. Most of the troops of the three Southern African Development Community (SADC) nations supporting the government of the Democratic Republic of Congo (DRC) withdrew following a series of peace agreements. This may lead to at least an attenuation of the divisions that have plagued the SADC in recent years due to Zimbabwe-led military support for the Kinshasa government. Additionally, South Africa launched an ambitious development initiative, the New Partnership for Africa's Development (NEPAD), to which it and several regional partners appear solidly committed. On the downside, Angola still has to address substantial problems of peace, Zimbabwe's political and economic situation has decayed further and the overspill of refugees and arms from the DRC remains a threat. The region is experiencing increasingly acute water scarcity, that is deepening existing widespread environmental degradation. Southern Africa also suffers chronically from the destabilising effects of famine and HIV/AIDS.

NEPAD – process vs progress

According to the World Food Programme, in 2002–03 the 14-member SADC region was suffering 'the largest single food crisis in the world today'. At least 13 million people faced starvation or acute food insecurity in the SADC region. Seven countries were affected by outright famine: Angola, Lesotho, Malawi, Mozambique, Swaziland, Zambia and Zimbabwe. To make matters worse, of the approximately 45m people globally who are HIV-positive, 70% live in the SADC region. The global HIV infection rate is some 1.2%, but is about 20.6% for SADC states. HIV/AIDS will reduce the regional consumer market, increase the premium paid to a shrinking pool of skilled workers, reduce productivity and increase turnover, recruitment and training costs, and raise absenteeism. It is estimated that, in poor households with an infected member, income may decline by as much as 40–60%. The social impact of HIV/AIDS is even less quantifiable than the economic impact but equally significant. AIDS is producing a burgeoning generation of orphans who lack social and familial support and who place an increasing and unsustainable burden on other family members and social services. The absence of familial support and guidance for AIDS orphans, particularly in communities in which the disease is highly stigmatised, is producing a generation of young people lacking a normative framework, making them increasingly susceptible to social delinquency, crime and insurgency.

In this dim light, it was timely for South African President Thabo Mbeki to seize the leadership of the southern African region and focus on economic development and the alleviation of poverty and disease. His brainchild, NEPAD, has significantly and positively altered the tenor of the continent's development debate, seeking to promote good governance in return for increased aid, investment and debt relief. South Africa's leading role reflects both its economic standing in Africa, where its GDP ($125 billion) is three times greater than the combined GDP of the rest of the SADC region (Angola, Botswana, DRC, Lesotho, Malawi, Mauritius, Mozambique, Namibia, Seychelles, South Africa, Swaziland, Tanzania, Zambia, Zimbabwe). It also tends to vindicate the faith and hope that the international community continues to place in South Africa's leadership and its continental example of internal transformation. Further, NEPAD underscores Mbeki's belief that only through a change in the external trade and aid environment can the continent make developmental progress. Such structuralism reveals his political upbringing as head of the African National Congress (ANC)'s Department of International Relations, and some 30 years spent in exile gathering international support for the ANC's domestic struggle against apartheid.

NEPAD was, along with global economic recovery and the fight against terrorism, one of the three agenda items for the G8 summit held in June 2002 in Kananaskis, Canada. Broadly modelled on the United States' post-Second World War Marshall Plan, NEPAD seeks annual investment of $64bn to achieve a 7% growth rate, so as to reverse African economic decline and arrest poverty. It is a bargain with the international community: in return for increased aid, investment and debt relief and improved trade access, Africa will commit itself to good governance and the rule of law. Although the global focus on Iraq threatens to eclipse Africa, and especially NEPAD, from the international spotlight, the ramifications of 11 September illuminated the importance of not allowing African states to collapse. Furthermore, NEPAD reinforces the need to reward performing states by, among other things, improving access to global markets through initiatives such as the US African Growth and Opportunity Act (AGOA) and the European Union (EU)'s Cotonou Arrangement (over which negotiations commenced in September 2002). While Western responses to African development needs are still schizophrenic – vacillating between protectionism through domestic subsidies and greater trade access for more aid – there has, in important respects, been much more generous and proactive engagement with Africa by the administration of US President George W. Bush than any of its predecessors, Clinton's included. Bush has met with 21 African heads of state since coming to office and has despatched five cabinet members to Africa. Bush signed into law, in August 2002, the second phase of AGOA ('AGOA II'), which doubled quantitative limits on duty-free African exports.

In evaluating NEPAD, process should be distinguished from substance. In terms of process, NEPAD witnessed a flurry of activity in 2002. A multitude of coordinating mechanisms were established, and the conference and summit circuit was clogged with NEPAD events, including the World Economic Forum (WEF) annual regional meeting held in Durban in June 2002. Internally, South African government ministries have allocated officials for NEPAD engagement, while NEPAD now has to feature in the business plans of South African diplomatic missions abroad. An outreach programme has been set up to provide points of entry for non-governmental organisations (NGOs), while a number of NEPAD business chapters are, at least in principle, now functional. Externally, by the start of 2003, there was coordination at eight different levels involving the NEPAD Secretariat based at the Development Bank of Southern Africa (DBSA) in Midrand near Johannesburg. Comprising seconded officials from the original five initiating states (Algeria, Egypt, Nigeria, Senegal and South Africa), the Secretariat is charged with both logistical support and programme facilitation with a wide range of institutions. In addition, NEPAD has recognised the need for engagement with civil society and business, and the importance of promoting internal discussion. Yet, just three African countries have thus far held parliamentary debates on NEPAD. Ten states were selected for a pilot outreach project during 2002. A NEPAD Business Group was also formed, involving, among others, the Corporate Council on Africa, the Commonwealth Business Forum and the International Chamber of Commerce.

Despite these nominal organisational successes, NEPAD so far has not adequately met four stiff challenges: the disputed nature of the embryonic African Peer Review Mechanism (APRM); the more tangible problem of Zimbabwe; organisational visibility; and organisational overstretch. The APRM remains contested with regard to its scope, depth and adherence. Only after considerable debate before and during the November 2002 Abuja meeting of the NEPAD Heads of State Implementation Committee were political and economic governance criteria accepted by 12 of the 18 states as part of the APRM. Furthermore, the APRM remains a voluntary mechanism and thus, by definition, fails to address the threat to NEPAD of non-performing states. The strongest test for the architects of NEPAD remains Zimbabwe. The regime of President Robert Mugabe represents the antithesis of all that African leaders have enshrined in their acceptance of NEPAD, yet Africa's most influential heads of state – Mbeki and Nigerian President Olusegun Obasanjo – have failed to acknowledge the connection between a collapsing Zimbabwe and a threat to NEPAD. Further, NEPAD is in constant danger of being overshadowed by global developments,

Africa

particularly in the Middle East. Africa virtually disappeared from the coverage of the WEF Summit in Davos in January 2003. Finally, NEPAD's credibility may be threatened by its proponents trying to take on too much in the political realm, such as attempting to influence global debates over Iraq, and losing track of priorities.

These question marks seemed to give rise to tentativeness with respect to NEPAD on the part of the G8. At the June 2002 Kananaskis Summit, while praising 'the imaginative effort that underlies NEPAD', the G8 members essentially adopted a 'wait and see' stance, committing themselves in their Africa Action Plan to a rather modest $6bn increment in aid through 2006 as an 'initial response'. Both African governments and NGOs registered disappointment. But the industrialised nations made it clear that primary responsibility for implementing NEPAD and attracting further support rested with African countries themselves, which would need to show 'a political and financial commitment to good governance and the rule of law, investing in their people and pursuing policies that spur economic growth and alleviate poverty'. This suggests that, at bottom, NEPAD's success hinges on reducing the costs of doing business in Africa. This demands, in turn, a closer working relationship with international and local business. To achieve its objectives, NEPAD may need to establish public–private partnerships, which indicates that the next phase of NEPAD activities is likely to fall increasingly outside the ambit of control of politicians, diplomats and bureaucrats and increasingly into the sphere of business people, investors, engineers, entrepreneurs and civil society. But the point remains that, with NEPAD, South Africa has taken the lead on regional development, and the region could well benefit.

South Africa's evolving foreign policy

In return for assistance in realising NEPAD's ambitious goals, South Africa might have been expected to use qualified support for a US-led strike against Iraqi President Saddam Hussein's regime as a bargaining chip. South Africa, however, has preferred to view Iraq in moral terms, reflecting a wider power dynamic in the international system and the need to restructure it. At the ANC party conference in Cape Town in December 2002, Nelson Mandela attacked the United States, saying its approach to Iraq was arrogant and marked an alarming indifference towards the UN. In more measured language, Mbeki also indicated, in January 2003, that there were no grounds for war against Iraq. To a degree, these statements reflect fears that an aggressively idealistic US foreign policy might one day threaten the sovereignty of African nations. In addition to its avowed 'human rights' foreign-policy orientation, underlying South Africa's strongly independent line with respect to Iraq and Zimbabwe is the ANC's latent anti-Western sentiment – shaped by a history of colonisation, the socialist background of many ANC leaders, some conservative Western leaders' historical ambivalence towards the ANC and, to some extent, religion and race. More strategically, South Africa's independent position may also in part be explained by its aspiration to assume Africa's seat on any future UN Security Council. But Pretoria also emphasised its interests in Iraqi trade and investment by sending two ministers to Baghdad in late 2002 and early 2003.

On 1 February 2003, UK Prime Minister Tony Blair and Mbeki met at Chequers, the British prime minister's country residence. Mbeki and Blair have been (perhaps uncomfortably) umbilically joined on the issue of Zimbabwe. Both share a degree of responsibility for extricating Zimbabwe from its crisis and both have much to gain from a partnered solution. Further, both leaders are committed to foreign policies that advance human rights, human dignity, good governance, economic development and the rule of law. Despite the UK's alignment with the US on Iraq, Mbeki may regard the UK as the most promising partner among the major powers. In any case, whatever their misgivings, Western powers are likely to remain engaged with South Africa, since it represents the continent's best chance of success and has grown more confident in its role as a stabilising regional force. South Africa's efficacious diplomatic attentiveness to the DRC conflict in 2002 and to NEPAD burnished its reputation as a regional actor. But more decisive diplomacy with respect to Zimbabwe will be needed to consolidate that reputation.

Zimbabwe unsaved

Zimbabwe is the region's most destabilising element. Mugabe may be on his way out, but he shows little sign of going quietly. Fresh from an extended Christmas holiday and shopping spree in Thailand, Singapore and Malaysia (the latter has been touted as a future country of refuge for the 78-year-old leader), he returned to his devastated economy in January 2003 amid reports of an exit strategy being plotted within the ruling Zimbabwe African National Union–Patriotic Front (ZANU–PF). High-ranking ZANU–PF officials reportedly approached the head of the opposition Movement for Democratic Chance (MDC), Morgan Tsvangirai. The deal floated was apparently designed to enable a coalition government to restore the economy and political stability by granting amnesty and exile to Mugabe and his cohorts in return for a place in government for the MDC and the holding of fresh elections. Yet Mugabe scotched any suggestion that he might accept retirement, saying: 'I will not go into exile. I grew up in Zimbabwe. I will die in Zimbabwe. I will be buried in Zimbabwe'. Indeed, in early 2003, Tsvangirai was being tried on dubious charges of plotting to assassinate Mugabe, suggesting that Mugabe was intent on stockpiling political ammunition against the MDC.

Africa

Time is running out for Mugabe, however. Six million Zimbabweans (more than half the population) faced food shortages in early 2003, and many could die as a result. Agricultural output dropped by 40% between June 2001 and June 2002 in what was once regarded as the breadbasket of Southern Africa. While drought played a part, this was primarily a result of Mugabe's so-called land redistribution programme, whereby he has encouraged his political supporters – often cast by ZANU–PF, for the most part fraudulently, as 'war veterans' – to confiscate land owned by white farmers by brutal, gratuitous and sometimes lethal force. As of early 2003, only 600 of 4,000 white farmers remained on their land. Three-quarters of the working-age population was unemployed, inflation was running at over 200% and rising, and the Zimbabwean dollar had collapsed, with the gap between the official exchange rate (Z$55 to US$1) and the unofficial rate (Z$1,800 to US$1) widening daily. The country's fiscal deficit for 2003 was estimated at US$1bn – half of the total budget.

Not surprisingly, however, the crisis in Zimbabwe appeared to fall between the cracks of international concern, as attention focused on Baghdad and Pyongyang. Western governments have remained engaged principally through the provision of humanitarian assistance – though this also had the perverse effect of cushioning Mugabe from the impact of his misrule – and the imposition of sanctions by the US, the EU and the Commonwealth. The latter, however, has not proven to be good public relations, and distanced the West. The exception is France, which finessed the EU travel ban on Mugabe by inviting him to the Franco-African summit in Paris in February 2003, citing the advantages of engagement over isolation in resolving Zimbabwe's problems. Mugabe attended, but despite French President Jacques Chirac's lip-service to human rights, France's main intention appeared to be to enlist African support for its position on Iraq. Nothing of substance was accomplished with respect to Zimbabwe. Indeed, France's invitation appeared to strengthen the African nations' stance in Mugabe's support. In mid-February, Obasanjo – purporting to speak for Mbeki as well – sent a letter to Australian Prime Minister John Howard, noting the Zimbabwean government's authorisation of compensation for appropriated land, recent dialogue with the Commercial Farmers Union and greater procedural transparency in administering the land programme, and requesting that Commonwealth sanctions be lifted. African nations also refused to attend the EU–Africa summit slated to be held in Lisbon on 5 April unless Mugabe was invited; EU nations would not bend, and the summit was cancelled.

On balance, it appears that the West has, for the time being, largely allocated responsibility for resolving the Zimbabwe crisis to South Africa. Pretoria has not completely met this challenge. Mbeki has shied away from pressuring Mugabe to moderate the brutal land-confiscation policies, economic dysfunction and political repression substantially responsible for

Zimbabwe's woes. The Zimbabwe crisis is further complicated by the fact that southern African governments refuse to work more closely with the MDC. One extreme, though unlikely, option remains direct military intervention by a major outside power or a coalition of states under the auspices of the EU or the UN in support of local democratic forces. Another possibility is a military coup: although the military has strongly backed ZANU–PF, its withdrawal from the DRC, difficulties in exploiting commercial opportunities there and Zimbabwe's continuing economic woes make dissent more likely. Concerted involvement by civil-society organisations, business interests and the media is a more attractive prospect. This could take the form of support for the MDC, Zimbabwean trade unions and other elements of civil society, which remain vocal, active and reasonably well organised.

The preferable answer to Zimbabwe's main problem, however, is still more energetic regional engagement. One possibility would be an agreement brokered by South Africa and perhaps Nigeria whereby Mugabe would stand aside in return for amnesty, a government of national unity between ZANU–PF and the MDC would be formed and fresh elections would be held under international and regional supervision. Further economic deterioration could increase illegal immigration from Zimbabwe into South Africa and worsen regional economic contagion, thus increasing Pretoria's incentive to act. Although Mugabe's misrule has predominantly affected black Zimbabweans, Mbeki's administration has consistently chosen to articulate the Zimbabwe crisis in terms of land redistribution from whites to blacks and therefore to assign responsibility for the solution principally to the United Kingdom, the former colonial power. South Africa's timidity may also reflect its unease with the rise of the union-based MDC in Zimbabwe, worries that South African blacks impatient with slow land reform in their own country will warm to Mugabe's land agenda if Pretoria is seen to oppose it, and the broader failure of the ruling ZANU–PF to complete the transition from liberation movement to political party.

Angola: demilitarisation, regional leadership and recovery

With its civil war ended, Angola is not the retrograde influence that it once was. Richly endowed with mineral wealth, as the second-largest African oil producer after Nigeria, the fourth-largest diamond producer worldwide and southern Africa's second-ranking economic power behind South Africa, Angola now has a chance to realise its potential. Yet it is also the world's 13th least developed nation. While there exists a wealthy elite – aided by a corrupt and cronyistic government – more than 4m (one-third) of its population is displaced, and 9m out of 13m people live on less than a dollar a day. More than one in 500 Angolans has been directly or indirectly

Africa

injured by landmines. Around 2m refugees in Angola live in appalling conditions on Luanda's surrounding hills. Only 40% of the population has access to safe water and sanitation; and life expectancy is a mere 44 years. This widespread humanitarian strife is graphic evidence of the high cost of war – even though the cost of defeat could have been much higher. Archbishop of Luanda Damiao Franklin ranks 'social justice' and 'the fight against poverty' as the first priorities for Angola. Former Angolan Army Chief of Staff, Joao de Matos, the man widely credited for defeating Savimbi, has highlighted the 'enormous challenges' facing his country. US Secretary of State Colin Powell's whistle-stop visit to Angola after the conclusion of the World Summit on Sustainable Development in September 2002 illustrated both the increasing importance of the southern African nation to US national interests – Angola supplied around 10% of American oil imports in 2002 – and the opportunities that arose after Savimbi's death in combat in February 2002. Asserting the US administration's support for economic and political reform, Powell publicly stressed the need not to squander the chance for reconciliation.

Despite Powell's warm comments and the United States' need in March 2003 to court Angola in the UN Security Council to ensure its support for a second resolution on Iraq, strategic economic interests primarily shape US policy towards Luanda. This reality could just as well circumscribe as expand its interest in the region. Portugal, the former colonial power, and other European players may be reluctant to encourage greater South African involvement in Angola, as it may be seen as a means of gaining a competitive advantage rather than improving the regional economy. These considerations merely underline the need for the most powerful regional players – Angola and South Africa – to take the initiative in generating greater regional harmony. Yet, as of early 2003, Angola had not proven itself as a fully functioning state. With the end of the war, it now has the opportunity. While there are substantial costs to demobilising and disarming 100,000 ex-União Nacional para a Independencia Total de Angola (UNITA) rebels and reintegrating an estimated 600,000 rebels and their family members, the process – helped by considerable foreign aid – has moved swiftly, with 39,000 former guerrillas having dispersed from government camps by November 2002. Against wartime military expenditures of up to 30% of the total government budget, peace will still yield a substantial economic dividend. It has also provided political benefits by relieving Angola of the burden of supporting the DRC government, alongside Zimbabwe and Namibia, in the Congo conflict. This had curtailed Angola's political capacity by creating a schism between those four states and the more reform-oriented South Africa, Botswana and Mozambique. A regional focus on Luanda's part could help heal this rift further. Having assumed the SADC chair following the organisation's annual regional summit in September 2002, Angola is in a good position to establish that focus. Some encouragement from South Africa would help. Many Angolans believe that the ANC has shown insufficient gratitude for the years of sanctuary and military assistance that Luanda provided during the apartheid era. Pretoria's brokerage of the Rwanda–DRC peace accord looked like a promising step, but South Africa's failure to publicly acknowledge Angola's role deepened residual resentment.

Southern Africa's prospects in 2003–04

Despite a few bright spots – peace in Angola, South Africa's more constructive foreign policy – southern Africa remains a bleak part of the world. Due to the political and economic incapacity of many of the region's countries, its prospects are to an extent dependent on the degree to which global strategic affairs divert world attention from the region. The main one in 2003 will be the nature, duration and outcome of the Iraq imbroglio. Any sustained surge in oil prices will have a marked adverse affect on SADC economies save for Angola's, particularly on the balance of payments, debt and inflation. Other developments in the international and multilateral arena that will affect southern Africa include: World Trade Organisation negotiations; the ability of SADC countries to take advantage of AGOA II; the level of debt relief provided by the International Monetary Fund and the World Bank under their Heavily Indebted Poor Countries (HIPC) programme; and the G8's follow-through on its Africa Action Plan in response to NEPAD.

The region's less contingent problems are closer at hand. Continued state collapse in Zimbabwe could lead to heightened refugee and humanitarian crises. Conversely, leadership change would open up a new horizon for political settlement and economic reconstruction. Given Mugabe's visceral disdain for direct political intervention by Western powers, any such eventuality would require a more proactive diplomatic stance by South Africa and perhaps Nigeria than they have demonstrated so far. In turn, Mbeki's political latitude vis-à-vis Zimbabwe may be influenced by two factors – one domestic, the other regional. The performance of the South African economy is important. South Africa's population growth requires economic growth of 6–8% to reduce unemployment. Although NEPAD sets a target of 7% economic growth and the government's own Growth Employment and Redistribution programme aims for 6% growth, South Africa is likely to achieve only half of this. Mbeki's diplomatic prestige hinges significantly on whether the political settlement that he midwifed in the DRC can be made to stick. Should the peace process fail to be converted into a binding and inclusive constitutional and political settlement, and the DRC is unable to retain its sovereign integrity, Mbeki is likely to feel risk-averse.

Africa

Some of the factors that could adversely impact on southern Africa are forces of nature. The El Niño effect, for instance, could make water even scarcer and hydro-political issues more contentious. But perhaps the single most important factor in propelling the region to higher levels of development is leadership and vision beyond emergent political and natural crises. The NEPAD initiative reflects the recognition of this fact by some regional leaders. But without the SADC's further demonstration of a concerted and tangible commitment to the principles and policies of NEPAD, rather than merely to summit-level rhetoric, the region will find it difficult to attract donors and therefore will continue to exhibit a highly uneven pattern of implementation, ranging from isolated and country-specific cases of progress to sustained regional decline.

Daylight in Central Africa?

Prospects for stability in Central Africa brightened slightly in 2002 as a result of two related processes. First, there were the two external agreements brokered by South African President Thabo Mbeki between Rwanda and Uganda, respectively, and the Democratic Republic of Congo (DRC) leading to the partial withdrawal of their forces, and, in turn, enabling other states that had been supporting Congolese President Joseph Kabila's government to withdraw their forces. Second, there was the December 2002 internal agreement between the Kinshasa government and various rebel groups. The two are linked in that the invasion of the DRC by Rwanda and Uganda not only led to the formation of some of these militias but also created the instability that enabled others to flourish.

Hopes remain centred on the internal political agreement between the DRC government and almost all of the rebel factions, armed and unarmed, that oppose it. Signed in South Africa in December 2002, it lays out a road map for the formation of a power-sharing administration in the DRC and for the holding of elections in 2005. Implementation of the agreements, however, has been halting owing to the contingent nature of the respective commitments to peace of three key states – the DRC, Rwanda and Uganda – and a low level of practical international support for the peace process. While none of the state and non-state parties to the agreements seems prepared to renounce the accords and return to all-out war, neither have they acted decisively to end the small-scale conflicts in eastern DRC that have paralysed relief work and efforts at economic reconstruction.

Changing motivations

The US-based International Rescue Committee reported that more than 2.5 million civilians, as distinct from combatants, had died from fighting and disease in eastern DRC alone between 1998 and mid-2002. The office of the UN High Commissioner for Refugees puts the number at three million. While the range of estimates admits of imprecision and broad criteria of the consequences of war – many of the deaths have been proximately caused by hunger – this scale of suffering makes the conflict in the DRC the worst in the world. A damning report by a UN expert panel on resource exploitation in the DRC, released in October 2002, argued that commercial gain by the rebel factions and their regional backers, Rwanda and Uganda, as well as by the DRC's military ally, Zimbabwe, had become a driving force in the conflict and recommended financial and travel restrictions on individuals and companies that it identified as playing a leading role in the exploitation. Rwandan President Paul Kagame has admitted that the war has been essentially self-financing. Indeed, it may not be in the financial interests of some of the parties to have a strong, stable government in Kinshasa earning revenues from natural resources to rebuild the country.

From such concerns about the social crisis and worsening resource exploitation, the need for intervention grew stronger in 2002. For South Africa, the DRC conflict was blocking progress on plans to revive the regional economy, encapsulated in the New Partnership for Africa's Development (NEPAD), as it was depriving Africa of one of its richest sources of minerals and hydroelectricity. Pretoria also recognised, in the face of Western lack of interest, that it was the only outside power with the economic and political capacity to improve the situation substantially. In facilitating 'Africa's first world war' – fuelled by genocide in Rwanda in 1994, the ouster of the late President Mobutu Sese Seko in 1997 and subsequent Congolese President Laurent-Desire Kabila's distancing himself from his original backers, Rwanda and Uganda – the system of regional alignments had drawn seven countries into the war, dividing states in Central and Southern Africa into antagonistic camps. Angola, Namibia and Zimbabwe, members of the Southern Africa Development Community (SADC), backed the DRC government, splitting the SADC into a Harare faction and a Pretoria faction and crippling the organisation. Rwanda and Uganda angled for Congolese territory for geopolitical and ethnic reasons. Burundian troops entered the DRC to stave off Burundian Hutu insurgencies allied with pro-Kinshasa Congolese groups. The conflict looked in early 2002 as though it might escalate again and in the process threaten several regimes with their own domestic preoccupations. Breaking the cycle of violence was in the interests of the regional powers, provided they could secure military and diplomatic terms that did not compromise their domestic power.

Africa

A major new factor in the equation was political change in the DRC government in Kinshasa. President Joseph Kabila, who assumed power unpromisingly after his father, Laurent Kabila, was assassinated in January 2001, wanted to unblock peace talks with the Rwandan and Ugandan-backed rebels in eastern DRC and set up a transitional government to which he would have to cede some, but not the most critical, of his executive powers. In attempting to do this, Kabila calculated that he would – if nothing else – regain some of the moral high ground that his father had won simply by virtue of replacing the kleptocratic Mobutu but then so extravagantly lost. Kagame and President Yoweri Museveni of Uganda were veterans of the trade-offs in Central African diplomacy. Despite their overt sponsorship of rebel militias in eastern DRC and the involvement of their own troops in pillaging minerals and timber from DRC, both Rwanda and Uganda had escaped serious censure from either the UN or their closest Western partners, the UK and the US.

By early 2002, though, attitudes were shifting. The US government made it was clear that it would not support credits from the International Monetary Fund (IMF) and the World Bank for Rwanda if it was not willing to withdraw its troops from eastern DRC, and at least some British officials supported this position. Museveni's continued opposition to political liberalisation and his army's inability to defeat a brutal rebellion in northern Uganda also raised questions in Washington about IMF and World Bank support for his government. In the south, the end of the civil war in Angola and the worsening economic situation in Zimbabwe persuaded those governments to rethink their military involvement in the DRC in favour of peace talks and a possible political agreement between the DRC's warring factions.

Tepid international engagement

Western powers – particularly France and the UK – were willing to give limited support to African diplomatic efforts in the DRC, much of it channelled through the European Union (EU). Belgium, the former colonial power, took a somewhat more unilateral approach, backed by rather grandiose promises of economic aid. But the EU did not field a large mediation team and, with so many troops committed to the Balkans, could not secure a substantial force of UN peacekeepers with the required robust mandate, dimming prospects for monitoring and verifying any peace accord resulting from the negotiations. The UN Mission d'Observation des Nations Unis au Congo (MONUC), had a book strength of 5,537 (of whom about 500 were military observers) throughout 2002, but numbers on the ground never actually rose above about 4,200. In December 2002, the UN Security Council agreed to expand the force to 8,700, but progress in securing budgetary commitments, troops and military hardware has been slow. Even that proposed force strength is far short of technical requirements. For example, Sierra Leone, which is smaller than Belgium, had a 20,000-strong UN mission, whereas the force sent to the DRC, which is the size of Western Europe, is a quarter of that strength. Yet, dealing with the DRC in the same manner as Sierra Leone would unrealistically require perhaps ten times the number of troops committed to the latter, and for a longer time. In the DRC, therefore, there remains a premium on mediation and outside political and economic pressure.

European efforts in the DRC were also held back by differences over strategy and over the causes of the conflict. Belgium and France regarded Rwanda and Uganda as predator states, backing rebel militias in the eastern DRC for national advantage. Britain argued that Rwanda and Uganda continued to have genuine security concerns about the DRC government's failure to rein in mainly Hutu militias linked to the 1994 genocide in Rwanda. Other EU members with economic interests in the region – Germany, Italy and Portugal – wavered between the two positions. No individual power, in the EU or on the UN Security Council, was prepared to lend determinative diplomatic and economic weight to the DRC conflict – comparable to, say, that which Britain lent to Sierra Leone's problems or Japan to Cambodia's – to consolidate local peacemaking efforts. The IMF and World Bank, for their part, declared themselves impressed by the Kinshasa government's emerging record on economic reform and indicated that they were prepared to make available some $2.5 billion in cheap loans to aid reconstruction. They would also back moves to cut Congo's foreign debt, made up mostly of politically motivated loans to the Mobutu regime. Such incentives, it was hoped, would concentrate minds in Kinshasa and also among the putative members of a transitional government.

They were also operating in a new and more hospitable regional diplomatic climate. Four sets of peace negotiations run by African regional organisations – in Burundi, the DRC, Somalia and Sudan – were in train. Western nations, led by the United States, were concerned that such conflicts could be exploited by terrorist cells able to trade profitably and clandestinely in battle zones. They were also aware of the way in which these conflicts overlap: that arms from Somalia can fuel violence in eastern DRC; and that diamonds from DRC can be used to launder money for terrorist networks. Much too was made of the DRC's uranium deposits at Shinkolobwe in the southeast of the country, the reported theft (albeit in 1998) of a rod of enriched uranium used at the University of Kinshasa's Atomic Research Centre, and British and American assertions that Iraq had attempted to purchase enriched uranium in Africa.

A new diplomatic calendar emerged by early 2002: the Inter-Congolese dialogue – negotiations for a power-sharing administration between government and rebels – would open early in the year with the aim of securing involvement by all the armed and non-armed groups. The other diplomatic track would entail bilateral negotiations between the Kinshasa

Africa

government and Rwanda, Burundi and Uganda, respectively, about security guarantees and the withdrawal of their troops from eastern DRC. The price of international support was a commitment by the Kinshasa government on political and economic reform aimed at halting endemic corruption in the mining sector that was further draining the state treasury. Such a reform strategy faced huge obstacles from entrenched domestic interests and the rampant militarily backed commercialism of the regional powers in Congo. On the ground, the dynamic driving the conflict was a three-cornered struggle between the Kinshasa government, Rwanda and Uganda for influence and assets in eastern DRC.

Pressure on Rwanda

By early 2002, the conflict was being fought mainly by proxies. Thus, while the struggle for control of a huge state that drew the armies of seven African states into the DRC has diminished, the overlapping micro-conflicts that they provoked still undermine the stability of the region and take an appalling human toll. These micro-conflicts were being fought mainly over minerals, farm produce, land and even tax revenues. The militias and businesses are linked to the armies of Rwanda, Uganda, Zimbabwe and the DRC government, yet the criminal networks in the DRC are sufficiently able to enrich themselves through mineral exploitation that they could stand on their own even if their foreign military sponsors withdrew. This effective concentration of resources, however, has devastated the region's traditional agricultural base. As the micro-conflicts continued, conditions for the Congolese people and neighbouring states worsened. The UN Office for the Coordination of Humanitarian Affairs reported on 31 July 2002 that the Great Lakes region was hosting 1.2m refugees and about 3.4m internally displaced people, an increase of roughly 5% from February 2002. UN agencies and voluntary organisations reported that mortality rates in eastern DRC remained among the world's worst. Accordingly, the peace negotiators contemplated the withdrawal of Rwandan, Ugandan and Zimbabwean troops as just the first step in the demilitarisation process. After that, a political accord between Congolese factions would be necessary to end the criminal commercial operations that were driving war and poverty.

Ameliorating this humanitarian and social crisis pivoted on the behaviour of Rwanda and Uganda in eastern DRC. A number of African commentators have been outraged that the UN and the West have allowed Rwanda and Uganda to get away with military aggression in the DRC, noting that comparable conduct was not tolerated in Kosovo and East Timor. By leveraging Western inaction with respect to the Rwandan genocide in 1994, Kagame has been able to stave off Western measures that might disadvantage Kigali. Since the Rwandans and the Ugandans were the original aggressors, this made resolution of the crisis impossible.

Further, unlike Sierra Leone or Côte d'Ivoire, where a former colonial power with a good relationship with the modern state was available to help, Belgium lacked the political and economic resources to do the same for the DRC. Finally, the immense size and intractability of the problem intimidated military planners.

Effective diplomatic pressure on Rwanda finally materialised in 2002 after several critical reports emerged on the operations of its troops and allies in eastern Congo. Investigations by UN human-rights rapporteurs and other agencies found that 100 people had been killed in the northern diamond centre of Kisangani in May 2002 by forces from the Rwandan-backed Rassemblement Congolais pour la Democratie-Goma (RCD-Goma). As a result, Kagame's claim that Rwandan troops in eastern DRC were combatting a massive security threat to the country's border – suspect to begin with – lost more credibility. The consensus is that, in reality, the Rwandans were in the DRC partly in self-defence against further Hutu aggression – and perhaps more ambitiously to strengthen the geopolitical position of the Kigali regime by dominating eastern DRC and establishing a 'Greater Tutsiland' – and partly for economic reasons. The EU and the US became more critical of Rwanda's operations in eastern DRC. And South Africa, Rwanda's closest regional partner, advised it to change course and restart negotiations. South Africa played a key brokering role between the DRC government and Rwanda, hosting the negotiations leading to the signing of a bilateral accord in Pretoria on 30 July. The agreement was based on the same expectations as the failed multilateral Lusaka Accord of July 1999: that the DRC government would disarm and handover the militia groups composed mainly of Hutu ex-Forces Armees Rwandaises (FAR) soldiers and the militia known as the Interahamwe, which, Kigali claims, were all involved in the 1994 genocide, and that Rwanda would withdraw its troops from the DRC.

The UN and South Africa were appointed joint guarantors of the agreement, and charged with verifying the identities of the ex-FAR and Interahamwe fighters, that the DRC government's support to them has ceased, and that all Rwandan troops have been withdrawn. There were no mechanisms to ensure compliance, so the accord depended strictly on the political will of the signatories. The problematic issue of Rwanda's military-commercial operations in eastern DRC was not covered in the accord. Within weeks of signing, Rwanda announced that it had withdrawn most of its military contingent of some 20,000 troops from the DRC. Much of the withdrawal occurred in front of UN and South African observers. But the DRC government accused Rwanda of disguising other elements of its military and leaving them in place elsewhere in the DRC, as well as insinuating several Rwandan military and intelligence officers into the ranks of the rebel RCD-Goma, which had established a provisional government in Goma claiming to have authority in Kivu Nord and Kivu

Sud and parts of Orientale province. International Crisis Group also reported that 5,000 Rwandan soldiers were covertly seconded to RCD-Goma. Even so, local Mai-Mai militias attacked Uvira in mid-October 2002. Immediately Rwanda re-dispatched its troops, arguing that the Mai-Mai attack was backed by the Kinshasa government and violated the accord. The Mai-Mai forces pulled back and the Rwandan withdrawal continued. But the political weight of Rwanda's proclaimed fear of genocidal Hutus and its willingness to use it as a pretext for military action means that the Pretoria agreement will remain difficult to implement.

Yet the return home of 20,000 troops added to political pressure that Kagame already faced due to the phased release of some 100,000 prisoners held after the 1994 genocide, slower economic growth in 2002 and Rwanda's transition to a multiparty political system. Some senior Rwandan officers also opposed the withdrawal strategy, and questioned redeployments of Rwandan troops further north in eastern DRC in the Ituri region, which had been dominated by militias allied to Uganda.

Uganda's strategic shift

Rwanda's pullback was made more secure by a strategic shift in 2002 in Uganda's approach to the DRC. This turned on several factors. First, Uganda enjoyed a degree of political credibility among the Congolese. While Museveni's government has added to the proliferation of armed factions in eastern DRC, and senior officers in the Ugandan People's Defence Force have struck commercial deals in the region belying their claims to have deployed troops across the border purely for military reasons, Uganda has also been the primary foreign sponsor of Jean-Pierre Bemba's Mouvement pour la Liberation du Congo (MLC). Unlike the Rwandan-backed RCD-Goma – widely denigrated as puppets of the Kagame government – the MLC has considerable legitimacy among the Congolese. Second, in 2002, Uganda needed to liberate military assets from the DRC for use in Sudan. Initially armed and trained by Sudan's Islamist government, Joseph Kony's Lord's Resistance Army used bases in southern Sudan to attack northern Uganda. In mid-2002, a limited rapprochement between Museveni and Sudanese President Omer Bashir allowed Uganda to send troops into southern Sudan to destroy the LRA's bases. Uganda's troops suffered heavy casualties, however, and LRA guerrillas launched several attacks on refugee camps in Uganda's Acholi region in July and August 2002. By the end of 2002, Museveni had set up a personal base camp in northern Uganda and staked his credibility on defeating the LRA. Finally, the nominal partnership between Uganda and Rwanda against the DRC government was becoming increasingly untenable. The two were in competition for economic gain from their respective presences in the DRC. Uganda's army had been defeated three times by Rwanda in clashes in Kisangani.

In 2002, these realities dictated a primarily political rather than a military strategy for Uganda. Its political standing as the MLC's backer afforded it a strong voice at the Inter-Congolese Dialogue held in March–April 2002 in Sun City, South Africa. With Angola, Uganda encouraged the MLC to sign a partial accord with Kabila's government to set up a power-sharing government. Uganda's apparent aim was to transform itself from rebel sponsor into state ally. This would allow it to pursue its economic interests in eastern DRC, albeit under greater constraints. Yet the DRC and Ugandan governments have been united only in their distrust of Rwanda. Their economic interests have been at variance, and so too has been their local political strategy. Uganda's troops were supporting the ethnic Hema in battles with the Lenda in eastern DRC. One of these battles erupted in Bunia in early August 2002 at a cost of 100 lives. Ugandan tanks were reported to have surrounded the governor's residence. But in the resulting melee, the UN mission asked Ugandan troops to keep order there in the absence of any other stabilising force.

In September 2002, in Luanda, Uganda agreed to withdraw all its troops from the DRC within 30 days. By 1 October, over 2,000 Ugandan troops had been withdrawn, and Uganda resumed full diplomatic relations with Kinshasa. Many of Uganda's soldiers from the DRC were employed immediately in operations against the LRA. Ituri province, however, remained an area of contention between Rwanda and Uganda, as both countries were amassing troops as well as rearming their local proxies there. In response, the Kinshasa government started to deploy its own militias in the area. In spite of the UK's mediation between Rwanda and Uganda, as of early 2003, relations between them remained tense. Uganda pledged to withdraw its last 1,000 soldiers from Congo by 20 March 2003. But on 6 March, Ugandan soldiers reoccupied Bunia, Ituri's capital, and several nearby airstrips and villages. As justification, Kampala cited an attack by Rwanda-backed rebels. Yet, while Uganda remains in Congo, Rwanda is unlikely to encourage its rebel proxies to join any transitional Congolese government.

Burundi's destabilising rebels

If external pressures have discouraged Ugandan military activities in the DRC, internal conflict has ultimately encouraged Burundian intervention. Burundian President Pierre Buyoya has pledged to stick to a power-sharing agreement (mediated by South Africa) with the Hutu Burundian opposition, stipulating that he forfeit the presidency to civilian opposition leader Domitien Ndayizeye in June 2003. Buyoya has had more difficulty negotiating with the opposition militias, Forces pour la Defence de la Democratie (FDD) and Forces Nationales de Liberation (FNL), which are making the more stringent demand of power-sharing in the Tutsi-dominated Burundian army. To pressure the Burundi government, the

FDD and FNL have run joint operations against government forces with pro-Kinshasa Hutu militias, while the Burundian Army has joined Rwanda and its allies in eastern DRC. Senior Congolese and Zimbabwean military officers have supplied and trained the FDD; in turn, the Burundian army has crossed into eastern DRC to attack FDD bases in south Kivu and Katanga.

In March 2002, in one of the most serious violations of the ceasefire, RCD-Goma troops backed by Rwanda and Burundi dislodged the FDD and the DRC's army from their garrison at Moliro, Katanga. Burundi maintained that the FDD was using Moliro to launch cross-border attacks in western Burundi, and that the DRC's army was supporting it. Both the DRC's army and RCD-Goma claimed Moliro under the Lusaka ceasefire agreement; the issue was subsequently resolved in favour of Congo by the UN Security Council. Reports of renewed Congolese military and intelligence support for the FDD after its military defeat at Moliro suggest that hardliners in Kinshasa still see the Burundian rebel movements as an important brake on further incursions by Congo's eastern neighbours. The upshot is that, until the FDD and the FNL are integrated into Burundi's political and military structure, they are likely to maintain a destabilising military presence in the DRC.

Tanzania has emerged as a candidate for brokering a deal. Given that traders linked to both the Congo government and rebels in eastern Congo use Dar es Salaam as an entrepot, Tanzania argues that it can strike a neutral stance. Shipments of arms through Tanzanian transit points like Mwanza airport and increasing traffic in contraband precious stones in Dar es Salaam may indicate a failure of regulation and perhaps corruption on the part of senior officials. The Burundian government also has long accused Tanzania of backing the FDD and the FDL. Even so, Tanzania has improved relations with Burundi. In March 2002, it allowed Burundian troops across the border to break up a FDD military headquarters after a series of raids by the Tanzanian army on Burundian rebels training in Tanzania, and in October 2002 hosted peace talks in Dar es Salaam between the Burundi government and opposition militias. Tanzania's army, having endured the burden of managing one of the largest concentrations of refugees in the world, also wants to contribute to a peacekeeping force in Burundi if the negotiations are successful, and it might play a similar role in the DRC.

Zimbabwe's stake

While the Burundian Hutu militias provide some tactical advantages to Kinshasa, Zimbabwe has been the DRC's key strategic military ally, with at least 10,000 troops stationed in Kasai Orientale, Katanga and Kinshasa. As the main confrontation between the Kinshasa government and the rebel sponsors, Rwanda and Uganda, developed into a complex series of smaller conflicts after 2000, Zimbabwe played a key role in training and supplying units of the FDD and the Armée pour la Liberation de Rwanda (ALIR), the product of a merger of ex-FAR soldiers and Interahamwe militiamen. Its military strategists also helped formulate the Congolese government's proxy-war strategy in eastern DRC, under which armed groups, such as the ALIR, FDD and the Mai-Mai, would be trained and equipped to counter RCD-Goma and Rwandan forces. By mid-2002, however, the mutual advantage accruing to Zimbabwe's strategic relationship with the DRC had shrunk.

From Kinshasa's perspective, the Zimbabwean presence was becoming a local political liability in the provinces of Kasai Occidental and Kasai Oriental. While the Kinshasa government, and Kabila in particular, had hoped to boost their political standing there, instead, in April 2002, the most popular opposition group in Kasai, Etienne Tshisekedi's Union pour la Democratie et le Progres Social (UDPS), formed an alliance with RCD-Goma. Further, the DRC's perceived cosiness with the internationally ostracised government of Zimbabwean President Robert Mugabe – which had been placed under sanctions by the EU, the US and the Commonwealth, subjected to travel bans and cut off from most sources of development finance – was not liable to improve its already dubious global image.

Zimbabwe, for its part, had intended to maintain its military relevance as a guarantor of the DRC government's security, but was increasingly reluctant to risk its troops and equipment in front-line battles with either Rwandan forces or their rebel allies in RCD-Goma. A more limited role of training and supplying pro-government forces made its previous scale of deployments unnecessary, and difficult to defend against allegations that Zimbabwe, like Uganda and Rwanda, was using its military alliance with the DRC as a pretext to exploit that country's resources. In early 2003, Zimbabwe's economy had also shrunk by more than one-third over a three-year period, worsening the domestic political crisis. In addition, although at one stage Zimbabwe's economic troubles were an incentive to stay in the DRC – the fruits of natural-resource exploitation enriched Mugabe's Zimbabwe African National Union–Patriotic Front (ZANU-PF) party and ensured that senior commanders remained loyal to him – the Mugabe government's efforts to maximise revenue from its military-commercial operations in the DRC had met with only limited success. In an attempt to hedge its retreat, Zimbabwe renegotiated its joint venture projects with Kinshasa in 2002, boosting profits and allowing private businesses to distance themselves from the Zimbabwean Army and thus increase their access to capital. A difficult question that remained unresolved was the magnitude of the DRC government's debt to Zimbabwe for military services rendered. Nevertheless, Zimbabwe started pulling out its troops in September 2002. By the end of the year its withdrawal was almost

Africa

complete, apart from a residual presence at strategic economic positions and a small number of soldiers undertaking some government security functions in Kinshasa.

Keys to stability: Angola and South Africa

The DRC government's strategy has shifted towards establishing a political accommodation with its opponents. The various withdrawals, however, have created a security vacuum in eastern DRC that the government is not equipped to fill on its own. Large areas, ethnic diversity and poor communications make security a problem even in the absence of conflict, especially for a government that has little control at any appreciable distance from Kinshasa. Accordingly, many people in the DRC have naturally looked to Kigali or to Kampala rather than to Kinshasa for protection. Without substantially more outside political and practical support than has been forthcoming, the absence of foreign forces could paradoxically prove destabilising. The UN will provide political support to the peace process, but even if MONUC (improbably) increases to its authorised strength of 8,700, it will be inadequate for anything more than monitoring and verification in such a large geographical area. Disarmament, for example, would not be possible.

Outside political brokers and security guarantors, then, are still required. They are difficult to find regionally because so many governments have been drawn into the DRC conflict. Zambia's mediating role and professed neutrality in that conflict resulted in its hosting the Lusaka peace negotiations in 1999, but its role was compromised by Angola's repeated claims that its senior officials were trading arms for diamonds with the Angolan rebel group União Nacional para Independência Total de Angola (UNITA). The DRC government also accused former Zambian President Frederick Chiluba's government of having clandestine links with Congolese businessman and politician Katebe Katoto. These accusations were given substance in July 2002, when new Zambian President Levy Mwanawasa told parliament that police were investigating a $100m contract between the Chiluba government and Katoto for arms that were never delivered. Mwanawasa's crackdown on his predecessor's financial networks did improve relations with the DRC and Angola. But Angola, reinvigorated as a regional player by the termination of its long civil war, and South Africa, determined to bring its diplomatic power in line with its economic dominance, are becoming more central to the DRC's regional calculations.

Angola, in particular, is reshaping its role as gendarme for the Congo basin. President José Eduardo dos Santos' government signed a ceasefire in April 2002 with UNITA following the death of its leader, Jonas Savimbi. The near-elimination of the UNITA threat at home and from its rear bases in the DRC gave Angola more flexibility in its military planning. As the dominant oil and gas producer in the region, Angola wants to wield more economic and diplomatic influence as the primary energy supplier in the SADC, of which it became chair in 2002. Furthermore, in May 2002, a UN Security Council mission in Luanda encouraged Angola's role as security guarantor, especially in negotiations to expel ex-FAR and Interahamwe forces from the DRC. In this vein, Angolan diplomats have kept open channels to Uganda and Rwanda, which aided negotiations at the April 2002 Inter-Congolese Dialogue in South Africa, and the subsequent withdrawal of Uganda's troops from Congo. On the economic front, Angola wants to expand economic relations with the DRC beyond its oil-distribution joint venture Sonangol-Congo and some diamond-mining operations in Tshikapa. As of January 2003, the biggest project under discussion was the rehabilitation of the railway from Katanga to Angola's Lobito port. Lobito would become the main exit port for the DRC's minerals, while the railway would also transport Angolan oil products to the southeastern province of Katanga.

More than any other state, South Africa stands to gain if Central Africa is stabilised. South Africa's potential economic interests in the DRC are not inconsiderable. South African mining concerns reopened negotiations with the DRC for concessions, and its electric power company Eskom is working on a plan to develop the DRC's massive hydroelectric potential. Trade in goods and services between South Africa and the DRC has been rising sharply in spite of – or perhaps because of – the conflict. If that trade is formalised, both governments' treasuries would gain. Until the Benguela railway is rehabilitated, most of the DRC's copper and cobalt will be transported by road to Durban on South Africa's east coast, which will pay economic dividends. More broadly, the DRC's resource-rich but at present dilapidated economy has a key potential role to play in NEPAD, which Mbeki has been aggressively promoting to Western states from which he hopes to secure funding. The plan is designed to promote stability and better governance in Africa to attract more investment and technology, and the DRC is simply too big and naturally well-endowed to be ignored.

Furthermore, durable political success in the DRC would enhance South Africa's influence in the African Union as well as its global prestige as a regional power, which has been hurt by its fecklessness on the Zimbabwe crisis. In 2002, Pretoria began to capitalise on the opportunities presented by the DRC challenge. South Africa sponsored the Inter-Congolese Dialogue, despite the DRC government's presumption that South Africa's strong relations with Rwanda would prejudice its role. Although the resulting partial accord sidelined Mbeki's proposals, South Africa persisted with efforts to bring Rwanda and its allies back into the diplomatic equation. The Congo–Rwanda accord signed in Pretoria on 30 July and mediated by Mbeki signalled South Africa's next diplomatic phase. South Africa hosted the launch of the African Union in July 2002, during which another round of negotiations between Kabila and Kagame

Africa

started. Pretoria also offered to send a battalion of 1,500 peacekeeping troops to Congo in support of MONUC's increased role. The July accord also gave South Africa leverage to press for widening the Inter-Congolese Dialogue's proposed power-sharing arrangements to include groups such as RCD-Goma and its ally, Tshisekedi's UDPS. In December 2002, South Africa was able to persuade almost all of the parties to sign the 'global accord' in Pretoria.

In the context of a global security environment in which major powers are consumed by more urgent counter-terrorism and counter-proliferation agendas, the formidable task of stabilising Central Africa has essentially devolved to regional powers, with a little political help from the UN. In 2002, they appeared to rise to the challenge. To continue the process of resurrecting a viable government in the DRC and establishing wider security there, South Africa, in particular, will need to stay diplomatically engaged in the DRC peace process. NEPAD, Mbeki's signature initiative, appears to provide strong motivation. Effective conflict-resolution in Burundi would also remove an obstacle to stable peace. Angola's relative domestic calm has afforded it a broader regional security policy, which it seems prepared to use to encourage peace in the DRC. Major economic powers and the international financial institutions still have an important subsidiary role to play in pressuring Rwanda and Uganda, and potentially Zimbabwe, not to revive territorial aggression or overreach commercially.

Geopolitical uncertainty remains

On account of the micro-conflicts, the withdrawal of the national military contingents solves only part of the problem. The Rwandans and Ugandans may in fact be happy enough to go because they believe that their political and financial objectives can now be met without deploying forces in the country. If so, the recent internal accord actually maintains Rwandan and Ugandan influence in Congo in that their proxies in the DRC will be playing a substantial role in government. Rwanda and Uganda could thus use their influence to promote a decentralised DRC state with a strong federal structure, which will give them effective control of much of the eastern DRC and its mineral wealth. But Rwanda may also ultimately conclude that a peaceful DRC is too big and potentially powerful a neighbour to remain a unitary state. Other governments may similarly conclude that peace and prosperity in the future could actually create regional problems, and that the 20-plus sub-national groups in the country may have more to gain from conflict than from peace. A new transitional government was to have been formed in March 2003, but this was delayed and jeopardised by rising violence in Ituri. The standing risk, then, is that one or more of the many parties to the war in Central Africa will decide that economic opportunism or ethnically fuelled hegemony is more important than the region's political and economic welfare.

Brittle West Africa

While the perennial problem states, Sierra Leone and Liberia, were relatively quiescent in 2002 – thanks, respectively, to a large United Nations presence and international pressure – the civil collapse of Côte d'Ivoire underlined the fragility of West African progress towards peace and democracy and of the state apparatuses in the region. For smaller countries, falling export earnings due to lower commodity prices have both promoted violence and disaffection and reduced the means that states have to combat them. In turn, the state's perceived fecklessness, as well as its corruption and intermittent brutality, has caused ordinary people to lose confidence in government and made them more inclined to support insurgents and factional leaders, out of desperation if nothing else. In this context, multiparty democracy can be as much a threat as a boon to stability. Further, porous borders, relatively sophisticated criminal networks and traditional cross-border ethnic and trading contacts facilitate the tranmission of security problems from one state into others; the connections among Liberia, Sierra Leone and Côte d'Ivoire constitute but one example. Major regional powers also have major problems. Nigeria, the region's major power, is unlikely to escape ethnic and religious violence around the time of the April 2003 elections. Senegal and Mali are notable exceptions to the region's anti-democratic cast, but even they are plagued by other troubles, such as civil war and debilitating refugee flows. Most West African countries are burdened with at least potential crises.

Ivorian rebels set the agenda

The ongoing conflict in Côte d'Ivoire originates from a combination of long-term economic stresses and politics based on ethnic patronage. President Henri Konan Bédié – who is from the Baoule tribe, the country's largest ethnic group, concentrated in the south and mainly Christian – exacerbated the situation by purging government of northerners and by establishing the exclusionary concept of Ivorité, or 'Ivorian-ness', as a criterion of political candidacy. From Felix Houphouet-Boigny, who as the country's first president produced over 30 years of relative prosperity and stability until his death in 1993, Bédié inherited a system which tried, however imperfectly, to balance ethnic groups against each other. But he did not maintain it. In the ensuing confusion, General Robert Guei, a disaffected soldier and a Guere from the west, staged a coup in December 1999. His motivations remain unclear. Although Guei was not a Muslim or a northerner, he had quarrelled with Bédié and indeed been sacked by him, and forged a tactical alliance with Alassane Ouattara, a Muslim politician

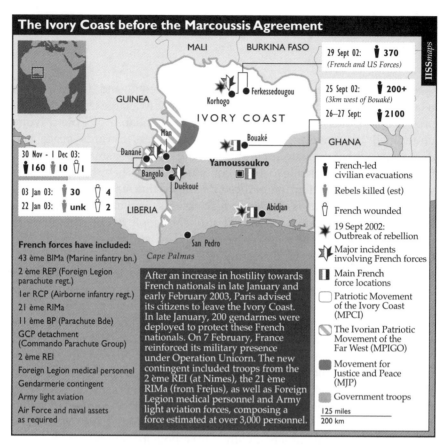

The Ivory Coast before the Marcoussis Agreement

MALI
BURKINA FASO

29 Sept 02: ▮ 370
(French and US Forces)

GUINEA

Ferkessedougou
Korhogo

25 Sept 02: ▮ 200+
(3km west of Bouaké)

26–27 Sept: ▮ 2100

IVORY COAST

Man
Bouaké

GHANA

30 Nov - 1 Dec 03:
▮ 160 ▮ 10 ⚰ 1

Danané
Bangolo
Duékoué

Yamoussoukro

03 Jan 03: ▮ 30 ⚰ 4

22 Jan 03: ▮ unk ⚰ 2

LIBERIA

Abidjan

▮ French-led
civilian evacuations

▮ Rebels killed (est)

⚰ French wounded

✷ 19 Sept 2002:
Outbreak of rebellion

⚔ Major incidents
involving French forces

▯ Main French
force locations

▯ Patriotic Movement
of the Ivory Coast
(MPCI)

◩ The Ivorian Patriotic
Movement of the
Far West (MPIGO)

▮ Movement for
Justice and Peace
(MJP)

▮ Government troops

French forces have included:

43 ème BIMa (Marine infantry bn.)

2 ème REP (Foreign Legion
parachute regt.)

1er RCP (Airborne infantry regt.)

21 ème RIMa

11 ème BP (Parachute Bde)

GCP detachment
(Commando Parachute Group)

2 ème REI

Foreign Legion medical personnel

Gendarmerie contingent

Army light aviation

Air Force and naval assets
as required

San Pedro

Cape Palmas

After an increase in hostility towards
French nationals in late January and
early February 2003, Paris advised
its citizens to leave the Ivory Coast.
In late January, 200 gendarmes were
deployed to protect these French
nationals. On 7 February, France
reinforced its military presence
under Operation Unicorn. The new
contingent included troops from the
2 ème REI (at Nimes), the 21 ème
RIMa (from Frejus), as well as Foreign
Legion medical personnel and Army
light aviation forces, composing a
force estimated at over 3,000 personnel.

125 miles
200 km

and former prime minister who has family links to Burkina-Faso and was
not considered to possess sufficient Ivorité, only to jettison him later. After
disputed October 2000 elections, Guei was unseated by Laurent Gbagbo
and fled to Benin. Gbagbo consolidated power by reinforcing Ivorité in
government and the military.

The rebellion broke out on 19 September 2002 with simultaneous attacks
in Abidjan, Bouaké and Korhogo, and the rebels swiftly seized control of
the northern half of the country. Many of the rebels are soldiers recruited
into the army by Guei, who had been resisting Gbagbo's efforts to remove
them; others had fled to Burkina-Faso in 2000 after falling out with Guei.
Guei was killed early in the rebellion in unclear circumstances.
The northern-based main rebel movement, the Mouvement Patriotique
de la Côte d'Ivoire (MPCI), agreed to a ceasefire in October 2002. But the
situation was complicated by the emergence of two new rebel groups in the
west, reportedly backed by Liberian and Sierra Leonean mercenaries, and
the presence of rebels of the Liberian United for Reconciliation and
Democracy (LURD), opposed to Liberian President Charles Taylor, fighting
on the government's side. There were also rumours of English-speaking

South African or Angolan mercenaries fighting for the government during the first few weeks of the rebellion. France has been reluctantly dragged into the conflict, increasing its troops in the country from 600 to 2,500, with the task of protecting some 20,000 French nationals and monitoring the ceasefire under what has been designated *Operation Unicorn.* French forces were also drawn into combat. In early 2003, these were to be supplemented by 1,250 Nigerian and Senegalese troops under an Economic Community of West African States (ECOWAS) mandate.

France has remained the principal diplomatic player in the conflict. It summoned the main political parties and rebel representatives to peace talks near Paris in January 2003 in the hope of pushing through a settlement in time for the Franco-African summit in late February. The result was the Marcoussis agreement, which sparked riots in the streets of Abidjan and an exodus of French residents. The negotiations required the ruling party to negotiate on an equal footing with rebels who seized control of half the country. Moreover, the peace deal takes away many of the powers enjoyed by Gbagbo's ruling party, Front Populaire Ivoirien (FPI). The agreement provides for the disarmament and reintegration of the rebels and the establishment of a government of national unity, to be led by Seydou Diarra, a respected northern businessman who was prime minister under Guei and chaired the National Reconciliation Forum. Gbagbo would remain as head of state and the FPI would retain the finance portfolio, while the main opposition Rassemblement des Républicains (RDR) and the former single party, the Parti Démocratique de la Côte d'Ivoire (PDCI), would take justice and foreign affairs respectively. According to the rebels, they were offered the defence and interior portfolios as a confidence-building gesture to encourage them to disarm. This was unacceptable to the crowds that rampaged through Abidjan for several days after the 25 January summit that ended the peace talks. Army spokesman Colonel Jules Yao Yao went on state television to describe the accord as humiliating to the armed forces, and support is growing for a military coup.

France appeared to lean on the negotiating parties in an attempt to get a settlement, and understandably opted for a quick fix that involved bringing the rebels into government and giving them some sensitive portfolios, as well as integrating their forces into the army. This was a fairly common solution, which – as with the defunct Lomé Accord for Sierra Leone – often does not work. It ignored the underlying problems, and blurred the distinction between a reasonably legitimate government and a group of violent insurrectionists. The Ivorian government and the French badly misjudged what ordinary people in Abidjan would accept. In February 2003, Gbagbo said that the Marcoussis agreement was only a series of proposals, and that, while he accepted 'the spirit' of the agreement, he would not implement it if it conflicted with the constitution.

Africa

France appeared to pin its hopes on RDR leader Ouattara, who has been barred by successive Ivorian governments from running for president. Ouattara was spirited away from the closed peace negotiations in the National Rugby Centre at Marcoussis for late-night talks with French Foreign Minister Dominique de Villepin at the Quai d'Orsay in Paris. But, as of April 2003, it was not clear how a peaceful solution could be found. Judging by recent history, the implications of an impasse for regional security are dire. The global preoccupation with Iraq's invasion of Kuwait in August 1990 was a key reason that Liberia was allowed to descend into brutal civil war after Charles Taylor's rebels invaded from Côte d'Ivoire in December 1989. As Côte d'Ivoire plunges into greater disorder, the world is again concentrating on Iraq. The United States initially refused outright to consider a proposal by Senegalese President Abdoulaye Wade that French and West African peacekeeping troops be put under a UN mandate, and then indicated to France that US cooperation at the UN with regard to Côte d'Ivoire depended on French support for war on Iraq. On 4 February 2003, however, the Security Council passed Resolution 1464, which endorses the Marcoussis agreement and welcomes the deployment of ECOWAS and French troops, which are, in any case, in the country at the invitation of the government. The resolution refers to Chapter VII of the UN Charter, and authorises ECOWAS to take any steps necessary for self-defence, freedom of movement and the protection of civilians imminently threatened with violence, though it does not cast the force in place as a UN 'blue-helmet' contingent.

If the peace process fails, a military stalemate between the government and the rebels is probable, in the absence of substantial outside assistance to the government. But while one-quarter of the country is Muslim and about one-fifth Christian, and much of the political grievance and violence is ethnically based, up to early 2003 no widespread ethnic or religious violence had materialised. Fatalities, while not negligible, were measured in the hundreds. Although a government of national unity had been nominally forged by April 2003, the rebels did not take their seats and FPI hardliners opposed the government. There remained at least some possibility that further negotiations and a more artful and equitable power-sharing arrangement could reintroduce a measure of stability in Côte d'Ivoire and stave off disarray comparable to that that had occurred in Liberia or Sierra Leone. Given that the Ivorian armed forces are part of the problem, however, an international military presence would probably be needed to guarantee any new political dispensation. An ECOWAS force the size of those deployed in Liberia and Sierra Leone is unlikely, as is a French contingent substantially larger than the one already in position. The critical issue is whether whatever small deployment ECOWAS and France can make available is adequate.

Nigeria's challenges

West Africa's other major flashpoint is Nigeria, where the north is predominantly Muslim and the south largely Christian. Tensions frequently arise when Muslim extremists take offence to supposed slights to Islam, and incite anger among gullible populations. This occurred in November 2002. The Miss World pageant was scheduled to be held in Abuja on 7 December, and had already aggravated Muslim sensibilities – all the more so when several contestants threatened to boycott the event in protest of the sentencing, under *sharia* law, of an alleged Muslim adulteress to death by stoning. When a 16 November newspaper article by a female fashion columnist, Isioma Daniel, suggested that the prophet Mohammed himself might have chosen a Miss World contestant as a bride, the deputy governor of the northern state of Zamfara issued a *fatwa* calling for Daniel's execution. Riots ensued in which some 220 people died, and the beauty pageant was forced to relocate to London. More broadly, while the large Christian population has dictated constitutional secularity, despite a probable Muslim majority, the latter has dictated government acquiescence to the application of *sharia* law in the north. This persistent religious tension is the source of continual and increasing communal violence in the north, and could be exacerbated by the war on terrorism.

President Olusegun Obasanjo was seeking a second four-year term in elections scheduled for 19 April 2003. A Baptist Yoruba from the southwest and a retired general, Obasanjo was Nigeria's military ruler in 1976–79. He was jailed in 1995 by the ruthless military dictator General Sani Abacha for allegedly plotting a coup and remains the only military ruler in the country's history to give up power voluntarily. He has strong support from politically dominant northern Muslims, yet is distrusted by many of his own tribe, who regard him as beholden to the military. Despite the pronounced religious division in Nigeria (estimated to be about 48% Muslim and 36% Christian), religion has not been and is not likely to be a crucially divisive issue in the national presidential elections. The two major parties – the People's Democratic Party (PDP) and the All Nigeria People's Party (ANPP) – of political necessity draw support from both north and south, Muslims and Christians. But sectarian unrest could attend elections at state level – particularly where Muslims are not numerous, yet Muslim candidates insist on the imposition of *sharia* law. Further, Nigeria has never achieved a successful handover of power from a civilian administration, and senior army officers will be watching the election closely. The army is no longer as homogeneous as it once was, however, and Obasanjo has worked hard to remove northerners from its senior ranks.

Although he lost the support of the northern power brokers who backed him in 1999, when he won a 63% majority, Obasanjo appeared in early 2003 to have established a solid support base. In the January PDP primary, the party nominated Obasanjo by a margin of 2,642 votes to 611 for former

Vice-President Alex Ekwueme, an Anglican Igbo from the eastern part of the country. All 21 PDP state governors (of a total of 36) were also re-nominated. Ekwueme challenged the result in the courts, alleging intimidation and demanding a re-run, but was unsuccessful. Obasanjo retained Vice-President Atiku Abubakar, an influential northern Muslim, as his running mate. Obasanjo's main opponent, former northern military ruler Major-General Muhammadu Buhari from the ANPP, has reconciled with his powerful former adversary ex-President Ibrahim Babangida, and may win financial backing from the family of late President Abacha. Obasanjo has alienated many Muslims through his opposition to the introduction of *sharia* law in northern states, and despite Atiku's best efforts they may rally solidly behind Buhari, who is known as a zealous Muslim. Chuba Okadigbo, Buhari's running mate, is an Igbo from the southeast, but may not help much with that constituency, given that he was found to have misused state funds as a senator in 2000.

Obasanjo and the PDP are likely to win the polls, although the far north will probably back Buhari. The Independent National Electoral Commission's lack of funds and clout is cause for concern. It is unlikely that the elections will be apprehended as free and fair enough to afford the winner a firm mandate. Any overly obvious attempt to rig the vote is likely to provoke a fresh outburst of the violence that has been a regular feature of the last four years of civilian rule, and Buhari's backing from Babangida and the army means he could prove a powerful adversary. Yet Babangida seems to be biding his time until 2007, when all the state governors must stand down and it will be easier to create a new political party. The upshot is that, for all its problems, Nigeria is liable finally to produce a reasonably orderly civilian change of government. This would improve its standing with Washington, which has suffered on account of corruption and Muslim extremism, and perhaps draw greater support for an improved relationship with the International Monetary Fund (IMF), which ended Nigeria's stand-by agreement in early 2002 due to excessive budget deficits and the government's inability to meet performance targets. In the longer term, however, lower oil prices could give rise to a major recession that could threaten civil order – particularly in the Niger Delta, a heavy oil-producing region and frequent site of violent ethnic clashes over the distribution of oil revenues.

On the diplomatic front, Nigeria is embroiled in a dispute with São Tomé & Principe over the terms for the licensing of offshore acreage in the two countries' shared Joint Development Zone. President Fradique de Menezes, who was elected in July 2001, pushed to renegotiate the contracts signed by his predecessor, Miguel Trovoada, after the IMF and the World Bank advised him that the deal was disadvantageous to São Tomé. These include a deal giving substantial oil rights to a US firm, Environmental Remediation Holding Company, which is now owned by Nigeria's Chrome

Energy, headed by prominent Igbo businessman Emeka Offor, who has close links to Atiku. Sao Tomé is also reviewing contracts with the US oil giant ExxonMobil and Norwegian seismic firm Petroleum Geo-Services, as well as the 60/40 asset split agreed in the Joint Development Zone treaty. Nigeria reacted to São Tomé's wavering by cancelling the entire deal in February 2003. But São Tomé has won a powerful ally in the United States, which is keen to import more non-OPEC African oil and reduce its dependence on the Gulf following the 11 September 2001 terrorist attacks.

Nigeria must also settle with Cameroon following the October 2002 International Court of Justice (ICJ) ruling awarding sovereignty over the Bakassi Peninsula (home to 200,000 Nigerians) to Yaoundé. The two sides have yet to settle on implementation of the decision, notwithstanding agreeing at UN-brokered talks before the verdict was announced that they would abide by the findings of the court. Despite a horrified reaction in Nigeria, the decision actually has much in Abuja's favour. The ICJ ruled that the Bakassi boundary was delimited by the Anglo-German agreement of March 1913, which is also used as the basis for some border rulings further north. Nigeria 'lost' Lake Chad as well as Bakassi, but largely 'won' the land boundary, 17,000 hectares versus 4,000 for Cameroon. Perhaps more importantly, Nigeria 'won' on the maritime boundary. Cameroon has been excluded from all the valuable deep-sea oil reserves it was aiming for, over which Nigeria now has undisputed sovereignty. Additionally, Nigeria's border treaties with Equatorial Guinea and São Tomé & Príncipe were vindicated and protected.

Mano River machinations

Regional concerns about Côte d'Ivoire and Nigeria and international worries about Iraq have taken some of the heat off Liberia's wily President Charles Taylor. He remains under heavy international scrutiny for harbouring al-Qaeda diamond buyers, as well as contravening UN sanctions on conflict diamonds. In addition, the rebel LURD was advancing towards the capital, Monrovia, in early 2003. But Taylor is adept at using regional mayhem to his advantage. He has called elections for 15 October 2003. Taylor's main opponent in the last poll, Ellen Johnson-Sirleaf, has indicated that the opposition is trying to form a multi-tribal coalition similar to the one that ousted President Daniel arap Moi in Kenya, but political conditions in Liberia are not conducive to free and fair elections. Taylor's main opponents live in exile, journalists are frequently imprisoned and harassed and the LURD challenge gives him a pretext for military repression. But the UN's review of sanctions against Taylor's government, slated for 7 May 2003, may generate momentum for a wider, more promising regional approach to controlling him.

Guinea's President Lansana Conté altered the constitution through a referendum in November 2001 to enable him to stand again in elections scheduled for December 2003. In 2002, however, he spent considerable time in a Morocco hospital receiving treatment for diabetes. He has no obvious successor, and the opposition has become more vocal in recent months. In mid-December, Conté carried out a major cabinet reshuffle after rumours circulated that he was already dead. The president of the opposition Rassemblement du Peuple de Guinée, Alpha Condé, had earlier declared his candidacy for the elections, but the other main opposition party, the Union pour le Progrès et le Renouveau, is weakened by tensions between its two leading members, Ba Mamadou and Siradiou Diallo. A document circulating in Conakry in December 2002 accused former Prime Minister Sidya Touré, who, in more harmonious times, was Alassane Ouattara's cabinet director in Côte d'Ivoire, of planning a coup – a campaign reminiscent of the smear tactics used against Condé, who served eight months of a five-year jail sentence in 2000–01 for threatening state security.

In war-torn Sierra Leone, President Ahmad Tejan Kabbah won a second five-year term in successful elections on 14 May 2002, but his health is failing (he is 71) and his government is being nursed through the reform process by aid organisations and donor countries, led by the UK. A donors' conference in Paris in November 2002 established a detailed set of targets and admonished the government to adhere to them. Rumours that Kabbah had offered to step down after two years were vigorously denied by Vice-President Solomon Berewa at election time, but may resurface and produce tensions. Institutions like the Truth and Reconciliation Commission (TRC) and the Special Court established to try suspected war criminals are making some progress in laying the foundations for a functioning civil society. But the election – hardly free and fair, albeit welcome – revealed some disturbing potential fissures. The Sierra Leone Army voted overwhelmingly for Lieutenant-Colonel Johnny Paul Koroma, who was installed as head of state following a military coup in 1997 and was allied with the brutal Revolutionary United Front (RUF). Koroma has re-invented himself as a born-again Christian and was elected to parliament. There is also scant indication that the government has learned much about good governance: it is still cronyistic and shows little sign of addressing the corruption and state aloofness from the larger population that underlie the conflict. In summer 2002, youth groups reminiscent of those that turned into the RUF were starting to form. The TRC and the Special Court could prove just as destabilising in practice as they are inspiring in theory. Finally, while the expensive UN Mission in Sierra Leone is being reduced from its peak of 20,000 troops, the Sierra Leonean military and police are not yet up to the task of managing security. In sum, Sierra Leone's hard-won peace could prove short-lived unless the security problems of the whole region, which provide opportunities for rebel holdouts and mercenaries to undermine internal security and effective governance, can be tackled.

Bitter economic medicine in Ghana

In Ghana, President John Agyekum Kufuor's New Patriotic Party administration will have to take some harsh decisions if it is to rebuild the shattered economy and repair damaged relations with development partners, especially the IMF and World Bank. The government discomfited donors when it came close to signing a highly dubious $1 billion loan deal in August with a mysterious group calling itself the International Finance Consortium – with no links to the World Bank's International Finance Corporation. The temptation was prompted by the previous government which, hoping to curry favour with the electorate, had put off badly needed price adjustments. Steep increases in value-added tax, petrol and water and electricity tariffs cannot be delayed much longer. Substantial cuts in the public-sector workforce – though probably not as high as the 60% floated by Economic Planning Minister Dr Paa Kwesi Nduom – will also be necessary. Further, as Finance Minister Yaw Osafo-Maafo pushes through the controversial privatisation programme, the sale of shares in Ghana Water Company, Ghana Airways and Ghana Commercial Bank will add to public unease over the direction of economic policy.

Ghana is also subject to political stresses and uncertainties. In the Muslim north, the King of the Dagombas, Ya-Na Yakubu Andani, was murdered in March 2002 along with 25 of his supporters. The opposition National Democratic Congress (NDC) has launched a campaign to win back power in the 2004 elections, with ex-President Jerry Rawlings backing former Vice-President John Atta Mills, who won landslide endorsement in December to the discomfort of party Chairman Obed Asamoah. The party's finances will come under severe strain, however, and NDC heavyweights like former Finance Minister Kwesi Botchwey, who lost the nomination battle to Atta Mills, may cut their losses and join the breakaway National Reform Party.

The Franc Zone

The crisis in Côte d'Ivoire has caused substantial economic and political damage to the Union Economique et Monetaire Ouest-Africaine. The closure of the border means Burkina-Faso has lost much of its customs revenue, and transport costs have been sharply increased by the detour via Ghana. Cotton exports from Mali, Burkina-Faso and northern Côte d'Ivoire have been particularly hard hit. Trade has been diverted to Ghana's Tema port, and also to Cotonou and to Lomé, where a plan for a container port first mooted in 2001 was only starting to receive funding from the US Trade and Development Agency in early 2003.

Togolese President Gnassingbé Eyadéma, whose seniority and 35 years as president earns him a measure of respect from the region's leaders, hosted Ivorian peace talks that led to a ceasefire but not to a wider deal. Although he has long-standing links to French President Jacques Chirac, a younger generation of diplomats at the Quai d'Orsay see him – and particularly his ineffectual role in the Côte d'Ivoire crisis – as something of an embarrassment. Eyadéma slipped a vote through parliament on 30 December altering the constitution to let him stand for another term in 2003. Sacked Prime Minister Agbéyomé Kodjo is now in Paris, deepening links with Togolese expatriates, while former National Assembly President Dahuku Péré, among the first heavyweights from the ruling Rassemblement du Peuple Togolais to come out against Eyadéma in recent years, is agitating in Lomé, and there are signs of discontent in the top ranks of the army.

The Ivorian crisis has also been a blow to Mali's President Amadou Toumani Touré, who was elected in May 2002 in widely praised elections and would like to increase his profile in the region. A former army general, he overthrew the dictator Moussa Traore in 2001 and handed back power to civilians the following year, winning universal admiration and launching him on a career as an international mediator. But the economy has been hard hit by the closure of the main freight route to Abidjan port, and local authorities are struggling with an influx of refugees from northern Côte d'Ivoire, many of them southern Baoulés who had been working in the north and fled in fear of revenge attacks. Touré is also struggling with the thankless task of reforming the monolithic cotton parastatal Compagnie Malienne de Développement de Textiles. The World Bank wants to introduce more competition, but this is likely to be unpopular.

Northwards along the Atlantic coast – farther from Côte d'Ivoire – there is greater stability but hardly tranquillity. While Senegal's President Abdoulaye Wade has impressed internationally, and in 2002 mediated between Madagascar's rival presidents, his diplomatic skills have proved unequal to the Ivorian crisis, and at home the Casamance rebellion continued unabated. The economy has benefited somewhat from an opening to new investors, notably Morocco, which has established the highly successful Air Senegal International joint venture between the Senegalese government and Royal Air Maroc. But power shortages remain a problem, as repeated failure to privatise the state electricity utility Senelec has left the sector in limbo. In Gambia, opposition to President Yahya Jammeh is increasing as economic stagnation deepens, and some opposition figures have charged that tax rises in the 2003 budget were designed specifically to drive out foreign workers. Sackings of senior officials and reports of coup plots in Guinea-Bissau remain routine, the latest in early December 2002, but the country – which has plenty of experience of army rebellion of its own – is clawing back some international status as a member of the six-nation ECOWAS contact group on Côte d'Ivoire. Parliamentary elections were set for 20 April 2003, in a bid to reassure donors that the country is returning to relative stability despite the sometimes erratic style of President Kumba Yala.

Further east, Niger continues to struggle with drought, floods and the economic effects of smuggling and low revenue collection. Finance Minister Ali Badjo Galmatié is under pressure from parliamentarians and trades unionists, but a greater worry is the army unrest in Diffa. December saw a mass escape of imprisoned mutineers, some with links to late President Ibrahim Baré Maïnassara. The Presidential Guard is thought to be loyal, but the town of Zinder remains openly sympathetic to the mutiny, which may also have an ethnic dimension.

The death in Libya in September 2002 of Chadian rebel leader Youssouf Togoïmi after a landmine explosion has removed a source of worry to President Idriss Déby, as the Doba petroleum project gears up to pump its first oil in July 2003. However, the Armée Nationale de Résistance, a loose grouping of Déby's tribal opponents, appears to have taken on the politico-military mantle of the Mouvement pour la Démocratie et la Justice au Tchad (MDJT). Led by former Army Chief of Staff Mahamat Garfa, it has claimed major victories in the south and southeast against the national army, using rear bases in Sudan and the Central African Republic. The MDJT itself is split, with hard-liners wanting to continue military action at all costs in the Tibesti region. Much will depend upon how useful the rebels are to Libyan President Muammar Gaddafi when Chadian oil starts flowing: he will want to maintain his influence in N'djamena at all costs.

Moving south, the Central African Republic (CAR), had appeared to be the test-bed for the embryonic regional mediation and peacekeeping ambitions of the Communauté Economique et Monetaire de l'Afrique Centrale (CEMAC), the central African franc zone. A CEMAC force of 370 – 200 having been supplied by Gabon – in Bangui, the CAR's capital, had been guarding key buildings, including the home of President Ange-Félix Patassé, whose ten-year rule had been marked by ineptitude, greed and brutality. This allowed the withdrawal of the troops sent by Patassé's ally Gaddafi, but a lasting settlement of the face-off between the CAR government and rebel leader General François Bozizé – whose troops control much of the north and centre of the country and who is supported by Chad – was not forthcoming. On 15 March 2003, General Bozizé and 1,000 troops seized the airport and presidential palace in Bangui while Patassé was at a conference in Niger. CEMAC peacekeepers, as well as regular soldiers (who had not been paid for months), abandoned their posts. Fifteen people died in the coup and looting subsequently prevailed. Bozizé imposed a curfew and had looters executed, but pledged to hold a 'national dialogue' with an eye towards a return to civil rule and to secure fresh loans from the IMF and World Bank. While CEMAC's institutional political capabilities continue to be relevant, this situation will determine the viability of the newly declared orthodoxy in Africa that rulers who come to power by force will not be recognised. Early signs were ominous: the foreign ministers of both Gabon and Congo-Brazzaville paid Bozizé ostensibly friendly visits.

There is little prospect of CEMAC intervening to promote genuine reconciliation in Congo-Brazzaville, where the conflict between government and Ninja rebels shows no sign of abating, with persistent human-rights abuses on both sides. French judges have continued to investigate the Beach affair – the May 1999 disappearance of over 350 refugees, mainly young ethnic Lari men, who arrived at Brazzaville dock by ferry from Kinshasa. President Denis Sassou Nguesso scored an overwhelming victory in the March 2002 presidential election, which gave his seizure of power in 1997 some measure of democratic legitimacy, and his Parti Congolais du Travail scored a decisive triumph in parliamentary elections in May 2002. But the polls, and the January 2002 referendum on a new constitution that gave him sweeping powers, were widely condemned. Former Deputy Governor of the Banque des Etats de l'Afrique Centrale Roger Rigobert Andély, appointed finance minister in August 2002, has international credibility. But, as of early 2003, he had not produced transparency in oil finance sufficient to satisfy the IMF. Paris, Congo-Brazzaville's closest partner among the major powers, seems in no hurry to move beyond the present limited bilateral cooperation in the country's economic recovery until Brazzaville can satisfy the Fund.

Cameroon's Paul Biya is keeping a low profile, but is expected to bring the presidential election forward by a year to 2003, following the opposition's poor showing in parliamentary polls in June 2002. He may well opt not to serve a full seven-year term. Potential successors include Prime Minister Peter Mafany Musonge, the Speaker of parliament Cavaye Yeguie Djibril, and the Secretary-General of the ruling Rassemblement Démocratique du Peuple Camerounais General Joseph Charles Doumba, who all produced healthy shows of support in their home regions in the parliamentary polls. But like other long-serving leaders, Biya will need assurances of immunity from prosecution for past misdeeds to ensure an easy transition into retirement. The fate of Cameroon's first president, Ahmadou Ahidjo, who died in exile, does not provide an attractive precedent.

2003: crisis management, political transition and oil

The major issues for West Africa in 2003 are essentially security-related. Left on its own, Côte d'Ivoire is likely to implode. The international community's response to events there may indicate whether the chronic instability of Liberia and Sierra Leone can be contained, or whether the region must continue to lurch from disaster to disaster. UN sanctions against the Liberian regime are due for renewal in May 2003, and the Security Council may take the opportunity then to consider a wider regional approach. But even a comprehensive and well-funded conflict prevention and development strategy would not guarantee stability because the central problem – institutionally weak states dependent on commodity exports being squeezed by globalisation pressures that create unrest and political tension that spread insecurity – is so daunting. The most that outside actors may be able to accomplish in the foreseeable future is manageable instability.

In any case, the most urgent task in West Africa is to secure the resources – in particular, ECOWAS troops – required to underpin Côte d'Ivoire's peace deal, or a future one if the current agreement breaks down. The focused engagement and military commitment of a major outside power – comparable to the UK's in Sierra Leone in 2000 – may be indispensable. France, the former colonial power, remains the logical candidate. Emboldened diplomatically by the new Gaullist majority in the National Assembly after 2002's parliamentary elections, France appeared in early 2003 to be treading with a somewhat surer step in Africa. While its performance in brokering the Marcoussis agreement is open to criticism, and the attendance of Mugabe at the 19–21 February Franco-African summit in Paris at France's invitation was scorned by other European powers, these developments do suggest that France is stepping 'back in Africa' after having its confidence shattered in Rwanda. But Chirac intended mainly to secure African support for France's position on Iraq, and did not deal substantively with Zimbabwe. It remains to be seen whether the French government is interested in developing any wider framework for its Africa policy, beyond the hyperactive crisis management that – of necessity – characterised de Villepin's first months in office. The real test of its effectiveness – and determinant of its staying power – will be diplomacy with respect to Côte d'Ivoire, the jewel in France's post-colonial crown.

Nigeria's fragile democracy may barely pass a test it has always failed in the past – the handover of power by a civilian administration. But the government of President Obasanjo is under considerable pressure to address the resentment of Muslims, communities in the oil-producing Niger Delta and other groups, as well as to repair relations with his neighbours. The economic slowdown in major countries will hit demand for many of the region's commodity exports. Though oil-producing economies may benefit from the crises in Iraq and Venezuela, the longer-term trend for crude prices is downward, as supply increases. At the global strategic level, 2003 will be critical in determining whether exploration now underway will make the Gulf of Guinea a global oil-and-gas province and raise the profile of littoral governments in the United States, which is looking to diversify its sources of supply away from Saudi Arabia and the Middle East. The African Oil Policy Initiative Group, which brings together such diverse interests as US independent Vanco Energy Company, with substantial deep-water acreage holdings in the Gulf of Guinea, and the Israeli Institute for Advanced Strategic and Political Studies, produced a report in 2002 recommending that the US establish a regional military base on São Tomé to ensure the security of the region and its oil. Despite considerable speculation, this now looks unlikely. Nevertheless, the US is expected to establish a logistics base and secure shore locations. This would confirm Washington's keen, if guarded, interest in engaging with reforming African states that can offer oil deals benefiting US firms in exchange for political backing and military aid.

Kenya 2002: Moi's Farewell

The 27 December 2002 general election in Kenya was a watershed in the country's history. After nearly four decades in power, the ruling Kenya African National Union (KANU) was defeated, winning only 65 of the 210 directly elected seats in the National Assembly, yielding to the National Alliance Rainbow Coalition (NARC). Despite this potentially refreshing change, however, Kenya continues to have chronic problems in regard to the HIV/AIDS epidemic and its relations with the Bretton Woods institutions. Possible bumps in Kenya's internal political transition could also affect its regional role, its partnership with the United States in the war on terrorism and its important role in the Sudanese and Somali peace processes.

The economic and social context
Kenyan President Daniel arap Moi came to power just as the easy options of the first 15 years of independence were running out, as the era of import-substitution industrialisation was giving way to the demands of structural adjustment and economic liberalisation. Economically, his presidency was a failure. The incomes of many Kenyans in real terms are now lower than they were when he came to power. Economic growth in the mid-1990s slipped far behind demographic growth, even as the population growth rate began to slow, falling from 4.2% in the mid-1970s to only 2.3% today. Most school-leavers were unable to find jobs in the formal economy. The government's own Economic Survey acknowledges that 56.5% of the population lives in poverty, whereas the top 10% control 48% of national income, making it one of the world's most economically unbalanced societies. For most of the 1980s and 1990s, the economy stagnated or even declined. Social problems have mounted. Although HIV incidence dropped from 13% to 10% between 1999 and 2003, HIV/AIDS now poses a serious threat not only to the country's economic growth but also to the coherence of many key institutions, including the military, the civil service and the teaching profession. Kenya's health infrastructure has deteriorated badly during the past two decades. Morale among doctors and nurses is

low; pay disputes have disrupted health care; and most rural clinics lack essential medicines.

Relations with the international financial institutions (IFIs) throughout Moi's last year remained poor. The World Bank and the International Monetary Fund (IMF)'s $300 million lending programmes were suspended in January 2000. In late July 2002, World Bank Kenya Director Menachem Katz announced that the Bank was not prepared to suggest any timetable for the resumption of aid. This decision forestalled the Central Bank's ambitious plan to stabilise interest and exchange rates by converting short-term debt into long-term borrowing, just as tax-policy reversals reduced government revenue by eight billion Kenyan Shillings (KSh) ($101m). Although IMF officials acknowledged 'substantive progress on a number of issues' in August 2002, the Bretton Woods institutions were waiting for further improvements – especially the privatisation of parastatals in the electricity, water and sugar industries, and of Telkom Kenya, the Kenya Railways Corporation and the Kenya Ports Authority. In his July 2002 budget speech, Finance Minister Chris Obure promised to concession the operations of Kenya Railways, to commercialise various port services, to introduce private-sector participation to Nairobi's water supply and to push through the privatisation of the Kenya Reinsurance Corporation and sell the remaining 35% government stake in the Kenya Commercial Bank. The Moi government, however, displayed little eagerness to privatise Telkom Kenya before the general election, given the political implications of cutting the corporation's workforce by 50%. The Bretton Woods institutions were determined not to repeat the pattern of the 1980s and 1990s, when relations with Kenya were restored after long and difficult negotiations only to be suspended again a short time later. The IMF made clear that new government directives and laws would not constitute sufficient proof that Kenya had addressed the problems that had led to the suspension of aid in January 2001. Decisive steps against corruption were required. Further discussions in October 2002 during the IMF's annual meeting failed to resolve the impasse.

Kenya and the United States

In recent years, Kenya has developed an elaborate network of ties and has arguably the most complex relationship with the US of any African state. The bombing of the US embassy in August 1998, in which over 200 Kenyans and 12 Americans lost their lives, established a bond between the two governments against terrorism. This has endured in spite of disputes over compensation for Kenyan victims of the attack. The relationship, reinforced by President George W. Bush's administration's war on terrorism, was strengthened further in the aftermath of the 28 November 2002 attack on the Israeli-owned Paradise Hotel near Mombasa, in which 13 Kenyans and three Israelis died. Supporters of al-Ittihad al-Islami, identified by the United States as a Somali terrorist organisation with links to al-Qaeda, are widely believed to have infiltrated some of the refugee camps in Kenya's Northeastern Province, and to have made their way to Mombasa and Eastleigh, the Somali quarter of Nairobi. In Coast Province, they may well have gained support among the thousands of unemployed youths, who have been hit by the decline of Kenya's tourist industry. Most Kenyans were appalled by the 11 September 2001 attacks on the World Trade Center and the Pentagon, and most support the US-led campaign against terrorism. But a few Kenyans – mostly Somalis – paraded through the streets of Nairobi in support of al-Qaeda after 11 September. The majority of the country's Muslim population is religiously moderate and law abiding, but in both the embassy bombing and the attack on the Israeli-owned hotel, a few Kenyans were implicated. In the 1990s, increasing numbers of youths turned to radical Islam as Kenya's tourist industry declined and left fewer employment opportunities.

Terrorist sleeper cells exist in Kenya – indeed, the two al-Qaeda Nairobi- and Mombasa-based cells involved in the 1998 embassy bombings were never completely rolled up. Screening of refugees is poor. Airport security is inadequate, Kenya's land borders are porous, and arms are easily available on the black market. The US has spent $3.1m on anti-terrorist training in Kenya since 1998, and after the Mombasa attack, contributed another $750,000 to improve airport security. Despite this expenditure, intelligence reports suggested that a team of Yemeni terrorists had arrived in Mombasa to prepare a possible attack on German Air Force personnel, who operate surveillance flights over southern Somalia. Although Kenya has weak counter-terrorism institutions, during 2002 Moi proved one of the US' most reliable allies in Africa. Kenya has important airport facilities in Nairobi and Mombasa, and the largest port facilities in the western Indian Ocean north of Durban. As the US prepared to go to war in the Persian Gulf, Moi confirmed its right to use the port of Mombasa as a supply and recreational base, and to airlift men and materiel to the Gulf through the Nairobi military airport. In September 2002, the US annual National Security Review designated Kenya as one of the US' four key partners in Africa, along with South Africa, Nigeria and Ethiopia. President Moi visited Washington in early December 2002, along with Prime Minister Meles Zenawi of Ethiopia, meeting with Bush and Secretary of State Colin Powell. Some Kenyans feared, however, that the preoccupation of the US and other major powers with counter-terrorism would mean a relaxation of support for democracy, good governance and economic reform in favour of 'hard' security concerns. The State Department argued that two sets of priorities should be seen as mutually reinforcing: the only guarantee of long-term stability in Kenya is the entrenchment of democracy and the rule of law.

In fact, Kenya has long been a focal point for the United States' support for democratisation and human rights. American ambassadors, starting with the maverick Smith Hempstone in 1989–93, have carefully balanced their support for greater political pluralism and multiparty politics against US strategic and economic interests in Kenya. The US is also anxious that Kenya, as the dominant economy in East Africa, should embrace the agenda of further economic liberalisation, press ahead with the downsizing of its parastatal sector and restore its good standing with the IMF and the World Bank. For their part, the Kenyan government and Kenyan businessmen are eager to take advantage of the trade opportunities provided by the US African Growth and Opportunity Act (AGOA), especially in the textile sector. Kenya's AGOA-eligible exports to the United States, however, amounted to only $36m in the first nine months of 2001, less than 1% of US–Africa trade. Bilateral US aid to Kenya came to $40m in 2002 and was budgeted at $47m in 2003.

Kenya and conflict resolution

For more than a decade, *Operation Lifeline Sudan* has been a vital conduit of humanitarian relief and food supplies to southern Sudan from its base in Kenya's Turkana District. Kenya also provides a haven to hundreds of thousands of Somali refugees in camps in Northeastern Province. In his last year in office, Moi played an important role in efforts to end the nearly two-decades-long civil war in Sudan, building on the US-led peace initiative of former Senator John Danforth. Danforth's exploratory peace mission to the region in November 2001 brought the two sides into discussion. Moi, as Chair of the Inter-Governmental Authority on Development (IGAD), which includes all of the countries of the wider Horn of Africa, then sponsored peace talks between Khartoum and the Sudan People's Liberation Movement/Army (SPLM/A) in Machakos, a city in southeast Kenya. Working closely with the United States, the Kenyans, led by General Lazaro Sumbeiwyo, achieved a major success when the two sides reached agreement on the Machakos Protocol on 20 July 2002, on the contentious issue of self-determination. The parties decided that a referendum should be held at the end of a six-year interim period to decide whether the south would remain part of Sudan or secede. In the meantime, it will not be subject to *sharia* law, which applies in the north.

The signing of the Machakos Protocol, however, intensified divisions in both camps between moderates and hardliners. As a result, the talks have nearly collapsed on a number of occasions. On 2 September 2002, two weeks into the second round of talks, the Sudanese government suspended its participation following the capture of the Sudanese town of Torit by the SPLA. Both Khartoum and the SPLM/A are beset by serious internal divisions over the peace negotiations. Key issues still to be resolved include arrangements for internal security, the conflict in the Nuba Mountains, the sharing of power and oil revenues, and structural reform of the state. The Northern Democratic Alliance, the SPLM/A's northern allies, have also not

Africa

been brought fully into the Machakos process. The third round of negotiations ended on 18 November 2002 with the signing of a new Memorandum of Understanding on power sharing and the extension of an earlier cessation of hostilities and the unrestricted access of aid agencies. The delegates failed to reach agreement on a further protocol on the sharing of political power and on the proportion of oil revenue that will go to a southern reconstruction fund. Kenya is also directly mediating government–SPLM/A peace talks, separate from the IGAD process, on the so-called marginalised areas of Sudan – Abyei, the Nuba Mountains and the Southern Blue Nile. Under Sumbeiwyo's chairmanship, negotiations occurred in Karen, outside Nairobi, in January and March 2003.

Kenya is deeply concerned about the situation in Somalia, its northeastern neighbour. It has a large Somali population of its own in Northeastern Province, in parts of Eastern and Coast Provinces, and in the Eastleigh quarter of Nairobi. The collapse of the Somali state has resulted in the influx of large numbers of refugees, and a serious decline in the security situation in much of northern Kenya. Journeys by road in this region have to be made in armed convoy. In the 1960s, the newly independent Kenyan government crushed Somali irredentism by forcing the pastoralists of the northeast into eight 'protected' villages, just as the British had crushed the Kikuyu tribe's Mau-Mau rebellion in the 1950s. The current insecurity is rapidly producing a similar result, as unarmed residents seek refuge in the few fortified towns at night. Kenya does not have the capacity to monitor the movement of asylum seekers across its borders and some of the refugees are deeply involved in cross-border trade in small arms and narcotics. Similar, although less serious security problems, exist in Turkana and West Pokot Districts, bordering on southern Sudan and the Karamojong region of Uganda. In these areas, small arms can be easily and cheaply acquired, and the AK-47 has replaced the spear as the weapon of choice among cattle rustlers, who raid the more settled, fertile and prosperous Trans Nzoia and Marakwet Districts.

In October 2002, Moi launched another IGAD initiative to bring peace to Somalia. Although some warlords initially complained that civil-society delegates far outnumbered backers of the military faction leaders and protested that two-thirds of the delegates on its intellectual advisory committee came from a single clan, the conference opened in Eldoret on 15 October. More than 800 Somali delegates, representing all of the rival factions – except Somaliland, which insisted it was independent – arrived to hear Moi appeal for peace. Representatives of the Transitional National Government (TNG) in Mogadishu, led by Prime Minister Hassan Abshir Farah, participated on an equal basis with the other factions. Although the conference hovered on the brink of collapse, it appears to represent the best prospect in a decade for establishing some sort of minimal national government. Moi's representative, former Minister of Agriculture Elijah

Mwangale, demonstrated little understanding of the suspicions and regional rivalries of the Somali groups, and seemed too willing to overturn unilaterally decisions that had been painstakingly negotiated. By December 2002, when the talks were suspended for the Kenyan election, the delegates had advanced little beyond their original declaration of 27 October, which was approved by 22 rival groups, including the TNG. The conference was mired in disputes over participation, mismanagement and alleged corruption. Factions breached the 27 October ceasefire several times and the TNG withdrew from the negotiations. Little substantive progress was made in phase two of the negotiations when the delegates formed smaller 'reconciliation committees' to discuss key issues, such as a new constitution, land disputes, the structure of a new government and disarmament and demobilisation.

Somali delegates and the members of the conference secretariat soon became disillusioned with Mwangale and expressed the view that the only way to salvage the conference was for Mwai Kibaki, the leader of the Democratic Party (DP), to win the election and appoint a new intermediary with an understanding of Somalia's problems. Ambassador Bethuel Kiplagat, a retired permanent secretary from Kenya's Ministry of Foreign Affairs, took over on 18 January 2003, and immediately sought to restore the credibility of the peace process. Foreign ministers of the 'frontline states' – Djibouti, Ethiopia and Kenya – reaffirmed their commitment to the process at their Addis Ababa meeting on 3 February 2003, and agreed to establish a mechanism to monitor violations of the declaration on the cessation of hostilities.

The succession issue

At the beginning of 2002, KANU's position appeared strong and unified, while the opposition parties were fragmented. The merger of KANU with the Luo-based National Development Party (NDP) in March 2002 seemed to guarantee a KANU victory in the December 2002 election. Following the merger, Raila Odinga, the new KANU's Secretary-General and a member of the Luo tribe, Kenya's third-largest, began to court KANU's large but disorganised central faction of moderate reformers in an effort to take control of the ruling-party apparatus. Recognising the danger, the courtiers around Moi started to push the candidacy of Uhuru Kenyatta – son of Jomo Kenyatta, Kenya's founding president and its most revered national figure, and a member of the Kikuyu tribe, Kenya's largest and most affluent group.

The succession issue was KANU's Achilles' heel. Although the ruling party was the only truly national political force, it remained a delicate coalition of rival factional groups held together by patronage and loyalty to Moi. His departure threatened the party's cohesion. For most of the 1990s, Moi's obvious successor was Vice-President George Saitoti. Saitoti's reputation, however, had been tarnished by his involvement in a scandal involving the diversion of KSh19.6bn ($250m) from the Treasury to Goldenberg International – an import–export company controlled by Kamlesh Pattni, a friend of Moi's – to defray KANU's costs in the 1992 election. Moreover, Moi had been angered by Saitoti's attempt in 1997 to impose his allies as KANU candidates in Kajiado District, which had precipitated a serious political revolt that cost KANU Kajiado South and put Kajiado Central in jeopardy. Moi did not reappoint Saitoti in January 1998, keeping the vice-presidency vacant for the next 18 months. When Saitoti began aggressively to court Kikuyu business leaders, establishing an independent power base, his relations with both Moi and Nicholas Biwott, the regime's *eminence grise,* deteriorated further. Meanwhile, the prospects of the other front-runner, Musalia Mudavadi, improved. As minister of finance from January 1993 to January 1998, he restored relations with the IFIs and slowly put the economy back on track. Mudavadi was one of the government's stars, a highly professional minister who was adept at dealing with the media, the IFIs and bilateral donors. Mudavadi had two additional advantages: as the government's senior representative among the Abaluhya of Western Province, he promised to bring to KANU the support of Kenya's second largest ethnic group at the expense of the Forum for the Restoration of Democracy (FORD)-Kenya; and he was distantly related to Moi, enjoying good relations with the powerful inner circle of Moi's Kalenjin tribe. By the beginning of 2002, Mudavadi had become the leading candidate to take over as president. Moi, however, was unhappy with both Saitoti and Mudavadi. Encouraged by his youngest son Gideon, Cooperative Bank Chairman Hosea Kiplagat and Assistant Minister William arap Ruto, Moi favoured Uhuru Kenyatta, whom he finally selected as his successor in July 2002.

The 41-year-old Kenyatta was politically inexperienced. He had sat in parliament for less than a year. Moi had nominated him to the National Assembly in October 2001, dismissing Mark Too, who had been talking too openly with opposition Kikuyu leaders. A month later, Moi had appointed Kenyatta to the Cabinet as Minister of Local Government. Defeated in Gatundu South in 1997 by 22,000 votes to 10,000, Kenyatta had never held elective office, although he had served as KANU chairman in Thika District from 1996 to 2002, and as head of the Disaster Relief Fund in 1999 and the Kenya Tourist Board in 2000–01. Kenyatta, however, had four factors in his favour: name; his family's money; his considerable personal charm; and, most importantly, Moi's backing. The strongest opposition to Moi's decision came from Odinga. He was 16 years older than Uhuru Kenyatta, had been a member of parliament (MP) for ten years and had contested the presidency himself in 1997. He had been in detention in 1982–86 and again in 1990–92. He was also a far more experienced politician. Moreover, Odinga felt that the Luo community's suffering during the first Kenyatta administration – especially the 1969 Kisumu massacre, when security forces killed over 100 people during Jomo Kenyatta's visit – made it politically untenable for the Luo people to vote for Uhuru Kenyatta. Odinga's arguments, however, left Moi unmoved. Odinga concluded that he had no alternative but to abandon KANU if Moi insisted on nominating Kenyatta. Odinga controlled a solid block of nearly 20 former NDP MPs. Having led them into KANU on 18 March 2002, he had no compunction about leading them out again a mere six months later. Moi and the inner circle calculated that Kikuyu voters, attracted by Kenyatta's nomination, would more than compensate for the loss of the Luos. Odinga, however, persuaded and cajoled non-Luo KANU reformers, middle-of-the-roaders and even a few members of the old-guard who felt slighted by Moi's decision to press for the democratic selection of party delegates. When Moi ignored their demands and attempted to rig the nomination process, the dissidents began to contemplate abandoning KANU.

Meanwhile, the ethnic-based parties of the opposition started to coalesce in opportunistic response to KANU's deterioration. Kenya's parties revolve essentially around personalities and patronage, so ideologically there was virtually nothing to distinguish them from one another or indeed from KANU. All of them rhetorically supported 'good governance', economic liberalisation, privatisation, the rule of law and respect for human rights, and were committed to poverty alleviation. The major opposition parties had learned from the 1992 and 1997 elections that divided they were not likely to wrest parliament from KANU. They had collectively won 103 constituencies to KANU's 107 in 1997. United, they had a better chance of victory. FORD-Kenya's Michael Kijana Wamalwa and Charity Ngilu, the Social Democratic Party (SDP)'s presidential candidate in 1997, had launched the National Party of Kenya (NPK). But Wamalwa was tottering on the brink of bankruptcy, suffered from serious kidney and liver problems, and had proved an ineffective chairman of the opposition-controlled Public Accounts Committee in 1994–97, while Ngilu was a woman, came from a marginal constituency and had never held government office. They recognised that they would have to give way to Kibaki, the DP leader.

Kibaki had more than four decades' experience at the forefront of Kenyan politics. He had served in parliament since 1963 and entered the Cabinet as Minister for Economic Development in 1966. From 1969–82, he had presided over Kenya's economic boom as minister of finance. From 1978–88, he had served as Moi's first vice-president, and even after his demotion had been too valuable to be dropped from the Cabinet, continuing as Minister of Health until Christmas Day 1991, when he had resigned to launch the Democratic Party. Since January 1998, Kibaki has been official leader of the opposition, supported by more MPs than Wamalwa and Ngilu combined. Quiet, but highly intelligent and with vast experience, Kibaki eschewed bombast and controversy. In many respects,

Africa

he appeared the perfect candidate to unite the rival opposition parties. But he was also widely regarded as an irresolute and tired old man of 71 whose presidential bid had come ten years too late.

Moi attempted to hold KANU together. Mudavadi was enticed back to the ruling party and made vice-president until the election. The dissidents, however, became increasingly irate as Moi intervened directly in the selection of delegates to secure Kenyatta's nomination. When Moi refused to guarantee free-and-fair elections or to re-run the delegates' selection process in Ukambani and other disputed regions, Odinga led Kalonzo Musyoka, Saitoti, Moody Awori and Maasai tribe political boss William ole Ntimama straight out of State House to announce to the waiting media that they were abandoning KANU for the Liberal Democratic Party (LDP). The formation of the LDP created a crisis for both KANU and the renamed opposition National Alliance for Kenya (NAK), which in late September had selected Kibaki as its presidential candidate and Wamalwa as its vice-president, with Ngilu taking the post of prime minister. These positions would have to be renegotiated if the LDP were to join the NAK alliance against KANU. Former Vice-President Saitoti had no intention of standing down for Kibaki, and Musyoka also had ambitions to be president. After a hard day of negotiations at Nairobi's Pan-Afric hotel between NAK and the LDP, the leaders had made little headway in reaching an agreed opposition slate when they went to address the public in Uhuru Park. Once again, Odinga pre-empted his former KANU colleagues, by declaring to the vast crowd 'Kibaki tosha': 'it has to be Kibaki'. Odinga's declaration reflected his recognition that Kibaki was the only person with sufficient multi-partisan stature to keep NARC together. Saitoti and Musyoka accepted Kibaki as NARC's presidential candidate. Odinga supplanted Ngilu as NARC's prime minister-in-waiting, while Musyoka, Awori and Ngilu were named as three deputy prime ministers-designate. Saitoti, former KANU Secretary-General Joseph Kamotho and William ole Ntimama – three members of the KANU old-guard – were left out in the cold. The best that they could hope for was to become members of a Kibaki Cabinet.

The electoral process

NARC candidates in the northern Rift Valley feared that KANU would outspend them by at least twenty-fold. KANU actually spent approximately KSh10m per seat, while NARC's candidates rarely raised more than KSh3m. Most opposition candidates had to dig into their own pockets and borrow from family and friends to cover their two major expenses: hiring four-wheel drive vehicles for the campaign; and paying party agents on election day. KANU pursued a traditional strategy, going door-to-door to hand out money. Chiefs and sub-chiefs played a less active role than in 1992 or 1997. Reforms had outlawed active participation in the campaign by members of the provincial administration, but in many areas they had remained a key element in KANU's election efforts. District commissioners came under less pressure than in the past two elections to mobilise their subordinates on behalf of the ruling party. Nevertheless, a dozen or so, especially the ones in Mombasa and Marakwet, were clearly partisan. Opposition candidates remained suspicious of both the district administration and the police, complaining that they were far from impartial in handling opposition and KANU complaints.

Uhuru Kenyatta sought to distance himself from the Moi regime, promising to tackle corruption and to bring the perspective of a younger generation of Kenyans to the country's problems. In a culture where old age remains respected, Kenyatta's appeal to youth did not arouse as much support as his advisers had anticipated. Indeed, even many young voters preferred Kibaki's 30 years' experience to Kenyatta's youth. Kenyatta's attempt to disassociate himself from Moi, moreover, was constrained by the fact that Kenyans knew that Moi had imposed him on the ruling party and would continue as party chairman, and even more by the fact that individuals, such as the president's son, Gideon, and Moi's close adviser, Biwott, remained very influential. Widespread corruption and the almost unchecked raiding of state coffers counted heavily against Kenyatta and undermined his message of KANU as the party of renewal. Even though some of the worst culprits were now leading figures in NARC, the corruption issue disproportionately damaged KANU. Economic conditions had deteriorated too long, the road, rail, education and health care infrastructures had decayed too far, and the level of corruption had become too blatant, for many voters to trust KANU. NARC's promises of reform, renewal and financial probity were more credible.

Moreover, Kibaki's quiet modesty and his vast political experience in the highest reaches of government overcame doubts among voters about his age and his reputation for laziness. KANU party leaders realised by early December 2002 that they stood little chance of victory against a united opposition. They decided that they could live with a Kibaki presidency. As a result, the ruling party did not launch its anticipated all-out campaign of bribery, rigging and intimidation; these were undertaken only in a spasmodic, half-hearted manner, which merely ensured its defeat. Nevertheless, the scale of Kibaki and NARC's victory was surprising. Kibaki defeated KANU's Uhuru Kenyatta by 61.3% to 31.6% of the popular vote. His victory was comprehensive. Kibaki exceeded the constitutional requirement of winning 25% of the vote in five of Kenya's eight provinces, reaching the 25% target in all eight provinces. The parliamentary results diverged only slightly from the presidential ones. Thus, NARC, with 62% of the popular vote, secured 57% of the seats in the National Assembly, while KANU with 31% and FORD-People with 7% of the popular vote won exactly the same proportion of seats in parliament. KANU was humiliated in Nyanza and Western Provinces. In Nyanza it failed to win a single seat

Africa

and in Western held on in only two constituencies – Nambale and Mount Elgon. Mudavadi's decision to stick with KANU rather than decamp to NARC was repudiated by the voters in KANU's former redoubt among the southern Abaluhya. In Eastern Province, the three largest communities – the Kamba, Meru and Embu – all voted decisively for Kibaki and NARC parliamentary candidates. KANU held on only in the northern parts of the province, among the semi-nomadic Boran, Galla and Somali electorates. Ukambani, in the southeast, also went solidly for Kibaki and NARC. And NARC won an overwhelming victory in the northern Kikuyu Districts of Central Province, the stronghold of Kibaki's DP in both 1992 and 1997.

Despite the enthusiasm that surrounded NARC's campaign, turnout in the election was surprisingly low, ranging from 67% in Central Province (the home of both Kibaki and Kenyatta) down to 45% in Coast Province and 42% in Nairobi. Nationally, the figure fell to 58% from 68.4% in 1997. Nevertheless, the election clearly constituted a major success for multiparty democracy in sub-Saharan Africa. President Kibaki sought to balance factional and ethnic factors with the need to have an experienced and loyal team. The new government, excluding the president, contained 14 NAK supporters (10 DP, three FORD-Kenya and one NPK), 11 LDP members and one civil servant (Attorney-General Amos Wako, who had held the same post in the Moi government since 1992). The new Cabinet had five Kikuyu members (six if Minister of Education Professor George Saitoti is counted as a Kikuyu rather than a Maasai), five Abaluhya (including Wako), four Luo, two Kalenjin, two Kamba, two Meru, two Mijikenda from Coast Province and two Maasai (if Saitoti is counted), one Embu and one Somali. This was a reasonably representative spread of the main ethnic communities. In provincial terms, the Cabinet was even more balanced, including five members from Central Province, five from Eastern Province, five from the Rift Valley, three from Nyanza, three from Western Province, two from Coast Province and one from Nairobi (Odinga) and Northeastern Province.

The Kibaki government's challenges

In his inaugural speech on 30 December, Kibaki castigated KANU's failure to advance development and economic growth, and promised to eradicate corruption and to increase spending on education, health and roads, restoring the agricultural sector as the dynamo of economic growth. Kibaki further dispelled doubts about his determination to rebuild Kenya in recalling parliament during his first week in government to get approval for full financing (KSh2.5bn or $35m) for his campaign pledge to institute free and compulsory primary education for all Kenyan children and to pass two tough anti-corruption bills. Drafting a new constitution before the end of 2003, as NARC has promised, is a more substantial challenge – though the Constitutional Review Commission's unexpected presentation of detailed proposals in late September 2002 provides some basis for optimism. In any case, the election itself broadly showed that multiparty democracy, which Moi's domination of the political scene had made essentially nominal since its inception in 1992, had worked in substance. A promising new era had started in Kenya's history.

Yet on the foreign-policy front, Moi had been a reasonably solid leader. Accordingly, there will be pressure from external actors for Kibaki to maintain Kenya's profile as a central player in regional security matters. The country has enjoyed generally good relations with its three most important neighbours – Ethiopia, Tanzania and Uganda. It was salutary that Tanzanian President Benjamin Mkapa and Ugandan President Yoweri Museveni both attended Kibaki's inauguration, warmly welcoming the new Kenyan leader. Regional relationships could improve further following the formation of a customs union slated for 30 November 2003 and the promotion of development activities in the Lake Victoria basin, which could bring better economic performance. Outside powers would also hope that Kibaki will continue to offer diplomatic support for the peace processes in Somalia and Sudan. This appears likely. Although domestic issues dominated the election campaign, newly appointed Kenyan Foreign Minister Stephen K. Musyoka indicated, on a trip to Washington in February 2003, that the new government had the political support to take an even more active role in promoting peace in Somalia and Sudan, and characterised the restoration of law and order in Somalia as one of Kenya's top foreign-policy interests.

Kenya, for all of its problems, has at least by default been the strongest force for stability among the nations of East Africa and the Horn. It has the region's strongest economy. Kenya has accommodated refugees, provided bases for non-governmental organisations (NGOs) and the UN operating in Sudan and Somalia, and extended important military cooperation to the US and European powers. From a counter-terrorism point of view, Kenya, along with Ethiopia, is the US' strongest partner in a potentially tough neighbourhood. US global security priorities and the apparent capacity of coalition partners to contain transnational terrorism through preventive means probably preclude deeper bilateral major-power engagement in East Africa in the near future. Bilateral aid concentrating on the security sector is likely to be maintained. Nevertheless, the US continues to regard Kenya as one of four 'anchor states' in sub-Saharan Africa, and has heightened concerns over the penetration of Kenya by al-Qaeda, as indicated by the Mombasa operation in November 2002. This suggests that Washington could have a standing, if secondary, interest in strengthening Kenyan institutions more broadly and in inoculating its Muslim population against radicalisation through longer-term development programmes. In January 2003, US military officials announced the formation of a joint task force with Kenya and five other Horn of Africa countries, backed by a 900-strong US military contingent

Africa

(including Special Forces) stationed in Djibouti, for disrupting terrorist operations in the region.

Given that KANU's corruption was a focus of IFI dissatisfaction as well as NARC's campaign, there are economic and political reasons for Kibaki's government to take pains to deliver on promises of better governance. At the same time, Kenya's political system remains based on tribal patronage. Thus, even if the new statutory standards and institutions urged by the IFIs are implemented, any immediate substantive advances are likely to be modest. Still, any visible improvement in Kenyan governance could spur Washington to use its influence in the IFIs to have aid to Kenya resumed. Indeed, after the elections, the IMF indicated that it could start lending again in June or July 2003 – which would likely trigger World Bank credits – and the US and the UK gave early signs of fresh development aid. As of April 2003, then, there appeared a reasonable chance that Kenya's December 2002 election would not only establish it as a better political model for other African states, but also preserve its strong putative role in maintaining regional stability and enhance its prospects for economic development.

Prospectives

A relatively swift and merciful war in Iraq would preserve the possibility that at least some of the Bush administration's more audacious visions can be realised. Should they be, the decision of the United States and the United Kingdom to go to war against the preponderance of world opinion will be substantively vindicated. But the manner in which the US, in particular, imposed its will is unlikely to be forgotten. The Iraq crisis has clearly damaged the United States' world standing. Many of the US' allies and partners, and to an even greater extent their populations, perceive American leadership as dangerously arrogant in its exercise of the United States' superior military power. On 18 March 2003 - the day after President George W. Bush issued his final ultimatum to Saddam Hussein - the Pew Research Center for the People and the Press released a telling survey covering eight US allies and counter-terrorism coalition partners in Europe. Whereas 50% or more of those surveyed in the UK, France, Germany, Italy, Spain, Poland and Turkey viewed the US favourably during the last year of the Clinton administration and substantially retained that view after the 11 September attacks, less than 50% in each country except Poland (at 50%) saw the US in a positive light in March 2003. While only 37% in Russia had approved of the US in 1999–2000, the figure jumped to 61% after 11 September, but plummeted to 28% in 2003. A majority of those polled in every one of those countries opposed war against Iraq. In a Gallup poll conducted in January 2003 - when inspections appeared promising - majorities in 12 of 22 European countries opposed war in Iraq under any circumstances; only in two - Ireland and The Netherlands - did majorities favour military action, and then only with UN sanction. On 1 April 2003, roughly two weeks into the war, a *Le Monde* poll indicated that 78% of the French public disapproved of American and British intervention in Iraq. Perhaps even more indicative of anti-war feeling among the French population was the fact that only 34% sided with the US and the UK in the conflict, while 25% supported Iraq.

Accompanying substantive disagreement was mistrust. When in March 2002 Washington chose to abandon diplomacy in the United Nations, sceptics sensed that previous and oft-repeated protestations that it wished to avoid war were disingenuous: that the US was willing to heed the UN only to the extent that it certified unshakable American intentions to oust Saddam. Beyond such perceptions and suspicions, the shambolic character of the diplomatic process that began with reinvigorated arms control and ended with armed conflict has diluted the international solidarity inspired by 11 September. In this light, the impassioned observation made by Leader of the House of Commons Robin Cook as he resigned from Prime Minister Tony Blair's Cabinet on 17 March 2003 in protest of Blair's decision to take Britain into war alongside the Americans, is worth noting. Said Cook: 'The reality is that Britain is being asked to embark on a war without agreement in any of the international bodies of which we are a leading partner – not NATO, not the European Union and, now, not the Security Council. To end up in such diplomatic weakness is a serious reverse. Only a year ago, we and the United States were part of a coalition against terrorism that was wider and more diverse than I would ever have imagined possible. History will be astonished at the diplomatic miscalculations that led so quickly to the disintegration of that powerful coalition'. On 19 March, Senator Robert Byrd of West Virginia echoed Cook's sentiments on the floor of the Senate: 'Today, I weep for my country. No more is the image of America one of strong, yet benevolent, peacekeeper. Around the globe, our friends mistrust us, our word is disputed, our intentions are questioned'.

These, of course, are exaggerations: regardless of the wisdom or imprudence of military intervention in Iraq, it will remain in the enlightened self-interest of most members of the international coalition to cooperate as robustly as ever on counter-terrorism, and indeed in the post-conflict reconstruction of Iraq. But the US did proceed in Iraq in perhaps greater isolation than in any military engagement since the Vietnam War.

Substance vs process

Perhaps the cruellest irony of the diplomatic debacle over Iraq is the fact that so many of those alienated by America's behaviour shared its basic attitude towards Saddam Hussein: that he was the scourge of his own people and a menace to his neighbours and needed to be disempowered. Thus, the Pew survey also indicated a measure of cognitive dissonance. While most people disapproved of the US' conduct, clear majorities in five of the eight countries surveyed – France and Germany as well as Britain, Italy and Poland – believed that the Iraqi people would be better off after the war, with only the Russians and Turks sceptical. This dissonance was moderated by the fact that majorities in only three countries believed that war would produce a more stable Middle East. But the larger problem was not the moral desirability of the immediate outcome of the war; on that there was at least rough agreement. The problem was rather that the US was preoccupied with substantive results at the expense of the diplomatic process, France and others with process at the expense of results. It goes almost without saying that both are essential to the smooth functioning of the international system. Both Paris and Washington should have shown a more balanced appreciation for each of these central aspects of international security.

The substance–process dichotomy also operated in the arms-control arena. Since before the withdrawal in late 1988 of arms inspectors from Iraq due to repeated Iraqi non-cooperation, most major powers considered Iraq to be in 'material breach' of a number of UN resolutions pertaining to its armaments, starting with UN Security Council Resolution 687, passed in April 1991 after the ceasefire in the first Gulf War and requiring Iraq to completely dismantle its weapons of mass destruction (WMD) programmes. Resolution 1441, unanimously passed on 8 November 2002, contemplated 'serious consequences' in the event of Iraq's 'further material breach' of UN resolutions. In effect, that meant Iraq's non-compliance with the weapons inspections requirements of the UN Monitoring, Verification and Inspection Commission (UNMOVIC) and the International Atomic Energy Agency (IAEA). Each of UNMOVIC Chairman Hans Blix's reports to the Security Council indicated that while Baghdad was broadly cooperating in terms of process, its compliance in terms of substance was, to various degrees and in various ways, lacking. In his presentation of technical intelligence on Iraq's WMD and missile programmes to the Security Council on 5 February 2003, US Secretary of State Colin Powell presented convincing evidence of the Iraqi regime's non-disclosure and non-compliance – effectively establishing a 'smoking gun' for 'material breach'. Blix's distinction between process and substance could be used to support both the pro-war and the anti-war position. But France, with strong Russian support, then effectively took the public position that as long as the Iraqi regime was extending procedural cooperation and improving substantive cooperation, its overall non-compliance would not dictate the use of force. The US viewed this as gratuitous and counter-productive encouragement to Saddam Hussein to conceal WMD and a dilution of the compellent effect of the US and British military mobilisation in the Gulf. When, in early March, France announced that it would veto any subsequent UN Security Council resolution authorising the use of force against Iraq, friction between France and Russia on one hand, and the US and the UK on the other, turned into outright diplomatic enmity.

The upshot of the ill will over Iraq is undoubtedly that the ability of coalition partners to function through multilateral institutions has been impaired. It goes almost without saying that it is not in the interest of international security or stability that either Europe or the US proceed as if it does not need the other, and therefore treat the hobbling of multilateral institutions apathetically. It is mainly differences in their tactical approaches to strategic problems and not in the basic values that guide solutions that have produced the present divisions. Both Americans and Europeans extol liberal democracy and would like to see it expand. Both favour open international trade, steady and stable energy supplies, countering WMD proliferation, easing humanitarian problems and containing rogue states inimical to these objectives. Europe and the US have an acute mutual self-interest in counter-terrorism cooperation at all levels. The US may not need much European military help, but the Iraq crisis shows that it does need Europe's political and logistical support to wield it most effectively. Thus, while the most exigent post-war tasks for the international community will be to establish a viable political framework for a unitary Iraq and to ensure the stability of the Middle East/Persian Gulf region, its broader preoccupation must be to repair the institutions that have been so badly damaged. Three in particular stand out: the UN; NATO; and the European Union (EU). The key players in weakening these institutions were the US and France – the leaders, respectively, of the pro-war and anti-war camps. They too must be the prime movers of the reconstruction of the institutions.

US policy vs French policy

The events of 11 September 2001 induced US makers of security policy to focus predominantly on consequences rather than probabilities in moving the US towards a system whereby all conceivable potential vulnerabilities would be eliminated or minimised. This mindset gave hawks – including those with a 'utopian' agenda for the Middle East whereby a liberated Iraq would become the ideal substitute for the increasingly sour partnership with Saudi Arabia and a political exemplar for the region – the opportunity to push Iraq to the top of the agenda. Immediately after the attacks, they successfully exploited the belief in the upper tier of US government that there was a better than even chance that Iraq had been involved in the attacks, and the more broadly held concern that Baghdad might in future supply WMD to terrorists. The stage was set for eventual confrontation with Iraq over Baghdad's WMD ambitions. Furthermore, the American obsession with vulnerability and the Bush administration's contempt for Bill Clinton's perceived failure to exploit the US' remarkable leverage in the Middle East during America's 'unipolar moment' meant that this time US diplomacy would proceed wilfully towards the objective of regime change.

Much of what motivates French policy on the Iraq issue is France's own wilful opposition to American wilfulness or, more broadly, hegemony. This is not new. During the Cold War, France opted out of NATO's integrated military command structure. In the 1990s, French leaders explicitly sought to enhance EU power to engender a 'multipolar world' to constrain the American 'hyperpower'. But in addition to France's general hostility to a unipolar world, a specific conviction that an invasion of Iraq would have highly negative consequences for Iraq, the wider Middle East and France itself added weight to its stance. Unlike some in Bush's inner circle, the French government does not believe that Iraq has strong operational links to al-Qaeda and, to the contrary, thinks that invading Iraq would inspire active al-Qaeda cells throughout Europe to stage more terrorist acts and ramp up recruitment. France is also highly sceptical about optimistic American plans to impose order and democracy on Iraq once Saddam's regime is defeated, and fears that the elimination of the current Iraqi leadership will not lead to democracy but to chaos. On both of these points, the French position is not very different from views widely held across Europe, where opposition to an invasion of Iraq ranges from 75 to 85% of public opinion. Instead, what distinguishes France's policy is its willingness to actively oppose war rather than acquiesce to US policy.

The United States' global military and economic dominance afford it substantial leverage to impose its will unilaterally to obtain a particular result. Hence the focus on substance. France's positions in the UN Security Council, NATO and the EU constitute its power multiplier. The fact that those institutions influence world affairs by imposing procedural restraints on the unilateral exercise of power, primarily through formalised supranational procedures, explains France's preoccupation with process. Because France derives such status from its role as one of only five permanent members of the Security Council – a body that France has sought to strengthen as a tool for promoting a more multipolar world – many analysts long assumed that Paris would not use its veto, lest that action undermine the Security Council's authority. In the event, the opposite logic appeared to prevail in Paris: failing to use a veto when convinced that much of the world opposed a war would for the French mean turning the Security Council into a rubber stamp for American policy, thus undermining its legitimising role. Within NATO, France also sought to prevent the Americans from dictating policy to Europe, blocking an American request for NATO to begin planning for a possible defence of Turkey upon the commencement of war on Iraq. Finally, while a strong proponent of unity within the EU, France acted vigorously to prevent the EU from lining up behind the US. Chirac's rapprochement with Germany on the 40th anniversary of the Elysée Treaty, and his supercilious outburst in February 2003 at the Central European EU candidates who had expressed support for the US – in which he suggested that their accession could be blocked – were efforts to prevent the EU's Common Foreign and Security Policy (CFSP) from becoming little more than an expression of American wishes. The political blowback, of course, was that in publicly accentuating the rift between pro-war and anti-war EU members, it appeared that there was no such policy worthy of the label.

Modes of reconciliation and rebuilding

Had the war shaped up as an unmitigated catastrophe, relations among EU, NATO and Security Council members could have become even worse. Resentment towards France and Russia among the US and other countries that backed the war could have deepened, as they would regard France and

Prospectives

Russia as having sabotaged the diplomatic and military efforts to disarm Iraq. In the worst case, French efforts to constrain the US could move Paris to try to build a European security and defence policy independent of US–NATO structures, and insist that all future international crises be settled through the UN. The US would bypass the Security Council on vital security matters. As of early April 2003, however, it appeared that US-led military action would have neither a pristine result nor a disastrous one. On one hand, Iraqi resistance was unexpectedly stiff and overt indigenous support for allied forces slow to materialise. On the other hand, there were few civilian casualties – at least compared to those in the first Gulf War – and little damage to oilfields or other critical infrastructure. Thus, after the conflict, neither the US nor France was likely to feel either embarrassed or vindicated. Rather, the two would probably emerge on roughly level political pegging. This situation should be conducive to the reconciliation and compromise needed to rebuild multilateral structures. The war will not have been bloodless, and there will remain Arab worries about American economic and political imperialism. Further, the US retains an institutional aversion to nation-building notwithstanding the 'utopian' cast of the Bush team, and may well be inhibited by domestic politics from following through on an aggressive revisionist agenda in the Middle East. The US, then, will require considerable political cover from the UN: as a neutral organising force for nation-building; as a trustworthy steward of Iraq's oil industry and a reactivated oil-for-food programme; and as a catalyst for drawing reconstruction aid – particularly from the EU.

Given Tony Blair's strong European vocation, notwithstanding his stance on Iraq, the UK will need such cover all the more. Indeed, the very fact that France used the UN Security Council to register its deep opposition to the war could make the UN the ideal post-conflict actor in terms of controlling damage to the relationship between Islam and the West. That said, France initially appeared defiant. Even after hostilities had begun, on 21 March 2003, Chirac proclaimed that it would block any UN resolution endorsing the war. At the same time, he stated that the UN was the only proper body for advancing Iraq's reconstruction. Conversely, in late March 2003, it became clear that the US would resist substantial UN authority over post-conflict Iraq – the buzz-phrase was 'a UN role, not UN rule' – not least for fear that France and Russia would attempt to curtail American plans for the establishment of an interim US-run administration and indigenous political structure. Chirac may never be invited to the White House again. Yet there was no doubt that Washington – partly at London's urging – would seek Security Council authorisation for any interim US-administered civilian government in Iraq. France and Russia will be inclined to challenge US domination of such a government, but given the US' political exigencies, there may be room for an effective compromise. It is virtually inevitable that the US will hesitate to consult the

UN Security Council in executing certain aspects of its security policy. Still, the weight and variety of its security burdens are likely to dictate a fair degree of pragmatism. For example, in late 2002 and early 2003, Washington's policy called for internationalising the North Korea crisis and co-opting Pyongyang precisely by referring the issue of the legality of its nuclear-weapons programme to the UN.

NATO was already in a somewhat palsied state after 11 September, enduring its second identity crisis in a decade. The Kosovo experience convinced many in the Pentagon that NATO was operationally counter-productive: the gap in capabilities meant that most of the sorties were carried out by US planes; and the process of North Atlantic Council (NAC) target approval produced the paralysis of 'war by committee'. When, in response to 11 September, European allies invoked Article 5 of the North Atlantic Treaty and rushed to offer combat forces, the US preferred to fight in Afghanistan mainly on its own, with some substantial help from UK forces. Afghanistan was, in some ways, an unfair test – having suffered a dramatic attack, it was never very likely that the US would organise its response under command of a multinational NATO headquarters. The Iraq crisis brought out NATO's potential marginalisation in starker relief. On account of Germany's at times haughty opposition to US Iraq policy, the US may withdraw its troops from German soil. Even more profoundly, the refusal of France and Belgium to approve the deployment of defensive equipment in Turkey and the Turkish parliament's refusal to allow US ground troops access to Turkish soil revealed a comprehensive lack of cohesion within the organisation. If the question before the Iraq crisis was whether NATO would be a unitary alliance or a set of military tools selectively available to 'coalitions of the willing', the post-Iraq question was whether a European institution operationally dominated by a United States now thoroughly contemptuous of France and Germany could continue to exist. There remain good European reasons for keeping NATO around. It will still be diplomatically and militarily useful in stabilising Eastern Europe which, given resurgent problems in the Balkans, is not yet out of the woods. NATO's value as a geopolitical bridge to Russia has been reinforced by NATO enlargement and Russia's new consultative role. And NATO administrative structures and political linkages can facilitate counter-terrorism cooperation in certain areas.

The transatlantic reasons for maintaining NATO are even stronger. As discomfited as 'old Europe' may be with the US' Iraq stance and vice-versa, core European countries are likely to continue to value strategic links with Washington for at least three reasons. First, Washington has an important residual role as a balancer and security guarantor for Europe. Second, steady and deep diplomatic relations enable France and other countries to influence US strategic policy across the globe. Third, France and Germany as well as the UK would seek to avoid Europe's irrelevance in military-strategic terms, which would be implied by the demise of NATO. From the American side, the US could more plausibly do without its European alliance, or with only the British, but such a prospect would pose problems of legitimacy both abroad and at home. Indeed, the more the US exercises its overwhelming power on its own, the more prominent a lightning rod it will be for anti-American reactions. At the very least, it needs an intact NATO as a fall-back option for the use of force in case the political heat becomes unbearable. Moreover, opinion polls consistently show that the American people do not want to be involved in military interventions without substantial allied support.

One focal point of mutual advantage for rebuilding US–Europe relations within NATO is the 21,000-strong NATO Response Force (NRF), proposed by none other than Rumsfeld and created at the December 2002 NATO summit in Prague. Even US military capabilities are finite, and they will be stretched by a war in Iraq that is proving tougher than expected, and for which President Bush requested $74.7 billion in supplemental funding after less than a week of hostilities. In future engagements, as in Iraq, considerable help at the 'high end' of most demanding strategic missions – for example, establishing a bridgehead, securing an airport, conducting a counter-terrorist commando raid or evacuating NATO-member nationals from a crisis area – will come reliably from Britain. But France has comparable experience – witness Côte d'Ivoire – and would also be a useful contributor. Energising the implementation of the NRF would re-concentrate transatlantic relations on pre-Iraq issues such as the military capabilities gap, security burden-sharing and, in particular, redefining NATO's mission rather than overseeing its dissolution. Before Iraq, there were two models for NATO. In the first, NATO itself would go to war, as it did over Kosovo, but this time outside the NATO area. Transatlantic divisions over Iraq cast serious doubt on the viability of this model. But the second model is quite feasible, whereby NATO remains a European security organisation and an important political forum, training institution and planning and logistical network from which 'coalitions of the willing' are assembled for military action outside Europe. Presumably, such coalitions would most often be US-led. But NATO and the EU are still working out arrangements for possible EU operations using NATO planning and assets. A strategically demanding EU-led humanitarian intervention in Africa – which generally does not feature prominently on the US' strategic radar screen – is quite conceivable.

The EU's Iraq problems also have both a transatlantic and European dimension. On 22 January 2003, Rumsfeld remarked to journalists that France and Germany constituted 'old Europe' and were not representative of the 'new Europe'. Another unnamed US defence official quipped that 'going to war without France is like going on a deer hunt without the accordion'. On 30 January 2003, the *Wall Street Journal* lent superficial credence to Rumsfeld's remarks by publishing a letter jointly signed by the leaders of eight European nations supporting US Iraq policy. Five – the UK, Spain, Denmark, Italy and Portugal – were EU members. The other three – the Czech Republic, Hungary and Poland – were formally approved for EU accession at the EU summit in Copenhagen in December 2002. Another letter signed by ten candidates for EU membership in support of the American position was also published. Chirac then warned that accession could be blocked for candidates who rejected French–German leadership on world affairs. Similarly, German Chancellor Gerhard Schröder told Social Democrat Party members that maintaining 'European sovereignty' meant unity on the Iraq issue, which would determine Europe's future for the next 10–15 years.

While reports of the demise of Germany and France as political forces in Europe have doubtless been exaggerated, it is clear that the divergence between those two core states, on one hand, and the UK and a significant number of other European countries, on the other, has enervated any EU aspiration to CFSP. Indeed, encouraged by the outraged reactions of Eastern European candidates to the threats of exclusion, UK Minister for Europe Denis MacShane in March 2003 called for a meeting of ministers for European affairs to produce a clear statement of principle that EU entry will not turn on anything resembling a test of allegiance to any existing member's foreign and security policy. From a broad perspective, the Iraq divisions within the EU simply illustrate the inherent limits of any CFSP among nations that also maintain independent foreign policies. Strongly nationalistic governments like the UK and France will inevitably disagree on some issues, especially when the use of force is involved. Thus, the Iraq debate may serve a generally useful function in lowering Brussels' sights to a more realistic level. As with NATO, general issues such as peacekeeping may be more amenable to consensus.

From a more acutely European perspective, the two letters illuminated the inexorable arithmetic of EU enlargement: in an expanded 25-member EU, with majority voting and composed of countries that tend to regard the US as their political and security guarantor, France and Germany are likely often to be in a minority on foreign-policy issues. This would explain Paris and Berlin's vehemence. Yet, if both an enlarged EU and a strong balancing voice for the EU in international affairs are to be salvaged from the Iraq crisis, the EU's strongest nations will have to reassure new members of Brussels' capacity and intention to protect them, so that they need not depend exclusively on the US. This means narrowing the military capabilities gap, establishing a European Rapid Reaction Force that is harmonised with the NRF and continuing close political engagement in the Balkans. These steps would merely re-energise initiatives that arose before the Iraq crisis and therefore would not appear to be European capitulation to American policy on Iraq. At the same time, Europe, in taking up a greater share of the global security burden, would be reaching out to the US and helping to repair transatlantic relations.

Building strategic consensus

The attitudes displayed during the Iraq crisis demonstrated the near total absence of strategic consensus between Europe (as a whole) and the United States. There is no common threat assessment and no common or agreed method for dealing with threats that emerge or are identified. There are sharply differing diplomatic approaches to many longstanding conflicts and crises, especially in the Middle East. There are deepening disagreements and inconsistent attitudes towards the use of force and the place of international law in settling disputes. France, in its preoccupation with process and the rule of law, undervalued force: Iraq's legal compliance would have been even more lacking had it not been for the US' willingness to back the inspections process with the credible threat of force. The US, in its zeal for ending Iraq's WMD threat, marginalised diplomatic and legal processes that generally render the use of force more acceptable: the perceived lack of UN backing for the Iraq war may make it more difficult for even a victorious US to convince the world that it did the right thing. In fact, the threat of force is not obsolete, and international law is not premature. Both derive maximum power and value from consensus. Insofar as consensus is engendered through institutions, rebuilding those that have been weakened via the Iraq ordeal should be a top strategic priority.

That rebuilding, however, cannot occur in the absence of an attempt to create a stronger transatlantic strategic consensus. No measure of tribute paid to the 'institutional prerogative' will replace the advantages to be gained from a common strategic approach. Yet that common strategic approach can best be crafted through institutions. Ideally, NATO could be resurrected to debate transatlantic views of security challenges, and the EU revivified to harmonise views among the UK, Spain, prospective new entrants and the sceptics led by France and Germany. The UN has never been good at authorising war, having formally blessed only three: Korea in 1950; Iraq in 1991; and Afghanistan in 2001. But it could promote and nurture debate on the unique challenges posed by transnational threats. The reality is that a few key European states need to engage the US productively on doctrinal issues relating to the use of force, and the US has to find a way of blending European views into a thicker transatlantically applied strategy.

In sum: the process of international decision-making must be made to better accommodate the substance of strategy, and vice-versa. This cannot be accomplished unless European and other powers somehow take account of and accommodate a psychological change in US foreign policy. The United States was a status-quo power during the Cold War, and during the decade thereafter at least attempted to moderate and slow radical transformations stemming from the end of the US–Soviet strategic confrontation. With the advent of the Bush administration's neo-conservative idealism, however, the US now seeks significant changes in the status quo. Its approach is selective: the US is quite willing to preserve the status quo between China and Taiwan. But some of the changes it does seek are so sweeping and audacious as to present the US as a revolutionary power. One aspect of this policy shift that discomfits other nations is its perceived lack of even-handedness. Washington seeks a catalytic alteration of the Arab world's geopolitical landscape and its political and institutional standards, but pushes for only incremental change in the Israeli–Palestinian conflict. Europeans and others have shown unease with many of the answers proposed by the strongest advocates of revolutionary change in doctrine (pre-emptive or preventive strikes) or in geopolitics (democratising the Middle East). But they have not yet engaged intellectually with the questions that have given rise to these suggested policies: the nature of today's transnational threats, and the unsustainability of the present political dispensations in many parts of the Middle East. To build a new strategic consensus with the US, they will have to do so. European nations, if they are to be formidable and persuasive interlocutors with the US, need to better and more calmly articulate what are quite understandable substantive concerns. If they so engage the US constructively through the very institutions that produced such divisiveness over Iraq, those institutions will perforce stand to recover their relevance and functionality.